Elements of Moral Cognition
*Rawls' Linguistic Analogy and the Cognitive
Science of Moral and Legal Judgment*

Is the science of moral cognition usefully modeled on aspects of Universal Grammar? Are human beings born with an innate "moral grammar" that causes them to analyze human action in terms of its moral structure, with just as little awareness as they analyze human speech in terms of its grammatical structure? Questions like these have been at the forefront of moral psychology ever since John Mikhail revived them in his influential work on the linguistic analogy and its implications for jurisprudence and moral theory. In this seminal book, Mikhail offers a careful and sustained analysis of the moral grammar hypothesis, showing how some of John Rawls' original ideas about the linguistic analogy, together with famous thought experiments like the trolley problem, can be used to improve our understanding of moral and legal judgment. The book will be of interest to philosophers, cognitive scientists, legal scholars, and other researchers in the interdisciplinary field of moral psychology.

John Mikhail is Professor of Law and Philosophy at Georgetown University.

Elements of Moral Cognition

*Rawls' Linguistic Analogy and the Cognitive
Science of Moral and Legal Judgment*

JOHN MIKHAIL

Georgetown University

CAMBRIDGE
UNIVERSITY PRESS

CAMBRIDGE UNIVERSITY PRESS
Cambridge, New York, Melbourne, Madrid, Cape Town,
Singapore, São Paulo, Delhi, Tokyo, Mexico City

Cambridge University Press
32 Avenue of the Americas, New York, NY 10013-2473, USA

www.cambridge.org
Information on this title: www.cambridge.org/9780521855785

First published 2011

Printed in the United States of America

A catalog record for this publication is available from the British Library.

Library of Congress Cataloging in Publication Data
Mikhail, John, 1969–
Elements of Moral Cognition / John Mikhail.
p. cm.
Includes bibliographical references and index.
ISBN 978-0-521-85578-5 hardback
1. Language and ethics.   2. Rawls, John, 1921–2002. Theory of justice.
3. Generative grammar.   4. Chomsky, Noam.   I. Title.
BJ44.M55   2009
170–dc22   2008050511

ISBN 978-0-521-85578-5 Hardback

To Sarah, Hannah, and Andrew; and to the memory of my parents,
Ramzy and Maryse Mikhail

*Homo homini lupus;** who has the courage to dispute it in the face of all the evidence in his own life and in history?
– Sigmund Freud, *Civilization and Its Discontents*

For when the Gentiles, which have not the law, do by nature the things contained in the law, these, having not the law, are a law unto themselves.... They show that what the law requires is written on their hearts, their conscience bearing witness....
– St. Paul, *Letter to the Romans*

What we have been saying would have a degree of validity even if we should concede that which cannot be conceded without the utmost wickedness, that there is no God, or that the affairs of men are of no concern to Him.
– Hugo Grotius, *On the Law of War and Peace*

---

* Man is to man a wolf.

Contents

List of Tables and Figures   *page* xi

Preface   xv

PART ONE: THEORY

1   The Question Presented   3

2   A New Framework for the Theory of Moral Cognition   13

   2.1   Nine Comparisons between Linguistics and Moral Theory   14

     2.1.1   The Main Questions   14

     2.1.2   The General Answers   15

     2.1.3   The Fundamental Arguments   17

     2.1.4   The Competence–Performance Distinction   17

     2.1.5   The Distinction between Operative and Express Principles   19

     2.1.6   Levels of Empirical Adequacy   21

     2.1.7   Two Additional Questions   23

     2.1.8   Commonsense and Technical Concepts of Language and Morality   24

     2.1.9   Theoretical Goals   26

   2.2   Preliminary Clarifications about Rawls' Linguistic Analogy   27

   2.3   Outline of Remaining Chapters   33

3   The Basic Elements of Rawls' Linguistic Analogy   42

   3.1   Eight Features of Rawls' Conception of Moral Theory   43

     3.1.1   The Argument for Moral Grammar   43

     3.1.2   The Problem of Descriptive Adequacy   48

     3.1.3   The Distinction between Descriptive and Observational Adequacy   49

3.1.4 The Distinction between Operative and
      Express Principles   50
3.1.5 The Distinction between Descriptive and
      Explanatory Adequacy   51
3.1.6 The Competence–Performance Distinction   51
3.1.7 The Theory-Dependence of the Competence–
      Performance Distinction   55
3.1.8 The Importance of Idealization   56
3.2 Further Clarifications about Terminology   57
3.3 Moral Theory as a Theory of I-Morality   63
3.4 Some Further Remarks about the Linguistic Analogy   67
3.5 The Contrast with Particularism   71

PART TWO: EMPIRICAL ADEQUACY

4   The Problem of Descriptive Adequacy   77
4.1 The Trolley Problems   78
4.2 The Properties of Moral Judgment   82
4.3 Framing the Problem of Descriptive Adequacy   85
4.4 Locating the Problem within the Framework of
    Cognitive Science   87
    4.4.1 Perceptual and Acquisition Models   88
    4.4.2 The Hypothetico-Deductive Method   91
4.5 Objections and Replies   94

5   The Moral Grammar Hypothesis   101
5.1 Some Initial Evidence   104
5.2 Simplifying the Problem of Descriptive Adequacy   106
    5.2.1 Twelve New Trolley Problems   106
    5.2.2 Twelve Considered Judgments   110
5.3 The Poverty of the Perceptual Stimulus   111
    5.3.1 Labeling the Stimulus   111
    5.3.2 Expanded Perceptual Model   111
5.4 Outline of a Solution   117
    5.4.1 Deontic Rules   117
    5.4.2 Structural Descriptions   118
    5.4.3 Conversion Rules   120
5.5 Intuitive Legal Appraisal   121

6   Moral Grammar and Intuitive Jurisprudence: A Formal Model 123
6.1 Three Simplifying Assumptions   124
6.2 Structural Descriptions I: Acts, Circumstances,
    and Intentions   125
    6.2.1 Acts and Circumstances   125
    6.2.2 K-Generation and I-Generation   130
6.3 Deontic Rules   132

6.3.1 The Principle of Natural Liberty 132
6.3.2 The Prohibition of Battery and Homicide 133
6.3.3 The Self-Preservation Principle 136
6.3.4 The Moral Calculus of Risk 137
6.3.5 The Rescue Principle 144
6.3.6 The Principle of Double Effect 148
6.4 Structural Descriptions II: A Periodic Table of Moral Elements 153
6.5 Conversion Rules 162
6.5.1 Temporal Structure 171
6.5.2 Causal Structure 172
6.5.3 Moral Structure 172
6.5.4 Intentional Structure 172
6.5.5 Deontic Structure 173
6.6 A Brief Note on Enlightenment Rationalism 174
6.7 Further Clarifications about Act Trees 175
6.8 Concluding Remarks 178

PART THREE: OBJECTIONS AND REPLIES

7 R. M. Hare, Peter Singer, and the Distinction between Empirical and Normative Adequacy 183
7.1 Hare's and Singer's Criticisms of Rawls' Linguistic Analogy 183
7.2 Empirical and Normative Adequacy in *Grounds* 191
7.3 Empirical and Normative Adequacy in *Outline* 195
7.4 Empirical and Normative Adequacy in *A Theory of Justice: Reflective Equilibrium* 197
7.4.1 The Main Contractual Argument of *A Theory of Justice* 198
7.4.2 The Concept of Reflective Equilibrium 202
7.5 Empirical and Normative Adequacy in *Independence* 213
7.6 Some Clarifications about Metaethics 217
7.7 Objections and Replies 221
7.8 Summary 227

8 Thomas Nagel and the Competence–Performance Distinction 228
8.1 Nagel's Criticisms of Rawls' Linguistic Analogy 228
8.2 Analysis of Nagel's Arguments 231
8.2.1 The Intuitions of Native Speakers Are Decisive in Linguistics 232
8.2.2 The Moral Intuitions of Ordinary Persons Are Not Decisive in Moral Theory 236
8.2.3 Whatever Native Speakers Agree on Is English 238
8.2.4 Whatever Ordinary Individuals Agree in Condemning Is Not Necessarily Wrong 240

8.2.5   The Plausibility of an Ethical Theory Can Change
        Our Moral Intuitions, but the Plausibility of a
        Linguistic Theory Cannot Change Our Linguistic
        Intuitions   248
8.2.6   In Linguistics, Unlike Ethics, the Final Test of a
        Theory Is Its Ability to Explain the Data   257
8.3   Objections and Replies   258
8.4   Summary   264

9   Ronald Dworkin and the Distinction between I-Morality
    and E-Morality   266
9.1   Dworkin's Analysis of Rawls' Linguistic Analogy   268
        9.1.1   The Natural Model versus the Constructive Model 269
        9.1.2   The Natural Model and Reflective Equilibrium Are
                Incompatible   271
9.2   Problems with Dworkin's Analysis   274
9.3   Dworkin's Misinterpretations of Rawls   276
        9.3.1   Subject Matter   277
        9.3.2   Goal   280
        9.3.3   Evidence   282
        9.3.4   Method   287
9.4   Objections and Replies   291
9.5   Brief Remarks about Moral Grammar and Human Rights   295
9.6   Summary   303

PART FOUR: CONCLUSION

10   Toward a Universal Moral Grammar   307

Appendix: Six Trolley Problem Experiments   319
Bibliography   361
Index   393

Tables and Figures

TABLES

1.1	Some Modern Authors Who Draw a Linguistic Analogy (1625–2000)	page 8
2.1	Seven Main Problems in the Theory of Moral Cognition	29
3.1	The Basic Elements of Rawls' Linguistic Analogy	59
3.2	The Heart of Rawls' Linguistic Analogy	67
4.1	Considered Judgments Elicited by Six Trolley Problems	86
5.1	Twelve Trolley Problems	106
5.2	Twelve Considered Judgments	111
5.3	The Poverty of the Perceptual Stimulus	115
6.1	Purposely and Knowingly Harmful Acts and Omissions	146
6.2	A Periodic Table of Moral Elements (Version 1)	154
6.3	A Periodic Table of Moral Elements (Version 2)	159
6.4	Manipulating Structural Features: Fourteen New Trolley Problems	163
9.1	Dworkin's "Natural" and "Constructive" Interpretations of Rawls' Conception of Moral Theory	278
A.1	Justifications for the Bystander and Footbridge Problems by 10 Subjects in Experiment 2 (Within-Subject Design)	332
A.2	Explaining Six Trolley Problems as a Function of the Principle of Double Effect	336
A.3	Explaining Six Trolley Problems as a Function of the Pauline Principle	338

FIGURES

4.1	Simple Perceptual and Acquisition Models for Language and Morality	89
5.1	Deontic Concepts and Deontic Logic: (a) Deontic Modality in Natural Language; (b) Square of Opposition and Equipollence	105

xi

5.2 Classifying the Stimulus: (a) Scheme; (b) Application to the
Bystander Problem 112

5.3 Two Inadequate Appraisal Theories: (a) Unanalyzed Link in
Haidt's (2001) Model of Moral Judgment; (b) Inadequacy of
Greene's (2001, 2002) Personal–Impersonal Distinction 113

5.4 Expanded Perceptual Model for Moral Judgment 114

5.5 Structural Descriptions of Action Plans in Footbridge and
Bystander Problems 118

5.6 Alternative Structural Descriptions of Action Plans in
Footbridge and Bystander Problems 119

6.1 Circumstances Alter Cases: (a) Variance in Six Trolley
Problem Experiments; (b) Six Structural Descriptions; (c) An
Illustration of Mill's (1843) "Mental Chemistry" 127

6.2 Computing Structural Descriptions 168

6.3 Moral Geometry: Varying Structural Descriptions of Four
Identical Sets of Act-Type Descriptions 174

7.1 Schematic Diagram of Rawls' Definition of Reflective
Equilibrium in Section 4 of *A Theory of Justice* 206

7.2 Schematic Diagram of Rawls' Account of the Problem of
Normative Adequacy in *A Theory of Justice* 209

8.1 Chomsky's (1964) Perceptual Model 253

8.2 Three Formats for Representing "Ian will throw the man
onto the track": (a) Tree Diagram; (b) Rewrite Rules; (c)
Labeled Brackets 254

9.1 Hohfeld's (1913, 1917) Fundamental Legal Conceptions 301

A.1 Moral Judgments of Two Act Types in Experiment 1
(Purposeful Battery vs. Knowing Battery) 322

A.2 Moral Judgments of Two Act Types in Experiment 1 by Gender
(Purposeful Battery vs. Knowing Battery) 322

A.3 Moral Judgments of Two Act Types in Experiment 2
(Purposeful Battery vs. Knowing Battery) 327

A.4 Moral Judgments of Two Act Types in Experiment 2 by Gender
(Purposeful Battery vs. Knowing Battery) 327

A.5 Moral Judgments of Two Act Types in Experiment 2
(Good Effects vs. Bad Effects) 328

A.6 Moral Judgments of Two Act Types in Experiment 2
by Gender (Good Effects vs. Bad Effects) 328

A.7 Moral Judgments of Two Act Types in Experiment 2
(Purposeful Battery vs. Implied Consent) 329

A.8 Moral Judgments of Two Act Types in Experiment 2 by Gender
(Purposeful Battery vs. Implied Consent) 329

A.9 Moral Judgments of Two Act Types in Experiment 3
(Purposeful Battery vs. Knowing Battery) 334

A.10 Moral Judgments of Two Act Types in Experiment 3
      (Good Effects vs. Bad Effects)   335
A.11 Moral Judgments of Two Act Types in Experiment 3
      (Purposeful Battery vs. Implied Consent)   335
A.12 Moral Judgments of Two Act Types in Experiment 4
      (Purposeful Battery vs. Knowing Battery)   339
A.13 Moral Judgments of Two Act Types in Experiment 4
      by Gender (Purposeful Battery vs. Knowing Battery)   340
A.14 Moral Judgments of Two Act Types in Experiment 5
      (Purposeful Homicide vs. Knowing Homicide)   344
A.15 Moral Judgments of Two Act Types in Experiment 5
      (Better Alternative vs. Knowing Homicide)   344
A.16 Moral Judgments of Two Act Types in Experiment 5
      (Disproportional Death vs. Knowing Homicide)   345
A.17 Moral Judgments of Two Act Types in Experiment 6
      (Purposeful Battery vs. Knowing Battery)   348

Preface

At first glance, Freud and St. Paul offer two competing accounts of human nature. On Freud's view, human beings are essentially predatory toward one another. On St. Paul's more optimistic conception, principles of justice and fairness spring from their nature as social creatures. The apparent conflict between these two familiar accounts can be reconciled, however, by means of a competence–performance distinction. Freud describes how humans often do in fact behave toward one another. Writing a decade before the most vicious mass murder machine in history was unleashed on its defenseless victims, he correctly observes that under some circumstances "men are not gentle, friendly creatures wishing for love, who simply defend themselves if they are attacked ... [but] savage beasts to whom the thought of sparing their own kind is alien." St. Paul focuses on different behaviors, however, and he also seems correct to infer from them that certain basic norms of conduct are engraved in the mind as a kind of innate instinct. This influential idea, although promoted by the Stoics and embraced by many Jewish and Christian writers, is neither exclusively Western nor inherently religious. Substantially the same notion can be found in the Hindu concept of *dharma*, the Confucian concept of *li*, and the writings of the Mu'tazilites and other Islamic rationalists, for example. Likewise, the hypothesis of an innate moral faculty is what supplies the foundation of the *jus gentium* or law of nations in its traditional, secular formulation. In 1625, Hugo Grotius set the tone for the modern scientific analysis of these subjects and thereby heralded the emancipation of ethics and jurisprudence from theology with his famous *etiamsi daremus* remark ("even if we should concede") in the Prolegomena to the *Law of War and Peace*, asserting that a natural moral law would exist even if there were no God, or human affairs were of no concern to him.

This book seeks to revive and develop aspects of the humanistic enterprise pioneered by Grotius and other Enlightenment philosophers by describing and explaining elements of moral cognition within a modern cognitive science framework. The linchpin is the analogy between rules of justice and rules of grammar, and the gnomon or measuring device is the trolley problem and other artfully designed thought experiments. Just as repeated observations of the gnomon's shadow gave birth to the science of astronomy by enabling ancient astronomers to compile and organize vast amounts of information about the daily and annual variation of the sun (Kuhn 1957), so too can repeated observations of the moral capacities of human nature as reflected in a variety of common moral judgments provide a secure foundation for moral theory. This, at any rate, is the guiding assumption of the research program described in these pages.

This book began as my Ph.D. dissertation, "Rawls' Linguistic Analogy: A Study of the 'Generative Grammar' Model of Moral Theory Described by John Rawls in *A Theory of Justice*," which was submitted to the Department of Philosophy at Cornell University in 2000. Most of the original research was done at Harvard University and the Massachusetts Institute of Technology from 1995 to 1999, beginning with a paper on moral competence I wrote for Noam Chomsky in the spring of 1995 and a series of illuminating conversations about moral theory I held with John Rawls later that summer, before the unfortunate event of his first stroke. The book also draws from the initial trolley problem studies I conducted at MIT from 1995 to 1999, when I was a visiting researcher in Elizabeth Spelke's Infant Cognition Lab. Many of the book's main ideas are therefore nearly 15 years old, although they have begun only recently to receive widespread attention, due in part to their popularization by other writers and to the growing use of trolley problems and similar cases to investigate the nature of human moral intuitions.

When I was in graduate school, moral psychology was not a thriving academic discipline, and moral philosophy was for the most part resolutely anti-empirical. As a result, I often found it difficult to persuade philosophers that combining some of Rawls' and Chomsky's theoretical insights with actual experiments on people's moral intuitions was a worthwhile dissertation topic. That would be psychology, not philosophy, is the essence of what I was told. Fortunately, things have now changed, and a new generation of philosophers that seeks to "introduce the experimental method of reasoning into moral subjects" (Hume) and thereby make contributions to cognitive science is receiving greater encouragement. Meanwhile, many psychologists now pursue research on moral cognition along the lines outlined in this book and related publications.

Legal theory has also undergone a transformation in the past decade. Many legal scholars now pay closer attention to the cognitive and brain sciences, and jurisprudence is gradually returning to its naturalistic roots as the attempt to systematize and explain the human sense of justice with the aid of a technical legal vocabulary (as both Adam Smith and Thomas Reid credited Grotius with doing; see *The Theory of Moral Sentiments*, VII.iv.37, and *Essays on the Active Powers of the Human Mind*, III). Likewise, cognitive scientists are increasingly drawing on the highly refined concepts of moral and legal theory in the design and analysis of their experiments. In light of all these developments, it is gratifying to observe that one of the primary motivations of the linguistic analogy – to help promote greater collaborative and interdisciplinary research on human moral capabilities – has already begun to be realized.

It seems unnecessary to observe that much has been learned in the past decade about the topics discussed in this book. In editing and revising the original manuscript for publication, I have not attempted to incorporate what has been accomplished during the intervening period in any systematic fashion. Rather, with a few exceptions, I have sought to preserve and extend the basic structure and argument of *Rawls' Linguistic Analogy* as much as possible, despite certain inherent limitations of this procedure. If I were to begin again today from scratch, I would probably write a very different book, one geared less toward fitting my own ideas about moral theory into the format of Rawls' brief remarks on the linguistic analogy in *A Theory of Justice* and more toward the independent development of a naturalistic moral psychology within broad scientific parameters. On balance, however, I continue to believe that there are significant advantages to the synthetic approach adopted here, which begins with certain well-known ideas of two seminal thinkers and seeks to integrate and build upon them.

In addition to Rawls and Chomsky, the framework within which this study unfolds draws heavily on the work of Alan Donagan, Philippa Foot, Alvin Goldman, Elizabeth Spelke, Judith Jarvis Thomson, and other highly original researchers, and some familiarity with the fields of linguistics and cognitive science, on the one hand, and moral theory and jurisprudence, on the other, is presupposed. Because I hope to reach a wide and diverse audience, I have nonetheless tried whenever possible to write in plain English and avoid unnecessary academic jargon. However unrealistic, my role models in this regard have been such lucid writers as Descartes, Hume, Mill, and Russell, and as Einstein would have it, my aim throughout the book, however imperfectly realized, has been to render things as simple as possible, but no simpler. At the same time, because of their exceptional value in the clarification and development of scientific ideas, I have not hesitated to utilize symbolic notations, mathematical formulas, structural diagrams, or technical terminology where this has seemed necessary or appropriate. I have also sought to bear in mind Rawls' wise observation that, in explicating commonsense morality, one must learn from one's predecessors and recognize that "morals is not like physics: it is not a matter of ingenious discovery but of noticing lots of obvious things and keeping them all in reasonable balance at the same time" (Rawls 1951b: 579–580; cf. Kant 1993/1788: 8). Hence the ample use throughout the book of quotations, historical illustrations, parenthetical references, and other pedagogical resources. In this respect, my greatest ambition for the book will be realized if it can stimulate further research and serve as an accessible and useful resource for students of law, philosophy, and cognitive science to advance these fields of inquiry.

***

I have incurred enormous debts in writing this book and the articles and chapters from which it draws. Indeed, the list of individuals from whom I have received assistance in this regard is embarrassingly long. Some of these debts stretch back decades, and many of those to whom I am most indebted are sadly no longer alive.

I would like first to thank the four members of my dissertation committee under whose formal direction I worked on this project from 1995 to 2000: Noam Chomsky, Richard Miller, Jason Stanley, and Allen Wood. I learned a great deal from each of them, and each gave generously of their time in helping me to finish the dissertation. Noam and Allen, in particular, deserve special thanks for the extraordinary support and guidance they have given me over the course of nearly two decades.

During the early stages of my research, David Lyons, Terry Irwin, and Nicholas Sturgeon offered penetrating criticisms of my original dissertation proposals. I remain grateful for their assistance and hope they find some return on that investment here. I would also like to thank the other faculty members of the Sage School of Philosophy at Cornell University from whom I received my initial graduate training in philosophy: Richard Boyd, Mark Crimmins, Gail Fine, Harold Hodes, Karen Jones, and Sydney Shoemaker. During the early stages of this project, Carl Ginet, Scott MacDonald, Henry Shue, and Zoltan Gendler Szabo made time for me and offered useful advice. Finally, I wish to thank a terrific group of fellow graduate students at Cornell, with whom I had many stimulating conversations that sharpened my understanding of philosophy, and moral philosophy in particular. In this regard, I am conscious of specific debts to Tom Bennigson, Travis Butler, Rebecca Copenhaver, Jennifer Dworkin, Stephen Gardiner, Eric Hiddleston, Keith McPartland, Thaddeus Metz, Joe Moore, David Robb, Susanna Siegel, Chris Sturr, Christie Thomas, Martino Traxler, Ralph Wedgwood, and Jessica Wilson.

My first papers on Rawls were written for Christine Korsgaard and T.M. Scanlon, both of whom supplied me with helpful feedback. Chris and Tim were also instrumental in enabling me to participate in the Harvard Workshop in Moral and Political Philosophy from 1994 to 1996, where I presented my ideas on Rawls' linguistic analogy for the first time. At Harvard, I also had the opportunity to take courses with Chris, Tim, Warren Goldfarb, Hilary Putnam, and Gisela Striker, and to engage in fruitful conversations about moral and legal theory with Anthony Appiah, Scott Brewer, Howard Gardner, Carol Gilligan, Duncan Kennedy, Fred Neuhouser, Robert Nozick, Derek Parfit, and Frederick Schauer. In June 1995, I had the pleasure of meeting John Rawls, and was lucky enough to discuss specific aspects of his work with him on several occasions thereafter. From 1995 to 1999, I served as a teaching Fellow for Seyla Benhabib, Cary Coglianese, and Kenneth Winston, and greatly benefited from conversations about ethics with all three. Finally, I received valuable input on this project from another exceptional group of fellow graduate students and visitors, including Carla Bagnoli, Sean Greenberg, Steven Gross, Erin Kelly, Thomas

Kelly, Rahul Kumar, Daniel Markovitz, Ian Proops, Faviola Rivera-Castro, Tamar Schapiro, Angela Smith, David Sussman, Alec Walen, and Leif Wenar. I thank all of these people for helping me to write this book and for making my tenure at Harvard such a rewarding experience.

In 1995, I took my first course in linguistics and cognitive science with Noam Chomsky. Shortly thereafter I became affiliated with MIT's Department of Brain and Cognitive Sciences, and over the next four years I was fortunate to receive critical feedback and assistance on this project from many linguists and cognitive scientists, including James Blair, Sylvain Bromberger, Stephen Chorover, Danny Fox, Ted Gibson, Dan Grodner, Kenneth Hale, Morris Halle, Alan Hein, Nancy Kanwisher, Jerrold Katz, Frank Keil, Howard Lasnik, Alec Marantz, Gary Marcus, Jon Nissenbaum, Camillo Padoa-Schioppa, Steven Pinker, Mary Potter, Liina Pylkkanen, Whitman Richards, Javid Sadr, Roger Shepard, Mriganka Sur, Tessa Warren, Kenneth Wexler, and Yaoda Xu. While at MIT, I frequently attended graduate courses in linguistics taught by Michel DeGraff, Irene Heim, Kai von Fintel, Alex Marantz, and David Pesetsky. I thank them for giving me this valuable opportunity. Despite a busy schedule, Sally McConnell-Ginet generously agreed to sit as proxy for Noam Chomsky during my final dissertation examination. She also provided many helpful comments on the penultimate draft of that manuscript, for which I am very grateful.

I owe a special debt to Elizabeth Spelke, with whom I had the good fortune to collaborate during the early stages of this enterprise. Liz has taught me a tremendous amount about cognitive science, and I am extremely grateful for her guidance and enthusiasm. I would also like to emphasize my extensive debt to Cristina Sorrentino, with whom I was privileged to work closely for several years in launching the empirical component of this project. Other alums of the Spelke Lab to whom I owe thanks include Kirsten Condry, Sue Hespos, Lori Markson, Lori Santos, Bill Turkel, and Fei Xu. All of these individuals, especially Liz and Cristina, were influential in helping me to devise and analyze the trolley problems discussed in Part Two.

My debts to Philippe Schlenker, Chris Moore, Rajesh Kasturirangan, and, above all, Matthias Mahlmann and Joshua Tenenbaum, are even greater, and indeed would be hard to overestimate. For well over a decade, I have maintained a running dialogue with each of them about the ideas contained in this book. These delightfully stimulating conversations have had a profound impact on how I understand the fields of linguistics, cognitive science, neuroscience, and ethics. I extend to all five of them my heartfelt thanks for their advice, comments, criticisms, and, most importantly, their friendship.

Making the transition from graduate school to law school was not always easy, but Stanford Law School proved to be the ideal intellectual environment in which to do so. I was fortunate to find generous mentors at Stanford who cultivated my legal skills while also encouraging the research I had begun in graduate school. It would be difficult to overstate how much I owe Tom Grey,

Pam Karlan, and Mark Kelman in this respect. For their support and encouragement, I would also like to thank Barbara Babcock, Joe Bankman, Richard Craswell, George Fisher, Barbara Fried, Hank Greely, Joe Grundfest, Larry Lessig, Mitch Polinsky, Jeff Strnad, Kathleen Sullivan, and Bob Weisberg. Among the friends and classmates whose patience I tested with my ramblings about the implications of cognitive science for jurisprudence, I am especially grateful to Fred Bloom, William Boyd, Kevin Collins, Cara Drinan, Kevin Driscoll, David Freeman Engstrom, Nora Freeman Engstrom, Roberto Gonzalez, Scott Hemphill, Josh Klein, Adam Kolber, Katherine McCarron, Sanjay Mody, Julian Davis Mortenson, John Ostergren, and Christian Turner. After law school, I was fortunate to clerk for Judge Rosemary Barkett on the U.S. Court of Appeals for the Eleventh Circuit and to work alongside a great group of co-clerks: Cecily Baskir, Jeff Bowen, Keith Donoghue, Morgan Doran, Ian Eliasoph, Hannah Garry, Angela Littwin, and Alan Pegg. I thank Judge Barkett and my co-clerks for taking a keen interest in my academic work and offering their ideas and suggestions.

Georgetown University Law Center has been a remarkably warm and hospitable environment in which to teach, write, and pursue interdisciplinary scholarship. For their generous support of the research that went into completing the final stages of this book, I wish to thank Deans Alex Aleinikoff and Judy Areen and Associate Deans Larry Gostin, Vicki Jackson, and Robin West. David Luban, Henry Richardson, Nancy Sherman, and Robin West have been extraordinarily kind and generous philosophical mentors, and I could not ask for more enthusiastic and supportive colleagues than Randy Barnett, Julie Cohen, David Cole, Dan Ernst, Chai Feldblum, James Forman, Steve Goldberg, Lisa Heinzerling, Emma Coleman Jordan, Greg Klass, Don Langevoort, Marty Lederman, Carrie Menkel-Meadow, Naomi Mezey, Julie O'Sullivan, Nina Pillard, Mitt Regan, Mike Seidman, David Vladeck, Ethan Yale, and Kathy Zeiler. Many other colleagues at Georgetown have offered assistance or encouraged me in a variety of ways. In particular, I would like to thank Chuck Abernathy, Lama Abu-Odeh, Jane Aiken, Tom Beauchamp, Norman Birnbaum, Sue Bloch, Gregg Bloche, Rosa Brooks, Peter Byrne, Alisa Carse, Steve Cohen, Wayne Davis, Michael Diamond, Richard Diamond, Viet Dinh, Robert Drinan, Peter Edelman, Jim Feinerman, Heidi Li Feldman, Steven Goldblatt, Chuck Gustafson, Bob Haft, Paul Heck, Kris Henning, Craig Hoffman, Bryce Huebner, John Jackson, Neal Katyal, Pat King, Lauri Kohn, David Koplow, Mark Lance, Chuck Lawrence, Richard Lazarus, Amanda Leiter, Adam Levitin, Judy Lichtenberg, David Lightfoot, Maggie Little, Wally Mlyniec, Jon Molot, Mark Murphy, Jim Oldham, Carol O'Neil, Les Orsy, Joe Page, Gary Peller, Terry Pinkard, Madison Powers, Nick Rosenkranz, Susan Deller Ross, Paul Rothstein, Peter Rubin, Alvaro Santos, Andy Schoenholtz, Jodi Short, Gerry Spann, Jane Stromseth, Peter Tague, Dan Tarullo, Jay Thomas, Philomila Tsoukala, Mark Tushnet, Rebecca Tusnhet, Carlos Vazquez, Pete Wales, and Si Wasserstrom.

The main arguments of this book have been presented at numerous workshops, seminars, conferences, and lectures, including legal theory workshops at Cardozo, Georgetown, Harvard, Illinois, Stanford, Virginia, and Yale law schools; philosophy talks at Cornell University, Dickinson College, Georgetown University, George Washington University, University of Berlin, University of British Columbia, University of New Mexico, and University of Toledo; graduate psychology seminars at Cornell University, MIT, and Stanford University; annual meetings of the American Association of Law Schools, American Philosophical Association, Cognitive Science Society, International Association for Philosophy of Law and Social Philosophy, Society for Philosophy and Psychology, and Society for Research in Child Development; philosophy and cognitive science conferences sponsored by the Air Force Office of Scientific Research, Brooklyn Law School, California Institute of Technology, Gruter Institute for Law and Behavioral Research, Harvard University Department of Psychology, Kellogg School of Management, MIT Computer Science and Artificial Intelligence Laboratory, Office of Naval Research, Princeton University Center for Human Values, Society for Evolutionary Analysis in Law, United Kingdom Arts and Humanities Research Council, University of Chicago Center for Law, Philosophy and Human Values, and Yale University Cowles Foundation for Economic Research; and invited lectures hosted by the MIT Culture and Technology Forum, MIT Department of Brain and Cognitive Sciences, Peter Wall Institute for Advanced Studies, Stanford University Department of Psychology, UCLA Center for Behavior, Evolution and Culture, and University of Maryland Cognitive Science Colloquium. I thank the organizers of these events as well as the many participants whose comments and criticisms helped to sharpen my understanding of various aspects of this research program.

This undertaking could not have been completed without additional support from a number of individuals and institutions. Joshua Greene supplied lengthy and detailed criticisms as a reviewer for Cambridge University Press and thereafter revealed his identity to initiate a fruitful exchange of ideas that continues to this day. I thank him along with a second, anonymous reviewer for their valuable input. Several other people read all or part of this manuscript in its early stages as a doctoral dissertation and gave me advice and encouragement, including Susan Dwyer, Gilbert Harman, Marc Hauser, Ray Jackendoff, James McGilvray, Julius Moravscik, Shaun Nichols, Jesse Prinz, Rebecca Saxe, Peter Singer, and M.B.E. Smith. For their outstanding editorial assistance, I wish to thank David Anderson, James Dunn, Catherine Fox, Helen Wheeler, and the other editors at Cambridge University Press, particularly Beatrice Rehl, who patiently shepherded this book to completion despite several unexpected delays. At various stages of this project, I relied on a talented group of research assistants, including Michael Dockery, Ben Dooling, Martin Hewett, Izzat Jarudi, Sean Kellem, Jennifer Rosenberg, and Amber Smith. In addition, I have benefited enormously from the expert assistance of research librarians at Cornell, Georgetown, Harvard, MIT, and Stanford. I also would like to acknowledge the generous financial support of Georgetown University Law Center, Stanford Law School, Peter Wall Institute of Advanced Studies, and the Air Force Office of Scientific Research, along with the helpful feedback of the students in my Law and Philosophy, Law, Mind, and Brain, and Law, Cognitive Science, and Human Rights seminars. Finally, I wish to express my deepest appreciation to my siblings and extended family. They have been unfailingly supportive of this endeavor from start to finish.

My greatest intellectual debt in connection with this project is owed to Noam Chomsky. As a graduate student, visitor, and teaching Fellow in his courses on the foundations of linguistic theory, I heard him lecture many times throughout the 1990s. These lectures were among the most stimulating academic experiences of my life. They sparked a love of philosophy, linguistics, and cognitive science that has stayed with me ever since. Even more importantly, over the course of several decades I have spent countless hours in personal conversations with him, discussing not only academic subjects, but also history, politics, activism, and life in general. To say I am grateful for these opportunities and humbled by the interest he has shown in my work would be an extreme understatement.

Many other friends, colleagues, and associates from a variety of disciplines and professions have helped me to write this book by discussing its central ideas with me and offering their comments, criticisms, and suggestions. With apologies to those I may have omitted, I would like in particular to thank Tom Abowd, Samir Abu-Absi, Matt Adler, Ralph Adolphs, David Albert, Larry Alexander, Ronald Allen, Ernie Alleva, Scott Atran, Jack Balkin, Susan Bandes, Zenon Bankowski, Jonathan Baron, Charles Barzun, Clark Barrett, Dan Bartels, Daniel Batson, Paul Bello, Gregory Berns, Mira Bernstein, Paul Bloom, Jeremy Blumenthal, Susanna Blumenthal, Alexander Bolyanatz, Rob Boyd, Michael Bratman, David Brink, Russ Burnett, Colin Camerer, Susan Carey, Peter Carruthers, Bill Casebeer, Michael Chandler, Jules Coleman, Fiery Cushman, Antonio Damasio, Jonathan Dancy, John Darley, Stephen Darwall, Peter DeScioli, Frans De Waal, Peter Ditto, John Doris, Emmanuel Dupoux, Matti Eklund, Jakob Elster, David Farber, Dan Fessler, John Martin Fischer, Alan Fiske, Simon Fitzpatrick, John Flavell, Rob Folger, Ken Forbus, Charles Fried, Mark Geistfeld, Tamar Gendler, Tracey George, Itzhak Gilboa, Herbert Gintis, John Goldberg, Matthew Goldberg, Alvin Goldman, Oliver Goodenough, Noah Goodman, Ryan Goodman, Geoffrey Goodwin, Alison Gopnik, Tom Griffiths, Chris Guthrie, Knud Haakonssen, Jonathan Haidt, Todd Handy, Brian Hare, Paul Harris, Deborah Hellman, Tony Honore, Norbert Hornstein, Heidi Hurd, Elisa Hurley, Douglas Husak, Pierre Jacob, Derek Jinks, Kent Johnson, Owen Jones, Craig Joseph, Paul Kahn, Frances Kamm, Jerry Kang, Robin Kar, Deborah Kelemen, Eldon Kerr, Melanie

Killen, Katie Kinzler, Toby Knapp, Nicola Knight, Joshua Knobe, Andrew Koppelman, Philipp Koralus, Kevin Kordana, Rob Kurzban, Doug Kysar, Nicola Lacey, Jason Lambert, Stephen Laurence, Brian Leiter, James Lenman, Neal Levy, Daphna Lewinsohn-Zamir, Jeff Lipshaw, Terje Lohndal, Tania Lombrozo, Eric Lormand, Eleanor Maccoby, Ken MacCrimmon, Edouard Machery, Maleiha Malik, Bertram Malle, Ron Mallon, Ruth Barcan Marcus, Mohan Matthan, Lester Mazor, Sarah McGrath, Steve McKay, Doug Medin, Andy Meltzoff, Robert Mnookin, Jorge Moll, Read Montague, Michael Moore, Christopher Morris, Jonathan Morris, Cynthia Moss, Thomas Nadelhoffer, Janice Nadler, Caleb Nelson, James Nickel, Jay Noonan, Alastair Norcross, Vanessa Nurock, Dennis Patterson, Michael Perry, Paul Pietroski, David Pizzaro, Thomas Pogge, Richard Posner, Danny Priel, Anne Pusey, Tage Rai, Peter Railton, Chandra Raman, Georges Rey, Paul Robinson, Evelyn Rosset, Hubert Rottleuthner, Jed Rubenfeld, Laura Schulz, Thomas Schuman, Micah Schwartzman, Amy Sepinwall, Scott Shapiro, Seana Shiffrin, Shinsuke Shimojo, Rick Shweder, Joan Silk, Ken Simons, Brian Simpson, Walter Sinnott-Armstrong, Steven Sloman, Steven Smith, Bryan Sokol, Larry Solan, Robert Solomon, Larry Solum, Luke Sotir, Dan Sperber, Chandra Sripada, Jeffrey Stake, Stephen Stich, Lynn Stout, Luke Swartz, David Tabachnick, Gillian Thomson, Judith Jarvis Thomson, Christian Thordal, J.D. Trout, Eliot Turiel, Bas Van Frassen, Peter Vranas, Michael Waldmann, Michael Walker, Wendell Wallach, Jonathan Weinberg, Catherine Wilson, John Witt, Andrew Woods, Amanda Woodward, Jen Wright, Ekow Yankah, Liane Young, Paul Zak, Eyal Zamir, and Ben Zipursky.

Without doubt, I owe the most to my wife, Sarah; my children, Hannah and Andrew; and my parents, Ramzy and Maryse Mikhail. Words cannot express how much they mean to me. With love, devotion, and gratitude, I dedicate this book to them.

***

Some portions of this book are drawn from previously published work, including the following articles: "Law, Science, and Morality: A Review of Richard Posner's 'The Problematics of Moral and Legal Theory,'" *Stanford Law Review* 54, 1057–1127 (2002); "Moral Heuristics or Moral Competence? Reflections on Sunstein," *Behavioral and Brain Sciences*, 28, 557–558 (2005); "Universal Moral Grammar: Theory, Evidence, and the Future," *Trends in Cognitive Sciences*, 11, 143–152 (2007); and "'Plucking the Mask of Mystery from Its Face': Jurisprudence and H.L.A. Hart," *Georgetown Law Journal*, 95, 733–779 (2007); "Scottish Common Sense and Nineteenth-Century American Law: A Critical Appraisal," *Law and History Review*, 26, 167–175 (2008); "Moral Grammar and Intuitive Jurisprudence: A Formal Model of Unconscious Moral and Legal Knowledge," *Psychology of Learning and Motivation*, 50, 27–100 (2009).

PART ONE

THEORY

The rules of justice may be compared to the rules of grammar; the rules of the other virtues, to the rules which critics lay down for the attainment of what is sublime and elegant in composition. The one, are precise, accurate, and indispensable. The other, are loose, vague, and indeterminate, and present us rather with a general idea of the perfection we ought to aim at, than afford us any certain and infallible directions for acquiring it.

– Adam Smith, *The Theory of Moral Sentiments*

I

The Question Presented

The peasant, or the child, can reason, and judge, and speak his language, with a discernment, a consistency, and a regard to analogy, which perplex the logician, the moralist, and the grammarian, when they would find the principle upon which the proceeding is founded, or when they would bring to general rules, what is so familiar, and so well sustained in particular cases.

   – Adam Ferguson, *An Essay on the History of Civil Society*

Is the theory of moral cognition usefully modeled on aspects of Universal Grammar? Noam Chomsky has suggested on a number of occasions that it might be (see, e.g., 1978, 1986a, 1988a, 1993a). In *A Theory of Justice,* John Rawls makes a similar suggestion and compares his own elaborate characterization of the sense of justice with the linguist's account of linguistic competence (1971: 46–53). A number of other philosophers, including Stephen Stich (1993), Alvin Goldman (1993), Susan Dwyer (1999), Matthias Mahlmann (1999), and Gilbert Harman (2000), among others, have ruminated publicly about the idea as well. Despite this, and despite the fact that the competence–performance distinction and other parts of Chomsky's basic theoretical framework have been successfully utilized in other areas of cognitive science, such as vision and musical cognition,[1] little sustained attention has been given to examining what a research program in moral cognition modeled on central features of Universal Grammar might look like, or how traditional philosophical questions about the nature of morality might be fruitfully addressed in these terms. The present study attempts to fill this gap.

---

[1] For visual cognition, see, for example, Gregory (1970), Marr (1982), and Richards (1988). For musical cognition, see, for example, Bernstein (1976), Lerdahl & Jackendoff (1983), and Jackendoff (1992: 165–183). For a recent attempt to apply parts of Chomsky's framework to the empirical investigation of logical cognition, see Macnamara (1986). I am indebted to Joshua Tenenbaum for many helpful discussions about possible applications of Chomsky's framework to the cognitive sciences and for directing me toward the essay on visual competence by Richards.

A natural place to begin taking a fresh look at the topic is Rawls' influential book *A Theory of Justice.* In the 1950s and 1960s Chomsky transformed the study of language and mind by arguing that all normal human beings are endowed with a genetic program for language acquisition. Chomsky drew attention to the fact that, prior to any formal instruction, once a child has mastered her native language, she is able to make a wide range of intuitive judgments about the properties and relations of expressions in her language, including whether any random sound sequence constitutes a grammatical sentence, whether a given expression is ambiguous, and whether one of two arbitrary expressions is a rhyme, paraphrase, entailment, or contradiction of the other. Chomsky argued that these and other linguistic behaviors would be inexplicable without presupposing the child's tacit knowledge of the grammar of her language. He reoriented theoretical linguistics toward the empirical investigation of the principles underlying this postulated knowledge, or what he labeled *linguistic competence;* and he thereby helped revive aspects of the rationalist tradition of Plato, Descartes, Leibniz, and Kant.

Rawls was one of the first philosophers to recognize the potential implications of Chomsky's project for moral philosophy. In Section 9 of *A Theory of Justice,* he pointed to several structural similarities between the descriptive part of ethics and theoretical linguistics, and he suggested that just as the latter studies aspects of linguistic competence, so the former should be directed toward investigating our *moral* competence, or what Rawls called there our "sense of justice" (1971: 46).[2] Rawls thus signaled his displacement of the narrower, semantic concerns of early twentieth-century analytic philosophers such as G. E. Moore (1903), A. J. Ayer (1946/1936), and Charles L. Stevenson (1944)[3] and a return to an older conception of ethics, assumed by nearly all

---

[2] Although Rawls uses related phrases, such as "morally competent" and "competent judge," in his early paper "Outline of a Decision Procedure for Ethics" (1951a), the term *moral competence* does not appear in his discussion of moral theory in Section 9 of *A Theory of Justice.* Instead, Rawls identifies his primary object of inquiry in Section 9 by means of different concepts, including "moral capacity," "moral conception," and "sense of justice." For example, instead of holding that the first task of moral philosophy is to describe moral competence, Rawls says "one may think of moral philosophy at first … as the attempt to describe our moral capacity; or, in the present case, one may regard a theory of justice as describing our sense of justice" (1971: 46). Instead of suggesting that an accurate description of moral competence may help resolve long-standing philosophical questions, Rawls writes: "if we can find an accurate account of our moral conceptions, then questions of meaning and justification may prove much easier to answer" (1971: 51). Finally, instead of imputing moral competence to all normal human beings, Rawls assumes "that each person beyond a certain age and possessed of the requisite intellectual capacity develops a sense of justice under normal social circumstances" and "that everyone has in himself the whole form of a moral conception" (1971: 46, 50). In my conversations with him, Rawls confirmed that moral competence, in a sense analogous to Chomsky's notion of linguistic competence, is an accurate description of the moral capacity, sense of justice, or moral conception he takes to be the moral philosopher's provisional object of inquiry in *A Theory of Justice.*

[3] For an early anticipation of this development, see generally Rawls (1951b).

of the leading philosophers and jurists of the Enlightenment, who placed the empirical study of the human mind and its various moral faculties and sentiments at the forefront of their inquiries.[4]

Although *A Theory of Justice* became highly influential, Rawls' linguistic analogy was not warmly received. Early reviews by R. M. Hare (1973), Thomas Nagel (1973), Ronald Dworkin (1973), and Peter Singer (1974) sharply criticized the idea that moral theory could or should be compared to linguistics. More recently, Norman Daniels (1979, 1980), Richard Brandt (1979, 1990), Joseph Raz (1982), and Bernard Williams (1985), among others, have objected to Rawls' idea as well.

Rawls did not defend the linguistic analogy in print after he first proposed it in *A Theory of Justice*. To a certain extent this seems understandable, given his diverse interests and the need to respond to so many criticisms more proximate to what emerged over time as his central, practical concerns. It may also reflect Rawls' tacit agreement with at least some of the objections to the linguistic analogy advanced by his critics.[5] What is quite surprising, however,

---

[4] Moral philosophy, moral psychology, and jurisprudence were not clearly distinct disciplines until at least the latter part of the nineteenth century, and most authors who examined one subject wrote extensively on the others as well. In particular, many of the leading Enlightenment treatises on moral philosophy, natural law, and the law of nations include important discussions of moral psychology. A partial list of such works from which this book draws, ordered chronologically by their date of initial publication (or, in some cases, by their date of original composition), includes the following: Hugo Grotius, *On the Law of War and Peace* (1625), Thomas Hobbes, *Leviathan* (1651), Samuel Pufendorf, *Elements of Universal Jurisprudence* (1660), John Locke, *Essays on the Law of Nature* (1660), Samuel Pufendorf, *On the Law of Nature and Nations* (1672), John Locke, *An Essay Concerning Human Understanding* (1689), G. W. Lebniz, *New Essays on Human Understanding* (1705), Joseph Butler, *Fifteen Sermons on Human Nature* (1726), Francis Hutcheson, *Illustrations on the Moral Sense* (1728), David Hume, *A Treatise of Human Nature* (1739–1740), Christian Wolff, *The Law of Nations Treated According to Scientific Method* (1740–1749), Francis Hutcheson, *A Short Introduction to Moral Philosophy* (1747), Jean-Jacques Burlamaqui, *The Principles of Natural and Politic Law* (1748), David Hume, *An Enquiry Concerning the Principles of Morals* (1751), Jean-Jacques Rousseau, *Discourse on the Origin of Inequality* (1754), Emile Vattel, *The Law of Nations; or Principles of the Law of Nature Applied to the Conduct and Affairs of Nations and Sovereigns* (1758), Adam Smith, *The Theory of Moral Sentiments* (1759), Jean-Jacques Rousseau, *On the Social Contract* (1762), Immanuel Kant, *Groundwork of the Metaphysics of Morals* (1785), Thomas Reid, *Essays on the Intellectual Powers of Man* (1785), Immanuel Kant, *Critique of Practical Reason* (1788), Thomas Reid, *Essays on the Active Powers of the Human Mind* (1788), Mary Wollestonecraft, *A Vindication of the Rights of Men* (1790), James Wilson, *Lectures on Law* (1790–1791), Mary Wollestonecraft, *A Vindication of the Rights of Woman* (1792), and James Mackintosh, *A Discourse on the Law of Nature and Nations* (1799). Compare Sidgwick (1988/1902: 160–161) (noting an "absence of distinction between the provinces of Ethics and Jurisprudence" in the history of moral philosophy prior to Grotius, which Grotius only partially abandoned). For some further discussion, see generally Haakonssen (1996) and Schneewind (1998); see also Mikhail (2007b, 2008c) and the references cited therein.

[5] Some of the alterations that Rawls made to the revised edition of *A Theory of Justice* appear to lend support to this assumption (compare Rawls 1999a: 40–46 with Rawls 1971: 46–53).

is that the debate over the analogy itself has been so one-sided. Until recently, there did not exist a single, sustained defense or critical examination of Rawls' idea in the entire philosophical literature.[6] At first glance, this seems strange. Chomsky's revolution in linguistics has generated a large following and has been thought by many philosophers and scientists to constitute a fundamentally new and promising approach to cognitive psychology and the study of the human mind (see, e.g., George 1989; Harman 1974; Kasher 1991; Otero 1994). Likewise, Rawls' work has been revolutionary in the context of recent moral, political, and legal philosophy, and it has also generated an enormous secondary literature (see, e.g., Wellbank, Snook, & Mason 1982; see generally Freeman 2003; Pogge 2007; Richardson & Weithman 1999). Coupled with the fact that Rawls considers (or at least once considered) moral theory to be a "type of psychology" (Rawls 1975: 7, 9, 22) and, in his most explicit methodological remarks in *A Theory of Justice,* repeatedly compares moral theory to generative linguistics (1971: 46–53), the absence of a detailed study of this comparison seems rather striking.[7]

It may be, of course, that so little has been written on the subject because there is so little of interest to say – in other words, because the analogy is so obviously inapt. This seems to be the general attitude of the critics to which I have referred (cf. Freeman 2007: 34–35). I am of the opposite opinion; and, while I certainly think that there are limits to how far the analogy can be usefully pressed, I believe that substituting moral competence for linguistic competence provides an illuminating perspective from which to view the aims and approach of moral theory.

---

[6] Although the gist of this statement was accurate when I first made it in 1995 as part of my original dissertation proposal, it no longer seems entirely appropriate. Stimulated partly by my previous work on the topic (see, e.g., Mikhail 2000, 2002a, 2002b; Mikhail & Sorrentino 1999; Mikhail, Sorrentino, & Spelke 1998), many important discussions of the linguistic analogy now exist in the literature. See, for example, Dubber (2006), Dupoux & Jacob (2007, 2008), Dwyer (2007, 2008), Dwyer & Hauser (2008), Greene (2005, 2008a, 2008b), Harman (1999, 2008), Hauser (2006), Hauser, Cushman, & Young (2008a, 2008b), Hauser et al. (2007), Jackendoff (2007), Kar (2006), Knobe (2005), Mahlmann (2005a, 2005b, 2007), Mahlmann & Mikhail (2005), Mallon (2008), Mikhail (2005, 2007a, 2007b, 2008a, 2008b), Nado, Kelly, & Stich (2006), Nichols (2005), Patterson (2008), Prinz (2007, 2008a, 2008b, 2008c), Roedder & Harman (2008a, 2008b), Sripada (2008a, 2008b), Sripada & Stich (2006), and Stich (2006). To the best of my knowledge, however, *Rawls' Linguistic Analogy* remains until now the only original book-length treatment of the topic.

[7] For two important statements, written over a century apart, of the importance for moral philosophers to attain a better empirical account of moral psychology, see Bain (1868) and Darwall, Gibbard, & Railton (1992). Compare Anscombe's (1958) important remarks about the need for philosophers to develop a more adequate "philosophical psychology." As Darwall, Gibbard, & Railton (1992: 188–189) observe, by the early 1990s many philosophers began to show renewed interest in moral psychology after a long period of relative neglect (see, e.g., Flanagan 1991; Miller 1992).

In what follows, therefore, I defend Rawls' claim that moral theory can be usefully modeled on aspects of Universal Grammar. My exposition falls into three main parts. In the remainder of Part One, I first introduce the linguistic analogy by identifying some key features of the theory of language to which the study of human morality might be usefully compared, and by drawing on those features to formulate a new analytical framework for the theory of moral cognition. I also examine what Rawls actually says about the nature of moral theory in *A Theory of Justice* and call attention to what, for our purposes, are his remarks' leading features. In Part Two, I attempt to clarify the empirical significance of Rawls' linguistic analogy and thereby place the theory of moral cognition on a sounder footing by formulating and stating a provisional solution to the problem of descriptive adequacy with respect to a range of commonsense moral intuitions, including those discussed in the trolley problem literature that began with the work of Philippa Foot (1967) and Judith Jarvis Thomson (1986). Finally, in Part Three I consider several influential early criticisms of Rawls' linguistic analogy and the conception of moral theory it presupposes – in particular, those of Hare, Singer, Nagel, and Dworkin – and argue that they are without force against the research program that Rawls describes in *A Theory of Justice,* and that I attempt to develop further here.

Before beginning, it may help to make some preliminary clarifications about the remarks that follow. The first concerns the place of the linguistic analogy within the history of philosophy. Rawls is by no means the only author who has compared the rules of justice with the rules of grammar. On the contrary, many other writers have made the same or similar comparisons. Moreover, as the quotations from Smith and Ferguson reveal, the linguistic analogy is, in fact, a traditional one. Indeed, when one looks, one finds that many of the most serious commentators who have attempted to explain the origin and growth of commonsense moral and legal knowledge have turned to the comparison with language for inspiration.[8]

Table 1.1 is a compilation of just some of the authors who, like Rawls, have compared the rules of justice with the rules of grammar, or the theory of morality with the theory of language, in one way or another during the modern period. As Table 1.1 reveals, the linguistic analogy has exercised the imagination not only of philosophers, but also of a wide range of scientists and scholars, including anthropologists, biologists, economists, linguists,

---

[8] As an historical matter, the analogy traces at least as far back as Aristotle's observation that the gift of speech and a sense of justice are what distinguish humans from other animals. See Aristotle, *The Politics,* 1253 a1–15: "[T]hat man is more of a political animal than bees or any other gregarious animal is evident. Nature ... makes nothing in vain, and man is the only animal who has the gift of speech. ... And it is [also] a characteristic of man that he alone has any sense of good and evil, of just and unjust, and the like, and the association of living beings who have this sense makes a family and a state."

TABLE I.I. *Some Modern Authors Who Draw a Linguistic
Analogy (1625–2000)*

Grotius 1625	Gilmore 1974
Hale 1668	Cover 1975
Pufendorf 1673	Donagan 1977
Hutcheson 1730	Chomsky 1978
Hume 1740	Much & Shweder 1978
Rousseau 1754	Quine 1978
Smith 1759	Smith 1979
Ferguson 1767	Perrot 1980
Kant 1783	Kohlberg 1981
Reid 1785	Shweder, Turiel, & Much 1981
Bentham 1789	Grey 1983
Wilson 1790	Gruter & Bohannan 1983
Paine 1791	Hampshire 1983
Von Savigny 1814	Friedman 1985
Feuerbach 1833	Kagan 1987
Mill 1861	Posner 1990
Bain 1868	Tienson 1990
Von Jhering 1869	Ellickson 1991
Darwin 1871	Flanagan 1991
Holland 1880	Fischer & Ravizza 1992
Pollock 1882	Neale 1992
Nietzsche 1887	Goldman 1993
Gray 1909	Johnson 1993
Cohen 1916	Quinn 1993
Piaget 1932	Stich 1993
Pareto 1935	Cosmides & Tooby 1994
Ross 1939	McKie 1994
Burke 1945	Pinker 1994
Ladd 1957	De Waal 1996
Ryle 1958	Stein 1996
Brandt 1959	Fletcher 1998
Oakeshott 1962	Gert 1998
Frankena 1963	Mikhail, Sorrentino, & Spelke 1998
Fuller 1964	Dwyer 1999
Nozick 1968	Harman 1999
Rawls 1971	Jackendoff 1999
Kroy 1973	Mahlmann 1999
Simpson 1973	Mikhail 2000

psychologists, sociologists, political scientists, and lawyers.[9] In light of this, one may wonder what is special about *Rawls'* linguistic analogy, as distinct from the various comparisons that others have drawn. My answer has several parts. First, Rawls stands out as the individual among this group who is perhaps most knowledgeable about both the history of moral philosophy and the theoretical foundations of generative linguistics.[10] Second, Rawls appears to have been the first philosopher to grasp the potential implications of the modern revival of Universal Grammar for ethics. Already in the 1960s one finds other philosophers, such as Robert Nozick (1968: 47–48), drawing inspiration from the competence–performance distinction and other aspects of Chomsky's framework. It was Rawls, however, who first organized and articulated an entire conception of moral theory on that basis. Third, *A Theory of Justice* is arguably the twentieth century's most important book of moral and political philosophy. Richard Rorty (1982: 216) is correct, I believe, to describe it as one of the few "genuine interuniversity paradigms" in an increasingly fragmented field.

A fourth reason why Rawls' linguistic analogy is worthy of special attention concerns how best to interpret the arguments of *A Theory of Justice*. It is a familiar observation that Rawls' text supports different readings and that various methodological and metaethical viewpoints can appear to be consistent with it (see, e.g., Brink 1989). Less attention has been given, however, to the fact that Rawls devotes one section of the book, Section 9, to clarifying how he conceives of the subject matter of moral philosophy, and to making explicit how he thinks the discipline should be pursued. Rawls' stated aims in Section 9 are "to prevent misunderstanding" about "the nature of moral

---

[9] Here I should perhaps clarify that not all of the authors listed in Table 1.1 approach the idea of a linguistic analogy from similar or even compatible theoretical standpoints. For example, Bentham's linguistic analogy arises out of his interest in the link between universal grammar and universal jurisprudence, whereas Von Savigny's does not. Reid holds that both rules of justice and rules of grammar are innate, whereas Mill draws a linguistic analogy to argue that morality is not innate, but learned. Likewise, Chomsky and Quine have quite different views about the apparent similarities and differences between language acquisition and moral development. I am grateful to Allen Wood for calling my attention to the need to highlight this point.

[10] Rawls' knowledge of the history of moral philosophy is well known and needs no elaboration here. Fortunately his lectures on this topic, along with his lectures on political philosophy, have been now published (see Rawls 2000, 2007; for a review of the former, see Mahlmann & Mikhail 2003). Rawls' familiarity with generative linguistics is less well known, but, as I will endeavor to explain, it is substantial and goes deeper than is often assumed (although it does appear inadequate in certain respects). On this point it is worth highlighting that Rawls spent several years helping to build the new Department of Linguistics and Philosophy at MIT in the early 1960s, at a time when Chomsky's new paradigm in linguistics and the philosophy of language and mind began to unfold (for some relevant background, see Pogge 2007). I am grateful to Sylvain Bromberger, Noam Chomsky, Charles Fried, Gilbert Harman, and John Rawls for sharing with me their personal recollections of this period, and for discussing with me the direct and indirect impact of Chomsky's work on Rawls.

theory" by "explaining in more detail the concept of a considered judgment in reflective equilibrium and the reasons for introducing it" (1971: 46). In spite of Rawls' efforts, however, uncertainty over the three key concepts in this statement – considered judgments, reflective equilibrium, and moral theory itself – has been widespread.

In my opinion, Rawls' remarks in Section 9 constitute one of the most powerful short statements about the nature of moral theory ever written. In part this is because of the comparisons between moral theory and generative grammar that Rawls draws. Nonetheless, I believe that a careful review of the secondary literature that has built up around such topics as reflective equilibrium and considered judgments suggests that much of this commentary appears to be misinformed about the development of these concepts in Rawls' philosophy and their counterparts in generative linguistics. By attempting to clarify these issues, I hope to contribute to a better understanding of the conception of moral theory presupposed by Rawls in *A Theory of Justice.*

These remarks lead to another important qualification. It is important to emphasize that all of the references to "Rawls' conception of moral theory" in this book refer *only* to Rawls' stated conception of moral theory during the period 1950–1975. My investigation here is limited to how the "early" Rawls conceives of the subject matter of moral theory – and specifically, the place of the linguistic analogy within that conception – as evidenced primarily by his four main statements on the topic during the early part of his career:

(i) Rawls' Ph.D. dissertation, *A Study in the Grounds of Ethical Knowledge* (1950) (henceforth *Grounds*)

(ii) Rawls' first published article, "Outline of a Decision Procedure for Ethics" (1951a) (henceforth *Outline*)

(iii) Section 9 of *A Theory of Justice,* entitled "Some Remarks on Moral Theory" (1971) (henceforth "Section 9")

(iv) Rawls' 1974 Presidential Address to the American Philosophical Association, "The Independence of Moral Theory" (1975) (henceforth *Independence*).

The naturalistic conception of moral theory that I ascribe to Rawls in these pages may or may not be one he still embraced toward the end of his career.[11] In any case, I believe that whether and, if so, why Rawls' conception of moral

---

[11] Many of Rawls' philosophical views changed over the course of his career. In particular, Rawls moved from conceiving of his theory of justice as part of a comprehensive moral doctrine to regarding it as a political conception of justice that is tied to the specific needs and characteristics of modern liberal democratic societies. Based on my conversations with Rawls, I believe that the naturalistic conception of moral theory outlined in Section 9 of *A Theory of Justice,* which I seek to develop in this book, is one that he continued to embrace in its essentials throughout his career. However, I do not defend this claim here, nor does any part of my argument depend on it. For Rawls' own interpretation of how his theory evolved over time, see generally Rawls (1980, 1985, 1993, 2001a, 2001b).

theory changed over time can be more profitably discussed once the prior question – whether the linguistic analogy and the conception of moral theory it implies are vulnerable to the objections leveled against them – is better understood.

I have said that one aim of this study is to contribute to a better understanding of *A Theory of Justice*. Although this is true, it is important to make clear that the discussion that follows is less about Rawls or Rawls' linguistic analogy *per se* than it is about the linguistic analogy itself – or, more precisely, about the conception of moral theory that Rawls describes in these early texts. My overriding objective is not to argue for a particular interpretation of *A Theory of Justice* but to develop the substantive research program Rawls describes in Section 9 – which I would characterize as Universal Moral Grammar, or more simply, as the scientific study of the moral sense. I agree with Stich (1993: 228) that the future of moral philosophy rests squarely within the cognitive and brain sciences. The theory of moral cognition, however, is at present neglected, underdeveloped, and maligned.[12] There are a variety of reasons for this unfortunate state of affairs. Some are historical and sociological, having to do with the rise of behaviorism, logical positivism, and psychoanalysis, and the struggle of professional philosophers and psychologists to define the boundaries of their respective disciplines. Others are more conceptual. In any event, what seems clear to me, and what I will argue here, is that many of the early criticisms of Rawls' linguistic analogy contributed significantly to this state of affairs. In point of fact, Rawls' early writings contain the germs of a scientific theory of moral cognition that far surpasses the work of psychologists like Jean Piaget (1965/1932) and Lawrence Kohlberg (1981, 1984) in terms of depth, coherence, and analytical rigor. Regrettably, however, some rather specious criticisms that were initially leveled against that

---

[12] Again, this statement seems less accurate today than when it first appeared in the introduction to *Rawls' Linguistic Analogy*. Indeed, in many respects it no longer seems accurate at all: moral psychology is currently experiencing a renaissance and has arguably become one of the most fruitful areas of research in both philosophy and the cognitive and brain sciences, broadly construed. A useful and stimulating collection of essays can be found in the three-volume anthology edited by Walter Sinnott-Armstrong (2008). In addition to these essays and the references listed in note 6, a partial list of notable recent contributions which have informed what follows includes Baron & Ritov (in press), Bartels (2008), Bartels & Medin (2007), Blair (2002), Bucciarelli, Khemlani, & Johnson-Laird (2008), Casebeer (2003), Cushman (2008), Cushman, Young, & Hauser (2006), Doris (2002), Doris & Stich (2005), Gazzaniga (2005), Greene & Haidt (2002), Greene et al. (2001), Haidt (2001), Haidt & Joseph (2004), Kelly et al. (2007), Killen & Smetana (in press), Koenigs et al. (2007), Lombrozo (2008), Machery (2007), Miller (2008), Moll, de Oliveira-Sousa, & Eslinger (2003), Nichols (2004), Nichols & Mallon (2006), Pinker (2008), Pizarro & Bloom (2003), Robinson, Kurzban, & Jones (2008), Saxe (2005), Schnall et al. (2008), Sinnott-Armstrong et al. (2008), Solum (2006), Sunstein (2005), Tetlock (2003), Valdesolo & DeSteno (2006), Waldmann & Dieterich (2007), Wellman & Miller (2008), Wheatley & Haidt (2005), Young et al. (2007), and Young & Saxe (2008). Extensive bibliographies can be found in Sinnott-Armstrong (2008) and Sunstein (2005), among others.

theory have resulted in its lying virtually dormant for the last several decades. Part of what I hope to accomplish in this book is to revive and update Rawls' theory, and to reintroduce it to the community of philosophers, cognitive scientists, and legal scholars, with an eye toward future research. In this sense the remarks that follow are as much of an attempt to formulate and defend a research program in moral cognition modeled on aspects of generative linguistics as they are an effort to add to the existing commentary on Rawls.

The scientific questions raised by Rawls' linguistic analogy are classic ones: What constitutes moral knowledge? Is it innate? Does the brain contain a module specialized for moral judgment? Does the human genetic program contain instructions for the acquisition of a sense of justice or moral sense? Questions like these have been asked in one form or another for centuries. In this book I take them up again, with the aim of clarifying them and developing Rawls' proposal in *A Theory of Justice* for how they should be investigated.

2

A New Framework for the Theory
of Moral Cognition

To search in our common knowledge for the concepts which do not rest upon particular experience and yet occur in all knowledge from experience, of which they as it were constitute the mere form of connection, presupposes neither greater reflection nor deeper insight than to detect in a language the rules of the actual use of words generally and thus to collect elements for a grammar (in fact both researches are very nearly related), even though we are not able to give a reason why each language has just this and no other formal constitution, and still less why any precise number of such formal determinations in general, neither more nor less, can be found in it.

– Immanuel Kant, *Prolegomena to Any Future Metaphysics*

In Chapter 1, I referred to aspects of Universal Grammar to which the theory of moral cognition might be usefully compared. In this chapter, I provide an initial statement of some of these comparisons and indicate which of them I take Rawls to have drawn and his critics to have misunderstood. In order to do so, it will be helpful to introduce and explain some technical terminology from Chomsky's framework, as well as some novel terminology of my own. The bulk of the chapter is therefore devoted to establishing a broad analytical framework for the theory of moral cognition and to clarifying certain philosophical issues that arise within this framework. At the end of the chapter, I draw on this conceptual scheme to provide a road map for the remainder of the book.

Three clarifications are worth making at the outset. First, throughout this chapter and the book as a whole, I often use phrases such as "generative linguistics," "linguistic theory," and "Chomsky's framework" as if they were indistinguishable. Obviously this is not the case: It is perfectly possible to be a linguist – indeed, a great linguist – and to disagree with Chomsky's particular theories of human language or its proper mode of inquiry. It is important to clarify, therefore, that all such references to linguistics in this book unless otherwise indicated are meant to refer *only* to the theoretical framework of

Universal Grammar and to those researchers working more or less within Chomsky's basic paradigm. Second, the following remarks are largely informal in nature. I make no sustained effort to defend the initial comparisons that I make in this chapter, merely to state them clearly, so as to clarify how I will be using certain terminology and to prepare the way for the more detailed discussions of the linguistic analogy that will occur in subsequent chapters. Finally, the comparisons identified in this chapter do not exhaust the interesting or relevant parallels between moral theory and linguistics, nor should they be taken to deny the existence of many important differences between these fields or their subject matters. They are merely some key initial comparisons that I have chosen to emphasize here, in an effort to focus attention on the linguistic analogy and to begin to draw out some of its potential implications for cognitive science, jurisprudence, and moral theory.[1]

2.1 NINE COMPARISONS BETWEEN LINGUISTICS AND MORAL THEORY

2.1.1 The Main Questions

Chomsky's (1986a: 3, 1991a: 6) approach to the study of language is organized around three main questions:

(1) (a) What constitutes knowledge of language?
     (b) How is knowledge of language acquired?
     (c) How is knowledge of language put to use?

In Chomsky's framework, the answer to (1a) is given by a particular *generative grammar* (or theory of *linguistic competence*): a theory of the steady state of the mind/brain of a person who "knows" or "cognizes" a particular natural language like English, Hebrew, Arabic, or Japanese. The answer to (1b) is given by *Universal Grammar* (UG), a theory of the initial state of the language faculty, assumed to be a distinct subsystem of the mind/brain devoted to language acquisition, along with an account of how the properties UG postulates interact with experience to yield knowledge of a particular language.[2] The answer

---

[1] I am grateful to Noam Chomsky for many illuminating conversations that have helped me to develop the framework presented in this chapter and the book as a whole. For helpful general introductions to the theory of Universal Grammar, see, e.g., Baker (2001), Cook & Newson (1996), Isac & Reiss (2008), Jackendoff (1994), and Pinker (1994). For more technical studies, see, e.g., Chomsky (1965, 1986, 1995) and Haegeman (1994).

[2] The terms *initial state* and *steady state* have technical meanings in theoretical linguistics that may be unfamiliar. Chomsky explains these terms in the following passage, which also usefully summarizes the research program of Universal Grammar as a whole:

> What many linguists call "universal grammar" may be regarded as a theory of innate mechanisms, an underlying biological matrix that provides a framework within which the growth of language proceeds. There is no reason for the linguist to refrain from imputing

to (1c) is, or would be, given by a theory of *linguistic performance:* a theory of how knowledge of language enters into the actual expression and interpretation of language specimens, as well as into interpersonal communication and other actual uses of language (Chomsky 1965: 4, 1988b: 3–4, 1991a: 6).

As I will attempt to show, the theory of moral cognition is usefully organized around three questions, close analogues to the fundamental questions in Chomsky's framework.

(2) (a) What constitutes moral knowledge?
    (b) How is moral knowledge acquired?
    (c) How is moral knowledge put to use?

An answer to (2a) would be given by a particular *generative moral grammar* (or theory of *moral competence*): a theory of the steady or acquired state of the mind/brain of a person who possesses a system of moral knowledge, or what one might refer to informally as a "sense of justice," "moral sense," "moral faculty," or "conscience." The answer to (2b) would be given by *Universal Moral Grammar* (UMG): a theory of the initial state of the moral faculty, assumed to be a distinct subsystem of the mind/brain, along with an account of how the properties UMG postulates interact with experience to yield a mature system of moral knowledge. The answer to (2c), if available, would be given by a theory of *moral performance:* a theory of how moral knowledge enters into the actual representation and evaluation of human acts and institutions and other forms of actual behavior.

2.1.2 The General Answers

Chomsky's general answer to (1a) is that a speaker's knowledge of language consists, in part, in her possession of a *grammar:* a complex system of unconscious principles or rules (1980: 51). His general answer to (1b) is that the system is acquired through the unfolding of a specific genetic program, under

existence to this initial apparatus of the mind as well. Proposed principles of universal grammar may be regarded as an abstract partial specification of the genetic program that enables the child to interpret certain events as linguistic experience and to construct a system of rules and principles on the basis of that experience.

To put the matter in somewhat different but essentially equivalent terms, we may suppose that there is a fixed, genetically determined initial state of the mind, common to the species with at most minor variations apart from pathology. The mind passes through a sequence of states under the boundary conditions set by experience, achieving finally a "steady state" at a relatively fixed age, a state that then changes only in marginal ways. The basic property of this initial state is that, given experience, it develops to the steady state. Correspondingly, the initial state of the mind might be regarded as a function, characteristic of the species, that maps experience into the steady state. Universal Grammar is a partial characterization of this function, of this initial state. The grammar of a language that has grown in the mind is a partial characterization of the steady state attained. (1980: 187–188)

the modest triggering and shaping effects of the environment (1980: 31). In Chomsky's framework, (1c) has two aspects: a *production problem* and a *perception problem*. The former is the problem of how people succeed in acting appropriately and creatively in linguistic behavior and performance. Chomsky's opinion is that serious investigation of this topic lies beyond the bounds of present-day science. He further conjectures that it may even be beyond the bounds of human intelligence in principle, having the status of a permanent mystery for creatures such as ourselves. The reason is that this "creative aspect of language use" (1966: 3–31, 1986b: 519) involves the exercise of free will and voluntary choice, which science is at least presently unable to explain. In any event, Chomsky expressly excludes the production half of (1c) from the set of fundamental questions he takes his theory of language to be addressing. Hence, his general answer to the production half of (1c) is that normal use of language consists in rule-governed yet nondeterministic behavior: in everyday speech production, language users exploit their knowledge of language in the freely chosen construction of linguistic expressions (1986b: 519, 1991b: 40).

The perception problem, also known as the *parsing problem,* is concerned with how the speaker-hearer is able to recognize the properties of form and meaning of linguistic expressions that she encounters. Chomsky's general answer to this question is that when a person is presented an expression in a particular situation, her rule-system assigns it a structural description that in some manner specifies those properties (1991a: 18).

Since (2a)–(2c) are empirical questions, of which there is little scientific understanding at present, whatever general comments one makes about them must be tentative. Nevertheless, for reasons that will become more apparent as we proceed, it seems reasonable to suppose in the case of (2a) that the normal individual's moral knowledge consists in part in her possession of what I will call a *moral grammar:* a complex and largely unconscious system of moral rules, concepts, and principles that generates and relates mental representations of various types. Among other things, this system enables individuals to determine the deontic status of a potentially infinite number and variety of acts and omissions. In the case of (2b), it seems reasonable to assume that this moral grammar is acquired through the unfolding of a specific genetic program, under the relatively modest triggering and shaping effects of the environment. Turning to (2c), it seems plausible to hold that a similar division between the production and perception components of the problem is a useful method of clarifying how moral knowledge is put to use. A solution to the *production problem* in the theory of moral performance would seek to determine how individuals succeed in applying their moral knowledge in their actual, day-to-day conduct. Here it seems possible that Chomsky is correct that, as far as science is concerned, this problem may turn out to be a permanent mystery for creatures like ourselves, since it involves concepts such as free will and voluntary choice that science is so far unable to explain. Given the largely spontaneous and involuntary nature of many human moral intuitions, however, the *perception problem* appears more tractable. Here the question is how individuals are able to recognize the moral properties of the acts and institutional arrangements they encounter. The general answer to this problem, at least in the case of human actions, appears to be substantially the same in case of moral perception as it is in the case of language or vision: when a person encounters or imagines a particular action, performed under a particular set of circumstances, her rule-system assigns it a structural description that in some manner specifies those properties.

2.1.3 The Fundamental Arguments

As we have seen, Chomsky's answer to (1a) largely equates an individual's knowledge of language with her possession of a particular mental grammar. His answer to (1b) holds that this grammar is acquired through the unfolding of a genetic program under the relatively modest triggering and shaping effects of the environment. These answers are supported by two fundamental arguments. Both have the logical form of what is often called an "abductive" argument (Peirce 1955/1901: 150–156) or an "inductive inference to the best explanation" (Harman 1965). The first is what I will refer to here as *the argument for linguistic grammar.* The second is what I will refer to here as *the argument from the poverty of the linguistic stimulus.* In Ray Jackendoff's (1994: 6) useful formulation, the former argument holds that the best explanation of "the expressive variety of language use" is the assumption that "the language user's brain contains a set of unconscious grammatical principles." The latter argument holds that the best explanation of how children acquire these principles is the assumption that "the human brain contains a genetically determined specialization for language."

The general answers to questions (2a) and (2b) may be defended by two similar arguments. The first is what I will refer to here as *the argument for moral grammar.* In its most general form, it holds that the best explanation of the properties of moral judgment is the assumption that the mind/brain contains a moral grammar. The second is what I will refer to here as *argument from the poverty of the moral stimulus.* In its most general form, it holds that the best explanation of how children acquire this grammar is the assumption that at least some of its core attributes are innate, in Descartes' and Chomsky's dispositional sense (see, e.g., Chomsky 1972: 173; Descartes 1985/1647: 303–305). Put differently, the argument from the poverty of the moral stimulus holds that at least part of the best explanation of how children acquire their unconscious moral knowledge is the assumption that the human genetic program includes instructions for the acquisition of a moral sense.

2.1.4 The Competence–Performance Distinction

In Chomsky's framework, the competence–performance distinction is a technical distinction that refers, in the first instance, to the difference between

(1a) and (1c). These two questions, although interrelated, must be sharply distinguished. (1c) asks a question about a speaker's actual behavior; (1a) represents a question about the knowledge or cognitive system that a speaker's observable behavior presupposes. The competence–performance distinction is, in the first instance, simply the difference between these two questions. A theory of linguistic competence provides an answer to (1a). A theory of performance seeks to provide an answer to (1c).

A less formal way to represent the difference between competence and performance is as the distinction between knowledge and behavior, or between what a person knows and what she does. Linguistic competence, in Chomsky's framework, denotes a person's *knowledge* of her language; linguistic performance refers to how, in actual situations, her knowledge of language gets put to *use*. It is uncontroversial that a speaker's actual linguistic behavior is affected by things other than her underlying competence: her memory structure, mode of organizing experience, perceptual mechanisms and attention span, and a wide range of additional factors. Linguistic competence is thus presupposed by, but is only one factor contributing to, actual performance or language use (Chomsky 1965: 3, 1980: 225).[3]

In my view, the competence–performance distinction is a useful means to distinguish different aspects of the research program illustrated by (2), as well to clarify different aspects of Rawls' linguistic analogy and how that analogy was received by Rawls' critics. In this book, therefore, I adopt this distinction and utilize it in the following manner. I will use the term *moral competence* to refer to an individual's moral knowledge and the term *moral performance* to refer to how that knowledge is put to use. I will say that a theory of moral competence provides an answer to (2a), and that a theory of moral performance, if available, would provide an answer to (2c).

It is important to grasp the significance of the competence–performance distinction. To a certain extent it reflects a division between

---

[3] Chomsky provides a helpful explanation of the competence–performance distinction in the following passage:

> The person who has acquired knowledge of a language has internalized a system of rules that relate sound and meaning in a particular way. The linguist constructing a grammar of a language is in effect proposing a hypothesis concerning this internalized system. The linguist's hypothesis, if presented with sufficient explicitness and precision, will have certain empirical consequences with regard to the form of utterances and their interpretations by the native speaker. Evidently, knowledge of language – the internalized system of rules – is only one of the many factors that determine how an utterance will be used or understood in a particular situation. The linguist who is trying to discover what constitutes knowledge of a language – to construct a correct grammar – is studying one fundamental factor that is involved in performance, but not the only one. This idealization must be kept in mind when one is considering the problem of confirmation of grammars on the basis of empirical evidence. There is no reason why one should not also study the interaction of several factors involved in complex mental acts and underlying actual performance, but such a study is not likely to proceed very far unless the separate factors are themselves fairly well understood. (1972: 26–27)

two fundamentally different approaches to the study of human nature: *mentalism* and *behaviorism*. Unlike psychological behaviorism, which at least in theory seeks to avoid all references to unobservable mental entities or processes (see, e.g., Skinner 1953; Watson 1925), generative linguistics is mentalistic in the technical sense: it represents a shift of focus from observable behavior to the cognitive structures of the mind entering into behavior (Chomsky 1965: 4, 1986a: 3). As Chomsky observes, the true novelty of his own theoretical approach is its mentalism: its shift of focus from performance to competence, from the study of language regarded from a purely behavioristic point of view to "the study of the system of knowledge of language attained and internally represented in the mind/brain" (1986a: 24). A grammar within a mentalistic framework is not a set of theoretical statements that purportedly describes observable behavior in some fashion; rather, it seeks to describe "exactly what one knows when one knows a language" (1986a: 24). Hence, by distinguishing (2a) and (2c), what I am attempting to do, in effect, is to shift (or begin to shift) the focus of moral theorists away from behaviorism and toward mentalism. In my judgment, the theory of moral cognition has not yet fully recovered from the damage that was done to it by behaviorism. Part of what I hope to accomplish in this book is to begin to repair this damage, by showing how a mentalistic approach to moral cognition might work.

2.1.5 The Distinction between Operative and Express Principles

Linguists do not assume that the normal language user is aware of the system of rules or principles that constitute her knowledge of language, or that she can become aware of them through introspection, or that her statements about them are necessarily accurate. On the contrary, as a result of empirical investigation, the rules of her language are assumed to lie beyond actual and even potential consciousness; moreover, it is taken for granted that her verbal reports and beliefs about her linguistic competence may be in error.

This leads to the following important point: in Chomsky's framework, a linguistic theory attempts to specify the *actual* properties of the speaker's linguistic competence, not what she may or may not report about them. The position linguists adopt in this regard is similar to the position adopted by theorists of visual perception, whose goal is to account for what a person actually sees and the cognitive mechanisms that determine what she sees, rather than to account for her own statements and explanations of what she sees and why (Chomsky 1965: 8).

To mark this difference, I will refer to it as the distinction between *operative* principles and *express* principles. In my view the same distinction should play an important role in moral theory. In this book I will attempt to capture it in the following terms. I will say that a person's *operative* moral principles are those principles that are actually operative in her exercise of moral judgment – the actual principles, in other words, of her moral competence. I will say that a person's *express* moral principles are those statements that a person verbalizes in the attempt to describe, explain, or justify her judgments. From this perspective moral theorists should not assume that the normal individual is aware of the operative principles that constitute her moral knowledge, or that she can become aware of them through introspection, or that her statements about them are necessarily accurate. On the contrary, they should be open to the possibility of discovering that just as normal persons are unaware of the principles guiding their linguistic or visual intuitions, so too are they often unaware of the principles guiding their moral intuitions. In any event, the important point is that, as with language or vision, the theory of moral cognition must attempt to specify what the properties of moral competence actually are, not what a person may report about them.

The distinction between operative and express principles is a traditional philosophical distinction. One finds reasonably clear expressions of it in the writings of many philosophers, including Leibniz (1981/1705), Hutcheson (1971/1728), Rousseau (1979/1762), Kant (1964/1785), Whewell (1845), Bradley (1962/1876), and Brentano (1969/1889), to name a few.[4] Hutcheson's manner of expressing the distinction in the opening pages of his *Illustrations on the Moral Sense* (1728) is especially elegant and perspicuous. Hutcheson writes:

Let this also still be remembered, that the natural dispositions of mankind may operate regularly in those who never reflected upon them nor formed just notions about them. Many are really virtuous who cannot explain what virtue is. Some act a most generous disinterested part in life who have been taught to account for all their actions by self-love as the sole spring. There have been very different and opposite opinions in optics, contrary accounts have been given of hearing, voluntary motion, digestion, and other natural actions. But the powers themselves in reality perform their several operations with sufficient constancy and uniformity in persons of good health whatever their opinions be about them. In the same manner our moral actions and affections may be in good order when our opinions are quite wrong about them. True opinions, however, about both, may enable us to improve our natural powers and to rectify accidental disorders incident unto them. And true speculations on these subjects must certainly be attended with as much pleasure as any other parts of human knowledge. (1971/1728: 106)

In this passage Hutcheson reminds his reader that the point of a theory of moral cognition is to describe the "regular operations" of the moral sense, not to determine whether a person "has formed just notions" about it, or can "explain what virtue is" (cf. Reid 1969/1785: 726). Despite its evident concern with being scientific, modern moral psychology has largely ignored Hutcheson's sensible warning not to conflate these distinctions. Indeed, under the apparent influence of behaviorism, the twentieth century's leading

---

[4] The crux of the distinction is familiar to lawyers in the somewhat different but nonetheless related contrast between *ratio decidendi* ("reason for deciding") and *obiter dictum* ("something said in passing") (see generally Mikhail 2002a).

moral psychologists, Piaget (1965/1932) and Kohlberg (1981, 1984), and their followers have concerned themselves primarily with charting the development of an individual's ability to express an articulate opinion about moral problems, and to give a coherent account of her own moral intuitions, rather than with providing a theory of the moral sense itself. While these abilities are important, they should not be confused with the primary subject matter of the theory of moral cognition. As is the case with a theory of language or a theory of vision, the theory of moral cognition must attempt to describe the operative principles of moral competence, not what an experimental subject may or may not report about them.

The specific relevance of the distinction between operative and express principles for our topic is that, unlike Piaget and Kohlberg, Rawls is careful not to conflate this distinction. On the contrary, he takes its significance fully into account. Indeed, this is one of the main reasons why I believe his conception of moral theory is superior to theirs and should be of special interest to cognitive scientists. A central element of Rawls' linguistic analogy is his recognition that the subject matter of generative linguistics is linguistic competence, not linguistic performance, and that a correct account of linguistic competence requires theoretical constructions that go well beyond anything a nonlinguist can formulate for herself. In *A Theory of Justice*, Rawls suggests a similar situation presumably holds in moral philosophy. Like Hutcheson, therefore, he warns us not to assume that a *theory* of her sense of justice is something that the normal individual can express on her own (see, e.g., Rawls 1971: 47, 491). Rawls' view of this matter appears sound. The distinction between operative and express principles, as it is defined here,[5] is simply taken for granted in the study of language, vision, musical cognition, face recognition, and other cognitive domains. There seems little reason to suppose that the situation should be any different for a cognitive capacity as complex as the moral sense.

2.1.6 Levels of Empirical Adequacy

The terms *observational adequacy, descriptive adequacy,* and *explanatory adequacy* were introduced into linguistics and cognitive science by Chomsky in the early 1960s. They have specific meanings in his framework that are somewhat different from their ordinary connotations. For our purposes these may be rendered as follows. A theory of language is *observationally adequate* with respect to the data of an observed corpus of utterances if it correctly describes that data in some manner or other, for example, by listing them. A

---

[5] The terms *operative principles* and *express principles* originate with the nineteenth-century philosopher, William Whewell (1845). I have adapted them to the present context, however, and am using them somewhat differently then he does. For a useful introduction to Whewell's moral philosophy, see Schneewind (1977), especially pp. 101–117.

linguistic theory is *descriptively adequate* with respect to a particular individual's system of linguistic knowledge to the extent that it correctly describes that system in its mature or steady state. A linguistic theory meets what Chomsky terms the condition of *explanatory adequacy* to the extent that it correctly describes the initial state of the language faculty and correctly explains how the properties of the initial state interact with the child's primary data to yield mature knowledge of language (Chomsky 1964: 28–29; 1965: 24–27; see also Haegeman 1994: 6–11).

To clarify, the distinction between descriptive and explanatory adequacy corresponds to the difference between (1a) and (1b). Hence, in Chomsky's framework, descriptively adequate means the same thing as "provides a correct description of linguistic competence" or "provides a correct answer to (1a)." Explanatorily adequate means the same thing as "provides a correct explanation of linguistic competence" or "provides a correct answer to (1b)."

Chomsky's distinction between the problems of descriptive and explanatory adequacy is potentially confusing because correct answers to *both* problems are *both* descriptive and explanatory in the usual sense. A solution to the problem of descriptive adequacy – that is, a correct answer to (1a) – is a *description* of the mature speaker-hearer's linguistic competence; at the same time it is an *explanation* of the speaker's linguistic intuitions. Likewise, a solution to the problem of explanatory adequacy – that is, a correct answer to (1b) – is a *description* of the initial state of the language faculty; at the same time it is an *explanation* both of the speaker-hearer's acquired competence and (at a deeper level) those same intuitions.[6]

---

[6] Chomsky explains the distinction between descriptive and explanatory adequacy in the following passage. As I explain in Chapter 3, Chomsky and other linguists often use the term "grammar" with an acknowledged systematic ambiguity, to refer both to the linguist's theoretical description of the speaker-hearer's knowledge of language and to that knowledge itself. To help the reader who may be unfamiliar with this practice, I have inserted what I take to be the type of grammar Chomsky has in mind (theoretical or mental) in brackets.

> In a good sense, the [theoretical] grammar proposed by the linguist is an explanatory theory; it suggests an explanation for the fact that (under the idealization mentioned) a speaker of the language in question will perceive, interpret, form, or use an utterance in certain ways and not in other ways. One can also search for explanatory theories of a deeper sort. The native speaker has acquired a [mental] grammar on the basis of very restricted and degenerate evidence; the [mental] grammar has empirical consequences that extend far beyond the evidence. At one level, the phenomena with which the [theoretical] grammar deals are explained by the rules of the [mental] grammar itself and the interaction of these rules. At a deeper level, these same phenomena are explained by the principles that determine the selection of the [mental] grammar on the basis of the restricted and degenerate evidence available to the person who has acquired knowledge of the language, who has constructed for himself this particular [mental] grammar. The principles that determine the form of [mental] grammar and that select a [mental] grammar of the appropriate form on the basis of certain data constitute a subject that might, following traditional usage, be termed "universal grammar." The study of universal grammar, so understood, is a study of the nature of human intellectual capacities. It tries to formulate the necessary and sufficient conditions that a system must meet to

Despite these potential misunderstandings, I believe that the concept observational, descriptive, and explanatory adequacy are a helpful means which to refer to different aspects of the research program illustrated by (. They are also a useful method of identifying and clarifying different aspects of Rawls' linguistic analogy and the arguments of Rawls' critics. Throughout this book, therefore, I will adopt these terms and utilize them in the following way. I will say that a moral theory is *observationally adequate* with respect to a set of moral judgments to the extent that it provides a correct description of those judgments in some manner or other, for example, by listing them. I will say that a moral theory is *descriptively adequate* with respect to the mature individual's system of moral knowledge to the extent that it correctly describes that system – in other words, to the extent that it provides a correct answer to (2a). Finally, I will say that a moral theory meets the condition of *explanatory adequacy* to the extent it correctly describes the initial state of the moral faculty and correctly explains how the properties of the initial state it postulates interact with experience to yield a mature system of moral competence – in other words, to the extent that it provides a correct answer to (2b).

2.1.7 Two Additional Questions

(1a)–(1c) do not exhaust the basic questions concerning human language about which scientists would like to achieve theoretical insight and understanding. In particular, Chomsky (1995b) identifies two additional questions:

(1) (d) How is knowledge of language physically realized in the brain?
    (e) How did knowledge of language evolve in the species?

Although (1d) and (1e) are the focus of much ongoing research, Chomsky (1995b: 17) has cautioned that they might be "beyond serious inquiry for the time being," much like many other far-reaching topics in the cognitive sciences. With respect to (1e), for example, although he is a leading proponent of a naturalistic approach to the study of language (the so-called biolinguistic perspective), Chomsky has been critical of those researchers, such as Pinker & Bloom (1990), who argue that the evolution of the human language faculty is best explained by Darwinian natural selection alone. Rather, along with other commentators such as Gould & Lewontin (1979), Lewontin (1990), and Darwin (1958/1859) himself, Chomsky has argued that a better explanation probably rests in some combination of selectional and nonselectional factors,

---

qualify as a potential human language, conditions that are not accidentally true of existing human languages, but that are rather rooted in the human "language capacity," and thus constitute the innate organization that determines what counts as linguistic experience and what knowledge of language arises on the basis of this experience. Universal grammar, then, constitutes an explanatory theory of a much deeper sort than particular [theoretical] grammar, although the particular [theoretical] grammar of a language can also be regarded as an explanatory theory. (1972: 27)

including various ecological and historical contingencies and the space of possible options afforded by physical laws (see, e.g., Chomsky 2000, 2002; see also McGilvray 2005).[7]

In a similar fashion, one can formulate the following two questions in the theory of moral cognition, in addition to the three questions already identified:

(2) (d) How is moral knowledge physically realized in the brain?
     (e) How did moral knowledge evolve in the species?

Many researchers began to investigate (2d) and (2e) (or broadly similar questions) from a naturalistic perspective during the last few decades of the twentieth century, including Blair (1995), Damasio (1994), and Damasio et al. (1994) in the case of (2d) and Alexander (1987), De Waal (1996), Trivers (1971), and Wilson (1975) in the case of (2e). More recently there has been an explosion of interdisciplinary research on these and related topics that shows no signs of abating (see, e.g., Sinnott-Armstrong 2008). Despite my keen interest in these issues, I will mostly put them aside in what follows, since within the framework I have articulated thus far any attempt to answer (2d) or (2e) would be premature. Just as posing well-framed and well-motivated questions about the neurophysiological and phylogenetic properties of human language largely depends on an adequate grasp of plausible answers to (1a)–(1c), so too, in my judgment, does the proper formulation of (2d) and (2e) largely depend on plausible answers to (2a)–(2c). Put differently, we cannot seriously ask how moral knowledge is realized in the brain or how it evolved in the species until what constitutes moral knowledge and how it is acquired and put to use by each individual are better understood.

2.1.8 Commonsense and Technical Concepts of Language and Morality

Chomsky draws a fundamental distinction between ordinary, common-sense, or pretheoretical concepts like language, knowledge of language, or linguistic competence, on the one hand, and various artificial or technical elaborations of those concepts, on the other. He suggests that all serious scientific approaches to the study of language must eventually replace the former concepts with technical substitutes, since the latter are more suitable for empirical study.

---

[7] As Chomsky (2000: 63) observes, "Darwin firmly denied that he attributed 'the modification of species exclusively to natural selection,' emphasizing in the last edition of *Origin of Species* that 'in the first edition of this work, and subsequently, I placed in a most conspicuous position – namely, at the close of the Introduction – the following words: "I am convinced that natural selection has been the main but not the exclusive means of modification." This has been of no avail. Great is the power of steady misrepresentation.'"

In Chomsky's case the technical concept most recently adopted (which simultaneously replaces both "language" and "knowledge of language," in their ordinary sense, and "linguistic competence," as this term was used by linguists during the two decades following publication of Chomsky's *Aspects of a Theory of Syntax*) is the concept *I-language*. A technical concept of language represents an instance of I-language, in Chomsky's view, if it characterizes a language as "some element of the mind of the person who knows the language, acquired by the learner, and used by the speaker-hearer" (1986a: 22). I-language thus refers to the language system in the mind/brain of a person who, in the ordinary sense, "knows" a language like English or Japanese. The "I" in I-language signifies at least three properties the I-language has: it is *internalized* in the sense that it is internal to the mind/brain. It is *intensional* in the sense that it may be regarded as a specific characterization of a function considered in intension that assigns a status to a range of events. It is *individualized* in the sense that the standpoint adopted toward I-language is that of individual psychology: I-languages are construed as something individual persons have, and different persons may be thought of as having in some sense different I-languages. A fourth reason the "I" in I-language is significant is that I-language represents an *idealization,* in several important respects (Chomsky 1986a: 3, 1986b: 513).

The general relevance for moral theory of Chomsky's distinction between commonsense and technical concepts of language emerges when we consider how a philosopher or scientist might go about replacing the more or less obscure, intuition-bound concepts ("sense of justice," "moral sense," "moral knowledge," "morality," "conscience," "moral competence," and so forth) in which her theoretical questions are initially posed with an artificially constructed technical concept, more suitable for scientific study.[8] An *I-morality* approach to moral theory would characterize its primary object of inquiry as some element of the mind/brain of a person who, we might ordinarily say, possesses a sense of justice ("moral sense," "moral knowledge," etc.). I-morality would thus refer, in its most neutral sense, to the moral system of the human mind/brain. The "I" in I-morality would signify at least four properties the system has: it is *internalized* in the sense that it is internal to the mind/brain. It is *intensional* in the sense that a theory of I-morality may be regarded as the characterization of a function considered in intension, which assigns a status to a range of events. It is *individualized* in the sense that the standpoint adopted toward I-morality is that of individual psychology: I-moralities are construed as something individual persons have, and different persons

---

[8] For instructive discussions of the conceptual difficulties in formulating a coherent account of the ordinary or intuitive concept of morality, see, e.g., Edel (1970: 285f.), Frankena (1976: 125–132, 168–183), Pareto (1935: 231f.), and Perry (1954: 86f.). As Perry aptly observes, "there is something which goes on in the world to which it is appropriate to give the name of 'morality'. Nothing is more familiar; nothing is more obscure in its meaning" (1954: 86).

may be thought of as having in some sense different I-moralities. Finally, I-morality represents an *idealization* in a number of important respects: it is a constructed model of a given biological object – the moral faculty of the human mind/brain.

The more specific relevance of I-morality for our topic is that while Rawls does not use this terminology in *A Theory of Justice,* he conceives of the subject matter of moral theory in precisely this way: that is, as a mental capacity that is internal, intensional, individual, and ideal, in the sense described. In my opinion, Rawls' remarks leave little doubt on this matter. Nonetheless, what appears to me equally true, and what I will argue below, is that many of Rawls' early critics appear to have misinterpreted him on just this point.

2.1.9 Theoretical Goals

Chomsky is often credited with asking more ambitious questions about the structure of language than his predecessors. While this is true, it is important to realize that, in another sense, his theoretical goals were more modest than theirs, and that it was the greater modesty of his goals that enabled him to ask more ambitious questions. In *Syntactic Structures,* Chomsky adapted a set of concepts from mathematical logic and distinguished three approaches to the metalinguistic problem of justifying grammars. He noted that the strongest requirement that could be asked of a linguistic theory is to provide what he called a *discovery procedure* for grammars: that is, a practical and mechanical method by which the linguist could actually construct the grammar, given a particular body of data (for example, a corpus of grammatical and ungrammatical utterances). Chomsky identified a weaker requirement of linguistic theory to be to provide a *decision procedure* for grammars: that is, a mechanical method for determining whether or not a proposed grammar is the *best* grammar of the language from which a given corpus is drawn. Finally, Chomsky identified an even weaker requirement of a linguistic theory to be to provide an *evaluation procedure* for grammars: that is, a mechanical method for determining which of two proposed grammars, G_1 and G_2, is the *better* grammar of the language from which a given corpus is drawn (1957: 49–60).

In *Syntactic Structures,* Chomsky adopted the position that it was unreasonable to expect a linguistic theory to provide anything more than an evaluation procedure for grammars. He thus adopted the weakest of the three positions described above. The notion that the overriding goal of linguistic theory is to evaluate which of two or more competing grammars is the better explanation of a given body of data has been a cornerstone of theoretical linguistics since that time.

In my view, the theory of moral cognition should follow Chomsky in distinguishing clearly and explicitly among possible theoretical goals. The strongest requirement that could be placed on a theory of moral cognition is that it provide what we might think of as a *discovery procedure* for moral principles: that is, a practical and mechanical method for actually constructing a correct set of moral principles on the basis of a given body of data (for example, a set of ordered pairs consisting of a moral judgment and a description of the circumstances that occasion it). A weaker requirement would be to demand that the theory provide a *decision procedure* for moral principles: that is, a mechanical method for determining whether or not a proposed set of moral principles is correct, or valid, or the best set of principles, with respect to a given class of judgments. Finally, a still weaker condition would be to require that the theory provide an *evaluation procedure* for moral principles: that is, a rational method of determining which of two or more proposed sets of principles is the better alternative, given a particular body of data.

The immediate significance of these distinctions for our topic emerges when we consider the evolution of Rawls' conception of metaethics from 1950 to 1971. In his early writings, Rawls explicitly rejects the notion that the appropriate goal of moral theory is to provide a discovery procedure for moral principles. In *Outline,* for example, he writes: "There is no way of knowing ahead of time how to find and formulate these reasonable principles. Indeed, we cannot even be certain that they exist, and it is well known that there are no mechanical methods of discovery" (1951a: 178). Hence Rawls' stated aim in *Outline* (as the title of that paper implies) is to construct a "decision procedure" for "validating or invalidating given or proposed moral rules," and he conceives of "the objectivity or the subjectivity of moral knowledge" to turn on whether such a procedure exists (1951a: 177). By 1971, when *A Theory of Justice* was published, Rawls' theoretical goals had apparently changed. His apparent objective in that book is to satisfy the weaker requirement of providing an evaluation procedure for moral principles, in particular to determine whether justice as fairness is a *better* theory of the sense of justice (I-morality) than utilitarianism (see, e.g., Rawls 1971: vii–viii, 17–18, 49–50, 52–53, 581). In my opinion, this is the most coherent way to interpret Rawls' metaethical commitments in *A Theory of Justice.* Nonetheless, as I will argue in Part Three, some of Rawls' early critics appear to have misunderstood this fundamental point.

2.2 PRELIMINARY CLARIFICATIONS ABOUT RAWLS' LINGUISTIC ANALOGY

Thus far I have identified the following questions in the theory of moral cognition:

(2) (a) What constitutes moral knowledge?
    (b) How is moral knowledge acquired?
    (c) How is moral knowledge put to use?
    (d) How is moral knowledge physically realized in the brain?
    (e) How did moral knowledge evolve in the species?

These five questions are simply the outline of a research program, all bones and no flesh. One of the primary aims of this book is to begin to sharpen these questions and to fill in some of the relevant details. The main advantage of introducing these problems and an appropriate terminology for pursuing them at this early stage of our investigation is that it affords the chance to make some initial clarifying remarks about the scope and limits of both Rawls' linguistic analogy and the research based on it that I seek to undertake here. It also enables me to summarize the remaining chapters of this book in a more perspicuous form.

What I am calling Rawls' linguistic analogy is actually a series of comparisons that Rawls makes in Section 9 of *A Theory of Justice* (1971: 46–53) between moral theory and parts of theoretical linguistics, as expressed primarily in the first few pages of Chomsky's *Aspects of the Theory of Syntax* (1965: 3–9). In my opinion Rawls' remarks have been widely misunderstood, due primarily to the failure of his readers to take seriously the distinctions that Rawls draws, implicitly in Section 9 and explicitly elsewhere (e.g., Rawls 1950, 1951a, 1975), between at least five general kinds of question that moral philosophy seeks to answer. The first are *empirical* questions about the *mature* or *steady* state of I-morality – roughly those questions corresponding to (2a). The second are *empirical* questions about the *initial* or *original* state of I-morality – namely, those questions corresponding to (2b). The third are *empirical* questions about how I-morality is put to use – that is, those questions corresponding to (2c). The fourth are *normative* questions about moral principles, in particular the question of which moral principles are justified. Finally, the fifth are *metaethical* questions about particular moral judgments and moral principles, such as the question *whether,* and if so *how,* they may be said on rational grounds to be justified.[9]

Rawls' fourth and fifth questions are not represented by (2a)–(2e). Instead, in Rawls' framework they correspond more closely to (2f) and (2g):

(2) (f) Which moral principles are justified?
     (g) How can moral principles be justified?

In what follows I will refer to (2a)–(2g) as *descriptive, explanatory, behavioral, neurocognitive, evolutionary, normative,* and *metaethical* questions, respectively (see Table 2.1). Following Chomsky, I will continue to refer to (2a) as *the problem of descriptive adequacy* and to (2b) as *the problem of explanatory adequacy.* Because it will be convenient to have analogous phrases to refer to (2f) and (2g), I will refer to them as *the problem of normative adequacy* and *the problem of metaethical adequacy,* respectively. Likewise, I will refer to

---

[9] All five questions must be distinguished from *practical* questions of political philosophy, such as the question that motivates *Political Liberalism:* How can a stable and just society of free and equal citizens live harmoniously when deeply divided by a plurality of incompatible and irreconcilable, though reasonable, comprehensive doctrines?

TABLE 2.1. *Seven Main Problems in the Theory of Moral Cognition*

No.	Problem	Theoretical Goal
(2a)	What constitutes moral knowledge?	Descriptive adequacy
(2b)	How is moral knowledge acquired?	Explanatory adequacy
(2c)	How is moral knowledge put to use?	Behavioral adequacy
(2d)	How is moral knowledge physically realized in the brain?	Neurocognitive adequacy
(2e)	How did moral knowledge evolve in the species?	Evolutionary adequacy
(2f)	Which moral principles are justified?	Normative adequacy
(2g)	How can moral principles be justified?	Metaethical adequacy

(2c)–(2e) as *the problem of behavioral adequacy, the problem of neurocognitive adequacy,* and *the problem of evolutionary adequacy,* respectively.[10]

Now, as I interpret it, Rawls' linguistic analogy is centered primarily on the comparison between the problem of descriptive adequacy in linguistics and the problem of descriptive adequacy in ethics, and, to a lesser extent, between the problem of explanatory adequacy in linguistics and the corresponding problem in ethics. The primary grounds on which the analogy is criticized, however, is its failure to solve (or to play a part in solving) the problem of *normative* adequacy. Therefore, the central issue between Rawls and his critics turns out to be, not the value of the linguistic analogy for moral theory, as one might initially assume, but the manner in which Rawls conceives the overall structure of an ethical theory, and in particular the relationship between its empirical and normative branches.[11]

In his early writings, Rawls' approach to moral theory appears to rest on two main assumptions about the relationship between the problems of descriptive

[10] In relying on the concepts of descriptive and explanatory adequacy, I largely follow Chomsky (1964, 1965). The remaining terms are constructed by analogy. Note that by defining the problem of metaethical adequacy to be how moral principles can be justified, Rawls departs from other familiar conceptions of metaethics, such as those conceptions that define metaethics to be the linguistic analysis of ethical concepts, or those conceptions that are concerned with the epistemological, metaphysical, or ontological status of moral truths or moral facts. I return to this topic in Chapter 6.

[11] Descriptive ethics, normative ethics, practical ethics, and metaethics are often held to be distinct fields of inquiry. However, what their exact boundaries are, and how much each draws from the others, are not entirely clear, or at least have never been clearly and convincingly stated. Hare's (1960: 100) observation that "no generally accepted terminology for making the necessary distinctions has yet emerged" arguably remains true today. For a series of recent taxonomies, see generally Lamont (1946), Rawls (1950, 1975), Hare (1952, 1960, 1963, 1973, 1981), Mandelbaum (1955), Nowell-Smith (1954), Brandt (1959), Stevenson (1963), Frankena (1963), Findlay (1970), Harman (1977), Scanlon (1982, 1992), Broad (1985), and Brink (1989).

and normative adequacy. First, Rawls assumes that there is an *order of priority* between these two problems, according to which the descriptive takes precedence over the normative. Second, Rawls assumes that a descriptively adequate moral theory constitutes a *presumptive* solution to the problem of normative adequacy, given the nature of the evidence that a descriptively adequate theory explains (see, e.g., Rawls 1951a: 182–184, 186–188; 1971: 46–53).

As I interpret him, Rawls employs the linguistic analogy primarily to clarify certain aspects of the problem of descriptive adequacy. In particular, Rawls draws on the theory of language to accomplish at least eight distinct but overlapping objectives. The first two objectives are (i) to formulate the problem of descriptive adequacy by (ii) defending the empirical assumption that the sense of justice is a cognitive system of sufficient coherence and complexity to make it interesting and worthwhile to describe. Rawls defends this assumption by means of what I refer to in this book as *the argument for moral grammar.* This argument may be usefully thought of as the moral analogue to the *argument for linguistic grammar.* In my terms – not Rawls' – the argument for moral grammar holds that the best explanation of the observable properties of moral judgment is the assumption that the mind/brain contains a moral grammar, or set of unconscious moral rules or principles.

As Norman Daniels (1979: 258, 1980: 22–23) observes, the argument for moral grammar can be restated in somewhat different but essentially equivalent terms as the claim that, like linguistic theory, moral theory is faced with a *projection problem*, that is, the problem of explaining how ordinary individuals are capable of applying their moral knowledge to new and often unprecedented cases. I explain this terminology at more length in Chapter 3 (see Section 3.1.1). For now, what is important to recognize is simply that the argument for moral grammar (or alternatively the recognition that moral theory is faced with a projection problem) constitutes the first feature of what I refer to in this book as Rawls' linguistic analogy.

As I interpret him, the six remaining elements of Rawls' linguistic analogy are meant primarily to clarify what the problem of descriptive adequacy involves. Like Chomsky, Rawls distinguishes between (iii) descriptive adequacy and observational adequacy, (iv) operative principles and express principles, (v) descriptive adequacy and explanatory adequacy, and (vi) moral competence and moral performance. He also draws on the framework of theoretical linguistics to explain (vii) the theory-dependence of the competence–performance distinction and (viii) the importance of idealization in addressing the problem of moral diversity and in solving problems of empirical adequacy more generally.[12]

---

[12] In this book for ease of expression I will sometimes use the term *empirical adequacy* in place of the phrase "descriptive and explanatory adequacy." In other words, an empirically adequate grammar in my usage refers to a grammar that satisfies both descriptive and explanatory adequacy, in the sense defined in the text. Empirical adequacy in its broadest sense also includes behavioral, neurocognitive, and evolutionary adequacy, of course, but my focus here will be descriptive and explanatory adequacy.

Thus far I have said little about (2f) and (2g), the problems of normative and metaethical adequacy. In *A Theory of Justice,* Rawls advances a straightforward answer to (2f). At least within the context of his main contractual argument for principles of social justice, the principles he purports to justify are those he calls *the special conception of justice*.[13] In the case of (2g), however, the situation is more complex. As I interpret him, Rawls presupposes a complicated answer to the general problem of justifying moral principles, which turns on at least three potentially unrelated ideas: first, that moral principles can be presumptively justified by showing that they are a solution to the problem of descriptive adequacy; second, that descriptively adequate moral principles can be further justified by showing that they are part of a solution to the problem of explanatory adequacy; and third, that moral principles that meet the demands of descriptive and explanatory adequacy can be justified to an even greater extent by showing that the adoption of such principles can be proven as a formal theorem in the theory of rational choice.[14] As I understand it, Rawls' notion of *reflective equilibrium* is intended to suggest that these three apparently disparate ideas can, in fact, be reconciled. In other words, Rawls assumes as a general matter that the same set of moral principles can be part of a single, comprehensive solution to the problems of descriptive, explanatory, and normative adequacy simultaneously.

Needless to say, this idea of Rawls' has been the source of considerable interest and debate. His perceived use of reflective equilibrium as a method for justifying moral principles has drawn sharp criticism from some philosophers and has been resourcefully defended by others. Rawls himself compares aspects of reflective equilibrium both with Nelson Goodman's (1983/1955) influential account of the justification of principles of deductive and inductive inference and with Chomsky's (1965) account of descriptive and explanatory adequacy (Rawls 1971: 18–22, 46–53; see also 120, 491). These comparisons have contributed to further uncertainty over whether Rawls conceives of moral theory as an empirical discipline – a branch of psychology – and, if so, whether its pretensions to normativity can be maintained.

[13] As I discuss in more detail in Chapter 6, the conception of social justice Rawls defends in *A Theory of Justice* comes in two forms, one general and one more specific. The two principles of the more specific conception – what Rawls calls the "special conception of justice" – are the following.

First Principle
   Each person is to have an equal right to the most extensive total system of basic liberties compatible with a similar system of liberty for all (1971: 250).

Second Principle
   Social and economic inequalities are to be arranged so that they are both (a) to the greatest benefit of the least advantaged and (b) attached to offices and positions open to all under conditions of fair equality of opportunity (1971: 83).

[14] For a helpful discussion of the rational choice element in *A Theory of Justice,* see generally Wolff (1977).

In my opinion, once the theory-dependence of the competence–performance distinction and the appropriately modest goal of moral philosophy to provide an evaluation procedure for moral principles are taken into account and given their due weight, Rawls' notion that the same set of moral principles can be part of a solution to (2a), (2b), and (2f) seems plausible. But this statement must not be interpreted too simply. As Rawls observes, reflective equilibrium is a name given to "the philosophical ideal" (1971: 50). It refers to the state of affairs that is reached once the theorist has discovered the principles to which her set of considered judgments conform and, in turn, the premises of those principles' derivation (1971: 20). As with any other science, the conclusions of moral theory are always provisional and hence may be modified as a result of further investigation. This emphasis on the provisional or presumptive character of moral theory is important. It implies that whether a moral theory is correct, and thus whether a given set of moral principles is justified, is always an open question. Nevertheless, the question of justification is largely settled at any given time, so far as it can be, by showing that a particular set of moral principles satisfies these three tests better than any available alternative. In this manner the theorist attempts to show that the principles that do in fact describe and explain human moral competence are also *rational,* in the sense that free and equal persons would choose to adopt them to govern their relations with one another, if they were given that choice.[15]

The fact that one of the three elements of the problem of metaethical adequacy is the requirement that justifiable principles be shown to be rational might seem like a sharp disanalogy with linguistics. Although I believe that this disanalogy is real, I would again caution against interpreting it too simply. It is true that linguists do not ask whether grammars are rational in the sense that Rawls has in mind. That is, they do not ask whether the principles of an empirically adequate grammar would also be chosen in a suitably characterized contractual situation. However, it is important to recognize that linguists do attempt to show that grammars of particular languages can be viewed, in a sense, as theorems derivable from principles of higher generality (i.e., Universal Grammar). Further, it is important to recall that, in *A Theory of Justice,* Rawls considers the original position to be not merely a procedure for proving the rationality of principles of justice, but also a model that explains how the sense of justice is acquired (see, e.g., 1971: 47, 120, 491). Moreover, Rawls evidently believes that by pursuing the problem of empirical adequacy,

[15] As Rawls makes clear in a passage of his dissertation that anticipates *A Theory of Justice,* his contract argument is hypothetical, not historical. Thus, he does not claim "that at any time in the past the rules of common sense have been explicitly discussed and voluntarily adopted in light of the principles, and the nature of man and society. This historical question is not to the point. But it is relevant to say that if men had explicitly discussed the adoption of common sense rules with the principles in mind, then they *would* have adopted those rules which in general they have. That is what I mean when I say that common sense is, in general, justifiable" (Rawls 1950: 107).

the problems of normative and metaethical adequacy may be transformed. This might help to explain his observation that "if we can find an accurate account of our moral conceptions, then questions of meaning and justification may prove much easier to answer. Indeed, some of them may no longer be real questions at all" (1971: 51). Rawls does not specify the conditions under which justifying moral principles may prove to be easier, or may no longer be a real question, but we can readily imagine what he has in mind. By solving the problem of descriptive adequacy, moral theorists may be led to frame, and then to solve, the problem of explanatory adequacy, thereby demonstrating that the morality of common sense is rooted in human nature, as many philosophers, jurists, and cognitive scientists have often assumed.

Having said this, it is important to emphasize that there are, and presumably always will be, many aspects of the problem of justification in ethics that have no clear analogue in linguistics. Even if we have described and explained the acquisition of moral competence, and even if we have discovered its evolutionary origin and its physical signatures in the brain, there will remain many questions that we might wish to ask that have no clear counterparts in the theory of grammar. For example, we may wish to ask whether the moral principles that have evolved in the species (assuming such principles exist) are compatible with the institutional requirements of modern life, and if not, whether our institutions should be changed. We might also wish to ask whether acting out of a sense of justice is conducive to a person's good or whether, as Nietzsche apparently thought, doing so is likely to be a psychological disaster for that person (cf. Scanlon 1982: 218). Above all, we will want to know whether the principles of moral competence are compatible with the requirements of rationality, in whatever sense of rationality seems appropriate. These are complex topics, which, except for a few peripheral remarks, I will not discuss here. Because I agree with Rawls about the importance of not giving way to the impulse to answer questions that one is not yet equipped to examine (Rawls 1975: 10), and because any serious discussion of these topics would be premature within the framework that I have described thus far, I must set them aside for now. I mention these issues only to forestall possible misinterpretations of the nature and scope of this inquiry. The point of this book is not to deny that there are significant differences between moral theory and linguistics. On the contrary, I not only accept, but insist, that these two disciplines, and the theoretical problems they seek to solve, are dissimilar in many fundamental respects.

2.3 OUTLINE OF REMAINING CHAPTERS

The remaining chapters of this book are intended to make a unified whole by supporting each other in the following way. Chapter 3 consists of an interpretation of Section 9 of *A Theory of Justice*. The main aim of this chapter is to call attention to the various features of Rawls' linguistic analogy described above. The conception of moral theory outlined thus far invites at least two kinds of questions. The first is exegetical: Is this conception correctly attributed to Rawls? The second is philosophical: Is this conception sound? Although these two inquiries are logically independent, they are not unrelated to one another. Rawls is among the clearest and most careful thinkers in the field. He has a deep knowledge of his subject matter as well as that of adjacent disciplines. Hence whatever theoretical positions he adopts are likely to be worthy of serious consideration (compare Singer's similar remarks about Sidgwick in Singer 1974). If it can be shown that the conception of moral theory described in this chapter is not merely a restatement of Chomsky's philosophy of linguistics in moral terms, but a restatement of Rawls' conception of moral theory in Chomsky's terms – or, rather, in terms that are intelligible to the community of researchers working more or less within the framework of Universal Grammar – then, insofar one believes, as I do, that Universal Grammar is on the right track, one's conviction that the conception is sound should be strengthened. To say this is not to make a mere appeal, or to rely uncritically, on either Rawls' or Chomsky's authority. Rather, it is to recognize that, like any other science, a theory of moral cognition is more likely to be sound insofar as it builds on the insights of its most successful predecessors, and insofar as it rests on assumptions that are shared by, or at least consistent with, what is known in adjacent fields. Hence, the primary aim of Chapter 3 is to show that the conception of moral theory Rawls describes in Section 9 can be accurately reformulated in the terminology we have adopted and, in fact, that it is even more compelling when restated within this general framework. To do this I first identify and explain the eight basic elements of Rawls' linguistic analogy described above. I then argue that Rawls' conception of moral theory is an I-morality conception in the sense defined in Section 2.1.8.

Let me now turn to a summary of Part Two. Here it helps to begin with some comments of a more general nature. Thus far I have referred to Rawls' conception of moral theory in exclusively favorable terms. I have suggested that Rawls was one of the first philosophers to grasp the potential implications of Universal Grammar for ethics, that *A Theory of Justice* contains one of the most powerful accounts of moral theory ever written, and that Rawls' early work contains the outline of an empirical theory of moral cognition that far surpasses the research programs of Piaget and Kohlberg in terms of depth, coherence, and scientific rigor. Remarks like these may lead the reader to assume that I believe that Rawls' conception of moral theory is somehow beyond criticism, or at least correct in its essentials. Any such assumption, however, would be inaccurate.

In my view, Rawls' early approach to moral theory suffers from at least three major shortcomings, at least from the perspective of someone like myself who wishes to draw on Rawls' early ideas to develop a fruitful research program in the cognitive science of moral judgment. The first shortcoming concerns how Rawls understands the relationship between the moral principles that apply to institutional arrangements and those that apply to the actions of individuals. According to Rawls, the first set of principles is primary, and the second set is derivative (1971: 108–110; cf. Hart 1973; Miller 1974). From a naturalistic point of view, this seems implausible. It seems more likely that the principles that generate considered moral judgments about the basic structure of society are themselves rooted in principles that apply to the acts of conspecifics, rather than the other way around.

The second weakness of Rawls' moral philosophy from a naturalistic perspective concerns his approach to moral psychology and cognitive development. In his early writings Rawls assumes that there are two major traditions in the theory of cognitive development, one stemming from classical empiricism and represented more recently by behaviorism and social learning theory, and the other deriving from classical rationalism and represented more recently by the social constructivism of Piaget and Kohlberg. Rawls places the utilitarians from Hume through Sidgwick, along with Freud, in the former category, and Rousseau, Kant, Humboldt, and J. S. Mill (at least in some of his moods) in the latter (1971: 458–461). While these groupings are conventional, I believe they are inadequate. To the extent that such classifications are helpful (which may be questioned), one must distinguish at least three traditions, not two. In addition to behaviorism and social constructivism, there is a genuine third alternative: the so-called *nativism* of Chomsky, Fodor, Spelke, and others, which is currently one of the major research paradigms in cognitive science and the philosophy of mind.

As this concept will be understood here, nativism is simply the view that early cognitive development is best understood, from a scientific point of view, as a process of biologically determined growth and maturation. As such, nativism assumes that while the acquisition of cognitive systems is triggered and shaped by appropriate experience, and thus depends crucially on cultural inputs, the specific properties of those systems are largely predetermined by the innate structure of the mind. So understood, nativism arguably has a stronger claim than constructivism does to having descended from the classical rationalism of philosophers such as Leibniz, Rousseau, Kant, and Humboldt. I will not take up this historical issue here (for some useful discussion, see, e.g., Chomsky 1966; Piatelli-Palmarini 1980; Spelke 1998). For our purposes what is important is simply to recognize that when Rawls evaluates different accounts of cognitive development in *A Theory of Justice,* he does not adequately consider nativism. I believe that the reasons for this apparent oversight are not too difficult to discern. We must keep in mind when *A Theory of Justice* was published. In 1971, neither academic philosophy nor academic psychology was particularly hospitable to genetic or biologically based accounts of moral or social development, or indeed of cognitive development more generally. Even in the case of language, Chomsky's "innateness hypothesis," as Putnam (1975) called it, was still highly controversial at the time. Moreover, the field of cognitive science as we think of it today was still in its infancy. For example, the first textbook in cognitive psychology did not appear until the late 1960s (Neisser 1967), and many leading journals had not yet begun publication. In general, during the period in which Rawls was writing *A Theory of Justice,* there simply did not yet exist a body of empirical literature or an established theoretical vocabulary on which Rawls could have relied to defend the claim that moral knowledge is innate, even if he had wished to do so.[16]

What I take to be the third inadequacy of Rawls' early approach to moral theory is his failure to take his own metaethical requirements seriously enough. In his early writings, Rawls sets admirably clear and ambitious computational goals for moral theory. For example, he frequently makes provocative observations such as the following: "We should strive for a kind of moral geometry with all the rigor which this name connotes" (1971: 121). Rawls also formulates reasonably clear and, in my view, compelling arguments to explain why moral philosophers interested in normative issues should largely postpone

---

[16] Indeed, even to find a phrase like "moral knowledge is innate" in recent literature is difficult. To do so, one must return to the Enlightenment. For example, Leibniz observes:

> [M]oral knowledge is innate in just the same way that arithmetic is, for it too depends on demonstrations provided by the inner light. Since demonstrations do not spring into view straight away, it is no great wonder if men are not always aware straight away of everything they have within them, and are not very quick to read the characters of the natural law which, according to St. Paul, God has engraved in their minds. However, since morality is more important than arithmetic, God has given to man instincts which lead, straight away and without reasoning, to part of what reason commands. (Leibniz 1996/ 1705: 94)

Likewise, Rousseu writes:

> Cast your eyes on all the nations of the world, go through all the histories. Among so many inhuman and bizarre cults, among this prodigious diversity of morals and characters, you will find everywhere the same ideas of justice and decency, everywhere the same notions of good and bad. ... There is in the depths of all souls, then, an innate principle of justice and virtue according to which, in spite of our own maxims, we judge our actions and those of others as good or bad. It is to this principle that I give the name *conscience.* (Rousseau 1979/1762: 288–289)

To clarify, I am not suggesting that Rawls actually wanted to argue that moral knowledge is innate but was prevented from doing so because he lacked an appropriate theoretical vocabulary. On the contrary, I believe that Rawls did *not* wish to make this type of argument. This is because his overriding aim was to promote consensus about principles of social justice, and presumably this would have been more difficult if he had also made strong claims about the naturalistic origins of these principles. As it was, Rawls' book generated stiff opposition from commentators who were uncomfortable with his occasional appeals to human nature.

These remarks are not entirely speculative: in my conversations with him, Rawls explained to me that he intended his theory to be consistent with, but not to require, assumptions about the innateness of the sense of justice because he wished to refrain from advancing a more controversial argument when a weaker one might achieve the same ends (cf. Rawls 1971: 495–496).

them until they have achieved the more modest goal of descriptive adequacy. Rawls' actual pursuit of these objectives, however, departs from the approach that he recommends to others. Thus, taking these points in reverse order, beginning in 1957 and continuing throughout the development of his account of justice as fairness, Rawls does not first show that his two principles of justice are descriptively adequate and proceed only afterward to the problem of justification. Rather, he takes their descriptive adequacy as more or less given, and he constructs the original position in order to justify and explain them.[17] Moreover, as many early commentators (e.g., Care 1969; Wolff 1977) observe, and as Rawls (e.g., 1971: 121, 581) readily concedes, Rawls does not actually attempt to prove any "theorems of moral geometry" in *A Theory of Justice* (1971: 126). Rather, his general mode of argument throughout the book is highly intuitive, a feature that draws the ire of many of. his sharpest critics (see, e.g., Hare 1973).

These remarks are not necessarily meant to be criticisms of Rawls. On the contrary, in light of his primary objectives in *A Theory of Justice* – to explicate and justify a comprehensive theory of social justice and to apply it to the basic institutional structure of a well-ordered society – Rawls' strategic choices and intuitive mode of argument seem highly appropriate, and indeed to some extent inevitable. In the first place, it does not seem reasonable to suppose that, for complex problems of social justice, there exists a finite yet complete system of principles that, together with the nonmoral facts, is capable of mechanically settling all possible disputes that might arise to the satisfaction of all relevant observers. Hence, the notion of a computational theory of social justice in this sense seems implausible (cf. Pound 1908). In addition, one must consider the vast ground that Rawls wished to cover. *A Theory of Justice* touches on a wealth of topics beyond those I have already mentioned. These range from constitutional liberties, justice between generations, and tax policy to civil disobedience and conscientious objection. The book also addresses the law of nations, natural duties and obligations, the theory of moral development, and even evolutionary stability. Rawls could not possibly have examined all of these topics in the manner he does while also proving "theorems of moral geometry" with "all the rigor which this name connotes" (1971: 126, 121). Hence, Rawls' actual mode of argument seems both appropriate and inevitable.

Nevertheless, one must recognize that these features of Rawls' work are real shortcomings from the point of view of the theory of moral cognition.

---

[17] See Rawls (1957), where Rawls introduces his two principles for the first time. He says: "*Given these principles,* one might try to derive them from a priori principles of reason, or offer them as known by intuition. These are familiar steps, and, at least in the case of the first principle, might be made with some success. I wish, however, to look at the principles in a different way" (1957: 655, emphasis added). In this essay and in his other early writings, Rawls does not show that his principles are descriptively adequate; rather, he takes their descriptive adequacy as more or less given, and he constructs an argument to justify and explain them.

Insofar as a philosopher or scientist seeks, as I do, to develop such a theory, and to integrate it into the cognitive and brain sciences, she must begin by focusing attention on much simpler problems than those that occupy Rawls in *A Theory of Justice*. In addition, she must start from empirically plausible assumptions about how the mind works. Finally, she must attempt to make her theory as analytically rigorous as possible.

The purpose of Part Two is to build on the conception of moral theory that Rawls outlines in Section 9 of *A Theory of Justice* while at the same time correcting for these perceived shortcomings. Specifically, I attempt to illustrate the worth of Rawls' linguistic analogy by showing how the conception of moral theory it presupposes can be transformed into a genuine empirical theory that takes the actions of individuals, rather than institutional arrangements, as its primary focus; that is broadly mentalist, modular, and nativist in its basic orientation; and that approaches the problem of descriptive adequacy in a manner consistent with the demanding computational requirements that Rawls articulates in his early writings.

In Chapter 4, I begin this process by taking a closer look at the family of trolley problems that originated with the work of Foot (1967) and Thomson (1986). In a series of experiments that began in the mid-1990s, my colleagues and I began testing these problems, and others like them based on the same basic template, on hundreds of individuals, both adults and children. Our central aim was to pursue the idea of a Universal Moral Grammar and to begin to investigate a variety of empirical questions that arise within this framework. Our basic prediction was that the moral intuitions elicited by at least some of these problems would be widely shared, irrespective of demographic variables such as race, sex, age, religion, national origin, or level of formal education. We also predicted that most individuals would be unaware of the operative principles generating their moral intuitions, and thus largely incapable of correctly describing their own thought processes. These predictions were confirmed, and our initial findings have now been replicated and extended with over 200,000 individuals from over 120 countries (see, e.g., Miller 2008; see generally Section 5.2.1).

After introducing the trolley problems and observing that the properties of the moral judgments they elicit appear to illustrate various aspects of the linguistic analogy, the remainder of Chapter 4 attempts to formulate the problem of descriptive adequacy with respect to these judgments, and to situate this problem within the framework of the contemporary cognitive sciences. Chapter 5 then sketches a provisional solution to this descriptive problem, which I label *the moral grammar hypothesis*. According to this hypothesis, a crucial feature of the trolley problems is that they suggest and can be used to prove that moral judgments do not depend solely on the superficial description of a given action, but also on how that action is *mentally represented,* a critical preliminary step in the evaluative process that jurists have frequently examined (see, e.g., Cardozo 1921; Hutcheson 1929; Oliphant 1928; Radin

1925; see also Grey 1983; Kelman 1981) but, surprisingly, many psychologists have unduly neglected. Hence the problem of descriptive adequacy in the moral domain must be divided into at least three parts, involving the description of (i) deontic rules, (ii) structural descriptions, and (iii) conversion rules. Although the difficulty that most people have in explaining or justifying their judgments implies that they are unaware of the principles that guide their moral intuitions, the judgments themselves can be explained by assuming that these individuals are intuitive lawyers, who possess tacit or unconscious knowledge of a rich variety of legal rules, concepts, and principles, along with a natural readiness to compute mental representations of human acts and omissions in legally cognizable terms. Put differently, the intuitive data can be explained by assuming that ordinary individuals implicitly recognize the relevance of categories like ends, means, side effects, and *prima facie* wrongs, such as battery, to the analysis of legal and moral problems. In particular, the key distinction that explains many of the standard cases in the literature is that the agent commits one or more batteries as a means of achieving his good end in the impermissible conditions (e.g., the Transplant and Footbridge problems), whereas these violations are merely subsequent and foreseen side effects in the permissible conditions (e.g., the Trolley and Bystander problems). Moreover, the structural descriptions that are implied by this explanation can be exhibited in a two-dimensional tree diagram, successive nodes of which bear a generation relation to one another that is asymmetric, irreflexive, and transitive (Goldman 1970a; see generally Mikhail 2000, 2002b, 2005; Mikhail, Sorrentino, & Spelke 1998).

In Chapter 6, I provide a more detailed and formal description of the mental operations implied by the moral grammar hypothesis. In particular, drawing on a diverse set of ideas and traditions, including deontic logic, lexical semantics, the philosophy of action, and the common law of crime and tort, I argue that the manner in which trolley problems are mentally represented can be described in terms of a hierarchical sequence of act-token representations, or *act tree* (Goldman 1970a; Mikhail 2000), which encodes the information relevant to determining a particular action's deontic status. On this basis I propose a novel computational analysis of trolley problem intuitions that appears capable of accounting, in explicit and rigorous fashion, for a broad range of these otherwise puzzling commonsense moral judgments. Finally, throughout Part Two I distinguish the moral grammar hypothesis from the alternative model of moral judgment advocated by researchers such as Joshua Greene and Jonathan Haidt (2002). Unlike Greene and Haidt, I argue that the critical issue in the theory of moral cognition is not whether moral intuitions are linked to emotions – clearly they are – but how to characterize the appraisal system those intuitions presuppose, and in particular whether that system incorporates elements of a sophisticated jurisprudence.

Let me turn next to a summary of Part Three. The main purpose of these chapters is to respond to what I take to be some rather unconvincing criticisms of Rawls' linguistic analogy that have not yet received adequate attention in the philosophical literature, in particular those of R. M. Hare, Peter Singer, Thomas Nagel, and Ronald Dworkin. In Chapter 7, I argue that philosophers such as Hare and Singer who have criticized Rawls' linguistic analogy on the grounds that the conception of moral theory it presupposes is too empirical or insufficiently normative appear to be operating with an unduly narrow and impoverished conception of moral philosophy. On the one hand, these critics apparently wish to exclude empirical questions about the nature and origin of commonsense moral knowledge from the domain of what they identify as moral philosophy. Yet, on the other hand, they appear to beg the very questions that Rawls' research program is designed to answer, inasmuch as they assume a broadly empiricist account of how moral knowledge is acquired. Moreover, neither Hare nor Singer appears to have grasped the relationship in Rawls' conception of moral theory between the problems of empirical and normative adequacy. In any event, they have failed to address Rawls' reasonable contention in *Outline* that a descriptively adequate moral theory constitutes a *presumptive* solution to the problem of normative adequacy, in light of the class of judgments that a descriptively adequate moral theory explains (Rawls 1951). Finally, I argue that their central objection to Rawls' method of explicating common moral intuitions, which I call their *objection from insufficient normativity,* fails to come to terms with Rawls' somewhat different, and more complex, approach to the relationship between empirical and normative adequacy in *A Theory of Justice,* as captured by his notion of reflective equilibrium.

In Chapter 8, I examine Thomas Nagel's brief objections to Rawls' linguistic analogy in his early review of *A Theory of Justice* (Nagel 1973). In particular, I use Nagel's objections as an opportunity to explore some of the implications of the competence–performance distinction for moral theory. I argue that Nagel's arguments are untenable as they stand and that, even if one charitably reconstructs them, they fail to constitute a compelling criticism of the conception of moral theory Rawls describes in *A Theory of Justice.* The main reason is that Nagel fails to acknowledge Rawls' reliance on the competence–performance distinction and to recognize the theory dependence of the corresponding distinction in linguistics. Once these points are properly understood, Nagel's criticisms do not seem persuasive. I defend a similar argument with respect to those philosophers, such as Norman Daniels (1979, 1980) and Richard Brandt (1979, 1990), who criticize Rawls by relying on what I call *the objection from prejudice,* according to which Rawls' conception of moral theory is flawed because it consists of a mere reshuffling of our prejudices. In response, I argue that this objection fails to acknowledge Rawls' legitimate and indeed indispensable use of the competence–performance distinction, in the form of his concept of a *considered judgment.* Rawls uses this concept to define the difference between a prejudice and a judgment in which moral capacities are likely to be displayed without distortion. Since, as a question of method, Rawls is entitled to draw this distinction and then seek empirical support for it within the framework of his theory, the objection from prejudice appears to be without force.

In Chapter 9, I examine Ronald Dworkin's discussion of Rawls' linguistic analogy in his influential book *Taking Rights Seriously*. Among other things, I contend that Dworkin's naturalist and constructivist interpretations of Rawls represent a false antithesis; neither is an accurate model of the conception of moral theory Rawls actually describes in *A Theory of Justice*. I argue that Dworkin's main error in this regard appears to be his mistaken assumption that a naturalistic approach to moral theory must be "realist" rather than "mentalist" (or what I describe in Chapters 3 and 8 as an "E-morality" conception of moral theory rather than an I-morality conception). In short, there is a credible, mentalistic alternative to Dworkin's untenable version of naturalism, which researchers interested in the idea of Universal Moral Grammar can seek to develop. Furthermore, this genuinely naturalistic alternative offers a sound basis on which to support and defend a robust conception of universal human rights.

In Part Four, I summarize the main points of the book and attempt to place Rawls' linguistic analogy within a broader historical and philosophical context. Finally, I conclude by arguing that the theory of moral cognition might be able to vindicate Rawls' guiding conviction that humankind possesses a shared moral nature if philosophers, linguists, cognitive scientists, and legal scholars would join forces and pursue the research program outlined in this book.

3

The Basic Elements of Rawls'
Linguistic Analogy

It may now be ask'd *in general,* concerning this pain or pleasure, that distinguishes moral good and evil, *From what principles is it derived, and whence does it arise in the human mind?* To this I reply, *first,* that 'tis absurd to imagine, that in every particular instance, these sentiments are produc'd by an *original* quality and *primary* constitution. For as the number of our duties is, in a manner, infinite, 'tis impossible that our original instincts should extend to each of them, and from our very first infancy impress on the human mind all that multitude of precepts, which are contain'd in the compleatest system of ethics. Such a method of proceeding is not conformable to the usual maxims, by which nature is conducted, where a few principles produce all that variety we observe in the universe, and everything is carry'd on in the easiest and most simple manner. 'Tis necessary, therefore, to abridge these primary impulses, and find some more general principles, upon which all our notions of morals are founded.

– David Hume, *A Treatise of Human Nature*

The main argument of this book is that Rawls was correct to assume in Section 9 of *A Theory of Justice* that the theory of moral cognition is usefully modeled on aspects of Chomsky's theory of Universal Grammar. In addition, I attempt to illustrate the worth of Rawls' linguistic analogy by showing how the conception of moral theory that Rawls describes in Section 9 can be developed into a substantive research program in moral psychology that uses thought experiments such as the trolley problem and other cases of necessity, and a Socratic, case-based method more generally, to investigate the nature and origin of human moral intuitions. Finally, in the last part of the book I argue that many of the early criticisms of Rawls' naturalistic conception of moral theory advanced by legal and moral philosophers such as Dworkin, Hare, Nagel, and Singer are unsound.

To achieve these objectives, we must first become clearer about what Rawls actually says about these issues in *A Theory of Justice.* Rawls opens Section 9 with a fundamental assumption: that under normal circumstances each person possesses a complex moral capacity, with which she develops a sense of justice. He then suggests that moral philosophy may be conceived, at least provisionally, as the attempt to describe the sense of justice, and he clarifies what he means by such a project by comparing it to the problem of describing the sense of grammaticalness that we have for the sentences of our native language.

For our topic there are at least eight main points to notice about the way Rawls characterizes moral theory in Section 9: (i) Rawls' apparent use of the argument for moral grammar to defend the empirical assumption that the sense of justice is a cognitive system of sufficient coherence and complexity to make it interesting and worthwhile to describe; (ii) Rawls' suggestion that moral philosophy may be conceived, at least provisionally, as the attempt to solve the problem of descriptive adequacy; (iii) the distinction Rawls appears to draw between the problems of descriptive and observational adequacy; (iv) the distinction Rawls appears to draw between express and operative principles; (v) the distinction Rawls appears to draw between the problems of descriptive and explanatory adequacy; (vi) Rawls' apparent use of a version of the competence–performance distinction; (vii) Rawls' apparent use of the linguistic analogy to emphasize the theory-dependence of the competence–performance distinction; and finally, (viii) Rawls' apparent use of the linguistic analogy to defend the importance of idealization.

In this chapter, I examine these eight features of Rawls' conception of moral theory. One main reason for doing so is to support the interpretation of the linguistic analogy that I defend in this book. Since the secondary literature on Rawls lacks a comparably extensive discussion, I hope that this effort will improve our general understanding of the conception of moral theory presupposed by Rawls in *A Theory of Justice*. In addition, the discussion that follows is meant to bring into sharper focus the substantive research program outlined in Section 2.1, which I then seek to develop further in Part Two. After identifying and provisionally explaining the basic elements of Rawls' linguistic analogy, I argue that Rawls' conception of moral theory is an I-morality conception in the sense defined in Section 2.1.8. I also make some further clarifying remarks about the linguistic analogy and briefly contrast the argument for moral grammar with moral particularism.

3.1 EIGHT FEATURES OF RAWLS' CONCEPTION OF MORAL THEORY

3.1.1 The Argument for Moral Grammar

Rawls begins Section 9 by assuming that each person possesses a complex moral capacity with which she develops a sense of justice:

Let us assume that each person beyond a certain age and possessed of the requisite intellectual capacity develops a sense of justice under normal social circumstances.

We acquire a skill in judging things to be just and unjust, and in supporting these judgments with reasons. Moreover, we ordinarily have some desire to act in accord with these pronouncements and expect a similar desire on the part of others. Clearly this moral capacity is extraordinarily complex. To see this it suffices to note the potentially infinite number and variety of judgments that we are prepared to make. The fact that we often do not know what to say, and sometimes find our minds unsettled, does not detract from the complexity of the capacity we have. (1971: 46)

For our topic, the most important thing to recognize about this passage – what philosophers have largely failed to recognize[1] – is that it contains the outline of what may be called an *argument for moral grammar*. This argument may be thought of as an application to the moral domain of a more general *argument for mental grammar,* in a sense that is familiar by now to many researchers in cognitive science and the philosophy of mind (see, e.g., Jackendoff 1994). As far as I am aware, the passage constitutes the first recent attempt by a contemporary philosopher to use this type of argument for the purpose of defending the existence and complexity of what traditionally was known as the moral faculty, moral sense, or conscience (see, e.g., Mikhail 2007b, 2008c).

The paradigm case of the argument for mental grammar is Chomsky's *argument for linguistic grammar.* Since the notion of a speaker's linguistic grammar is *the* central theoretical construct of modern linguistics (Jackendoff 1994: 15) and lies at the heart of Rawls' linguistic analogy, it may be helpful to begin by reviewing the structure of Chomsky's argument and its role in linguistic inquiry before examining Rawls' apparent use of a parallel argument in the moral domain.

The argument for linguistic grammar turns on what is sometimes called the "expressive variety of language use" (Jackendoff 1994: 6), and, as we have seen, it has the form of an abductive argument or an inference to the best explanation (Harman 1965; Peirce 1955/1901). The argument holds that the best explanation of certain observable phenomena is the presence of a *grammar,* or system of principles or rules, in the mind of the normal language user, on which she unconsciously relies in behaving as she does. Without this assumption, it is argued, the subject's observable behavior would be largely inexplicable.

The argument begins with a fairly simple set of empirical observations. A mature speaker of a language has encountered a limited set of utterances in her lifetime. On the basis of this finite experience, she can construct an infinitely large set of new utterances that are immediately acceptable to other speakers of her language. The mature speaker also possesses the ability to make a wide range of intuitive judgments about the properties and relations of sound, form, and meaning of novel expressions in her language, including whether

---

[1] When I wrote *Rawls' Linguistic Analogy,* the only exceptions I could find in a fairly extensive literature search were Daniels (1980) and Williams (1985).

any random sequence of sounds constitutes a grammatical sentence; whether a given sentence is ambiguous; whether, given two arbitrary sentences, one is a paraphrase, rhyme, or entailment of the other; and a number of additional properties and relations (Chomsky 1975a: 61–62; see also Chomsky 1957, 1964).

As a simple illustration of these claims, consider the following expressions:

(3) (a) colorless green ideas sleep furiously
    (b) furiously sleep ideas green colorless
    (c) invisible blue rainbows bark lovingly
    (d) lovingly bark rainbows blue invisible
    (e) the little boys' camp is on fire
    (f) they are flying planes
    (g) I wonder who the men expected to see them
    (h) the men expected to see them
    (i) the man is tall
    (j) is the man tall
    (k) the man who is here is tall
    (l) is the man who here is tall
    (m) is the man who is here tall
    (n) John is too stubborn to talk to Bill
    (o) John is too stubborn to talk to
    (p) Jane appeared to Mary to like herself
    (q) Jane appeared to Mary to like her
    (r) Jane appealed to Mary to like herself
    (s) Jane appealed to Mary to like her

Every fluent speaker of English knows or when suitably prompted can recognize that (a) and (c) but not (b) and (d) are grammatical; that (e) and (f) are ambiguous; that in (g) but not (h) the pronoun "them" may be referentially dependent on "the men"; that (j) is a well-formed question of (i); that (m) is a well-formed question of (k), but (l) is not; that (n) implies that John won't talk to Bill, but (o) implies that an arbitrary person, X, won't talk to John; and that each of (p) –(s) has a different combination of who is to like whom: in (p) Jane likes Jane; in (q) Jane likes Mary or some unspecified third party; in (r) Mary is to like Mary; in (s) Mary is to like Jane or a third party (Chomsky 1957: 15, 1986a: 8–14; Jackendoff 1994: 23). They can do this even though they may never have heard these utterances before and might otherwise never encounter or produce them. Moreover, they can exhibit these behaviors even though they probably cannot explain sophisticated concepts like referential dependence or otherwise provide a coherent theoretical account of their own practice.

For the linguist, intuitive judgments like these possess at least two crucial properties. The first is that they extend to expressions that are *novel,* in the sense of having no point-for-point relationship to any previously encountered or produced. The second is that the judgments, or more exactly, the expressions the judgments are about, are *unbounded in scope:* the number of these expressions is, in point of fact, indefinitely large.

Although seemingly innocuous, these two properties carry with them far-reaching consequences. The novelty and unboundedness of linguistic judgment imply that once the speaker has mastered her native language, she has the capacity to make, not just a wide range of judgments, but (in Rawls' phrase) "a potentially infinite number and variety" (1971: 46) of judgments about the properties and relations of expressions in her language. This fact, however, is significant. Coupled with the finite storage capacity of the brain, it implies that each of these expressions cannot be stored in her mind individually. Instead, her mind must contain a recipe or program of some sort – a grammar – that can build, out of a finite list of words and phrase patterns, the unlimited set of expressions she is able to produce, understand, and interpret (Chomsky 1957: 13f.; see also Jackendoff 1994: 10; Pinker 1994: 22; Quine 1972: 443; Strawson 1972: 455).

Rawls' argument for moral grammar is contained primarily in the following sentence: "To see [the extraordinary complexity of our moral capacity], it suffices to note the potentially infinite number and variety of judgments that we are prepared to make" (1971: 46). Rawls' inference in this sentence turns on the simple but important observation that, like linguistic judgment, moral judgment is potentially novel and unbounded. These properties suffice to establish what Rawls calls the "complexity" of our moral capacity. Rawls' argument is incomplete, but we can imagine how an argument might be constructed that would support his conclusion by somewhat similar reasons as those we encountered in the linguistic case. An individual who possesses an adequately developed sense of justice is prepared to make a potentially unlimited number and variety of intuitive moral judgments about the moral properties of various acts, agents, and institutional arrangements, including judgments in entirely new situations, which are dissimilar from the finite number of situations she has previously encountered. Since the storage capacity of the brain is finite, it follows that each of these judgments (or more exactly, each of the mental representations of those situations which these judgments are about) cannot be stored in her mind individually. Instead, her brain must contain, with respect to moral judgment, something more complex: some kind of cognitive system, perhaps characterizable in terms of principles or rules, that can construct or generate the unlimited number and variety of representations her exercise of moral judgment presupposes.

The argument for moral grammar may be reformulated as the claim that moral theory faces a *projection problem*. In *Fact, Fiction, and Forecast,* Nelson Goodman (1983/1955: 84) utilizes this term to refer to the general problem of defining the relationship in any science "between evidence or base cases on the one hand, and hypotheses, predictions or projections on the other." In *Syntactic Structures,* Chomsky discusses the same problem as it occurs in linguistics; but, in addition, Chomsky makes the crucial observation that the relationship between the linguist's grammar and her corpus parallels the behavior of the native speaker in this respect. Here is how Chomsky puts the point:

> On what basis do we actually go about separating grammatical sequences from ungrammatical sequences? ... I would like to point out that several answers that immediately suggest themselves could not be correct. First, it is obvious that the set of grammatical sentences cannot be identified with any particular corpus of utterances obtained by the linguist in his field work. Any grammar of a language will *project* the finite and somewhat accidental corpus of observed utterances to a set (presumably infinite) of grammatical utterances. In this respect, a grammar mirrors the behavior of the speaker who, on the basis of a finite and accidental experience with language, can produce or understand an indefinite number of new sentences. Indeed, any explication of the notion 'grammatical' ... can be thought of as offering an explanation for this fundamental aspect of linguistic behavior. (1957: 15, emphasis original)

As Daniels (1980: 22–23) observes, Rawls' reference in Section 9 to the "potentially infinite number and variety of moral judgments that we are prepared to make" (1971: 46) implies that moral theory is confronted with a projection problem of its own.[2] The problem in moral theory is to determine what enables normal persons, once they reach a certain age and level of development, to *project* their partial and limited experience with human actions and institutions to the potentially unlimited number of novel acts and institutional arrangements they are prepared, morally speaking, to evaluate. Presumably most persons are capable of accomplishing, and do accomplish, this projection; given the stability, predictability, and other systematic properties of at least some of their judgments, it seems reasonable to assume that, despite being intuitive, their basis is a system of principles or rules. Hence the moral philosopher like the linguist has a job to do: to extract and state with full explicitness those principles and rules.

Rawls' observation is not new; at least since Aristotle, philosophers have recognized that a striking feature of moral judgment is its characteristic variety and lack of repetition. With few exceptions, no two situations that occasion moral judgment are exactly alike. Each is a potentially brand new

---

[2] "I believe Rawls, in introducing this analogy, intends us to see a similarity to the 'projection problem' in syntactic theory. People who have encountered only finitely many sentences can make judgments of grammaticality (actually, of acceptability) about indeterminately many sentences, which suggests we should look for general principles or rules when we seek to characterize their syntactic competency. Similarly, people who have encountered only finitely many moral situations can make indeterminately many judgments. In both cases people may cite principles which they appeal to in forming judgments of grammaticality (acceptability) or rightness or justice, but such principles may not, in fact, be the principles which would be needed to explain their linguistic or moral competency" (Daniels 1980: 22–23).

combination of agents, acts, events, and circumstances, occurring for the first time in the history of the universe (for parallel remarks about language, see Pinker 1994: 22; for morality, see, e.g., James 1890: vol. 2, 672–675). What distinguishes Rawls is his assumption that this situational or "particularistic" aspect of moral judgment is not incompatible with the existence of moral rules, as some philosophers, such as Jonathan Dancy (1983) and John McDowell (1979), have mistakenly assumed (see Section 3.5). On the contrary, Rawls recognizes that, as is the case with grammaticality judgments, the novelty and unboundedness of moral judgment (together with its other systematic properties) *implies* the existence of rules.

3.1.2 The Problem of Descriptive Adequacy

Once the argument for linguistic grammar has been used to defend the assumption that a speaker's knowledge of language consists in her possession of a grammar, two further questions suggest themselves to the linguist. The first question is, What exactly are the properties of this grammar or system of rules? This question is equivalent to (1a). The second question is, Given a particular answer to the first question, how does such a system develop in the individual? This question is equivalent to (1b). Although both questions are the subject of ongoing research, enough detailed properties of the speaker's grammar are now known – in fact, enough were recognized right away – to favor one of two general types of answer to the second question. Given the richness and complexity of the postulated grammar, coupled with the poor and degenerate information available to the language learner, it is concluded that a significant component of the acquired grammar must be innate. Hence what Chomsky has termed the rationalist flavor of contemporary linguistic theory (see, e.g., Chomsky 1966).

The significance of this sequence of question for our topic is that Rawls conceives of the structure of moral theory in a similar way. Having attributed a sense of justice or moral grammar to normal individuals, Rawls immediately turns his attention to the task of characterizing or describing it:

Now one may think of moral philosophy at first (and I stress the provisional nature of this view) as the attempt to describe our moral capacity; or in the present case, one may regard a theory of justice as describing our sense of justice. This enterprise is very difficult. For by such a description is not meant simply a list of the judgments on institutions and actions that we are prepared to render, accompanied with supporting reasons when these are offered. Rather, what is required is a formulation of a set of principles which, when conjoined to our beliefs and knowledge of the circumstances, would lead us to make these judgments with their supporting reasons were we to apply these principles conscientiously and intelligently. A conception of justice characterizes our moral sensibility when the everyday judgments we do make are in accordance with its principles. These principles can serve as part of the premises of an argument which arrives at the matching judgments. We do not understand our sense of justice until we know in some systematic way covering a wide range of cases what these principles are. Only a deceptive familiarity with our everyday judgments and our natural readiness to make them could conceal the fact that characterizing our moral capacities is an intricate task. The principles which describe them must be presumed to have a complex structure, and the concepts involved will require serious study. (1971: 46)

Just what Rawls has in mind by a description of the sense of justice will be examined in Chapter 4. What I wish to call attention to here is simply the general significance of the paragraph as a whole. It suggests that Rawls thinks there is a conceptual distinction, and an order of priority, between at least two parts of moral philosophy. Moreover, it suggests that, in Rawls' view, the part that takes precedence is a descriptive enterprise, or, in other words, a type of moral psychology. That the proper sequence of inquiry in moral philosophy begins with the problem of descriptive adequacy – with empirical questions about aspects of human psychology – is a feature of Rawls' stated conception of moral theory whose importance cannot be overemphasized. Rawls' linguistic analogy is misunderstood unless one clearly grasps this point.[3]

3.1.3 The Distinction between Descriptive and Observational Adequacy

In the paragraph under discussion, Rawls contrasts two types of description, the first of which is "a list of the judgments on institutions and actions that we are prepared to render, accompanied with supporting reasons when these are offered," and the second of which is "a set of principles which, when conjoined to our beliefs and knowledge of the circumstances, would lead us to make these judgments with their supporting reasons were we to apply these principles conscientiously and intelligently" (1971: 47). The contrast parallels the distinction that Chomsky draws in *Syntactic Structures* and elsewhere between two conceivable kinds of linguistic grammar: one that merely presents an inventory of all morpheme (or word) sequences that constitute grammatical sentences in a language, the other that consists of a finite set of rules or principles capable of mechanically enumerating each of the infinite set of well-formed strings in a language, and assigning it an appropriate structural description (Chomsky 1957: 18). From a formal point of view, each type of grammar may be regarded as a deductive system: a collection of statements, rules, or axioms capable of describing, defining, or (in the logical sense) *generating* all and only the well-formed utterances in a language (Chomsky 1957: 13–17, 1975a: 113; Halle 1962: 334). Only the second type of grammar, however, is interesting to a linguist. The former implies that when a speaker-hearer assigns a grammatical status to the expressions she encounters, she

---

[3] The conception traces in its essentials to *Grounds* and *Outline*. Another clear statement may be found in *Independence*. I return to this topic in Chapter 7.

does so merely by consulting a huge checklist of sentences. Hence it implies, absurdly, that her knowledge of language consists of nothing more than her having internalized this infinitely long list.

Rawls' characterization of the problem of describing the sense of justice suggests that he thinks that moral philosophy confronts a similar situation and should distinguish between *descriptive adequacy* and *observational adequacy* in the linguist's technical sense. An adequate description of the sense of justice, Rawls observes, cannot be a mere inventory of particular judgments. An individual's capacity for moral judgment is infinite; her memory capacity, however, is finite. A mere inventory of judgments would imply that her sense of justice consists of an infinitely long list. Hence a descriptively adequate theory of her sense of justice must amount to more than a mere list.

3.1.4 The Distinction between Operative and Express Principles

We have seen that two important features of Rawls' conception of moral theory are the assumption that each person develops a sense of justice under normal circumstances[4] and the claim that the provisional aim of moral philosophy is to describe or characterize this particular mental capacity. We have also briefly reviewed how Rawls uses the argument for moral grammar to defend this assumption and clarifies what he means by a description of the sense of justice by distinguishing different forms such a description might take.

It is at this point in his discussion, not before, that Rawls turns his reader's attention toward the linguistic analogy:

A useful comparison here is with the problem of describing the sense of grammaticalness that we have for the sentences of our native language. In this case, the aim

---

[4] We saw earlier that Rawls rests his conception of moral theory on the assumption that "each person beyond a certain age and possessed of the requisite intellectual capacities develops a sense of justice under normal social circumstances" (1971: 46). The qualification "under normal social circumstances" may seem unimportant, but in fact it is quite significant. Historically, skepticism toward the idea of a universal moral faculty has often found expression in the specious objection that such a faculty might not develop in certain individuals in certain nonstandard but imaginable circumstances. For example, in *The Province of Jurisprudence Determined,* John Austin advances two general arguments against "the hypothesis of a moral sense," the first of which is that it implies the existence of a moral sense even in "a child abandoned in the wilderness immediately after its birth and growing to the age of manhood in estrangement from human society" (Austin 1954/1832: 89). Likewise, in *Leviathan,* Hobbes' apparent reason for insisting that "Justice, and Injustice are none of the Faculties neither of the Body, nor Mind" is that "If they were, they might be in a man that were alone in the world, as well as his Senses, and Passions. They are Qualities, that relate to men in Society, not in Solitude" (Hobbes 1968/1651: 188). Rawls' qualification may be considered an effective rejoinder to objections such as Hobbes' and Austin's. For examples of children whose language faculty failed to develop normally due to extreme deprivation of the same general type that Hobbes and Austin appear to have in mind, see generally Pinker (1994: 290–296) and the literature cited there.

is to characterize the ability to recognize well-formed sentences by formulating clearly expressed principles which make the same discriminations as the native speaker. This is a difficult undertaking which, although still unfinished, is known to require theoretical constructions that far outrun the ad hoc precepts of our explicit grammatical knowledge. A similar situation presumably holds in moral philosophy. There is no reason to assume that our sense of justice can be adequately characterized by familiar common sense precepts, or derived from the more obvious learning principles. A correct account of moral capacities will certainly involve principles and theoretical constructions which go much beyond the norms and standards cited in everyday life. (1971: 47)

For our topic, the first point to notice about this passage is that Rawls recognizes that linguistic grammars "require theoretical constructions that far outrun the ad hoc precepts of our explicit grammatical knowledge" and warns that "there is no reason to assume that our sense of justice can be adequately characterized by familiar common sense precepts" (1971: 47). He therefore concludes that "a correct account of moral capacities will certainly involve principles and theoretical constructions which go much beyond the norms and standards cited in everyday life" (1971: 47). This suggests that Rawls distinguishes between *operative principles* and *express principles,* in the sense defined in Section 2.1.5.

3.1.5 The Distinction between Descriptive and Explanatory Adequacy

A further point worth highlighting about the preceding passage is the doubt Rawls expresses about whether the sense of justice can be "derived from the more obvious learning principles" (1971: 47). Rawls distinguishes, at least implicitly, between a description of the sense of justice and a description of how the sense of justice is acquired – in other words, between *the problem of descriptive adequacy* and *the problem of explanatory adequacy,* in the sense defined in Section 2.1.6. Moreover, his skepticism about the more obvious learning principles implies that Rawls thinks that familiar processes of association, internalization, socialization, and the like may be inadequate explanations of moral development, hence that a version of the argument from the poverty of the stimulus might be defensible in the moral domain.

3.1.6 The Competence–Performance Distinction

Let us set aside for now the foregoing pair of distinctions between operative and express principles (Section 3.1.4) and descriptive and explanatory adequacy (Section 3.1.5); the issues they raise are complex, and exploring them further here would lead us far afield. Consider instead the next element of Rawls' linguistic analogy. Rawls' next paragraph introduces the concept of a *considered judgment,* which he describes as follows:

[C]onsidered judgments ... enter as those judgments in which our moral capacities are most likely to be displayed without distortion. Thus in deciding which of our judgments to take into account we may reasonably select some and exclude others. For example, we can discard those judgments made with hesitation, or in which we have little confidence. Similarly, those given when we are upset or frightened, or when we stand to gain one way or the other can be left aside. All these judgments are likely to be erroneous or to be influenced by an excessive attention to our own interests. Considered judgments are simply those rendered under conditions favorable to the exercise of the sense of justice, and therefore in circumstances where the more common excuses and explanations for making a mistake do not obtain. The person making the judgment is presumed, then, to have the ability, the opportunity, and the desire to reach a correct decision (or at least, not the desire not to). Moreover, the criteria that identify these judgments are not arbitrary. They are, in fact, similar to those that single out considered judgments of any kind. And once we regard the sense of justice as a mental capacity, as involving the exercise of thought, the relevant judgments are those given under conditions favorable for deliberation and judgment in general. (1971: 47–48)

For our topic, the most important thing to recognize about this passage – again, something Rawls' commentators have largely neglected[5] – is that Rawls appears to be drawing a distinction between *moral performance* (a person's actual exercise of moral judgment in concrete situations) and *moral competence* (the mental capacity or cognitive system underlying those judgments) in approximately the sense introduced by Chomsky in *Aspects of a Theory of Syntax* (1965: 4); and to be identifying competence, not performance, as the moral philosopher's proper object of inquiry.

Since the competence–performance distinction is a technical distinction, which has often been misunderstood (see, e.g., Harman 1967; but cf. Harman 1973), it may be helpful to explain how the distinction operates in Chomsky's framework as a means of clarifying Rawls' apparent use of it in the moral case. As we have seen, Chomsky's approach to the study of language is organized around the following central questions:

(1) (a) What constitutes knowledge of language?
       (b) How is knowledge of language acquired?
       (c) How is knowledge of language put to use?

In Chomsky's framework the argument for linguistic grammar establishes a provisional or presumptive answer to (1a). We reviewed earlier how that argument proceeds: Under normal conditions, once a speaker has mastered her native language, she is able to understand it, communicate with it, and use it for a wide variety of purposes. Among these uses are a potentially unlimited range of common as well as esoteric perceptual judgments about the properties and relations of novel expressions in the language. The fundamental empirical assumption of contemporary linguistics is that in making these judgments

---

[5] Although the literature on considered judgments is vast, Daniels (1980) is the only writer I could find in an extensive literature search while writing *Rawls' Linguistic Analogy* who discusses the competence–performance distinction in this connection.

(as in language use generally), the speaker must be relying on a tacit knowledge of the grammar of her language, understood to be her internalized grasp of a complex, abstract system of rules. In the absence of such knowledge, it is argued, the exhibited behaviors would be largely inexplicable.

Once linguists take the assumption of a speaker's linguistic grammar to be adequately established, their attention naturally turns more directly toward (1a). This question asks what exactly the properties of the postulated grammar are. To understand the competence–performance distinction, one must pay close attention to the difference between (1a) and (1c). The latter asks a question about a speaker's actual behavior. The former represents a question about the mental grammar or cognitive system the speaker's observable behavior presupposes. In Chomsky's framework the distinction between competence and performance is, in the first instance, simply the difference between these two questions. A theory of linguistic competence provides an answer to (1a). A theory of performance seeks to provide an answer to (1c).

A less formal way to represent the difference between competence and performance is in terms of the distinction between knowledge and behavior, or between what a person knows and what she does. Linguistic competence denotes a person's *knowledge* of her language; linguistic performance refers to how her knowledge of language actually gets put to *use* in specific circumstances. It seems clear that a speaker's actual linguistic behavior is affected by things other than her underlying competence, such as her memory structure, mode of organizing experience, perceptual mechanisms and attention span, and so on. Linguistic competence is thus presupposed by, but only one factor contributing to, actual performance or language use (Chomsky 1965: 3, 1980: 225).

Rawls' use of the competence–performance distinction in the paragraph under discussion is suggested by his method of filtering judgments to identify a class of considered judgments against which conjectured principles may be checked, thereby focusing attention on "those judgments in which our moral capacities are most likely to be displayed without distortion." This parallels rather closely the linguist's method of proceeding, which is to simplify and idealize actual linguistic behavior to the point at which hypothetical performance may be reasonably assumed to directly reflect underlying competence. A competence–performance distinction is also implied by Rawls' use of epistemological terms like "erroneous," "correct," "distortion," and "mistaken," along with phrases like "the exercise of the sense of justice," which conceptually dissociates an underlying mental capacity from its actual exercise.

It is important to emphasize that, in Chomsky's framework, a generative grammar is not a model of performance; it does not represent, in other words, a theory of behavior, of how speaker-hearers do or might in fact proceed to perceive or produce linguistic expressions. Rather, a generative grammar is a theory of linguistic competence. It attempts "to characterize in the most neutral possible terms the knowledge of the language that provides the basis for actual use of language by a speaker-hearer" (Chomsky 1965: 9). To discover the properties of competence, theoretical linguists do, in a sense, study actual behavior. However, to minimize the role of exogenous factors, they idealize behavior in various ways. Hence, they take their primary object of study to be "an ideal speaker-listener, in a completely homogeneous speech community, who knows its language perfectly and is unaffected by such grammatically irrelevant conditions as memory limitations, distractions, shifts of attention and interest, and errors (random or characteristic) in applying his knowledge of the language in actual performance" (Chomsky 1965: 3). And they employ other simplifying devices as well.

Rawls' approach to moral competence appears to be similar. To describe the sense of justice, he suggests, moral philosophers must be free to introduce contingent assumptions and simplifying devices as they please. In particular, they must be free to replace their *actual* object of inquiry – the moral capacity or sense of justice of real, identifiable individuals – with the model of an ideal moral observer; and to select, from among the moral judgments people *actually* make, a class of considered judgments against which philosophical theories may be checked.[6]

Rawls' reliance on idealization – his use of constructs like considered judgments and the ideal observer – has seemed controversial to some observers (see, e.g., Brandt 1979; Copp 1984; Grice 1978; Hare 1973; Posner 1999; Raz 1982). In fact, it is just standard science. Any serious attempt to delineate the structure of a cognitive system must seek reasonable ways to reduce the complexity of that system and to identify its fundamental properties. It is instructive to note the common ground Rawls shares with Robert Nozick in this regard. To describe the cognitive structures underlying the ordinary exercise of moral judgment, Nozick observes,

one needs a distinction similar to that which linguists make between linguistic competence and linguistic performance. The actual judgments which a person makes will depend on various limitations common to all persons, and upon some special to him (or at any rate, not common to all); e.g., limitations of attention span, of memory, limitations on the complexity of information which can be manipulated and processed, limitations on the amount of time he is willing to spend thinking about moral problems. The actual judgments he makes will also depend upon various exogenous factors; e.g., whether he has a headache, whether there's noise which

---

[6] To avoid misunderstanding, I should perhaps note that how the competence–performance distinction is drawn in moral philosophy, on the one hand, and in linguistics, on the other, may be quite different. What counts as a considered judgment in each case is a complex, theory-internal matter that each discipline must work out for itself. Moreover, it is obvious that the specific criteria to be employed will be dissimilar in important respects. Nonetheless, the rationale for invoking the distinction is basically the same in each domain: to focus attention on "those judgments in which our ... capacities are most likely to be displayed without distortion" (Rawls 1971: 47), so that actual behavior (performance) may be reasonably taken to reflect an underlying cognitive competence.

prevents him from thinking as clearly as he otherwise would, whether he's inter-
rupted while thinking and loses some thought which he doesn't later remember. We
may think of the structure we have been discussing either as a model of an idealized
moral judge in idealized circumstances (i.e., ignoring the various limitations and
exogenous factors), or as *one component* of an adequate psychological model of the
person. (1968: 47–48, emphasis original)

Nozick's observations are exactly to the point. They also help to illuminate the
role of considered judgments in Rawls' framework, which many critics appear
to have misunderstood. One thing well understood about science, whether
the subject is language, vision, economics, or anything else, is that idealization, simplification, and carefully controlled artificiality are often required
for systematic study to get off the ground. There seems little reason to question whether the situation should be any different for a cognitive capacity as
complex as the moral sense.

3.1.7 The Theory-Dependence of the Competence– Performance Distinction

The seventh element of Rawls' linguistic analogy is the theory-dependence of
the competence–performance distinction. As Rawls observes, the conception
of moral theory discussed thus far is an oversimplification. One main reason is that when moral theorists attempt to solve the problem of descriptive
adequacy, the set of moral judgments they originally take to be an accurate
reflection of moral competence may change. Rawls' next comparison with
linguistics helps to illustrate this point:

Moral philosophy is Socratic: we may want to change our present considered judgments once their regulative principles are brought to light. And we may want to do
this even though these principles are a perfect fit. A knowledge of these principles
may suggest further reflections that lead us to revise our judgments. This feature
is not peculiar to moral philosophy, or to the study of other philosophical principles such as those of induction or scientific method. For example, while we may
not expect a substantial revision of our sense of correct grammar in view of a linguistic theory the principles of which seem especially natural to us, such a change
is not inconceivable, and no doubt our sense of grammaticalness may be affected to
some degree anyway by this knowledge. But there is a contrast, say, with physics. To
take an extreme case, if we have an accurate account of the motions of the heavenly
bodies that we do not find appealing, we cannot alter these motions to conform to
a more attractive theory. It is simply good fortune that the principles of celestial
mechanics have their intellectual beauty. (1971: 49)

In this passage, Rawls correctly insists that the revisability of considered
judgments in light of an adequate theoretical account of moral competence
is not something peculiar to the theory of moral cognition. On the contrary,
it is a common feature of ethics, linguistics, the philosophy of induction,
and other disciplines devoted to what he calls "the study of principles which

govern actions shaped by self-examination" (1971: 48–49). The point of considered judgments, as we have seen, is for the theorist to single out a class
of moral judgments in which the sense of justice is most likely to be displayed without distortion, so that actual behavior (moral performance) may
be presumed to be an accurate reflection of the properties of an underlying cognitive faculty (moral competence). Considered judgments are themselves a theoretical construct; by acknowledging that the moral theorist may
want to modify the set of judgments that she initially takes to be considered
judgments "once their regulative principles are brought to light" (1971: 49),
Rawls makes an allowance for the possibility that even this prior idealization is inadequate. He thus allows for the possibility that, over the course
of her inquiry, the set of moral judgments that the moral theorist assumes
are those judgments "in which our moral capacities are most likely to be
displayed without distortion" (1971: 47) may change.

3.1.8 The Importance of Idealization

Rawls' eighth and final comparison between moral theory and linguistics in
Section 9 concerns the issue of idealization:

> I shall not … ask whether the principles that characterize one person's considered
> judgments are the same as those that characterize another's. I shall take for granted
> that these principles are either approximately the same for persons whose judg-
> ments are in reflective equilibrium, or if not, that their judgments divide along a few
> main lines represented by the family of traditional doctrines that I shall discuss.
> (Indeed, one person may find himself torn between opposing conceptions at the
> same time.) If men's conceptions of justice finally turn out to differ, the ways in
> which they do so is a matter of first importance. Of course we cannot know how
> these conceptions vary, or even whether they do, until we have a better account of
> their structure. And this we now lack, even in the case of one man, or a homoge-
> neous group of men. Here too there is likely to be a similarity with linguistics: if we
> can describe one person's sense of grammar we shall surely know many things about
> the general structure of language. Similarly, if we should be able to characterize
> one (educated) person's sense of justice, we would have a good beginning toward a
> theory of justice. We may suppose that everyone has in himself the whole form of a
> moral conception. (1971: 50)

For our topic, perhaps the most important thing to notice about this passage
is how Rawls uses the notion of idealization to address the problem of moral
diversity. In approaching this problem, Rawls adopts a standard feature of scientific method, which is to resist asking more complicated questions until simpler and logically prior questions are fairly well understood. He thus refrains
from prejudging the issue of diversity until enough is known to be able to discuss the matter seriously. In addition, he makes the simplifying assumption
that investigating the moral competence of a single, idealized individual will
reveal something about human beings generally.

Rawls' reliance on idealization to address the problem of diversity has seemed controversial to some observers. It is difficult to understand how they would have the theory of moral cognition otherwise proceed. It is not in dispute that a descriptively adequate moral grammar is something that moral theory now lacks, even in the case of the moral competence of *one* idealized individual. Moreover, the convergence of considered moral opinion, as evidenced by the Universal Declaration of Human Rights, Rome Statute of the International Criminal Court, and other human rights instruments, along with the existence of peremptory norms (*jus cogens*) in international law generally (see Hannikainen 1988; Henkin 1990; Sadat 2002), is remarkable and goes well beyond anything imaginable in the corresponding case of language. The systems of linguistic intuition that children in diverse cultures acquire are not only discrepant, but in the normal course of events mutually unintelligible. For example, a child who grows up speaking English is typically unable to locate the word boundaries of foreign languages like Arabic or Japanese. Nothing comparable exists in the moral domain. Although moral diversity appears to be a real phenomenon, even the most superficial comparison of language and morality thus suggests that the development of moral competence is *more* constrained than the development of linguistic competence. Yet, even in the case of language, it makes sense from a scientific point of view to assume that there is a single human language, as Chomsky, Pinker, and others have often explained. If there is a "single mental design" (Pinker 1994: 430) underlying all known human languages, then it is not clear why it should be troubling, in a cognitive domain where much less is known, but where superficial observation implies an even greater convergence, to begin investigation from the simplifying assumption, or null hypothesis, that human beings share a common moral nature.

3.2 FURTHER CLARIFICATIONS ABOUT TERMINOLOGY

Let us take stock and summarize the main points of our discussion thus far. As we have seen, Rawls organizes his conception of moral theory around the assumption that each individual develops a sense of justice under normal circumstances, an assumption he takes to be the best explanation of the moral version of the projection problem – roughly, the ability of normal persons to make systematic and stable moral judgments about an indefinite number of cases of first impression. Rawls takes describing the sense of justice to be the provisional aim of moral philosophy. He distinguishes different forms such a description might take, and he suggests that a descriptively adequate moral grammar should take the form of a fully explicit, deductive theory – a *generative* grammar, in approximately Chomsky's sense (Chomsky 1964: 9, 1965: 4, 1986a: 3).

Rawls compares the problem of describing the sense of justice with the linguist's problem of describing linguistic competence. He emphasizes that both inquiries are difficult and require theoretical constructions that go beyond the familiar precepts of common sense. He distinguishes descriptive and explanatory adequacy, in the linguist's technical sense. Finally, he uses the notion of a considered judgment to draw a distinction between moral performance and moral competence, and he takes the provisional object of moral theory to be the developed moral capacity of an ideal moral observer, a theoretical construct that is analogous in some respects to the ideal speaker-listener of linguistic theory.

Table 3.1 is a useful summary of these eight elements of Rawls' linguistic analogy, together with certain key statements of them in Rawls' text. As Table 3.1 suggests, Rawls' remarks about moral theory in Section 9 contain almost the entire outline of a generative grammar model of moral cognition. The main points of comparison between Rawls' stated framework and generative linguistics are straightforward. Both take as their fundamental empirical assumption the existence of a particular cognitive system or mental grammar. Both seek to describe that grammar accurately, hence to construct a scientific theory that approximates a "generative" grammar, so far as is possible in each case. Both take a special class of intuitions to be evidential; the provisional aim of theory is to explain or explicate them. Both distinguish between competence and performance. Finally, both adopt the standpoint of individual psychology and take their primary object of inquiry to be the competence of a single, idealized individual.

Table 3.1 represents the heart of Rawls' linguistic analogy. As we shall see, it is also the key to understanding why many of the published criticisms of that analogy – in particular those of Hare, Singer, Nagel, and Dworkin – are unsound.

Before exploring the empirical significance of Rawls' linguistic analogy in Part Two and then considering the details of these criticisms in Part Three, it will be useful to clarify some of the terminology found in Table 3.1. To begin with, Chomsky does not label the argument for mental grammar by that name; the phrases "argument for mental grammar" and "argument for linguistic grammar" are originally Jackendoff's (1994). I have temporarily adopted them, as a useful expository device to characterize the first important feature of Rawls' linguistic analogy: what I have called Rawls' *argument for moral grammar*. Since all three phrases – mental grammar, linguistic grammar, moral grammar – remain potentially misleading, however, and since the notion of a speaker's linguistic grammar, in particular, has been the source of controversy among philosophers, it may be useful to begin by clarifying several different meanings that "grammar" has within Chomsky's theoretical framework.

What generative linguists mean by "grammar" should not be confused, in the first instance, with what ordinary persons or nonlinguists might refer to by that term: namely, a *traditional* or *pedagogical* grammar such as the kind used to teach language to children in "grammar school." A pedagogical grammar typically provides paradigms of regular constructions, lists of prominent

TABLE 3.1. *The Basic Elements of Rawls' Linguistic Analogy*

Element	Key Remarks in *A Theory of Justice*
Argument for Moral Grammar	"To see [the extraordinary complexity of our moral capacity] it suffices to note the potentially infinite number and variety of judgments that we are prepared to make." (p. 46)
Problem of Descriptive Adequacy	"One may think of moral philosophy at first … as the attempt to describe our moral capacity; or, in the present case, one may regard a theory of justice as describing our sense of justice." (p. 46)
Descriptive vs. Observational Adequacy	"By such a description is not meant simply a list of the judgments on institutions and actions that we are prepared to render. … What is required is a formulation of a set of principles which, when conjoined to our beliefs and knowledge of the circumstances, would lead us to make these judgments … were we to apply these principles conscientiously and intelligently." (p. 46)
Operative vs. Express Principles	"There is no reason to assume that our sense of justice can be adequately characterized by familiar common sense precepts … A correct account of moral capacities will certainly involve principles and theoretical constructions which go much beyond the norms and standards cited in everyday life." (p. 47)
Problem of Explanatory Adequacy	"There is no reason to assume that our sense of justice … can be derived from the more obvious learning principles." (p. 47)
Competence vs. Performance	"Considered judgments … enter as those judgments in which our moral capacities are most likely to be displayed without distortion." (p. 47)
Theory-Dependence of Competence– Performance Distinction	"[W]e may want to change our present considered judgments once their regulative principles are brought to light. … A knowledge of these principles may suggest further reflections that lead us to revise our judgments." (p. 49)
Idealization	"I shall not … ask whether the principles that characterize one person's considered judgments are the same as those that characterize another's. I shall take for granted that these principles are either approximately the same … or, if not, that their judgments divide along a few main lines represented by the family of traditional doctrines that I shall discuss." (p. 50)

exceptions to these constructions (irregular verbs, etc.), and descriptive commentary at various levels of detail and generality about the form and meaning of expressions in a language (Chomsky 1986a: 6). By contrast, a *theoretical* grammar, in Chomsky's framework, is a scientific theory: it seeks to provide a complete theoretical characterization of the speaker-hearer's knowledge of her language, where this knowledge is interpreted to refer to a particular set of mental states and structures.

The difference between a theoretical grammar and a pedagogical grammar is one important distinction to bear in mind in order to avoid confusion about how the term "grammar" operates in theoretical linguistics. A second, more fundamental distinction is between a *theoretical* grammar and a *mental* grammar. In Chomsky's early work, primarily for ease of expression, the term "grammar" was often used with an acknowledged systematic ambiguity to refer both to the linguist's theoretical description of the speaker-hearer's knowledge of language and to that knowledge itself. In the section of *Aspects of the Theory of Syntax* Rawls cites (1965: 3–9), for instance, Chomsky uses "grammar" in the sense of theoretical grammar when he explains: "A grammar of a language purports to be a description of the ideal speaker-hearer's intrinsic competence" (1965: 4). Chomsky uses "grammar" in the sense of *both* theoretical and mental grammar, by contrast, on different occasions in the following statement:

Obviously, every speaker of a language has mastered and internalized a generative grammar that expresses his knowledge of his language. This is not to say that he is aware of the rules of the grammar or even that he can become aware of them, or that his statements about them are necessarily accurate. Any interesting generative grammar will be dealing, for the most part, with mental processes that are far beyond the level of actual or potential consciousness; furthermore, it is quite apparent that a speaker's reports about his behavior and his competence may be in error. Thus a generative grammar attempts to specify what the speaker actually knows, not what he may report about his knowledge. Similarly, a theory of visual perception would attempt to account for what a person actually sees and the mechanisms that determine this rather than his statements about what he sees and why, though these statements may provide useful, in fact, compelling evidence for such a theory. (1965: 8–9)

To the extent one is unaware of, or does not adequately attend to, the distinction between a theoretical grammar and a mental grammar, the first statement in this passage may seem confusing. A theoretical grammar – a set of propositions that, in Chomsky's framework, purports to be a complete description of a speaker-hearer's linguistic competence – is a complicated scientific theory. How then is it possible (let alone "obvious") that every mature speaker of language has mastered and internalized such a theory? How can a speaker's linguistic competence be equated with her knowledge of such a theory?

The confusion reflected in these questions represents a failure to distinguish adequately between a theoretical and a mental grammar. The grammar referred to in the first and second sentences is not a linguistic theory, but a biological object: a set of states and structures of the mind/brain. Chomsky's contention and that of other linguists is that, despite its inaccessibility to consciousness, every normal speaker of a language possesses such an object. The grammar referred to in the third and fourth sentences, on the other hand, is a scientific theory; its stated aim is to specify the properties of this object.

I suspect that similar confusions in moral theory can be avoided by distinguishing a *theoretical* moral grammar from the *mental* moral grammar the theorist seeks to characterize; and by following Chomsky on certain other conceptual and terminological points as well. For example, the basic concept of the research program introduced in Chapter 2 is that of *moral knowledge*. This concept is the source of potential confusion that should be avoided. When one asks what constitutes moral knowledge or how moral knowledge is acquired, the phrase "moral knowledge" functions in much the same way "knowledge of language" functions in Chomsky's research program. Since the latter phrase has itself been a source of disagreement, it will be useful to examine how Chomsky understands the significance of this concept as a means of clarifying its counterpart in the moral domain.

The basic concept in Chomsky's framework, which identifies the subject of inquiry, is that of "knowing" a language. The basic concept, however, is equally that of "having" or "possessing" a language (see, e.g., Chomsky 1991a: 6). English contains the locution "know a language," and English speakers commonly say things like "John knows French" or "John knows seven languages." Nonetheless, languages other than English often describe the situation differently: John is said to "have" or "possess" a language, or a language is said to be something "in" him, or perhaps to be something he "speaks." This variety of locution is largely irrelevant to the objectives of linguistic inquiry, however, because to know a language, or to possess or be capable of speaking a language, is to be in a certain mental or cognitive state. Specifically, it is for one's language faculty to be in a certain state, which persists as one, relatively steady component of otherwise transitory mental states (Chomsky 1980: 48).

To clarify how "knowledge of language" functions in the five main questions of his research program, therefore, Chomsky draws an implicit distinction between *having* or *possessing* a particular mental structure and *lacking* such a structure. He equates knowledge of language with possession of "a certain mental structure consisting of a system of rules and principles that generate and relate mental representations of various types," a situation he contrasts with "the concept of mental capacities as lacking structured vehicles." Chomsky takes one important version of the latter conception to be Wittgenstein's apparent denial that there are processes in the brain "correlated with association or with thinking." On such a Wittgensteinian alternative, Chomsky observes, nothing physiological corresponds to certain psychological phenomena, hence it follows that "there can be no theory of mental structures and processes that attempts to formulate the properties of these nonexistent physiological mechanisms." The linguist, psychologist, or philosopher of mind is thus left with only an essentially behaviorist project: a descriptive study of behavior or potential behavior (Chomsky 1980: 48–50; see generally Botha 1989: 52–55).

Chomsky's analysis of "knowledge of language" in terms of having a mental structure of the kind envisaged is a departure, in certain respects, from ordinary English usage. Fidelity to ordinary usage, however, is in Chomsky's view a matter of limited importance. As we have seen (Section 2.1.8), Chomsky draws a fundamental distinction between ordinary, commonsense, or pretheoretic concepts like "language" or "knowledge of language," on the one hand, and various technical replacements of those concepts, on the other. His view is that all serious scientific approaches to the study of language must seek to replace the ordinary or commonsense concepts with artificially constructed technical concepts, more suitable for empirical study.

The technical concept currently used most often by linguists working within the framework of Universal Grammar is the concept *I-language* (see, e.g., Isac & Reiss 2008). As Chomsky defines it, a concept of language is an I-language conception if it characterizes a language as "some element of the mind of the person who knows the language, acquired by the learner, and used by the speaker-hearer" (1986a: 22). I-language thus refers to the language system in the mind/brain of a person who (in the ordinary sense) "knows" a language like Arabic, Hebrew, or Japanese. The "I" in I-language signifies at least three properties the I-language has: it is *internalized* in the sense that it is internal to the mind/brain. It is *intensional* in the sense that a theory of I-language may be regarded as a specific characterization of a function considered in intension that assigns a status to a range of physical events. It is *individualized* in the sense that the standpoint adopted toward I-language is that of individual psychology: I-languages are construed as something individual persons have, and different persons may in some sense be thought of as having different I-languages. Finally, a fourth reason the "I" in I-language is significant is that, as already explained, I-language represents an *idealization,* in a number of respects (Chomsky 1986a: 3, 1986b: 513).

Chomsky distinguishes I-language from two other technical definitions of language: *E-language* and *P-language.* On an E-language definition, a language is understood to be a set of objects of some kind – for instance, a collection of actions or behaviors, utterances, or linguistic forms paired with meanings – and the set is taken to exist outside and independently of the mind/brain. The "E" in E-language is thus intended to suggest two properties such technical definitions possess: the construct is *extensional* in that it takes language to be a set of objects of some kind, and it is *externalized,* in the sense that the language, so defined, is external to and independent of the properties of the mind/brain (Chomsky 1986a: 19–20, 1986b: 510).

Chomsky also distinguishes I-language from what he calls *P-language* concepts of language, such as those adopted by Katz, Bever, and Soames, who take the subject matter of linguistics to be an abstract, Platonic object. In

Katz's Platonistic framework, for instance, sentences are construed as being timeless, spaceless, abstract objects, like numbers: objects "whose existence is independent of mind and matter but which must count as real along with mental and material objects" (Katz 1981: 12). Whereas in Chomsky's framework, I-language represents a constructed idealization of a given biological object, in Katz's framework, the abstract objects of P-language

> are not idealizations at all. They do not represent anything physical or psychological. They are not a means of simplifying the laws of a discipline. Rather, abstract objects are another ontological kind from the physical and psychological objects that are represented in ideal objects. Like the actual objects of empirical science, they are the things of which the statements in a science are true. (Katz 1981: 56)

In P-language frameworks, then, linguistics is not seen, as Chomsky sees it, as a branch or form of psychology, but instead, like mathematics, as an independent, nonempirical discipline (see generally Katz 1981; see also Botha 1989: 73–74).

3.3 MORAL THEORY AS A THEORY OF I-MORALITY

As we saw in Section 2.1.8, the significance for moral theory of technical concepts of language such as I-language, E-language, and P-language emerges most clearly when one considers how to replace various pre-theoretical concepts of morality with technical counterparts more suitable for scientific study. An *I-morality* approach to moral theory would take its primary subject matter to be whatever mental states and properties are implicated by ordinary uses of pre-theoretic concepts such as the sense of justice, moral sense, and the like. I-morality would thus refer to the moral system of the human mind/brain, whatever it turns out to be. The "I" in I-morality would signify at least four properties the system has: it is *internalized* in the sense that it is internal to the mind/brain. It is *intensional* in the sense that a theory of I-morality may be regarded as the characterization of a function considered in intension, which assigns a status to a range of physical events. It is *individualized* in the sense that the standpoint adopted toward I-morality is that of individual psychology: I-moralities are construed as something individual persons have, and different persons may in some sense be thought of as having different I-moralities. Finally, I-morality represents an *idealization* in a number of important respects: it is a constructed model of a given biological object – the moral faculty of the human mind/brain.

Likewise, an I-morality approach to moral theory may be usefully contrasted with two other approaches: E-morality and P-morality. An *E-morality* approach to moral theory would be any approach that characterizes its primary object of inquiry as a set of objects or facts or truths of some kind – for example, a collection of behaviors, or customs, or social practices, or the fact that slavery is unjust or breaking promises is wrong – and takes that set to exist outside and independently of the mind/brain. The "E" in an E-morality would thus refer to two things: first, that the central theoretical concept in an E-morality approach to moral theory is *extensional,* in that E-morality is taken to denote a set of objects or facts of some kind, and, second, that the concept is *externalized,* in the sense that, so defined, E-morality is external to and independent of the mind/brain. Likewise, a *P-morality* approach to moral theory would be any approach that conceives of itself as a Platonized version of an E-morality approach, thus differing from the latter only in its assumptions about the ontological realm to which moral facts or truths belong.

Whether or not there is a significant correspondence between what Chomsky takes to be E-language and P-language approaches to linguistics, on the one hand, and what I have identified as E-morality and P-morality approaches to moral theory, on the other, is something that we need not consider here.[7] For our purposes the important point is simply that, whereas in an I-morality framework the central theoretical concept is a constructed idealization of a given cognitive system, and moral theory is identified as a branch of psychology, in E-morality and P-morality approaches neither condition obtains.

The particular significance of I-morality for our topic is that, although Rawls does not use this terminology, he conceives of the subject matter of moral theory in exactly this way: as a mental object that is internal, intensional, individual, and ideal, in the sense described. In my opinion Rawls' remarks in Section 9 leave little room for doubt on this matter; but since the point is crucial for understanding how his linguistic analogy has been misinterpreted, it is perhaps worthwhile to call attention to several more relevant passages from Section 9 and elsewhere in his corpus during the period we are considering (1950–1975).

Consider first the question of idealization. As we have seen, Rawls is a strong advocate of the use of idealization in moral theory. To describe the sense of justice, he insists, moral philosophers must be free to introduce contingent assumptions and simplifying devices as they please. In particular, they must be free to replace their actual object of inquiry with the model of an ideal moral observer; and to rely on a value-laden process of sifting through the moral judgments people actually make to arrive at a class of considered judgments against which their theories may be checked.[8] In addition,

---

7 Robert Nozick (1981: 744) briefly discusses this issue when he observes: "Katz argues that it is a mistake for linguistics to be oriented toward the task of delineating an explanatory psychological mechanism, rather than the (Platonist) task of characterizing language as an abstract object; this proposal for linguistics, whatever its merits there, would correspond to utilizing a moral structure to delineate the realm of moral truths, rather than as a component in a psychological theory to help explain a person's moral judgments." More recently, in a series of papers Susan Dwyer (2007, 2008, in press) has developed a sophisticated and illuminating account of the relationship between I-morality and E-morality.

8 Rawls has indicated to me in conversation that he has always considered his conception of moral theory to be a type of ideal observer theory, similar in this respect to Roderick Firth's (1952).

they should avoid grappling with the question of moral diversity until the sense of justice of at least *one* idealized individual is better understood. As we have seen, throughout Section 9, Rawls' defense of this kind of simplification and idealization is clear and unequivocal. Here is another representative passage:

> I wish ... to stress the central place of the study of our substantive moral conceptions. But the corollary to recognizing their complexity is accepting the fact that our present theories are primitive and have grave defects. We need to be tolerant of simplifications if they reveal and approximate the general outlines of our judgments. Objections by way of counterexamples are to be made with care, since these may tell us only what we know already, namely that our theory is wrong somewhere. The important thing is to find out how often and how far it is wrong. All theories are presumably mistaken in places. The real question at any given time is which of the views already proposed is the best approximation overall. To ascertain this some grasp of the structure of rival theories is surely necessary. It is for this reason that I have tried to classify and to discuss conceptions of justice by reference to their basic intuitive ideas, since these disclose the main differences between them. (1971: 52)

Once again, in this paragraph Rawls adopts a standard feature of scientific method toward his subject matter, which is to resist demanding too much of a theory and preoccupying oneself with the more complicated aspects of a problem until its simpler, idealized elements are better understood. Rawls emphasizes the importance of methodological considerations like these on numerous occasions, especially in *The Independence of Moral Theory* (1975), to which we return.

Consider next the issue of individual psychology and the fact that I-morality denotes a cognitive system, an object internal to the mind/brain. That Rawls adopts this standpoint toward the sense of justice is a clear and unambiguous feature of his conception of moral theory during the period 1950–1975. As we have seen, Rawls characterizes the sense of justice as "a mental capacity" and takes it to be something "each person beyond a certain age and possessed of the requisite intellectual capacity develops under normal social circumstances" (1971: 46). He proceeds from the assumption that "everyone has in himself the whole form of a moral conception" (1971: 50). These statements and many others like them reveal that Rawls takes the subject matter of moral theory to be an aspect of individual psychology. Elsewhere in Section 9, Rawls reiterates the point:

> I wish to stress that a theory of justice is precisely that, namely, a theory. It is a theory of the moral sentiments (to recall an eighteenth century title) setting out the principles governing our moral powers, or, more specifically, our sense of justice. There is a definite if limited class of facts against which conjectured principles can be checked, namely our considered judgments in reflective equilibrium. ... This is the conception of the subject adopted by most classical British writers through Sidgwick. I see no reason to depart from it. (1971: 50–51)

That Rawls takes moral theory to be a theory of I-morality is further confirmed by the general character of his remarks in Chapter VIII of *A Theory
of Justice,* particularly those remarks relating to the work of developmental
psychologists like Freud, Piaget, and Kohlberg, and of evolutionary biologists
like Darwin, Lorenz, and Trivers (see generally 1971: 453–512). This chapter
of Rawls' book follows the general point of view of "The Sense of Justice"
(Rawls 1963b), the opening passages of which also worth recalling in this
context:

> In *Emile* Rousseau asserts that the sense of justice is no mere moral conception
> formed by the understanding alone, but a true sentiment of the heart enlightened
> by reason, the natural outcome of our primitive affections. In the first part of this
> paper, I set out a psychological construction to illustrate the way in which Rousseau's
> thesis might be true. ... Throughout, I think of a sense of justice as something which
> persons have. One refers to it when one says, for example, that cruel and unusual
> punishments offend one's sense of justice. It may be aroused or assuaged, and it is
> connected not only with such moral feelings as resentment and indignation but also,
> as I shall argue, with such natural attitudes as mutual trust and affection. The psy-
> chological construction is designed to show how the sense of justice may be viewed
> as the result of a certain natural development; it will be useful in understanding why
> the capacity for a sense of justice is the fundamental aspect of moral personality in
> the theory of justice. (Rawls 1963b: 281–282)

Several of Rawls' remarks in *Independence* also lend support to the conclusion that he conceives of moral theory to be a theory of I-morality. We will
return to these passages below, in our discussion of Hare and Dworkin.

Consider finally the intensional aspect of I-morality: the fact that a theory
of I-morality may be regarded as a specific characterization of a function considered in intension. That Rawls conceives of moral principles in this way, as
analogous to functions in the technical sense, is also a clear element of his
conception of moral theory during the period 1950–1975. In *Grounds,* for
example, Rawls explains that moral principles "are analogous to functions.
Functions, as rules applied to a number, yield another number. The principles, when applied to a situation yield a moral rule. The rules of common
sense morality are examples of such secondary moral rules" (Rawls 1950: 107;
see also 308–310). Rawls' characterization of the problem of explication in
both *Grounds* and *Outline* also supports this interpretation, as do his remarks
in *A Theory of Justice* about the deductive character of the argument for his
two principles of justice (e.g., 1971: 19–20, 46, 118–121, 580–581).

One may reasonably question how deeply Rawls is committed to conceiving the sense of justice in computational, mentalist, and broadly naturalistic
terms. I will return to this issue in Chapter 9 and consider some of its implications for Rawls' interpretation of *A Theory of Justice* as a type of natural rights
argument (see, e.g., 1971: 28, 32, 505–506, n. 30). For now, because our limited aim in this chapter is to elucidate the basic elements of Rawls' linguistic

TABLE 3.2. *The Heart of Rawls' Linguistic Analogy*

Linguistic Theory	Moral Theory
(1a) What constitutes I-language? (Descriptive adequacy)	(2a) What constitutes I-morality? (Descriptive adequacy)
(1b) How is I-language acquired? (Explanatory adequacy)	(2b) How is I-morality acquired? (Explanatory adequacy)
(1c) How is I-language put to use? (Behavioral adequacy)	(2c) How is I-morality put to use? (Behavioral adequacy)

analogy, I simply note that the fact that Rawls' conception of moral theory appears to be an I-morality conception allows us to replace the commonsense concept of moral knowledge in (2) with the technical concept of I-morality. This in turn enables us to distill the essence of Table 3.1 and restate it in the somewhat different format of Table 3.2.

Table 3.2 does not exhaust Rawls' linguistic analogy. But it represents the true heart of that analogy. Like Chomsky, Rawls takes his primary object of inquiry to be a mental object of some sort: a set of principles or properties of the human mind/brain. Moreover, he recognizes that any serious under-standing of moral development – more philosophically, of the origin of our moral ideas – presupposes a clearer understanding of the moral principles that the normal mind acquires. For example, in Section 75 of *A Theory of Justice* ("The Principles of Moral Psychology") Rawls writes:

[I]t seems likely that our understanding of moral learning cannot far exceed our grasp of the moral conceptions that are to be learned. Analogously, our understand-ing of how we learn language is limited by what we know about its grammatical and semantic structure. Just as psycholinguistics depends upon linguistics, so the theory of moral learning depends upon an account of the nature of morality and its various forms. Our common sense ideas about these matters do not suffice for the aims of theory. (1971: 491)

Finally, Rawls recognizes both the difficulty and the scientific status of the entire enterprise. Indeed, he recognizes that these two characteristics are closely related (see, e.g., 1971: 46–47, 50–52; cf. 1951a: 185–186).

3.4 SOME FURTHER REMARKS ABOUT THE LINGUISTIC ANALOGY

Table 3.2 does not merely represent the heart of Rawls' linguistic analogy. It also captures what is essential to many of the linguistic analogies others have drawn, including many of the authors in Table 1.1. Surprising as it may seem, even these limited comparisons appear to be a sufficient basis for defending

Rawls' linguistic analogy against many of the criticisms that have been leveled against it, a point that may simply reflect the deep aversion to empirical moral psychology on the part of many of Rawls' critics. Turning to these criticisms at this point in our discussion, however, would be premature. Before doing so, it will be useful to make some further clarifying remarks in this chapter, and then to begin to investigate the empirical significance of the linguistic analogy in Part Two.

To begin with, it should be noted that one traditional form of philosophical skepticism is irrelevant for the research programs represented by (1) and (2). This form of skepticism concerns the legitimacy of using the term "knowledge" to describe the normal individual's system of linguistic or moral principles. A skeptic of this sort demands to know whether the systems in question, and the particular intuitive judgments they yield, meet certain a priori conceptual requirements that, it is insisted, any claim to knowledge must satisfy: for example, that the knowledge in question conform to the formula "justified true belief" or be analyzable into one of Gilbert Ryle's two forms, "knowledge how" or "knowledge that" (Ryle 1949). As far as the empirical study of cognitive systems is concerned, these questions are primarily verbal. The term "cognition" ("cognize," etc.) may be substituted for "knowledge" ("know," etc.) in (1) and (2), without substantive effect. Either way, the same fundamental questions arise, can be posed as scientific problems, and – by those interested in studying them, at least – must be squarely faced.[9]

Second, it is important to emphasize that both the argument for moral grammar and the argument for linguistic grammar are nondemonstrative. Chomsky (1965: 8) thinks it is "obvious" that every speaker of language possesses a linguistic grammar. Quine (1972: 443) contends that the speaker's possession of a system of linguistic rules "is evident" from the infinitude of her repertoire. Jackendoff (1994: 6) claims that the expressive variety of language use "implies" that the mind/brain contains a set of grammatical rules or principles. And Katz's and Fodor's contention (1963: 481–482) is that the conclusion that a speaker's knowledge of language takes the form of linguistic rules "follows" from her infinite use of finite means. Meanwhile, as we have seen, Rawls' claim (1971: 46) is that, in order to defend the assumption that each person possesses a moral grammar, "it suffices" to note the novelty and unboundedness of moral judgment. Remarks like these may lead one to assume that the form of inference at work in both the argument for linguistic grammar and the argument for moral grammar is deductive or conceptual, but this would be a mistake. The arguments are an attempt at *scientific* explanation; we are not compelled to accept them by means of conceptual analysis or logic. Alternative explanations are logically possible.

---

[9] For the application of this argument to knowledge of language, see Chomsky (1975b: 5f., 1986a: 3f.). For related remarks in connection with moral theory, see Rawls (1971: 51–52, 1975: 7f.); see also Ross (1988/1930: 39–41) and Quinn (1993: 117).

The arguments claim only to be more reasonable or adequate explanations of a given body of evidence than their rivals; this, of course, is what is meant by characterizing them as abductive arguments, or inferences to the best explanation.

A number of technical distinctions are important for understanding how linguists working within Chomsky's framework face (1b), the problem of language acquisition. Several of them are worth introducing here in anticipation of our attempt to flesh out the empirical significance of the linguistic analogy in Part Two. The first such distinction is between the *psychological* and *logical* versions of the problem of language acquisition. The former refers to the issue of "real-time acquisition": how a child actually acquires her knowledge of language in various stages "over a period of time, the earlier stages forming the basis of the later ones" (Botha 1989: 13; see also Hornstein & Lightfoot 1981). In early work on generative grammar, Chomsky and Halle adopted the position that this psychological or "realistic" version of the problem was too complex to be addressed meaningfully without reliance on a certain amount of idealization and simplification.[10] Hence to pursue (1b), they introduced an idealization, *instantaneous language acquisition,* thereby turning the real or psychological problem into a logical one. The logical version of the problem thus becomes the problem of a simple input–output situation. A child who initially does not possess a mature grammar constructs one for herself on the basis of a certain amount of data; the data are the input, her grammar is the output. The logical problem is to determine how on the basis of this limited set of data, the child chooses or "projects" only the acquired grammar from among an indefinitely large class of nonacquired and mutually incompatible grammars consistent with that data set.

Simply formulating the logical problem invokes a second important conceptual distinction, which is the contrast between the *innate* and *environmental* components in language acquisition. The environmental component represents the linguistic data available to the child. The innate component represents that part of the acquired grammar for which the environmental component contains insufficient evidence. It is because the environmental component available to the child is informationally so poor and degenerate, and the resulting grammar is so rich and complicated, that Chomsky postulates a relatively large innate component to bridge this gap.

---

[10] "We have been describing acquisition of language as if it were an instantaneous process. Obviously, this is not true. A more realistic model of language acquisition would consider the order in which primary linguistic data are used by the child and the effects of preliminary 'hypotheses' developed in the earlier stages of learning on the interpretation of new, often more complex, data. To us it appears that this more realistic study is much too complex to be undertaken in any meaningful way today and that it will be far more fruitful to investigate in detail, as a first approximation, the idealized model outlined earlier, leaving refinements to a time when this idealization is better understood" (Chomsky & Halle 1968: 331). I am indebted to Botha (1989: 14) for drawing my attention to this passage.

In Chomsky's framework, *poverty of stimulus* and *degeneracy of stimulus* are quasi-technical terms that are sometimes used to characterize the nature of the linguistic experience available to the child acquiring language. Chomsky considers the available database degenerate insofar as it is comprised of expressions that are not well-formed, including false starts, slips of the tongue, changes of plan in mid-course, endings that do not match beginnings, and other similar departures from well-formedness. He considers the database impoverished, by contrast, to the extent that it contains *no* relevant evidence for certain properties and principles of the grammars acquired by children (see, e.g., Chomsky 1986a: 7–9; see generally Botha 1989: 19–20).

Chomsky and the other linguists and cognitive scientists working within his framework have uncovered many properties of acquired grammars for which the linguistic evidence is poor. One leading example is the structure-dependence of rules. In the absence of explicit instruction or direct evidence, young children nonetheless use computationally complex, structure-dependent rules instead of computationally simple rules that involve only the predicates "leftmost" or "rightmost" in a linear sequence of words. To take a specific example, consider again the following expressions.

(3) (g) I wonder who the men expected to see them
    (h) the men expected to see them

Both (3g) and (3h) contain the expression "the men expected to see them." But only in (3g) may the pronoun "them" be referentially dependent on the antecedent "the men." Children as young as 3–5 appear to know facts like these – consequences of what is known as "binding theory" – without relevant experience to differentiate the cases (Chomsky 1986a: 7–8). Hence Chomsky observes:

Such facts pose a serious problem that was not recognized in earlier work: How does every child know, unerringly, to interpret the clause differently in the two cases? And why does no pedagogic grammar have to draw the learner's attention to such facts (which were, in fact, noticed only quite recently, in the course of the study of explicit rule systems in generative grammar)? (1986a: 7–8)

The proposed answer is that the principles of binding theory belong to Universal Grammar. That is, they are part of the innate intellectual equipment that every child brings to the task of acquiring her language (Chomsky 1986a; see generally Baker 2001; Cook & Newson 1996).

It is important to recognize that the argument for linguistic grammar and the argument from the poverty of the linguistic stimulus are conceptually distinct. Logically speaking, the second argument comes into play only when the first has already been established and a (putatively) descriptively adequate linguistic grammar has been formulated. Similar logic applies in the moral domain. We cannot seriously address the topic of innate moral principles until a set of moral principles is produced and shown to be descriptively adequate. Put differently, we cannot even formulate (2b) until a presumptively adequate answer to (2a) is in hand. This is one reason why I have said very little about the argument from the poverty of the moral stimulus thus far, and why the main empirical focus of this book is descriptive rather than explanatory adequacy. As Rawls (1975: 10) correctly observes, we must resist the temptation to answer questions before we are adequately prepared to do so.

3.5 THE CONTRAST WITH PARTICULARISM

This seems like a useful place to say a brief word about the contrast between the argument for moral grammar and *moral particularism*. In "Ethical Particularism and Morally Relevant Properties," Jonathan Dancy (1983: 530) characterizes particularism as the view that "ethical decisions are made case by case, without the comforting support or awkward demands of moral principles." In that paper Dancy defends particularism, hence argues for what he calls "the non-existence of moral principles" (1983: 530). Elsewhere, Dancy characterizes particularism as the view that conceives of the virtuous person

as someone who has been perfectly trained, and thereby equipped with a full range of sensitivities to the sorts of considerations that can matter morally. These sensitivities have no content of their own. They are … simply the ability to recognize whatever morally relevant features we come across for what they are, case by case. … [The] person is not conceived as someone equipped with a full list of moral principles and an ability to correctly subsume each new case under the right one. There is nothing that one brings to the new situation other than a contentless ability to discern what matters where it matters, an ability whose presence in us is explained by our having undergone a successful moral education. (Dancy 1993: 50)

The main reason for mentioning particularism at this juncture is to clarify what may be controversial about the argument for moral grammar. As I interpret Dancy's formulations of particularism in these passages, which I shall take as definitive of the doctrine for the purposes of this brief discussion, particularism is incompatible with the argument for moral grammar. According to the argument for moral grammar, the properties of moral judgment imply that the mind/brain contains or possesses a set of moral principles. According to particularism, no such principles exist: the capacity for moral judgment is nothing more than a "contentless ability," and moral judgments are made on a case-by-case basis, without the use of principles or rules. Which of these two views is correct? The issue would seem to be one of considerable importance, certainly for someone attracted to the conception of moral theory outlined in Section 2.1. If the capacity for moral judgment is nothing more than a "contentless ability," then there would seem to be little point in organizing the theory of moral cognition around the assumption that the mind/brain contains a system of moral principles and in directing one's efforts toward the problems of describing and explaining them, since, by hypothesis, no such system exists. Understood in this light, then, particularism can be conceived as a skeptical challenge to the research program described in Section 2.1 and developed throughout this book.

Now, as I interpret Rawls, he rejects particularism in no uncertain terms, although he does recognize that the nonexistence of moral rules or principles is a logically possible alternative to the view he wishes to defend (see, e.g., 1971: 341). His main reason for reaching this conclusion is the argument for moral grammar. Is Rawls correct? Is the argument for moral grammar sound? While a detailed investigation of this topic must be deferred until Part Two, here I will simply reiterate and amplify my provisional claim that both of these questions should be answered affirmatively. The novelty and unboundedness of moral judgment, together with its frequent predictability, stability, and other systematic properties, implies the existence of a moral grammar, because to explain how an individual is able to project her finite experience to entirely new cases, we must assume that she is guided, implicitly, by a system of principles or rules. Without this assumption, her ability to make these novel judgments – and our ability to predict them – would be inexplicable. Logically speaking, it is conceivable that her moral capacity could consist of a list of principles, one for each new case she encounters (more exactly, the list might be a set of ordered pairs, consisting of a moral judgment and a description of the circumstances which occasioned it). The observation that moral judgment is not only novel but also potentially unbounded is meant to call even this logically possible explanation into question. If we make the simplifying assumption that her capacity for moral judgment is literally infinite, then, given the finite character of the storage capacity of the brain, it follows that her moral capacity must be something more complex than a mere list. Together with the other properties of moral judgment (e.g., its stability, frequent predictability, amenability to constituent manipulation, rapid and highly automatic character, etc.), we are left with the assumption that this "something" amounts to a system of principles or rules.

So understood, the argument for moral grammar is a traditional philosophical argument. A version of the argument, for example, can be found in the passage from Hume's *Treatise* that appears at the start of this chapter (1978/1740: 473). As I interpret this passage, Hume, like Rawls, proposes a kind of "infinite use of finite means" (Chomsky 1965; Humboldt 1971/1836) argument with respect to moral judgment. Specifically, Hume observes that the indefinite or unbounded extent of human moral judgment implies the existence of general moral principles, since the primary alternative – one instinct or precept for each of an infinite number and variety of judgments – is philosophically absurd. A similar argument can be found in many books on jurisprudence and legal theory. This is perhaps not surprising, given the fact that lawyers and judges have long been interested in explaining how a potentially infinite number and variety of fact situations can be captured in advance by a finite system of legal rules and principles. See, for example, Levi (1949), Pound (1939), and Stone (1968).[11]

These remarks allow me to clarify what may be an apparent ambiguity about Rawls' argument for moral grammar. As I interpret him, Rawls' argument is meant to show only that the indefinite extent of a person's capacity for moral judgment (i.e., its potential novelty and unboundedness), together with its other systematic properties, implies that she is guided, implicitly, by a set of general principles or rules. It is not meant to show, nor does it, that these principles are the same for all persons. It is true, as we have seen, that Rawls also makes the further simplifying assumption that the proper subject matter of moral theory is the moral competence of a single, idealized individual. But that is a methodological maneuver only; it is not the same thing as defending the empirical claim, by means of the argument from the poverty of the moral stimulus, that all humankind shares a common moral nature, in the form of a Universal Moral Grammar. That claim, understood as a hypothesis of natural science, goes far beyond anything Rawls actually defends in *A Theory of Justice*.[12] This more ambitious hypothesis can be pursued within a modern scientific framework, however. We turn our attention to this task in Part Two.

---

[11] For discussion of this phenomenon in the context of the codification of the substantive criminal law and its corollary, the general prohibition against retroactive criminal punishment, see, for example, Fletcher (1998), Hall (1947), and Moore (1993). For discussion of the same phenomenon in the law of torts, see, for example, Green (1928) and Hilliard (1859); but compare the Proposed Final Draft No. 1 of the Restatement (Third) of Torts, Section 8, comment c (embracing particularism and citing Dancy).

[12] I am grateful to Richard Miller for helping to clarify my views on this issue.

PART TWO

EMPIRICAL ADEQUACY

Two things fill the mind with ever new and increasing wonder and awe, the oftener and more steadily we reflect on them: the starry heavens above me and the moral law within me. ... But though wonder and respect can indeed excite to inquiry, they cannot supply the want of it. What, then, is to be done in order to set inquiry on foot in a useful way appropriate to the sublimity of its objects? Examples may serve for warnings here, but also for imitation. The observation of the world began from the noblest spectacle that was ever placed before the human senses and that our understanding can undertake to follow in its vast expanse, and it ended in – astrology. Morals began with the noblest attribute of human nature, the development and cultivation of which promised infinite utility, and it ended in – fanaticism or superstition. So it goes with all crude attempts in which the principal part of the business depends on the use of reason, a use which does not come of itself, like that of the feet, from frequent exercise, especially when it concerns attributes which cannot be so directly exhibited in common experience. Though late, when the maxim did come into vogue of carefully examining every step which reason had to take and not to let it proceed except on the path of a well-considered method, the study of the structure of the world took an entirely different direction and therewith attained an incomparably happier result. The fall of the stone and the motion of a sling, resolved into their elements and the forces manifested in them treated mathematically, finally brought that clear and henceforth unchangeable insight into the structure of the world which, as observations continue, we may hope to broaden but need not fear of having to retract.

   This example recommends to us the same path in treating of the moral capacities of our nature and gives hope of a similarly good issue. We have at hand examples of the morally judging reason. We may analyze them into their elementary concepts, adopting, in default of mathematics, a process similar to that of chemistry, i.e., we may, in repeated experiments on common sense, separate the empirical from the rational, exhibit each of them in its pure state, and show what each by itself can accomplish. Thus we shall avoid the error of a crude and unpracticed judgment and (something far more important) the extravagances of genius, by which, as by the adepts of the philosopher's stone, visionary treasures are promised and real treasures are squandered for lack of methodical study and knowledge of nature. In a word, science (critically sought and methodically directed) is the narrow gate that leads to the doctrine of wisdom, when by this is understood not merely what one ought to do but what should serve as a guide to teachers in laying out plainly and well the path to wisdom which everyone should follow, and in keeping others from going astray. It is a science of which philosophy must always remain the guardian; and though the public takes no interest in its subtle investigations, it may very well take an interest in the doctrines which such considerations first make clear to it.

> – Immanuel Kant, *Critique of Practical Reason*

4

The Problem of Descriptive Adequacy

How does it happen that the prevailing public opinion about what is right and what is moral is in so many respects correct? If such a philosopher as Kant failed in the attempt to find the source of our knowledge of right and wrong, is it conceivable that ordinary people succeeded in drawing from this source? And if it is not, how does it happen that they have so often arrived at the proper conclusions without having the necessary premises? One cannot possibly explain the fact by saying that the correct view was established long ago. ... But this difficulty ... is easily resolved. We only have to reflect that much of what is present in our store of knowledge contributes toward the attainment of new knowledge without our being clearly conscious of the process. ... Thus it has often been observed that for thousands of years men have drawn right conclusions without bringing the procedure and the principles which form the condition of the formal validity of the inference into clear consciousness by means of reflection. ... In spite of their false conception of the true fundamental principles, these still continue to operate in their reasoning. But why do I go so far for examples? Let the experiment be made with the first "plain man" who has just drawn a right conclusion, and demand of him that he give you the premises of his conclusion. This he will usually be unable to do and may perhaps make entirely false statements about it. On requiring the same man to define a notion with which he is familiar, he will make the most glaring mistakes and so show once again that he is not able rightly to describe his own thinking.

– Franz Brentano, *The Origin of the Knowledge of Right and Wrong*

The central problem of the research program outlined in Part One is the problem of descriptive adequacy. In Part Two, I take a closer look at what solving this problem involves. I begin by introducing a set of thought experiments that appears to elicit considered judgments in Rawls' sense, namely, the family of trolley problems arising out of the work of Philippa Foot (1967) and Judith Jarvis Thomson (1986). I then discuss some of the findings of the original trolley problem experiments that I conducted in the mid-1990s with my colleagues Cristina Sorrentino and Elizabeth Spelke at the Massachusetts

Institute of Technology. I also attempt to clarify the empirical significance of the linguistic analogy by formulating, and proposing a solution to, the problem of descriptive adequacy with respect to these judgments. In addition, I endeavor to situate this problem within the framework of the contemporary cognitive sciences, thereby placing the theory of moral cognition on a sounder footing. My primary aim throughout Part Two is to continue to develop the substantive research program that Rawls sketches in Section 9 of *A Theory of Justice*. At the same time, I wish to shed further light on Rawls' overall conception of moral philosophy, and thereby to anticipate some of the criticisms of the linguistic analogy that I examine in Part Three.

4.1 THE TROLLEY PROBLEMS

Our discussion of the linguistic analogy thus far has been highly abstract. Before turning to some influential criticisms of that analogy, it will be useful to focus our attention on a set of considered judgments and a specific attempt to explicate them. This will enable us to examine various aspects of the problem of descriptive adequacy in more detail. Once we have done so, we will be in a better position to assess the significance of the linguistic analogy and to decide whether the criticisms of it, and of Rawls' conception of moral theory more generally, are sound.

Consider the following examples, versions of which have been discussed at length in the literature (see, e.g., Foot 1967; Harman 1977; Thomson 1986; see generally Fischer & Ravizza 1992). For our purposes they can be conceived as loosely analogous to the set of linguistic expressions that we listed in Chapter 3 (see Section 3.1.1). Since these fact patterns can be easily manipulated to produce a "potentially infinite number and variety" of new cases (Rawls 1971: 46), each of which appears capable of eliciting considered judgments in Rawls' sense, the examples appear to support Rawls' assumption that the mind/brain contains a moral grammar. The fact that most individuals have considerable difficulty explaining these judgments illustrates the distinction between operative and express principles, and lends weight to Rawls' assumption that the principles needed to describe that grammar are complex, involving theoretical constructions that "go much beyond the norms and standards cited in everyday life" (1971: 47). Finally, in light of Nagel's (1986: 174) apt observation that moral intuitions about cases like these often "begin to fail above a certain level of complexity," the examples also can be used to illustrate the relevance of the competence–performance distinction for moral theory.

(4) (a) **Scarce Resources: Alice**

Alice is a doctor in a hospital's emergency room when six accident victims are brought in. All six are in danger of dying but one is much worse off than the others. Alice can just barely save that person if she devotes all of her resources to him and lets the others die. Alternatively, Alice can save the other five if she is willing to ignore the patient who is most seriously injured.

Is it morally permissible for Alice to save the most seriously injured patient?

(b) Transplant: Bob

Bob is a transplant surgeon. He has five patients in the hospital who are dying, each in need of a separate organ. One needs a kidney, another a lung, a third a heart, and so forth. Bob can save all five if he takes a single healthy person and removes her heart, lungs, kidneys, and so forth, to distribute to these five patients. Just such a healthy person is in Room 306. She is in the hospital for routine tests. Having seen her test results, Bob knows that she is perfectly healthy and of the right tissue compatibility. If Bob does nothing, she will survive without incident; the other patients will die, however. The other patients can be saved only if the person in Room 306 is cut up and her organs distributed. In that case there would be one dead but five saved.

Is it morally permissible for Bob to cut up the person in Room 306?

(c) Trolley: Charlie

Charlie is driving a train when the brakes fail. Ahead five people are working on the track, with their backs turned. Fortunately, Charlie can switch to a side track, if he acts at once. Unfortunately, there is also someone on that track with his back turned. If Charlie switches his train to the side track, he will kill one person. If Charlie does not switch his train, he will kill five people.

Is it morally permissible for Charlie to switch his train to the side track?

(d) Passenger: Denise

Denise is a passenger on a train whose driver has just shouted that the train's brakes have failed, and who then fainted from the shock. On the track ahead are five people; the banks are so steep that they will not be able to get off the track in time. The track has a side track leading off to the right, and Denise can turn the train onto it. Unfortunately there is one person on the right-hand track. Denise can turn the train, killing the one; or she can refrain from turning the train, letting the five die.

Is it morally permissible for Denise to switch the train to the side track?

(e) Bystander: Edward

Edward is taking his daily walk near the train tracks when he notices that the train that is approaching is out of control. Edward sees what has happened: the train driver saw five workmen men ahead on the tracks and slammed on the brakes, but the brakes failed and the driver fainted. The train is now rushing toward the five men; the banks are so steep that they will not be able to get off the track in time. Fortunately Edward is standing next to a switch, which he can throw, that will turn the train onto a side track. Unfortunately, there is one person standing on the side track, with his back turned. Edward can throw the switch, killing the one; or he can refrain from doing this, letting the five die.

Is it morally permissible for Edward to throw the switch?

(f) Footbridge: Frank

Frank is on a footbridge over the train tracks. He knows trains and can see that the one approaching the bridge is out of control. On the track under the bridge there are five people; the banks are so steep that they will not be able to get off the track in time. Frank knows that the only way to stop an out-of-control train is to drop a very heavy weight into its path. But the only available, sufficiently heavy weight is a large man wearing a backpack, also watching the train from the footbridge. Frank can shove the man with the backpack onto the track in the path of the train, killing him; or he can refrain from doing this, letting the five die.

Is it morally permissible for Frank to shove the man?

When experimental subjects are presented with these scenarios, they judge Alice's saving the one more seriously injured patient in the Scarce Resources problem, Bob's cutting up the patient in the Transplant problem, and Frank's shoving the man in the Footbridge problem to be impermissible. However, they also judge it to be permissible for Charlie to turn the train in the Trolley problem, Denise to switch the train to the side track in the Passenger problem, and Edward to throw the switch in the Bystander problem (see, e.g., Cushman, Young, & Hauser 2006; Hauser et al. 2007; Mikhail 2000, 2002b, 2007a; Mikhail, Sorrentino, & Spelke 1998; see generally Appendix 1). These responses confront us with a potentially surprising contrast between the Scarce Resources, Trolley, Passenger, and Bystander problems, on the one hand, and the Transplant and Footbridge problems, on the other. In the former scenarios, saving five people at the cost of sacrificing one person is thought to be permissible. In the latter two scenarios, by contrast, achieving the same outcome is held to be impermissible.

These facts lead us to speculate about the cognitive mechanisms that are used to respond to these six scenarios. In particular, they invite the following question: what are the operative principles of moral competence that are responsible for these divergent responses? The problem is more difficult than it initially may seem. On the one hand, comparatively simple deontological and consequentialist moral principles (e.g., "If an act causes death, then it is wrong," "If the consequences of an act are better than the consequences of any of available alternative, then it is required," etc.) are incapable of explaining the pattern of intuitions elicited by these problems. For example, a simple deontological principle forbidding any act of killing would generate the intuition that both Charlie's switching tracks in the Trolley problem and Edward's switching tracks in the Bystander problem are impermissible. Yet these actions are judged to be permissible. Likewise, a simple utilitarian principle requiring agents to perform actions with the best foreseeable consequences would presumably generate the intuition that Bob's cutting up the patient in the Transplant problem and Frank's throwing the man into the train's path in the Footbridge problem are obligatory, or at least permissible; yet these actions are judged to be impermissible.

On the other hand, conditional principles whose antecedents simply restate those action-descriptions found in the stimulus (e.g., "If an act is of the type 'throwing the switch,' then it is permissible"; "If an act is of the type 'throwing the man,' then it is impermissible") are also descriptively inadequate. This is because they yield inaccurate predictions of how these action-descriptions will be evaluated when they are embedded in materially different circumstances. For example, when the costs and benefits in the Bystander problem are manipulated, so that an action described as "throwing the switch" will save five million dollars of new railroad equipment at the cost of killing one person, individuals judge the action so described to be impermissible. Likewise, when the circumstances of the Footbridge problem are modified so that the action described as "throwing the man" is presumed to involve consensual touching, subjects judge the action to be permissible (see Appendix 1). In general, it is easy to show that the action-descriptions used in these problems are "morally neutral" (Nelson 1980), in the sense that the permissibility judgments they elicit are circumstance-dependent.

Since the circumstances of an action can vary indefinitely (e.g., D'Arcy 1963; Donagan 1977; Green 1928; Hilliard 1859; Lyons 1965; Stone 1968), the conclusion to which we quickly are led by considerations like these is that any attempt to explain the moral intuitions elicited by these examples by means of a simple stimulus–response model is doomed at the start. Instead, a descriptively adequate model must be more elaborate and must involve complex, structure-dependent rules, whose basic operations are defined in relation to abstract categories that are only indirectly related to the stimulus.

Philosophers, psychologists, and legal scholars have analyzed many different rule systems that might adequately explain these intuitions, including rules that depend on a variety of familiar distinctions, such as killing versus letting die, action versus inaction, act versus omission, doing versus allowing, positive versus negative rights, and intended versus foreseen effects (see, e.g., Fischer and Ravizza 1992; Quinn 1993; Steinbock 1980; Thomson 1986). As those researchers who actually have attempted to do so are keenly aware, however, it is not easy to formulate clear and unambiguous proposals that are capable of providing intuitively satisfying explanations of these and similar intuitions.

In addition to the question of which principles or rules are descriptively adequate, there is a more intriguing question: How are the relevant principles or rules acquired? Until now, little experimental research has been done to investigate, first, when children or adolescents begin to distinguish various cases like the six examples in (4), and second, the nature of the evidence available to them prior to that time. If the relevant principles can be shown to emerge and become operative in the course of normal development, but to be neither explicitly taught nor derivable in any obvious way from the data of experience, then there would appear to be at least some evidence supporting an argument from the poverty of the stimulus in the moral domain.[1]

It is important not to confuse the problem of explanatory adequacy presented by thought experiments like these with the problem of *descriptive* adequacy. The latter problem is logically prior to the former. We cannot seriously formulate the problem of explanatory adequacy with respect to trolley problem intuitions, or any other moral intuitions, until we have a better sense of their structure and what a solution to the problem of descriptive adequacy actually involves (Mikhail 2008a; cf. Chomsky 1975b). In attempting to discover which principles or rules explicate these judgments, therefore, we are not prejudging the issue of whether those principles or rules are innate. Rather, we are trying to put ourselves in the position of being able to ask *whether* they are innate.[2]

4.2 THE PROPERTIES OF MORAL JUDGMENT

The moral judgments elicited by the problems in (4) are *intuitive:* they are not made by a conscious application of moral rules or principles, so far as this may

[1] To the best of my knowledge, the first experiment to use trolley problems to investigate the moral judgment of children was Mikhail & Sorrentino (1999). In that study the Trolley and Transplant problems were presented to 16 children (seven girls and nine boys) between the ages of 8 and 12. Each child was asked to evaluate only one scenario: eight children were given a version of the Transplant problem and eight were given a version of the Trolley problem. Six of eight children judged the doctor's cutting up the patient in the Transplant problem to be impermissible; by contrast, all eight children judged switching the train to the side track in the Trolley problem to be permissible. These findings, which were presented to the Society for Research in Child Development in 1999, suggest that the operative principles that generate the intuitive responses to these problems and similar cases emerge at early stages of cognitive development. More research is necessary, however, to get a better handle on this issue. For some further discussions of moral nativism that helped to inform *Rawls' Linguistic Analogy*, see, e.g., Chomsky (1986b); Cummins (1996a, 1996b); Dwyer (1999); Harman (1999); Kagan & Lamb (1987); Mikhail, Sorrentino, & Spelke (1998).

[2] Having emphasized that one should not prejudge this issue, it is also important to note that the examples in (4) have not been chosen randomly or without design. On the contrary, I think that trolley problems are some of the best cases, perhaps *the* best cases, for moral theorists to investigate, particularly those researchers interested in moral nativism. In particular, these problems are much better than the examples used by either Kohlberg (1981) or Piaget (1965/1932), in part because they appear to elicit considered judgments in Rawls' sense, whereas the moral dilemmas used by Piaget and Kohlberg often do not. I return to this point in Chapter 7.

be determined by observation or introspection.[3] Nonetheless, the judgments appear to be *principled,* as evidenced by the fact that, despite being relatively immediate and spontaneous, they are stable, stringent, and highly predictable.[4] Moreover, the judgments appear to be highly structured, amenable to constituent manipulation, and intuitively consistent with judgments rendered in structurally similar scenarios. In addition, the judgments are typically made with a high degree of certitude and, indeed, are often experienced as being "objective" rather than a matter of subjective taste or preference from a phenomenological perspective (cf. Mandelbaum 1955: 51–59; Ross 1988/1930: 39–41; Thomson 1990: 32). We thus appear led to the hypothesis that, as is the case with grammaticality judgments, which also possess similar properties, the moral judgments elicited by (4) involve the use of unconscious principles or algorithms.

When experimental subjects are asked to justify or explain their judgments, they appear unable to express the principles on which their judgments are based (see, e.g., Cushman, Young, & Hauser 2006; Hauser et al. 2007; Mikhail 2000, 2002b, 2007a; Mikhail, Sorrentino, & Spelke 1998; see generally Appendix 1). We are thus led to a further surprising hypothesis: some of the operative principles of moral grammar appear to function below actual or even potential consciousness, at least in this context. The content of these principles, in other words, appears to be nonintrospectible.[5]

---

[3] The meaning of *intuitive* as it is used in this context should not be misunderstood. It is not a temporal notion and does not mean the same thing as "immediate," "impulsive," or "instinctive." Intuitive moral judgments are those which satisfy a simple criterion: they are not determined by the systematic and conscious use of ethical principles. An intuitive judgment may be relatively fast or automatic, but it also can be made after thoroughly studying the relevant circumstances and carefully assessing the likely consequences of different alternatives. The important condition is simply that the judgment is not made by consciously applying ethical principles (see Rawls 1951a: 183).

[4] The four key terms in this sentence are being used here in the following sense. Judgments are *spontaneous* when they are not consciously originated. Spontaneous judgments are unintentional and nonvoluntary; they seem to "happen" to us, rather than being the result of any conscious decision or intention. The *immediacy* of a moral judgment refers to a slightly different property: its speed. Judgments are immediate when they occur very soon after encountering a moral situation. *Stability* refers to a judgment's invariance over time. If an individual is presented with a moral situation on two or more occasions, and each presentation elicits the same moral response, her judgments are said to be stable. Finally, judgments are *stringent* to the degree they are difficult or even impossible to convince ourselves, or to be convinced, out of. No amount of reflection after the fact enables us to change our mind. For discussion, see generally Rawls (1950, 1951a, 1963b, 1971, 1975). An interesting affirmation of the compatibility of the intuitive and systematic properties of moral judgment can be found in F. H. Bradley's essay *My Station and Its Duties* (Bradley 1962/1876; see especially pp. 193–199).

[5] Once again, the inferences drawn in this and the preceding paragraph are abductive. Inspired by Helmholtz (1962/1867), perhaps, many nineteenth-century writers held that moral judgment involves unconscious inference. In addition to Brentano (1969/1889: 33–35; cf. Brentano 1973/1952: 143–147), other notable examples include Bain (1868), Bradley

The last of these observations may not be entirely clear or persuasive. To see the basic point, it helps to consider what some of the participants in our experiments said when they were asked to justify or explain their judgments about the six problems in (4). One individual who was given both the Bystander and Footbridge problems said:

> Very odd. I don't know why I chose differently in the second scenario. The end result is the same. I just went with my gut response – and now am intrigued with how to reconcile them.

A second person said:

> It's amazing that I would not throw a person but would throw a switch to kill a person.

Finally, a third person said:

> My reaction is intuitive and I realize not logically justifiable. I am reluctant to grade life and thus equate the value of one life as being less than five, even though I know this can be done.

In sharp contrast with Kohlberg's (1981, 1984) findings concerning the relevance of demographic variables like age, race, gender, and level of formal education, but in line with our predictions, our subjects' deontic judgments were widely shared, irrespective of these factors. As these remarks imply, however, our subjects' *express* principles were widely divergent. Moreover, our subjects were consistently incapable of articulating the operative principles on which their judgments were based. They often said things that were incompatible with their own judgments, or even internally incoherent. Finally, they often appeared puzzled by the nature and strength of their intuitions, together with how those intuitions changed as a result of minor alterations in the stimuli that were made in order to evoke distinct mental representations.

The distinction between *operative* and *express* principles – between those principles actually used in the exercise of moral judgment and their articulated counterparts (i.e., those principles verbalized by experimental subjects in an attempt to justify or account for their judgments) – appears to vitiate, or at least seriously compromise, certain key elements of Piaget's and Kohlberg's theoretical paradigms, which have dominated moral psychology in the twentieth century. Both Piaget's stage theory of moral development and Kohlberg's subsequent elaboration of it are theories that primarily track the development of a person's ability to *express* or *articulate* moral beliefs or moral principles. While this is obviously an important skill, which may track to some extent the ability to engage in more complex acts of moral reasoning,

---

(1962/1876), Holmes (1991/1881), Mill (1972/1861), Sidgwick (1981/1907), Spencer (1978/1897), and Whewell (1852). Unfortunately, like much other accumulated wisdom in the theory of moral cognition, this penetrating insight gradually disappeared with the rise of behaviorism.

it does not necessarily reveal the properties of I-morality. On the contrary, our subjects' responses to trolley problems clearly indicate that a person's introspective verbal reports and general viewpoint about her moral knowledge may be in error. The important point is that, as is the case with a theory of language or vision, a theory of moral cognition must attempt to specify what the properties of I-morality actually are, not what a person may or may not introspect about them.

4.3 FRAMING THE PROBLEM OF DESCRIPTIVE ADEQUACY

The descriptive problem Rawls identifies is the construction of a set of clear and precise principles or rules that, when applied rigorously and consistently to a representation of the facts and circumstances of the six problems in (4), would lead individuals to make the same judgments that they already make intuitively. In this way, he suggests, we may hope to discover something about the cognitive machinery that is used to represent and evaluate these six scenarios.

To formulate this problem more precisely, we might begin with some provisional definitions. By the *deontic status* of an act, let us mean the status assigned to that act by the sense of justice, or (mental) moral grammar. As an idealization, we may assume that the deontic status of an act is exhausted by three possibilities – *forbidden, permissible, obligatory* – leaving other traditional deontic categories, such as *indifferent* and *supererogatory,* to one side.[6]

The six problems in (4) are deliberately described in a manner that limits the number of options available to the agent in each scenario. Each scenario is followed by a question that asks the respondent to decide whether a given course of conduct is morally permissible. For now let us use the term *possible act* to refer to each of these (explicit or implicit) possible courses of conduct available to agents in the six problems in (4).

Our theoretical task is to construct a system of principles or rules that can account for the deontic status that individuals intuitively assign to possible acts in these six problems. The basic facts our system must account for, we might suppose, are those represented in Table 4.1.

As Rawls (1971: 46) observes, Table 4.1 is not itself an adequate description of the sense of justice with respect to the six problems in (4); rather, Table 4.1 represents facts about these problems that an adequate description

---

[6] We thus stipulate, in effect, that the three main deontic operators belong to the theory of moral competence, while the less formal concepts of everyday discourse ("right," "wrong," "acceptable," "impermissible," "morally required," etc.) belong to the theory of moral performance. In this way we draw a distinction similar to the one that linguists make between *grammatical* and *acceptable* utterances. The former belong to the theory of linguistic competence, while the latter belong to the theory of linguistic performance (e.g., Chomsky 1965: 10ff.; Haegeman 1994: 6ff.). I return to this topic in Chapter 7.

TABLE 4.1. *Considered Judgments Elicited by Six Trolley Problems*

Problem	Possible Act	Deontic Status
(4a)	Alice's saving the most seriously injured patient	Forbidden
(4b)	Bob's cutting up the person in Room 306	Forbidden
(4c)	Charlie's switching his train to the side track	Permissible
(4d)	Denise's switching the train to the side track	Permissible
(4e)	Edward's throwing the switch	Permissible
(4f)	Frank's shoving the man	Forbidden

must *explain*. In each of these six problems, we are presented with a scenario in which an agent has open to him or her a series of possible acts. We intuitively assign a deontic status to (a representation of) one of these possible acts. Rawls suggests that this phenomena may be usefully compared to our being presented with six linguistic expressions, each of which we intuitively assign a grammatical status. The general question we face is: On what basis do we assign a deontic status to the possible acts at issue in the six problems in (4)? Again, this question may be thought of as comparable to the question faced by the linguist: on what basis do we assign a grammatical status to the linguistic expressions we encounter?

The limited information contained in Table 4.1 is inadequate to account for the judgments given in the third column. Only a brief characterization of possible acts is given. Likewise, no mention is made of the consequences of each possible act. These omissions are deliberate. They suggest that no adequate rule system of the kind we require can be written on the limited basis of the information contained in Table 4.1. This table must therefore be expanded by incorporating additional information that is extracted in some manner or other from the information that is contained in or implied by the six problems in (4).

What additional information shall we use? How we answer this question seems likely to tell us something about the cognitive machinery that is used in representing and evaluating the six problems in (4). Put differently, it seems likely to tell us something about the fundamental constructs that the sense of justice – the (mental) moral grammar – employs.

Some obvious candidates come readily to mind. Situations occasioning moral judgment are typically thought to be mentally represented and evaluated in terms of abstract categories like *agent, patient, act, consequence, motive, intention, circumstance, proximate cause,* and other familiar concepts that are the stock in trade of philosophers, lawyers, and jurists. But which specific constructs does the system of moral cognition in fact use? In what manner, that is, according to what principles or rules, does it use them? The answers to questions like these would begin to satisfy the demand that Rawls identifies: the demand for a descriptively adequate moral grammar.

4.4 LOCATING THE PROBLEM WITHIN THE FRAMEWORK OF COGNITIVE SCIENCE

Act, consequence, motive, intention, and the like are concepts largely drawn from ordinary thought and ordinary language. In short, they risk being "obscure and intuition-bound notions" of the type that Chomsky (1957: 5, 1965: 4, 1975a: 58) suggests may be incapable of playing the role required of them by a *generative* grammar: the requirement of perfect explicitness.

If these and other fundamental moral concepts are incapable of being explicated and applied in a relatively precise manner, then the likelihood that a theoretical grammar of the kind envisaged would be illuminating is slim indeed. Can the relevant concepts be given a precise enough characterization to allow an effort to construct a theoretical grammar, at least with respect to our moral judgments in (4), to proceed? It makes little sense to answer this question in the abstract, in advance of actual inquiry. A more reasonable course of action, it seems, would be to engage in specific, concrete attempts to define and utilize the concepts in question, in the construction of a grammar of the kind envisaged.

Fortunately there is no need to reinvent the wheel; the philosophical and legal literatures are replete with complex, detailed analyses of many of the concepts in question.[7] In attempting to incorporate these analyses into our framework, however, it is imperative to keep in mind the scope and limits of our inquiry. Our topic is limited to the manner in which a particular cognitive system, the system of moral cognition, represents and evaluates possible acts in (4). We are interested in a question of fact. Evidently individuals do assign a deontic status to each of the six possible acts in (4); our question is what role mental constructs like act, consequence, and so on play in this process.

One traditional formulation of the immediate object of moral judgment takes that object to be a particular mental construction, imposed by the mind on the otherwise undifferentiated data of sense, whose primary constituents include the following two constructs: *moral agent* and *voluntary act or omission.* On this view, the representational objects on which moral judgment operates are not events or states of affairs, but acts or omissions; specifically, those acts or omissions that can be imputed to *moral* agents and can

---

[7] For act, see, e.g., Bennett (1995), Coval & Smith (1986), D'Arcy (1963), Davidson (1980), Davis (1979), Donagan (1977), Ginet (1990), Goldman (1970a, 1970b), Holmes (1991/1881), Lyons (1965), Terry (1884), Thomson (1986), and White (1968). For consequence, see, e.g., Anscombe (1958), Bergstrom (1966), D'Arcy (1963), Donagan (1977), Scheffler (1988), and Terry (1884). For circumstance, see, e.g., Bergstrom (1966), D'Arcy (1963), and Donagan (1977). For alternative, see, e.g., Bergstrom (1966), Lyons (1965), and Mandelbaum (1955). For agency, see, e.g., Bradley (1962/1876), Coval & Smith (1986), and Quinn (1993). For motive, see, e.g., Lawrence (1972). For intention, see, e.g., Anscombe (1957), Donagan (1977), Holmes (1991/1881), Lawrence (1972), and Sidgwick (1981/1907). For cause, see, e.g., Donagan (1977), Hart & Honore (1959), Mackie (1974), and Wright (1985).

be characterized as *voluntary*. What occupies a central place in any theoretical explanation of moral judgment, then, is a complex mental construction consisting, in part, of a compound of the form *voluntary act or omission of a moral agent*. Only events that are mentally represented in this form are taken to be the natural and appropriate objects of deontic judgment.[8]

In what follows we will adopt this traditional view but modify it in various respects. These modifications will be explained as our attempt to construct a fragment of moral grammar that is capable of explaining our judgments in (4) proceeds. At this point, however, it seems useful to clarify the issues involved by setting our question within the general framework of the contemporary study of human cognitive faculties and their properties (cf. Chomsky 1964: 25).

4.4.1 Perceptual and Acquisition Models

As we saw in Part One, the moral grammar approach to moral cognition relies on two fundamental arguments: the argument for moral grammar and the argument from the poverty of the moral stimulus (see Section 2.1.3). The argument for moral grammar holds that the properties of moral judgment imply that the mind contains a moral grammar: a complex and possibly domain-specific set of rules, concepts, and principles that generates and relates mental representations of various types. Among other things, this system enables individuals to determine the deontic status of an infinite variety of acts and omissions. The argument from the poverty of the moral stimulus holds that the manner in which this grammar is acquired implies that at least some of its core attributes are innate, where "innate" is used in a dispositional sense to refer to cognitive systems whose essential properties are largely predetermined by the inherent structure of the mind, but whose ontogenetic development must be triggered and shaped by appropriate experience and can be impeded by unusually hostile learning environments (Chomsky 1986a; Gallistel 1999; Jackendoff 1994). Both arguments are abductive and presuppose a familiar set of idealizations and simplifying assumptions (Chomsky 1965, 1986a; Rawls 1971). Moreover, both arguments have direct parallels in the case of language, and, like their linguistic counterparts, they can be depicted graphically by simple perceptual and acquisition models (Figure 4.1).

The perceptual and acquisition models depicted in Figure 4.1 illustrate how a philosopher or scientist who wishes to pursue the research program that Rawls describes in Section 9 of *A Theory of Justice* might begin to utilize a set of considered judgments as evidence for hypotheses about what

---

[8] Traditional formulations like this recur throughout the history of jurisprudence and moral philosophy. One exceptionally clear statement of the distinction between act and event may be found in Joseph Butler, *A Dissertation upon the Nature of Virtue* (1983/1736).

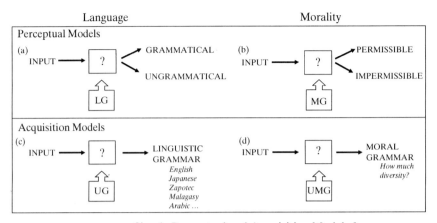

FIGURE 4.1. Simple Perceptual and Acquisition Models for
Language and Morality

constitutes moral knowledge and how it is acquired. In early work on generative grammar, Chomsky (1964: 26) clarified the objectives of linguistic theory by developing the idea that verbal behavior can be studied as an input-output relation. Chomsky distinguished two devices or models that a linguistic theory must specify: a *perceptual model* corresponding to the first main question of generative linguistics ("What constitutes knowledge of language?") and an *acquisition model* corresponding to the second main question ("How is knowledge of language acquired?"). In an abstract format that is suitably modified for our purposes, Chomsky's perceptual model is reproduced in Figure 4.1(a).

Implicit in Rawls' linguistic analogy (1971: 47) is a comparison between two types of judgment: the judgment that a linguistic expression is grammatical or ungrammatical, and the judgment that a given action is permissible or impermissible (or that a given institutional arrangement is just or unjust). Figure 4.1(b) represents what, for our purposes, is a suitably general model of the kind of perceptual behavior Rawls describes.

The question that motivates *Syntactic Structures* (1957: 14) and Chomsky's other early work is: On what basis do we actually go about distinguishing grammatical from ungrammatical sentences? Our question is similar: On what basis do we actually go about distinguishing permissible from impermissible acts? Provisional answers are provided by a linguistic grammar (LG) and moral grammar (MG), respectively.[9]

---

[9] The foregoing account is a potentially misleading characterization of the motivation of *Syntactic Structures* and Chomsky's other early work. For one thing, it ignores the distinction between *strong generation* and *weak generation* (see Section 8.2.5), along with the distinction between grammaticality and acceptability judgments and the

Turning to the two acquisition models in Figure 4.1, while the argument from the poverty of the stimulus implies that some linguistic knowledge is innate, the variety of human languages provides an upper bound on this hypothesis; what is innate must be consistent with the observed diversity of human languages (Figure 4.1[c]). Hence Universal Grammar (UG) must be rich and specific enough to get each child over the learning hump, but flexible enough to enable her to acquire different grammars in different linguistic contexts (Chomsky 1964, 1986a; Pinker 1994). In the case of moral development (Figure 4.1[d]), whether models incorporating parametric variation will likewise enter into the best explanation of Universal Moral Grammar (UMG) – the innate function or acquisition device that maps the child's early experience into the mature state of her moral competence – is yet to be determined. What is needed are answers to two questions: first, what are the properties of the moral grammars people do in fact acquire, and, second, how diverse are they? Although it is plausible to suppose that some aspects of moral judgment are innate, it seems clear that cultural factors also have a significant influence (see, e.g., Nader 1997; Nichols 2004; Nisbett & Cohen 1996; Prinz 2007; Shweder, Mahapatra, & Miller 1987).

Consider Figure 4.1(b) as a model for explaining the behavior involved in the perceptual judgments elicited by the six problems in (4). From an information-processing perspective, these problems consist of a series of statements describing possible acts and their circumstances, the deontic status of which our subjects are evidently capable of evaluating. Hence, we may reasonably assume the mind/brain contains a device or mechanism of some sort capable of sorting the acts in question into those that are permissible and those that are not. What might this device be? This question may be rephrased in the idiom of contemporary cognitive science. For each of these problems, experimental subjects are presented with a specific proximal stimulus, in the form of a series of utterances (or, if the scenarios are read by the subjects themselves, in the form of patterns of scrawls of ink on a page).[10] The subjects then engage in a specific behavior: that is, they answer the question. Given that both input and output are determinate, a nontrivial but feasible problem emerges. What "background information" (Lashley 1951; cf. Chomsky 1959) must be attributed to the perceiving organism to account for these effects, given these particular inputs?

phenomena of "semi-grammatical" utterances and degrees of grammaticalness more generally (see, e.g., Chomsky 1961). Further, it mistakenly implies that generative linguists are mainly preoccupied with discovering a formal solution to the problem of descriptive adequacy. In fact, their main concern has been to make progress on understanding language acquisition. Still, the foregoing account is a useful way to frame this aspect of the linguistic analogy at an appropriate level of generality for our purposes.

[10] Likewise, if, instead of reading these vignettes, subjects were to watch the events unfold in a movie, scripted enactment or computer simulation of some sort, with or without an accompanying narration, then the relevant input would consist of a different mix of visual and/or auditory stimuli. The independence of moral cognition from particular sensory modalities is an intriguing topic, which I set aside for the time being.

Extending our earlier definition somewhat, let us continue to refer to this as the *problem of descriptive adequacy.* In Figure 4.1(b), the background information is conceived as a mechanism or device of some sort – technically a *function* – with a sequence of words as its input and the answers "permissible" or "impermissible" as its output. At a first approximation, to solve the problem of descriptive adequacy with respect to the six problems in (4) the theory that describes this mechanism must do at least two things. First, it must be capable of determining whether each of the possible acts in (4) is permissible or impermissible. Second, it must do so in a manner that provides a correct account of our subjects' moral knowledge and explains their moral intuitions.

4.4.2 The Hypothetico-Deductive Method

How should we attempt to solve this problem? The method that Rawls (1971: 46) recommends is the *hypothetico-deductive method* (see, e.g., Carnap 1966; Hempel 1966; Nagel 1961). We formulate hypotheses about the background information, each of which may be thought of as a moral principle or set of principles. We test a hypothesis by taking it to be one of the premises of a deductive argument, whose further premises include, among other auxiliary hypotheses, our knowledge and beliefs about the action in question, and whose conclusion is a moral judgment. In this way, Rawls suggests, we attempt to discover whether "a conception of justice characterizes our moral sensibility," by determining whether "the everyday judgments we do make are in accordance with its principles" (1971: 46).

To see clearly what is involved in this method, some additional terminology drawn from the philosophy of science may be helpful. The pattern of explanation we are considering is *deductive-nomological explanation,* or explanation by the deductive subsumption under general laws ("covering laws"). The phenomenon we ultimately wish to explain is a mental event, the behavioral effect of a given input. But the conclusion of our argument is not that event or behavior, but a *statement* describing what we take to be instructions sent to various behavioral/performance systems by the system of moral competence. Following Hempel (1966: 50–51), the former may be termed the *explanandum phenomenon;* the latter, the *explanandum sentence.* In Hempel's terms, then, the explanation we seek may be conceived as a deductive argument whose premises, the explanans, consist of a set of laws, $L_1 \ldots L_n$, plus other factual statements, $C_1 \ldots C_n$, and whose conclusion is the explanandum sentence, E. Thus we can represent the logical form of the argument schematically as follows:

(5) (a) $L_1 \ldots L_n$ $\Bigg\}$ Explanans Sentences

        $C_1 \ldots C_n$

        $\overline{\text{E}}$ Explanandum Sentence

Returning to Rawls, the method he recommends in Section 9 may be restated in the following terms. To solve the problem of descriptive adequacy, we formulate hypotheses about the relevant background information, each of which may be thought of as an explanans sentence of the form:

(5) (b) If possible act, A, has features $F_1 ... F_n$, then A has deontic status D

We test a hypothesis by taking it to be one of the premises of a deductive argument, whose other premises include a collection of additional explanans sentences characterizing A, and whose conclusion is an explanandum sentence that assigns A a deontic status. The former statements may be thought of as a set of affirmative propositions of the form:

(5) (c) A has feature F_1
      A has feature F_2
      A has feature F_3
      ...
      A has feature F_n

The latter may be thought of as an affirmative proposition of the form:

(5) (d) A has deontic status D

Schematically, then, the argument (5b)–(5d) may be represented as follows:

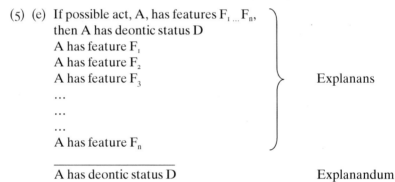

(5) (e) If possible act, A, has features $F_1 ... F_n$,
      then A has deontic status D
      A has feature F_1
      A has feature F_2
      A has feature F_3 Explanans
      ...
      ...
      ...
      A has feature F_n

      A has deontic status D   Explanandum

Now, for our purposes, it is useful to note that the set of propositions comprising (5c) may be expressed, if one wishes, as a single, comprehensive proposition:

(5) (f) A has features $F_1 ... F_n$.

Since this is the case, and since (5b) is a conditional statement, the method Rawls advocates may be rewritten in the form of a mixed hypothetical syllogism (5g), specifically, the form traditionally known as *modus ponendo ponens:*

(5) (g) If A has features, $F_1 ... F_n$, then A is forbidden
      A has features $F_1 ... F_n$

      A is forbidden

The significance of this formula for our topic is that the logical structure of the explanation of moral judgment with which we are concerned is identical with the pattern of explanation found in both the traditional model of common law adjudication, wherein a legal rule or *ratio decidendi* is applied to a particular fact pattern to yield a specific legal judgment (see, e.g., Holmes 1870; Pound 1908; Terry 1884), and the traditional study of conscience, wherein the judgment of conscience, or *conscientia,* is conceived as a mental act that proceeds from the first principles of practical reason, or *synderesis* (see, e.g., Crowe 1977; D'Arcy 1961; Greene 1991, 1997; Potts, 1980).[11] As we have seen, it is also identical to the hypothetico-deductive model of explanation in the natural sciences (see, e.g., Carnap 1966: 3–18). Hence, from a logical point of view, Rawls' characterization of the problem of descriptive adequacy, the traditional model of common law adjudication, the medieval theory of conscience, and the hypothetic-deductive model of scientific explanation are functionally equivalent. These comparisons are significant for understanding the relationship between Rawls' conception of moral theory, on the one hand, and common law theory, natural law theory, and natural science, on the other, a group of topics to which we will return in Chapter 9.

In short, the method Rawls advocates in Section 9 for attempting to solve the problem of descriptive adequacy is the hypothetico-deductive method. According to this method: (i) hypotheses about the relevant background information, and statements about features of actions, are jointly interpreted (along with further auxiliary hypotheses) as explanans sentences; (ii) moral judgments are interpreted as explanandum sentences; and (iii) the connection between the former and the latter is interpreted as one of deductive entailment. Put differently, Rawls suggests that we test a description of moral competence by taking it to be the major premise of a hypothetical syllogism, whose minor premise is the structural description of an action and whose conclusion is a considered judgment. In this way we attempt to discover whether a set of moral principles is descriptively adequate, by determining whether a given range of moral judgments, which we antecedently identify as considered judgments, are in accordance with its principles.[12]

---

[11] Although the medieval concept of synderesis appears to be an important historical antecedent to the idea of an innate moral grammar, John Macnamara (1990) is the only cognitive scientist I have discovered who discusses this concept in the context of moral development. I am grateful to Terry Irwin for suggesting that I investigate the medieval distinction between synderesis and conscientia, and for directing me to the valuable study by Potts (1980).

[12] This analytic or regressive method of explicating commonsense moral judgments by searching for principles from which they can be deduced is substantially similar to the method employed by Kant (1964/1785) and Sidgwick (1981/1907). On Kant, see, e.g., Paton (1948: 25–29, 1964: 15–16); Sullivan (1989: 19–20); and Wolff (1963: 44–56; 1973: 52–55). On Sidgwick, see, e.g., Schneewind (1963: 137–156, especially 140, 147–148) (cited in Rawls 1971: 51); see also Schneewind (1977). Chomsky's approach to the task of explicating the intuitive concept *grammatical* can also be characterized as analytic or regressive in this sense. See, e.g., Moravcsik (1967); cf. Chomsky (1975a). On the topic of Chomsky's

4.5 OBJECTIONS AND REPLIES

Thus far I have been assuming that trolley problems are useful cases with which to begin pursuing the research program outlined in Section 2.1. At this point it seems worthwhile to pause and consider some initial objections to this assumption. This may help to prevent misunderstanding about what I take to be the significance of these problems and other similar thought experiments.

Consider three objections to the trolley problems: they are (i) unfamiliar and (ii) artificial, and the judgments they elicit are (iii) highly uncertain. Commentators often criticize the use of trolley problems in moral theory on these grounds (see, e.g., Hare 1981; Sunstein 2005). While I agree, at least to some extent, that the six problems in (4) possess these characteristics, I disagree that this prevents them from being useful in theory construction. The main reason is that the data used in linguistics and other cognitive sciences also often possess these characteristics.

Consider (i), the concern about unfamiliarity. That trolley problems are unfamiliar – that few persons have ever had to make or witness decisions of this sort – is sometimes thought to be a reason for not trusting our intuitions about them (see, e.g., Hare 1981; Sunstein 2005; cf. Kaplow & Shavell 2002). Yet why is this a good reason, by itself, for not trusting our intuitions? The same logic does not hold in linguistic inquiry. On the contrary, Chomsky's most famous examples,

(3) (a) colorless green ideas sleep furiously
    (b) furiously sleep ideas green colorless

are also entirely unfamiliar before being encountered. Nonetheless, native speakers of English do have sharp (or at least discernible) grammatical intuitions about these expressions: in particular, although both of them are nonsensical, only the first is syntactically acceptable (or syntactically "well-formed").

The same point holds for many of the most revealing cases in linguistic inquiry. The actual expressions that linguists rely on to discover linguistic structure, for example,

(3) (r) sincerity may frighten the boy
    (s) sincerity may admire the boy
    (t) the boy may frighten sincerity
    (u) Who did Mary tell Bill that Albert wanted her to ask Sam to talk to about the situation in Central America? (Chomsky 1965; Harman 1989)

are almost always unfamiliar before one encounters them. That does not change the fact that normal speakers have spontaneous and stable intuitive

---

"Kantian" epistemology in general, see also Kolhberg (1981: 181). As I observe in Section 8.3, however, Kohlberg appears to misinterpret Chomsky in several key respects.

judgments about these expressions, hence that they comprise evidence that a theory of I-language must, if possible, explain.

There is another more important point to make about (i). The potential novelty or unfamiliarity of the expressions that linguists investigate is not incidental to the research program of Universal Grammar. Rather, the emphasis on novel constructions is crucial. The most characteristic feature of human language is precisely the native speaker's ability to produce and interpret sentences of her language, *including indefinitely many that are previously unfamiliar to her.* It is just this property that refutes behavioristic conceptions of language, such as those of Quine (1960) and Skinner (1957), which attempt to reduce knowledge of language to a system of habits. And it is just this property, coupled with facts about the limited storage capacity of the brain, that underwrites the argument for linguistic grammar (cf. Jackendoff 1994).

The same logic appears to hold in the case of moral judgment. The potential novelty of trolley problem intuitions does not tell against their being taken as behavioral data by researchers interested in pursuing the research program outlined in Chapter 2. Quite the contrary: the fact that normal persons have a "natural readiness" (Rawls 1971: 46) to make intuitive judgments about these cases, despite their novelty, implies that any behaviorist-inspired account of moral judgment, which seeks to characterize the sense of justice as a mere "habit system," or perhaps as a learned ability to imitate the judgments of others, must be mistaken. Behaviorism in ethics fails for the same reason that behaviorism in linguistics fails: it is simply unable to account for the fact that the operation of a specific mental capacity, in an identifiable cognitive domain, is characterized by potential novelty and unboundedness.

Much of the foregoing applies equally well to (ii). It is certainly true that trolley problems are often highly artificial. They are unusual scenarios, rarely if ever encountered in everyday life. Moreover, they are typically invented by philosophers to make a point about general philosophical theories or principles, such as Utilitarianism or the Principle of Double Effect. The relevant question, however, is whether the artificiality of these cases, as such, necessarily detracts from their significance for moral theory: in other words, whether their artificiality is itself a reason for being skeptical about the moral intuitions they elicit. I do not believe it is. Once again, a clear appreciation of the linguistic analogy sheds light on this question. Consider again (3a) and (3b):

(3) (a) colorless green ideas sleep furiously
    (b) furiously sleep ideas green colorless

Chomsky invented these expressions for a specific reason: to reveal an important concealed ambiguity in the notion of *grammaticalness* or *meaningfulness,* as used by Quine (1961/1953) and others to refer to intuitively well-formed or acceptable linguistic expressions (see, e.g., Chomsky 1957: 15). Chomsky's point was that the notion of a semantically based definition of grammaticality was too coarse-grained; what he called attention to by means of examples like

(3a)–(3b) is that native speakers do recognize a distinction between syntax and semantics, however difficult it is to capture that difference in the form of a theoretical system. But the obvious artificiality of (3a) and (3b) did not hinder this argument; on the contrary, the argument was in a sense enabled by it. Chomsky's observation had been overlooked or ignored in part because the examples needed to exemplify it are somewhat rare and unusual, from the point of view of everyday uses of language. Hence, (3a) and (3b) needed to be constructed, for the purpose of showing that native speakers possess a type of knowledge of linguistic structure that had previously gone unnoticed, or at least had been underemphasized.

Whether thought experiments like the trolley problems can be equally revealing about the structure of moral knowledge is, of course, an open question. I am inclined to think they can be. In *The Methods of Ethics,* for example, Sidgwick repeatedly claims that the morality of common sense is "unconsciously utilitarian" (1981/1907: 453; see also 450, 456). The observed pattern of responses to the trolley problems suggests that Sidgwick's view, and, in fact, all simple forms of consequentialism, are mistaken insofar as they purport to be descriptively adequate. By contrast, the same evidence lends support to Kant's contention in the *Groundwork* that ordinary human reason utilizes the categorical imperative (or another means-sensitive principle, e.g., battery as a means is prohibited) as a standard of moral judgment, even if it does not conceive of that principle "abstractly in its universal form" (1964/1785: 71).

The significance of these observations will become clearer as we proceed, but perhaps it will be useful in this context to consider another criticism of the trolley problems, advanced by R. M. Hare (1981). Hare writes: "the point is that one has no time to think what to do, and so one relies on one's immediate intuitive reactions; but these give no guide for what critical thinking would prescribe if there were time for it" (1981: 139). This is precisely *not* the point. The relevant question is not what particular moral agents, ourselves or others, would actually *do* in these circumstances. Rather, the interesting question is why disinterested third parties (i.e., experimental subjects) *perceive* or *judge* trolley problems in the way that they do, even in relaxed settings where they have plenty of time to rely on all of their moral capacities, including their capacities for critical thinking. Trolley problems are thought experiments in the science of moral perception and moral cognition. As such, they appear particularly well suited to perform their designated task – far better, in my view, than many of the experimental probes used by Piaget (1965/1932) and Kohlberg (1981, 1984) in their own studies of moral psychology.

There is a further point to make about (ii). As Rawls observes, in attempting to construct an adequate description of a cognitive faculty as complex as the moral sense, one must rely on a fair bit of simplification, artificiality, and idealization. The aim must be, as Rawls rightly says, to focus our moral sensibilities and to put before our intuitive capacities "limited and manageable questions for judgment" (Rawls 1971: 53). There is no such thing as the longest sentence in English; linguists, however, do not make a practice of studying extremely long and complex constructions, which are difficult to process. Likewise, moral theorists must be willing to study instances of moral judgment that are relatively simple and artificial.

The six trolley problems in (4), at least, seem to be appropriately simple in this sense. They are not so unusual or artificial that they render the capacity for moral judgment inoperative. Nor are they the kind of fairy tale or fantastic example that Donagan (1977: 35–36) justly warns against, for which no credible causal explanation can be given. Nonetheless, the intuitive judgments that these problems trigger appear to qualify as considered judgments in Rawls' sense. They are intuitive, stable, spontaneous, and impartial, and made with a high degree of certitude. They appear to be judgments in which our moral capacities are displayed without distortion. Furthermore, they appear to withstand "all relevant philosophical arguments" (Rawls 1971: 49), as illustrated by the fact that several decades of intensive analysis in the academic literature have left them essentially unchanged. Hence, they even appear to qualify as *rational* in Brandt's (1979: 10) and Hare's (1981: 214) sense: they survive maximum criticism of facts and logic.

In sum, with respect to the general objection that the trolley problems are novel or artificial, the response is that these are not good reasons to disregard the moral intuitions they elicit, any more than the novelty or artificiality of a particular linguistic expression is a good reason for disregarding the intuitive data about that expression. Indeed, while the general objection sounds initially plausible, and while it has become especially popular in some circles (see, e.g., Kaplow & Shavell 2002; Sunstein 2005), on reflection it seems altogether specious. Exotic and unfamiliar stimuli are used in theory construction throughout the cognitive sciences. For example, the discovery that infants perceive objects in accordance with principles of cohesion, contact, and continuity utilizes novel displays that depart from previous experience and violate ordinary expectations (e.g., Spelke, Breinlinger, & Jacobson 1992). Or consider such contrivances as "blicket detectors" (Gopnik & Sobel 2000), rotating three-dimensional line drawings (Shepard & Metzler 1971), or, as we have seen, nonsense expressions such as "colorless green ideas sleep furiously" (Chomsky 1957), which linguists sometimes use to discover linguistic structure. In any psychology experiment, the decisive question is not whether the stimulus is unfamiliar or artificial, but whether it reveals something interesting about how the mind works. While some moral dilemmas may indeed be too outlandish to satisfy this criterion, the determination must be made on a case-by-case basis. The particular trolley problems in (4) appear to satisfy this test.

Let me turn finally to the issue of uncertainty. The first point to make in connection with this issue is that one must distinguish at least two senses in which a moral judgment might be uncertain. First, the judgment might lack *certitude,* in that it is not formulated with sufficient confidence (Rawls

1950: 57–60, 1951a: 182). Second, the judgment might be emotionally troubling in some manner, insofar as it causes some type of anxiety or psychological disturbance.

In light of our experiments, it seems clear that most of the familiar trolley problem intuitions are not uncertain in the first sense. In particular, most individuals appear to be quite confident about the deontic status they would assign to the possible acts involved in the six cases in (4). In this respect their behavior mirrors that of most academic researchers, whose intuitions about these cases are also marked by a high degree of certitude (see, e.g., Foot 1967; Thomson 1986, 1990; see generally Fischer & Ravizza 1992). There appears, therefore, to be a wide convergence of considered opinion about the specific deontic judgments listed in Table 4.1.

The second meaning of uncertainty concerns the fact that some trolley problem intuitions are, or at least may be, emotionally disturbing. If it is permissible to throw the switch in the Bystander problem, for example, then this implies that there may be circumstances in which an actor might knowingly kill an innocent person for the sake of a greater good. This conclusion might be difficult to swallow, and it might naturally lead someone to question whether her initial reaction to the Bystander problem is correct, or otherwise to feel uneasy about her intuitions. This type of emotional uncertainty, however, must be distinguished from whether the deontic status of an action is itself uncertain (although both types of uncertainty can, of course, coexist in a given case).

A different meaning of uncertainty concerns whether a moral intuition can *become* uncertain, or perhaps be altered or abandoned, by modifying the circumstances of the relevant action. Some philosophers, such as Nozick, have suggested that this phenomenon poses a problem for the effort to formulate a deductive theory of moral judgment (see, e.g., Nozick 1968: 5; cf. Donagan 1977: 71–74). However, the objection does not seem persuasive, or at least has not been adequately explained. In any event, this seems like another case in which the linguistic analogy can help to clarify a potential misconception. For the simple fact is that adding or deleting information to a linguistic expression can also affect the intuitive acceptability of that expression. To see this point, consider again two of Chomsky's (1986a: 11) examples:

(3) (v) John is too stubborn to expect anyone to talk to Bill
     (w) John is too stubborn to visit anyone who talked to Bill

Intuitively, (3v) and (3w) are acceptable sentences, whose meanings are fairly straightforward. Here (3v) means that John is too stubborn for him (John) to expect an arbitrary person, X, to talk to Bill; (3w) means that John is too stubborn for him (John) to visit an arbitrary person, X, who talked to Bill. Suppose, however, we delete "Bill" from each sentence, yielding (3x) and (3y):

(3) (x) John is too stubborn to expect anyone to talk to
     (y) John is too stubborn to visit anyone who talked to

Here (3x) remains both meaningful and grammatical: it means that John is so stubborn that someone (e.g., the reader) would not expect an arbitrary person, X, to talk to him (John). However, (3y) does not mean, by analogy, that John is so stubborn that someone would not visit an arbitrary person, X, who talked to him (John). On the contrary, (3y) is gibberish (Chomsky 1986a: 11).

The relevant point is simply that (3v)–(3y), while evidently closely related, are unique expressions. Likewise, each of the several trolley problems that researchers have discussed, including the six cases in (4), represents a unique action and its circumstances. The question that moral theorists must confront is why these problems occasion certain moral judgments and not others. Why the process of adding further information to these action-descriptions can modify those judgments is a separate, albeit related, question. I believe it can be adequately answered only when relatively simple trolley problems, such as those in (4), are better understood.

In sum, I do not believe that it is advisable, when attempting to formulate a descriptively adequate moral grammar, to begin one's investigation with examples that are much more complex, realistic, or difficult to process than the six trolley problems in (4). On the contrary, as I shall suggest in Chapter 5, it seems useful to render these problems in an even more idealized and stylized form if the underlying structure of these moral intuitions is to be discovered. It is certainly true that altering the specific circumstances of the six problems in (4) might make them less artificial and more realistic. Depending on what information is added, these alterations might also cause the corresponding judgments to fluctuate. However, these facts do not pose a problem for the research program outlined in Section 2.1. Rather, they exemplify the projection problem that this research program is attempting to solve.

Finally, this seems like a good place to clarify the distinction between considered judgments and what Rawls calls "considered judgments *in reflective equilibrium*" (1971: 51, emphasis added). It is important not to conflate these two notions. The moral judgments occasioned by the six problems in (4) appear to be considered judgments, in Rawls' sense. In particular, they appear to satisfy all of the operational tests that Rawls identifies for a moral judgment to qualify as a member of this set: that is, they are intuitive, stable, spontaneous, and impartial, and made with a high degree of certitude. In general, they seem likely to be judgments in which our moral capacities are displayed without distortion. Still, the judgments do *not* qualify as considered judgments in reflective equilibrium. That is because we do not yet know the principles to which the judgments conform, and the premises of those principles' derivation (Rawls 1971: 20). To turn these judgments into considered judgments in reflective equilibrium, we must not merely "reflect" on them, in the ordinary sense of that word; rather, we must solve the problem of descriptive adequacy. To do this, as we have seen, it is necessary to formulate hypotheses about the premises of our subjects' perceptual and cognitive inferences, and to test these hypotheses by taking them to be part of the premises of a deductive argument, whose additional premises include the structural description or fact pattern of an action, and whose conclusion is a considered judgment. In other words, we must construct a *derivation* of the explanandum sentence. This is the challenge taken up in Chapters 5 and 6.

5

The Moral Grammar Hypothesis

It is the merit of the Common Law that it decides the case first and determines the principle afterwards. Looking at the forms of logic, it might be inferred that when you have a minor premise and a conclusion, there must be a major, which you are also prepared then and there to assert. But in fact lawyers, like other men, frequently see well enough how they ought to decide on a given state of facts without being very clear as to the *ratio decidendi*.... It is only after a series of determinations on the same subject matter, that it becomes necessary to "reconcile the cases," as it is called, that is, by a true induction to state the principle which has until then been obscurely felt.
  – Oliver Wendell Holmes, Jr., "Codes, and the Arrangement of Law"

In Chapter 4, I introduced a family of trolley problems and began to discuss some of their implications for the cognitive science of moral judgment. In the next two chapters, I outline a provisional solution to the problem of descriptive adequacy with respect to these cases, which I refer to as the *moral grammar hypothesis*. The guiding assumption of this hypothesis is that ordinary individuals are intuitive lawyers, who possess tacit or unconscious knowledge of a rich variety of legal rules, concepts, and principles, along with a natural readiness to compute mental representations of human acts and omissions in legally cognizable terms (Mikhail 2007a, 2008a; see also Alter, Kernochan, & Darley 2007; Cushman, Young, & Hauser 2006; Haidt 2001; Robinson, Kurzban, & Jones 2008; Solum 2006; Wellman & Miller 2008; Young & Saxe 2008). Put differently, the guiding assumption of this hypothesis is the classical rationalist idea, suitably reinterpreted, that certain basic moral and legal notions and precepts are engraved in the mind, presumably as a kind of innate instinct (Leibniz 1981/1705: 94; Rousseau 1979/1762: 288–289; see also Cudworth 1996/1731; Descartes 1985/1647; Hume 1983/1751; Kant 1993/1788; Reid 1969/1788; Smith 1976/1759).
  In Section 5.1, I begin by describing some of the evidence that supports the moral grammar hypothesis. The rest of Chapter 5 is then devoted to sharpening this hypothesis and to developing a more controlled scientific framework

for studying trolley problems and similar judgment tasks within this empirical paradigm. Section 5.2 shifts attention from the six problems in Chapter 4 to a more carefully controlled set of trolley cases and the intuitive judgments they elicit. Section 5.3 discusses the problem of perceptual underdetermination illustrated by these cases and draws out some of its implications for social psychology and the neuroscience of moral intuition. Section 5.4 then outlines a provisional solution to the problem of descriptive adequacy with respect to these cases, which includes the assumption that ordinary individuals possess tacit or unconscious knowledge of specific deontic rules, including the prohibition of intentional battery, the prohibition of intentional homicide, the Rescue Principle, and the Principle of Double Effect. Finally, Section 5.5 briefly considers an alternative explanation of the trolley problems that is defended by Joshua Greene and colleagues (2001, 2002, 2008a,b). In Chapter 6, I provide a more detailed and formal description of some of the mental operations implied by the moral grammar hypothesis, thereby showing that the moral data can be turned into what Rawls calls "considered judgments in reflective equilibrium" (1971: 46).

Because some readers might find the efforts at formalization in these two chapters to be tedious or unnecessary, it seems useful to make a few additional remarks about this issue at the outset. Cognitive science was transformed by subjecting linguistic and visual phenomena to precise, formal analysis. The theory of moral grammar holds out the prospect of doing the same for aspects of ordinary human moral cognition, perhaps thereby lending support to the Enlightenment assumption that at least some aspects of intuitive moral judgment are "capable of demonstration" (Locke 1991/1689: 549; cf. Hume 1978/1740; Kant 1993/1788; Leibniz 1981/1705). The alleged computational properties of moral cognition, however, must be shown and not merely asserted.

As Rawls (1971: 46) emphasizes, the first step in this inquiry is to identify a class of considered judgments and a set of rules or principles from which they can be derived. As I have observed elsewhere (see, e.g., Mikhail 2007a, 2008a), recent sustained efforts to explain human moral judgment in this framework suggests that untutored adults and even young children are intuitive lawyers, who are capable of drawing intelligent distinctions between superficially similar cases, although their basis for doing so is often obscure. If this is correct, then future research in moral psychology should begin from this premise, moving beyond pedagogically useful examples such as the trolley problem and other cases of necessity to the core concepts of universal fields like torts, contracts, criminal law, property, agency, equity, procedure, and unjust enrichment, which investigate the rules and representations implicit in common moral intuitions with unparalleled care and sophistication. Chomsky (1957) emphasized that rigorous formulation in linguistics is not merely a pointless technical exercise but rather an important diagnostic and heuristic tool, because only by pushing a precise but inadequate formulation to an unacceptable conclusion can we gain a better understanding of the relevant data and of the inadequacy of our existing attempts to explain them. Likewise, Marr (1982: 26) warned against making inferences about cognitive systems from neurophysiological findings without "a clear idea about what information needs to be represented and what processes need to be implemented" (cf. Mill 1987/1843: 36–38). Cognitive scientists who take these ideas seriously and who seek to understand human moral cognition must devote more effort to developing computational theories of moral competence, in addition to studying related problems, such as its underlying mechanisms, neurological signatures, cultural adaptations, or evolutionary origins. As I attempt to show in the remainder of Part Two, the formalization of common legal notions can play an important part in this process.

Because the enterprise this chapter engages, the search for considered judgments in reflective equilibrium, is controversial in some quarters, a further clarification may be helpful before we proceed. Moral judgment is a flexible, context-dependent process, which cannot be accurately described by simple consequentialist or deontological principles, and which is clearly subject to framing effects and other familiar manipulations (Doris 2002; Kahneman & Tversky 1984; Kelman, Rottenstreich, & Tversky 1996; Schnall et al. 2008; Sunstein 2005; Valdesolo & DeSteno 2006; Unger 1996; Wheatley & Haidt 2005). For example, as the literature on protected values has shown, how trade-offs among scarce resources are described can often influence how they are evaluated (Baron & Spranca 1997; Bartels 2008; Bartels & Medin 2007; Fiske & Tetlock 1997; Tetlock 2003). Facts like these are sometimes taken to imply that moral intuitions are so malleable that the project of reflective equilibrium is quixotic. From our perspective, however, these phenomena simply reinforce the need to draw a competence–performance distinction in the moral domain and thus to take a position, fallible and revisable to be sure, on which moral judgments reflect the ideal operations of a core human competence and which are the result of various psychological limitations, performance errors, or other exogenous factors (Nozick 1968; Rawls 1971; cf. Chomsky 1965; Macnamara 1986; Marr 1982). Hence the importance of jury instructions, rules of evidence, and other familiar methods of directing attention to precisely formulated questions and preventing irrelevant or prejudicial information from having a distorting effect on one's judgments. Unlike some researchers (e.g., Baron & Ritov, in press), who define any deviation from utilitarianism as a cognitive "bias" – and who thus appear committed to holding that even the most basic rules of criminal and civil law reflect pervasive cognitive errors, insofar as they do not merely track outcomes, but also rely heavily on concepts like proximate causes, goals, means, side effects, and mental states generally – the approach taken here assumes that at least some of these rules are a natural benchmark with which to describe human moral cognition, at least to a good first approximation. Whether these legal norms are built into the very fabric of the human mind is one of cognitive science's deepest and most persistent questions. Our immediate concern, however, is not ontogenesis but descriptive adequacy, because without a clear understanding of the learning target in this domain, one cannot formulate, let alone endorse, one or another learning theory. Despite their obvious limitations, trolley problems are a useful heuristic for this purpose, and their artificiality is a virtue, not a vice, in this regard. These hypothetical cases must be supplemented with more realistic probes drawn from other branches of law, policy, and everyday life, however, if moral competence is to be adequately understood.

5.1 SOME INITIAL EVIDENCE

In Section 5.2, I describe a new set of trolley problems and thereafter attempt to supply a principled explanation of them within the framework we have outlined thus far. Before doing so, however, it may be useful to summarize some of the available evidence that appears to lend support to the moral grammar hypothesis and to the research program of UMG more generally. Initial evidence for this basic approach comes from multiple sources, including developmental psychology, comparative linguistics, legal anthropology, and cognitive neuroscience. While none of this evidence is univocal or conclusive, collectively it provides at least modest support for the hypothesis that humans possess an innate moral faculty that is analogous, at least in some respects, to the language faculty postulated by Chomsky and other linguists.

First, developmental psychologists have discovered that the intuitive jurisprudence of young children is complex and exhibits many characteristics of a well-developed legal code. For example, three-to-four-year-old children use intent or purpose to distinguish two acts with same result (Baird 2001; Nelson 1980). They also distinguish "genuine" moral violations (e.g., battery, theft) from violations of social conventions (e.g., wearing pajamas to school) (Smetana 1983; Turiel 1983). Four-to-five-year-olds use a proportionality principle to determine the correct level of punishment for principals and accessories (Finkel, Liss, & Moran 1997). Five-to-six-year-olds use false factual beliefs but not false moral beliefs to exculpate (Chandler, Sokal, & Wainryb 2000).

Second, every natural language appears to have words or phrases to express basic deontic concepts, such as *may, must, must not,* or their equivalents (Bybee & Fleischman 1995). These concepts comprise the basic categorization scheme of most human moral, legal, and religious systems, and their natural domain of application is the voluntary acts and omissions of moral agents (cf. Section 4.4). Moreover, deontic logic is formalizable (Prior 1955, 1958; Von Wright 1951, 1963). The three primary deontic operators may be placed in the traditional *square of opposition and equipollence,* similar to those for quantified and modal forms (Figure 5.1).

Third, prohibitions of murder, rape, and other types of aggression appear to be universal or nearly so (Brown 1991), as do legal distinctions based on

(a)

Forbidden	Permissible	Obligatory
"must not"	"may"	"must"
haram	*mubah*	*wajib*
verboten	*zulassig*	*obligat*
ne...pas	*pouvoir*	*devoir/il faut*
(neg)	*poder*	*deber*
interdictum	*licitus*	*debitum*
far inte	*matte*	*bora*
myen a tway	*to tway*	*ya hay/tway*
swanelo	*sibaka*	*mwila*
... ...	......	... ...

(b)

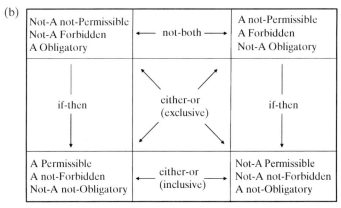

Key: Equipollence relations (i.e., logical equivalences) are expressed in the four corners. "A" stands for *act*; "not-A" stands for *omission*.

FIGURE 5.1. Deontic Concepts and Deontic Logic: (a) Deontic Modality in Natural Language; (b) Square of Opposition and Equipollence

causation, intention, and voluntary behavior (Fletcher 1988; Mikhail 2002a). Further, comparative legal scholars have suggested that a few basic distinctions capture the "universal grammar" of all systems of criminal law (Fletcher 1998, 2007; Green 1998).

Finally, functional imaging and patient studies have led some researchers to conclude that a fairly consistent network of brain regions is involved in moral cognition, including the anterior prefrontal cortex, medial and lateral orbitofrontal cortex, dorsolateral and ventromedial prefrontal cortex, anterior temporal lobes, superior temporal sulcus, and posterior cingulate/precuneus region (Greene & Haidt 2002; Moll et al. 2005). These findings, however, are both preliminary and controversial. Moreover, some of the moral judgment tasks on which they rely seem poorly motivated, since they involve stand-alone sentences with allegedly moral or nonmoral content ("The elderly are useless," "Stones are made of water"), rather than acts of conspecifics that can be carefully manipulated to test specific theories of mental representation. Nonetheless, these probes will likely become more refined as the scientific understanding of moral competence improves.

5.2 SIMPLIFYING THE PROBLEM OF DESCRIPTIVE ADEQUACY

5.2.1 Twelve New Trolley Problems

The provisional aim of moral theory is to solve the problem of descriptive adequacy (Rawls 1971, 1975; cf. Chomsky 1957, 1965). To simplify this problem, it is useful to shift our attention from the six problems we discussed in Chapter 4 to the 12 problems in Table 5.1, which, building on previous work (Foot 1967; Harman 1977; Thomson 1985), I designed in order to investigate the mental computations underlying the ordinary exercise of moral judgment (Mikhail 2000, 2002b). They may be taken to serve as inputs into the perceptual model in Figure 4.1(b) that we seek to describe (see Section 4.4.1).

In a series of experiments that began in the mid-1990s, my colleagues and I began testing these cases, and others like them based on the same basic template, on hundreds of individuals, both adults and children. The participants included several groups of American adults, several groups

TABLE 5.1. *Twelve Trolley Problems*[a]

---

1. **Bystander:** Hank is taking his daily walk near the train tracks when he notices that the train that is approaching is out of control. Hank sees what has happened: the driver of the train saw five men walking across the tracks and slammed on the brakes, but the brakes failed and the driver fainted. The train is now rushing toward the five men. It is moving so fast that they will not be able to get off the track in time. Hank is standing next to a switch, which he can throw, that will turn the train onto a side track, thereby preventing it from killing the men. There is a man standing on the side track with his back turned. Hank can throw the switch, killing him; or he can refrain from doing this, letting the five die. Is it morally permissible for Hank to throw the switch?

2. **Footbridge:** Ian is taking his daily walk near the train tracks when he notices that the train that is approaching is out of control. Ian sees what has happened: the driver of the train saw five men walking across the tracks and slammed on the brakes, but the brakes failed and the driver fainted. The train is now rushing toward the five men. It is moving so fast that they will not be able to get off the track in time. Ian is standing next to a *heavy object,* which he can throw *onto the track in the path of the train,* thereby preventing it from killing the men. *The heavy object* is a man, standing *next to Ian* with his back turned. Ian can throw the *man,* killing him; or he can refrain from doing this, letting the five die. Is it morally permissible for Ian to throw the *man?*

3. **Expensive Equipment:** Karl is taking his daily walk near the train tracks when he notices that the train that is approaching is out of control. Karl sees what has happened: the driver of the train saw *five million dollars of new railroad equipment lying* across the tracks and slammed on the brakes, but the brakes failed and the driver fainted. The train is now rushing toward the *equipment*. It is moving so fast that *the equipment* will be *destroyed*. Karl is standing next to a switch, which he can throw, that will turn the train onto a side track, thereby preventing it from *destroying the equipment*. There is a man standing on the side track with his back turned. Karl can throw the switch, killing him; or he can refrain from doing this, letting the *equipment be destroyed*. Is it morally permissible for Karl to throw the switch?

4. **Implied Consent:** Luke is taking his daily walk near the train tracks when he notices that the train that is approaching is out of control. Luke sees what has happened: the driver of the train saw *a man* walking across the tracks and slammed on the brakes, but the brakes failed and the driver fainted. The train is now rushing toward the *man*. It is moving so fast that *he* will not be able to get off the track in time. Luke is standing next to *the man, whom* he can throw *off the track out of the path of the train*, thereby preventing it from killing the *man*. The *man* is *frail and* standing with his back turned. Luke can throw the man, *injuring* him; or he can refrain from doing this, letting the *man* die. Is it morally permissible for Luke to throw the man?

5. **Intentional Homicide:** Mark is taking his daily walk near the train tracks when he notices that the train that is approaching is out of control. Mark sees what has happened: the driver of the train saw five men walking across the tracks and slammed on the brakes, but the brakes failed and the driver fainted. The train is now rushing toward the five men. It is moving so fast that they will not be able to get off the track in time. Mark is standing next to a switch, which he can throw, that will turn the train onto a side track, thereby preventing it from killing the men. There is a man on the side track. Mark can throw the switch, killing him; or he can refrain from doing this, letting the men die. *Mark then recognizes that the man on the side track is someone who he hates with a passion. "I don't give a damn about saving those five men," Mark thinks to himself, "but this is my chance to kill that bastard."* Is it morally permissible for Mark to throw the switch?

6. **Loop Track:** Ned is taking his daily walk near the train tracks when he notices that the train that is approaching is out of control. Ned sees what has happened: the driver of the train saw five men walking across the tracks and slammed on the brakes, but the brakes failed and the driver fainted. The train is now rushing toward the five men. It is moving so fast that they will not be able to get off the track in time. Ned is standing next to a switch, which he can throw, that will temporarily turn the train onto a side track. There is a heavy object on the side track. If the train hits the object, the object will slow the train down, giving the men time to escape. The heavy object is a man, standing

(continued)

TABLE 5.1 *(continued)*

on the side track with his back turned. Ned can throw the switch, preventing the train from killing the men, but killing the man. Or he can refrain from doing this, letting the five die. Is it morally permissible for Ned to throw the switch?

7. **Man-in-Front:** Oscar is taking his daily walk near the train tracks when he notices that the train that is approaching is out of control. Oscar sees what has happened: the driver of the train saw five men walking across the tracks and slammed on the brakes, but the brakes failed and the driver fainted. The train is now rushing toward the five men. It is moving so fast that they will not be able to get off the track in time. Oscar is standing next to a switch, which he can throw, that will temporarily turn the train onto a side track. There is a heavy object on the side track. If the train hits the object, the object will slow the train down, giving the men time to escape. *There* is a man standing on the side track *in front of the heavy object* with his back turned. Oscar can throw the switch, preventing the train from killing the men, but killing the man; or he can refrain from doing this, letting the five die. Is it morally permissible for Oscar to throw the switch?

8. **Costless Rescue:** Paul is taking his daily walk near the train tracks when he notices that the train that is approaching is out of control. Paul sees what has happened: the driver of the train saw five men walking across the tracks and slammed on the brakes, but the brakes failed and the driver fainted. The train is now rushing toward the five men. It is moving so fast that they will not be able to get off the track in time. Paul is standing next to a switch, which he can throw, that will turn the train onto a side track, thereby preventing it from killing the men. Paul can throw the switch, saving the five men; or he can refrain from doing this, letting the five die. Is it morally *obligatory* for Paul to throw the switch?

9. **Better Alternative:** Richard is taking his daily walk near the train tracks when he notices that the train that is approaching is out of control. Richard sees what has happened: the driver of the train saw five men walking across the tracks and slammed on the brakes, but the brakes failed and the driver fainted. The train is now rushing toward the five men. It is moving so fast that they will not be able to get off the track in time. Richard is standing next to a switch, which he can throw, that will turn the train onto a side track, thereby preventing it from killing the men. There is a man on the side track with his back turned. Richard can throw the switch, killing him; or he can refrain from doing this, letting the men die. *By pulling an emergency cord, Richard can also redirect the train to a third track, where no one is at risk. If Richard pulls the cord, no one will be killed. If Richard throws the switch, one person will be killed. If Richard does nothing, five people will be killed.* Is it morally permissible for Richard to throw the switch?

10. **Disproportional Death:** Steve is taking his daily walk near the train tracks when he notices that the train that is approaching is out of control. Steve sees

what has happened: the driver of the train saw *a man* walking across the tracks and slammed on the brakes, but the brakes failed and the driver fainted. The train is now rushing toward the man. It is moving so fast that he will not be able to get off the track in time. Steve is standing next to a switch, which he can throw, that will turn the train onto a side track, thereby preventing it from killing the man. There *are five men* standing on the side track with their backs turned. Steve can throw the switch, killing the *five men;* or he can refrain from doing this, letting the *one man* die. Is it morally permissible for Steve to throw the switch?

11. **Drop Man:** Victor is taking his daily walk near the train tracks when he notices that the train that is approaching is out of control. Victor sees what has happened: the driver of the train saw five men walking across the tracks and slammed on the brakes, but the brakes failed and the driver fainted. The train is now rushing toward the five men. It is moving so fast that they will not be able to get off the track in time. Victor is standing next to a switch, which he can throw, that will drop a heavy object into the path of the train, thereby preventing it from killing the men. The heavy object is a man, who is standing on a footbridge overlooking the tracks. Victor can throw the switch, killing him; or he can refrain from doing this, letting the five die. Is it morally permissible for Victor to throw the switch?

12. **Collapse Bridge:** Walter is taking his daily walk near the train tracks when he notices that the train that is approaching is out of control. Walter sees what has happened: the driver of the train saw five men walking across the tracks and slammed on the brakes, but the brakes failed and the driver fainted. The train is now rushing toward the five men. It is moving so fast that they will not be able to get off the track in time. Walter is standing next to a switch, which he can throw, that will *collapse a footbridge overlooking the tracks* into the path of the train, thereby preventing it from killing the men. *There* is a man standing on *the* footbridge. Walter can throw the switch, killing him; or he can refrain from doing this, letting the five die. Is it morally permissible for Walter to throw the switch?

---

[a] Italics in Table 5.1 identify salient differences between the following minimal pairs: Bystander-Footbridge, Bystander-Expensive Equipment, Footbridge-Implied Consent, Bystander-Intentional Homicide, Loop Track-Man in Front, Bystander-Costless Rescue, Bystander-Better Alternative, Bystander-Disproportional Death, Drop Man-Collapse Bridge. Experimental subjects were not shown these markings.

of American children, one group of recent Chinese immigrants to the United States, and two groups of master's students at Harvard University's Kennedy School of Government. Collectively these individuals hailed from a diverse set of countries and regions, including Belgium, Canada, China, Colombia, Denmark, Egypt, Finland, France, Germany, India, Iran, Israel, Italy, Japan, Lebanon, Mexico, Puerto Rico, South Africa, and South Korea. The main objective of our research was to pursue the idea of a Universal Moral Grammar and to begin to study a variety of empirical questions that arise within this framework. Our basic prediction was that the moral intuitions elicited by the first two problems in Table 5.1 (the Bystander and Footbridge problems) would be widely shared, irrespective of demographic variables such as race, sex, age, religion, national origin, or level of formal education (see Mikhail 2000, 2002; Mikhail, Sorrentino, & Spelke 1998). We also predicted that most individuals would be unaware of the operative principles generating their moral intuitions, and thus they would be largely incapable of correctly describing their own thought processes (Mikhail, Sorrentino, & Spelke 1998). These predictions were confirmed, and our initial findings have now been replicated and extended with over 200,000 individuals from over 120 countries (see, e.g., Hauser et al. 2007; Miller 2008; Pinker 2008; Saxe 2005). The result is perhaps the first qualitatively new data set in the history of the discipline, which has transformed the science of moral psychology and opened up many new and promising avenues of investigation (see, e.g., Bartels 2008; Bucciarelli, Khemlani, & Johnson-Laird 2008; Cushman 2008; Cushman, Young, & Hauser 2006; Dupoux & Jacob 2007; Greene et al. submitted; Koenigs et al. 2007; Lombrozo 2008; Machery 2007; Moore, Clark, & Kane 2008; Nichols & Mallon 2006; Sinnott-Armstrong et al. 2008; Waldmann & Dieterich 2007; Young et al. 2007).[1]

5.2.2 Twelve Considered Judgments

The modal responses to these 12 cases are listed in Table 5.2. Although the variance in these intuitions is an important topic, which I discuss elsewhere (see, e.g., Mikhail 2002a, 2007a), in both this chapter and Chapter 6 I focus on the modal responses themselves and make the simplifying assumption that these judgments are considered judgments in Rawls' sense, that is, "judgments in which our moral capacities are most likely to be displayed without distortion" (1971: 47). Hence, I take them to be categorical data that a descriptively adequate moral grammar must explain.

---

[1] When our trolley problem studies began in Liz Spelke's MIT lab in the mid-1990s, Petrinovich and colleagues (1993, 1996) had already begun using trolley problems as probes, which another lab member (Laurie Santos) brought to our attention only several years after the fact. From our perspective, the Petrinovich experiments were poorly conceived, however, because they asked participants to supply behavioral predictions ("What would you do?") rather than clearly identified moral judgments ("Is X morally permissible?"). In the context of jury trials, the former instruction has long been held to be reversible error (see, e.g., Eldredge 1941; Epstein 2004), while the latter more closely approximates the key theoretical issue of reasonableness or justifiability under the circumstances.

TABLE 5.2. *Twelve Considered Judgments*

Problem	Act	Deontic Status
Bystander	Hank's throwing the switch	Permissible
Footbridge	Ian's throwing the man	Forbidden
Expensive Equipment	Karl's throwing the switch	Forbidden
Implied Consent	Luke's throwing the man	Permissible
Intentional Homicide	Mark's throwing the switch	Forbidden
Loop Track	Ned's throwing the switch	Forbidden
Man-in-Front	Oscar's throwing the switch	Permissible
Costless Rescue	Paul's throwing the switch	Obligatory
Better Alternative	Richard's throwing the switch	Forbidden
Disproportional Death	Steve's throwing the switch	Forbidden
Drop Man	Victor's throwing the switch	Forbidden
Collapse Bridge	Walter's throwing the switch	Permissible

5.3 THE POVERTY OF THE PERCEPTUAL STIMULUS

5.3.1 Labeling the Stimulus

For convenience, let us label each of these cases a *complex action-description.* Let us say that their two main constituents are a *primary act-token description* and a *circumstance description.* The primary act-token description consists of a *primary act-type description* and a *primary agent-description.* The circumstance description also includes *secondary act-type descriptions.* Hence, our scheme for classifying the input may be rendered by Figure 5.2(a), and the results of applying it to an example like the Bystander problem can be given by Figure 5.2(b). Clearly it is unproblematic to classify the remaining cases in Table 1 in these terms.

5.3.2 Expanded Perceptual Model

With this terminology we may now make a simple but crucial observation about the data in Table 5.2. Although each of these rapid, intuitive, and highly automatic moral judgments is *occasioned* by an identifiable stimulus, how the brain goes about interpreting these complex action descriptions and assigning a deontic status to each of them is not something revealed in any obvious way by the surface structure of the stimulus itself. Instead, an intervening step must be postulated: an intuitive appraisal of some sort that is imposed on the stimulus prior to any deontic response to it. Hence, a simple perceptual model, such as the one implicit in Haidt's (2001) influential model of moral

(a)

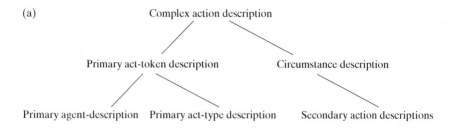

(b)

Primary act-token description	Hank to throw the switch
Circumstance description	Hank is taking his daily walk over the train tracks when he notices that the train that is approaching is out of control. Hank sees what has happened: the driver of the train saw five men walking across the tracks and slammed on the brakes, but the brakes failed and the driver fainted. The train is now rushing toward the five men. It is moving so fast that they will not be able to get off the track in time. Hank is standing next to a switch, which he can throw, that will turn the train onto a side track, thereby preventing it from killing the men. There is a man standing on the side track with his back turned. Hank can throw the switch, killing him; or he can refrain from doing this, letting the five die
Primary agent description	Hank
Primary act-type description	throw the switch
Secondary act-type descriptions	1. will turn the train onto a side track 2. preventing it from killing the men 3. killing him 4. refrain from doing this 5. letting the five die

FIGURE 5.2.   Classifying the Stimulus: (a) Scheme; (b) Application
to the Bystander Problem

judgment, appears inadequate for explaining these intuitions, a point that can be illustrated by calling attention to the unanalyzed link between eliciting situation and intuitive response in Haidt's model (Figure 5.3(a); cf. Mikhail 2007a, 2008b). Likewise, an ad hoc appraisal theory, such as the personal/ impersonal distinction that underlies Greene's (2005; Greene and Haidt 2002; Greene et al. 2001) initial explanation of the trolley problems, also fails to explain the data (Figure 5.3(b); cf. Mikhail 2002a, 2007a, 2008b; see also

(a)

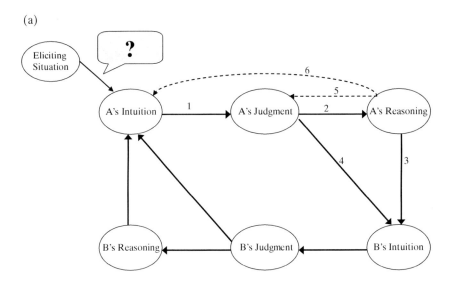

Figure 1. The social intuitionist model of moral judgment. The numbered links, drawn for Person A only, are 1) the intuitive judgment link, 2) the post-hoc reasoning link, 3) the reasoned persuasion link, and 4) the social persuasion link. Two additional links are hypothesized to occur less frequently: 5) the reasoned judgment link, and 6) the private reflection link. (Reprinted with alteration from Haidt 2001.)

(b)

Problem	Personal / Impersonal	Deontic Status	"A moral violation is personal if it is (i) likely to cause serious bodily harm, (ii) to a particular person, (iii) in such a way that the harm does not result from the deflection of an existing threat onto a different party. A moral violation is impersonal if it fails to meet these criteria." (Greene & Haidt 2002: 519)
Bystander	Impersonal	Permissible	
Footbridge	Personal	Forbidden	
Expensive Equipment	Impersonal	Forbidden	
Implied Consent	Personal	Permissible	
Intentional Homicide	Impersonal	Forbidden	
Loop Track	Impersonal	Forbidden	
Man-in-Front	Impersonal	Permissible	
Costless Rescue	Impersonal	Obligatory	
Better Alternative	Impersonal	Forbidden	
Disproportional Death	Impersonal	Forbidden	
Drop Man	Impersonal	Forbidden	
Collapse Bridge	Impersonal	Permissible	

FIGURE 5.3. Two Inadequate Appraisal Theories: (a) Unanalyzed Link in Haidt's (2001) Model of Moral Judgment; (b) Inadequacy of Greene's (2001, 2002) Personal–Impersonal Distinction

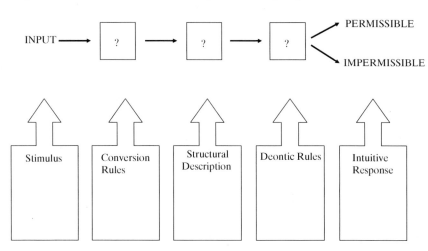

FIGURE 5.4. Expanded Perceptual Model for Moral Judgment

Greene 2008a, 2008b for recognition of this problem). Instead, an adequate model must be more complex and must look more like Figure 5.4.

The expanded perceptual model in Figure 5.4 implies that moral judgments do not depend merely on the superficial properties of an action-description, but also on how that action is *mentally represented,* a critical preliminary step in the evaluative process that jurists have frequently examined (e.g., Cardozo 1921; Hutcheson 1929; Oliphant 1928; Radin 1925; see also Grey 1983; Kelman 1981), but, surprisingly, many social psychologists and neuroscientists have unduly neglected. The point can be illustrated by Table 5.3, which supplies an exhaustive list of the primary and secondary act-type descriptions that are directly derivable from the stimuli in Table 5.1. As Table 5.3 reveals, it is not just difficult, but *impossible,* to explain the data in Table 5.2 by relying on these primary and secondary act-type descriptions alone. Strictly speaking the impossibility covers only the Bystander, Intentional Homicide, Loop Track, and Man-in-Front problems, since these are the only cases whose primary and secondary act-type descriptions are completely equivalent. It is therefore logically possible to formulate ad hoc hypotheses that could handle the remaining eight cases. For example, each case could be explained by an elaborate conditional whose antecedent simply restates the primary and secondary act-types contained in the stimulus. Presumably, with enough effort, even such an unimaginative theory as this could be falsified, but, in any case, the point I am making should be apparent. Clearly the brain must be generating action representations of its own that go beyond the information given. That is, much like a given patch of retinal stimulation or the acoustic stream in speech perception, the stimulus here evidently consists merely of clues for the formation of an unconscious percept that the perceiver first constructs using her own internal resources and then projects back onto the stimulus, creating an illusion of qualities

TABLE 5.3. *The Poverty of the Perceptual Stimulus*

Problem	Act-Type Descriptions		Deontic Status
	Primary	Secondary	
Bystander	throw switch	1. will turn the train onto a side track 2. preventing it from killing the men 3. killing him 4. refrain from doing this 5. letting the five die	Permissible
Footbridge	throw man	1. throw onto the track into the path of the train 2. preventing it from killing the men 3. killing him 4. refrain from doing this 5. letting the five die	Forbidden
Expensive Equipment	throw switch	1. will turn the train onto a side track 2. preventing it from killing the man 3. killing them 4. refrain from doing this 5. letting the man die	Forbidden
Implied Consent	throw man	1. throw off the track out of the path of the train 2. preventing it from killing the man 3. injuring him 4. refrain from doing this 5. letting the man die	Permissible
Intentional Homicide	throw switch	1. will turn the train onto a side track 2. preventing it from killing the man 3. killing him 4. refrain from doing this 5. letting the man die	Forbidden
Loop Track	throw switch	1. will turn the train onto a side track 2. preventing it from killing the men 3. killing him 4. refrain from doing this 5. letting the five die	Forbidden
Man-in-Front	throw switch	1. will turn the train onto a side track 2. preventing it from killing the men 3. killing him 4. refrain from doing this 5. letting the five die	Permissible
Costless Rescue	throw switch	1. will turn the train onto a side track 2. preventing it from killing the men 3. saving the five men 4. refrain from doing this 5. letting the five die	Obligatory

(continued)

TABLE 5.3 (*continued*)

Problem	Act-Type Descriptions		Deontic Status
	Primary	Secondary	
Better Alternative	throw switch	1. will turn the train onto a side track 2. preventing it from killing the men 3. killing him 4. refrain from doing this 5. letting the man die 6. pulling an emergency cord 7. redirect the train to a third track	Forbidden
Dispropor-tional Death	throw switch	1. will turn the train onto a side track 2. preventing it from killing the man 3. killing the five men 4. refrain from doing this 5. letting the one man die	Forbidden
Drop Man	throw switch	1. will drop a heavy object into the path of the train 2. preventing it from killing the men 3. killing him 4. refrain from doing this 5. letting the five die	Forbidden
Collapse Bridge	throw switch	1. will collapse a footbridge overlooking the tracks into the path of the train 2. preventing it from killing the men 3. killing him 4. refrain from doing this 5. letting the five die	Permissible

that the latter does not in fact possess (cf. Descartes 1985/1647: 303; Hume 1983/1751: 88; see also Chomsky 2000; Fodor 1985; Helmholtz 1962/1867; Marr 1982; Rey 2006). Hence an adequate scientific explanation of the data in Table 2 must specify at least three elements: (i) the deontic rules operative in the exercise of moral judgment, (ii) the structural descriptions over which those computational operations are defined, and (iii) the conversion rules by which the stimulus is transformed into an appropriate structural description.

Figure 5.4 is a schematic diagram of these three problems. As Figure 5.4 depicts, one central aspect of the problem of descriptive adequacy is to discover the deontic rules that are operative during the exercise of moral judgment. However, a second and in some sense preliminary aspect of the problem, which many researchers have thus far ignored, is to determine how the stimuli that occasion these judgments are mentally represented. This second problem may be described as how a complex action-description is converted or transformed into what I will call a *complex act-token representation*.

For ease of expression, I refer to the rules governing these transformations as *conversion rules*. I refer to them as conversion rules instead of transformation rules in order to preserve the connotation of the latter term in the original framework of transformational generative grammar. I assume for now that there may be different types of conversion rules and that linguistic transformations are just one of these. A third problem illustrated by Figure 5.4 that must be explained, then, is how a complex action-description is converted to a complex act-token representation by means of linguistic transformations and other conversions.

5.4 OUTLINE OF A SOLUTION

In this section, I outline a provisional solution to each of the three main aspects of the problem of descriptive adequacy with respect to the 12 considered judgments in Tables 5.1 and 5.3. A more detailed and formal explication of these judgments is then presented in Chapter 6.

5.4.1 Deontic Rules

Trolley problems are what jurists call cases of necessity (see, e.g., Epstein 2006; Prosser 1971), and they can be solved by assuming individuals are intuitive lawyers who possess a natural readiness to compute mental representations of human acts in legally cognizable terms. In particular, we can explain an indefinitely large class of such cases by postulating tacit or unconscious knowledge of a variety of specific legal rules, including the prohibition of intentional battery, the prohibition of intentional homicide, the Rescue Principle, and the Principle of Double Effect. The prohibition of intentional battery forbids purposefully or knowingly causing harmful or offensive contact with another individual or otherwise invading her physical integrity without her consent (e.g., Prosser 1941). The prohibition of intentional homicide forbids purposefully or knowingly killing another individual (e.g., LeFave 2003; LeFave & Scott 1972). The Rescue Principle is a familiar principle of common morality – but not the common law (e.g., Grey 1983: 157) – that forbids one from failing to prevent an easily preventable death or other serious misfortune, where this can be accomplished without risking one's own life or safety, or without violating other fundamental moral precepts (Donagan 1977; Scanlon 1998; Singer 1972; Weinrib 1980). Finally, the Principle of Double Effect is a complex principle of justification, narrower in scope than the traditional necessity defense, which holds that an otherwise prohibited action, such as battery or homicide, that has both good and bad effects may be permissible if the prohibited act itself is not directly intended, the good but not the bad effects are directly intended, the good effects outweigh the bad effects, and no morally preferable alternative is available (e.g., Fischer & Ravizza 1992).

5.4.2 Structural Descriptions

All of these principles require clarification, but, taken together and suitably formalized, they can be invoked to explain the relevant pattern of intuitions in a relatively straightforward manner. For example, the key distinction that explains many of the standard cases in the literature is that the agent commits one or more distinct batteries prior to and as a means of achieving his good end in the impermissible conditions (e.g., Transplant, Footbridge, Loop Track, Drop Man), whereas these violations are subsequent side effects in the permissible conditions (e.g., Trolley, Bystander, Man-in-Front, Collapse Bridge). The structural descriptions implied by this explanation can be exhibited in a two-dimensional tree diagram, or *act tree,* successive nodes of which bear a generation relation to one another that is asymmetric, irreflexive, and transitive (Donagan 1977; Goldman 1970a; Mikhail 2000; Mikhail, Sorrentino, & Spelke 1998). Figure 5.5 illustrates two provisional descriptions of this type that use boldface to highlight the crucial distinction in the Footbridge and Bystander problems between battery as a means and battery as a side effect.

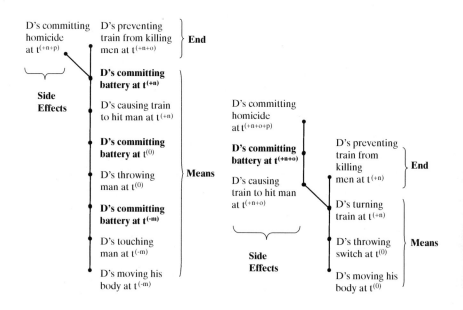

Footbridge   Bystander

FIGURE 5.5. Structural Descriptions of Action Plans in Footbridge and Bystander Problems

In Figure 5.6, these act trees are given a different and somewhat more elaborate interpretation that *inter alia* uses italics to identify the various act-type representations that are isomorphic to act-type descriptions in the stimulus, exhibits the underlying causative structures from which these representations derive, supplies a more fine-grained serial ordering of these and other representations according to dimensions of time and lexicalization, and locates morally salient representations such as battery and homicide as early as possible in the relevant computations within the constraints set by other parameters (see also Section 6.7; cf. Mikhail 2000: 170–171).

The moral grammar hypothesis holds that when people encounter trolley problems, they unconsciously compute structural descriptions of the relevant action plans that can be adequately described by act trees such as those in Figures 5.5 and 5.6. (For an alternative descriptive format, see Section 6.6.) Note that in addition to providing a basis for explaining the relevant intuitions, this hypothesis has further testable implications. For example, we can

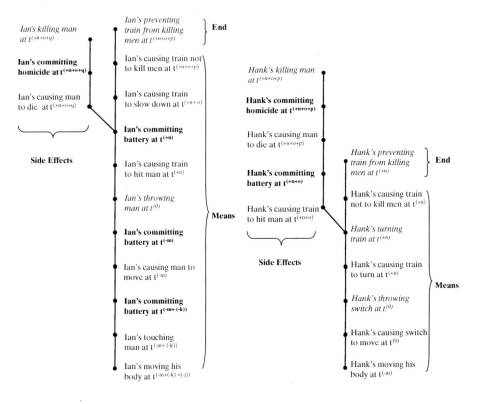

Footbridge   Bystander

FIGURE 5.6. Alternative Structural Descriptions of Action Plans in Footbridge and Bystander Problems

investigate the structural properties of these representations by asking subjects to evaluate probative descriptions of the relevant actions. Descriptions using the word "by" to connect individual nodes of these act trees in the downward direction (e.g., "D turned the train by throwing the switch," "D killed the man by turning the train") will generally be deemed acceptable; by contrast, causal reversals using "by" to connect nodes in the upward direction ("D threw the switch by turning the train," "D turned the train by killing the man") will generally be deemed unacceptable. Likewise, descriptions using connectors like "in order to" or "for the purpose of" to link nodes in the upward direction along the vertical chain of means and ends ("D threw the switch in order to turn the train") will generally be deemed acceptable. By contrast, descriptions of this type linking means with side effects ("D threw the switch in order to kill the man") will generally be deemed unacceptable. In short, there is an implicit geometry to these representations, which many neo-emotivist theories of moral cognition neglect (see, e.g., Greene 2005; Greene & Haidt 2002; Sunstein 2005), but which an adequate theory must account for.

5.4.3 Conversion Rules

The main theoretical problem implied by the foregoing account is how people manage to compute a full structural description of the relevant action plan that incorporates properties like ends, means, side effects, and prima facie wrongs like battery, even when the stimulus contains no direct evidence for these properties. This is a distinct poverty of stimulus problem, involving perception rather than acquisition (Fodor 1985), similar in principle to determining how people manage to recover a three-dimensional representation from a two-dimensional stimulus in the theory of vision (e.g., Marr 1982) or to recognize the word boundaries in unmarked auditory patterns in the theory of language (e.g., Chomsky and Halle 1968; Jackendoff 1994). In our case, the question is how, and why, individuals make the particular inferences they do about the various agents and actions in our examples, even when we deliberately deprive them of direct evidence of those agents' mental states and other morally salient properties.

In Chapter 6, I explain how these properties can be recovered from the stimulus by a sequence of operations that are largely mechanical. The main steps in this process include (i) identifying the various action descriptions in the stimulus, (ii) placing them in an appropriate temporal order, (iii) decomposing them into their underlying causative and semantic structures, (iv) applying certain moral and logical principles to these underlying structures to generate representations of good and bad effects, (v) computing the intentional structure of the relevant acts and omissions by inferring (in the absence of conflicting evidence) that agents intend good effects and avoid bad ones, and (vi) deriving representations of morally salient acts like battery and situating them in the correct location of one's act tree. Although each of these operations is relatively simple in its own right, the overall length, complexity, and abstract nature of these computations, along with their rapid, intuitive, and at least partially inaccessible character, lend at least modest support to the hypothesis that they depend on innate, domain-specific algorithms. However, this argument is not conclusive (see, e.g., Nichols 2005; Prinz 2008a,b,d; Sripada 2008a,b; Sripada & Stich 2006), and more research is needed to clarify the relevant conceptual and evidentiary issues.

5.5 INTUITIVE LEGAL APPRAISAL

An important alternative to the moral grammar hypothesis is defended by Joshua Greene and his colleagues (see, e.g., Greene 2005, 2008a,b; Greene & Haidt 2002; Greene et al. 2001). On their view, moral intuitions result from the complex interplay of at least two distinct processes: domain-specific, social-emotional responses that are inherited from our primate ancestors, and a uniquely human capacity for "sophisticated abstract reasoning that can be applied to any subject matter" (Greene & Haidt 2002: 519). The evolutionary rationale behind this approach seems compelling; however, Greene's distinction between "personal" and "impersonal" harms is far too crude to achieve descriptive adequacy (see Section 5.3.2). Ordinary legal casebooks – repositories of centuries of moral problems and the intuitions they elicit – are full of plausible counterexamples. By contrast, concepts like *battery, end, means,* and *side effect* are computational formulas that have stood the test of time. Not only are they capable of predicting human moral intuitions in a huge number and variety of actual cases, but they also can help to explain the *variance* one finds in unusual permutations of the trolley problem (see Section 6.2.1). Moreover, as we will see in Chapter 6, these concepts can be broken down into clear cognitive components, thereby providing links to other domains, such as theory of mind (see, e.g., Knobe 2005; Saxe, Carey, & Kanwisher 2004). For example, the moral grammar hypothesis may be used to predict that individuals with disorders such as autism and Asperger's syndrome may have difficulty distinguishing certain pairs of trolley problems, and to pinpoint the exact source of this difficulty; likewise, the computations exhibited here and in Chapter 6 may sharpen our understanding of a diverse range of neuropsychological phenomena, from psychopathy, sociopathy, and various forms of brain damage to the asymmetrical attribution of intentions underlying the so-called side-effect effect (Knobe 2003a, 2003b, 2005; Leslie, Knobe, & Cohen 2006). Finally, Greene's conception of personal harm "in terms of 'ME HURT YOU', and as delineating roughly those violations that a chimpanzee can appreciate" (Greene & Haidt 2002: 519) appears to rest on the assumption that the psychological patterns associated with human deontological judgment are qualitatively similar to the thought processes of chimpanzees. Yet it seems clear that adequately specifying the kinds of harm humans intuitively grasp requires a technical legal vocabulary (see, e.g.,

Alter, Kernochan, & Darley 2007; Brown 1991; Chandler, Sokal, & Wainryb 2000, Finkel, Liss, & Moran 1997; Fletcher 1998; Harman 1977; Mackie 1977; Mikhail 2002b, 2008a; Nelson 1980; Robinson & Darley 1995; Robinson, Kurzban, & Jones 2008; Smetana 1983; Young & Saxe 2008), whereas the same is not true (or at least has not yet been shown) of our primate ancestors. The critical issue is not whether moral intuitions are linked to emotions – clearly they are – but how to characterize the appraisal system that those intuitions presuppose, and in particular whether that system incorporates elements of a sophisticated jurisprudence.

6

Moral Grammar and Intuitive Jurisprudence:
A Formal Model

A critic who wished to say something against that work [*Groundwork of the Metaphysic of Morals*] really did better than he intended when he said that there was no new principle of morality in it but only a new formula. Who would want to introduce a new principle of morality and, as it were, be its inventor, as if the world had hitherto been ignorant of what duty is or had been thoroughly wrong about it? Those who know what a formula means to a mathematician, in determining what is to be done in solving a problem without letting him go astray, will not regard a formula which will do this for all duties as something insignificant and unnecessary.
  – Immanuel Kant, *Critique of Practical Reason*

[In] our science, everything depends upon the possession of the leading principles, and it is this possession which constitutes the greatness of the Roman jurists. The notions and axioms of their science do not appear to have been arbitrarily produced; these are actual beings, whose existence and genealogy have become known to them by long and intimate acquaintance. For this reason their whole mode of proceeding has a certainty which is found no where else, except in mathematics; and it may be said, without exaggeration, that they calculate with their notions.
  – F. C. Von Savigny, *Of the Vocation of Our Age for Legislation and Jurisprudence*

The demand is not to be denied: every jump must be barred from our deductions. That this is so hard to satisfy must be set down to the tediousness of proceeding step by step.
  – Gottlob Frege, *The Foundations of Arithmetic*

The central aim of this chapter is to provide a more detailed and formal description of the mental operations that are implied by the moral grammar hypothesis outlined in Chapter 5. In a comprehensive study, each of these operations would need to be described in a format suitable for explicit derivations, and many details, complications, and objections would need to be addressed. In what follows, I will be content merely to sketch some of the main

123

ideas in quasi-formal terms, leaving further refinements, extensions, and clarifications for another occasion. My primary objective is to demonstrate that a
computational theory of moral cognition, which explains an interesting and
illuminating range of common moral intuitions, can indeed be formulated. By
accomplishing this task, I also wish to supply a concrete illustration of a set of
"considered judgments in reflective equilibrium" (Rawls 1971: 46, 51), thereby
preparing the ground for responding to Rawls' critics in Part Three.

6.1 THREE SIMPLIFYING ASSUMPTIONS

Because we seek to explicate 12 distinct judgments, we must construct 12 separate derivations. To make this task more manageable, we rely on the following idealizations and simplifying assumptions. First, we assume that ordinary
individuals possess unconscious knowledge of the basic principles of deontic
logic illustrated in Figure 5.1(b) (see Section 5.1). We also assume that the
sole deontic primitive in our model is the concept *forbidden,* leaving the concepts *permissible* and *obligatory,* and the various logical expressions in Figure
5.1(b), to be defined by implication.[1]

Second, we assume that the form of our derivations is given by the following schema:

(6) A has deontic status D ≡ A has features $F_1 ... F_n$
     A has features $F_1 ... F_n$
     A has deontic status D.

In other words, we attempt to state necessary and sufficient conditions for
assigning a deontic status to a given act or omission. As noted in Section 6.3.1,
this renders our model a logically closed system, and, given our choice of primitive, it is equivalent to assuming that the correct closure rule is a Residual
Permission Principle.

Third, we replace the letter 'A' in (6) with the following formula:

(7) $[S's V\text{-ing at } t^{(\alpha)}]^C$

The syntax of this formula calls for comment. Drawing on Goldman (1970a)
and Ginet (1990), we take the central element of what we call the *normal form*
of a *complex act-token representation* to be a gerundive nominal, whose grammatical subject is possessive (cf. Bentham's preference for nominalization in
Ogden 1932). Following Katz (1972), we use the symbol 'at t' to denote some
unspecified position on an assumed time dimension, and we use superscripts

---

[1] To generate the various expressions in Figure 5.1(b), one needs just two logical connectives,
because out of '~' (*not*) and any one of '·' (*and*), 'v' (*or*), '⊃' (*if-then*), or '≡' (*if and only if*),
the others may be defined. For example, given two propositions, P and Q, and the connectives '~' and 'v', one may define '(P.Q)' as an abbreviation for '(~((~P) v ((~Q)))'; '(P⊃Q)' as
an abbreviation for '((~P) v Q)'; and '(P≡Q)' as an abbreviation for '(P⊃Q).(Q⊃P)'.

on occurrences of 't' to refer to specific positions on this dimension. We assume that superscripts can be either variables or constants. We take 't' with the superscript constant 'o', that is, '$t^{(o)}$', to function as an indexical element in a complex act-token representation, serving to orient the temporal relationships holding between it and other such representations (cf. Katz 1972: 312).

Superscript variables ('n', 'm', etc.) denote members of the set of natural numbers. They appear in superscripts with prefixes '+' and '−', indicating the number of positive or negative units from the origin point ('$t^{(o)}$') of the time dimension. For example, '$t^{(+n)}$' means 'n units to the right of the origin', whereas '$t^{(-n)}$' signifies 'n units to the left of the origin'. Thus, '$t^{(-n)}$', '$t^{(o)}$', and '$t^{(+m)}$' in the following series of representations imply that Hank's seeing what happened occurs before his throwing the switch, which occurs before his killing the man:

(8) (a) [Hank's seeing what happened at $t^{(-n)}$]
    (b) [Hank's throwing the switch at $t^{(o)}$]
    (c) [Hank's killing the man at $t^{(+m)}$]

There is an important convention this notation incorporates, which is to date an action by its time of *completion*. Strictly speaking, an act that begins at $t^{(o)}$ and ends at $t^{(+n)}$ is performed neither at $t^{(o)}$ nor $t^{(+n)}$, but in that period of time bounded by them. We simplify this situation by following the traditional legal rule of dating an action by when it is completed (Salmond 1966/1902: 360). Doing so enables us to avoid many problems, such as locating "the time of a killing," that have been identified in the literature (Thomson 1970a; cf. Fodor 1970; Fried 1978; Jackendoff 1987; Pinker 2007). Finally, since acts always occur in particular circumstances, we need a notation for designating those circumstances. Hence, we enclose these representations in square brackets, followed by the superscript 'C' to denote the circumstances in which act-tokens are performed.[2]

6.2 STRUCTURAL DESCRIPTIONS I: ACTS, CIRCUMSTANCES, AND INTENTIONS

6.2.1 Acts and Circumstances

It is at this point that turning more directly to legal theory and the philosophy of action is useful for our topic. Together with aspects of Goldman's (1970a) theory of level-generation, the substantive law of crime and tort

[2] Our notation for designating act-token representations can be elaborated in simple ways, as needed. For example, we can exhibit more complex temporal relations by relying on conventions for adding and subtracting in algebra. Thus, '$t^{(+n+(-m))}$' signifies 'n − m units to the right of the origin', while '$t^{(-n+(-m)+(-o))}$' signifies 'n + m + o units to the left of the origin'. Likewise, our generic reference to circumstances, 'C', can be replaced with one or more sets of circumstances, '{C1, C2, C3 ... Cn}'. See generally Katz (1972); Mikhail (2000).

provides us with the necessary conceptual tools for explaining the 12 considered judgments in Table 5.2, as well as an indefinitely large class of structurally similar judgments.

From a common legal point of view, an *act* is simply a voluntary bodily movement that occurs in a particular set of circumstances (Holmes 1991/1881; Terry 1884; cf. ALI 1965; Goldman 1970a). Those circumstances, in turn, may be regarded as a body of information that obtains at the time that the act or its omission occurs. In *De inventione,* Cicero supplies a classic list of seven probative questions that can be asked about the circumstances of any particular action:

> *Quis? Quid? Ubi? Quibus auxiliis? Cur? Quomodo? Quando?*
> Who? What? Where? By what aids? Why? How? When?

Cicero's list, which is presumably illustrative rather than exhaustive, has been the subject of philosophical analysis for centuries (see, e.g., Aquinas 1952/1274: 653; cf. Kenny 1963: 160). For our purposes, its significance rests in the fact that the answers elicited by these questions can transform one description of an action into another, and that the resulting set of descriptions can be arranged into hierarchical tree structures, successive nodes of which bear a generation relation to one another that is asymmetric, irreflexive, and transitive (Goldman 1970a; see also Anscombe 1957; Davidson 1963; Donagan 1977; Moore 1993; Ryle 1968; cf. Geertz 1973 on "thick description"). When properly constructed, these expository diagrams enable us not only to predict moral intuitions with surprising accuracy, but also to see at a glance a variety of structural relationships, including those we might have overlooked or ignored.

For example, act trees can be used not only to identify the basic differences between the Footbridge and Bystander problems, but also to explain the *variance* one finds in highly refined manipulations of these cases, such as the Loop Track, Man-in-Front, Drop Man, and Collapse Bridge problems. As Figure 6.1(a) indicates, the intuitive data in these six cases form a remarkably consistent pattern, with permissibility judgments increasing linearly across the six conditions. Moreover, as Figure 6.1(b) illustrates, these results can be tentatively explained as a function of the properties of each problem's structural description. Other things equal, acts are more likely to be judged permissible as counts of battery committed as a means decrease from three (Footbridge) to two (Drop Man) to one (Loop Track), and as these violations become side effects and additional structural features come into play. In Man-in-Front, the agent's goal presumably is to save the men by causing the train to hit the object but not the man, yet the actual result (not shown) is likely to involve hitting the man before the object; hence, from an *ex post* perspective, the agent will commit a battery prior to and as a means of achieving his good end. Likewise, in Collapse Bridge, one or more counts of battery must necessarily occur before the good end is achieved. By contrast, in Bystander, battery and homicide are

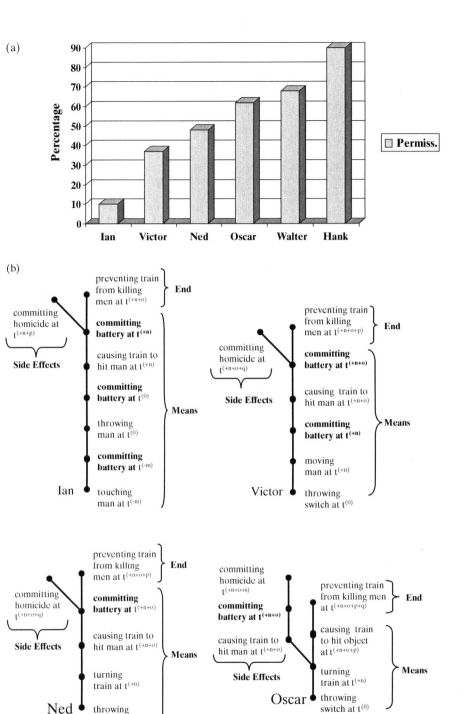

FIGURE 6.1. Circumstances Alter Cases: (a) Variance in Six Trolley
Problem Experiments; (b) Six Structural Descriptions; (c) An Illustration
of Mill's (1843) "Mental Chemistry" (Data in [a] from Mikhail 2002b,
2007a; see also Appendix 1.)

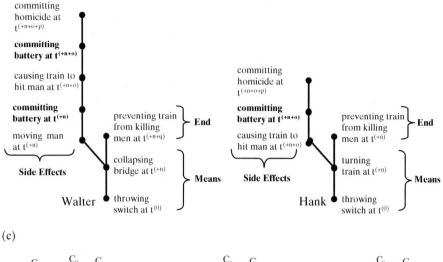

(c)

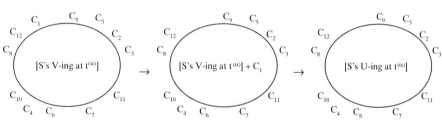

Figure 6.1 *(continued)*

side effects that occur only after the good end has been secured by turning the train onto the side track (Mikhail 2007a).

Diagramming action plans is an important tool for solving the problem of descriptive adequacy, and it was a major part of the effort that began with the earliest work on moral grammar to identify the precise structural properties of the mental representations that are elicited by thought experiments such as the trolley problems (see, e.g., Mikhail 2000; Mikhail, Sorrentino, & Spelke 1998; cf. Bentham 1948/1789: 79; Locke 1991/1689: 550–552). In what follows, I seek to build on this foundation by explaining how iterated applications of a general computational principle, which combines an act-token representation with its circumstances to yield another act-token representation, can be utilized together with a variety of legal rules, concepts, and principles to explain how the brain computes the complex structural descriptions of a given action and its alternatives. All of these structural descriptions can be exhibited by act trees, but, as I suggest in Section 6.4, other graphic devices, such as a table of recurring elements, can also be fruitfully utilized in this endeavor.

Formally, this general computational principle can be rendered in various ways, including the following:

(9) (a) $[\text{S's V-ing at } t^{(\alpha)}]^C \rightarrow [\text{S's U-ing at } t^{(\beta)}]$

(b) $[\text{S's V-ing at } t^{(\alpha)}] + C \rightarrow [\text{S's U-ing at } t^{(\beta)}]$

(c) $[\text{S's V-ing at } t^{(\alpha)} + C] \rightarrow [\text{S's U-ing at } t^{(\beta)}]$

(d) $[\text{S's V-ing at } t^{(\alpha)}]^{\{C_1, C_2, C_3 \dots Cn\}} \rightarrow [\text{S's V-ing at } t^{(\alpha)} + C_1]^{\{C_2, C_3 \dots Cn\}}$

(e) $[\text{S's V-ing at } t^{(\alpha)} + C_1]^{\{C_2, C_3 \dots Cn\}} \rightarrow [\text{S's U-ing at } t^{(\beta)}]^{\{C_2, C_3 \dots Cn\}}$

(9a) provides that a complex act-token representation can yield another act-token representation. In this formula, '$\rightarrow$' functions as a rewrite rule that permits the object on the left side of the arrow to be replaced by the object on the right side. (9b) uses the '+' symbol to express a similar proposition, indicating that a circumstance can be added to an act-token representation to yield another act-token representation. (9c) is similar, but more precise, because it signifies that a circumstance becomes material, so to speak, by combining with an act-token representation within its corresponding brackets. Finally, (9d) and (9e) reveal how, in two distinct steps, the process might unfold in a generic case. First, a particular circumstance, C_1, is selected from the set of circumstances surrounding an act-token representation, S's V-ing at $t^{(\alpha)}$, and conjoined with the latter (9d). Next, the combination of these two elements yields a new act-token representation, S's U-ing at $t^{(\beta)}$ (9e). The set of circumstances surrounding this transformation remains intact throughout, except that C_1 is no longer an element of this set.

As Bentham (1948/1879: 77) observes, the basic mental processes we seek to describe can be illustrated by drawing on the etymology of the word *circumstance – "circumstantia,* things standing round: objects standing around another object" – and thus conceiving of "the field of circumstances, belonging to any act" to be "a circle, of which the circumference is no where, but of which the act in question is the centre." Moreover, as Mill (1987/1843: 39–40) observes, the relevant phenomena can be conceived as a kind of "mental chemistry," in which simple ideas combine to generate more complex ones in a process loosely analogous to chemical combination (Figure 6.1 (c); cf. Kant 1993/1788: 169–171; D'Arcy 1963: 57–61). The particular diagrams used to exhibit these transformations are inessential, of course, and one should avoid getting carried away with metaphors that risk obscuring rather than illuminating the relevant mental operations. What matters is simply to recognize that any adequate scientific theory of moral intuition must seek to explain how the brain converts complex action-descriptions and other sensory inputs into complex act-token representations as a necessary precondition of moral judgment. The general computational principle we have identified is a plausible component of one such proposal, but, even so, it obviously cannot do the job on its own. As I argue below, however, this principle, together with other elements of moral grammar, can be used to explain the 12 cases in Table 5.1, along with a potentially infinite number and variety of other cases.

6.2.2 K-Generation and I-Generation

Modifying Goldman's (1970a) analysis to suit our topic, let us begin by defining two generation relations that might hold between pairs of act-token representations.

Definition of K-Generation

Given two act-token representations, [S's V-ing at $t^{(\alpha)}$] and [S's U-ing at $t^{(\beta)}$], and a set of known circumstances, C, [S's V-ing at $t^{(\alpha)}$]^C *K-generates* [S's U-ing at $t^{(\beta)}$] if and only if:

(a) $V \neq U$

(that is: [S's V-ing] and [S's U-ing] are syntactically distinct)

(b) $\beta - \alpha \geq 0$

(that is: [S's U-ing at $t^{(\beta)}$] is either time-identical or subsequent to [S's V-ing at $t^{(\alpha)}$])

(c) [S's V-ing at $t^{(\alpha)}$ + C] $\rightarrow$ [S's U-ing at $t^{(\beta)}$]

(that is: the conjunction of [S's V-ing at $t^{(\alpha)}$] and C yields [S's U-ing at $t^{(\beta)}$])

Definition of I-Generation

Given two act-token representations, [S's V-ing at $t^{(\alpha)}$] and [S's U-ing at $t^{(\beta)}$], and a set of known circumstances, C, [S's V-ing at $t^{(\alpha)}$]^C *I-generates* [S's U-ing at $t^{(\beta)}$] if and only if:

(a) [S's V-ing at $t^{(\alpha)}$]^C K-generates [S's U-ing at $t^{(\beta)}$]

(b) [S's U-ing at $t^{(\beta)}$] = [GOAL] v [S's U-ing at $t^{(\beta)}$] I-generates [GOAL]

(that is: [S's U-ing at $t^{(\beta)}$] is the goal, or I-generates the goal, of an action plan)

Comment: These provisional definitions of K-generation and I-generation are meant to provide a sufficient basis for our limited objectives of accounting for the fact that individuals ordinarily distinguish at least two types of effects that are caused by a moral agent: (i) effects that are *knowingly* caused (K-generation), and (ii) effects that are *intentionally* or *purposely* caused (I-generation). For simplicity, we assume here that the latter are a proper subset of the former; hence, we do not attempt to account for cases in which an agent intends to accomplish ends that she believes are unlikely to occur. Instead, we simply assume that all of the effects that are intentionally or purposefully caused by an agent are also knowingly caused by her.

In Anglo-American jurisprudence, "intent" is often defined or used broadly to include knowledge. For example, the American Law Institute's Restatement (Second) of Torts uses "intent," "intentional," and related terms "to denote that the actor desires to cause consequences of his act, or that he believes that the consequences are substantially certain to result from it" (ALI 1965: 15; cf. Lefave & Scott 1972: 196–197). Likewise, Sidgwick holds that "[f]or purposes of exact moral or juristic discussion, it is best to include under the term of 'intention' all the consequences of an act that are foreseen as certain or probable" (1981/1907: 202). Ordinary language often exhibits a different and more precise understanding of intention, however, and distinguishes intended and foreseen effects in a variety of contexts (Anscombe 1958; Bratman 1987; Finnis 1995; Kenny 1995), including the trolley problems, if our hypothesis is correct. By defining K-generation and I-generation in the foregoing manner, then, we depart from certain conventional accounts of intention and attempt instead to explicate the familiar distinction between ends and means, on the one hand, and known or foreseen side effects, on the other.

Bentham (1948/1789: 84) succinctly captures the distinction between I-generation and K-generation when he explains that a consequence may be "directly or lineally" intentional, when "the prospect of producing it constituted one of the links in the chain of causes by which the person was determined to do the act," or merely "obliquely or collaterally" intentional, when "the consequence was in contemplation, and appeared likely to ensue in case of the act's being performed, yet the prospect of producing such a consequence did not constitute a link in the aforesaid chain." The definition of I-generation tracks Bentham's notion of direct intention; it can also be regarded as a rule for generating the adverb "purposely" (or "intentionally" in one of its ambiguous meanings) and conjoining it to an act-token representation that otherwise lacks this mental state element. The definition of K-generation corresponds with Bentham's notion of collateral intention; it can also be regarded as a rule for generating the adverb "knowingly" and conjoining it to an act-token representation that otherwise lacks this mental state element.

The recursive aspect of the definition of I-generation (i.e., provision [b]) is meant to provide a computational interpretation of the principle Kant takes to be analytic: A rational agent who wills the end necessarily wills the known means (Kant 1964/1785: 84–85). The key insight here is that once the end, goal, or final effect of a causal chain has been identified, each of the previous links of that chain can be sequentially transformed from a representation of a mere *cause* of its subsequent effects to a representation of a *means* of its subsequent ends. In this manner we can explain how the brain imputes intentional structure to what previously was only a projection of causes and effects. The end, goal, or final effect of an action is presupposed in this process. Later we explain how one can compute the end, goal, or final effect of a complex act-token representation on the basis of information about its good and bad effects (see Section 6.5.4).

For present purposes, we do not define a separate notion of C-generation (i.e., causal generation; see Goldman 1970a) or distinguish it from K-generation. Nor do we incorporate an explicit causal requirement in our definition of K-generation. Doing so would complicate our model, and it seems unnecessary given our immediate aims. Instead, we simply assume that each agent in Table 5.1 both causes and knows the stipulated effects of his actions. The reference to *known* circumstances in the definition of K-generation is thus taken to mean that these circumstances, including relevant causal conditionals, are known to the agents themselves (as well as to the participants in our experiments, in a secondary sense of the term). In a fully adequate grammar, these assumptions would need to be scrutinized, and a separate notion of C-generation would presumably need to be analyzed, defined, and incorporated into our definition of K-generation to account for the fact that individuals ordinarily distinguish both the effects that are objectively caused by an agent and those that she knowingly caused. We leave this task for another occasion, with the expectation that by drawing on a sophisticated body of work on causation (e.g., Alicke 1992; Hart & Honore 1959; Mackie 1974; Pearl 2000; Wright 1985), a computational theory of C-generation can be integrated into the foregoing framework.

6.3 DEONTIC RULES

The two notions we have defined, K-generation and I-generation, provide a principled basis for distinguishing what an agent knowingly does from what she purposely does, at least in a provisional way suitable for our aims. We need more conceptual tools, however, to explain the data in Table 5.2. An adequate moral grammar must include several more concepts and principles.

6.3.1 The Principle of Natural Liberty

One of these principles is a so-called *closure rule* (Stone 1968; see also Raz 1970), which renders our idealized model closed or complete. From a logical point of view, there are two main possibilities: (i) a *Residual Prohibition Principle,* which assumes that all permissible acts and omissions are defined and states that "whatever is not legally permitted is prohibited," and (ii) a *Residual Permission Principle,* which assumes that all forbidden acts and omissions are defined and states that "whatever is not legally prohibited is permitted."[3] The first alternative, which appears in Aristotle's discussion of law,[4] is essentially authoritarian, since it leaves little or no room for individual choice. The second alternative, which underwrites the legal maxims *nullum crimen sine lege* (no crime without law) and *nulla peona sine lege* (no penalty without law) and characterizes modern liberalism, is essentially libertarian,

---

[3] A *Residual Obligation Principle* is not a genuine third alternative, because it is logically equivalent to the Residual Prohibition Principle (cf. Figure 5.1 [b]).

[4] See Aristotle, *Nichomachean Ethics,* 1138a6–8 (observing that "the law does not expressly permit suicide, and what it does not expressly permit it forbids").

since it implies unrestricted freedom within the domain of acts that are neither obligatory nor forbidden.

The Residual Permission Principle may also be called a *Principle of Natural Liberty*, and it is this essentially libertarian principle, rather than the essentially authoritarian Residual Prohibition Principle – or, alternatively, the altogether unrestrained notion of natural liberty that one finds in legal writers like Hobbes, Blackstone, and Bentham – on which the system we describe here rests. In particular, we follow a long line of modern writers on moral philosophy, natural jurisprudence and the law of nations (e.g., Burlamaqui 2006/1748: 284; Kant 1991/1797: 63–64; Locke 1980/1690: 9; Spencer 1978/1897: 61–62; Wilson 1967/1790–1791: 587–588; cf. Mill 1978/1859: 9–10) in adopting a more restricted, yet still expansive, precept of natural liberty as our preferred closure rule, which can be rendered as follows: *If an act has features $F_1 \ldots F_n$, then it is forbidden; otherwise, it is permissible.* More formally, the principle can be restated as the following conjunction of conditionals, which is simply a theorem of our model that can be derived from the schema in (1) together with the equipollence relations in Figure 4:

Principle of Natural Liberty

$[[\text{S's V-ing at } t^{(a)}]^C$ has features $F_1 \ldots F_n] \supset [[\text{S's V-ing at } t^{(a)}]^C$ is forbidden].
$\sim[[\text{S's V-ing at } t^{(a)}]^C$ has features $F_1 \ldots F_n] \supset [[\text{S's V-ing at } t^{(a)}]^C$ is permissible]

In his discussion of the principles of natural duty in *A Theory of Justice,* Rawls mentions but does not elaborate on the fact that a complete system of moral principles will contain a principle asserting its completeness (1971: 340). The Principle of Natural Liberty may be regarded, for our purposes, as one plausible version of this principle.

6.3.2 The Prohibition of Battery and Homicide

Any normative system seeking to achieve descriptive adequacy must presumably include a set of basic legal prohibitions. In particular, it must include or otherwise account for a small number of absolute or near-absolute prohibitions against various forms of trespass, such as battery, assault, rape, murder, fraud, deceit, and so on. In my judgment, the theoretical debates over the past two centuries surrounding the inadequacies of utilitarianism and intuitionism – at least when these moral theories are applied to the actions of individuals – make this conclusion rather clear. Whether or not precepts like these can be derived in turn from a small number of fundamental principles, or even from a single "supreme" principle, such as the categorical imperative or the Golden Rule, is a topic that we need not consider here.

For our purposes, two familiar prohibitions are relevant: battery and homicide. In a moral grammar that is capable of serving as premises of a derivation, each of these trespasses would need to be clearly and comprehensively defined. Here I will merely state provisional definitions that are suitable for our limited purposes.

First homicide: The American Law Institute's Model Penal Code defines homicide in part as an act that consists in "purposely, knowingly, recklessly, or negligently causing the death of another human being" (ALI 1985/1962, Section 210.1). Modifying this definition to suit our purposes by detaching its adverbial component, let us assume that the act-type *commits homicide* can be defined[5] simply as causing the death of a person. Formally, this can be stated as follows:

Definition of Homicide

[S commits homicide at $t^{(\alpha)}]^C =_{Df}$ [S's V-ing [EFFECT (Person, Death)] at $t^{(\alpha)}]^C$

There is an implicit causation element in this definition that requires further analysis, but we set aside this issue here. By combining this definition with the notions of I-generation and K-generation, we can now distinguish the following two types of homicide.

Representation of Purposeful Homicide

[S's V-ing at $t^{(\alpha)}]^C$ *I-generates* [S's committing homicide at $t^{(\beta)}]$

Representation of Knowing Homicide

[S's V-ing at $t^{(\alpha)}]^C$ *K-generates* [S's committing homicide at $t^{(\beta)}]$

In our model, the first expression formalizes the complex act-type *purposely committing homicide*. The second expression formalizes the complex act-type *knowingly committing homicide*. As we shall see, the second formula appears operative in 10 of our 12 cases. By contrast, the only case that appears to involve the first formula is the Intentional Homicide problem.

Next, battery: Prosser (1941: 43) defines battery in part as "unpermitted, unprivileged contact with [a] person." The Restatement (Second) of Torts (ALI 1965: 25) offers a more elaborate definition, which reads in part: "An actor is subject to liability for battery if (a) he acts intending to cause a harmful or offensive contact with the person of the other or a third person, or an imminent apprehension of such contact, and (b) a harmful contact with the person of the other directly or indirectly results." Modifying these accounts to suit our objectives, let us assume that the act-type *commits battery* can be defined simply as causing harmful contact with a person without her consent.[6]

---

[5] On the standard form of definition used here, see generally Hempel (1955: 4). For its application to legal definitions, see Stone (1968: 169–172).

[6] I focus here on harmful battery rather than offensive battery, since only the former is relevant for our purposes. On the latter, see generally the Restatement (Second) of Torts, Sections 18–20.

Formally, this definition can be stated as follows:

Definition of Battery

[S commits battery at $t^{(a)}]^C = _{Df}$ [S's V-ing [EFFECT (Person, Contact-$_H$, ~Consent)] at $t^{(a)}]^C$

The concept of *contact* as it is used in this definition needs to be explained. In the common law of torts, protection against unwanted physical contact encompasses all forms of direct touching and "extends to any part of the body, or to anything which is attached to it and practically identified with it" (Prosser 1971: 34). Moreover, it includes any "touching of the person, either by the defendant or any substance put in motion by him" (Hilliard 1859: 191). Hence, the ordinary concept of contact is inadequate in some circumstances and must be replaced with a more expansive concept. Although we need not draw the precise contours of this broader concept here, it is important to recognize that a salient contact occurs not only when a person is (i) touched or (ii) moved by an agent, but also when she is (iii) touched by an object that is being touched by an agent, (iv) touched by an object that was previously moved by an agent, without the intervention of a more proximate cause, or (v) moved by an object that was previously moved by an agent, without the intervention of a more proximate cause. None of these effects necessarily trigger a representation of battery, but each is sufficient to generate a representation of the contact necessary for battery, at least within the confines of our model.

For example, the contact requirement can be met by shoving or grabbing another person, but also by kicking the umbrella she is holding, snatching a plate from her hand, throwing a rock at her, spitting on her, or pulling a chair out from under her as she sits down, thereby causing her to fall (see, e.g., Epstein 2004). In our 12 cases, the requirement is satisfied by throwing a person (as in the Footbridge and Implied Consent problems), moving a person and thereby causing him to come into contact with a train (as in the Drop Man and Collapse Bridge problems), or redirecting a train so that it comes into contact with a person (as in the Bystander, Expensive Equipment, Intentional Homicide, Loop Track, Man-in-Front, Better Alternative, and Disproportional Death problems). Depending on how the implicit causation element of battery is interpreted, the requirement might also be satisfied in the Costless Rescue problem. I ignore this issue here, along with the broader question of whether battery can occur by omission, which some commentators have denied, even when the resulting harm or offense is intentional (see, e.g., the Restatement (First) of Torts, Sections 2, 13, 18, 281, 284, and Topic 1, Scope Note).

Our definition of battery also requires that the contact be *harmful.* Hence this concept must also be analyzed, and sufficient conditions for generating a representation of it must be provided. Once again, for our purposes it is sufficient to adopt with only minor changes the concept of harm utilized by the

Restatement (Second) of Torts, which provides a useful framework in this regard. First, we use the word "harm" and its cognates, without further qualification, to denote any kind of detriment to a person resulting from any cause (ALI 1965: 12). That is, we interpret harm broadly to include any "detriment or loss to a person which occurs by virtue of, or as a result of, some alteration or change in his person, or in physical things" (ALI 1965: 13). Second, we use the narrower notion of *bodily* harm to refer to any physical impairment of a person's body, including physical pain, illness, or alteration of the body's normal structure or function to any extent. Third, we understand the harmful contact element of battery to require bodily harm, in the sense defined. Finally, we stipulate that a harmful contact occurs whenever contact with a person *results* in bodily harm, whether or not it does so directly, immediately, or purposely. In other words, we assume that the harmful effect of an I-generated contact need not be I-generated itself for the I-generated contact to be considered harmful (cf. Bentham 1948/1789: 83).

Although these analyses could be improved, they are sufficient for our limited aims. By combining our definition of battery with the notions of I-generation and K-generation, we can now formally distinguish the following two types of battery:

Representation of Purposeful Battery

[S's V-ing at $t^{(\alpha)}$]^C *I-generates* [S's committing battery at $t^{(\beta)}$]

Representation of Knowing Battery

[S's V-ing at $t^{(\alpha)}$]^C *K-generates* [S's committing battery at $t^{(\beta)}$]

In our model, the first expression formalizes the complex act-type *purposely committing battery*. The second expression formalizes the complex act-type *knowingly committing battery*. The second formula appears operative in 10 of our 12 cases. By contrast, the first formula appears operative in only four cases, all of which are judged to be impermissible: Footbridge, Intentional Homicide, Loop Track, and Drop Man.

6.3.3 The Self-Preservation Principle

The concept of *consent* in our definition of battery, which usually operates instead as an affirmative defense (see, e.g., ALI 1965: Sections 49–62), also calls for comment. Crucial as this concept is, I do not attempt to analyze it here, beyond stating one sufficient condition for its application. What is important for our purposes is to have a principled basis for distinguishing Luke's throwing the man in the Implied Consent problem from Ian's performing the same action in the Footbridge problem (along with numerous other cases of simple battery, in which harmful contact occurs without any possible justification). Intuitively the relevant difference is that the man *would* consent to being thrown in the Implied Consent problem, since his own life is being saved. To generate this representation, we may assume that the moral grammar includes the following principle:

Self-Preservation Principle

[EFFECT (Person, Contact$_{-H}$)] $\supset$ [EFFECT (Person, Death)] $\rightarrow$ [EFFECT (Person, Contact$_{-H}$, ~Consent)]

Roughly, the Self-Preservation Principle affords a presumption that, if a harmful contact with a person necessitates killing her, then she would not consent to it. This presumption may, of course, be rebutted in certain contexts, such as triage, euthanasia, or physician-assisted suicide, but I set aside these potential complications here.

6.3.4 The Moral Calculus of Risk

If our hypothesis is correct, then the "background of excitation" (Lashley 1951) that must be attributed to the participants in our experiments to explain their considered judgments must include not only principles of deontic logic (Section 6.1), a general computational principle capable of transforming one act-token representation into another (Section 6.2.1), a set of rules for distinguishing K-generation and I-generation (Section 6.2.2), a closure rule (Section 6.3.1), and a set of presumptively prohibited acts (Section 6.3.2). Among other things, it also must include a moral calculus of some sort for specifying, ranking, and comparing the probabilities of an action's good and bad effects.

In our simple model, we account for the first of these three necessary operations by postulating three primary bad effects: (i) death of a person, (ii) bodily harm to a person, and (iii) destruction of a valuable thing. Formally these three postulates can be rendered as follows:

Postulate #1:

[EFFECT [(Person, Death)] $\rightarrow$ [BAD EFFECT]

Postulate #2:

[EFFECT [(Person, Harm$_{-B}$)] $\rightarrow$ [BAD EFFECT]

Postulate #3:

[EFFECT [(Thing$_{-V}$, Destroy)] $\rightarrow$ [BAD EFFECT]

The first postulate states that an effect that consists of the death of a person is a bad effect, and may be rewritten as such. In this formula, '$\rightarrow$' is a rewrite rule that converts the object on the left side of the arrow to the object on the right side. The second and third postulates apply the same rule to bodily harm to a person and the destruction of a valuable thing, respectively.

We also make the simplifying assumption that the only good effects in our model are those that consist of the negation of a bad effect. That is, we postulate that each bad effect has a corresponding good effect: namely, the prevention of that bad effect. In addition, we postulate a second, derivative type of bad effect that consists of the prevention of a good effect. Formally, these two postulates can be rendered as follows:

Postulate #4:

[EFFECT [neg [BAD EFFECT]]] → [GOOD EFFECT]

Postulate #5:

[EFFECT [neg [GOOD EFFECT]]] → [BAD EFFECT]

Postulate #4 states that an effect that consists of the negation of a bad effect is a good effect, and may be rewritten as such. Postulate #5 states that an effect that consists of the negation of a good effect is a bad effect, and may be rewritten as such. In Section 6.5.3, I provide an alternative formal interpretation of these principles and explain how they can be applied directly to the underlying semantic structures of certain causative constructions in the stimulus, thereby showing how these structures can be transformed into richer representations that encode both good and bad effects.

The second operation we must explain is how to generate a moral ranking of an action's good and bad effects. In our model, we postulate a simple ordinal ranking of bad effects, according to which (i) the death of a person is morally worse than bodily harm to a person, and (ii) bodily harm to a person is morally worse than the destruction of a valuable thing. Formally these two postulates can be rendered as follows:

Postulate #6:

[EFFECT [(Person, Death)] $<_m$ [EFFECT [(Person, Harm$_{-B}$)]

Postulate #7:

[EFFECT [(Person, Harm$_{-B}$)] $<_m$ [EFFECT [(Thing$_{-V}$, Destroy)]

In these formulas, '$<_m$' symbolizes what we call the *morally-worse-than* relation. Postulate #6 states that an effect that consists of the death of a person is morally worse than an effect that consists of bodily harm to a person. Postulate #7 states that an effect that consists of bodily harm to a person is morally worse than an effect that consists of destruction of a valuable thing.

In our model, the morally-worse-than relation is assumed to be asymmetric, irreflexive, and transitive. If 'A', 'B', and 'C' are three effects, then the following can be validly inferred: if A is morally worse than B, then B is not morally worse than A (asymmetry); A is not morally worse than A (irreflexivity); if A is morally worse than B, and B is morally worse than C, then A is morally worse than C (transitivity). We also assume that each bad effect is morally worse than its corresponding good effect. Hence, we assume that (i) the death of a person is morally worse than its prevention, (ii) bodily harm to a person is morally worse than its prevention, and (iii) destruction of a valuable thing is morally worse than its prevention. Formally these three postulates can be rendered as follows:

Postulate #8:

[EFFECT [(Person, Death)] $<_m$ [EFFECT [neg (Person, Death)]]

Postulate #9:

[EFFECT [(Person, Harm$_{-B}$)] $<_m$ [EFFECT [neg (Person, Harm$_{-B}$)]]

Postulate #10:

[EFFECT [(Thing$_{-V}$, Destroy)] $<_m$ [EFFECT [neg (Thing$_{-V}$, Destroy)]]

Finally, we postulate that the life of one person has the same moral worth as that of another. We also assume that these values can be aggregated to arrive at an ordinal (although not necessarily cardinal) ranking of multiple effects, each of which consists of the death of one or more persons. Letting '∀' stand for the universal quantifier, letting 'x' and 'y' stand for positive integers, and letting '>' and '≤' stand for the *is-greater-than* and *is-less-than-or-equal-to* relations (which, unlike the morally-worse-than- relation, are mathematical concepts, not normative ones), these assumptions imply two further postulates:

Postulate #11:

$\forall$(x, y) [[x > y] ≡ [(x Persons, Death)] $<_m$ [(y Persons, Death)]]

Postulate #12:

$\forall$(x, y) [[x ≤ y] ≡ ~ [(x Persons, Death)] $<_m$ [(y Persons, Death)]]

Similar formulas could presumably be constructed for the two other bad effects in our model: bodily harm to a person and the destruction of a valuable thing. However, certain complications would have to be addressed in each case. For example, even if one assumes that the physical security of one person has the same moral worth as that of another, it does not follow that bodily harm to five persons is morally worse than bodily harm to one person; to reach this conclusion, both the type and the extent of the harm must be held constant. For different types of harm, at least, a separate ranking is necessary, and problems of incommensurability can arise (Fiske & Tetlock 1997; Hallborg 1997; Tetlock

2003). Likewise, it is conceivable, but not obvious, that valuable things can be monetized or otherwise ranked to permit judgments of their comparative moral worth. Nor is it clear that the destruction of a more expensive object is always morally worse than that of a less expensive one. A comprehensive moral grammar would need to confront issues like these, but since this is not necessary for our purposes, we can set them aside.

The third operation we must explain is how to compute and compare the probabilities of an action's good and bad effects. In our model, we draw upon the common law of torts to sketch a provisional account of how this operation is performed. On this account, the reasonableness and hence justifiability of a given risk of unintentional harm can be calculated as a function of five variables: (i) the magnitude of the risk, R_M; (ii) the value of the principal object, V_P, which may be thought of as the life, safety, or property interests of the individual in question; (iii) the utility of the risk, R_U; (iv) the necessity of the risk, R_N; and (v) the value of the collateral object, V_C, which may be thought of as the actor's own purpose in imposing the given risk (Terry 1915; cf. Restatement [Second] of Torts, Sections 291–293). In particular, justifiability depends on whether R_M multiplied by V_P is greater than (i.e., morally worse than) the combined product of R_U, V_C, and R_N:

Moral Calculus of Risk

$$(R_M) \, (V_P) > (R_U) \, (V_C) \, (R_N)$$

The Moral Calculus of Risk is similar to the famous Hand Formula for calculating negligence liability, according to which negligence depends on whether the probability that a given accident will occur, P, multiplied by the injury or loss resulting from the accident, L, is greater than the cost or burden of preventing the accident, B; that is, on whether $PL > B$ (see, e.g., Epstein 2004; Hurd & Moore 2002). Whereas the Hand Formula is comprised of three variables, however, the Moral Calculus of Risk relies on five. Three of these variables are probabilities, while two of them are evaluative components that measure the comparative moral worth of the principal and collateral objects. We have already explained how the two evaluative variables can be specified and compared by means of a simple ordinal ranking of the various good and bad effects in our model. It will be useful, however, to say a further word about the three probability variables.

The *magnitude of the risk* is the probability that the principal object will be harmed in some manner; in our case, this is simply the probability that an agent will K-generate one of our three bad effects: death of a person, bodily harm to a person, or destruction of a valuable thing. The *utility of the risk* is the probability that the collateral object – the agent's purpose – will be achieved; in our model, this usually refers to the probability of K-generating a *good* effect (e.g., preventing the train from killing the men). The sole exception is the Intentional Homicide problem, where the agent's purpose is to achieve a bad effect. The *necessity of the risk* is the probability that the agent's purpose would *not* be achieved without risk to the principal object; in our model, this variable typically measures the likelihood that a good effect (e.g., preventing the train from killing the men) could not be achieved without K-generating a bad side effect. The sole exception is the Better Alternative problem, where risking the bad side effect is unnecessary due to the availability of a safer alternative: turning the train onto the empty third track.

The complement to the necessity of the risk is the *gratuitousness of the risk:* the probability that the agent's purpose *would* be achieved without the risk to the principal object, or, in other words, that the risk to the principal object is useless or unnecessary. A completely gratuitous risk is one in which the necessity of the risk is 0 and the gratuitousness of the risk is 1; conversely, a completely necessary risk is one in which the gratuitousness of the risk is 0 and the necessity of the risk is 1. More generally, the gratuitousness of the risk, R_G, can be given by the formula, $1 - R_N$. Likewise, the necessity of the risk can be given by the formula, $1 - R_G$.

By substituting $(1 - R_G)$ for R_N in the Moral Calculus of Risk and by performing some simple algebra, a marginal version of the same formula can be stated as follows:

Marginal Calculus of Risk

$$(R_M) (V_P) > (V_C) (R_U) - (V_C) (R_U) (R_G)$$

What the Marginal Calculus of Risk makes transparent, which both the Hand Formula and, to a lesser extent, the Moral Calculus of Risk tend to obscure, is that a narrow calculation of the expected benefit of the agent's conduct, the value of the collateral object multiplied by the probability of success, is not the correct measure against which to compare the expected cost to the potential victim. Rather, what matters is the expected benefit of the *necessary risk,* that is, the difference between the expected benefit of the agent's conduct *with* the unnecessary risk and the expected benefit of the agent's conduct *without* the unnecessary risk. What matters, in other words, is how much the unavoidable risk of harm to the potential victim increased the likelihood that the actor's goal would be achieved. (The actor does not get credit, as it were, for the avoidable risk.) To make this calculation, one must first discount the expected benefit of the agent's conduct by its gratuitous risk, and then subtract the resulting value from the expected benefit, narrowly construed.

For ease of reference, in what follows I will refer to the value of the agent's expected benefit when it is discounted by its gratuitous risk, which can be given by either "$(R_U) (V_C) (R_N)$" or "$(V_C) (R_U) - (V_C) (R_U) (R_G)$," as the agent's *discounted expected benefit.* I will refer to the agent's expected benefit when this value includes its unnecessary risk, which is given by "$(V_C) (R_U)$," as the agent's *simple expected benefit.* Finally, I will refer to the likely harm to the injured victim resulting from the agent's conduct, which is given by "$(R_M) (V_P)$," as the *expected cost* of the agent's conduct.

With this terminology, we can now clarify an important aspect of the simple model of moral grammar outlined in this chapter and prior publications
(e.g., Mikhail 2007a), which is that it generally assumes that the magnitude,
utility, and necessity of the risk are to be given a value of 1, rather than some
other, more realistic value. That is, our model assumes that when ordinary
individuals evaluate the trolley problems, they accept the stipulation that certain actions "will" have certain effects without discounting those effects by
their intuitive probability.

Clearly this assumption is unrealistic. There is good reason to think that
people might be discounting the stipulated outcomes by their relative likelihood. For example, they might assign a relatively low utility of the risk to
throwing the man in the Footbridge problem, but a relatively high utility of the
risk to throwing the switch in the Bystander problem. If this is correct, then the
perceived wrongfulness of the former could be the result of two independent
yet interacting factors, using battery as a means and doing something whose
expected cost exceeds its discounted expected benefit, neither of which is operative in the Bystander problem. Indeed, it seems entirely possible to explain
the Footbridge problem data on cost-benefit grounds alone. Holding all other
factors constant, one need only postulate that people intuitively recognize that
the utility of the risk of throwing the man is less than 0.2, or, put differently,
that there is a less than one in five chance that this action will manage to prevent the train from killing the men. In that case, expected costs would exceed
discounted expected benefits, and the conduct would be unjustifiable on that
basis alone. By contrast, the intuitive mechanics of the Bystander problem are
different: there is no apparent basis for doubting that the utility of the risk of
turning the train to the side track is 1 (or nearly so). Nor is there any reason to
doubt that the necessity of the risk is also 1 (or nearly so), as long as the stipulation that this situation is unavoidably harmful, with no latent possibility of
preventing harm to all parties involved, is deemed to be credible. Hence, the
discounted expected benefit in this case is equivalent to simple expected benefit, which itself equals the value of the five lives that are saved.

The same logic can be applied to other familiar thought experiments. In the
Transplant problem, for instance, in which five patients are dying of organ failure, but a doctor can save all five if she removes the organs from a sixth patient
and gives them to the other five (Foot 1967), the utility of the risk might not
be 1, but something much less than 1. Transplant surgery, after all, is a complicated business. Things can go wrong. It is also *expensive*. So, unlike the Trolley
or Bystander problems with which it is usually compared, the discounted
expected benefit of this arduous and expensive set of operations might be considerably less than it first appears. It is conceivable, although perhaps unlikely,
that individuals perceive the expected costs of these operations to exceed their
discounted expected benefits, and make their judgments accordingly.

Could all of the familiar trolley problem data be explained in terms of a
sophisticated cost-benefit analysis, and are the complex structural descriptions

we have proposed therefore unnecessary? Several factors weigh against this possibility. First, simple linguistic experiments, such as the "by" and "in order to" tests, support the hypothesis that people spontaneously compute structural descriptions of these problems that incorporate properties like ends, means, side effects, and prima facie wrongs, such as battery (Mikhail 2007a). Moreover, this hypothesis is corroborated by the finding that even young children distinguish genuine moral violations, such as battery, from violations of social conventions (Smetana 1983; Turiel 1983; cf. Nichols 2004) and that even infants are predisposed to interpret the acts of moral agents in terms of their goals and intentions (Gergely & Csibra 2003; Hamlin, Wynn, & Bloom 2007; Johnson 2000; Meltzoff 1995; Woodward, Sommerville, & Guajardo 2001). It is also reinforced by a variety of recent studies at the interface of moral cognition and theory of mind (e.g., Knobe 2005; Sinnott-Armstrong et al. 2008; Wellman & Miller 2008; Young & Saxe 2008). So there appears to be substantial independent evidence supporting this aspect of the moral grammar hypothesis.

Second, although we have identified a potentially important confound in the Footbridge and Bystander problems, one should not assume that it operates in all of the cases in Table 5.1. For example, while one might be tempted to attribute the data in Figure 6.1(a) to different utilities of the risk – it is easier to stop an onrushing train with a heavy object, such as a brick wall (Man-in-Front), than with a man (Loop Track), after all, just as one is more likely to do so with a bridge (Collapse Bridge) than with a man (Drop Man) – not all of the variance in these six cases can be explained in this manner. Whatever its value, the utility of the risk of moving a man in the path of a train, for instance, is presumably equivalent in the Footbridge and Drop Man problems. Hence the variance in these cases must be due to some other factor, which repeated applications of the battery prohibition can explain (see Figure 6.1[b]).

Third, the structural descriptions we have proposed for the Transplant, Footbridge, Loop Track, and Drop Man problems share a single, crucial property: in each case an agent's good end cannot be achieved without committing battery as a means to this objective (Mikhail 2007a). It seems both implausible and unparsimonious to deny that this property enters into the relevant computations, particularly since it presumably operates in countless instances of ordinary battery, that is, run-of-the-mill cases that do not involve any possible justification of necessity.

Finally, while it seems reasonable to assume that individuals perceive the utility of the risk in the Transplant problem to be considerably less than 1, it also seems plausible to infer that the utility of this risk is perceived to be considerably greater than that of the structurally similar Footbridge problem. Successful transplants, after all, are much more probable than using a man to stop or slow down an onrushing train. Yet roughly the same proportion of individuals (around 90 percent) judges these actions to be impermissible

(Mikhail 2007a). While this does not necessarily imply that these actions are held to be morally equivalent – the Footbridge problem, for example, could be held to involve reckless behavior in a way that the Transplant problem does not – it does suggest that the Moral Calculus of Risk may play a subordinate operative role in these problems, whereas a more dominant role is played by the prohibition of purposeful battery.

The precise role of the Moral Calculus of Risk in intuitive moral judgments and its relation to other moral principles is obviously an important topic, which requires careful and thorough investigation that goes beyond the scope of this chapter. We will return to it briefly in Sections 6.3.5, 6.3.6, and 6.4. Here I will simply make the following clarifications, as a way of summarizing the foregoing remarks and anticipating that subsequent discussion. In our model, we generally make the simplifying assumption that the magnitude, utility, and necessity of the risk in the 12 cases in Table 5.1 are to be given a value of 1, rather than another more realistic value. The lone exception is the Better Alternative problem, for which the perceived necessity of the risk of throwing the switch is assumed to be 0, and thus the discounted expected benefit is also held to be 0. In the other 11 cases, we assume that the necessity of the risk is 1; hence, in these cases, the discounted expected benefit is assumed to be equivalent to the simple expected benefit.

6.3.5 The Rescue Principle

The Rescue Principle is a familiar precept of common morality – but not the common law –that has been defended by many writers, including Bentham (1948/1789), Scanlon (1998), Singer (1972), Unger (1996), and Weinrib (1980). Briefly, it holds that failing to prevent a preventable death or other grave misfortune is prohibited, where this can be achieved without risking one's own life or safety, or without violating other more fundamental precepts. It may be presumed to contain a *ceteris paribus* clause, the precise details of which need not detain us here.

The central element of the Rescue Principle in its core application is simple and intuitive: *Failing to rescue a person in grave danger is forbidden.* In this section, I briefly describe how this principle can be explicated merely by concatenating elements we have already defined.

First, we need a formula to represent an omission or "negative act" (Bentham 1948/1789: 72). To do this, we place the negation symbol in front of a complex act-token representation, thus taking the *normal form* of a *complex omission-token representation* to be given in (10):

(10) $\sim[S\text{'s V-ing at } t^{(a)}]^C$

As before, we assume that any expression obtainable by substituting permissibly for the individual variables in the normal form of a complex omission-token representation is also a complex omission-token representation. For example, '~[Hank's throwing the switch at $t^{(a)}]^{C}$' symbolizes an omission, which can be paraphrased as "Hank's neglecting to throw the switch at time t in circumstances C," "Hank's not throwing the switch at time t in circumstances C," "It is not the case that Hank throws the switch at time t in circumstances C," and so forth.

Second, to interpret this formula, we adopt the standard convention of using brackets to restrict the scope of the negation symbol. Thus, '[~[Hank's throwing the switch at $t^{(a)}]^{C}$ has features $F_1 \ldots F_n$]' is a statement that refers to an omission and affirms that it has certain features. By contrast, '~[[Hank's throwing the switch at $t^{(a)}]^{C}$ has features $F_1 \ldots F_n$]' does not refer to an omission; rather, it is the negation of a statement that affirms that a complex-act-token representation has certain features. It can be paraphrased as "It is not the case that Hank's throwing the switch at time t in circumstances C has features $F_1 \ldots F_n$," or "Hank's throwing the switch at time t in circumstances C does not have features $F_1 \ldots F_n$."

By relying on our formula for omission, together with the other concepts we have already explicated, we can now individuate 12 different purposely harmful acts and omissions and 12 different knowingly harmful acts and omissions, each of which can be formally described using the resources of our model. These 24 expressions are listed in Table 6.1, where they are divided into four groups: (i) purposely harmful acts, (ii) purposely harmful omissions, (iii) knowingly harmful acts, and (iv) knowingly harmful omissions.

With the aid of the expressions in Table 6.1, one can consider various formulations of the Rescue Principle and ascertain which, if any, are descriptively adequate. I will not pursue this inquiry here, beyond making the following general observations. First, while a simple rescue principle that forbids *any* knowingly harmful omission is capable of explaining the intuition that Paul has a duty to throw the switch in the Costless Rescue problem, it clearly conflicts with all those cases in Table 5.1 in which harmful omissions are held to be permissible. Likewise, a simple rescue principle that forbids any act of (i) letting die, (ii) failing to prevent bodily harm to a person, or (iii) failing to prevent the destruction of a valuable object can also be shown to be inadequate. The first conflicts with the Footbridge problem (among others), while the second and third can easily be falsified by designing two new problems in which killing five persons is set against preventing bodily harm to one person and destroying a valuable object, respectively. Among other things, this implies that an adequate rescue principle must be a *comparative* rather than a *noncomparative* principle, which compares an act or omission with its alternatives (Lyons 1965; Mikhail 2002a). It further suggests, although it does not entail, that an adequate rescue principle must occupy a subordinate position in a "lexically ordered" scheme of principles, in which at least some negative duties to avoid harm are ranked higher than at least some positive duties to

TABLE 6.1. *Purposely and Knowingly Harmful Acts and Omissions*

Purposely Harmful Acts

[S's V-ing at $t^{(\alpha)}]^C$ *I-generates* [S's committing homicide at $t^{(\beta)}$]

[S's V-ing at $t^{(\alpha)}]^C$ *I-generates* [S's committing battery at $t^{(\beta)}$]

[S's V-ing at $t^{(\alpha)}]^C$ *I-generates* [S's U-ing at $t^{(\beta)}$ [BAD EFFECT]]

[S's V-ing at $t^{(\alpha)}]^C$ *I-generates* [S's U-ing at $t^{(\beta)}$ [EFFECT (Person, Death)]]

[S's V-ing at $t^{(\alpha)}]^C$ *I-generates* [S's U-ing at $t^{(\beta)}$ [EFFECT (Person, Harm$_{-B}$)]]

[S's V-ing at $t^{(\alpha)}]^C$ *I-generates* [S's U-ing at $t^{(\beta)}$ [EFFECT (Thing$_{-V}$, Destroy)]]

Purposely Harmful Omissions

~[S's V-ing at $t^{(\alpha)}]^C$ *I-generates* [S's committing homicide at $t^{(\beta)}$]

~[S's V-ing at $t^{(\alpha)}]^C$ *I-generates* [S's committing battery at $t^{(\beta)}$]

~[S's V-ing at $t^{(\alpha)}]^C$ *I-generates* [S's U-ing at $t^{(\beta)}$ [BAD EFFECT]]

~[S's V-ing at $t^{(\alpha)}]^C$ *I-generates* [S's U-ing at $t^{(\beta)}$ [EFFECT (Person, Death)]]

~[S's V-ing at $t^{(\alpha)}]^C$ *I-generates* [S's U-ing at $t^{(\beta)}$ [EFFECT (Person, Harm$_{-B}$)]]

~[S's V-ing at $t^{(\alpha)}]^C$ *I-generates* [S's U-ing at $t^{(\beta)}$ [EFFECT (Thing$_{-V}$, Destroy)]]

Knowingly Harmful Acts

[S's V-ing at $t^{(\alpha)}]^C$ *K-generates* [S's committing homicide at $t^{(\beta)}$]

[S's V-ing at $t^{(\alpha)}]^C$ *K-generates* [S's committing battery at $t^{(\beta)}$]

[S's V-ing at $t^{(\alpha)}]^C$ *K-generates* [S's U-ing at $t^{(\beta)}$ [BAD EFFECT]]

[S's V-ing at $t^{(\alpha)}]^C$ *K-generates* [S's U-ing at $t^{(\beta)}$ [EFFECT (Person, Death)]]

[S's V-ing at $t^{(\alpha)}]^C$ *K-generates* [S's U-ing at $t^{(\beta)}$ [EFFECT (Person, Harm$_{-B}$)]]

[S's V-ing at $t^{(\alpha)}]^C$ *K-generates* [S's U-ing at $t^{(\beta)}$ [EFFECT (Thing$_{-V}$, Destroy)]]

Knowingly Harmful Omissions

~[S's V-ing at $t^{(\alpha)}]^C$ *K-generates* [S's committing homicide at $t^{(\beta)}$]

~[S's V-ing at $t^{(\alpha)}]^C$ *K-generates* [S's committing battery at $t^{(\beta)}$]

~[S's V-ing at $t^{(\alpha)}]^C$ *K-generates* [S's U-ing at $t^{(\beta)}$ [BAD EFFECT]]

~[S's V-ing at $t^{(\alpha)}]^C$ *K-generates* [S's U-ing at $t^{(\beta)}$ [EFFECT (Person, Death)]]

~[S's V-ing at $t^{(\alpha)}]^C$ *K-generates* [S's U-ing at $t^{(\beta)}$ [EFFECT (Person, Harm$_{-B}$)]]

~[S's V-ing at $t^{(\alpha)}]^C$ *K-generates* [S's U-ing at $t^{(\beta)}$ [EFFECT (Thing$_{-V}$, Destroy)]]

prevent harm (Rawls 1971: 40–45; cf. Foot 1967; Russell 1977).[7] In particular, on the basis of the Footbridge, Intentional Homicide, Loop Track, and Drop Man problems, one may infer that purposeful homicide and, at a minimum, purposeful battery that results in knowing homicide, are each lexically prior to the Rescue Principle – at least in circumstances other than a potential catastrophe or "supreme emergency" (Rawls 1999b; Walzer 1977; cf. Nichols & Mallon 2006).

Determining the precise nature of a descriptively adequate rescue principle is beyond the scope of this chapter. Instead, we merely state the following relatively simple yet demanding version of the principle as it relates the death

---

[7] A lexical order is not entailed because, as Rawls (1971: 40–45) observes, there are other ways to solve the priority problem.

of a person, which appears to be consistent with the data in Table 5.2, along with some further natural extensions:

Rescue Principle (provisional version, applied to least harmful alternative)

~[S's V-ing at $t^{(\alpha)}]^C$ *K-generates* [S's U-ing at $t^{(\beta)}$ [EFFECT [neg [neg [(Person, Death)]]]]] ⊃ ([~[S's V-ing at $t^{(\alpha)}]^C$ is forbidden] ≡

(a) ~[[S's V-ing at $t^{(\alpha)}]^C$ *I-generates* [S's committing homicide at $t^{(\beta)}$]]
(b) ~[[S's V-ing at $t^{(\alpha)}]^C$ *I-generates* [S's committing battery at $t^{(\beta)}$]]
(c) ~[[S's V-ing at $t^{(\alpha)}]^C$ *K-generates* [S's U-ing at $t^{(\beta)}$ [BAD EFFECT]] $<_m$ [S's V-ing at $t^{(\alpha)}]^C$ *K-generates* [S's U-ing at $t^{(\beta)}$ [EFFECT [neg [BAD EFFECT]]]]])

Several aspects of this provisional formula merit attention. First, the principle is formulated as a comparative rather than a noncomparative principle; specifically, it compares one type of knowingly harmful omission with its least harmful alternative, the precisely relevant act-token being omitted under the circumstances, and it forbids the former just in case the latter does not possess certain features. Second, the principle holds that an omission that K-generates the double negation of the death of a person is forbidden just in case its least harmful alternative neither (a) I-generates homicide, (b) I-generates battery, nor (c) K-generates bad effects that are morally worse than the negation (i.e., prevention) of the bad effects that it K-generates. This sounds exceedingly complex, but in plain English it simply means that the only justifications for knowingly letting a person die in our simple model are that doing so constitutes purposeful homicide, purposeful battery, or knowing homicide whose (discounted) expected benefits do not exceed its expected costs. More simply, preventing death is obligatory in our model unless doing so requires purposeful homicide, purposeful battery, or unjustified costs. The principle thus explains the Costless Rescue problem, yet it is also consistent with the other eleven problems in Table 5.1. Third, the principle is limited to the *knowingly* harmful omission of letting die. While one could expand the principle to include *purposely* harmful omissions, such as the deliberate letting die that Rachels (1975) depicts in the second of his famous Bathtub examples, in which a man purposely refrains from saving his drowning cousin in order to receive a large inheritance, this is unnecessary for our purposes: in light of our theory of how intentional structure is computed (Section 6.5.4), we may safely assume that none of the omissions in Table 5.1 is represented as purposely harmful (with the possible exception of the Intentional Homicide problem, where the actor's bad intent conflicts with a default rule of good intentions that we assume operates in this context; see Section 6.5.4). Fourth, the principle implies that pursuing the greater good in the Bystander, Implied Consent, Man-in-Front, and Drop Man problems is not only permissible, but obligatory, a strong assumption that is consistent with, but goes beyond, the data in Table 5.2. A weaker explanation might seek to accommodate a principle of pacifism, according to which knowing homicide is never obligatory, at least in the type of circumstances at issue here (cf. Thomson 1985: 280).

Fifth, the principle incorporates the assumptions we made in Section 6.3.4 about the magnitude, utility, and necessity of the risk. Condition (c) merely specifies the Moral Calculus of the Risk under those assumptions, as does restricting the scope of the principle to the least harmful alternative. We return to the significance of this restriction in Section 6.3.6. Sixth, the fact that condition (b) is given as purposeful battery, rather than purposeful battery that results in knowing homicide, reflects the stronger of two possible explanations from a deontological perspective of what constitutes an independent and adequate ground for precluding a duty to rescue that is consistent with the data in Table 5.2. A weaker assumption would appeal to purposeful battery that results in knowing homicide as the operative analysis of the Footbridge, Loop Track, and Drop Man problems. Finally, the presence of conditions (a) and (b) in the principle reflects the presumed lexical priority in common morality of at least some negative duties to avoid harm over some positive duties to prevent harm, and the possibility of justifying breaches of the latter, but not the former, by the Moral Calculus of Risk. Put differently, the Rescue Principle as it is formulated here is both consistent with and closely related to the Principle of Double Effect, a topic to which we now turn.

6.3.6 The Principle of Double Effect

The Principle of Double Effect (PDE) is a complex principle of justification, which is narrower in scope than the traditional necessity defense because it places limits on what might otherwise be justified on grounds of necessity. Historically the principle traces to Aquinas' attempt to reconcile the prohibition of intentional killing with the right to kill in self-defense. Denying any contradiction, Aquinas observed: "One act may have two effects only one of which is intended and the other outside of our intention" (1988/1274: 70). On Aquinas' view, the right to kill in self-defense is thus apparently limited to cases in which death is a side effect of defending oneself against attack. It does not apply when the attacker's death is directly intended.

Our question here is not whether the PDE is a sound principle of normative ethics, but whether it is descriptively adequate, or at least captures the implicit logic of common moral intuitions to a useful first approximation (cf. Harman 1977; Nagel 1986). In other words, our practical concern is whether the PDE can be strategically utilized to identify elements of moral grammar and other building blocks of intuitive jurisprudence. Likewise, because our main objective is to construct a computational theory of moral cognition along the lines of Marr's (1982) first level, we are not concerned here with how the PDE or whatever mental operations it implies are actually implemented in our psychology, nor with whether those operations are modular in Fodor's (1983) sense, or otherwise informationally encapsulated (for some interesting discussion of these topics, see, e.g., Dupoux & Jacob 2007; Greene 2008b; Hauser, Cushman, & Young 2008a, 2008b; Mallon 2008; Nichols 2005; Patterson 2008; Prinz 2008a, 2008b; Sripada 2008a, 2008b; Stich 2006). We merely assume that they are implemented in some manner or other, and that our analysis will help guide the search for underlying mechanisms, much as the theory of linguistic and visual perception has improved our grasp of the cognitive architecture and underlying mechanisms in these domains.

Many different versions of the PDE exist in the literature (see, e.g., Woodward 2001; cf. Mikhail 2000: 160–161). According to the version we will develop here, the principle holds that an otherwise prohibited action, such as battery or homicide, which has both good and bad effects may be permissible if the prohibited act itself is not directly intended, the good but not the bad effects are directly intended, the good effects outweigh the bad effects, and no morally preferable alternative is available. In this section, we briefly describe how this principle can be rendered in a format suitable for premises of a derivation. Moreover, as we did with the Rescue Principle, we explain how this can be accomplished merely by concatenating elements we have already defined. In this manner, we show how what appears on the surface to be a rather complex moral principle can be broken down into its relatively simple psychological constituents.

At least six key terms in the PDE must be explained: (i) *otherwise prohibited action,* (ii) *directly intended,* (iii) *good effects,* (iv) *bad effects,* (v) *outweigh,* and (vi) *morally preferable alternative.* In our model, we interpret these concepts as follows.

First, we use the notions of I-generation, homicide, and battery to explicate the meanings of *otherwise prohibited action* and *directly intended.* While there are four prima facie wrongs in our simple model – purposeful homicide, purposeful battery, knowing homicide, and knowing battery – only the first two are directly intended under the meaning we assign them here, which equates "directly intended" with "I-generated." As a result, these two actions cannot be justified by PDE, as we interpret it here. By contrast, knowing homicide and knowing battery *can* in principle be justified by the PDE. Unless they are justified in this manner, however, knowing homicide and knowing battery are forbidden.[8] There is no circularity, therefore, in referring to them as "otherwise prohibited actions" that can be justified under certain limited circumstances.

---

[8] Because our model is concerned only with explicating the data in Table 5.2, we need not consider other possible justifications or excuses, such as self-defense, duress, or mental illness.

Formally, these four prima facie prohibitions can be stated as follows:

Prohibition of Purposeful Homicide

[S's V-ing at $t^{(\alpha)}]^C$ I-generates [S's committing homicide at $t^{(\beta)}] \supset [[$S's V-ing at $t^{(\alpha)}]^C$ is prohibited]

Prohibition of Purposeful Battery

[S's V-ing at $t^{(\alpha)}]^C$ I-generates [S's committing battery at $t(\beta)] \supset [[$S's V-ing at $t^{(\alpha)}]^C$ is prohibited]

Prohibition of Knowing Homicide

[S's V-ing at $t^{(\alpha)}]^C$ K-generates [S's committing homicide at $t^{(\beta)}] \supset [[$S's V-ing at $t^{(\alpha)}]^C$ is prohibited]

Prohibition of Knowing Battery

[S's V-ing at $t^{(\alpha)}]^C$ K-generates [S's committing battery at $t(\beta)] \supset [[$S's V-ing at $t^{(\alpha)}]^C$ is prohibited]

In these formulas, we use the predicate *prohibited,* rather than the predicate *forbidden,* to differentiate the function of these prima facie prohibitions in our model from those all-things-considered deontic rules that assign a status of forbidden to complex act-tokens, if they have certain features.

Second, the PDE requires that the good effects but not the bad effects must be directly intended. Because we equate the meaning of "directly intended" with "I-generated," and because we have already specified the only good and bad effects in our model, it is simple enough to combine these representations in a manner that explicates the meaning of this condition. Formally these two requirements can be rendered as follows:

Good Effects Directly Intended

[S's V-ing at $t^{(\alpha)}]^C$ I-generates [S's U-ing at $t^{(\beta)}$ [GOOD EFFECT]]

Bad Effects Not Directly Intended

~[[S's V-ing at $t^{(\alpha)}]^C$ I-generates [S's U-ing at $t^{(\beta)}$ [BAD EFFECT]]]

Third, the PDE requires that the good effects outweigh the bad effects. Because we have already stipulated that the only good effects in our model consist of the negation of a bad effect, and because we have already relied on the morally-worse-than relation to provide an ordinal ranking of bad effects, this condition can also be straightforwardly explained, at least insofar as we limit our attention to the 12 cases in Table 5.1. The key observation is that the good effects of an action can be said to outweigh its bad effects just in case the bad effects that the action *prevents* are morally worse than the bad effects that the action *causes*. Here it should be recalled that the only good effects in our simple model consist in the negation (or prevention) of certain specified bad effects (Section 6.3.4). Consequently, this condition can be formalized as follows:

Good Effects Outweigh Bad Effects (full version)

[[S's V-ing at $t^{(\alpha)}$]^C K-generates [S's U-ing at $t^{(\beta)}$ [BAD EFFECT]] $<_m$ [S's V-ing at $t^{(\alpha)}$]^C K-generates [S's U-ing at $t^{(\beta)}$ [EFFECT [neg [BAD EFFECT]]]]]

Good Effects Outweigh Bad Effects (abbreviated version)

[BAD EFFECT$_P$] $<_m$ [BAD EFFECT$_C$]

The first formula, which we already encountered in the Rescue Principle, holds that the bad effects K-generated by a complex act-token representation are morally worse than the negation of those bad effects that are also K-generated by that act-token representation. The second formula abbreviates and incorporates a new notation for stating the same proposition, using "BAD EFFECT$_P$" to refer to the bad effects an actor knowingly prevents and "BAD EFFECT$_C$" to refer to the bad effects that she knowingly causes. Because the second formula shifts our focus from the (good) effect that consists of the negation of a bad effect to the bad effect that an actor knowingly prevents, the two sides of the relation are exchanged (cf. Sections 6.3.4, 6.3.5).

Finally, the PDE demands that no morally preferable alternative be available. This is an important condition of the PDE that is often overlooked or ignored, causing the principle to seem unduly lax because it appears to justify knowingly harmful acts as long as their good effects outweigh their bad effects, without further qualification. Among other things, to understand this condition we need to know the meaning of "morally preferable" and "alternative." In our model, we explicate this condition as follows. First, we take the alternative to a given action to refer in the first place to *omission* rather than *inaction,* that is, to the failure to perform a specific act-token, rather than the failure to do anything at all (cf. Section 6.3.5). Second, we interpret the no-morally-preferable-alternative condition to require comparing a given action to its *least harmful* omission. In all but one of our examples, there is only one possible alternative to the given action, hence the least harmful omission is identical with failing to perform that action. In the Better Alternative problem, by contrast, there are two possible alternatives, only one of which is the least harmful. Third, to decide which of several possible omissions is least harmful, we fall back on two comparative measures we have already explicated: (i) the morally-worse-than relation and (ii) the Moral Calculus of Risk. Finally, to decide whether the least harmful omission is *morally preferable* to the given action, we rely not only on (i) and (ii), but also (iii) the presumed lexical priority of the prohibition of purposeful homicide to the prohibition of knowing homicide, and the presumed lexical priority of the prohibition of purposeful battery (or, alternatively, the prohibition of purposeful battery that results in knowing homicide) to the Rescue Principle (cf. Section 6.3.5). By drawing on (i)–(iii), the computations for deciding whether a morally preferable alternative exists can be made without introducing any new evaluative concepts into our model, which thus can be kept as parsimonious as possible.

Formally, the comparison-to-the-least-harmful-omission component of the no-morally-preferable-alternative condition can be rendered for our purposes as follows:

No Less Harmful Alternative (full version)

$\sim$[S's V-ing at $t(\alpha)$]^c K-generates [S's U-ing at $t(\beta)$ [BAD EFFECT$_{LHA}$]] $<_m$
[S's V-ing at $t(\alpha)$]^c K-generates [S's U-ing at $t(\beta)$ [BAD EFFECT]]]

No Less Harmful Alternative (abbreviated version)

[BAD EFFECT$_{LHA}$] $<_m$ [BAD EFFECT$_C$]

The first formula holds that the bad effect K-generated by the least harmful alternative to a complex act-token representation is morally worse than the bad effect K-generated by that act-token representation. In this formula, "BAD EFFECT$_{LHA}$" refers to the bad effect of the least harmful alternative (which must be calculated separately, of course, a task whose complexity grows with the increase of available alternatives and may become computationally intractable or inefficient beyond a certain point, one plausible source of so-called omission bias; cf. Baron & Ritov, in press). The second formula abbreviates the same proposition, again using "BAD EFFECT$_C$" to refer to the bad effects that are caused.

The PDE has been the subject of intense scrutiny in the literature in recent years. Nonetheless, this discussion has often obscured both its virtues and limitations, and the foregoing analysis indicates one reason why. Many writers have assumed that the "natural application" (Quinn 1993: 179) of the PDE is to state conditions under which actions are prohibited. This way of putting the matter seems potentially misleading. The PDE is not a direct test of whether an action is right or wrong; rather, its status is that of a second-order priority rule (Rawls 1971) or ordering principle (Donagan 1977) whose proper application is to state the only conditions under which otherwise prohibited actions are (or may be) permissible. Put differently, the principle's natural application is to serve as a principle of justification, which states necessary and sufficient conditions for a presumptively wrong action to be justified. As such, it constitutes a precise explication of yet another commonsense principle: *A knowingly harmful action that would otherwise be wrong may be justifiable, if but only if no better option exists.*

6.4 STRUCTURAL DESCRIPTIONS II: A PERIODIC TABLE
OF MORAL ELEMENTS

All of the foregoing definitions could presumably be improved, but they are satisfactory for our purposes. By utilizing these concepts, we can now construct a "periodic table" of moral elements, which identifies the key recurring properties of the structural descriptions elicited by the 12 cases in Table 5.1, and which can be used to explain their deontic status (Table 6.2).

Like any graphic device for displaying certain properties or relations, the layout of Table 6.2 is meant to provide a systematic arrangement of its essential information. Beginning at the top and working down, the table is divided into three main columns: Problem, Structural Features, and Deontic Status, respectively. Broadly speaking, this layout matches that of Tables 4.1, 5.2, and 5.3, as well as the other schemas and models we have previously used to develop the moral grammar hypothesis. The table's main value from this vantage point is the ability to predict the deontic status of a given act or omission based entirely on its structural features and those of its available alternatives. All of these features are included in the Structural Features column. From another perspective, the table can simply be viewed as an alternative method for exhibiting part of the structural description of a given action, for which act trees are also a useful method.[9]

The Structural Features column is itself divided into three groups. The first group includes three of the six purposely harmful features that can be I-generated in our model: homicide, battery, or a bad effect. The last of these, it will be recalled, is a broad category that can include either death of a person, bodily harm to a person, or destruction of a valuable thing (Section 6.3.4). For convenience, I have listed only the Bad Effect category itself in Table 6.2 (using "BE" to refer to this category), even though this results in some redundancy. A different table might list all six features, or perhaps only the three bad effects themselves (cf. Table 6.3). Because the notion of I-generation is meant to incorporate and replace what are commonly referred to as ends or means, these notions are included parenthetically in the heading of this first group of properties.

The second group of properties includes three of the six knowingly harmful features that can be K-generated in our model: homicide, battery, or a bad effect. Because the notion of K-generation is meant to incorporate and serve as a replacement for what are commonly referred to as side effects, this notion is included parenthetically in the heading of this group of properties. Finally, the third group includes the three remaining conditions of the PDE not already encompassed by the first group: (i) good effects are directly intended, (ii) good effects outweigh bad effects, and (iii) no less

---

[9] Note, however, that Table 6.2 conveys both more and less information than the act trees in Figures 5.5 and 6.1(b). The computations required by the PDE are exhibited, for example, but temporal information is not.

TABLE 6.2. *A Periodic Table of Moral Elements (Version 1)*

Problem	Structural Features									Deontic Status
	I-generates (End or Means)			K-generates (Side Effect)			Remaining Conditions of PDE			
	Homicide	Battery	BE	Homicide	Battery	BE	E/M = GE	$BE_P <_m BE_C$	$BE_{LHA} <_m BE_C$	
Bystander										
Act (throw switch)				X	X	X	X	X	X	Permissible
Omission				X	X	X	X			?
Footbridge										
Act (throw man)	X			X	X	X	X	X	X	Forbidden
Omission				X	X	X	X			*Obligatory*
Expensive Equipment										
Act (throw switch)				X	X	X	X			Forbidden
Omission						X	X	X	X	*Obligatory*
Implied Consent										
Act (throw man)					X	X	X	X	X	Permissible
Omission				X	X	X	X			?

Intentional Homicide

Act (throw switch)	X	X	X	X		X	X	Forbidden
Omission			X	X		X	X	*Obligatory*

Loop Track

Act (throw switch)		X	X	X	X	X	X	Forbidden
Omission			X	X	X	X		*Obligatory*

Man-in-Front

Act (throw switch)		X	X	X	X	X	X	Permissible
Omission			X	X	X	X		?

Costless Rescue

Act (throw switch)		X	X			X	X	Obligatory
Omission				X		X		*Forbidden*

Better Alternative

Act (throw switch)		X	X	X		X		Forbidden

(continued)

TABLE 6.2. (continued)

Problem	I-generates (End or Means)			K-generates (Side Effect)			E/M = GE	Remaining Conditions of PDE		Deontic Status
	Homicide	Battery	BE	Homicide	Battery	BE		$BE_p <_m BE_C$	$BE_{LHA} <_m BE_C$	
Alt.1 (pull cord)							X	X	X	*Obligatory*
Alt.2 (do nothing)				X	X	X	X			*Forbidden*
Disprop. Death										
Act (throw switch)				X	X	X	X			Forbidden
Omission				X	X	X	X		X	*Obligatory*
Drop Man										
Act (throw switch)		X		X	X	X	X	X	X	Forbidden
Omission				X	X	X	X	X		*Obligatory*
Collapse Bridge										
Act (throw switch)				X	X	X	X	X	X	Permissible
Omission				X	X	X	X			?

156

harmful alternative. Table 6.2 uses "E/M = GE" to label the first condition (where "E/M" is itself an abbreviation of "End or Means"), "$BE_P <_m BE_C$" to label the second condition, and "$BE_{LHA} <_m BE_C$" to label the third condition.

Each problem in Table 6.2 has two or more rows, one each for an act and its alternatives. Since 11 of our 12 cases afford only one alternative, the set of alternatives is generally listed as *omission*. The sole exception is the Better Alternative problem, whose alternatives are given as "Alt. 1" and Alt. 2" and listed in descending order from least to most harmful, in order to facilitate the required comparison with that act's least harmful alternative. While the prevalence of single-alternative acts in Table 6.2 might suggest otherwise, it is important to emphasize that trolley problems are exceptional in this regard. In most real-life situations, there are many alternatives to a given action (i.e., many possible omissions), and in these situations identifying the least harmful alternative will take on much greater importance than it does here, a point of considerable significance for civil litigation (see, e.g., Grady 1989).

The last column lists the deontic status of each act and omission. The judgments gleaned directly from experiments are given in normal type face, while those that were not, but which can be logically derived from them, are italicized. Because the principles of deontic logic imply that both the doing and the forbearing of a given action can be permissible without contradiction, but the same is not true of the other two deontic operators (Mikhail 2008b), one cannot simply infer the deontic status of omissions in the Bystander, Implied Consent, Man-in-Front, and Collapse Bridge problems. They are thus marked as open questions, which could of course be investigated empirically.

Turning to the table's individual cells, the presence or absence of an "X" in each cell indicates the presence or absence of a given feature. As indicated, the only case in which the first (I-generates homicide), third (I-generates bad effect), or seventh (good effects are directly intended) features are atypical is the Intentional Homicide problem. No other problem involves death or another bad effect as a means or an end. By contrast, the second feature (I-generates battery) is implicated in four cases, all of which are forbidden: namely, the Footbridge, Intentional Homicide, Loop Track, and Drop Man problems. Next, 11 structural descriptions include one or more knowingly harmful acts (K-generates homicide, battery, or bad effect). The only exception is the Costless Rescue problem. Likewise, 11 structural descriptions include one or more knowingly harmful omissions. The only exception is the Better Alternative problem.[10] Finally, the three residual conditions of the PDE are satisfied in eight cases. In four of these cases – the Bystander, Implied Consent, Man-in-Front, and Collapse Bridge problems – these

---

[10] Here one should recall that for the purposes of this study we have assumed that each I-generated homicide, battery, or bad effect is also K-generated (Section 6.2.2). Hence these cells are checked in both the first and second groups in the Intentional Homicide problem.

conditions can be invoked to explain why otherwise prohibited actions are held to be justified.

Table 6.2 is not the only way to exhibit structural features in a tabular format. Another instructive example is Table 6.3. On this layout, which closely resembles but in some ways improves upon the basic conceptual scheme of both the first and second Restatements of Torts and the Model Penal Code, structural features are divided into four groups: Homicide, Battery, Other Bad Effect, and Justification. The first three groups are each divided into two subgroups: Purpose and Knowledge. These labels replace their technical counterparts in Table 6.2, as do the three subgroups of the Justification category: Good, Useful, and Necessary.

Table 6.3 has several advantages over Table 6.2. As indicated, one advantage is that how structural features are now labeled largely comports with a common type of legal analysis. Moreover, the exceptions to this pattern tend to be virtues rather than vices. For example, Table 6.3 implies that one can commit battery by omission. This stipulation is potentially at odds with the first and second Restatements of Torts, which includes a voluntary act requirement for battery (cf. Section 6.3.2). Still, this layout enables us to exhibit certain priority rules that might otherwise go unnoticed, as I explain below. Likewise, Table 6.3 avoids relying on the intuitive but often misleading terms, "killing" and "letting die," while nonetheless identifying two distinct ways each of these acts can occur in our model, resulting in four different possibilities in all: purposely killing, knowingly killing, purposely letting die, and knowingly letting die. The table thus reinforces Thomson's (1985: 283–284) apt observation that "'kill' and 'let die' are too blunt to be useful tools" for solving the trolley problems, and that one therefore ought to look "within" these acts "for the ways in which the agents would be carrying them out."

A further advantage of Table 6.3 is that its justifications closely track the Moral Calculus of Risk (Section 6.3.4). As such, they largely reflect the commonsense analysis of unintentional harm that underlies the common law of negligence. Ordinarily, when a reasonable person seeks to justify a knowingly or foreseeably harmful or risky act, she asks the following questions: Is it good? (That is, is the act directed toward a good or worthwhile end?) Is it useful? (That is, does the act promote utility, insofar as the harm avoided outweighs the harm done?) Is it necessary? (That is, is there a less harmful alternative?) These questions not only capture the core residual features of the PDE; they also are basically utilitarian, much like the traditional necessity defense. This is to be expected, since the residual features of the PDE and the necessity defense are largely identical within the confines of our model. It is important to recognize, however, that neither the PDE nor the traditional necessity defense is utilitarian in the conventional sense; rather, each is a species of "negative utilitarianism" (Popper 1945; Smart 1958), which justifies the lesser of two evils, but not knowingly harming another individual simply because doing so maximizes aggregate welfare.

TABLE 6.3. *A Periodic Table of Moral Elements (Version 2)*

Problem	Structural Features									Deontic Status
	Homicide		Battery		Other Bad Effect		Justification			
	Purpose	Knowledge	Purpose	Knowledge	Purpose	Knowledge	Good	Useful	Necessary	
Bystander										
Act (throw switch)		X		X			X	X	X	Permissible
Omission		X		X			X			?
Footbridge										
Act (throw man)	X	X		X			X	X	X	Forbidden
Omission		X		X			X			*Obligatory*
Expensive Equipment										
Act (throw switch)		X		X			X			Forbidden
Omission						X	X	X	X	*Obligatory*
Implied Consent										
Act (throw man)		X		X			X	X	X	Permissible
Omission		X		X			X			?

(continued)

159

TABLE 6.3 (continued)

Problem	Structural Features									Deontic Status
	Homicide		Battery		Other Bad Effect		Justification			
	Purpose	Knowledge	Purpose	Knowledge	Purpose	Knowledge	Good	Useful	Necessary	
Intentional Homicide										
Act (throw switch)	X	X	X	X				X	X	Forbidden
Omission		X		X						*Obligatory*
Loop Track										
Act (throw switch)	X	X	X	X			X	X	X	Forbidden
Omission		X		X			X			*Obligatory*
Man-in-Front										
Act (throw switch)		X		X			X	X	X	Permissible
Omission		X		X			X			?
Costless Rescue										
Act (throw switch)							X	X	X	Obligatory
Omission		X		X						*Forbidden*
Better Alternative										
Act (throw switch)		X		X			X	X		Forbidden

Alt. 1 (pull cord)				X	X	X	*Obligatory*
Alt. 2 (do nothing)	X					X	*Forbidden*
Disprop. Death							
Act (throw switch)	X		X		X		Forbidden
Omission	X		X		X	X	*Obligatory*
Drop Man							
Act (throw switch)	X	X	X		X		Forbidden
Omission	X		X		X		*Obligatory*
Collapse Bridge							
Act (throw switch)	X		X		X	X	Permissible
Omission	X		X		X		?

Perhaps the biggest advantage of Table 6.3 is that it aligns structural features in a regular order that reflects the apparent lexical priority of some prohibitions over others in common morality. In particular, prohibited acts are prioritized over prohibited omissions, and purposeful harms are prioritized over knowing harms. In addition, homicides as a group are prioritized over batteries as a group, which in turn are prioritized over bad effects as a group. Further, unlike Table 6.2, the Bad Effect category in Table 6.3 is limited to the destruction of a valuable thing in order to avoid unnecessary overlap with those bad effects that are already implicit in the homicide (death of a person) and battery (bodily harm to a person) categories, respectively. The result is that each individual cell in Table 6.3 represents a prohibition that is presumably lexically prior (subsequent) to the cells to the right (left) of it. Likewise, with respect to act and omission, each cell represents a prohibition that is lexically prior (subsequent) to the one immediately below (above) it. Finally, this layout naturally suggests a series of novel experiments that can be used to test, refine, and, if necessary, revise these assumptions, while rounding out our analysis of the behavior of structural features by considering them in all logically possible permutations. In particular, a new set of probes can be designed that systematically manipulate as far as possible each of the 18 variables (9 columns × 2 rows) into which the Structural Features column is divided (see, e.g., Table 6.4). Together with sophisticated techniques for measuring neurological activity, reaction time, implicit bias, and other familiar psychological phenomena, these probes can be used to improve our understanding of moral competence beyond that which has been previously contemplated.[11] I will not pursue these lines of inquiry further here; instead, I simply identify them as objects of future research that grow directly out of the foregoing analysis.

6.5 CONVERSION RULES

As we have seen, for the PDE or another extensionally equivalent principle to be operative in moral cognition, the mind/brain must have the resources to compute representations of an agent's ends, means, side effects, and available alternatives. It also must incorporate a calculus of some sort capable of identifying, ranking, and computing the probabilities of an act's good and

[11] For example, some readers might wonder why all of our stimulus materials have thus far used only Anglophone male names. One objective of doing so is precisely to study the potential prejudicial effect of other names – and their associated sexual, racial, religious, or other identities – on intuitive moral judgment. Regrettably, it is not unreasonable to assume that "Helen," Isabel," "Karen," or "Lydia" will yield different data than "Hank," "Ian," "Karl," or "Luke" (or that both might yield different data than, e.g., "Fawzy," "Hussein," "Mourid," or "Naguib"). To understand this phenomena and thus integrate the theory of moral grammar with research on implicit bias (see, e.g., Banaji et al. 2007; Kang 2005), one must first establish a descriptive baseline from which comparisons can be made. I return to the distinction between considered judgments and prejudices in Section 8.3.

TABLE 6.4. *Manipulating Structural Features: Fourteen New Trolley Problems*[a]

1a. Bystander: Purposely Homicidal Omission (not throwing the switch, for purpose of letting die): Adam is taking his daily walk near the train tracks when he notices that the train that is approaching is out of control. Adam sees what has happened: the driver of the train saw five men walking across the tracks and slammed on the brakes, but the brakes failed and the driver fainted. The train is now rushing toward the five men. It is moving so fast that they will not be able to get off the track in time. Adam is standing next to a switch, which he can throw, that will turn the train onto a side track, thereby preventing it from killing the men. There is a man standing on the side track with his back turned. Adam can throw the switch, killing him; or he can refrain from doing this, letting the five die. *Adam then recognizes that the men walking across the tracks are individuals whom he hates with a passion and wants to see dead. "I don't give a damn [am indifferent/care deeply] about that guy on the side track," Adam thinks to himself, "but this is my chance to sit by and watch those bastards get killed."* Is it morally permissible [*obligatory*] for Adam to throw the switch?

1b. Bystander: Purposely Homicidal Act and Omission (throwing the switch for the purpose of killing; not throwing the switch, for the purpose of letting die): Bob is taking his daily walk near the train tracks when he notices that the train that is approaching is out of control. Bob sees what has happened: the driver of the train saw five men walking across the tracks and slammed on the brakes, but the brakes failed and the driver fainted. The train is now rushing toward the five men. It is moving so fast that they will not be able to get off the track in time. Bob is standing next to a switch, which he can throw, that will turn the train onto a side track, thereby preventing it from killing the men. There is a man standing on the side track with his back turned. Bob can throw the switch, killing him; or he can refrain from doing this, letting the five die. *Bob then recognizes that both the men walking across the tracks and the man on the side track are individuals whom he hates with a passion and wants to see dead. "Wow, this is my lucky day," Bob thinks to himself, "this is my chance either to kill that jerk on the side track or to sit by and watch those bastards get killed."* Is it morally permissible [*obligatory*] for Bob to throw the switch?

2a. Footbridge: Purposely Homicidal Act (throwing the man for the purpose of killing): Charles is taking his daily walk near the train tracks when he notices that the train that is approaching is out of control. Charles sees what has happened: the driver of the train saw five men walking across the tracks and slammed on the brakes, but the brakes failed and the driver fainted. The train is now rushing toward the five men. It is moving so fast that they will not be able to get off the track in time. Charles is standing next to a heavy object, which he can throw onto the track in the path of the train, thereby preventing it from killing the men. The heavy object is a man, standing next to Charles with his back turned. Charles can throw the man, killing him; or he can refrain from doing this, letting the five die. *Charles then recognizes that the man standing next to him is someone whom he hates with a passion and wants to see dead.*

(continued)

TABLE 6.4 *(continued)*

"I don't give a damn [am indifferent/care deeply] about saving those five men," Charles thinks to himself, *"but this is my chance to kill that bastard."* Is it morally permissible for Charles to throw the man?

2b. Footbridge: Purposely Homicidal Omission (not throwing the man, for the purpose of letting die): Donald is taking his daily walk near the train tracks when he notices that the train that is approaching is out of control. Donald sees what has happened: the driver of the train saw five men walking across the tracks and slammed on the brakes, but the brakes failed and the driver fainted. The train is now rushing toward the five men. It is moving so fast that they will not be able to get off the track in time. Donald is standing next to a heavy object, which he can throw onto the track in the path of the train, thereby preventing it from killing the men. The heavy object is a man, standing next to Donald with his back turned. Donald can throw the man, killing him; or he can refrain from doing this, letting the five die. *Donald then recognizes that the men walking across the tracks are individuals whom he hates with a passion and wants to see dead.* *"I don't give a damn [am indifferent/care deeply] about this guy next to me,"* Donald thinks to himself, *"but this is my chance to sit by and watch those bastards get killed."* Is it morally permissible [*obligatory*] for Donald to throw the man?

2c. Footbridge: Purposely Homicidal Act and Omission (throwing the man for the purpose of killing; not throwing the man, for the purpose of letting die): Edward is taking his daily walk near the train tracks when he notices that the train that is approaching is out of control. Edward sees what has happened: the driver of the train saw five men walking across the tracks and slammed on the brakes, but the brakes failed and the driver fainted. The train is now rushing toward the five men. It is moving so fast that they will not be able to get off the track in time. Edward is standing next to a heavy object, which he can throw onto the track in the path of the train, thereby preventing it from killing the men. The heavy object is a man, standing next to Edward with his back turned. Edward can throw the man, killing him; or he can refrain from doing this, letting the five die. *Edward then realizes that both the men walking across the tracks and the man standing next to him are individuals whom he hates with a passion and wants to see dead.* *"Wow, this is my lucky day,"* Edward thinks to himself, *"this is my chance either to kill this jerk standing next to me or to sit by and watch those bastards get killed."* Is it morally permissible [*obligatory*] for Edward to throw the man?

3a. Expensive Rescue (destroying an expensive thing as a side effect of saving life): Fred is taking his daily walk near the train tracks when he notices that the train that is approaching is out of control. Fred sees what has happened: the driver of the train saw *a man walking* across the tracks and slammed on the brakes, but the brakes failed and the driver fainted. The train is now rushing toward the *man*. It is moving so fast that *he* will *not be able to get off the track* *in time*. Fred is standing next to a switch, which he can throw, that will turn the train onto a side track, thereby preventing it from *killing the man*. There is *five million dollars of new railroad equipment* lying across the side track. Fred can throw the switch, *destroying the equipment;* or he can refrain from doing this, letting the *man die*. Is it morally permissible [*obligatory*] for Fred to throw the switch?

3b. Inexpensive Rescue (destroying an inexpensive thing as a side effect of saving life): George is taking his daily walk near the train tracks when he notices that the train that is approaching is out of control. George sees what has happened: the driver of the train saw *a man walking* across the tracks and slammed on the brakes, but the brakes failed and the driver fainted. The train is now rushing toward the *man*. It is moving so fast that *he* will *not be able to get off the track in time*. George is standing next to a switch, which he can throw, that will turn the train onto a side track, thereby preventing it from *killing the man*. There is *an old wagon worth about five hundred dollars* lying across the side track. George can throw the switch, *destroying the wagon;* or he can refrain from doing this, letting the *man die*. Is it morally permissible [*obligatory*] for George to throw the switch?

4a. Substituted Consent (harmful contact as a means of saving life; prevent suicide): Jack is taking his daily walk near the train tracks when he notices that the train that is approaching is out of control. Jack sees what has happened: the driver of the train saw a man walking across the tracks and slammed on the brakes, but the brakes failed and the driver fainted. The train is now rushing toward the man. It is moving so fast that he will not be able to get off the track in time. Jack is standing next to the man, whom he can throw off the track out of the path of the train, thereby preventing it from killing the man. The man is frail and standing with his back turned. *Jack believes he is trying to commit suicide by walking in front of the train.* Jack can throw the man, injuring him; or he can refrain from doing this, letting the man die. Is it morally permissible [*obligatory*] for Jack to throw the man?

4b. Hypothetical Consent (harmful contact as a means of saving life; remove obstruction): Quinn is taking his daily walk near the train tracks when he notices that the train that is approaching is out of control. Quinn sees what has happened: the driver of the train saw *five men* walking across the tracks and slammed on the brakes, but the brakes failed and the driver fainted. The train is now rushing toward the *men*. It is moving so fast that *they* will not be able to get off the track in time. Quinn is standing next to *a switch*, which he can throw, that will turn the train onto a side track, thereby preventing it from killing the *men*. There is a man standing *in front of the switch* with his back turned. *To reach the switch in time, Quinn will need to grab and throw the man out of the way, thereby injuring him.* Quinn can throw the man, injuring him, *and then throw the switch, saving the men;* or he can refrain from doing this, letting the five die. Is it morally permissible [*obligatory*] for Quinn to throw the man?

(continued)

TABLE 6.4 *(continued)*

8a. Suicidal Rescue (knowingly killing oneself as a side effect of saving life): Thomas is taking his daily walk near the train tracks when he notices that the train that is approaching is out of control. Thomas sees what has happened: he driver of the train saw five men walking across the tracks and slammed on the brakes, but the brakes failed and the driver fainted. The train is now rushing toward the five men. It is moving so fast that they will not be able to get off the track in time. Thomas is standing next to *the tracks and can throw himself in front of the train,* thereby preventing it from killing the men. *Doing so will put his own life at risk, however, and almost surely kill him.* Thomas can throw himself in front of the train, *killing himself,* but saving the five men; or he can refrain from doing this, letting the five die. Is it permissible [*obligatory*] for Thomas to throw *himself in front of the train?*

10a. Efficient Risk (destroying a valuable thing as a side effect of saving a more valuable thing): Upton is taking his daily walk near the train tracks when he notices that the train that is approaching is out of control. Upton sees what has happened: the driver of the train saw *five million dollars of new railroad equipment lying* across the tracks and slammed on the brakes, but the brakes failed and the driver fainted. The train is now rushing toward the *equipment.* It is moving so fast that *the equipment* will be *destroyed.* Upton is standing next to a switch, which he can throw, that will turn the train onto a side track, thereby preventing it from *destroying the equipment.* There is *an old wagon worth about one hundred dollars lying across* the side track. Upton can throw the switch, *destroying the wagon;* or he can refrain from doing this, letting *the equipment be destroyed.* Is it morally permissible [*obligatory*] for Upton to throw the switch?

10b. Inefficient Risk (destroying a valuable thing as a side effect of saving a less valuable thing): Xavier is taking his daily walk near the train tracks when he notices that the train that is approaching is out of control. Xavier sees what has happened: the driver of the train saw *an old wagon worth about five hundred dollars lying* across the tracks and slammed on the brakes, but the brakes failed and the driver fainted. The train is now rushing toward the *wagon.* It is moving so fast that *the wagon* will be *destroyed.* Xavier is standing next to a switch, which he can throw, that will turn the train onto a side track, thereby preventing it from *destroying the wagon.* There is *five million dollars of new railroad equipment lying across* the side track. Xavier can throw the switch, *destroying the equipment;* or he can refrain from doing this, letting *the wagon be destroyed.* Is it morally permissible for Xavier to throw the switch?

11a. Drop Equipment (destroying a valuable thing as a means of saving life): Yale is taking his daily walk near the train tracks when he notices that the train that is approaching is out of control. Yale sees what has happened: the driver of the train saw five men walking across the tracks and slammed on the brakes, but the brakes failed and the driver fainted. The train is now rushing toward the five men. It is moving so fast that they will not be able to get off the track in time. Yale is standing next to a switch, which he can throw, that will drop a heavy object into the path of the train, thereby preventing it from killing the men. The heavy object is *five million dollars of new railroad equipment, which* is standing on a footbridge overlooking the tracks. Yale can throw the switch, *destroying the equipment;* or he can refrain from doing this, letting the five die. Is it morally permissible [*obligatory*] for Yale to throw the switch?

12a. Collapse Bridge: Destroy Equipment (destroying a valuable thing as a side effect of saving life): Zach is taking his daily walk near the train tracks when he notices that the train that is approaching is out of control. Zach sees what has happened: the driver of the train saw five men walking across the tracks and slammed on the brakes, but the brakes failed and the driver fainted. The train is now rushing toward the five men. It is moving so fast that they will not be able to get off the track in time. Zach is standing next to a switch, which he can throw, that will collapse a footbridge overlooking the tracks into the path of the train, thereby preventing it from killing the men. There is *five million dollars of new railroad equipment* standing on the footbridge. Zach can throw the switch, *destroying the bridge and equipment;* or he can refrain from doing this, letting the five die. Is it morally permissible [*obligatory*] for Zach to throw the switch?

---

a Italics in Table 6.4 identify salient differences between the given problem and its correspondingly numbered problem in Table 5.1. The bracketed terms suggest alternative formulations of the given scenario, the effects of which could be investigated experimentally.

bad effects. In *Rawls' Linguistic Analogy,* I sought to provide a basis for generating these representations by formalizing five commonsense moral postulates: (i) the death of a person is bad, (ii) preventing a bad effect is good, (iii) failing to prevent a bad effect is bad, (iv) good is to be done and pursued, and evil avoided, and (v) from a moral point of view, the life of one person is worth the same as that of another (Mikhail 2000: 163–169). Nevertheless, I did not provide complete account of the relevant conversion rules. Such an account is needed, however, because a key theoretical question implied by the moral grammar hypothesis is how the brain manages to compute a full structural description that incorporates properties like ends, means, side effects, and prima facie wrongs, such as battery, even when the stimulus contains no direct evidence for these properties.

As Figure 6.2(a) implies, this problem may be divided into at least five parts. To compute an accurate structural description of a given act and its alternatives, the systems that support moral cognition must generate complex representations that encode pertinent information about their temporal, causal, moral, intentional, and deontic properties. An interesting question

(a) Conversion Rules

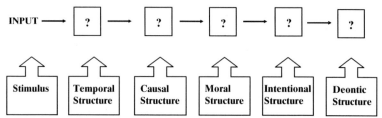

(b) Stimulus

Hank is taking his daily walk over the train tracks when he notices that the train that is approaching is out of control. Hank sees what has happened: the driver of the train saw five men walking across the tracks and slammed on the brakes, but the brakes failed and the driver fainted. The train is now rushing toward the five men. It is moving so fast that they will not be able to get off the track in time. Hank is standing next to a switch, which he can throw, that will turn the train onto a side track, thereby preventing it from killing the men. There is a man standing on the side track with his back turned. Hank can throw the switch, killing him; or he can refrain from doing this, letting the five die. Is it morally permissible for Hank to throw the switch?

(c) Temporal Structure

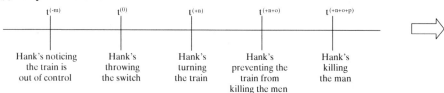

(d) Causal Structure

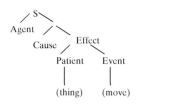

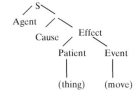

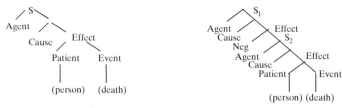

FIGURE 6.2. Computing Structural Descriptions

Semantic structure of "Hank let the men die"

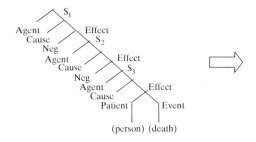

Causal chain generated by not throwing switch in *Bystander*

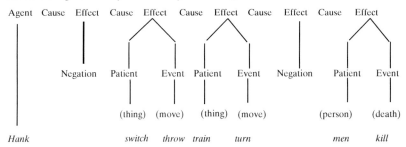

First causal chain generated by throwing switch in *Bystander*

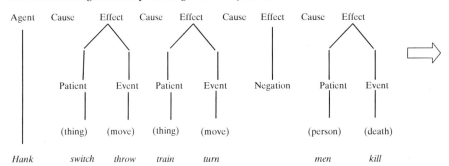

Second causal chain generated by throwing switch in *Bystander*

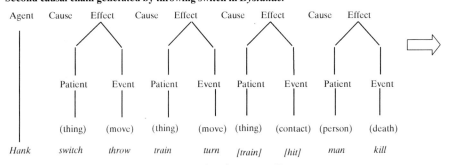

FIGURE 6.2 (*continued*)

(e) Moral Structure

Moral transformation of "Hank killed the man"

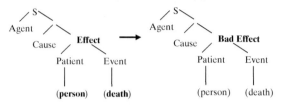

Moral transformation of "Hank prevented the train from killing the men"

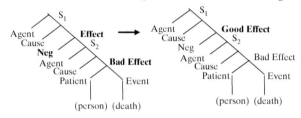

Moral transformation of "Hank let the men die"

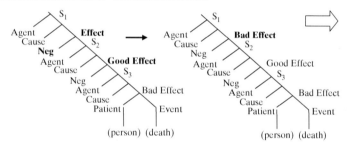

(f) Intentional Structure

Computing intentional structure of act with good and bad effects

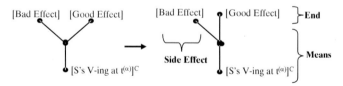

Computing intentional structure in trolley problems

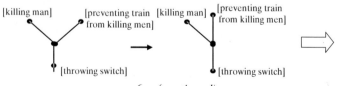

FIGURE 6.2 *(continued)*

(g) Deontic Structure

Partial derivation of representation of battery in *Footbridge*

1. [Ian's throwing the man at $t^{(0)}$]^C	
2. [Ian's throwing the man at $t^{(0)}$]	Given
3. [Ian throws the man at $t^{(0)}$]	2; Linguistic Transformation
4. [Ian throws the man at $t^{(0)}$] ⊃ [Ian touches the man at $t^{(0)}$]	Analytic
5. [Ian touches the man at $t^{(0)}$]	3, 4; Modus Ponens
6. [The man has not expressly consented to be touched at $t^{(0)}$]	Given
7. [The man has not implicitly consented to be touched at $t^{(0)}$]	Given; Abductive inference
8. [Ian throws the man at $t^{(0)}$] ⊃ [Ian kills the man at $t^{(+n)}$]	Given
9. [[Ian throws the man at $t^{(0)}$] ⊃ [Ian kills the man at $t^{(+n)}$]] ⊃ [the man would not consent to being touched at $t^{(0)}$, if asked]	Self-Preservation Principle
10. [the man would not consent to be touched at $t^{(0)}$, if asked]	8, 9; Modus Ponens
11. [Ian touches the man without his express, implied, or hypothetical consent at $t^{(0)}$]	5, 6, 7, 10
12. [Ian touches the man without his express, implied, or hypothetical consent at $t^{(0)}$] ⊃ [Ian commits battery at $t^{(0)}$]	Definition of battery
13. [Ian commits battery at $t^{(0)}$]	11, 12; Modus Ponens
14. **[Ian's committing battery at $t^{(0)}$]**	Linguistic Transformation

FIGURE 6.2 (*continued*)

is whether these computations must be performed in any particular order. Offhand, it might seem that the order is irrelevant; however, this impression appears to be mistaken. In fact, it seems that these computations must be performed in the order depicted in Figure 6.2(a), at least in our 12 cases, because to recognize the deontic structure of these actions, one must already grasp their intentional structure; to recognize their intentional structure, one must already grasp their moral structure; to recognize their moral structure, one must already grasp at least part of their causal structure; and finally, to recognize their full causal structure, one must already grasp their temporal structure. These assumptions reflect some classical philosophical ideas about the relevant mental operations. But how exactly does each individual manage to extract the relevant cues from an impoverished stimulus (Figure 6.2 [b]) and convert what is given into a full structural description? The process appears to include the following main steps.

6.5.1 Temporal Structure

First, the mind/brain must identify the relevant action-descriptions in the stimulus and order them serially according to their relative *temporal* properties (Figure 6.2 [c]). Presumably this task is accomplished by relying on auxiliary verbs ("can," "will," etc.) and other temporal clues in the stimulus, but I set aside for now a closer examination of these operations.

6.5.2 Causal Structure

Second, the mind/brain must identify the *causal* structure of the relevant action-descriptions by decomposing these causative constructions into their underlying semantic properties (Figure 6.2 [d]). In addition, presumably by relying on temporal information, it must compute the full causal structure of the relevant acts and omissions by combining these percepts into ordered sequences of causes and effects ("causal chains"), supplying missing information where necessary (cf. Kant 1965/1787). Figure 6.2 (d) illustrates the three chains at issue in the Bystander problem, linking (i) Hank's not throwing throw the switch to the effect of letting the men die, (ii) Hank's throwing the switch to the effect of preventing the train from killing the men, and (iii) Hank's throwing the switch to the effect of killing the man. In (iii), causing the train to hit the man is placed in brackets because this percept is not derived directly from the stimulus, but must be inferred from how objects interact with one another, presumably in accord with certain core knowledge of contact mechanics (Carey & Spelke 1994; Spelke, Breinlinger, & Jacobson 1992). In other words, the brackets identify one location in the causal chain where the mind/brain supplies the missing information that killing the man requires causing the train to come into contact with him.

6.5.3 Moral Structure

Third, the mind/brain must compute the *moral* structure of the relevant acts and omissions by applying the following rewrite rules to the causal structures in Figure 6.2 (d): (i) an effect that consists of the death of a person is bad, (ii) an effect that consists of the negation of a bad effect is good, and (iii) an effect that consists of the negation of a good effect is bad. As a result, these causal structures are transformed into richer representations that encode good and bad effects (Figure 6.2 [e]). Moreover, since the second and third operations can be attributed to simple logical reasoning, and the first can be attributed, at least indirectly, to an instinct for self-preservation – the same likely source as that of the Prohibition of Homicide (Section 6.3.2) and the Self-Preservation Principle (Section 6.3.3) – we presumably can explain this entire process merely by appealing to a common sociobiological instinct (cf. Darwin 1981/1871: 85–87; Hobbes 1968/1651: 189; Leibniz 1981/1705: 92; Proudhon 1994/1840: 170–174; Pufendorf 2003/1691: 53).

6.5.4 Intentional Structure

Fourth, the mind/brain must apply a presumption of good intentions, or what might be called a presumption of innocence, to the structures generated up to this point, thereby converting them into new structures that represent the *intentional* properties of the given action. That is, taking an act-token representation with both good and bad effects as a proximal input, one must (in the absence of countervailing evidence) generate its intentional structure by identifying the good effect as the *end* or *goal* and the bad effect as the *side effect* (cf. Section 6.2). This operation also can be represented graphically (Figure 6.2 [f]). Note that some procedure of this general type must be postulated to explain how the mind/brain computes ends, means, and side effects, since – crucially – there is no goal or mental state information in the stimulus itself. In Figure 6.2 (f), the presumption of good intentions acts as a default rule which says, in effect, that unless contrary evidence is given or implied, one should assume that S is a person of good will, who pursues good and avoids evil – another principle commonly held to be an innate instinct (see, e.g., Hume 1978/1740: 438; cf. Aquinas 1988/1274: 49; St. Germain 1874/1518: 39). By relying on this principle, one perhaps can explain how the mind/brain regularly computes representations of *mens rea,* even though goals and mental states are never directly observable.

6.5.5 Deontic Structure

Fifth, because the foregoing steps are necessary but not sufficient to explain the data in Table 5.2, the mind/brain must supply some additional structure to the foregoing representations. What additional structure is necessary? One key insight of the moral grammar hypothesis is that adequate structural descriptions must also incorporate prima facie legal wrongs, such as battery or homicide. For example, in the Footbridge problem one must derive a representation of battery by inferring that (i) the agent must *touch* and *move* the man in order to throw him onto the track in the path of the train, and (ii) the man would not *consent* to being touched or moved in this manner because of his desire for self-preservation (and because no contrary evidence is given). Utilizing standard notation in deductive logic (e.g., Leblanc & Wisdom 1993), this line of reasoning argument can be also formalized (Figure 6.2 [g]).

Furthermore, because merely recognizing that the 12 cases in Table 5.1 implicate the legal categories of battery and homicide does not yet enable us to explain the data in Table 5.2, these violations must also be situated in the correct location of their associated structural descriptions, thereby identifying whether they are a means, end, or side effect. Figure 6.3 illustrates the outcome of this process for the four cases that we encountered in Section 6.2.1 whose act-type descriptions are completely equivalent.

Finally, once accurate structural descriptions of a given act-token representation and its alternatives (or at least the least harmful alternative of this potentially infinite set) are generated, the correct deontic rules must be applied to these descriptions to yield a considered judgment. Moreover, as we have observed (Section 6.3.4), the magnitude, utility, and necessity of the risk, and the comparative moral worth of the principal and collateral objects, must also be calculated and incorporated into these evaluations. This chapter has avoided

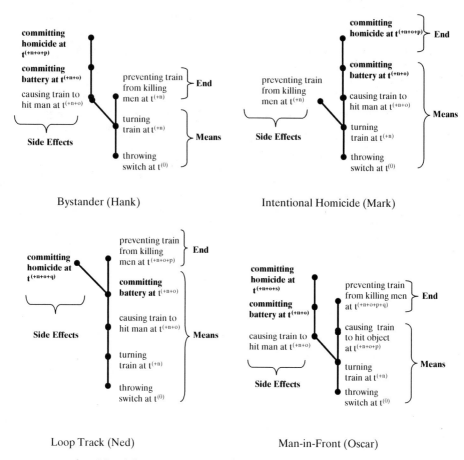

Bystander (Hank)　　　　　　　　　Intentional Homicide (Mark)

Loop Track (Ned)　　　　　　　　　Man-in-Front (Oscar)

FIGURE 6.3. Moral Geometry: Varying Structural Descriptions of Four Identical
Sets of Act-Type Descriptions

many of the complexities that arise in this context, but they must be squarely
confronted by any theory which purports to be descriptively adequate.

6.6 A BRIEF NOTE ON ENLIGHTENMENT RATIONALISM

One often hears that the Enlightenment project of justifying commonsense morality, by providing it with a rational foundation, is dead (see, e.g.,
MacIntyre 1981; Rorty 1992; Williams 1985). What exactly is meant by claims
like this is not altogether clear. In any event, it seems clear that by formalizing
the conversion rules we have identified, and by utilizing them together with (i)
a presumed set of linguistic transformation rules and (ii) a few other fundamental ordering principles (some of which are discussed below), the structural

descriptions exhibited in Tables 6.2 and 6.3 and Figures 5.5, 6.1 (b), and 6.3 can be mechanically generated. If so, then the problem of descriptive adequacy with which we began may be answered in purely computational terms, merely by applying the deontic rules we identified in Section 6.3 to these structural descriptions. In this sense, at least, the Enlightenment assumption that common moral knowledge "depends on demonstrations" (Leibniz 1996/1704: 92; cf. Locke 1991/1689: 549), would appear capable of being vindicated, as would Rawls' (1971: 46, 121, 126, 581) somewhat similar conception.

To put the matter in different and more general terms, by ascribing the moral knowledge outlined in this chapter to ordinary individuals, we can predict and explain their moral intuitions in a wide range of actual cases, including otherwise puzzling thought experiments like the trolley problems. Because this imputed knowledge is *intuitive* and not fully open to conscious introspection, we can also explain why few if any individuals appear capable of providing adequate justifications of their judgments, even though those judgments do, in fact, appear to depend on demonstrations. The explanation, simply put, is that moral judgment depends on *unconscious* demonstrations, that is, on mental computations that are not consciously accessible. In this respect, the human moral faculty can be usefully compared to other cognitive capacities, such as language, vision, object perception, and face recognition, all of which also involve unconscious computation. At least since Helmholtz (1962/1867) introduced the concept of "unconscious inference" to explain the mental computations underlying visual perception, one of the principal objectives of cognitive science has been to describe and explain the unconscious premises of human perceptual and cognitive inferences. Unlike many of their nineteenth-century predecessors (see, e.g., Bradley 1962/1876; Brentano 1969/1889; Holmes 1991/1881; Sidgwick 1981/1874; Spencer 1978/1897), however, many contemporary scholars have largely abandoned this project in the domain of moral cognition. The analogy between rules of justice and rules of grammar provides a useful opportunity to reexamine this situation, particularly insofar as human language is clearly understood to depend on "mental processes that are far beyond the level of actual or even potential consciousness" (Chomsky 1965: 8; cf. Gray 1972/1909: 136–137). From the perspective of the linguistic analogy, the dissociation between moral judgments and justifications that we have uncovered is not surprising; indeed, it is consistent with the nontransparent character of mental activity generally. Consequently, we may reasonably infer on the foregoing basis that just as normal persons are typically unaware of the principles guiding their linguistic intuitions, so too are they often unaware of the principles guiding their moral intuitions.

6.7 FURTHER CLARIFICATIONS ABOUT ACT TREES

To prevent misunderstanding, it seems useful at this point to make some further clarifications about the "act tree" method of diagramming structural

descriptions. The act trees in Figures 5.5, 5.6, 6.1(b), and 6.3 have been constructed according to the following principles. At the base of each tree in
Figure 5.5 is an act-token representation that corresponds to what Goldman
(1970a) and Moore (1993), following Danto (1965), often call a *basic action,*
and what Austin (1954/1832), Holmes (1991/1881), and Terry (1884), along
with the first and second Restatements of Torts, often call simply an *act.* As
a general matter, this representation always takes the form "[S's (voluntarily)
moving S's body at t$^{(a)}$]." As Goldman explains, the intuitive idea lying behind
the notion of a basic action is that "A person's action often has far-reaching
effects in the world, but whatever one does in the world at large must come, in
one way or another, from one's body, especially from the movements of one's
body" (1970a: 18). Holmes makes a similar point: "An act is always a voluntary
muscular contraction, and nothing else" (1991/1881: 91). In our framework, we
make the simplifying assumption that when individuals mentally represent
the various actions described in the trolley problems, they represent those
actions as having been generated out of a basic action, in this sense. The act
trees in Figures 6.1(b) and 6.3 do not include representations of basic actions,
but they should be thought of as implicitly incorporated there nonetheless.

At the opposite end of the basic action is the *end* or *goal.* In many of the
cases we have examined in this chapter, the relevant goal takes the following
general form: "[S's preventing the train from killing the men/man at t$^{(a)}$]." In
other cases, including countless real-life examples, of course, the goal is or
would be different.

For the sake of simplicity, I have assumed that all of the act-token representations on these trees are K-generated by the basic action, and in an informal
sense can therefore be accurately described as having been done "knowingly"
(cf. Section 6.2.2). The vertical line of act-token representations connecting the
basic action to the goal consists of those act-token representations that are also
I-generated. Each of these I-generated actions can be described as having been
done "purposely" (or "intentionally," in one of its ambiguous meanings), but it
is important to recognize that ordinary language is often an uncertain guide in
these contexts (see, e.g., Knobe 2003a, 2003b, 2005; Machery 2007). For example, our act tree for the Bystander problem yields a prediction that experimental subjects will find it more natural or acceptable to say "Hank intentionally
caused the train to turn" than "Hank intentionally killed the man on the side
track," but folk intuitions on this matter are not decisive for our purposes, and
they must be carefully interpreted in any event, particularly when experimental subjects are not given an opportunity, as they should be, to distinguish purposely and knowingly harmful actions (cf. Guglielmo & Malle 2008).

All of the act-token representations on our act trees, whether K-generated
or I-generated, are ordered serially, according to (i) time and (ii) lexicalization, in that order. Thus, the act-token representations are first ordered
according to "time of completion," as explained previously (see Section 6.1).
Within each time frame, those act-token representations that have been

lexicalized appear above the structures out of which they are transformed (cf. Fodor 1970). This explains why, for example, "[Hank's killing the man at $t^{(\alpha)}$]" appears above "[Hank's causing the man to die at $t^{(\alpha)}$]" in Figure 5.6, rather than the other way around. Finally, in each act tree, those act-token representations involving battery or homicide are rendered in boldface to signify their moral salience. In Figures 5.6 and 6.3, these representations appear as early as possible in the relevant computations, within the constraints set by other parameters. By contrast, this restriction is occasionally relaxed in Figures 5.5 and 6.1(b). As this variation suggests, more research is needed to clarify the precise rules governing these operations, which this chapter purports merely to sketch rather than exhaustively describe.

It is important to emphasize that our act trees make a number of predictions that can be verified experimentally. For instance, we can obtain further evidence that individuals are mentally representing the trolley problems in this manner by utilizing a number of familiar tests, such as the "by" test, the "in order to" test, and the "for the purpose of" test (see generally Goldman 1970a). Any statement of the general form "[[S V-ed at $t^{(\alpha)}$] by [U-ing at $t^{(\beta)}$]]" should be acceptable just in case a direct line can be drawn on the tree from [S's U-ing at $t^{(\beta)}$] to [S's V-ing at $t^{(\alpha)}$] in the upward direction, with the possible exception of cases of lexicalization, which sound somewhat odd. Likewise, any statement of the general form "[[S V-ed at $t^{(\alpha)}$] in order to [U at $t^{(\beta)}$]]" or any statement of the general form "[[S V-ed at $t^{(\alpha)}$] for the purpose of [U-ing at $t^{(\beta)}$]]" should be acceptable just in case [S's V-ing at $t^{(\alpha)}$] I-generates [S's U-ing at $t^{(\beta)}$]. Hence, the following judgments in the Bystander problem, for example, are presumably entailed by the specific construction of these act trees (where, adapting standard linguistic practice, '*' means semantically odd or ill-formed).

(11) (a) Hank killed the man by throwing the switch
(b) Hank threw the switch by moving his body
(c) Hank killed the man by turning the train
(d) Hank threw the switch in order to turn the train
(e) Hank threw the switch in order to prevent the train from killing the men
(f) Hank turned the train in order to prevent the train from killing the men
(g) Hank threw the switch for the purpose of turning the train
(h) Hank turned the train for the purpose of preventing the train from killing the men
(i) Hank prevented the train from killing the men by turning the train
(j) Hank prevented the train from killing the men by throwing the switch
(k) * Hank threw the switch in order to kill the man
(l) * Hank threw the switch for the purpose of killing the man

(m) * Hank moved his body by throwing the switch
(n) * Hank threw the switch by turning the train
(o) * Hank prevented the train from killing the men in order to kill the
man
(p) * Hank prevented the train from killing the men by committing
battery
(q) * Hank threw the switch in order to commit homicide
(r) * Hank turned the train for the purpose of causing the train to hit
the man

This list is merely illustrative, not exhaustive. As we shall see in Chapter
9, moreover, a similar list of acceptable (i.e., valid) and unacceptable (i.e.,
invalid) statements involving fundamental legal conceptions, such as *rights,
duties, liberties*, and the like can also be generated in this context by drawing
on the work of Terry (1884), Salmond (1966/1902), Hohfeld (1913, 1917), and
other analytical jurists (see generally Herget 1990) and by synthesizing these
efforts with the elements of moral grammar and intuitive jurisprudence we
have investigated thus far. This synthesis points to an important conceptual
link between moral grammar and human rights, a topic to which we return
(Section 9.5).

6.8 CONCLUDING REMARKS

The model outlined in this chapter remains incomplete in many respects,
some of which have been highlighted along the way. For example, compen-
sating for an apparent overemphasis on the role of emotions and heuristics in
recent literature, I have avoided discussing these and other important topics
in order to analyze a set of basic computations in ordinary moral cognition,
whose subtlety, complexity, and explanatory power are often underestimated.
The foregoing model is merely one component of an adequate moral psychology, however, and it must be integrated with general theories of affect,
emotion, memory, motivation, prejudice, probabilistic reasoning, situation-
ism, and a range of other cognitive systems and processes, particularly causal
cognition and theory of mind, all of which have been fruitfully investigated
in recent years. Moreover, the chapter does not supply any formal proofs,
of course, and many gaps remain in the derivations I have sketched. Still,
it seems clear from what has been achieved here that a complete theory of
the steps converting proximal stimulus to intuitive response by means of an
unconscious structural description could be given along the foregoing lines.
In principle, a computer program could be devised that could execute these
rapid, intuitive, and highly automatic operations from start to finish. The
model outlined here thus goes some way toward achieving the first of Marr's
(1982) three levels at which any information-processing task may be understood, the level of computational theory, because the abstract properties of
the relevant mapping have been defined and its adequacy for the task at hand

has been demonstrated. The model thus appears to be a significant advance in our understanding of intuitive moral judgment.

At the same time, we have discovered how certain fundamental legal conceptions can be utilized in this endeavor to explain an interesting range of moral intuitions, which prior experimental studies have indicated may be universal, or nearly so. By postulating latent knowledge of these and other basic legal norms, we can accurately predict human moral intuitions in a huge number and variety of actual cases. How this knowledge is acquired and put to use in different cultural, social, and institutional contexts thus emerge as pressing questions for law, philosophy, the social sciences, and the cognitive and brain sciences, broadly construed. As difficult to accept as it may seem, there are grounds for thinking that much of this knowledge may be innate or rooted in universal human instincts, as many cognitive scientists, philosophers, and jurists have often assumed. The argument is not conclusive, however, and more cross-disciplinary research is needed to clarify the relevant conceptual and evidentiary issues.

In short, the fragment of moral grammar presented in this chapter allows us to restate and explain, in a purely mechanical way, the considered judgments with which we began, thereby making progress toward achieving the state of affairs Rawls calls a reflective equilibrium (1971: 20, 46–51). I will not show the full proofs of this proposition here, nor attempt to state the elements of this moral grammar more clearly, nor consider possible complications or objections. Instead, I wish to turn now to some familiar objections to the linguistic analogy and the naturalistic conception of moral theory it presupposes. Having identified the basic elements of Rawls' linguistic in Part One, and having clarified the empirical significance of Rawls' conception of moral theory in Part Two, we are now in a good position to examine the arguments of Rawls' critics and to determine the extent to which they are cogent.

PART THREE

OBJECTIONS AND REPLIES

The problem which we must put at the center of ethics is a purely psychological one. For, without doubt, the discovery of the motives or laws of any kind of behavior, and therefore of moral behavior, is a purely psychological affair. Only the empirical science of the laws which describe the life of the soul can solve this problem. One might wish to derive from this a supposedly profound and destructive objection to our formulation of the problem. For, one might say, "In such case there would be no ethics at all; what is called ethics would be nothing but a part of psychology!" I answer, "Why shouldn't ethics be a part of psychology?" Perhaps in order that the philosopher have his science for himself and govern autonomously in this sphere? He would, indeed, thereby be freed of many burdensome protests of psychology. If he laid down a command, "*Thus* shall man act," he would not have to pay attention to the psychologist who said to him, "But man *cannot* act so, because it contradicts psychological laws!" I fear greatly that here and there this motive, though hidden, is at work. However, if one says candidly that "there is no ethics," because it is not necessary to label a part of psychology by a special name, then the question is merely terminological.

It is a poor recommendation of the philosophical spirit of our age that we so often attempt to draw strict lines of division between the sciences, to separate ever new disciplines, and to prove their autonomy. The true philosopher goes in the opposite direction; he does not wish to make the single sciences self-sufficient and independent, but, on the contrary, to unify and bring them together; he wishes to show that what is common to them is what is most essential, and that what is different is accidental and to be viewed as belonging to practical methodology. *Sub specie aeternitatis* there is for him only *one* reality and *one* science.

Therefore, if we decide that the fundamental question of ethics, "Why does man act morally?" can be answered only by psychology, we see in this no degradation of, nor injury to, science, but a happy simplification of the world-picture. In ethics we do not seek independence, but only the truth.
— Moritz Schlick, *Problems of Ethics*

7

R. M. Hare, Peter Singer, and the Distinction between Empirical and Normative Adequacy

I fully subscribe to the judgment of those writers who maintain that of all the differences between man and the lower animals, the moral sense or conscience is by far the most important. This sense, as Mackintosh remarks, "has a rightful supremacy over every other principle of human action"; it is summed up in that short but imperious word *ought*, so full of high significance. It is the most noble of all the attributes of man, leading him without a moment's hesitation to risk his life for that of a fellow-creature; or, after due deliberation, impelled simply by the deep feeling of right or duty, to sacrifice it in some great cause. Immanuel Kant exclaims, "Duty! Wondrous thought, that workest neither by fond insinuation, flattery, nor by any threat, but merely by holding up thy naked law in the soul, and so extorting for thyself always reverence, if not always obedience; before whom all appetites are dumb, however secretly they rebel; whence thy original?"
        – Charles Darwin, *The Descent of Man*

In Part One, I introduced Rawls' linguistic analogy and drew on the work of both Rawls and Chomsky to formulate a new analytic framework for the theory of moral cognition, modeled on aspects of Universal Grammar. In Part Two, I sought to clarify the empirical significance of the linguistic analogy by formulating, and stating a provisional solution to, the problem of descriptive adequacy with respect to a class of considered moral judgments, including the original trolley problems devised by Foot and Thomson. In Part Three, I turn my attention to some influential criticisms of Rawls' linguistic analogy and argue that they lack force against both Rawls' conception of moral theory and the research program outlined in Parts One and Two.

7.1 HARE'S AND SINGER'S CRITICISMS OF RAWLS' LINGUISTIC ANALOGY

A useful place to begin is by examining R. M. Hare's objections to Rawls' linguistic analogy. Hare begins his 1973 essay, "Rawls' Theory of Justice," by distinguishing four topics that any moral philosopher is likely to discuss: (i) "philosophical methodology," (ii) "ethical analysis," (iii) "moral methodology," and (iv) "normative moral questions." According to Hare, philosophical methodology concerns "what philosophy is supposed to be doing and how it does it." Ethical analysis relates to "the meaning of moral words or the nature and logical properties of the moral concepts." Moral methodology addresses "how moral thinking ought to proceed, or how moral arguments or reasonings have to be conducted if they are to be cogent." Finally, normative moral questions are questions such as "what we ought or ought not to do, what is just or unjust, and so on" (Hare 1973: 81).

Hare's central claim is that "through misconceptions about (i), Rawls has not paid enough attention to (ii), and that therefore he has lacked the equipment necessary to handle (iii) effectively; so that what he says about (iv), however popular it may prove, is unsupported by any firm arguments" (1973: 81–82).[1] Hare organizes his review around these four topics. His explicit remarks on Rawls' linguistic analogy are contained in his discussion of (ii). I will examine Hare's specific objection to that analogy in a moment. But first some general remarks about Hare's review are in order.

In Part One, we saw that in Section 9 of *A Theory of Justice* Rawls organizes his conception of moral theory around the assumption that each normal human being possesses a moral sense or sense of justice, the existence of which he defends by the argument for moral grammar. Rawls takes describing this sense of justice to be the provisional aim of moral philosophy. He distinguishes different forms that such a description might take, and he suggests that a descriptively adequate moral grammar should take the form of a fully explicit scientific theory – a generative grammar, in approximately Chomsky's sense.

Rawls compares the problem of describing the sense of justice with the linguist's problem of describing linguistic competence. He emphasizes that both inquiries are difficult and require theoretical constructions that go beyond the familiar precepts of common sense. He distinguishes between a description of the sense of justice and a description of how the sense of justice is acquired – in other words, between descriptive adequacy and explanatory adequacy, in the linguist's technical sense. Finally, Rawls draws a distinction between moral performance and moral competence, taking his primary object of inquiry to be the moral competence of a single, idealized individual.

Hare's review is striking, in the first instance, for the number of these features of Rawls' stated conception of moral theory that he ignores or fails to recognize. Hare does not discuss Rawls' assumption that each person possesses a moral sense or sense of justice, nor Rawls' argument for moral grammar; on the

---

[1] This passage is a direct quotation, except that I have substituted "(i)–(iv)" for Hare's original "(1)–(4)."

contrary, the terms "moral sense" and "sense of justice" do not appear in his review. Hare does not appear to recognize the distinctions Rawls draws among different levels of empirical adequacy, or between operative and express principles. He does not acknowledge Rawls' use of a competence–performance distinction, nor how Rawls uses the linguistic analogy to clarify both the theory-dependence of that distinction and the importance of idealization.[2] Nor, finally, does Hare discuss Rawls' historical claim that Rawls' conception of moral theory is how the subject matter of moral philosophy was traditionally conceived by most classical British writers through Sidgwick.

Hare's most direct criticism of Rawls' linguistic analogy is contained in the following passage:

There are significant passages where Rawls compares moral philosophy with mathematics and linguistics. The analogy with these sciences is vitiated by the fact that they do not yield substantial conclusions, as moral philosophy is supposed, on Rawls' view, to do, and in some sense clearly should. It is quite all right to test a linguistic theory (a grammar) against what people actually say when they are speaking carefully; people's *linguistic* 'intuitions' are indeed, in the end, authoritative for what is correct in their language. The kind of interplay between theory and data that occurs in all sciences can occur here, and it is perfectly proper for the data to be the utterances of native speakers. But the only 'moral' theories that can be checked against people's actual moral judgments are anthropological theories about what, in general, people *think* one ought to do, not moral principles about what one ought to do. That these latter can be so checked is not, indeed, what Rawls is suggesting in this passage; but do not the whole drift of his argument, and the passage quoted above, suggest it? (Hare 1973: 85–86, emphasis original, internal citations omitted)

According to Hare, Rawls' linguistic analogy is "vitiated" by the fact that linguistics does not yield the kind of "substantial" conclusions that it is reasonable to expect of moral philosophy. What Hare means by this remark is not entirely clear. Given what he says elsewhere in the passage and in his review

---

[2] For example, Hare writes:

Rawls states quite explicitly how he thinks moral philosophy should be done: "There is a definite if limited class of facts against which conjectured principles can be checked, namely our considered judgments in reflective equilibrium" (p. 51). It is clear from the succeeding passage that Rawls does not conceive of moral philosophy as depending primarily on the analysis of concepts in order to establish their logical properties. Rather, he thinks of a theory of justice as analogous to a theory in empirical science. It has to square with what he calls the 'facts', just like, for example, physiological theories. But what are these facts? They are what people will *say* when they have been thinking carefully. (Hare 1973: 82, emphasis original)

The fact that Hare takes these observations to be cogent criticisms of Rawls suggests that he misunderstands Rawls' use of the competence–performance distinction and, in particular, the distinction between operative and express principles. In effect, what Rawls takes to be the facts against which conjectured principles may be checked are not what people *say* when they have been thinking carefully, but what they *cognize* when they have been thinking carefully. The difference between these two alternatives is crucial.

as a whole, however, Hare's point appears to be that a research program in moral theory modeled on linguistics as Rawls advocates would fail to be prescriptive or normative ("authoritative for what is correct"), as both Hare and, Hare suggests, Rawls think a moral theory clearly should be.

If this is an accurate interpretation of Hare's objection, then it seems that Hare has misunderstood the main point of Rawls' linguistic analogy. Moreover, it suggests that Hare has a surprisingly impoverished conception of the proper scope and limits of moral philosophy. The comparisons that Rawls draws in Section 9 of *A Theory of Justice* are not comparisons between linguistics and an undifferentiated set of questions called "moral philosophy," where the latter is interpreted to refer exclusively to normative ethics, as Hare understands this topic, and to exclude scientific questions about the nature and origin of commonsense moral knowledge. Rather, as we have seen, Rawls' conception of moral theory is more complex. In Section 9 and elsewhere, Rawls distinguishes at least five problems that moral philosophy seeks to solve, which I have labeled the problems of descriptive adequacy, explanatory adequacy, behavioral adequacy, normative adequacy, and metaethical adequacy, respectively (see Table 2.1). The analogy with linguistics is centered primarily on the comparison between the first two problems, descriptive and explanatory adequacy, and their counterparts in linguistics. Hare's criticism of the linguistic analogy is itself vitiated by his failure to grasp these points.

In my view, confusion over these issues has been widespread in the philosophical literature. Some version or other of Hare's criticism that Rawls' conception of moral theory is too empirical or insufficiently normative can be found in many leading philosophers' responses to Rawls. Peter Singer, for instance, objects to Rawls' linguistic analogy on the grounds that "the historical task of moral philosophy" is

to develop theories that serve as guides to conduct. So long as there are grounds for hoping that discussion, argument, and the careful consideration of moral theories can help us to decide how to act, the importance of this historical task cannot be denied. Sidgwick, obviously, was engaged on this task. Can the same be said for Rawls? In a sense, yes. Rawls clearly intends his theory to be a guide to conduct; yet, at the same time, his use of the reflective equilibrium idea means that he is on the verge of slipping off into an altogether different activity, that of systematizing the considered judgments of some unspecified moral consensus. This latter task, while it may be of some interest, is, like the linguistic and scientific investigations on which it is modeled, a descriptive task from which, without supplementation from other sources, no normative or action-guiding consequences can be derived. We cannot test a normative theory by the extent to which it accords with the moral judgments people ordinarily make. Insofar as Rawls frequently does seem to be testing his own theory in this way, the theory fails to be normative and Rawls cannot be regarded as pursuing the same task as Sidgwick and most other moral philosophers. (Singer 1974: 515)

Similar concerns about the insufficiently normative or authoritative character of Rawls' conception of moral theory can be found in many other influential philosophers, including Dworkin, Daniels, Williams, and Brandt.

I believe this criticism is misguided, for at least the following reasons. First, those authors who have criticized Rawls on this basis appear to be operating with an unduly narrow and impoverished conception of moral philosophy and are simply refusing to join Rawls in recognizing the centrality of the problem of empirical adequacy in the history of their discipline. In *The Descent of Man,* for example, Darwin (1981/1871: 71) observes that the classical philosophical question – "whence thy original?" – that stimulates his own inquiry into the moral sense from the side of natural history "has been discussed by many writers of consummate ability." Darwin then explains this reference by referring to Alexander Bain's list in *Mental and Moral Science* (1868) of "twenty-six British authors who have written on this subject, and whose names are familiar to every reader" (Darwin 1981/1871: 71). Bain's list consists of Hobbes, Cumberland, Cudworth, Clarke, Wollaston, Locke, Butler, Hutcheson, Hume, Price, Smith, Hartley, Reid, Stewart, Brown, Paley, Bentham, Mackintosh, James Mill, Austin, Whewell, Ferrier, Mansel, J. S. Mill, Bailey, and Spencer (Bain 1868: 543–725). There seems little doubt that when Rawls refers to "the conception of the subject adopted by most classical British writers through Sidgwick" (1971: 51), it is this group of writers, with the addition of Sidgwick and perhaps a few other additions or subtractions, that Rawls has primarily in mind; and there is little question that most of these writers considered empirical questions about the nature and origin of moral knowledge, along with related topics concerning the existence, character, and origin of the human moral faculty, moral sense, or conscience, to be central problems – if not *the* central problems – in moral philosophy (see, e.g., Hume 1978/1739–1740, 1983/1751; Price 1948/1758; Smith 1976/1759; see generally Mackintosh 1830; Schneewind 1977, 1990, 1998; Sidgwick 1988/1902, 1981/1907; Stewart 1876/1793).

Moreover, many of the philosophers who have criticized Rawls on the ground that his conception of moral theory is too empirical or insufficiently normative have often underestimated or ignored the complexity of Rawls' approach to the problem of metaethical adequacy, that is, the problem of how moral principles can be justified (Section 2.2). In the first place, they have generally neglected Rawls' plausible contention in *Outline* (and *Grounds*) that there is a natural order of priority between the problems of descriptive and normative adequacy, and that a solution to the former problem constitutes at least a presumptive solution to the latter problem, given the properties of the considered judgments that a descriptively adequate moral theory purports to explicate.[3] In addition, they have also largely neglected Rawls' sensible observation that metaethical questions about meaning and justification may prove easier to answer once solutions to the problems of descriptive and explanatory

---

[3] Despite an extensive literature search, when I wrote *Rawls' Linguistic Analogy* I could not find a single critic who objected to Rawls' conception of moral theory on these grounds, yet who also discussed Rawls' claim in *Outline* that a solution to the problem of descriptive adequacy is presumptively normative in light of the properties of the judgments it purportedly explains. I put *Grounds* in parentheses in the text to signal that I am not

adequacy are achieved (1971: 50–51). More generally, they have not seriously engaged with the complexity and plausibility of Rawls' concept of reflective equilibrium and its implication, building on the work of Nelson Goodman (1983/1955) to which we return (Section 7.4.2), that the set of considered judgments in reflective equilibrium can, in principle, yield principles that are both descriptively and normatively adequate.

Finally, from a cognitive science perspective, what is perhaps most noteworthy about the writers who have pressed this criticism – what I call the *objection from insufficient normativity* – against Rawls is that they often beg the very empirical questions that Rawls' conception of moral theory, or the research program outlined in Parts One and Two at any rate, is ultimately designed to answer. In particular, these critics often simply take for granted that some version of behaviorism or social learning theory is the correct account of how commonsense moral knowledge is acquired (see, e.g., Brandt 1979, 1982; Hare 1952, 1973, 1981; Singer 1974; Williams 1985; see generally Mikhail 2007b).

Because this last point may be the most important, it seems appropriate to illustrate it with a specific example. In his influential commentary on Rawls' concept of reflective equilibrium, Singer (1974) questions Rawls' fundamental assumption that each person develops a moral sense or sense of justice under normal circumstances, suggesting Rawls is "led to" make this assumption because of a mistaken conception of the proper aims of moral philosophy. Singer (1974: 516) thinks moral philosophy should begin from what he calls "the opposite assumption," namely, that "all the particular moral judgments" human beings intuitively make are likely to result from their upbringing or other features of their environment. Here is how Singer puts the criticism:

[F]rom the start [Rawls] thinks of moral philosophy in the wrong way. Thus he says: 'Now one may think of moral philosophy at first (and I stress the provisional nature of this view) as the attempt to describe our moral capacity' (p. 46). Even if this is only provisional, it is a misleading starting point. It leads to the assumption that we have a certain moral capacity, and that at least some of the moral judgments we make will, after consideration, remain as fixed points against which theories can be tested. Why should we not rather make the opposite assumption, that all the particular moral judgments we intuitively make are likely to derive from discarded religious systems, from warped views of sex and bodily functions, or from customs necessary for the survival of the group in social and economic circumstances that now lie in the distant past? In which case it would be best to forget all about our particular moral judgments, and start again from as near as we can to self-evident moral axioms. (Singer 1974: 516)

making the unreasonable suggestion that Rawls' critics should be faulted for failing to track down his dissertation. *Outline* is another matter, however, since Rawls repeatedly makes clear that the conception of moral theory on which he relies in *A Theory of Justice* follows the general point of view of this essay (see, e.g., 1971: 46, 579).

There are at least three interrelated points to make about this remarkable passage. First, as a description of Rawls, Singer gets things backwards: as we saw in Chapter 3, Rawls' characterization of moral philosophy *follows from* the assumption that human beings possess a moral capacity. Moreover, Rawls *defends* this assumption when he points to observable properties of moral judgment, including its spontaneity, novelty, and unbounded scope, from which the assumption is inferred. Like Chomsky, for whom the argument for linguistic grammar helps to frame the aims of linguistic theory, Rawls suggests "our natural readiness" to make moral judgments, and their "potentially infinite number and variety," point toward regarding "the sense of justice as a mental capacity," a capacity whose structure is "extraordinarily complex" and hence a topic for investigation (Rawls 1971: 46; see generally Section 3.1.1). In questioning Rawls' assumption that human beings possess a moral capacity, Singer simply fails to speak directly to those properties of moral judgment that Rawls actually invokes, however tentatively, in his own defense.

Second, Singer's criticism of Rawls is question-begging. Singer thinks that moral philosophy should begin from certain factual assumptions about the origin of moral judgments, while criticizing Rawls for making different empirical assumptions. But, like any theorist, Rawls is entitled to begin his enterprise from whichever assumptions he thinks are valid, so long as he is prepared to defend them with arguments and evidence. We will return to this topic in Chapter 8.

Third, Singer apparently thinks that the assumption that human beings possess a moral capacity is necessarily incompatible with the "opposite" claim that "all the particular judgments" they intuitively make "are likely to derive" from the various sources he cites, but this view is mistaken. The claim that human beings possess a moral capacity does not imply that their moral intuitions do not also derive from their environment in some manner, as I shall explain momentarily. As with language, the two issues are distinct.

Singer's tacit assumption that the *exclusive* origin of a child's moral knowledge is her surrounding environment, what one might call his *extreme environmentalism,* is a pervasive and influential one. The same basic premise, which is found elsewhere in G. H. Mead's claim that "minds and selves are essentially social products" (1956: 116) and in Emile Durkheim's claim that "society is the only source of morality" (Piaget 1965/1932: 327, citing Durkheim's *L'Education Morale*), informs many existing research programs in moral development, including those approaches inspired by the social constructivism of Piaget and Kohlberg. But the assumption, at least as Singer expresses it, appears badly confused, a point that becomes clear when one considers what a comparable assumption would imply in the case of language. Suppose Singer or someone skeptical of Universal Grammar asserted the following proposition:

From the start Chomsky thinks of linguistics in the wrong way. Thus he thinks of linguistics as the attempt to describe our linguistic capacity. This is a misleading starting point. It leads to the assumption that we have a certain linguistic capacity, and that at least some of the linguistic judgments we make will, after consideration, remain as fixed points against which theories can be tested. Why should we not rather make the opposite assumption, which is that all the particular linguistic judgments we intuitively make are likely to derive from the early training we receive from the environment? In which case it would be best to forget all about our particular linguistic intuitions, and start again from as near as we can to self-evident axioms.

There obviously are many problems with an argument like this. Here I simply will concentrate on what appears to be its main fallacy. The fact that a person's linguistic intuitions "derive" in some manner from her environment is obvious and uncontroversial. A child who grows up in England or the United States will learn English; if the same child had grown up in Egypt or Israel, she would speak fluent Arabic or Hebrew. This observation, however, is not usefully contrasted with an allegedly "opposite" assumption that the child's linguistic intuitions are a body of scientific evidence against which conjectured theories of her linguistic capacities can be checked. On the contrary, the two propositions are perfectly compatible. Indeed, it is precisely their compatibility, in effect, that motivates the study of Universal Grammar in the first place, whose main objective is to explain the phenomena of language acquisition within the boundary conditions set by experience and by the facts of linguistic diversity. The same logic presumably holds in the moral domain. The fact that people acquire moral beliefs that in some manner reflect the circumstances of their upbringing appears obvious and uncontroversial. The interesting question, from scientific point of view, concerns the character of the morality acquisition system (Universal Moral Grammar) that maps this early experience into the mature or steady state of each individual's moral competence. In implicitly denying that human beings possess such a system, Singer appears to be adopting an extreme version of epistemological empiricism, which, although popular among many midcentury Anglo-American moral philosophers (see generally Mikhail 2007b), seems both at variance with modern science and empirically untenable.

In the remainder of this chapter, I do not pursue all of the foregoing lines of inquiry. Instead, I focus my attention on the relationship between the problems of empirical and normative adequacy in Rawls' conception of moral theory, limiting the scope of my investigation as I have throughout this book to the early part of Rawls' career (1950–1975). I begin by examining how Rawls approaches this topic in *Grounds* and *Outline*. Then I turn my attention to *A Theory of Justice,* focusing in particular on how the concept of reflective equilibrium appears to function in the conception of moral theory that Rawls elaborates there. Finally, I examine Rawls' response to the objection from insufficient normativity in *Independence* (Rawls 1975). My primary aim is to show that Rawls' approach to the problem of metaethical adequacy is plausible and compelling, and that theorists who are inclined to pursue the research program outlined in Parts One and Two need not avoid doing so on the ground that it is insufficiently normative.

7.2 EMPIRICAL AND NORMATIVE ADEQUACY IN *GROUNDS*

The distinction in Rawls' conception of moral theory between the problem of descriptive adequacy and the problem of normative adequacy traces in its essentials to Rawls' Ph.D. dissertation, *A Study in the Grounds of Ethical Knowledge* (1950) (hereafter cited as *Grounds*). There Rawls conceives the structure of an ethical theory to be comprised of two main parts: *explication* and *justification*. Rawls identifies the former as an empirical inquiry, whose aim is the explanation or "real" rational reconstruction of a specified class of commonsense moral judgments.[4] He identifies the latter as the problem of discovering or describing a method of verifying the soundness of such judgments. Rawls does think such a method exists; moreover, he thinks the method in question is, in a highly specified sense, *rational*. Although he does not employ the term himself, then, in terms of the philosophical positions of the 1950s, Rawls appears to interpret his own approach to ethics as at least weakly "cognitivist": the aim of his inquiry as a whole is "to evidence the falsity of those views which deny the possibility of the use of reason in the solution of moral problems" (Rawls 1950: Abstract).

In *Grounds,* Rawls explains his rationale for identifying explication as one of the two main parts of ethical theory as follows. He begins with what he takes to be the only two remaining credible ethical theories, some form of utilitarianism and some form of intuitionism (not excluding the possibility, he says, that they may be combined in various ways) (1950: 17). He then does something interesting: to exhibit the proper form an ethical theory should take (a question on which he temporarily suspends judgment), he canvasses a number of well-known objections to utilitarianism and intuitionism.

Rawls' three refutations of utilitarianism are taken from Butler (1983/1736), Broad (1930), and Ross (1939). Rawls takes Butler's criticisms to reveal that "one of the aims of ethical theory was to find the principles in accordance on [*sic*] which this [moral] faculty judged, and that any theory could be refuted by showing that it failed to do this by pointing out actual instances which conflict with it." From Broad, Rawls discerns that at least one of the aims of ethical theory "is to state the principles by which we actually appraise moral conduct." And from Ross, he concludes that "among the relevant facts by which a moral theory is tested are the judgments of daily life" (1950: 20, 22).

---

4 In his helpful commentary on Kant, Robert Paul Wolff (1973: 52–55) distinguishes two different conceptions of the rational reconstruction of common moral intuitions: a *real rational reconstruction*, which "seeks to uncover the principles which actually, though perhaps unconsciously, guide our moral judgment," and a *virtual rational reconstruction,* which "proceeds as though our moral judgments involved appeal to underlying principles, but ... does not assume that such an appeal actually takes place." On Wolff's view, Kant was engaged in the former activity in Chapter One of the *Groundwork*. As I interpret his remarks on explication, Rawls is also engaged in the project of real rather than virtual rational reconstruction in *Grounds*.

On this basis Rawls concludes that the first task of ethics consists of finding a successful explication of our commonsense moral judgments. Pursuing the matter, he first defines those persons whose judgments should be taken as relevant, whom he calls *reasonable men*. He then defines those judgments of reasonable men that are to be the object of study, which he calls *rational judgments*. Next, he specifies more clearly what he means by explication: it is "a set of principles (directives) such that if used and applied intelligently to the cases at hand will lead the user of it to make the same judgments as that judgment on the case that would be made by reasonable men judging rationally in the sense defined" (1950: Abstract). Finally, he clarifies the relationship between explication and the second part of moral philosophy, justification, which he describes as "the general problem of the justification of those principles which have been found to constitute successful explications" (1950: Abstract, 2). Explication is thus characterized as a heuristic device likely to yield justifiable principles. As Rawls explains, "there is reason to suppose that the rational judgments of reasonable men are the most likely repository of such principles" (1950: Abstract).

In *Grounds*, Rawls clarifies the notion of explication in a number of relevant respects. To explicate an idea or concept, he says, is similar, although not identical, to providing an *analysis* of the idea or concept, in the sense of the logical analysis of philosophers like Russell and Moore. An analysis is "an enumeration of the properties of those objective complexes to which the name expressing the concept is actually applied in ordinary or scientific language. Thus, for example, the analysis of the concept expressed by the term 'cause' consists in stating the properties of those complexes which are actually called 'causes'" (1950: 71). In a somewhat similar fashion, an explication of a concept

will mean a listing of the properties of a complex, together with the necessary rules of application, such that, a person who fully understands them both, will be led, by their use, to employ the term expressing the concept on exactly the same occasions, and in exactly the same way, as that term is used in the data with which the explication is concerned. For example: if the data is the rational judgments of reasonable men, and if the concept is that expressed by the term 'good', then an explication of the concept good will be a listing of the complex of characters of those things actually called 'good' in the rational judgments of reasonable men, together with such rules and instructions which enable any intelligent person understanding them to make his usage of the term 'good' exactly coincide with the use and application of it in the data under consideration. (1950: 72–73)

Rawls next adds an important observation about the intuitive application of complex concepts:

The meaning of explication may be stated another way: ordinarily the use of elaborate concepts is intuitive and spontaneous, and therefore terms like 'cause', 'event', 'good', *are applied intuitively or by habit, and not by consciously applied rules.* The concept expressed by the term will be said to be explicated whenever the explication offered will lead, if mechanically followed by anyone understanding it, to the same applications of the term as one is led to by one's intuitive feelings. Sometimes, instead of using the term 'explication', one can use the phrase 'rational reconstruction', and one can say that a concept is rationally reconstructed whenever the correct rules are stated which enable one to understand and explain all the actual occasions of its use. (1950: 73, emphasis added)

Rawls stresses that successful explications are extremely difficult, as evidenced by the then-recent attempts by philosophers of science like Hempel and Carnap to explicate two intuitively simple concepts: *confirmation* and *probability*. As Rawls observes, these efforts spawned a whole area of inquiry into induction, whose purpose was to formulate rules of inductive logic. Likewise, he explains,

with ethical terms like 'justice', 'good', 'virtue', we must expect that the correct explication will lead to a lengthy and detailed investigation. ... It is this somewhat unexpected complication which shows the short-sightedness of those who try to convict such analysis of verbal quibbling, and who fail to see in it anything more than the playing with words. They do not understand it as the careful study of the use of a term expressing a concept in an effort to find a correct explication of it, and thereby formalize the implicit rules and principles which have developed over the centuries of experience and practice. It is a profitable inquiry, and not easy. (1950: 75)

Crucially, Rawls insists it is *not* a task of the explication of a normative concept to capture what its user *intends* to assert. Despite the fact that many moral philosophers have engaged in this activity – Rawls mentions specifically Moore and Ross, and it is easy to think of more recent counterparts – Rawls diagnoses it as an "unnecessary inquiry which it is helpful to avoid" (1950: 76). His complete explanation of this point is worth quoting in full:

[A]n explication does not attempt to analyze either what people intend to assert by the use of a word, or what is before their minds when making an assertion containing it. It is concerned only with the statement of a set of principles which if used and applied by an intelligent person will enable him to judge in accordance with the rational judgments of reasonable men. Put another way: an explication may be successful even if it can be established with certainty that everyone would reject it as a statement of what they intend to assert. A rational reconstruction has nothing to do with consciously felt meanings. Its data is the objectively known judgments as these are made in different situations. It is to be applied to nothing else whatsoever. Therefore, the validity of an explication is not put into question by considering what we intend to assert; but only by showing that the use of it would lead to judgments not in conformity with the opinions of reasonable men. Explications consider not the sense of ethical terms; but objectively determinable judgments alone. (1950: 77)[5]

---

[5] Rawls adds that while intentions and consciously felt meanings are not the proper data of ethical theory, they still can provide useful clues for the construction of successful explications. So, even though they play no direct role in the confirmation or disconfirmation of a proposed explication, intentions and felt meanings may serve as hints for discovery (1950: 77).

Rawls says that in defining explication, and so ethical theory, in this way, he is attempting "a strategic maneuver." No methodological failure has plagued moralists more, he observes, "than the lack of an appeal to objectively established data (such as the rational judgments of reasonable men), and the consequent reference to feelings, intentions, and subjectively apprehended meanings" (1950: 78). Rawls identifies the delimitation in question as a mere consequence of applying to ethical theory the distinction between *methodological* and *metaphysical* physicalism. "The latter is a doctrine made familiar by the writings of the earlier behaviorists, and particularly known for its denial of the existence of consciousness and its identification of thought with physiological processes." The former "is a principle which embodies an essential rule of scientific method, namely, the insistence that the theories and principles of a science be established or refuted wherever possible by objective data which can be checked by the community of investigators, together or individually" (1950: 78).[6]

Rawls adds a further clarification about the nature of explication: it does not set out to study the physical *causes* of moral judgments, as does "the sociology of morals," but merely to explicate moral judgments, in the sense of formulating rules and principles that, if followed intelligently, would lead one to the same intuitions as those being explicated. This leads to the following important point: explication does not seek to decide whether considered moral judgments are determined by the intuition of nonnatural properties, or by reason, or by emotions, feelings, or instincts, or by cultural or environmental factors. This question may receive illumination along the way, but "an explication is successful even if it mentions none of these things, provided that it states rules leading to conformity with common intuitions." Once again, Rawls identifies this feature of explication as "a strategic maneuver." The point is "to avoid difficult questions about psychological and sociological causes, moral emotions, subjective states of mind and the like," in the course of attempting to find, as easily and directly as possible, "justifiable norms for selecting between different lines of conduct" (1950: 80; for somewhat similar remarks on the difference between a computational and causal account of language and vision, respectively, see generally Chomsky 1986a and Marr 1982).

Finally, Rawls entertains and dismisses the criticism that explications are circular because an explication constructed from a class of intuitive judgments will naturally fit them. He replies that it is simply no objection that explications deliberately fit a certain class of judgments, since this is precisely their point. Moreover, since no mechanical construction of an explication from any class of judgments is possible, and since an explication that is initially

---

[6] Rawls' distinction between methodological and metaphysical *physicalism* appears somewhat similar to Chomsky's (2000) distinction between methodological and metaphysical *naturalism*. The comparison merits further inquiry, but I do not pursue this topic here.

suggested by a small class of judgments may turn out to be more comprehensive by accounting for many more judgments outside that initial class, the circularity objection is without force.[7]

7.3 EMPIRICAL AND NORMATIVE ADEQUACY IN *OUTLINE*

The same general conception of moral philosophy, as comprised of two main problems, the problem of descriptive adequacy and the problem of normative adequacy, forms the basis of Rawls' first publication, *Outline of a Decision Procedure for Ethics* (1951a) (hereafter cited as *Outline*). In this paper, which is both a condensed version of his Ph.D. thesis and the first published sketch of the conception of moral theory described in Section 9 of *A Theory of Justice* (see 1971: 46, n. 24), Rawls substitutes the phrase "considered judgments of competent judges" for what he calls the rational judgments of reasonable men in *Grounds*. He makes other terminological changes as well. Nonetheless, the central role played by the distinction between these two problems remains substantially the same.

Rawls' position on the priority of the problem of descriptive adequacy to the problem of normative adequacy in *Outline* is nearly identical with the view that he expresses in *Grounds*. So, too, is his view of the relevance of the problem of descriptive adequacy. Rawls characterizes the explication of a given class of considered judgments as "a heuristic device" likely to yield "reasonable and justifiable principles" (1951a: 184). A solution to the problem of descriptive adequacy thus constitutes a presumptive solution to the problem of normative adequacy. Rawls writes:

If reasonable principles exist for deciding moral questions, there is a presumption that the principles of a satisfactory explication of the total range of the considered judgments of competent judges will at least approximate them. On the basis of this presumption the explication of these judgments is designed to be a heuristic device for discovering reasonable principles. Therefore, while explication is an empirical inquiry, it is felt that it is likely to be a way of finding reasonable and justifiable principles in view of the nature of the class of judgments which make up its range. (1951a: 184)

The details of Rawls' account of the problem of descriptive adequacy in *Outline* are also broadly equivalent to those in *Grounds*. Rawls again divides his discussion of explication into three parts. First, he defines a class of persons whose judgments he takes to be relevant, which he refers to as the class

---

[7] Interestingly, the first published commentary on *Outline* (Mardiros 1952) raises the very same circularity objection that Rawls here anticipates. In my judgment, Rawls' reply to the objection appears to be sound: the circularity in question is real enough, but it is a familiar and innocuous feature of the explication of an intuitive concept, whether it is *grammatical* (Chomsky 1957: 15), *valid inductive inference* (Goodman 1983/1955: 64), or, in Rawls' case, *sound moral judgment*.

of *competent moral judges* (or, alternatively, *competent judges*). Second, he defines the class of moral judgments he takes to be relevant, which he refers to as *considered moral judgments* (or, alternatively, *considered judgments*). Third, he specifies more precisely what he means by explication:

Consider a group of competent judges making considered judgments in review of a set of cases which would be likely to arise in ordinary life. Then an explication of these judgments is defined to be a set of principles, such that, if any competent man were to apply them intelligently and consistently to the same cases under review, his judgments, made systematically nonintuitive by the explicit and conscious use of the principles, would be, nevertheless, identical, case by case, with the considered judgments of the group of competent judges. The range of an explication is specified by stating precisely those judgments which it is designed to explicate, and any given explication which successfully explicates its specified range is satisfactory. (1951a: 184)

As he did in *Grounds,* Rawls clarifies further the meaning of explication in *Outline.* He does so both negatively, by stating some of the things an explication is not, and positively, by affirming some of its positive characteristics. On the negative side, Rawls explains that an explication is neither an analysis of the meaning of ethical terms, nor concerned with capturing what people intend to assert when making moral judgments. Nor is it a theory of the actual causes of those judgments. Finally, it is not an attempt to determine whether moral judgments are best understood as the intuition of nonnatural properties, the expression of an emotion, or the deterministic outcome of one's upbringing. On the positive side, Rawls explains that an explication must be a set of principles that are "capable of an interpretation that the average competent man can grasp." The principles must be "general directives ... such that, when applied to specific cases, they yield preferences expressed in considered judgments." Finally, to be fully successful, an explication must be comprehensive, in the sense that "it must explicate ... all considered judgments ... with the greatest possible simplicity and elegance." The requirement of simplicity "means that, other things being equal, an explication is more or less satisfactory according to the number of principles which it uses; and although this demand is difficult to state precisely, it is clear that nothing is gained if we require a separate principle for each case or for each class of cases" (1951a: 186).

Two further observations about Rawls' characterization of the problem of descriptive adequacy in *Outline* are worth emphasizing. First, Rawls characterizes explication as an *empirical* inquiry. Explications are falsifiable: there is "one way of showing an explication to be unsatisfactory, and that is to show that there exist considered judgments of competent judges on specifiable cases for which it either fails to yield any judgments at all or leads one to make judgments inconsistent with them" (1951a: 185).

Second, successful explications are *difficult.* Rawls writes:

There is no way of knowing ahead of time how to find and formulate these reasonable principles. Indeed, we cannot even be certain that they exist, and it is well known that there are no mechanical methods of discovery. ... Whether such an explication exists or not, one cannot know at present, and opinions vary; but the belief that such an explication does exist is perhaps a prerequisite for the finding of it, should it exist, for the reason that one who does not so believe is not likely to exert the great effort which is surely required to find it. (1951a: 178, 186)

In Chapter 3, we saw that Rawls emphasizes the difficulty of solving the problem of descriptive adequacy in Section 9 of *A Theory of Justice.* We see here that the same emphasis may be found in both *Outline* and *Grounds.* The observation is thus a recurring feature of Rawls' conception of moral theory during the period of his career (1950–1975) with which we are concerned.[8]

In sum, the distinction between the problem of descriptive adequacy and the problem of normative adequacy is a central feature of Rawls' conception of moral philosophy in both *Grounds* and *Outline.* However, the fact that Rawls distinguishes these two problems, and privileges the former over the latter, does not imply that he is not interested in the problem of normative adequacy. On the contrary, it seems clear that Rawls is ultimately concerned with the latter problem (see, e.g., 1951a: 177). Nonetheless, Rawls also believes in a natural *order of priority* between these two problems. According to Rawls, the most reasonable method of solving the problem of normative adequacy is to attempt to solve the problem of descriptive adequacy first. Hence the problem of descriptive adequacy is in this sense both logically and methodologically prior to the problem of normative adequacy.

7.4 EMPIRICAL AND NORMATIVE ADEQUACY IN *A THEORY OF JUSTICE:* REFLECTIVE EQUILIBRIUM

To understand how the problems of empirical and normative adequacy are related to each other in *A Theory of Justice,* we need to examine Rawls' notion of *reflective equilibrium.* Thus far, apart from a few expository passages, I have deliberately refrained from elaborating on the meaning of this concept. Because unnecessary confusion about the significance of reflective equilibrium, above all else, has resulted in Rawls' linguistic analogy being misunderstood, I have sought to explain and illustrate how the basic elements of that analogy are independent of this concept. Having done so, and having now located the source of the distinction between empirical and normative adequacy in *Grounds* and *Outline,* we are in a better position to examine

---

[8] Despite Rawls' observation, philosophers often implicitly underestimate the difficulty of the problem of descriptive adequacy. See, for example, Daniels (1980: 25) and Kagan (1989: 11).

Rawls' remarks about reflective equilibrium and to determine their relevance for our topic.

The first and most important thing to notice about reflective equilibrium is that it is not a term of ordinary language, but an invented, technical term – a term of art, in the traditional sense. Like all invented terms, then, it has whatever meaning its author gives it. In *A Theory of Justice,* Rawls defines reflective equilibrium in Sections 4 and 9 and mentions it in passing on only four other occasions. He also briefly clarifies its meaning in *Independence* (Rawls 1975). Despite this, it is not uncommon in the literature on Rawls to find commentators investing reflective equilibrium with original, unwarranted connotations of their own. Of the authors I shall discuss, Dworkin and Daniels seem to fall into this pattern quite frequently.

Reflective equilibrium makes its first appearance in Section 4 of *A Theory of Justice* ("The Original Position and Justification," pp. 17–22), where it is defined as a hypothetical state of affairs that is reached in the course of attempting to justify the original position by resolving expected discrepancies between our considered judgments and the principles yielded by a candidate description of the initial situation. In Rawls' theory, *original position* and *initial situation* are also technical terms. Accordingly, the Section 4 definition of reflective equilibrium cannot be understood without a clear grasp of the meanings of these concepts. For this, a brief summary of the main, contractual argument of *A Theory of Justice* is required.

7.4.1 The Main Contractual Argument of *A Theory of Justice*

Rawls' main contractual argument in *A Theory of Justice* may be understood, for our purposes at any rate,[9] as an attempt to propose and defend a particular solution to a specific version of the problem of normative adequacy that is a viable alternative to utilitarianism and intuitionism. Rawls characterizes his proposal as a "workable and systematic moral conception" that is implicit in the contract tradition of Locke, Rousseau, and Kant. As compared with its two main rivals, it better "approximates our considered judgments of justice" and "constitutes the most appropriate moral basis for a democratic society" (Rawls 1971: viii).

Like moral conceptions generally, a conception of justice enunciates a set of rules or procedures by which ethical questions are to be answered and ethical disputes resolved. What singles out a conception of justice, according to Rawls, is the kind of questions and disputes that fall under its

---

[9] Rawls' complete argument in *A Theory of Justice* is rich and complicated, and the brief summary offered in this section is thus selective in its points of emphasis. Many important themes and distinctions are ignored. My aim is to present a suitably clear picture of the essentials of the book's theoretical structure, primarily as they pertain to the meaning of reflective equilibrium and, more broadly, to the research program outlined and developed in Parts One and Two.

jurisdiction. In its widest sense, justice is ascribed not only to laws, institutions, and social systems, including those within and among nation-states, but also to particular actions, attitudes, and dispositions of individual persons. Rawls, however, limits the scope of his inquiry to a conception of *social* justice. Human society, which is "a cooperative venture for mutual advantage," produces by its collaborative effort a net surplus of advantages and benefits. A conception of social justice provides a set of principles "for choosing among the various social arrangements which determine this division of advantages and for underwriting an agreement on the proper distributive shares" (1971: 4).

Rawls distinguishes between various *conceptions* of justice and the *concept* of justice, the latter of which may be thought of as "specified by the role which ... these different conceptions have in common" (1971: 5). From the concept of justice it is possible to derive certain substantial requirements that just institutional arrangements must satisfy, for example, that "no arbitrary distinctions are made between persons in the assigning of basic rights and duties" and that "the rules determine a proper balance between competing claims to the advantages of social life" (1971: 5). However, the mere concept of justice leaves important questions unsettled, such as how to interpret the notions of an arbitrary distinction and a proper balance. For these, a particular conception of justice is required.

Rawls narrows his topic in two more fundamental respects. First, he focuses on a special case of the problem of justice, which he calls "the primary subject of justice" or the "basic structure of society" (1971: 7). This problem concerns how the major social institutions – the political constitution and the primary economic and social arrangements – should assign basic rights and duties and determine the division of the advantages of social cooperation. Second, Rawls limits his attention to *ideal* rather than *non-ideal* theory. Thus, he seeks principles which would govern a "well-ordered society," which is designed to advance the good of its members and to be regulated by a public, and publicly accepted, conception of justice (1971: 4–5, 8–9).

Rawls' main argument in *A Theory of Justice* may be characterized, then, as an argument for a particular conception of social justice, the principles of which are to answer moral questions and resolve moral disputes about the basic structure of a well-ordered society. The complete argument is complex and includes numerous idealizations and simplifying devices. One guiding idea, borrowed from social contract theory, is nonetheless straightforward. Rawls' proposed conception of justice is not deduced from a presumed self-evident or a priori proposition, nor is it arrived at by an analysis of moral concepts or of the meanings of ethical terms. Instead, its principles are the object of a rational choice made by persons in a hypothetical contractual arrangement, and the fact that certain principles and not others would be chosen under such an arrangement constitutes at least *one* argument for their being a solution to the problem of normative adequacy.

Rawls' contract argument, as Lyons (1975: 150) usefully labels it, consists of two parts: first, a characterization of an initial contractual arrangement, and, second, a conception of justice that, it is claimed, would be chosen in that situation. As Rawls observes, the two parts are logically independent. It is possible to object to one part but not the other. Thus one might reject the particular conditions and constraints Rawls imposes on the initial contractual situation, or alternatively, one might accept Rawls' characterization of the initial situation but argue that the principles he derives from it are invalid (Rawls 1971: 15, 54).

The bulk of *A Theory of Justice* is devoted to working out and defending a solution to the choice problem presented by this contractual arrangement. As is well known, the conception of justice he advocates comes in two forms, one general and one more specific. The two principles of the specific conception – what Rawls calls the *special conception of justice* – are as follows:

First Principle

Each person is to have an equal right to the most extensive total system of basic liberties compatible with a similar system of liberty for all. (1971: 250)

Second Principle

Social and economic inequalities are to be arranged so that they are both (a) to the greatest benefit of the least advantaged and (b) attached to offices and positions open to all under conditions of fair equality of opportunity. (1971: 83)

To understand the contract argument for the special conception of justice, it is important to explain some terminology that Rawls employs in connection with the first part of the argument. Rawls draws a fundamental distinction between the idea of an initial contractual arrangement and particular interpretations of that idea. The former, which Rawls names the *initial situation,* may be thought of as a common feature of contract views generally. The initial situation in turn admits of many possible interpretations, each of which gains expression in the form of a set of conditions and constraints imposed there. These usually include a description of the contracting parties, such as their motives and nature, the extent to which they are rational, their knowledge of themselves, and so on. It also includes a general description of their deliberative circumstances, such as the historical information available to them and the formal constraints under which they deliberate (1971: 18, 121).

The name Rawls gives to his own preferred interpretation of the initial situation is the *original position.* Among its most salient features are the following. Most famously, the parties in the original position are presumed to operate behind a "veil of ignorance" that temporarily prevents them from knowing their identities, their natural talents and skills, their conception of the good, and their social circumstances generally. The deliberators do, however, possess full knowledge of all the general facts and scientific laws relevant to the determination of principles of justice they must make (1971: 136–138). Moreover, they are presumed to be rational, in the sense of being able to choose the most effective means to given ends, and in the sense of being able, despite the absence of information about their particular ends, to rank their alternative ends self-interestedly in accordance with a postulated preference for more, rather than less, primary social goods (1971: 14, 142–143). They are also presumed to be mutually disinterested, meaning that the parties are conceived as taking no interest in one another's interests (1971: 13, 127).

A number of other important features characterize the original position as well. For instance, one of the objective circumstances of the parties in the original position is moderate scarcity: demand outruns supply, and resources are neither abundant enough to make cooperation superfluous, nor scarce enough to make it futile (1971: 127). As for candidate principles presented to the parties, they must meet certain formal requirements even to be eligible for consideration. Rawls arranges these requirements under five headings: generality, universality, publicity, order, and finality. Taken conjointly, these five conditions exclude the several variants of egoism as serious candidates for a suitable conception of justice. The traditional conceptions, however, do satisfy these conditions, hence the formal constraints do not prejudge the issue between Rawls' theory and its main rivals (1971: 130–136). Finally, Rawls assumes that it is rational for the parties in the original position to adopt a "maximin" rule, which instructs them to prefer principles whose worst possible outcome is superior to that of alternative principles (1971: 152–153).

According to Rawls, the original position is "the most philosophically favored interpretation" of the initial situation (1971: 18, 122). By this he means that the restrictions imposed on the initial situation are more reasonable and widely accepted than any alternative set of conditions. They are so not only from the standpoint of rational choice, but also from the standpoint of moral theory: that is, the conditions and constraints embodied in the original position are not only reasonable, but also morally defensible in that "the principles that would be chosen, whatever they turn out to be, are acceptable from a moral point of view" (1971: 120). The original position thus constitutes a model of what Rawls calls *pure procedural justice:* the principles it generates are held to be normatively valid principles of justice because they are the outcome of a procedure that has been characterized in such a way as to give them moral force (1971: 85f., 136). In particular, the initial situation is interpreted so as to respect the freedom, equality, and rational self-interest of the contracting parties. This feature of the original position is captured by the name Rawls gives to his conception of justice: *justice as fairness.* It conveys the idea that the principles of justice are the product of an agreement that is itself fair (1971: 11–12, 136; see also Rawls 1957, 1958).

It is this aspect of procedural fairness that is thought to lend the original position its justifying force. That is, Rawls contends that the intuitively fair and plausible nature of the conditions and constraints embodied in the original position constitutes a provisional justification of the set of principles chosen there (1971: 18). The justification is only *provisional* because there is more

to establishing the procedural fairness of the original position than showing
that the conditions imposed there *seem* fair and reasonable. Additionally, we
defend the fairness of a particular interpretation of the initial contractual situation by determining whether

> the principles which would be chosen match our considered convictions of justice or
> extend them in an acceptable way. We can note whether applying these principles
> would lead us to make the same judgments about the basic structure of society which
> we now make intuitively and in which we have the greatest confidence; or whether,
> in cases where our present judgments are in doubt and given with hesitation, these
> principles offer a resolution which we can affirm on reflection. (1971: 19)

To test a proposed description of the initial situation, then, we measure
the consequences of its principles against our pretheoretical moral intuitions
about the basic structure of society in like cases. The intuitions in question
are what Rawls calls "our considered convictions of justice," that is, those
judgments "we now make intuitively and in which we have the greatest confidence" (1971: 19–20). If, on reflection, the principles chosen in the contractual
situation can be shown to cohere with our considered convictions about these
same cases, then we possess further evidence of the fairness of our proposed
interpretation of the initial situation, hence further grounds for having satisfied the requirements of pure procedural justice.

7.4.2 The Concept of Reflective Equilibrium

Thus far I have not yet said anything specific about how reflective equilibrium fits into this picture. It first enters Rawls' discussion in Section 4 in the
explicit service of the contract argument, as a state of affairs that is reached
in the course of resolving expected discrepancies between our considered
judgments and the principles generated by a candidate description of the initial situation, in an effort to justify the original position. Later, in Section 9,
Rawls characterizes reflective equilibrium somewhat differently, not merely
as a state of affairs achieved in the course of justifying the original position,
but also as a state of affairs that results after a person has been given the
opportunity to evaluate and reflect on competing theoretical descriptions of
her sense of justice, and has either revised her initial judgments or held fast to
them. Significantly, Rawls does not emphasize the difference between these
two accounts of reflective equilibrium. Instead, the Section 9 account is presented as if it were a resumption and elaboration of the earlier discussion in
Section 4. Yet, as we shall see, there appear to be at least superficial differences between these two accounts.

The Section 4 Account
We can begin to understand the Section 4 account by recognizing the role that
reflective equilibrium plays in support of the contract argument. According to

the contract argument, the two principles of justice are justified because they would be chosen in a suitably characterized contractual situation (1971: 11, 118–119, 136, 579). This justificatory strategy, as we have seen, is procedural: in the absence of an independent criterion for justice, we construct a procedure whose fairness ensures an outcome that is likewise just or fair. The original position is itself justified as the most suitable interpretation of the initial situation in two ways: first, by grounding its conditions in intuitively plausible and commonly shared presumptions, and, second, by testing its consequences against our considered judgments of justice (1971: 86, 111, 136).

In Section 4, reflective equilibrium is introduced as a state of affairs toward which we strive in attempting this second sort of justification of a proposed description of the initial situation. Presumably, when we test a proposed description, we discover discrepancies between our considered judgments, on the one hand, and the consequences of the principles generated by the description under consideration, on the other. We advance toward reflective equilibrium by attempting to resolve these differences.

Here it is helpful to distinguish our motivation for advancing toward reflective equilibrium from our manner of doing so. According to Rawls, the reason *why* we want equilibrium, and why we don't simply settle for whichever principles a plausible set of contractual conditions generates, is that we may have stronger convictions about certain specific issues of social justice than we do about what constitutes a fair contractual arrangement. For example, consider our firm convictions, which Rawls cites, that religious intolerance and racial discrimination are unjust (1971: 19). Because of the strength of these convictions, we may reasonably be suspicious of an otherwise plausible description of the initial situation whose consequent principles fail to honor them. If our convictions are strong enough, we may go so far as to invalidate such a description. *How* we advance toward reflective equilibrium is thus by modifying either the description or the considered judgments, for the latter, like the former, are merely provisional fixed points that may be changed. We go back and forth like this, sometimes conforming the description to our judgments, sometimes our judgments to the description and its consequent principles, until at last we "find a description of the initial situation that both expresses reasonable conditions and yields principles which match our considered judgments duly pruned and adjusted" (1971: 20). When this happens reflective equilibrium is achieved, and the description constitutes a temporarily stable conception of the original position. The conception is only temporarily stable because, as its name implies, reflective equilibrium is a state that is always subject to further reflection and change. Nonetheless, according to Rawls, once the state of reflective equilibrium is reached, the claim that the original position is the philosophically most favored interpretation of the initial situation is then fully justified – both because the constraints it imposes are independently plausible and because its principles conform to our considered judgments of justice. Since the original position is fully justified, by transitivity the principles of justice it yields are also justified. Rawls describes the entire process as follows:

In searching for the most favored description of this [initial] situation we work from both ends. We begin by describing it so that it represents generally shared and preferably weak conditions. We then see if these conditions are strong enough to yield a significant set of principles. If not, we look for further premises equally reasonable. But if so, and if these principles match our considered convictions of justice, then so far well and good. But presumably there will be discrepancies. In this case we have a choice. We can either modify the account of the initial situation or we can revise our existing judgments, for even the judgments we take provisionally as fixed points are liable to revision. By going back and forth, sometimes altering the conditions of the contractual circumstances, at others withdrawing our judgments and conforming them to principle, I assume that eventually we shall find a description of the initial situation that both expresses reasonable conditions and yields principles which match our considered judgments duly pruned and adjusted. This state of affairs I refer to as reflective equilibrium. It is an equilibrium because at last our principles and judgments coincide; and it is reflective since we know to what principles our judgments conform and the premises of their derivation. At the moment everything is in order. But this equilibrium is not necessarily stable. It is liable to be upset by further examination of the conditions which should be imposed on the contractual situation and by particular cases which may lead us to revise our judgments. Yet for the time being we have done what we can to render coherent and to justify our convictions of social justice. We have reached a conception of the original position. (1971: 20–21)[10]

For our topic, three points about how Rawls characterizes reflective equilibrium in this passage are especially worth emphasizing. First, reflective equilibrium is not, strictly speaking, a method or technique, as Dworkin and other commentators have often described it (see Chapter 9), but rather *a state of affairs*. Specifically, it is the state of affairs that is achieved once a description of the initial situation has been reached "that both expresses reasonable conditions and yields principles which match our considered judgments duly pruned and adjusted" (Rawls 1971: 20).

Second, the word "reflective" appears to play the same role in Rawls' definition of reflective equilibrium as the word "generative" plays in Chomsky's notion of a generative grammar. In Chomsky's framework "generative" simply means "explicit" (see, e.g., Chomsky 1965: 4). In other words, a linguistic grammar qualifies as a *generative* grammar when its principles can be explicitly stated by the linguist in a format suitable for functioning as the premises of a derivation. This is essentially the same meaning Rawls assigns to a

---

[10] Rawls (1971: 20) adds the following footnote to this paragraph, the significance of which I address below: "The process of mutual adjustment of principles and considered judgments is not peculiar to moral philosophy. See Nelson Goodman, *Fact, Fiction, and Forecast* (Cambridge, Mass., Harvard University Press, 1955), pp. 65–68, for parallel remarks concerning the justification of the principles of deductive and inductive inference."

reflective equilibrium. It refers to the fact that once we have found a correct description of the initial situation, "we know to what principles our judgments conform and the premises of their derivation" (1971: 21).

Third, Rawls holds that any proposed description of the initial situation is merely provisional and open to modification as a result of further investigation, hence not necessarily stable. This emphasis on the provisional nature of the original position is important: it implies that it is always an open question whether the initial situation has been accurately characterized, and thus whether our convictions of social justice are justified. Rawls emphasizes the provisional or contingent character of reflective equilibrium (understood as the state of affairs that obtains when the initial situation has been accurately characterized) throughout Section 4. For example, he says, "there is no point at which an appeal is made to self-evidence in the traditional sense either of general conceptions or particular convictions" and elaborates: "I do not claim for the principles of justice proposed that they are necessary truths or derivable from such truths. A conception of justice cannot be deduced from self-evident premises or conditions on principles; instead, its justification is a matter of the mutual support of many considerations, of everything fitting together into one coherent view" (1971: 21).

Rawls' definition of reflective equilibrium in Section 4 may be summarized by means of the simple diagram in Figure 7.1. According to Rawls' definition, a reflective equilibrium is the state of affairs that is reached when the moral theorist knows the principles to which her chosen set of considered judgments conform, and the premises of those principles' derivation.[11] When this state of affairs has been reached, the theorist has arrived at a conception of the original position. A considered judgment is justified when it is derivable from the original position. At that point – although not until then – the considered judgment may be called a considered judgment in reflective equilibrium. If we inquire after the relationship holding among reflective equilibrium, the justification of considered judgments, and the original position, therefore, the answer is that, in Rawls' stated framework, these concepts are merely different ways of saying the same thing.

---

[11] Here it should be noted that I am taking the liberty of resolving an apparent ambiguity in Rawls' definition of reflective equilibrium. Rawls writes: "It is an equilibrium because at last our principles and judgments coincide; and it is reflective since we know to what principles our judgments conform and the premises of their derivation" (1971: 21). What is the antecedent of "their" in the phrase "their derivation"? If the antecedent is "judgments," then Rawls would be saying that a reflective equilibrium is reflective because we know "to what principles our judgments conform and the premises of the derivation of those judgments," which would appear to be redundant. Hence it seems preferable to interpret the intended antecedent of "their" as the principles themselves. On this reading, Rawls would be saying that a reflective equilibrium is reflective because we know "to what principles our judgments conform and, in turn, the premises of the derivation of those principles."

```
Original Position          ⎫
....                       ⎪
....                       ⎪
Rawls' Two Principles of Justice    ⎬  Reflective Equilibrium
....                       ⎪
....                       ⎪
                           ⎪
_____            ⎪
Considered Judgments       ⎭
```

FIGURE 7.1. Schematic Diagram of Rawls' Definition of Reflective Equilibrium in Section 4 of *A Theory of Justice*

The Section 9 Account

In Section 9, Rawls characterizes reflective equilibrium in more elaborate terms. The Section 9 definition is more revealing for a number of reasons, perhaps the most significant of which is its precise location in Rawls' text. For it is only after comparing the problem of descriptive adequacy in ethics with the problem of descriptive adequacy in linguistics, and only after distinguishing moral competence and moral performance by identifying considered judgments as those judgments in which our moral capacities are likely to be displayed without distortion, that Rawls reintroduces the notion of reflective equilibrium first discussed in Section 4. "The need for this idea," Rawls now explains, "arises as follows":

According to the provisional aim of moral philosophy, one might say that justice as fairness is the hypothesis that the principles which would be chosen in the original position are identical with those that match our considered judgments and so these principles describe our sense of justice. But this interpretation is clearly oversimplified. In describing our sense of justice an allowance must be made for the likelihood that considered judgments are no doubt subject to certain irregularities and distortions despite the fact that they are rendered under favorable circumstances. When a person is presented with an intuitively appealing account of his sense of justice (one, say, which embodies various reasonable and natural presumptions), he may well revise his judgments to conform to its principles even though the theory does not fit his existing judgments exactly. He is especially likely to do this if he can find an explanation for the deviations which undermines his confidence in his original judgments and if the conception presented yields a judgment which he finds he can now accept. From the standpoint of moral philosophy, the best account of a person's sense of justice is not the one which fits his judgment prior to his examining any conception of justice, but rather the one which matches his judgments in reflective equilibrium. As we have seen, this state is reached after a person has weighed various proposed conceptions and he has either revised his judgments to accord with one of them or held fast to his initial convictions (and the corresponding conception). (1971: 48)

On casual glance, this definition of reflective equilibrium seems to repeat the Section 4 definition we reviewed earlier. Rawls' use of the phrase "As we have seen" in the last sentence of the paragraph reinforces this impression.

However, the account of reflective equilibrium that Rawls provides in this paragraph differs from the Section 4 definition in what seem like crucial respects. While in Section 4 reflective equilibrium is a state of affairs that is reached in the course of evaluating proposed interpretations of the initial situation and identifying one interpretation, the original position, as the most favored, here reflective equilibrium is a state of affairs that is reached in the course of evaluating competing descriptions of the sense of justice. Likewise, while in Section 4 justice as fairness is the contractual thesis that the principles of justice are justified because they are chosen in the original position, thereby qualifying as justifiable on the basis of the notion of pure procedural justice, here justice as fairness is the hypothesis that these same principles describe the sense of justice. In short, whereas in Section 4 the general problem Rawls appears to be discussing is the *normative* problem of justifying principles of justice, in Section 9 Rawls' topic appears to be the *descriptive* problem of describing and explaining the sense of justice.

The apparent discrepancy in the definitions of reflective equilibrium that Rawls provides in Sections 4 and 9 raises a number of important questions about the significance of his theory of justice as a whole. In terms of the conceptual distinctions we have drawn in this book, perhaps the most pressing of these questions may be stated as follows. In *A Theory of Justice,* Rawls certainly seems to be defending a solution to the problem of normative adequacy. This seems like the only reasonable interpretation of many statements he makes throughout the book, such as his remarks on the notion of pure procedural justice in Sections 14 and 20 and his remarks on justification in Sections 4 and 87. Yet, as we have seen, Rawls also repeatedly describes justice as fairness as a solution to the problem of descriptive and explanatory adequacy. This characterization is not limited to Section 9: in Section 20, for example, Rawls explains that the original position "is not intended to explain human conduct except insofar as it tries to account for our moral judgments and helps to explain our having a sense of justice. Justice as fairness is a theory of our moral sentiments as manifested by our considered judgments in reflective equilibrium" (1971: 120). We are thus led to ask whether, and if so how, these apparently divergent aims can be reconciled, and what role the notion of reflective equilibrium is supposed to play in this process.

Resolving the Discrepancy: Reflective Equilibrium
But are Rawls' aims necessarily divergent? Hare, Singer, and other commentators who have criticized Rawls' conception of moral theory for being too empirical and insufficiently normative apparently think so. I would counter that to assume that there must be an irresolvable tension between the normative and empirical aspects of Rawls' approach is to miss the point of Rawls' reference to Goodman in Section 4. The theme of those pages of *Fact, Fiction and Forecast* where Rawls directs his reader when he first defines reflective equilibrium in Section 4 is the justification of induction. Goodman's main

point in that discussion is that philosophers should be wary of expecting too much from the theory of induction. They should stop plaguing themselves with certain spurious questions about justification and should relax the distinction between *justifying* principles of induction and *describing* ordinary, reliable inductive practice:

> We no longer demand an explanation for guarantees that we do not have, or seek keys to knowledge that we cannot obtain. It dawns upon us that the traditional smug insistence upon a hard-and-fast line between justifying induction and describing ordinary inductive practice distorts the problem. And we owe belated apologies to Hume. For in dealing with the question how normally accepted inductive judgments are made, he was in fact dealing with the question of inductive validity. (Goodman 1983/1955: 64–65)

How do Goodman's remarks in this passage bear on the tension between Rawls' two definitions of reflective equilibrium in Sections 4 and 9? In a word, they imply that the tension is only apparent. There is no necessary inconsistency in assuming that a set of moral principles can be part of a solution to the problems of empirical and normative adequacy simultaneously.

To see this point, it helps to examine how Rawls conceives of the problem of normative adequacy in diagrammatic form (Figure 7.2). In *A Theory of Justice,* Rawls' two principles of justice are what he takes to be a solution to the problem of descriptive adequacy (with respect to one component of I-morality, namely, the sense of social justice). His contract argument is intended to show that these principles would be chosen in the original position, thereby proving that they are rational. At the same time, Rawls conceives of the original position as a provisional solution to the problem of *explanatory* adequacy, insofar as it represents an acquisition model that helps explain the fact that normal persons possess a sense of justice (1971: 120). Hence, when Rawls equates justice as fairness *both* with the claim that his two principles would be chosen in the original position, thereby being part of a solution to the problem of normative adequacy, *and* with the empirical hypothesis that those principles constitute an accurate description and explanation of the sense of justice, thereby solving the problems of descriptive and explanatory adequacy, he is not necessarily being inconsistent. A set of moral principles can, in principle, be descriptive, explanatory, and normative simultaneously. Indeed, according to Rawls, this is the philosophical ideal.[12] It is part of what it means to justify the morality of common sense, by showing that it has a rational foundation.

---

[12] "[J]ustice as fairness can be understood as saying that the two principles previously mentioned would be chosen in the original position in preference to other traditional conceptions of justice, for example, those of utility and perfection; and that these principles give a better match with our considered judgments on reflection than these recognized alternatives. Thus justice as fairness moves us closer to the philosophical ideal; it does not, of course, achieve it" (1971: 49–50).

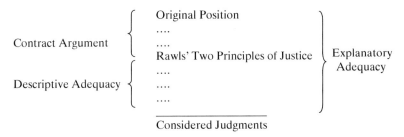

FIGURE 7.2. Schematic Diagram of Rawls' Account of the Problem of Normative
Adequacy in a *Theory of Justice*

Now, it is important to avoid misinterpreting the diagram in Figure 7.2. It is
potentially misleading for several interrelated reasons. In the first place, it fails
to take into account the theory-dependence of the competence–performance
distinction. As we have seen, Rawls emphasizes that moral theorists may want
to change what they presently take to be considered judgments once those
judgments' regulative principles are brought to light. So it is important not to
be misled by the static appearance of the diagram in Figure 7.2. A reflective
equilibrium is not necessarily stable. As its name implies, it is always subject
to further reflection and change (Rawls 1971: 20–21; cf. Nagel 1973: 2–3).

Second, it is important not to be misled by Rawls' reference to Goodman
and the problem of justifying induction. It is tempting to conclude that just
as "the problem of justifying induction is not something over and above the
problem of describing or defining valid induction" (Goodman 1983/1955: 65),
so too, according to Rawls, is the problem of justifying moral principles not
something over and above the problem of describing or defining what one
takes, pre-theoretically, to be instances of valid moral reasoning. As we
observed in Chapter 2, however, this interpretation of Rawls runs the risk
of ignoring the third aspect of the problem of normative adequacy in ethics, which has no clear analogue in the case of either induction or linguistics;
namely, the requirement of rationality, understood to be the suitability of
moral principles as the object of rational choice. Neither induction nor linguistics requires the principles of an adequate theory to be rational in this
special sense.

Finally, Figure 7.2 is an oversimplification because it fails to make allowance for the possibility that when a person is presented with an intuitively
appealing account of her sense of justice, her sense of justice may itself be
transformed as a result of reflecting on this account. This is the basis for the
distinction that Rawls draws between *narrow* and *wide* reflective equilibrium,
which Rawls first explains in the following passage, also from Section 9:

There are ... several interpretations of reflective equilibrium. For the notion var-
ies depending upon whether one is to be presented with only those descriptions
which more or less match one's existing judgments except for minor discrepancies,

or whether one is to be presented with all possible descriptions to which one might plausibly conform one's judgments together with all relevant philosophical arguments for them. In the first case we would be describing a person's sense of justice more or less as it is although allowing for the smoothing out of certain irregularities; in the second case a person's sense of justice may or may not undergo a radical shift. Clearly it is the second kind of reflective equilibrium that one is concerned with in moral philosophy. (1971: 49)

In this passage, Rawls uses the phrase "second kind of reflective equilibrium" to refer to what he calls "wide reflective equilibrium" in *Independence*. By invoking this second kind of equilibrium, he allows for the possibility that when a person is given the opportunity to reflect on a plausible theory of her sense of justice, her sense of justice may "undergo a radical shift." Although he does not elaborate on this observation, its meaning and motivation seem fairly clear. Rawls' overriding aim in *A Theory of Justice* is not merely to convince his reader that justice as fairness is a better overall account of the sense of justice than its two main rivals, utilitarianism and intuitionism. He clearly wants to do this, and thereby to convince readers inclined toward these alternatives that their understanding of their own sense of justice may be mistaken. Yet he also wishes to suggest that reflecting on a moral theory may cause a person's sense of justice to be transformed. For example, in the case of utilitarianism, he makes room for the possibility that reading a book like *A Theory of Justice* will cause a person whose existing sense of justice "does not take seriously the distinction between persons" (1971: 27) to change her mind.

In *Independence,* Rawls revisits the distinction between narrow and wide reflective equilibrium in the following passage, in which the terms "narrow" and "wide" are used for the first time:

[B]ecause our inquiry is philosophically motivated, we are interested in what conceptions people would affirm when they have achieved wide and not just narrow reflective equilibrium, an equilibrium that satisfies certain conditions of rationality. That is, adopting the role of observing moral theorists, we investigate what principles people would acknowledge and accept the consequences of when they have had the opportunity to consider other plausible conceptions and to assess their supporting grounds. Taking this process to the limit, one seeks the conception, or plurality of conceptions, that would survive the rational consideration of all feasible conceptions and all reasonable arguments for them. We cannot, of course, actually do this, but we can do what seems like the next best thing, namely, to characterize the structures of the predominant conceptions familiar to us from the philosophical tradition, and to work out the further refinements of these that strike us as most promising. (Rawls 1975: 8)

This account of the distinction between narrow and wide reflective equilibrium is virtually identical to Rawls' initial account of the same distinction in Section 9 of *A Theory of Justice*. Indeed, there are only two discernible differences between the two accounts. First, "considering all possible descriptions to which one might plausibly conform one's judgments" in Section 9 becomes considering "other plausible conceptions" in *Independence*. Second, considering conceptions of justice "together with all relevant philosophical arguments for them" in Section 9 becomes conducting a "philosophically motivated" inquiry and searching for an equilibrium that "satisfies certain conditions of rationality" by assessing the "supporting grounds" of different moral conceptions in *Independence*. Otherwise the two explanations are identical.

Carefully identifying the differences between the two explanations may seem pedantic, but doing so allows us to register an important concern about the dominant interpretation of reflective equilibrium in the philosophical literature, which traces to influential work by Norman Daniels (see, e.g., Daniels 1979, 1980; see generally Daniels 1996). In his 1980 paper, "On Some Methods of Ethics and Linguistics," which is one of the most extensive and helpful early commentaries on Rawls' linguistic analogy in the literature, Daniels' stated objective is "to free wide equilibrium from an unnecessary or, at least, overstated analogy to linguistic method" (1996: 66). Yet, a revealing footnote to the paper makes clear that Daniels is not concerned to "free" moral theory from comparisons to E-language or P-language interpretations of linguistics, such as (in the case of the latter) Jerrold Katz's, but only from I-language interpretations, such as Chomsky's. Specifically, Daniels' criticism of the linguistic analogy is "restricted to approaches to syntactics that view it as a branch of psychology, broadly construed. These are the approaches Rawls has in mind in proposing the analogy, but alternative approaches, such as the one indicated in Jerrold Katz's recent work, reject the psychologizing of linguistics" (1996: 79 n. 17).

Daniels' main thesis is that it is "wide equilibrium ... not narrow, that is of interest to the moral philosopher – and for just those reasons that distinguish it from syntactics" (1996: 66). Significantly, however, Daniels defines these two forms of reflective equilibrium differently than Rawls does. Rawls does not take the difference between wide and narrow reflective equilibrium to map onto the distinction between an I-morality conception of moral theory and some other conception, according to which moral theory is not conceived as part of psychology, broadly construed. On the contrary, he considers both narrow and wide reflective equilibrium to be states of affairs that are achieved in the course of "investigating an aspect of human psychology, the structure of our moral sensibility" (Rawls 1975: 7). By contrast, Daniels effectively stipulates that the target of wide reflective equilibrium is not the human moral sense or sense of justice, or indeed any other aspect of human psychology. What Daniels actually produces in this paper, therefore, is neither a coherent criticism of the linguistic analogy, nor a coherent criticism of the conception of moral theory Rawls actually describes in *A Theory of Justice,* but a terminological sleight of hand. Daniels simply redefines narrow and wide reflective equilibrium in a manner that dissociates the latter from an I-morality interpretation of moral theory. He then draws on this new definition to reject the linguistic analogy, first by arguing that wide reflective equilibrium (as he defines it) is at odds with the scientific methods of linguistics in various respects, and then by concluding, on the foregoing basis, that "the heart of the analogy to the case of descriptive syntactics is gone" (1996: 72). The main effect of all this theoretical maneuvering is to obscure a substantive difference between Daniels and Rawls over a fundamental issue, namely, the proper subject matter of moral theory, and the significance of the problem of descriptive adequacy with respect to it.

Daniels is free to define (or redefine) technical terminology in any way he wants, of course. He is also at liberty to disagree with Rawls and "most classical British writers through Sidgwick" (Rawls 1971: 51) that the proper subject matter of moral theory is an aspect of human nature: the structure of human moral sensibility. But he owes it to his readers to make clear that this is what he is doing. Instead of this, Daniels simply assumes that descriptive adequacy is a narrow psychological inquiry that "is not of central interest to moral philosophy" (1996: 69) – essentially the same strategy of avoidance that we encountered with Hare and Singer – and thereby constructs a mere pseudo-argument against the linguistic analogy. Moreover, like Hare and Singer, he frequently begs the very questions about the nature and origin of human moral intuitions that a research program in moral theory inspired by the linguistic analogy is meant to answer in the first place (see, e.g., Daniels 1996: 70–72).

Returning to the main thread of the chapter and summarizing the results of our investigation thus far: The distinction between the problem of empirical adequacy and the problem of normative adequacy appears to be a stable feature of Rawls' conception of moral theory in *Grounds, Outline,* and *A Theory of Justice.* In *Grounds* and *Outline,* Rawls' conception of the problem of empirical adequacy appears to be limited to the problem of descriptive adequacy. In these two early texts, Rawls adopts the view that there is an order of priority between the problem of descriptive adequacy and the problem of normative adequacy, the descriptive inquiry taking precedence over the normative. He also assumes that a solution to the problem of descriptive adequacy constitutes a presumptive solution to the problem of normative adequacy, given the character of the evidence that a descriptively adequate set of principles explains. In *A Theory of Justice,* Rawls' approach to the problem of metaethical adequacy appears to be more complex. Specifically, as I read him, Rawls makes at least five major modifications to his approach to metaethical adequacy in *A Theory of Justice.* First, he includes the problem of *explanatory* adequacy (i.e., the problem of how moral knowledge is acquired) among the fundamental problems that he thinks a comprehensive moral theory should solve.[13] Second, he introduces the contract argument and the notion of pure procedural justice as means of showing that the principles of justice as fairness are rational. Third, he follows Goodman in defining reflective equilibrium in

[13] Rawls' concern with this problem first emerges most clearly in "The Sense of Justice" (1963b). It is elaborated at greater length in Part Three of *A Theory of Justice,* particularly chapter 8.

a manner that allows for solutions to the problems of empirical and normative adequacy to be mutually dependent. Fourth, he makes certain reasonable
allowances for the theory-dependence of the competence–performance distinction. Finally, Rawls adopts the weakest of the three metaethical standpoints described in Section 2.1.9, according to which the overriding goal of
a moral theory is to construct an *evaluation procedure* for moral principles.
Consequently, Rawls remains satisfied with the relatively modest claim that
justice as fairness is a *better* overall account of the sense of justice (I-morality)
than either utilitarianism or its other rivals. As Rawls puts it, his limited claim
in this regard is that justice as fairness is "more reasonable than" any of its
rivals, hence that it is "justifiable with respect to them" (1971: 17).

7.5 EMPIRICAL AND NORMATIVE ADEQUACY
IN *INDEPENDENCE*

Rawls' fourth important statement about the nature of moral theory during
the early part of his career (1950–1975) may be found in *The Independence
of Moral Theory,* Rawls' 1974 Presidential Address to the American
Philosophical Association (1975) (hereafter cited as *Independence*). In this
essay, which appeared after many of the first critical reviews of *A Theory
of Justice,* including Hare's and Singer's, were initially published, Rawls
reaffirms the importance of descriptive adequacy for moral philosophy.
Furthermore, although he makes some minor modifications to the account
of metaethical adequacy presented in *A Theory of Justice,* his basic attitude
toward that problem and the relationship between empirical and normative
adequacy appears to remain essentially the same, at least at the level of detail
that concerns us here.

In *Independence,* Rawls distinguishes moral theory from moral philosophy
and takes the former to be one of the latter's main parts. Rawls defines moral
theory as the attempt to characterize "the structure of our moral sensibility"
and to trace the basis of an individual's "substantive moral conceptions" in
her "natural attitudes" and "moral psychology" (1975: 5, 7). The crucial fact
about moral theory, so understood, is its relative independence from a number of traditional philosophical problems. As Rawls puts it, moral theory

is independent from the other parts of philosophy. The theory of meaning and epistemology, metaphysics and the philosophy of mind, can often contribute very little. In
fact, preoccupation with the problems that define these subjects may get in the way
and block the path to advance. To be sure, no part of philosophy is isolated from the
rest; and so the same is true of that part of moral philosophy I call moral theory. But
the study of substantive moral conceptions and their relation to our moral sensibility
has its own distinctive problems and subject matter that requires to be investigated
for its own sake. At the same time, answers to such questions as the analysis of moral
concepts, the existence of objective moral truths, and the nature of persons and personal identity, depend on an understanding of these structures. Thus the problems of

moral philosophy that tie in with the theory of meaning and epistemology, metaphysics and the philosophy of mind, must call upon moral theory. (1975: 5–6)

According to Rawls, the moral theorist attempting to solve the problems of empirical and normative adequacy, as he has defined them, is neither forced to assume that there is one authoritative or correct moral conception, nor to presuppose the existence of objective moral truths. On the contrary, she may – and, Rawls says, she should – set aside such notoriously difficult problems as the objective or ultimate truth of a given set of moral judgments or moral principles. Preoccupation with these issues, he writes, "may get in the way and block the path to advance" (1975: 5). Since we will have occasion to refer to this passage again (see Section 9.3.3), Rawls' full explanation of this theoretical perspective is worth quoting at length:

Let us consider first a way in which moral theory is independent from epistemology. I suggest that for the time being we put aside the idea of constructing a correct theory of right and wrong, that is, a systematic account of what we regard as objective moral truths. Since the history of moral philosophy shows that the notion of moral truth is problematical, we can suspend consideration of it until we have a deeper understanding of moral conceptions. But one thing is certain: people profess and appear to be influenced by moral conceptions. These conceptions themselves can be made a focus of study; so provisionally we may bracket the problem of moral truth and turn to moral theory: we investigate the moral conceptions that people hold, or would hold, under suitably defined conditions.

In order to do this, one tries to find a scheme of principles that match people's considered judgments and general convictions in reflective equilibrium. This scheme of principles represents their moral conception and characterizes their moral sensibility. One thinks of the moral theorist as an observer, so to speak, who seeks to set out the structure of other people's moral conceptions and attitudes. Because it seems likely that people hold different conceptions, and the structure of these conceptions is in any case hard to delineate, we can best proceed by studying the main conceptions found in the tradition of moral philosophy and in leading representative writers, including their discussions of particular moral and social issues. We may also include ourselves, since we are ready to hand for detailed self-examination. But in studying oneself, one must separate one's role as a moral theorist from one's role as someone who has a particular conception. In the former role we are investigating an aspect of human psychology, the structure of our moral sensibility; in the latter we are applying a moral conception, which we may regard (though not necessarily) as a correct theory about what is objectively right and wrong. (1975: 7)

Rawls' remarks in these passages raise a number of important philosophical issues. We will return to many of them in Chapter 9 when we consider Ronald Dworkin's objections to Rawls' linguistic analogy. The main point I wish to emphasize here is simply the manner in which, when taken together with other aspects of Rawls' approach to metaethical adequacy, Rawls' remarks constitute a plausible rejoinder to Hare, Singer, and his other critics who object that his conception of moral theory is too empirical and insufficiently normative.

Rawls appears to have a ready answer to his critics, which simply put is that it is *their* conception of moral theory – in which the empirical and the normative are sharply dissociated, and terms like "objectively valid" (Singer 1974: 495) or "substantial," "authoritative," and "anthropological" (Hare 1973: 85–86) do philosophical work, but are often left undefined – that seems overly simple and inadequate. Indeed, both here and in his other core texts on moral theory, Rawls advances at least eight overlapping reasons why philosophers should not avoid engaging with the problems of empirical and normative adequacy as he has framed them simply because those problems are considered to be "a type of psychology" (1975: 7, 9, 22). Rather than examine these reasons at length, in what follows I shall simply paraphrase them and cite to some of the relevant passages in Rawls' texts.

First, the history of moral philosophy shows that one of the central topics in normative ethics, the truth (or "objective" truth) of moral judgments and principles, is obscure and difficult to formulate coherently. By contrast, the problems of empirical and normative adequacy as they have been defined here are real and easily identifiable problems. Moreover, they are distinguishable from these other, more obscure problems. Hence the moral theorist can and should suspend consideration of the problem of objective moral truth and focus attention instead on finding a scheme of principles that can explain the set of considered judgments in reflective equilibrium (Rawls 1975: 7; cf. 1951a: 177–186; 1971: 50–52).

Second, if we can make progress in solving the problems of empirical and normative adequacy, then certain questions of normative ethics and metaethics, such as the meaning and justification of moral judgments and moral principles, may prove easier to answer, or indeed may no longer be real questions at all (1971: 51–52). Further, such questions as the analysis of moral concepts and the nature of persons and personal identity may also depend on solutions to the problems of empirical and normative adequacy (1975: 6). In this sense, further progress in moral philosophy may turn on the success of moral theory (1971: 51–52; 1975: 7, 21–22).

Third, some degree of conformity with common moral intuitions is frequently taken by philosophers to be a necessary, albeit not sufficient, condition for a moral theory to be true. Hence it is natural to seek an explicit theoretical description and, if possible, justification of the morality of common sense, in the form of a solution to the problems of empirical and normative adequacy. The alternative is to continue to rely on deeply felt, but poorly understood, moral intuitions, and to do so in an ad hoc, unsatisfying manner in order to evaluate the strengths and weaknesses of competing moral theories (1950: 20–22).[14]

---

[14] The assumption that conformity to considered judgments is a necessary condition for normative adequacy is what motivates Part Two of *A Theory of Justice,* where Rawls attempts to show that justice as fairness provides a better match with our considered judgments than utilitarianism does when both are applied to particular problems of social justice.

Fourth, solving the problems of empirical and normative adequacy might be the only way to constructively address the issue of moral diversity and moral relativism. By pursuing these problems, we may be able to discover that human beings share, and are willing to acknowledge, moral principles that are rich enough to afford a constructive basis of mutual accommodation in those areas where disagreements persist (1975: 9).

Fifth, moral theory currently lacks solutions to the problems of empirical and normative adequacy. Moreover, just as adequate theories in other cognitive domains, such as language, enable us to ask new questions about the nature of those domains, so too might solving these problems help us to understand and ask new questions about the nature of morality (1971: 50).

Sixth, philosophical subjects such as semantics, metaphysics, epistemology, and the philosophy of mind (as these were conceived in 1975)[15] often can contribute very little to solving the problems of empirical and normative adequacy. Further, preoccupation with the issues that define these subjects might get in the way and block the path to advance (1975: 5–6).

Seventh, the problems of empirical and normative adequacy are traditional philosophical projects. In particular, they are a continuation of the Enlightenment project that used to be called (among other things) the theory of moral sentiments (1971: 50–51).

Finally, the problems of empirical and normative adequacy have their own distinctive questions and subject matter that deserve to be investigated for their own sake (1975: 6).

By assembling these eight reasons in this manner, I do not mean to suggest that all of them are equally clear or persuasive. On the contrary, I think that some of Rawls' arguments are stronger than others, and that at least several of them admit of significant challenges. My main point is simply that, in light of these initial arguments, the burden of persuasion is not on Rawls but on his critics. During the early part of his career (1950–1975), at least, Rawls fully accepts the interpretation of moral theory that Hare, Singer, and his other critics assume is so damaging to attribute to him. Moreover, none of their specific criticisms seem particularly troubling for the naturalistic conception of moral theory that Rawls actually describes in these early texts. This

---

[15] It is important to recall that *Independence* was delivered as an address to the American Philosophical Association in 1974. Hence what Rawls meant by referring to these subjects is presumably different than one might expect today. To take one obvious example: by the philosophy of mind, Rawls probably did not mean to refer to the type of nativist, modular, and representationalist theory of mind defended by Chomsky in *Reflections on Language* (1975b) and *Rules and Representations* (1980) or by Fodor in *The Language of Thought* (1979) and *The Modularity of Mind* (1983), none of which were published at the time. Today, however, Chomsky's and Fodor's influential (and importantly different) conceptions of nativism, modularity, and representationalism are part of mainstream debates in cognitive science and the philosophy of mind. See, for example, Carruthers et al. (2005, 2006, 2007), George (1989), Loewer & Rey (1992), and McGilvray (2005).

explains, I believe, the confident manner in which Rawls responds to the objection from insufficient normativity in *Independence*. For, in truth, his early critics were merely raising objections that Rawls had long since considered and accommodated.[16]

7.6 SOME CLARIFICATIONS ABOUT METAETHICS

I have been arguing that Rawls' approach to the problem of metaethical adequacy in his early writings constitutes a plausible rejoinder to the argument from insufficient normativity. On the one hand, Rawls' original assumption in *Grounds* and *Outline* that descriptive adequacy is a necessary condition of normative adequacy, hence that a solution to the problem of descriptive adequacy constitutes a presumptive solution to the problem of normative adequacy, seems like a plausible starting point for moral theory. Quite apart from the more elaborate metaethical apparatus of *A Theory of Justice,* therefore, Rawls' earliest conception of moral theory possesses the resources to respond effectively to those critics who would reject it outright because it appears to be insufficiently normative. At the same time, Rawls' more sophisticated conception of metaethical adequacy in *A Theory of Justice* and *Independence,* manifested in the notion of reflective equilibrium, supplies a much stronger defense against the objections raised by Hare and Singer. Indeed, when one combines the theory-dependence of the competence–performance distinction (Sections 2.1.4, 3.1.6; see also Chapter 8) and the appropriately modest goal of moral theory to provide an evaluation procedure for moral principles (Sections 2.1.6, 3.4; see also Chapter 9) together with the concept of reflective equilibrium and the relaxation of the distinction between empirical and normative adequacy it implies (Section 7.4), the result is a powerful and compelling conception of moral theory that seems capable of providing an effective response to the argument from insufficient normativity, albeit not one that is fully conclusive.

At this point it seems useful to discuss some of the broader metaethical commitments of both Rawls' conception of moral theory and the research program outlined in Parts One and Two. It also seems like a good opportunity to consider some specific objections to the responses to Hare and Singer

---

[16] To give one further illustration, Rawls goes to great lengths in both *Grounds* and *Outline* to answer the very question – *Whose* considered judgments are probative? – that Singer and Hare later press against him when they refer to "the considered judgments of some unspecified moral consensus" (Singer 1974: 515) and the "cosy unanimity" of "Rawls and his coterie" (Hare 1973: 82, 85). These criticisms were surely not troubling for Rawls when he encountered them, because he anticipated and responded to them nearly 25 years earlier. In Part I, Section 3 of *Grounds,* for example, Rawls spends 15 pages discussing whose considered judgments should be taken as probative for the purposes of an explication (see 1950: 30–45, entitled "Whose Judgments?"), anticipating many of the specific challenges that Hare and Singer would later raise against him in their critical responses to *A Theory of Justice.*

that I have given on behalf of Rawls. In this section I begin with the first topic, Rawls' broader metaethical commitments, before turning to the metaethical import of the moral grammar hypothesis. My remarks will necessarily be brief and superficial, but hopefully they will help to clarify at least some issues that might otherwise remain obscure.

As I interpret it, Rawls' conception of moral theory represents a deliberate and self-conscious departure from the way moral philosophy was usually studied and taught from around 1930 to 1960, the heyday of noncognitivism. At the most general level, the noncognitivists divided ethics into three main parts: descriptive ethics, normative ethics, and metaethics. They took questions of descriptive ethics to be questions of fact about the moral beliefs or behaviors of particular individuals or groups, and they viewed this inquiry as falling primarily within the domain of the social sciences, such as psychology, sociology, and anthropology. They took normative ethics to consist of questions about the moral status of particular agents, actions, institutions and states of affairs, but they held that its answers were fundamentally "non-cognitive" in character because they did not admit of truth-value in the manner of genuinely empirical statements. Finally, they took metaethics to consist of the linguistic or conceptual analysis of ethical terms: "right," "good," "ought," and so on (see, e.g., Ayer 1936; Reichenbach 1952).

On the noncognitivists' view, normative ethics was not a scientific enterprise, nor even a form of rational inquiry. The moral judgments of both philosophers and other individuals were viewed simply as expressions of emotion or subjective preference. Hence metaethics was really the only branch of ethics that the professional philosopher could legitimately spend her time investigating. This conclusion followed from the division of labor implied by the foregoing account of descriptive ethics: because the genuinely empirical or fact-finding branch of ethics belonged to the social scientist, it was the conceptual or linguistic branch that properly belonged to the professional philosopher.

How does Rawls' conception of moral theory fit into this familiar taxonomy? As we have seen, in his early writings Rawls appears to reject several main elements of the noncognitivists' account of ethics. In the first place, he rejects the noncognitivists' denial of a place for reasoned analysis in normative ethics. Second, Rawls also effectively rejects the division of labor implicit in the noncognitivists' account, wherein it is the job of the social scientist, but not the philosopher, to pursue the tasks of descriptive ethics. Instead, Rawls advocates a return to an older conception of ethics, assumed by all the leading Enlightenment moralists, who placed the structure of intuitive moral reasoning, and thus the properties of the human moral faculty, at the forefront of their inquiries. At least during the early part of his career, therefore, Rawls takes the "aim of philosophical ethics" to be giving "an account of ethical reasoning" (1951b: 579), and he emphasizes "the central place of the study of our substantive moral conceptions" in this endeavor (1971: 52). Moreover, he does not shrink from identifying this inquiry as a "type of psychology" (1975: 7, 9, 22).

At the same time it is important to recognize that Rawls in effect anticipates and accommodates some of noncognitivism's strongest criticisms. Thus, beginning with *Grounds,* throughout the early part of his career Rawls consistently avoids discussing the "truth value" or "meaning" of moral judgments, relying instead on the key concept of *justification* when formulating the problem of normative adequacy. In addition, Rawls largely sets aside the correspondence of moral judgments to mind-independent moral facts and other similar metaphysical questions because they are not relevant to the main problems of ethical theory as he defines them. Some philosophers have claimed that, as a result of these maneuvers, Rawls simply bypasses traditional metaethics (see, e.g., Rorty 1982: 216; cf. Darwall, Gibbard, & Railton 1992: 142). If metaethics is taken to refer to the linguistic analysis of ethical terms, or to the investigation into the nature of mind-independent moral truths or moral facts, then the observation seems valid, since it is true that Rawls does not engage in these types of inquiry. If, however, metaethics is taken to denote foundational questions about the *subject matter* of ethics (see, e.g., Scanlon 1982, 1992; cf. Darwall, Gibbard, & Railton 1992: 125–130), then the charge that Rawls bypasses metaethics seems less convincing. For it is simply not true that Rawls ignores foundational questions about the subject matter of ethics. Rawls does not take the principal question of normative ethics to be "Which moral judgments and moral principles are true?" but rather "Which moral judgments and moral principles are justified?" Likewise, he does not take the principal question of metaethics to be "How can moral judgments and moral principles be true?" or "How can moral judgments and moral principles correspond to an external moral reality?" but rather "How can moral judgments and moral principles be justified?" From this perspective, Rawls does not bypass metaethics; he merely conceives of the proper aim and organization of an ethical theory in a manner quite unlike many of his philosophical contemporaries, and more in keeping with the conception of moral theory adopted by Aristotle and "most classical British writers through Sidgwick" (1971: 51; cf. Rawls 1951b: 579–580; 1950: 336–346).

In light of these remarks, let me turn now to some of the broader metaethical implications of the research program outlined in Parts One and Two and say a brief word about this topic, as I presently understand it. On the vexed question of moral realism, understood here to be "a thesis about the metaphysical status of moral claims" that affirms the existence of mind-independent moral facts or moral truths, that is, "moral facts and true moral claims whose existence and nature are independent of our beliefs of what is right and wrong" (Brink 1989: 7), it seems useful to begin by reiterating that the conception of moral theory presupposed and elaborated in this book is an *I-morality* conception, according to which I-morality is understood to be the moral analogue of *I-language* (see generally Sections 2.1.8, 3.3). This implies that the main theoretical concept of the research program outlined in Parts One and Two is an idealized model of a particular faculty or cognitive system of the human mind/brain. From this naturalistic perspective, many of the dominant questions of twentieth-century metaethics, such as whether moral judgments of the form "x is wrong" and the like are best interpreted as empirical propositions, descriptions of nonnatural properties, expressions of emotion, universalizable imperatives, or statements about the speaker's own state of mind (see, e.g., Ayer 1936; Hare 1952, 1963; Moore 1903; Prichard 1912; Ross 1930, 1939; Stevenson 1944, 1963; see generally Darwall, Gibbard, & Railton 1992; Harman 1977; Foot 1986; Melden 1958; Sayre-McCord 1988; Urmson 1968; G. Warnock 1967; M. Warnock 1978), do not necessarily arise, at least not in any conventional manner. Thus, they can be profitably set aside. As Rawls suggests, these questions *may* receive illumination along the way, but a naturalistic theory of moral cognition can be successful even if it neglects to address these questions or provide insight into them. Here too there is a comparison with linguistics. Linguists and cognitive scientists do not generally linger over whether judgments of the form "x is grammatical" possess any of these or similar characteristics. In particular, as Chomsky (1980: 27) explains, "the question of truth, conformity to an external reality, does not enter [into knowledge of language] in the way it does in connection with our knowledge of the properties of objects." The linguistic analogy thus permits us to assume as a working hypothesis that so-called moral properties such as *wrongness, permissibility,* and the like can be usefully compared to linguistic properties like *grammaticality* in terms of their phenomenological, ontological, metaphysical, and epistemological qualities, and to get on with the difficult task of supplying an explication of these complex concepts in Rawls' and Chomsky's sense (Rawls 1950: 68–85; 1951a: 184–186; cf. Chomsky 1957: 13–14, 1975a: 61–65).

　　Viewed from this perspective, Hume was correct: properties like permissibility and grammaticality "are not qualities in objects but perceptions in the mind" (Hume 1978/1740: 469). They do not refer in any determinate sense to things that exist in the world apart from the projections of human psychology and the cognitive capacities that support these projections. In other words, insofar as these properties are "part of the fabric of the world" (Mackie 1977: 15), they are properly located in the human Umwelt, the subjective universe of the organism, rather than in anything independent of or external to it. This does not mean that an I-morality conception of moral theory is necessarily incompatible with a more robust, mind-independent interpretation of moral realism, any more than an I-language conception of linguistics is necessarily incompatible with a more robust, mind-independent interpretation of linguistic facts. It simply means that, like the I-language linguist, the I-morality moral theorist attempts to investigate the main questions of her research program within an *internalist* framework, without recourse to mind-independent moral facts. As an initial matter, therefore, it seems plausible to identify an I-morality conception of moral theory with the antirealist position Gilbert Harman adopts in *The Nature of Morality* (1977), the subjectivist position J. L. Mackie defends in *Ethics: Inventing Right and Wrong* (1977), and the projectivist and quasi-realist positions Simon Blackburn elaborates in *Spreading the Word* (1984) and *Essays in Quasi-Realism* (1993), and to contrast it with the realist positions defended by Richard Boyd (1988), David Brink (1989), Michael Moore (1982, 1992), Nicholas Sturgeon (1984), and other prominent moral realists (see generally Sayre-McCord 1988). A sustained examination of these and related metaethical topics falls outside the scope of this book, however, and thus must be reserved for another occasion.

7.7 OBJECTIONS AND REPLIES

Finally, let me turn to some possible objections to the responses to Hare, Singer, and other commentators that I have given on behalf of Rawls in this chapter. Consider first Rawls' claim that a solution to the problem of descriptive adequacy constitutes a presumptive solution to the problem of normative adequacy. Is it true that this contention is plausible? Isn't the response offered here on behalf of Rawls simply negating Hare's point without argument? After all, isn't this presumptive normativity precisely the assumption that Hare is challenging?

A full answer to these questions would require examining Rawls' use of the competence–performance distinction, particularly his concept of considered judgments, which is the topic of Chapter 8. Here I will simply call attention to Rawls' own reply to the objection in *Outline*. In *Outline,* Rawls assumes for the sake of argument that one already possesses an adequate explication of considered judgments. He then asks why one should accept these principles as justifiable. Rawls offers four answers, the first of which is the most relevant for our purposes:

The first reason for accepting them has already been touched upon: namely, since the principles explicate the considered judgments of competent judges, and since these judgments are more likely than any other judgments to represent the mature convictions of competent men as they have been worked out under the most favorable existing conditions, the invariant in what we call "moral insight," if it exists, is more likely to be approximated by the principles of a successful explication than by principles which a man might fashion out of his own head. Individual predilections will tend to be canceled out once the explication has included judgments of many persons made on a wide variety of cases. Thus the fact that the principles constitute a comprehensive explication of the considered judgments of competent judges is a reason for accepting them. That this should be so is understandable if we reflect, to take the contrary case, how little confidence we would have in principles which should happen to explicate the judgments of men under strong emotional or physical duress, or of those mentally ill. Hence the type of judgments which make up the range of the explication is the first ground for accepting the principles thereof. (1951a: 187–188)

Although his reasoning is perhaps too compressed, Rawls' basic argument in this passage seems plausible. As I discuss at greater length in Chapter 8, Rawls selects considered judgments judiciously, relying on criteria that make it reasonable to assume that those judgments accurately reflect an underlying moral competence. Hence the fact that a set of moral principles solves the problem of descriptive adequacy is at least *one* defeasible reason for taking those principles to be justifiable. Here it must be recalled that, for Rawls, the notion of justifiability is a comparative notion. In this passage, Rawls thus suggests that if a moral theorist considers two theories, T_1, explicating what she takes to be considered judgments, and T_2, explicating what she takes to be judgments made under conditions of mental illness, emotional, or physical duress, or other adverse circumstances, and she asks whether T_1 or T_2 is more likely to contain justifiable moral principles, then the answer seems clear and obvious. Consequently, Rawls maintains that a descriptively adequate moral theory is presumptively normative, in light of the data that the former explains.

Does this argument imply that Rawls is a "subjectivist" about morality, as Peter Singer (1974) contends? After considering different interpretations of reflective equilibrium, and after settling on an interpretation according to which the validity of a moral theory depends on whether it successfully describes the human moral capacity, Singer remarks:

If I am right in attributing this version of the reflective equilibrium idea to Rawls, then Rawls is a subjectivist about morality in the most important sense of this often-misused term. That is, it follows from his views that the validity of a moral theory will vary according to whose considered moral judgments the theory is tested against. There is no sense in which we can speak of a theory being objectively valid, no matter what considered moral judgments people happen to hold. If I live in one society, and accept one set of considered moral judgments, while you live in another society and hold quite a different set, very different moral theories may be "valid" for each of us. There will then be no sense in which one of us is wrong and the other right. This point is not affected by whether there is one unique reflective equilibrium for all men or not (a question upon which Rawls refuses to speculate). Even if everyone shared the same considered moral judgment, this would only mean that a theory might have intersubjective validity: it would not make for objective validity. People might have judged differently, and then a different moral theory would have been "valid." (1974: 494–495)

Whatever its merits against other targets, Singer's objection misses the mark against Rawls' conception of moral theory and the research program outlined in Parts One and Two. First, as a branch of cognitive science, moral theory is avowedly "subjectivist," insofar as it takes its field of inquiry to be an aspect of human psychology. As a scientific theory, it is purely explanatory; it presumes that human beings possess a certain moral capacity, and it seeks to ascertain the principles that enter into the nature, origin, and use of this capacity. Its basic standard of epistemic justification is therefore identical with that of other scientific disciplines: conformity to ill-defined but pragmatically acceptable standards of nondemonstrative inference. As with any nontrivial scientific theory, the conclusions of moral theory will be vastly underdetermined, so as a matter of logic there will be infinitely many empirically inequivalent theories that are consistent with all of the available evidence. As such, the "validity" of a particular moral theory simply depends on whether, and, if so, how well, it explains the data defined by its object of inquiry, in comparison with alternative theories.

In this passage, Singer grants that a "Rawlsian" moral theory might have "intersubjective validity" if it turns out that everyone shares the same set of considered judgments in reflective equilibrium. However, he argues that even such a remarkably successful theory would not possess "objective validity" because people "might have judged differently, and then a different moral theory would have been 'valid'" (1974: 494–495). But what is this notion of "objective validity" that Singer expects a moral theory to satisfy? Is it "contingent on human beings and the world they live in retaining the salient characteristics which they have," as Hart (1961: 195) describes the conventional assumption of most naturalistic moral theories? Or is it meant to apply to creatures with brains, nervous systems, or other features quite unlike our own? Clearly these are matters that warrant further explanation. Yet what is striking about Singer's criticism in this passage is that it appears to rest, at bottom, on a complex, controversial, and possibly unintelligible metaethical requirement that Singer seems content to leave entirely unanalyzed. Singer criticizes Rawls for making a philosophical mistake without any recognition or apparent awareness that it is his own conception of moral theory that may be untenable because it expects more than one can reasonably deliver. In any case, it is important to see that how one should interpret the notion of objective validity and how it relates to more modest epistemological goals are precisely the types of question that Rawls rightly insists should not stand in the way of the problems of descriptive and normative adequacy as he has framed them, which are perfectly intelligible and which present both difficult challenges and fruitful opportunities in their own right.

Consider next a different set of objections to Rawls' conception of metaethical adequacy. Suppose for the sake of argument that one has discovered a set of moral principles or axioms that successfully explicates a class of considered judgments in reflective equilibrium. Suppose further that these principles can themselves be derived from a contract among rationally self-interested parties in the original position, hence that their adoption can be proven as a formal theorem in the theory of rational choice. From a logical point of view, therefore, the principles satisfy the two tests of normative adequacy we have identified: they can generate considered judgments in reflective equilibrium, and they can be derived from the original position (see Sections 2.2, 7.4). The principles are only provisional, of course, because further reflection might yield a different conception of which judgments are considered judgments, whether these derivations are valid, whether the original position is correctly characterized, and so forth. Nonetheless, for the time being, one has arrived at a stable equilibrium that satisfies the tests Rawls has identified.

Now the main objection is this: Why should these principles, which by hypothesis are a logical solution to the problem of *normative* adequacy, also be held to be part of a solution to the problems of *descriptive* and *explanatory* adequacy, as we have defined them? Put differently, why should one assume that these principles are not only normatively justified, but also part of an accurate description of how some component of the human mind works? The question can be reframed with reference to Figures 7.1 and 7.2 (see Section 7.4.2). Why should one assume that this putative solution to the problem of normative adequacy looks like Figure 7.2 instead of Figure 7.1? The former incorporates a significant role for descriptive and explanatory adequacy, but why should one assume that these empirical enterprises are part of the normative project of justifying moral principles? Finally, to a certain extent the same challenge can be put in the provocative terms Richard Posner (1999: 6) uses to criticize the influence of moral philosophy on legal analysis: why should one grant that these moral principles describe real, scientifically valid entities, rather than simply being "epiphenomenal"?

There are several responses one might give to these skeptical challenges. Beginning with Posner's challenge, it is certainly true that one can consistently adopt an antirealist perspective (in this sense) toward these principles, thereby refraining to give them mentalistic import. Yet the claim that these moral principles are epiphenomenal is unclear and must be disambiguated. Does the skeptic like Posner simply mean to assert that a neuroscientist could describe the mental activity underlying these judgments without reference to moral or legal concepts like the prohibition of purposeful battery but only in terms of, say, reductions of deoxyhemoglobin in various regions of the cerebral cortex? If so, the claim is true, but uninteresting. The same deflationary account of computational theories could be given in other cognitive domains, where the compatibility and interrelatedness of different levels of scientific description is simply taken for granted. For example, the theory of visual perception can be formulated abstractly, in terms of mental representations and computations, or more concretely, in terms referring to the properties of specific cells in the visual cortex, but it does not follow that the more abstract vocabulary is dispensable (see, e.g., Marr 1982: 24–27, discussing the impact different levels of description have on understanding perceptual information processing). On the other hand, if Posner wishes to argue that the *best* scientific explanation of moral judgments makes no reference to moral or legal concepts, then the claim seems implausible on naturalistic grounds. For example, as I argued in Part Two, recent attempts to explain trolley problem intuitions using the methods of cognitive neuroscience cannot begin to match range of relevant data that scientists can predict by assuming that ordinary individuals are intuitive lawyers, who possess unconscious knowledge of specific rules and principles of tort and criminal law (see generally Sections 5.3, 5.5, and 6.4, especially Figure 5.3 [b] and Tables 6.2 and 6.3). Similarly, neuroscientists cannot successfully explain linguistic phenomena such as the ability of normal language users to recognize whether a novel expression is acceptable without reference to grammatical principles and the representational categories – morphemes, phonemes, phrase structures, and so on – over which they compute. In these and other respects, the need for a good computational the-ory is evident, and the "epiphenomenal" quality of the jurist's and linguist's theoretical vocabularies are on a par.

Moreover, those critics who wish to refrain from assigning mentalistic import to descriptively adequate moral principles would seem to owe us a positive account of their ontological status. Do they exist in some kind of Platonic universe or heavenly realm of juristic concepts? The existence of extensionally equivalent grammars in other domains is well understood (see, e.g., Quine 1972; Chomsky 1975b). Why then should one care whether a par-ticular axiomatization is employed in this domain? On the psychologically realistic approach to moral grammar I have adopted, the answer is that only one set of axioms is a genuine property of I-morality. That is, the correct moral grammar is a true description of some aspect of human cognition, formulated at a suitable level of abstraction, which presumably can be related in principle to other levels of scientific description, perhaps involving neurocognitive or biochemical properties (cf. Chomsky 1980). A skeptic who wishes to reject psychological realism about moral grammars, and to adopt instead a nomi-nalist or instrumentalist standpoint toward these explanations (for example, an E-morality or P-morality standpoint; see Section 3.3), is certainly free to do so. But the mere possibility of these alternative perspectives on the ontol-ogy of moral grammars does not constitute a sound *objection* to an I-morality conception of moral theory. This is especially true in light of the fact that the I-morality theorist is likely to possess converging evidence from a variety of sources – comparative linguistics, developmental psychology, legal anthro-pology, cognitive neuroscience, and so forth – that supports and reinforces her theory of the nature, acquisition, and use of these principles.

The foregoing remarks are rather abstract. To make the discussion more concrete, consider again the formal model of moral grammar and intuitive jurisprudence sketched in Chapter 6. The deontic rules described in that chapter (see generally Section 6.3) were held to be part of a tentative solution to the problem of descriptive adequacy with respect to the data in Table 5.2. Yet, in light of the meaning of reflective equilibrium uncovered in this chap-ter, these rules can also be regarded, at least provisionally, as a solution to the problem of *normative* adequacy. That is, they are presumptively justifiable principles, insofar as they explicate a set of considered judgments in reflective equilibrium. Further, we might assume for the sake of argument, contrary to at least some plausible empirical arguments (see, e.g., Prinz 2008a, 2008b; but cf. Dwyer 2008), that at least some of these rules are neither explicitly taught nor otherwise derived from the surrounding environment. Therefore, they are part of an instantiation of UMG and enter into a solution to the problem of explanatory adequacy. Finally, we can also assume *arguendo* that these rules, and indeed much of the substantive law of crime and tort generally, would be chosen by free, equal, and rationally self-interested parties in the original position to govern their relations with one another.

If this much is sound, then we can now restate each of the three main objections we have been considering in this section and consider them in light of this concrete example. First, why should one accept that these rules are normatively adequate? Second, why should one accept that these rules are objectively valid? Third, why should one accept that these rules are descriptively adequate and thus psychologically real?

In each case the answer seems relatively straightforward, if we adopt the standpoint Rawls recommends. First, it is important to emphasize that the claim that these rules are normatively adequate is merely a presumptively sound working hypothesis, fallible and revisable in the face of sufficient counterevidence. Still, the claim seems warranted in light of the fact that the rules do appear to constitute a successful explication of a set of considered judgments in reflective equilibrium. Furthermore, no alternative theory has been proposed that can do likewise and thereby explain the same phenomena. In addition, the considered judgments that make up the range of the explication appear to be widely shared by demographically diverse populations (see, e.g., Hauser et al. 2007; Mikhail 2007a; Miller 2008). Finally, it seems noteworthy that the same judgments are found less frequently in individuals who are subject to various performance-based errors (for example, deliberate emotional manipulation), as well as those persons suffering from brain lesions and other forms of mental defect (see, e.g., Valdesolo & Steno 2006; Koenigs et al. 2007). While not dispositive, these findings reinforce the assumption that the relevant data are correctly classified as considered judgments in reflective equilibrium.

Second, on the issue of objectivity, the main response is that the concept of objective validity on which critics like Singer rely is obscure and needs to be clarified. In the absence of such clarification, the skepticism implied by this objection may simply illustrate "the harm of expecting too much" (Rawls 1950: 336). Moreover, while the specific notion of objective validity at issue may be an inappropriate and unattainable ideal for moral philosophy, the deontic rules described in Chapter 6 do appear to possess an impressive degree of intersubjective validity. This is a significant and highly desirable finding, particularly because the data appear to be considered judgments in reflective equilibrium in Rawls' sense.

Finally, with respect to the concern about descriptive adequacy and psychological realism, the response is first, that the rules satisfy all the tests for descriptive adequacy outlined in Chapter 4, and second, that there appears to be considerable additional evidence from various branches of cognitive science that suggests that the rules in question are psychologically real. In the case of the prohibition of purposeful battery, for example, this specific rule not only enters into the best explanation of the trolley problems, but it also appears to be implicated in a wide range of other behavioral, developmental, and neuroscientific studies of human moral cognition (see, e.g., Cushman et al. 2006; Greene et al. 2001, 2009; Hamlin, Wynn, & Bloom 2007; Koenigs et al. 2007; Sinnott-Armstrong et al. 2008; Smetana 1983; Young & Saxe 2008).

Moreover, the same presumably holds for the other deontic rules described in Chapter 6. Therefore, although as a logical matter one need not assign mentalistic import to these rules, it seems justifiable on empirical grounds to assume that these rules and the mental computations they imply are both descriptively adequate and psychologically real.

7.8 SUMMARY

Returning to Hare and Singer and summarizing the main argument of this chapter: If Hare's criticism that linguistics does not yield "substantial" or "authoritative" conclusions and Singer's related complaint that Rawls thinks of moral philosophy "in the wrong way" are taken to mean that Rawls' conception of moral theory is inadequate because it is not directed toward solving the traditional problems of normative ethics, then it seems that Hare and Singer have misunderstood the scope and limits of Rawls' linguistic analogy. That analogy makes sense only if one is already concerned with the traditional philosophical questions about the nature and origin of moral knowledge which occupy "most classical British writers through Sidgwick" (Rawls 1971: 51). Put differently, the analogy makes sense only if one already grasps the problem of metaethical adequacy as Rawls conceives of it, including the place of explication and empirical moral psychology within that conception. The parallels Rawls draws are not between linguistics and a set of undifferentiated questions called "moral philosophy," but something more specific: the problem of empirical adequacy in two cognitive domains. Hare's and Singer's criticisms of Rawls' linguistic analogy are themselves vitiated by their apparent failure to grasp these basic points.

Hare, Singer, and other critics who object to Rawls' conception of moral theory on the grounds that it is insufficiently normative have given no indication in their published criticisms of Rawls that they understand the full complexity of Rawls' approach to the problem of metaethical adequacy. Nor, so far as I am aware, have they identified and defended a more cogent metaethical alternative. Unless such an account is actually produced and shown to be superior to the one Rawls adopts in *A Theory of Justice,* Rawls' account would appear to be the most defensible version currently available in the literature. It takes a theory to beat a theory. As is the case with any scientific theory, the best that a theory of moral cognition can hope to achieve is to be better than any of its alternatives.

8

Thomas Nagel and the Competence–
Performance Distinction

It appears to me that in Ethics, as in all other philosophical studies, the difficulties and disagreements, of which its history is full, are mainly due to a very simple cause: namely to the attempt to answer questions, without first discovering precisely *what* question it is which you desire to answer. I do not know how far this source of error would be done away, if philosophers would *try* to discover what question they were asking, before they set about to answer it; for the work of analysis and distinction is often very difficult: we may often fail to make the necessary discovery, even though we make a definite attempt to do so. But I am inclined to think that in many cases a resolute attempt would be sufficient to ensure success; so that, if only this attempt were made, many of the most glaring difficulties and disagreements in philosophy would disappear.

– G. E. Moore, *Principia Ethica*

8.1 NAGEL'S CRITICISMS OF RAWLS' LINGUISTIC ANALOGY

Thomas Nagel's criticisms of Rawls' linguistic analogy may be found in his 1973 review of *A Theory of Justice,* "Rawls on Justice" (Nagel 1973). Nagel begins by summarizing Rawls' conception of moral theory in broad terms:

Rawls believes that it will be more profitable to investigate the foundations of ethics when there are more substantive ethical results to seek the foundations of. Nevertheless, in Section 9 he expounds a general position that helps to explain his method of proceeding. Ethics, he says, cannot be derived from self-evident axioms nor from definitions, but must be developed, like any other scientific subject, through the constant interaction between theoretical construction and particular observation. In this case the particular observations are not experiments but substantive moral judgments. It is a bit like linguistics: ethics explores our moral sense as grammar explores our linguistic competence. (1973: 2)

228

In a footnote Nagel then adds the following criticism of the linguistic analogy:

This seems to me a false analogy, because the intuitions of native speakers are decisive as regards grammar. Whatever native speakers agree on is English, but whatever ordinary men agree in condemning is not necessarily wrong. Therefore the intrinsic plausibility of an ethical theory can impel a change in our moral intuitions. Nothing corresponds to this in linguistics (*pace* Rawls' suggestion on p. 49), where the final test of a theory is its ability to explain the data. (1973: 2 n. 1)

As was the case with Hare, Nagel's brief remarks in this passage are noteworthy in the first instance insofar as they ignore many of the basic elements of Rawls' linguistic analogy that we identified in Part One. The overall impression that Nagel's discussion creates, especially for the reader who has little or no familiarity with generative linguistics, is that the analogy is badly misconceived. This impression is no doubt reinforced by the brevity of Nagel's remarks and the fact that his only direct statement on the topic is relegated to a footnote. As we have seen, however, Rawls' remarks in Section 9 of *A Theory of Justice* contain almost the entire outline of a "generative" or computational approach to the theory of moral cognition. Indeed, there are many significant points of comparison between Rawls' and Chomsky's theoretical frameworks. Both frameworks take their fundamental assumption to be the existence of a particular mental grammar. Both seek to describe or characterize this grammar as accurately as possible, thus making the description qualify as a generative grammar, in approximately Chomsky's sense. Both adopt the standpoint of individual psychology. Both take ordinary intuitions to be evidential; the central aim of the descriptive study is to explain or explicate them. Finally, both frameworks draw a distinction between competence and performance, and take competence, not performance, to be the primary object of inquiry. In the first instance, therefore, Nagel's discussion is noteworthy for failing to call attention to these and other features of the comparison Rawls actually makes.

Turning more directly to Nagel's substantive criticisms of Rawls' linguistic analogy, Nagel makes a number of distinct claims in the foregoing passage. Collectively they seem at first glance to be plausible and to establish not just one but several important differences between moral theory and linguistics. Nonetheless, closer examination suggests that Nagel's criticisms fail to state a compelling objection to the conception of moral theory that Rawls actually describes in Section 9. Moreover, this conclusion holds even if one reconstructs Nagel's criticisms in a more defensible form.

There are at least three plausible reconstructions of the criticisms Nagel makes in this passage. The first is that Rawls' linguistic analogy overstates the theory-dependence of the competence–performance distinction in linguistics and understates the theory-dependence of the competence–performance distinction in ethics. The second is that the analogy is inapt because native speakers are not likely to alter their linguistic performance as a result of reflecting on linguistic theory, whereas the same situation does not hold in the case of moral theory. Finally, Nagel could simply be arguing that there is an aspect to the problem of normative adequacy that has no analogue in linguistics. While all three claims seem plausible, the first two represent empirical issues that cannot be decided on a priori grounds. They do not, therefore, constitute a compelling objection to the conception of moral theory that Rawls describes in Section 9. On the contrary, it is only by getting on with the business of "explor[ing] our moral sense as grammar explores our linguistic competence" (Nagel 1973: 2) that the properties of moral competence and the theory-dependence of the competence–performance distinction in the moral domain can be discovered. Thus, Rawls' linguistic analogy is not false at all, insofar as it enables us to see more clearly what the project of describing and explaining moral competence involves. As for the third criticism, Rawls appears to share the view that the problem of normative adequacy has no precise analogue in linguistics, and we have adopted the same view here (see Section 2.2). Hence the relevance of Nagel's objection, so interpreted, seems limited.

In this chapter, I defend these conclusions by first distinguishing the several propositions that Nagel either asserts or implies in the foregoing passage. I then argue that Nagel's criticisms are unsound as they stand. In doing so, I attempt to clarify the significance of the competence–performance distinction in linguistics. I also discuss Rawls' use of the concept of a considered judgment to capture the corresponding distinction in ethics. Finally, I attempt to reconstruct Nagel's arguments in a more plausible form. I consider and reject several possible reconstructions, settling on the three interpretations mentioned above. I then argue that, so understood, Nagel's criticisms remain unsound.

Before proceeding, it seems useful to make two initial clarifications about the objectives of this chapter and how it is organized. First, while the chapter might seem to imply, implausibly, that Nagel is unfamiliar with the competence–performance distinction, this is not at all what I am suggesting.[1] The main burden of the chapter is simply to argue that Nagel's stated criticisms of Rawls' linguistic analogy are unsound because they fail to make suitable allowances for Rawls' use of the competence–performance distinction and because they underestimate the theory-dependence of the corresponding distinction in linguistics. In fact, given his healthy respect for commonsense moral knowledge and his understanding of how the science of human language has unfolded over the past few decades, I suspect that Nagel would agree with most if not all of the claims advanced in this chapter, and perhaps accept that his dismissal of the linguistic analogy was therefore premature. At any rate, these are among the main objectives I hope to achieve in this chapter.

[1] I am grateful to Jason Stanley for suggesting that an early draft of this chapter gave rise to this impression.

The second clarification concerns how the chapter is organized. In what follows I begin by distinguishing the several propositions that Nagel either asserts or implies in his brief criticism of Rawls' linguistic analogy. I then examine these propositions, point by point, often in considerable detail. The reader might reasonably wonder what the point of this exercise is if, as I have implied, effective replies to Nagel can be stated more succinctly, perhaps even in a few sentences. Why spend a whole chapter elaborating a mere footnote? My response is twofold. First, despite its obvious importance, there remains relatively little sustained discussion in the literature about implications of the competence–performance distinction for moral theory.[2] Nagel's footnote thus offers a useful opportunity to examine certain aspects of this distinction, both as it is apparently used by Rawls and as it has been developed by Chomsky and other linguists. Second, one of the main aims of this book is to remedy a certain casualness with which both critics and proponents have approached the linguistic analogy. For some reason the strengths and weaknesses of the analogy have seemed too obvious to many commentators for them to belabor. As a result, arguments and counterarguments have not always been formulated with sufficient care. Nagel's footnote seems to me to be a good example of this tendency. In my opinion, it possesses a specious plausibility that does not withstand careful analysis. By studying Nagel's objections in considerable detail, then, I hope to fill a gap in the literature and thereby to elevate our understanding of the linguistic analogy to a more sophisticated level.

8.2 ANALYSIS OF NAGEL'S ARGUMENTS

Having made these preliminary remarks, let me turn now to an analysis of Nagel's criticisms of the linguistic analogy. We can begin by distinguishing the several propositions that Nagel either explicitly asserts or implies:

(12) (a) Rawls' linguistic analogy is a false analogy.
   (b) The intuitions of native speakers are decisive in linguistics.
   (c) The moral intuitions of ordinary persons are not decisive in moral theory.
   (d) Whatever native speakers agree on is English.
   (e) Whatever ordinary individuals agree in condemning is not necessarily wrong.
   (f) The intrinsic plausibility of an ethical theory can impel a change in our moral intuitions.

---

[2] In *Rawls' Linguistic Analogy*, I made a stronger claim at this juncture about the inadequate attention given to this topic (see Mikhail 2000: 243). Once again, the statement seems less accurate today than it did at that time, since many important discussions of the linguistic analogy now exist in the literature (see Chapter 1, note 6). Still, the competence–performance distinction remains surprisingly underexamined, a deficiency I attempt to remedy here.

(g) Nothing corresponds to (f) in linguistics. That is, the intrinsic plausibility of a linguistic theory cannot impel a change in our linguistic intuitions.

(h) Rawls' suggestion (1971: 49) that the intrinsic plausibility of a linguistic theory can impel a change in our linguistic intuitions is false.

(i) In linguistics the final test of a theory is its ability to explain the data.

(j) In ethics the final test of a theory is not its ability to explain the data.

According to Nagel, (12a)–(12j) are true statements, and (12f) follows in some manner from (12b)–(12e). Further, (12a) – Nagel's main assertion – follows from the conjunction of (12b)–(12j). That is, (12a) is the conclusion of an argument that is supported in some manner by (12b)–(12j).

Nagel's arguments have been taken by some philosophers (e.g., Daniels 1989: xliii) to be a plausible challenge to the idea that moral theory can be usefully compared with linguistics. In the precise form in which they appear, however, Nagel's arguments are unsound. (12b), (12d), and (12g) are false statements about linguistics. (12h) is a mistaken objection against Rawls. (12c), (12e), (12f), and (12i), although true, are strictly speaking irrelevant because they do not address any comparisons that Rawls actually draws. Finally, (12f) does not follow from the conjunction of (12b)–(12e),[3] nor does (12a) follow from the conjunction of (12b)–(12j). Despite the confident impression created by his brief remarks, therefore, Nagel has not managed to formulate a sound objection to the conception of moral theory that Rawls describes.

Let us examine each of these points in turn.

8.2.1 The Intuitions of Native Speakers Are Decisive in Linguistics

Nagel's first substantive claim, that "the intuitions of native speakers are decisive as regards grammar" (1973: 2 n. 1), is an inaccurate description of the role that linguistic intuitions of native speakers play in theoretical linguistics for at least three reasons. The first is the competence–performance distinction. The second is the related technical distinction linguists draw between grammaticality and acceptability judgments. Finally, the third is the fact that linguists do not consider either the acceptability judgments of native speakers or the grammaticality judgments of linguists, or both, to exhaust possible sources of evidence for the construction of (theoretical) linguistic grammars, as Nagel's

---

[3] By "does not follow from," I do not mean truth-functionally: as I have indicated, (12f) is true, hence it follows truth-functionally from the conjunction of (12b)–(12e). The point I am making is that (12f) is not adequately supported by (12b)–(12e), as Nagel's use of "therefore" is presumably meant to suggest.

claim implies. On the contrary, they consider these judgments to be only one of several possible sources of evidence.

Consider first the competence–performance distinction. As we saw in Part One, a generative grammar is not a model of performance or actual behavior; in other words, it does not represent a theory of how language users actually manage to perceive or produce linguistic expressions. Rather, a generative grammar is a theory of linguistic competence. It attempts "to characterize in the most neutral possible terms the knowledge of the language that provides the basis for actual use of language by a speaker-hearer" (Chomsky 1965: 9). Uncontroversially, a speaker's actual linguistic behavior is affected by things other than her underlying competence: her memory structure, perceptual apparatus, mode of organizing experience, attention span, and a wide range of additional nonlinguistic factors. A speaker's knowledge of language is thus presupposed by, but only one factor contributing to, her actual behavior or language use.

To discover the properties of linguistic competence (I-language), linguists do, of course, study actual behavior. However, to minimize the influence of exogenous factors, they idealize behavior in various ways. Hence they take as their primary object of study to be the I-language of "an ideal speaker-listener, in a completely homogeneous speech community, who knows its language perfectly and is unaffected by such grammatically irrelevant conditions as memory limitations, distractions, shifts of attention and interest, and errors (random or characteristic) in applying his knowledge of the language in actual performance" (Chomsky 1965: 3). And they rely on other idealizations and simplifying assumptions as well.

This leads us to the distinction between grammaticality and acceptability judgments. To clarify and develop the competence–performance distinction, linguists draw a fundamental conceptual distinction between utterances that are *grammatical* and those that are *acceptable*. The former is the key theoretical concept and belongs to the theory of linguistic competence. Although not insignificant, the latter is somewhat less important and belongs to the theory of linguistic performance. Within the framework of generative linguistics, a sentence is grammatical if it is formed in accordance with the rules of the grammar of that language, as formulated by the linguist. A sentence is acceptable if it seems natural to, or conforms to the linguistic intuition of, the native speaker (Chomsky 1965: 10–15). Here is how one leading textbook puts the point:

'Grammaticality' is a theoretical notion. A sentence is grammatical if it is formed according to the grammar of English as formulated by the linguist. 'Acceptability', on the other hand, is the term which characterizes the native speaker's intuitions. ... The native speaker who judges a sentence cannot decide whether it is grammatical. He only has intuitions about acceptability. It is for the linguist to determine whether the unacceptability of a sentence is due to grammatical principles or whether it may be due to other factors. (Haegeman 1994: 7–8)

A classic illustration of the distinction between grammaticality and acceptability judgments is the set of sentences that involve nested or center-embedded constructions. Consider, for example, the following expressions:

(13) (a) The girl is my sister.
    (b) The girl who the boy knocked down is my sister.
    (c) The girl who the boy who the cat tripped knocked down is my sister.
    (d) The girl who the boy who the cat who the dog chased tripped knocked down is my sister.

For the linguist, each sentence in (13) is grammatical: that is, each can be generated by descriptively adequate grammatical rules. Not all of these sentences are acceptable to native speakers, however. On the contrary, (13c) and (13d) are confusing and difficult to process without careful analysis. They are clearly unnatural, and they are unlikely to be produced or encountered in normal conversation. Hence, for most native speakers, they qualify as unacceptable.

One reason Nagel's statement that "the intuitions of native speakers are decisive as regards grammar" (1973: 2 n.1) is inadequate is that it fails to accurately characterize the expressions in (13). If Nagel's statement were true, then the linguist would have no basis for attributing the intuitive unacceptability of (13c) and (13d) to the memory and other processing limitations that typically accompany nested or center-embedded expressions. Nor would she have an interest in constructing a rule system capable of generating these expressions. The point here is a general one, widely followed throughout the cognitive sciences: only by distinguishing the various factors underlying intuitive judgments, and thus by being discriminating toward those judgments, can descriptively adequate theories of cognition be formulated.

Nagel's neglect of the technical distinction between grammaticality and acceptability judgments is a common mistake among commentators on Rawls' linguistic analogy. This includes some philosophers who, unlike Nagel, believe that the linguistic analogy is a *good* analogy. For example, Bernard Gert begins his book *Morality: Its Nature and Justification* by observing:

A useful analogy for knowledge of morality is knowledge of the grammar that all competent speakers of a language have. Even though almost no competent speaker can explicitly describe the grammatical system, they all know it in the sense that they use it when speaking themselves and in interpreting the speech of others. If presented with an explicit account of the grammar, competent speakers have the final word on its accuracy. ... [T]he appropriate test of a grammar is to determine if it allows speaking in a way that all competent speakers regard as acceptable and rules out speaking in a way that is recognized as unacceptable by all who are competent speakers of a language. An explicit account of a grammar must accurately describe the way competent speakers actually use the language. (Gert 1998: 4–5)

Gert's statement contains at least three related mischaracterizations of linguistics. Taking them in reverse order, the first is his remark that an "explicit account of a grammar must accurately describe the way competent speakers *actually use* the language" (Gert 1998: 5, emphasis added). This confuses competence and performance. Put otherwise, it confuses the difference between two questions a theory of language seeks to answer. Recall that generative linguistics is organized around three questions:

(1) (a) What constitutes knowledge of language?
    (b) How is knowledge of language acquired?
    (c) How is knowledge of language put to use?

According to Gert, the aim of a descriptive grammar is to answer the question posed by (1c). This is a mistake: in linguistics, a descriptively adequate grammar seeks to provide an answer to (1a).

The second inaccuracy in Gert's formulation is his statement that "the appropriate test of a grammar is to determine if it allows speaking in a way that all competent speakers regard as acceptable" and "rules out speaking in a way that is recognized as unacceptable" (1998: 4–5). This statement conflates the distinction between grammaticality and acceptability. As we have just seen, however, the distinction is crucial for constructing an accurate theoretical account of linguistic expressions and the properties of rule systems that generate them.

Gert's third mistake is related to the first two. Gert asserts that "competent speakers have the final word" on the "accuracy" of an "explicit account of the grammar" (1998: 4–5). This statement is false for the same reason that (12b) is false. The subject matter of linguistic theory is a biological object: a set of states and properties of the mind/brain. Linguists and other cognitive scientists, not native speakers, have the final word on the accuracy of a grammar with respect to this object. The appropriate test of a linguistic grammar is not whether it accurately describes how competent speakers actually use their language (although such behavior may, of course, be evidential). Instead, the appropriate test is whether it accurately describes the properties of this object.

This brings me to the third overarching reason why Nagel's statement in (12b) is false as a description of the role the linguistic intuitions of native speakers play in theoretical linguistics. Linguists do not consider either acceptability judgments or grammaticality judgments to exhaust their potential sources of evidence for the construction of (theoretical) linguistic grammars, as (12b) implies. On the contrary, they consider these judgments to be only one of several possible sources of evidence. For example, other potential evidence includes data from other languages, data about the chemical or electrical activity of the brain, clinical data from autopsies, and data from aphasics and other individuals with various mental deficits. Moreover, like other scientists, linguists cannot delimit ahead of time what kinds of evidence might bear on their hypotheses (see, e.g., Chomsky 1980: 48–52). Insofar as (12b) implies otherwise, it is simply mistaken.

I have been arguing that both Nagel's statement in (12b) and Gert's similar assertion misrepresent the role of the competence–performance distinction in generative linguistics. It is natural to ask what relevance this has for our analysis of the linguistic analogy and of Rawls' conception of moral theory as a whole. The answer is that it suggests that generative linguistics possesses a theoretical dimension that brings its aims and methods much closer to the type of inquiry that Rawls and others envision for moral theory. As we have seen, Chomsky's theory of language is *mentalistic* in the technical sense: its subject matter is not "the intuitions of native speakers" (Nagel 1973: 2 n.1) or "the way competent speakers actually use the language" (Gert 1998: 5), but rather the essential properties of I-language itself. While all of these behaviors constitute potential *evidence* for I-language, they do not define the subject matter of linguistics. To think otherwise is to confuse evidence with subject matter, as Chomsky (1972), Harman (1989), and others have often emphasized.[4]

8.2.2 The Moral Intuitions of Ordinary Persons Are Not Decisive in Moral Theory

Nagel's second assertion, that the moral intuitions of ordinary persons are not decisive in moral theory, is not explicit but implied. Strictly speaking, this proposition is true. As a criticism of Rawls, however, it misses the mark, because Rawls does not assume that the moral intuitions of ordinary persons are decisive in moral theory. In addition, Nagel's assertion depends on a presumed contrast between (12b) and (12c). As we have seen, however, (12b) is mistaken. The implicit contrast Nagel draws between (12b) and (12c) thus

---

[4] Harman (1989: 490) explains the essential point as follows:

> Many psychologists refuse to take linguistics to be part of psychology and do not count Chomsky as a psychologist. This refusal no doubt arises from not seeing how to use developments in linguistics to help design the sorts of experiments psychologists think they have to do. It is unclear why these psychologists conclude that linguistics is not psychology rather than that psychology should stop depending on a particular conception of experiment. Psychology is the science of mind. Its identity is determined by its subject matter, not by an arbitrary choice of experimental design. Hypotheses in linguistics are supported by such evidence as that the proper noun cannot serve as antecedent to the pronoun in *Jack talked to him.* To suppose that such data do not count as 'evidence' for purposes of psychology is simply to turn one's back on the most successful part of the subject.

> Psychologists sometimes confuse subject matter and evidence, a confusion that is manifested, for example, in the phrase 'behavioral sciences'. Behavior may serve as evidence relevant to theories in cognitive science, but it is not what those theories are about. As Chomsky said years ago, physics is not the science of meter readings and psychology is not the science of behavior.

appears to be based on a misconception of the evidentiary role of ordinary intuitions in generative linguistics.

There are three interrelated reasons why (12c) is true, which are essentially the same reasons we encountered in the linguistic case. First, in both Rawls' stated framework and the research program outlined in Parts One and Two, a moral theory is not a model of actual behavior, but a theory of moral competence (I-morality). Second, in both of these frameworks, the moral intuitions of "ordinary men" are not taken to be "decisive" (Nagel 1973: 2 n. 1), because the only intuitions taken to be evidential are what Rawls calls *considered judgments*. The notion of a considered judgment is a *technical* concept in Rawls' framework, corresponding in relevant respects to the notion of a grammaticality judgment in theoretical linguistics. Considered judgments are thus quite different from the moral intuitions of ordinary persons, as that class of intuitions is commonly understood. Third, even the set of considered judgments does not exhaust the possible sources of evidence for the theoretical construction of moral grammars. As with linguistics and other cognitive sciences, there are many other potential sources of evidence: anthropological and developmental data, data from the chemical or electrical activity of the brain, data about patients with brain damage and various forms of mental illness, and so forth. The point is general, and it follows as soon as we accept Rawls' implicit suggestion that the proper subject matter of moral theory is I-morality. Because the theory of I-morality is an empirical theory, the moral theorist *qua* scientist cannot enumerate ahead of time all of the possible sources of evidence that might bear on her investigation.[5]

Thus far I have confined my attention to a literal interpretation of (12b) and (12c), which is how someone unfamiliar with linguistics seems likely to interpret Nagel's remarks. Jason Stanley (personal communication) has suggested that there is a different interpretation of (12b) worth considering in this context. By "intuitions of native speakers," Stanley observes, Nagel could mean to refer to the grammaticality judgments of native speakers. In that case we could reinterpret (12b) to mean the following:

(12) (b′) The grammaticality judgments of native speakers are decisive in linguistics.

There are at least two problems with (12b′), both of which we have already encountered. First, linguists use the term "grammaticality judgment" in such a way that, strictly speaking, native speakers do not have grammaticality

---

[5] Hence Rawls was mistaken if his oft-quoted remark that there is "a definite if limited class of facts against which conjectured principles can be checked, namely, our considered judgments in reflective equilibrium" (1971: 51) was meant to imply otherwise. Rawls amends and revises this remark in *Independence* by noting that "even the totality of the particular judgments are not assigned a decisive role" in the construction of moral theories (1975: 8). Daniels (1996) takes the latter comment to imply that Rawls' moral theory is not a branch of psychology, but this inference is mistaken (see Section 7.4.2).

judgments (Chomsky 1965: 10–15; Haegeman 1994: 7–8). Second, the notion of a grammaticality judgment, or for that matter any type of an intuitive judgment, being "decisive" within a scientific framework seems misplaced. Stanley concedes the latter point, but he observes that (12b′) could be rephrased as (12b″) to account for the fact that there are multiple sources of evidence for the construction of linguistic grammars:

>   (12)   (b″) Grammaticality judgments, together with the relevant biological facts about the brain, are decisive in linguistics.

Stanley observes that (12b″) is both true and highly relevant to a critical appraisal of Rawls' linguistic analogy because we can also reformulate (12c) to read:

>   (12)   (c′) The considered moral judgments of ordinary persons, together with the relevant biological facts about the brain, are not decisive in moral theory.

Stanley suggests that there is a real difference between (12c′) and (12b″), which could be the disanalogy that Nagel has in mind. While this suggestion seems plausible, it still does not amount to a cogent criticism of Rawls, nor does it conflict with anything Rawls actually says. More importantly, Stanley's reconstruction of Nagel's criticism does not constitute a serious challenge to the research program based on the linguistic analogy outlined in Parts One and Two. To evaluate Stanley's proposal, we must first decide how to interpret the phrase "moral theory" in (12c′). Does it refer in the first instance to the problem of empirical adequacy, or to the problem of normative adequacy? If it refers to the former, then (12c′) looks to be false in whatever sense (12b″) is true. If it refers to the latter, then (12c′) appears to be true, but irrelevant, since neither Rawls nor I contend that the problem of normative adequacy has a precise analogue in generative linguistics. Either way, then, Stanley's proposed reconstruction does not seem to call into question the conception of moral theory at issue, although it does help to clarify some potential misunderstandings of that conception.[6]

8.2.3   Whatever Native Speakers Agree on Is English

Nagel's statement that "whatever native speakers agree on is English" (1973: 2 n.1) could merely be a reiteration of (12b). Alternatively it could be meant to express a separate, novel observation. In either case, the statement overlooks two important features of generative linguistics, both of which we have already encountered.

First, as we have just seen, linguists distinguish between grammaticality and acceptability judgments. The former are the principal body of evidence

---

[6] To be fair, Rawls does not always distinguish the different aspects of moral theory as carefully and consistently as I have tried to do here. Nevertheless, his conception of moral theory does appear to possess the conceptual resources to be defended along the foregoing lines.

for the construction of linguistic grammars, but "whatever native speakers agree on" appears to refer to the latter. On this interpretation, therefore, Nagel's remark appears inapt, for the reasons we have just discussed.

Second, as we saw in Part One, no direct role is played in linguistics by informal, pretheoretic, or commonsense notions of language like English or French, apart from expository passages.[7] Although these informal concepts serve reasonably well for ordinary life, they are inadequate for scientific investigation for at least two reasons that Chomsky and other commentators have often explained. First, concepts like English have a "crucial socio-political dimension" having to do with empires, nation-states, colors on maps, and various other scientifically irrelevant factors:

We speak of Chinese as "a language," although the various "Chinese dialects" are as diverse as the several Romance languages. We speak of Dutch and German as two separate languages, although some dialects of German are very close to dialects that we call "Dutch" and are not mutually intelligible with others that we call "German." A standard remark in introductory linguistics courses is that a language is a dialect with an army and a navy (attributed to Max Weinreich). That any coherent account can be given of "language" in this sense is doubtful; surely, none has been offered or ever seriously attempted. Rather, all scientific approaches have simply abandoned these elements of what is called "language" in common usage. (Chomsky 1986a: 15)

Second, informal concepts of language also have "equally obscure normative and teleological elements," a fact that becomes clear if we ask what language a child or a foreigner learning English is speaking:

Consider the way we describe a child or a foreigner learning English. We have no way of referring directly to what that person knows. It is not English, nor is it some other language that resembles English. We do not, for example, say that the person has a perfect knowledge of some language L, similar to English but still different from it. What we say is that the child or foreigner has a "partial knowledge of English," or is "on his or her way" toward acquiring knowledge of English, and if they reach the goal, they will then know English. Whether or not a coherent account can be given of this aspect of the commonsense terminology, it does not seem to be one that has any role in an eventual science of language. (Chomsky 1986a: 16)

---

7 It is important to recognize that statements like "The SVO hypothesis, which we postulated as part of English grammar, cannot be an absolute linguistic universal: it is part of the grammar of English (and other languages) but not that of Japanese" (Haegeman 1994: 14), which one often finds in linguistic textbooks and which apparently refer to common public languages, are not counterexamples to this assertion. These passages are expository in nature and, if necessary, could be rewritten as follows: "The SVO hypothesis, which we postulated as a part of the (theoretical) linguistic grammar that seeks to describe the (mental) linguistic grammar of those persons commonly described as 'knowing English', cannot be an absolute linguistic universal: it is part of the (theoretical) grammar that seeks to describe the (mental) grammar of persons commonly described as 'knowing English' (and other languages) but not that of persons commonly described as 'knowing Japanese'." Obviously, this kind of prose is tedious and unnecessary. Thus, linguists often refer to languages in their pretheoretic sense, particularly in pedagogical settings, where the risk of misunderstanding is slight (see generally Chomsky 1986a, 1986b).

As Chomsky observes, the terms in which scientific questions are initially posed do sometimes rely on informal or intuitive concepts. For example, when biologists study how dolphins swim or how ants communicate, they might initially use the terms "swim" and "communicate" in more or less the same sense in which they are used in ordinary discourse. However, these intuitive concepts will often quickly give way to more precise empirical concepts that are better suited to scientific inquiry and that depart in crucial ways from ordinary meanings. "Living," "force," "work," and "energy," for instance, often mean very different things in the natural sciences than they do in ordinary discourse (Chomsky 1993b: 181–182).

The relevant point is that Nagel does not adequately differentiate commonsense and technical concepts of language and morality (cf. Sections 2.1.8 and 3.9). "Whatever ordinary men agree on is English" (Nagel 1973: 2 n. 1) is how a layperson might view the study of grammar, but it is an inaccurate picture of the scientific aims of theoretical linguistics. Linguists are not primarily interested in the question: What is English? Rather, their primary questions are (1a)–(1c). These questions may be rephrased in a variety of different ways: What is human language? What is Universal Grammar? What are the properties of the steady and initial states of the language faculty? Likewise, in the research program outlined in Parts One and Two, the corresponding questions are (2a)–(2c) (see Section 2.1.1). These questions can also be reformulated in different ways: What is human morality? What is Universal Moral Grammar? What are the properties of the steady and initial states of the moral faculty? What instructions, if any, are included in the human genetic program for the acquisition of a moral sense or sense of justice? These are the main empirical problems in the cognitive science of moral and legal judgment, at least within the framework we have developed here. From this perspective, the faulty analogy with languages like English, as the latter is understood by folk psychology, need not arise.

8.2.4 Whatever Ordinary Individuals Agree in Condemning Is Not Necessarily Wrong

Nagel's observation that "whatever ordinary men agree in condemning is not necessarily wrong" (1973: 2 n. 1) is perhaps meant to reiterate (12c). Alternatively, perhaps it is meant to be a separate observation. In any event, the proposition is true but, again, irrelevant, insofar as it is meant as a criticism of Rawls' framework or the research program outlined in Parts One and Two. The same three reasons we encountered in our discussion of (12c) apply in this context as well: (i) the competence–performance distinction, (ii) the technical meaning that Rawls assigns to considered judgments, and (iii) the fact that Rawls' topic is moral competence (I-morality).

These three reasons are, as I have said, interrelated. They are simply the consequences of applying the competence–performance distinction to the moral domain. Nagel's failure to recognize this distinction or to acknowledge Rawls' related use of the concept of a considered judgment is a common mistake among philosophers who have discussed the linguistic analogy (cf. Daniels 1980: 34 n. 7). Casual remarks about the moral intuitions or common beliefs of ordinary individuals may be found throughout the literature on this topic. For example, in his review of *A Theory of Justice,* Stuart Hampshire writes:

The point of a moral theory, and so of philosophical ethics, is to find some very general guiding principles that explain the apparently unconnected moral beliefs that constitute a prevailing morality. Rather as a linguist and philologist may look for the general principles that determine word order and the structure of sentences in English, so the philosophical moralist looks for the general principles, or the single principle, that explain the apparently diverse arrangements that we would consider unjust and therefore wrong. If we do succeed in finding such principles, which fit the facts of our ordinary moral beliefs fairly well except in a few marginal cases, then we can use the principles as a guide in doubtful cases; just as we would use general principles of grammar as a guide in doubtful cases when our intuitions fail us or are uncertain. (Hampshire 1972: 34)

Likewise, T. H. Irwin observes:

Rawls compares the task of moral theory to the task of linguistics, suggesting that they both aim at descriptive adequacy. In linguistics, "the aim is to characterize the ability to recognize well-formed sentences by formulating clearly expressed principles which make the same discriminations as the native speaker." The corresponding moral theory will seek principles that generate the common beliefs and remove the puzzles created by the common beliefs. (Irwin 1981: 199)

At first glance, Hampshire's and Irwin's remarks seem unobjectionable. However, they are imprecise and misleading in at least one important respect: they ignore the distinction between moral performance and moral competence. Put differently, these commentaries are notable insofar as they fail to incorporate the crucial difference in Rawls' conception of moral theory between ordinary intuitions or common beliefs and *considered judgments.* Rawls assigns a technical meaning to the latter concept that is largely absent from formulations like Hampshire's and Irwin's. Since this point has often been overlooked and its neglect has sometimes resulted in misunderstanding, a brief review of the meaning of considered judgments seems in order.

The Meaning of "Considered Judgments"
Like the distinction between the problem of descriptive adequacy and the problem of normative adequacy, Rawls' use of a version of the competence–performance distinction in the form of the concept of a considered judgment traces in its essentials to his Ph.D. dissertation (Rawls 1950). In *Grounds,* Rawls divides ethical theory into two parts, explication and justification. He

describes the former as an empirical inquiry, whose aim is the rational reconstruction of a specified class of commonsense moral judgments, which he
calls "the rational judgments of reasonable men" (1950: Abstract). In *Outline,*
Rawls gives a new name to these judgments, calling them "the considered
judgments of competent judges" (1951a: 183). In *A Theory of Justice,* he refers
to them simply as the class of "considered judgments" (1971: 18–22, 47–48).
Terminology aside, Rawls' reason for identifying a class of judgments against
which conjectured principles can be checked appears to be substantially the
same in *Grounds, Outline,* and *A Theory of Justice.* As he explains in *A
Theory of Justice,* the point of doing so is to focus attention on "those judgments in which our moral capacities are most likely to be displayed without
distortion" (1971: 47).

In *Grounds,* Rawls clarifies what he means by the rational judgment of
reasonable men in several respects. He begins by defining the concept *reasonable men.* Rawls first characterizes this idealization as "the class of the average, rational, and right-thinking and fair men, irrespective of wealth, social
stratification, nationality, race, creed or religion," whose members may be
thought of "as possessing a normally developed human nature and as having
capacities which it is reasonable to expect of an average man." Rawls then
enumerates what he takes to be "the four defining properties of the average
right-thinking and fair-minded man": (i) "that he be of a certain age so that
his intellectual and emotional nature be fully developed"; (ii) that he possess
"knowledge and education, at least so much as one could reasonably expect
an average intelligent person to have acquired in the normal course of living";
(iii) "that he can be depended on to be reasonable, if not on all, then at least
on most occasions"; and (iv) that he possess "a certain amount of sensitivity
for the feelings and interests of other people; and a certain sympathy and
understanding for human suffering" (1950: 30–44).

Having explained whose judgments are relevant, Rawls turns to the next
question: Which judgments of reasonable men are relevant? (1950: 45). Rawls
writes:

[T]his question naturally arises, since many judgments which we make are not
meant to be taken seriously, and many others, we readily admit, do not deserve to
be conscientiously considered. Some judgments are made jokingly, and others from
prejudice, bias, or anger, and no one would insist that such utterances are to be put
on a par with calm and considered opinions. One can say, then, that those judgments
which are of weight are those which are spontaneous, stable, impartial, and certain.
These are far more likely to represent our mature convictions on moral questions.
(1950: 45)

Rawls spends 15 pages defining the meaning of the four key terms in this passage: "spontaneous," "stable," "impartial," and "certain." These definitions
form the heart of his concept of a rational or considered judgment. In my opinion they also reveal that, already by 1950, Rawls possessed an intuitive understanding of the competence–performance distinction and its implications for

moral theory and cognitive science that goes well beyond anything discernible in the work of Piaget (1965/1932) or Kohlberg (1981, 1984), arguably the twentieth century's two most influential moral psychologists. Given the importance and relative inaccessibility of these passages, I will quote from them at length.

(i) Rawls begins with the notion of *spontaneity*. By a spontaneous judgment, he says,

I mean one which, superficially at least, results from a direct inspection of the situation itself, and which appears to be determined by a direct and instantaneous contemplation of it. This notion may be clarified if one considers examples of judgments which are not spontaneous by definition. Thus, if a person were to look to the judgment of another person, and were to say just what that person said, or just what he thought that person would say, then his judgment would not be spontaneous. It would be determined, and obviously so, by factors independent of his direct contemplation of the situation itself. Again: if a person were to have worked out in advance an ethical theory of his own, or were to have adopted that of some one else's (well-established or otherwise), and if he were to determine his judgments by the criteria supplied by this theory, then his judgments would not be spontaneous, but determined by the theory and not by his direct inspection of the case confronting him. Less likely instances of non-spontaneous judgments would be contained in a series of appraisals determined by a flip of a coin, or the drawing of a card.

A spontaneous judgment, then, is one in which the judgment is apparently determined by the situation itself, and by the felt reaction to it as a result of direct inspection; and it is one which is not determined by the conscious application of some rule, criterion, or theory. One model of a spontaneous judgment might be the kind that we make when we see unexpectedly some object of great natural beauty. We have no preconceived ideas about it, but, upon seeing it, we spontaneously exclaim that it is beautiful. A spontaneous judgment will be similar in this respect, but will be made concerning virtuous actions, various goods of life, and the like. (1950: 45–46)

(ii) The second property that Rawls identifies is *stability*. According to Rawls, this concept refers to

a certain constancy from time to time and from person to person. One can well imagine our spontaneous judgments to fluctuate from day to day, and from person to person. We might consider the same thing reprehensible one day and admirable the next. By a stable judgment, then, I shall mean one that reflects an enduring disposition to judge in the same way so far as the personal history of an individual is concerned; and also one that reflects a disposition which is shared among the group of persons whose judgments are being considered. A judgment is thus stable in two senses: it endures throughout a period of personal history, and is shared by the class in question. (1950: 49)

Having thus distinguished what we might call *subjective stability* and *intersubjective stability,* Rawls adds the following important remark about stability in general:

The importance of this property is plainly very great; because it is obvious that the study of ethics, so far as it is a rational attempt to explicate common sense morality, could not exist unless there were more or less permanent patterns of judgment and appraisal to serve both as material for theoretical construction and as a body of data against which the validity of the theory could be tested. Stability amongst the patterns of common sense moral appraisal serves the same part for ethical theory that the unchanging patterns of physical events serve for physical theory. It is the daily observed rhythms and structures of nature which first attract attention and stimulate the mind to fashion a theoretical construct to explain them; and it is the belief in a kind of order, simple enough for us to understand, that encourages the investigator to push ahead. Similarly, the stable patterns of moral appraisal in daily life which are summed up by common sense moral rules (such as one should not tell falsehoods, one should repay kindnesses), encourage the moralist to discover, if possible, those more general rules [which] will explain or explicate the entire range of stable common sense judgments. Without such stability, it is doubtful whether any science could begin; and certainly without it, the data against which an explication could be tested would not exist. (1950: 49–50)

(iii) The third property that Rawls examines is *impartiality*. Rawls first discusses this property in conjunction with the notion of a moral judgment's being "cool," in the sense of Butler's phrase "in a cool hour" (1950: 52). By cool, Rawls explains,

I intend to exclude such judgments that are hastily made in moments of emotional duress, such as fits of anger, from revenge, or from fear, and the like. Everyone recognizes the likelihood of these judgments being distorted and everyone has had the experience of regretting what he has said on such occasions. And no one would urge that such utterances are likely to express our mature and considered convictions. To rule out such appraisals is to discard those which we generally recognize to be often ill-founded and unfair. (1950: 53)

Having explained the notion of a cool judgment, Rawls turns to impartiality itself, a concept that he finds more difficult to characterize. One of its features "is an awareness of all of the relevant interests involved." An impartial judgment "will not unwittingly, much less deliberately, overlook any particular interest," but on the contrary, "each one will be given its due weight" (1950: 53).[8] Rawls emphasizes that an impartial judgment need *not* be one that is made without accompanying emotion or feeling. What is important, he suggests, is that those judgments which are accompanied by a *distorting* emotional factor be excluded. Thus he observes:

Anger, revenge, jealousy, fear and the like are likely to distort. But an impartial judgment may arise together with righteous indignation, sympathy, and strong

---

[8] Rawls notices a tension between his definitions of impartiality and spontaneity, in that the former suggests conscious reliance on principles, while the latter excludes it. Seeking to reconcile the two definitions, he observes: "Since we have ruled out the weighing of interests in terms of some rule or theory, we must consider an impartial judgment ... as one wherein the decision is arrived at intuitively and according to one's feelings as one contemplates the total complex of interests concerned. The effort of thought will be to construct in imagination the

feelings for the welfare of other people. Further, an impartial judge need not be a person without interests and aspirations of his own; nor should he be without personal knowledge of those interests which he is required to adjust. It is customary to speak of an impartial spectator as one who just watches what happens, but doesn't care in any way concerning the outcome. But a man may be impartial and care a great deal. It depends on the cause of his concern, whether it is some private interest of his (gain in wealth and the like), or whether it is his concern for the achievement of a just resolution of conflicts. A person who wants to be just, is more likely to be impartial than one who does not. So in excluding certain emotions and interests as likely to distort, I do not intend to exclude them all. An impartial appraiser of moral situations will not be emotionless but deeply concerned about a just solution of the problem; and he is not without direct acquaintance with the interests requiring resolution. Those emotions and interests which disqualify a judgment are only those which are readily admitted to work for unfairness. (1950: 54–55)

Summarizing his discussion of impartiality, Rawls writes that "an impartial and cool judgment is one in which there is no distorting emotional factor, and in which all the relevant interests have been conscientiously reviewed in imagination, and a decision spontaneously given which, to the best of the agent's knowledge, is not unwittingly or deliberately biased by a likelihood of winning personal gain." It seems evident, he concludes, that a judgment lacking these qualities "would not be a reliable guide to a person's mature moral convictions, and therefore they are not arbitrarily or capriciously excluded" (1950: 54).

(iv) The last feature that Rawls takes to be definitive of rational judgments is *certainty*. Rawls contrasts the *feeling* of certainty (or what he labels *certitude* in *Outline*) with certainty, strictly speaking: the former is the psychological state of feeling confident or certain about the truth of a given proposition, whereas the latter is a logical relation between a proposition and its evidence. Judgments marked by certitude are his primary concern:

[T]he judgments we are interested in are those which we feel to be certain. They express our deep-seated intuitive convictions which remain on reflection. ... [T]hese judgments are those about which we feel certain and about which we simply have an intuitive assurance. This feeling of certainty is understood to be known like any other feeling; and it is assumed that everyone is able to tell whether a judgment is accompanied by it. A certain judgment, on the definition, means one that is uttered with the felt conviction that it is certain. (1950: 57–58)

Rawls adds a further revealing clarification about certitude that anticipates one of the meanings he later gives to the concept of a considered judgment in reflective equilibrium. A judgment characterized by certitude, he explains, "means one wherein the feeling of certainty remains after criticism and reflection. The feeling of conviction is not temporary, but remains with us

pattern of interests to be adjusted; while the decision is left to one's spontaneous response as one sees it" (1950: 53).

after criticism. For example, if we compare our judgment with a theory like utilitarianism, and if there is a conflict, then we think that there must be something wrong with the theory, not with the judgment" (1950: 58).

In short, Rawls characterizes the rational judgments of reasonable men in *Grounds* in terms that reflect his underlying commitment to the idea that it is possible to provide a rational reconstruction of the morality of common sense and that only a highly specific idealization of the intuitive moral judgments that people actually make is genuinely probative in that endeavor. If one wants to, one could summarize Rawls' idealization in a sentence: The "rational judgments of reasonable men" are the set of spontaneous, stable, and impartial moral judgments that are felt to be certain by average persons whose intellectual and emotional capacities are normally developed, irrespective of morally irrelevant factors like race, religion, wealth, or social status.

In *Outline,* Rawls changes the name of his preferred class of judgments to "the considered judgments of competent judges" (1951a: 183). He makes other terminological and substantive changes, as well. Nonetheless, his overall approach to these judgments remains essentially the same as it was in *Grounds.* Rawls first defines a *competent judge* as a person who possesses an average degree of intelligence, knowledge, reasonableness, and sympathy (1951a: 178–180). He then identifies several properties that a moral judgment must possess in order to qualify as a *considered judgment.* According to Rawls, such a judgment must be intuitive, stable, impartial, informed, and made with certitude. Finally, it also must concern an actual conflict of interest and not be made under duress of any kind (1951a: 181–183).[9]

The Objection from Prejudice

Carefully reviewing Rawls' definition of a considered judgment as we have done in the foregoing section is important. A clear appreciation of the meaning and underlying rationale of this concept reveals not only that the concern expressed by Nagel in (12e) is unfounded, but also that many of the philosophical criticisms of Rawls' use of considered judgments (see, e.g., Copp 1984; Daniels 1979, 1980; Dworkin 1973; Hare 1973; Nielson 1977; Raz 1982; Singer 1974; Williams 1985; Wolff 1977) appear to be unwarranted as well. For example, Norman Daniels observes:

> The effect [of Rawls' method] is that a set of principles gets 'tested' against a determinate and relatively fixed set of moral judgments. We have, as it were, foundationalism without foundations. Once the foundational claim is removed, however, we have nothing more than a person's moral opinion. It is a 'considered' opinion, to be sure, but still only an opinion. Since such opinions are often the result of self-interest, self-deception, historical and cultural accident, hidden class bias, and so on, just systematizing some of them hardly seems a promising way to provide a justification for them or for the principles that order them. (Daniels 1979: 265)

[9] The specific characteristics that enter into Rawls' definitions of competent judges and considered judgments are elaborate, and they repay careful study. These criteria are reproduced in full in *Rawls' Linguistic Analogy* (see Mikhail 2000: 267–269).

In a similar vein, David Lyons argues that Rawls' approach to considered judgments is flawed because it seems

to move us in a circle, between our current attitudes and the principles they supposedly manifest. We seem to be 'testing' principles by comparing them with given 'data'. Because the latter (our shared, considered moral judgments) are impartial, confidently made, and so on, we can, indeed, regard them as reliably reflecting our basic moral convictions. But we can still wonder whether they express any more than arbitrary commitments or sentiments that we happen now to share. (Lyons 1975: 146)

Likewise, Richard Brandt objects to what he calls Rawls' "method of intuitions" by observing that it is "only an internal test of coherence, what may be no more than a reshuffling of our moral prejudices" (1979: 21–22). Finally, in his book, *Ethics and the Limits of Philosophy,* Bernard Williams criticizes Rawls' linguistic analogy and his effort to explicate common moral intuitions in a chapter entitled "Theory and Prejudice" (Williams 1985: 93–119).

Based on the meaning Rawls actually gives to considered judgments, I believe that objections like these – different versions of what might be called *the objection from prejudice* – are misplaced. For the fact is that none of the judgments that are held to be the result of the delegitimizing factors to which Daniels and others critics refer would qualify as a considered judgment in Rawls' sense that are held by the moral theorist to be the result of the factors to which Daniels, Lyons, and Brandt refer would not qualify as a considered judgment in Rawls' sense. The whole point of the concept of a considered judgment in Rawls' framework is to distinguish between presumptively sound moral judgments and prejudices. Rawls *defines* considered judgments to be those judgments "in which our moral capacities are most likely to be displayed without distortion" (1971: 47). Moreover, he goes to great lengths to identify criteria on the basis of which the moral theorist can assert with some confidence that the judgments she seeks to explicate are *non*-arbitrary, *non*-prejudicial, and *non*-distorted judgments. In the absence of specific criticisms of those criteria, or of their application in concrete cases, wholesale skepticism directed toward the notion of considered judgments seems out of place.

Returning to Nagel and summarizing the main point of this section, Nagel's observation that "whatever ordinary men agree in condemning is not necessarily wrong" (1973: 2 n. 1) is true, but irrelevant, because it overlooks the role of the competence–performance distinction in Rawls' framework. Put differently, Nagel's remark neglects the distinction that Rawls draws between what ordinary individuals condemn and *considered judgments.* Rawls assigns a technical meaning to the latter concept. Once that meaning is properly understood, Nagel's objection appears to be without force. For similar reasons, the objection from prejudice appears misguided, insofar as it, too, fails to make allowances for Rawls' use of the competence–performance distinction.

8.2.5 The Plausibility of an Ethical Theory Can Change Our Moral Intuitions, but the Plausibility of a Linguistic Theory Cannot Change Our Linguistic Intuitions

I will return to the objection from prejudice in Section 8.3. Let me turn now to Nagel's statement that "the intrinsic plausibility of an ethical theory can impel a change in our moral intuitions" (1973: 2 n. 1) and examine the contrast he implies with linguistic theory in this regard.

Consider first Nagel's tacit assumption that the intrinsic plausibility of a linguistic theory cannot impel a change in our linguistic intuitions. To evaluate this proposition, we need to know the referent of "our linguistic intuitions." Is it the acceptability judgments of native speakers or the grammaticality judgments of linguists? The difference is crucial, if for no other reason than that most native speakers are not in the position to assess the intrinsic plausibility of a linguistic theory – the theory is simply too complicated to be grasped by nonspecialists. On the first interpretation, therefore, the relevance of Nagel's assumption seems limited. Does it follow that "our linguistic intuitions" refers to the grammaticality judgments of linguists? One apparent problem with this interpretation, as I see it, is that Nagel's assumption would clearly be false: it amounts to denying that the competence–performance distinction in linguistics is theory-dependent. Put differently, the assumption would be true only if the linguist's grammaticality judgments could never change, that is, if she could not decide for theoretical reasons that an intuition she once took to reveal the properties of I-language was not, in fact, probative evidence after all. Yet counterexamples to this generalization are easy to find; indeed, one can find them in virtually any linguistics textbook. For example, Haegeman (1994: 7) explains the theory-dependence of the competence–performance distinction by means of the following examples:

(14) (a) Bill had left. It was clear.
      (b) [That Bill had left] was clear.
      (c) It was clear [that Bill had left].
      (d) Once that it was clear [that Bill had left], we gave up.
      (e) Once that [that Bill had left] was clear, we gave up.

As Haegeman observes, in (14b) the bracketed sentence *Bill had left* is the subject of the complex sentence [*That Bill had left*] *was clear*. *Bill had left* is a subordinate clause, introduced by *that,* a subordinating conjunction. Likewise, in both (14c) and (14d), *that Bill had left* is a subordinate clause. As these examples illustrate, an adequate grammar must satisfy the general requirement of being capable of generating complex sentences in which one clause is part of another (Hageman 1994: 7–8).

All of this seems straightforward and uncontroversial. The analysis becomes more significant when we consider an expression like (14e). As Haegeman observes, (14e) is odd and *unacceptable* for most native speakers. However, the expression is *grammatical* because it is formed according to the same general rule that is postulated to account for the formation of (14b)–(14d) (1994: 8).

Whether or not Hageman's interpretation of this phenomenon is accurate, the relevant point is that the grammaticality of (14e) is a theory-dependent judgment that the linguist must make. It is therefore likely to be the subject of dispute among linguists and, in any event, can certainly change over time. As Haegeman explains:

Faced with intuitions such as that for (14e), the linguist might decide to modify the grammar he has formulated in such a way that the sentence (14e) is considered to be ungrammatical. He may also decide, however, that (14e) is grammatical, and that the unacceptability of the sentence is due to independent reasons. For instance, (14e) may be argued to be unacceptable because the sentence is hard to process. In the latter case the unacceptability is not strictly due to linguistic factors but is due to the more general mechanisms used for processing information.

The native speaker who judges a sentence cannot decide whether it is grammatical. He only has intuitions about acceptability. It is for the linguist to determine whether the unacceptability of a sentence is due to grammatical principles or whether it may be due to other factors. It is the linguist's task to determine what it is that makes (14e) unacceptable. This entails that there may be disagreement between linguists as to whether certain unacceptable sentences are grammatical or not. The disagreement is not one of conflicting judgments of the sentence (although these may also exist), but it is one of analysis. The linguist will have to determine to what degree the unacceptability of a sentence is to be accounted for in terms of the grammar. (Haegeman 1994: 8, numeration altered)

Haegeman's observations bear directly on the point at issue. If we interpret Nagel's tacit assumption that the intrinsic plausibility of a linguistic theory cannot cause our linguistic intuitions to change to refer to the grammaticality judgments of linguists, then the assumption appears to be false because it effectively denies that the competence–performance distinction is theory-dependent. That distinction, however, *is* theory-dependent in just the way Haegeman describes. As a result, it seems we must search for another interpretation of (12g).

Now, there is another, more sophisticated interpretation of (12g), which is worth considering in this context. It draws on Nagel's criticism in (12h) of the following passage in *A Theory of Justice*, in which Rawls appears to affirm the theory-dependence of the competence–performance distinction.

Moral philosophy is Socratic: we may want to change our present considered judgments once their regulative principles are brought to light. And we may want to do this even though these principles are a perfect fit. A knowledge of these principles may suggest further reflections that lead us to revise our judgments. This feature is not peculiar to moral philosophy, or to the study of other philosophical principles such as those of induction or scientific method. For example, while we may not expect a substantial revision of our sense of correct grammar in view of a linguistic theory the principles of which seem especially natural to us, such a change is not inconceivable, and no doubt our sense of grammaticalness may be affected to some degree anyway by this knowledge. But there is a contrast, say, with physics. To take an extreme case, if we have an accurate account of the motions of the heavenly bodies that we do not find appealing, we cannot alter those motions to conform to a more attractive theory. It is simply good fortune that the principles of celestial mechanics have their intellectual beauty. (Rawls 1971: 49)

According to Nagel, Rawls is mistaken to assume in this passage that "our sense of correct grammar" is revisable in light of theoretical discoveries. If this phrase is taken to refer to a linguist's *theoretical* grammar, then Nagel's claim is clearly false. If "our sense of correct grammar" is taken to refer more narrowly to the grammaticality judgments of linguists, however, then Nagel's claim is also false; as we have seen, the linguist's grammaticality judgments are revisable in just the way considered judgments are revisable, namely, in light of a compelling theory that describes and explains them. We should therefore consider the following alternative. Perhaps what Nagel has in mind is that even if native speakers could reflect on the intrinsic plausibility of a linguistic theory (thus, in effect, could become linguists), they are not likely to alter their intuitions about which expressions in their language are acceptable or well formed as a result of reflecting on a linguistic grammar, whereas the same situation does not hold in moral theory. In other words, what is different about the relationship between linguistic theory and linguistic intuitions, on the one hand, and between moral theory and moral intuitions, on the other, is that only the latter relationship is truly dynamic and interactive. The idea here might be put in terms of the relative malleability or "hardness" of the intuitive data in linguistics, as compared with moral theory. Grammaticality judgments are relatively fixed and hard, whereas permissibility judgments are relatively malleable and soft (cf. Fischer & Ravizza 1992: 12–16). Consequently, the theory of linguistic competence is quite different from the theory of moral competence in this regard.

If this is the contrast Nagel has in mind, then admittedly it does seem plausible. Offhand, it seems unlikely that linguistic intuitions and moral intuitions are equally revisable in light of theoretical reflection. The issue is an empirical one, however, and it would be a mistake simply to assume without further analysis that commonsense moral intuitions are infinitely or even highly malleable. For example, the trolley problem experiments summarized in Part Two seem to suggest that at least some considered judgments are highly stable, stringent, and spontaneous for creatures like us. Moreover, these intuitions appear to emerge relatively early in the course of a moral development and to persist throughout adulthood, quite independently of one's familiarity with moral theory (see generally Chapters 5 and 6; see also Appendix 1). So one should be cautious about making strong and potentially unwarranted assumptions about the power of philosophical reflection to alter deeply held moral intuitions (cf. Posner 1999; see also Mikhail 2002a). More to the point, since the malleability of considered judgments (and so of moral competence itself) is an empirical issue, it cannot be decided one way or another without actual investigation. Hence, if this is the contrast Nagel has in mind, then, while (12g) may turn out to be true, it cannot constitute a compelling objection to the conception of moral theory Rawls actually describes in Section 9 of *A Theory of Justice*. On the contrary, it is only by getting on with the business of "explor[ing] our moral sense as grammar explores our linguistic competence" (Nagel 1973: 2) that the properties of moral competence, and thus the extent to which the competence–performance distinction is theory-dependent, can be discovered. Hence Rawls' linguistic analogy is not false at all, insofar as it enables us to see more clearly what the project of describing and explaining moral competence involves.

Permissibility Judgments versus Acceptability Judgments
To amplify these remarks, it seems useful to consider some further implications for moral theory of the linguist's distinction between grammaticality and acceptability judgments. Like other researchers (e.g., Dwyer 1999), I suspect that moral theorists would do well to adopt a similar terminology to clarify whether certain properties of moral intuitions are, in their considered estimation, the result of endogenous or exogenous factors. For example, moral theorists could distinguish the *permissibility* of an action from its *acceptability*. The former concept would belong to the theory of moral competence, whereas the latter concept would belong to the theory of moral performance. By exploiting this terminology, moral theorists may be able to discover whether the intuitive acceptability of a particular act or institutional arrangement can be explained by principles of moral grammar or should be attributed to other psychological mechanisms that are used for processing information.

To make matters more concrete, consider again the trolley problem intuitions discussed in Part Two. In Chapters 5 and 6, I outlined a fragment of moral grammar that I claimed is capable of generating these intuitive judgments. Moreover, I assumed that these judgments were considered judgments in Rawls' sense, that is, judgments in which the acquired moral capacities of the participants in our experiments were displayed without distortion. However, this assumption certainly could be mistaken. After all, the assumption is highly theory-dependent. Indeed, it is partly *because* the moral grammar hypothesis outlined in Chapters 5 and 6 implies that all or most normal adults possess tacit knowledge of deontic rules like the prohibition of purposeful battery, the Rescue Principle, and the Principle of Double Effect that I took the trolley problem intuitions to be considered judgments in Rawls' sense. Yet consider now the perspective of a theorist who disagrees with all of this and prefers an alternative hypothesis. How can she formulate her hypothesis while at the same time accounting for our data? The competence–performance distinction, and the permissibility–acceptability distinction in particular, provide her with useful conceptual resources to handle this situation. The theorist who wishes to explain away these data can argue that these mere acceptability judgments (as she might classify them), although real enough, are not strictly the product of moral principles, but of other factors. As we saw (Section 6.3.4), the intuitive unacceptability of Ian's throwing the man in the Footbridge problem, for instance, might simply be due to the absurdity of thinking that a man, however large, can stop an onrushing train, rather than to the fact that this action constitutes three counts of purposeful battery. If throwing the man onto the track really *could* stop the train, so the argument might run, then perhaps it is permissible after all. Conversely, a theorist who thinks that the moral grammar hypothesis outlined in Chapter 6 is approximately correct might classify the intuitive unacceptability of Ian's throwing the man as a genuine permissibility judgment. She might note that Ian's throwing the man is structurally analogous to Bob's cutting up the patient in the Transplant problem, along with countless other cases of purposeful battery that are likewise felt to be unacceptable. That superficially distinct cases can be explained by a few fundamental principles might serve to strengthen her initial theoretical convictions.

My point is that there is a genuine counterpart in ethics to the distinction between grammaticality and acceptability judgments, which moral theorists can use to interpret the results of their experiments. Linguists are not content with mere observational adequacy – that is, with merely classifying their data accurately. Rather, they attempt to advance principled explanations of their data. Yet it seems clear that each such explanation must presuppose, at least tacitly, certain controversial empirical claims about the properties of cognitive architecture and systems of mental representation. To make one's way through the study of language, some version of the competence–performance distinction is absolutely essential. The same appears to be true of other areas of cognitive science, such as vision, motor control, musical cognition, and face recognition. There seems little reason to assume that the theory of moral cognition should be any different.

Strong Generation versus Weak Generation

A second point worth mentioning in this context, which provides a more sophisticated interpretation of (12g), relates to the efforts of practicing linguists to achieve explanatory adequacy and turns in part on the distinction between strong and weak generation (Chomsky 1965: 60–62). Until now, I have examined Rawls' linguistic analogy without explicit reference to this distinction, because it has not been particularly relevant. To gain a better appreciation of the theory-dependence of the competence–performance distinction, however, a brief discussion of this distinction and its role in linguistic theory may be helpful.

Perhaps the easiest way to introduce the distinction between strong and weak generation is to return our attention to the simple perceptual and acquisition models for language and morality that we encountered in Part Two. In Chapter 4 I observed that, in his early work on generative grammar, Chomsky clarified the objectives of linguistic theory by distinguishing two

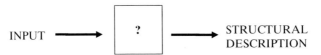

FIGURE 8.1. Chomsky's (1964) Perceptual Model

models that a linguistic theory must specify: a perceptual and an acquisition model (Chomsky 1964: 25f.). I also suggested that, in a suitably modified form, Chomsky's perceptual model could be diagrammed in the manner of Figure 4.1(a) (see Section 4.4.1). This simple input-output model is probably what most of Rawls' readers imagined when they first encountered his linguistic analogy in *A Theory of Justice* (Rawls 1971: 47). Figure 4.1(a), however, is an oversimplification of the perceptual processes that linguists and psycholinguists actually investigate. Moreover, it is not the perceptual model that Chomsky proposed at all. Instead, Chomsky's actual model looked more like Figure 8.1.

Although some comments in *Syntactic Structures* might tempt one to conclude otherwise, the actual goal of a descriptively adequate grammar is not primarily to divide all possible linguistic expressions into grammatical and ungrammatical utterances. As Chomsky emphasizes, this enterprise is of rather limited theoretical interest. Rather, the actual goal insofar as descriptive adequacy is concerned is to formulate a grammar that generates the correct *structural descriptions* of linguistic expressions, as illustrated by Figure 8.1.[10]

What is meant by the correct "structural description" of a linguistic expression? Here it helps to consider a specific example, such as the following expression:

(15) (a) Ian will throw the man onto the track.

(15a) is a grammatical sentence. When we consider its components, the units that first come to mind are its eight words: "Ian," "will," "throw," "the," "man," "onto," "the," and "track." These eight words, however, are not the immediate constituents of (15a). Rather, they are its ultimate constituents, which are organized hierarchically into larger structural units (phrases). These phrase structures can be represented in at least three different formats, including a *tree diagram* (Figure 8.2[a]), *rewrite rules* (Figure 8.2[b]), or *labeled brackets* (Figure 8.2[c]), each of which encodes information concerning the structure of (15a). For example, these structural descriptions indicate that the string *the track* is a syntactic unit, whereas the string *onto the* is not. Likewise, they indicate that *the track* is a noun phrase (NP), whose main element, or head, is the noun *track*. They also indicate that *onto the track* is a prepositional phrase (PP), the head of which is a preposition, *onto,* followed by an NP, *the track* (cf. Haegeman 1994: 34–36).

---

[10] The following three paragraphs are patterned on Haegeman (1994: 34–36).

(a)

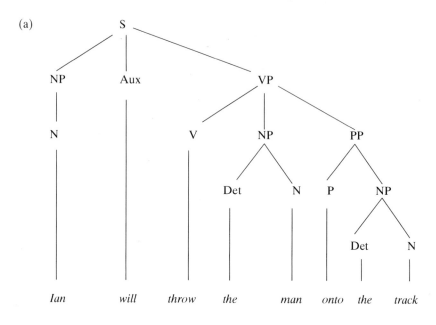

(b) (i)   S → NP - AUX - VP
     (ii)   NP → (Det) – N
     (iii) VP → V - NP - PP
     (iv)   PP → P - NP
     (v)   N → *Ian, man, track*
     (vi)   V → *throw*
     (vii) AUX → *will*
     (viii) P → *onto*
     (ix)   Det → *the*

(c) [s [NP [N Ian]] [AUX will] [VP [V throw] [NP [Det the] [N man]] [PP [P onto]
     [NP [Det the][N track]]]]].

FIGURE 8.2. Three Formats for Representing "Ian will throw the man onto the
track": (a) Tree Diagram; (b) Rewrite Rules; (c) Labeled Brackets

The structural descriptions in Figure 8.2 allow linguists to describe various syntactic operations that might be performed on the expression in (15a).
Consider, for instance, the following examples:

(15) (b) Onto the track, Ian will throw the man.
      (c) The man, Ian will throw onto the track.
      (d) Throw the man onto the track, Ian will (in fact).

For native English speakers, (15b)–(15d) are more or less intuitively acceptable and are thought to be paraphrases of (15a). In order to capture the

relationship between (15a) and (15b)–(15d), linguists might assume that (15b)–(15d) have the same underlying structure as (15a). They might then account for (15b)–(15d) by holding that these expressions can be generated by movement rules that operate on this underlying structure. In each of (15b)–(15d), one of the underlying constituents identified in Figure 8.2 has been moved to the beginning of the sentence, by an operation called *preposing*. Specifically, the PP *onto the track,* the NP *the man,* and the VP *throw the man* have been preposed in (15b), (15c), and (15d), respectively. Yet one cannot indiscriminately prepose any random string of words to generate one well-formed expression out of another (Haegeman 1994: 35). On the contrary, the rule for preposing appears to be structure-dependent, as the following examples illustrate:

(15) (e) * Man onto the, Ian will throw the track.
     (f) * Throw the, Ian will man onto the track.

Another operation that provides evidence for phrase structure in syntax is question-formation. Linguists typically distinguish two types of question, *yes-no questions* and *constituent questions.* These terms refer to the type of answer in each case. Ordinarily one expects a *yes* or a *no* to a question like (16a); by contrast, the remaining questions in (16) are constituent questions. Each of (16b)–(16h) illustrates one of the seven questions that, as we saw in Chapter 6, jurists and philosophers traditionally have asked about the circumstances of a particular action (see Section 6.2.1; cf. Haegeman 1994: 36).

(16) (a) Will Ian throw the man onto the track?
     (b) Who will Ian throw onto the track?
     (c) What will Ian throw onto the track?
     (d) Where will Ian throw the man?
     (e) By what aid will Ian throw the man onto the track?
     (f) Why will Ian throw the man onto the track?
     (g) How will Ian throw the man onto the track?
     (h) When will Ian throw the man onto the track?

The important point about formal operations such as preposing and question-formation is this: linguists are not primarily interested in either the grammaticality or acceptability of (15a)–(15d), nor do they spend their time trying to formulate a grammar that entails these facts. Rather, what interests them are the properties of their underlying structures. It is these properties, rather than the grammaticality of these expressions, that a descriptively adequate grammar must account for. This difference, between a grammar capable of generating a set of grammatical expressions and a grammar capable of generating a set of correct *structural descriptions* of such expressions, is the basis of Chomsky's distinction between strong and weak generation. According to Chomsky, a grammar *weakly generates* a set of grammatical expressions and *strongly generates* a set of structural descriptions of those expressions (1965: 60–62).

What does all this imply for Nagel's criticisms of Rawls' linguistic analogy? The answer is that it points to an important feature of the notion of a grammaticality judgment that might otherwise be missed. Earlier we noted Haegeman's remark (1994: 7–8) that the native speaker who judges a sentence cannot decide whether it is grammatical, but rather can have only intuitions about acceptability. This comment might have come across as somewhat heavy-handed, a misguided attempt by linguists to set themselves up as experts about the grammaticality of sentences whose well-formed character is intuitively obvious to everyone. As the distinction between weak and strong generation illustrates, however, the concept of a grammaticality judgment has a far wider scope than the rather thin issue of whether a particular string of words seems intuitively natural or well formed. The intuitions of a trained linguist, someone who spends her professional career studying the underlying structure of sentences, extend to *those structures* as well. For example, they might include the intuition that Figure 8.2(a) is the correct tree diagram of (15a), rather than some other diagram. The actual debates that occupy linguists are different and more complex than these, of course, because of their focus on explanatory adequacy. Still, the point I am making should be fairly clear. In its broadest sense, the grammaticality judgment of a linguist encompasses the full structural description of an expression like (15a), not merely its intuitive acceptability. Moreover, this broader notion of a grammaticality judgment is heavily theory-dependent, and the intrinsic plausibility of a linguistic theory can cause these intuitions about underlying structure to change. Hence, Nagel is quite wrong to imply otherwise, if what he has in mind are the grammaticality judgments of linguists. These intuitions are theory-dependent and therefore change all the time. Each new book or theoretical paper on linguistic structure is, in effect, a proposal that at least some of the prior grammaticality judgments of scientific researchers were mistaken, and should be modified accordingly.

I believe that a similar situation exists in moral theory and should be given greater emphasis. To begin with, the notion of a permissibility judgment should be widened to include the moral theorist's intuitions about the correct *structural descriptions* of actions, as well as their deontic status. Further, these structural descriptions should become a more central focus of inquiry, as I sought to illustrate in Chapters 6.[11] Finally, researchers should remain open to the possibility that the intrinsic plausibility of a moral grammar might cause their moral intuitions, broadly construed, to change. In the case of trolley problem intuitions, for example, a skeptic inclined to view them with suspicion should be open to being persuaded otherwise, insofar as these intuitions can be successfully embedded within a fruitful explanatory framework.

---

[11] Rawls makes a potentially similar proposal in *Independence* when he suggests that considered judgments can include judgments "at all levels of generality, from those about particular situations and institutions up through broad standards and first principles to formal and abstract conditions on moral conceptions" (1975: 8).

8.2.6 In Linguistics, Unlike Ethics, the Final Test of a Theory Is Its Ability to Explain the Data

In the previous section, I began by noting that the meaning of "our linguistic intuitions" in Nagel's assertion in (12g) is ambiguous. I then argued that regardless of whether this phrase refers to the acceptability judgments of native speakers or to the grammaticality judgments of linguists, (12g) does not state a convincing objection to Rawls' linguistic analogy. The main reasons are the competence–performance distinction and the fact that linguists disagree with one another not only about whether particular grammars are empirically adequate, but also over the nature of the linguistic evidence itself. Further, I argued that this state of affairs should not be surprising. We know enough or should know enough about the philosophy of science to realize that this type of theoretical disagreement is natural and inevitable. No well-developed science is characterized by a total consensus about the evidence for which a successful theory must account. On the contrary, working scientists understand and take for granted that observations and evidence are theory-dependent. Because competing empirical theories are often incompatible with one another, what counts as probative evidence or theoretical confirmation is often fluid and contestable as well.

The final premise of Nagel's argument should be understood in this light. Nagel contends that "the final test of a theory in linguistics is its ability to explain the data" (1973: 2 n. 1), and he contrasts linguistics with moral theory in this regard. This statement is ambiguous and depends in the first place on what is meant by "the data." If this phrase is interpreted with the theory-dependence of scientific evidence in mind, then the statement seems unobjectionable.[12] In that case, however, it seems clear that no relevant contrast with moral theory would thereby be drawn.

Moreover, there is an additional ambiguity lurking beneath the parallel assertion that the final test of an ethical theory is not its ability to explain the data, which concerns the meaning of "ethical theory" itself. Does it refer to the same enterprise that Rawls labels "moral theory" in *A Theory of Justice* and *Independence,* or to something else? If it's the latter, then Nagel and Rawls would appear to be talking past one another. By contrast, if it's the former, then Nagel's claim would appear to be untenable. Nagal and Rawls would then be in genuine disagreement, but Nagel's claim would imply that the final test of a proposed solution to the problem of empirical adequacy is not its ability to explain the data. Yet what else could be the final test of a proposed solution to this problem, other than its ability to explain the relevant data? For that matter, what else could be the final test of any scientific theory, other than its ability to best explain the relevant data?

---

[12] As Chomsky (1988a: 241–242) emphasizes, however, one must be careful not to conflate data coverage with explanatory depth.

Nagel might respond to this question in a number of ways, but it is not clear that any of them are availing. For instance, he could observe that what counts as the relevant data in science is theory-dependent. In addition, he could point out that what counts as explanation in science is often controversial and likewise theory-dependent. More specifically, he could point out that given any fixed body of data, there will always be an indefinite number of different theories that are incompatible with each other but equally capable of explaining the data – in other words, that empirically equivalent alternatives to any scientific theory always exist and, as a result, scientific theories are always logically underdetermined. Nagel could resort to any of these related observations to counter the response that, under the interpretation at issue, (12j) is clearly false.

The problem with all of these replies, of course, is that they are inconsistent with the spirit of (12j). Recall that Nagel's aim is to establish a *contrast* between ethical theory and linguistics. All of the foregoing characteristics are well-established features of normal science. They apply equally well to any form of empirical inquiry, including linguistics. Hence, the significance of Nagel's initial contention would be unclear under this interpretation.

In sum, insofar as (12i) and (12j) are true, they either fail to draw a meaningful contrast with linguistics or reduce to the claim that an analogy that Rawls does *not* draw is a "false analogy" (Nagel 1973: 2 n. 1). As such, they do not amount to a coherent objection to the linguistic analogy as we have interpreted it here.

8.3 OBJECTIONS AND REPLIES

I have argued that the competence–performance distinction in general, and the role of considered judgments in Rawls' framework in particular, implies that both Nagel's criticisms of Rawls' linguistic analogy and the objection from prejudice are misplaced. This argument invites a number of challenges, and in this section I consider and respond to several of them.

Consider first the case of children who are brought up to be racist (see, e.g., Kagan 1989: 13–14). Isn't it legitimate to worry that their moral judgments would not be considered judgments in Rawls' sense, hence that their moral intuitions would be excluded from the class of judgments that the moral theorist seeks to explain? Alternatively, if the moral theorist does exclude their judgments, isn't it legitimate to worry that she does so only because these individuals do not share the theorist's own moral beliefs?

A related objection would push the same issue further back along the evolutionary timeline. Suppose that human moral capacities have evolved in such a way that humans are inherently racist or ethnocentric. Isn't Rawls overlooking this possibility? In general, isn't the moral theorist who sets out to provide an empirically adequate account of I-morality making strong empirical assumptions about the properties of that system that beg crucial questions right from the start?[13]

---

[13] I am grateful to Jason Stanley and Allen Wood for pressing these objections.

While these concerns are understandable, I do not believe that they pose a serious problem for the theory of moral cognition outlined in Parts One and Two. In the first place, if a moral judgment is taken to be an expression of racism or prejudice, then it would not qualify as a considered judgment in Rawls' sense. Second, while it is certainly legitimate to ask whether the considered judgments explicated by a moral theorist are in some sense peculiar to her (cf. Sidgwick 1981/1907: 338), or likewise to ask whether the judgments of some individuals or groups are being excluded for illegitimate reasons, there can be no general objection to Rawls' conception of moral theory on these grounds. The moral theorist who wishes to pursue the research program outlined in Parts One and Two is entitled to begin her investigation from the assumption that a principled distinction between considered judgments (i.e., judgments in which moral capacities are displayed without distortion) and prejudices (i.e., judgments in which moral capacities are distorted in some manner) can be drawn. Put differently, she is entitled to begin her inquiry from the assumption that there really is such a thing as human moral competence and that this system can be characterized in terms of "regular operations" and "accidental disorders" just as Hutcheson (1971/1728: 106) and other philosophers of the Enlightenment thought (cf. Section 2.1.5). The theorist must remain open, of course, to discovering that her assumptions will turn out to be false. And a different theorist may wish to begin from different assumptions. Hence the objections are correct insofar as they mean to imply that the moral theorist who sets out to answer (2a)–(2c) in the manner outlined in this book is basing her investigation on potentially controversial empirical claims that could turn out to be mistaken. But, again, the theorist is entitled to construct her theory in this way. All nontrivial empirical theories depend on potentially controversial empirical assumptions. Hence there can be no principled objection to the competence–performance distinction on these grounds.

These remarks are somewhat abstract. To make them more concrete, consider again the moral judgments elicited by the trolley problems in (4) and Table 5.1 (Sections 4.1 and 5.2.1). In Chapter 6, I constructed a fragment of moral grammar capable of explicating these considered judgments. Significantly, the principles of that grammar made no mention of what I take to be morally irrelevant information, such as race, gender, religious affiliation, and so forth. Suppose, however, that a cognitive scientist tested the following problems on a group of children and discovered that the italicized manipulations had a significant effect:

(17) (a) Alice is a doctor in a hospital's emergency room when six accident victims, *five black and one white,* are brought in. All six are in danger of dying but one, *the white person,* is much worse off than the others. Alice can just barely save him if she devotes all of her resources to him and lets others die. Alternatively, Alice can save the other five if she is willing to ignore the patient who is most seriously injured.

Is it morally permissible for Alice to save the one more seriously injured patient?

(b) Bob is a transplant surgeon. He has five *Christian* patients in the hospital who are dying, each in need of a separate organ. One needs a kidney, another a lung, a third a heart, and so forth. Bob can save all five if he takes a single healthy person and removes her heart, lungs, kidneys, and so forth, to distribute to these five patients. Just such a healthy person is in Room 306. She is *a Muslim,* in the hospital for routine tests. Having seen her test results, Bob knows that she is perfectly healthy and of the right tissue compatibility. If Bob does nothing, she will survive without incident; the other patients will die, however. The other patients can be saved only if the person in Room 306 is cut up and her organs distributed. In that case there would be one dead but five saved.

Is it morally permissible for Bob to cut up the person in Room 306?

(c) Charlie is driving a train when the brakes fail. Ahead five *women* are working on the track with their backs turned. Fortunately Charlie can switch to a side track, if he acts at once. Unfortunately there is *a man* on that track with his back turned. If Charlie switches his train to the side track, he will kill one person. If Charlie does not switch his train, he will kill five people.

Is it morally permissible for Charlie to switch his train to the side track?

(d) Denise is a passenger on a train whose driver has just shouted that the train's brakes have failed, and who then fainted of the shock. On the track ahead are five people, *all Arabs;* the banks are so steep that they will not be able to get off the track in time. The track has a side track leading off to the right, and Denise can turn the train onto it. Unfortunately there is one person, *a Jew,* on the right-hand track. Denise can turn the train, killing the one; or she can refrain from turning the train, letting the five die.

Is it morally permissible for Denise to switch the train to the side track?

(e) Edward is taking his daily walk near the train tracks when he notices that the train that is approaching is out of control. Edward sees what has happened: the train driver saw five *Americans* ahead on the tracks and slammed on the brakes, but the brakes failed and the driver fainted. The train is now rushing toward the five men; the banks are so steep that they will not be able to get off the track in time. Fortunately, Edward is standing next to a switch, which he can throw, that will turn the train onto a side track. Unfortunately, there is one person, *an Asian,* standing on the side track, with his back turned. Edward can throw the switch, killing the one; or he can refrain from doing this, letting the five die.

Is it morally permissible for Edward to throw the switch?

(f) Frank is on a footbridge over the train tracks. He knows trains and can see that the one approaching the bridge is out of control. On the track under the bridge there are five people; the banks are so steep that they will not be able to get off the track in time. Frank knows that the only way to stop an out-of-control train is to drop a very heavy weight into its path. But the only available, sufficiently heavy weight is a large *German* man wearing a backpack, also watching the train from the footbridge. Frank can shove the man with the backpack onto the track in the path of the train, killing him; or he can refrain from doing this, letting the five die.

Is it morally permissible for Frank to shove the man?

Presented with these probes, most experimental subjects will presumably respond in the same way as they do to the original trolley problems in (4). The reason is transparent: there are no morally relevant differences between (4) and (17). Suppose, however, that an investigator tests the two sets of questions on a group of children and discovers that their judgments are at odds with one another. Confronted with data like this, the investigator has at least three options: (i) she can assume that the children possess the same principles of I-morality that her previous experiments have led her to postulate in others, and she can classify their responses as performance errors, distortions, or prejudices; (ii) she can assume that the children possess *different* principles of I-morality than the principles she previously assumed were possessed by others, and she can classify their responses as an accurate reflection of the former principles; or (iii) she can infer that these children have no moral principles (i.e., no I-morality) at all.

Which option should the theorist choose? I do not believe there is a simple answer to that question. Different researchers, proceeding from different assumptions about human nature, might answer the question differently.[14] The important point, however, is that it is an *empirical* question. Whichever decision the moral theorist makes, further investigation may reveal that she was wrong, hence that she must revise her initial assumptions accordingly. But one cannot simply stipulate at the outset that there are no such things as considered judgments, hence that no principled distinction between a valid moral judgment and a prejudice can be drawn, as some philosophers have implied (e.g., Singer 1974: 516). To do so is to use the term "prejudice" in such

---

[14] My own inclination in such a situation would be to pursue option (i) rather than (ii) or (iii). As I explain below, one problem with the objection from prejudice is that it seems to preclude pursuing (i), since it undermines the theorist's ability to draw a principled distinction between considered judgments and prejudices.

a way as to distort its meaning. Rawls makes this point clearly and forcefully in another early text, his 1951 review of Stephen Toulmin's *An Examination of the Place of Reason in Ethics* (1950). Rawls warns against the mistake made by writers

who assert that all moral evaluations are the result of prejudices. ... A prejudice is a recognizable kind of attitude which can be contrasted with other kinds of attitudes. To call all moral evaluations "prejudices" is to use the word "prejudice" in such a way as to make its use pointless. (1951b: 573)

Rawls' remarks are exactly to the point. The distinction between a valid moral judgment and a prejudice is deeply rooted in ordinary language and common sense. It is certainly conceivable that the distinction does not withstand analysis. However, the moral theorist who believes otherwise, as Rawls clearly does, is entitled to begin her investigation from the assumption that a principled basis for the distinction can be found (cf. Kamm 1998: 469).

Much the same reasoning applies, I believe, to whether moral capacities have evolved in such a way that humans are inherently racist or ethnocentric in various ways. This discouraging hypothesis certainly could be true. It is certainly conceivable that the natural foundations of moral judgment are somehow designed to take race, gender, or other similar variables into account when making moral evaluations. If so, then what common sense takes to be prejudices might be largely innate or inborn. The task facing parents, teachers, and moral educators generally would then presumably be to correct for these natural biases.

On the other hand, the hypothesis could be false: all normal human beings could be born with an innate predisposition to know or recognize that fundamental moral categories are universal. As Kohlberg (1981: 16) puts the proposal, "the recognition that moral judgment demands a universal form" could be "a universal a priori intuition of humanity."[15] More simply, it could be a species instinct of some sort. And, of course, there

---

[15] In fact, Kohlberg rejects this proposal, as the following passage makes clear:

From my developmental perspective, moral principles are active reconstructions of experience; the recognition that moral judgment demands a universal form is neither a universal a priori intuition of humanity nor a peculiar invention by a philosopher but, rather, a portion of the universal reconstruction of judgment in the process of development from Stage 5 to Stage 6. An analogy to grammar may clarify this point. Kantian moral intuitionists see their task as like that of Chomsky, who attempts to delimit the principles, the deep structure transformations, which define competent syntax in any language. In grammar, the codification of these principles does not, however, transform syntax itself. Chomsky speaks the same syntax he spoke at age five. It is for this reason that he is able to hold a Kantian epistemology of grammar. There is only one grammatical system of intuition, known to all children of five. In contrast, I am arguing that the codification of principles is an active reconstruction of morality, that Stage 6 principled morality is a radically different morality rather than a codification of conventional Stage 4 morality. The task of both the psychologist and the philosopher, then, is

are many other possibilities. The relevant point, for our discussion, is that these are factual questions. Different theorists, proceeding from different assumptions about human nature, will wish to approach them differently. If the objection from prejudice is meant simply to call attention to the fact that, with his notion of a considered judgment, Rawls appears to be making potentially controversial empirical assumptions that have yet to be validated and may turn out to be false, then the point is well taken. As I interpret them, however, Brandt, Kagan, Lyons, and the other philosophers who have raised this objection appear to be saying something different. They appear to be casting doubt on any conception of moral theory that even purports to draw a competence–performance distinction and thus takes a (provisional) stand on whether the commonsense or pretheoretic distinction between a valid moral judgment and a prejudice can be vindicated. This objection I take to be illegitimate. The moral theorist is entitled to begin her investigation of commonsense moral knowledge from whatever empirical assumptions she thinks are valid. She then faces the burden of gathering empirical evidence to support those assumptions. In the course of doing so, she must remain willing to revise her initial hypotheses on the basis of counterevidence. But all of this is standard science and should be no cause for controversy. Hence if the proponents of the objection from prejudice are intending to make this second, methodological point, then the objection seems misplaced. Unless one is prepared to advance specific criticisms of the criteria Rawls uses to identify considered judgments or of

> very different in the sphere of morality than in grammar. If my position is correct, the only "competent moral speakers" are the rare individuals at Stage 6 (or, more tolerantly, at Stages 6 and 5), and normative ethical codifications and metaethical explanations of conventional moral speech will miss their true task. Like neo-Kantian intuitionists, ordinary-language moral philosophers, particularly formalists such as Hare, think their task is to analytically define and clarify ordinary (Stage 4) moral language. If the form of ordinary moral language is, however, qualitatively different from that of the language of a normative ethical philosopher, the problem is different. (1981: 16)

Kohlberg's remarks in this passage are noteworthy in several respects. First, he conflates the distinction between competence and performance when he writes, "Chomsky *speaks* the same syntax he spoke at age five" (1981: 16, emphasis added). Second, he mischaracterizes linguistic development when he says "there is only one grammatical system of intuition, known to all children of five" (1981: 16). This statement is false if it refers to the *acquired* I-languages of five year-olds, which obviously vary depending on cultural factors. On the other hand, if what Kohlberg means to refer to is UG, then by hypothesis this system is "known" or possessed by all children at birth, although it may not manifest itself until later in development. More generally, the passage nicely illustrates the essentially behaviorist character of Kohlberg's approach to moral psychology: as he explains, his theory tracks the development of a person's ability to engage in certain verbal behaviors (i.e., to become a "competent moral speaker") rather than the development of moral cognition itself. Put differently, Kohlberg's theory is concerned primarily with express principles, not operative principles, unlike Rawls and "most classical British writers through Sidgwick" (Rawls 1971: 51 n. 26).

the particular judgments he selects to belong to that class, the objection from prejudice would seem to be without force.[16]

8.4 SUMMARY

Let me summarize the main results of this chapter. I began by observing that Nagel's objections possess a certain amount of initial plausibility and that some philosophers have implied that they constitute a significant challenge to Rawls' linguistic analogy. However, I then argued that careful analysis reveals that Nagel does not manage in his footnote to formulate a cogent criticism of the analogy Rawls actually draws. This conclusion holds, I suggested, even if we attempt to reconstruct Nagel's stated criticisms in a more defensible form.

In my opinion, there are three plausible criticisms Nagel could be making in his footnote that warrant careful scrutiny. The first is that Rawls overstates the theory-dependence of the competence–performance distinction in linguistics and understates the theory-dependence of the same distinction in ethics. The second is that native speakers are not likely to alter their linguistic

---

[16] I have been arguing that the very meaning of "considered judgment" in Rawls' framework implies both that (12e) and the objection from prejudice are misplaced. Both Jason Stanley and Noam Chomsky have suggested to me that there is another reading of (12e) that deserves consideration. Perhaps by (12e) Nagel really means to assert (12e'):

> (12e') Whatever is condemned by the considered judgments of ordinary individuals is not necessarily wrong.

This statement certainly seems to be true, but I do not see how it can constitute a coherent objection to Rawls' linguistic analogy. In the first place, Rawls assumes, as we have seen, that the distinction between moral competence and moral performance, as manifested in the notion of a considered judgment, is theory-dependent. So Rawls would presumably insist on (12e'). Moreover, the significance of the word "necessarily" in (12e') is obscure and, in any event, destroys the parallel with (12e). Stanley suggests that (12e') has an analogue in linguistics, namely:

> (12e") Whatever is deemed ungrammatical by the tutored grammaticality judgments of an ordinary speaker is necessarily ungrammatical in the idiolect of that speaker.

I have several problems interpreting (12e"). First, as we have seen, linguists use "grammaticality judgment" in such a way that, strictly speaking, (12e") is a contradiction in terms. But beyond that, the whole notion of a grammaticality judgment being "necessarily" anything seems out of place. As Chomsky observes, in the study of natural language there are no such things as "well-formed formulas," strictly speaking. In light of this, I am unclear what is meant by Stanley's notion of a "necessarily ungrammatical" sentence. Finally, (12e") seems in danger of losing sight of the fact that concepts like "grammaticality judgment" in Chomsky's framework and "considered judgment" in Rawls' framework are simply useful ways of talking about *evidence*. The general problem with all of these propositions, then, is that they tacitly assume that the subject matter of Rawls' conception of moral theory is to determine "what is necessarily wrong." Yet, as we saw in Chapter 7, this is exactly the kind of normative question Rawls seeks to avoid, because preoccupation with it may get in the way of solving the problems of empirical and normative adequacy.

performance by reflecting on grammar, whereas the analogous situation does not hold in moral theory. Finally, the third is that there is an aspect to the problem of justifying moral principles that has no analogue in linguistics.

Depending on how these claims are interpreted, they could turn out to be true. But, even so, they cannot constitute compelling objections to Rawls' conception of moral theory. As far as the first two criticisms are concerned, their cogency turns on empirical questions that cannot be decided on a priori grounds. Hence Rawls' linguistic analogy is not false at all, insofar as it enables us to gain a better understanding of the project of describing and explaining moral competence. As far as the third criticism is concerned, Nagel's observation (so interpreted) appears to be sound. If one attributes this argument to Nagel, however, then there is no real disagreement between Nagel and Rawls on this point, since Rawls shares the view that the problem of justification in ethics is, in the final analysis, different from the problem of justification in linguistics. Hence the relevance of Nagel's third criticism, as a criticism of Rawls, seems to be limited. In short, even if one reconstructs Nagel's objections to Rawls' linguistic analogy in their most defensible form, those objections appear to be unsound.

9

Ronald Dworkin and the Distinction between I-Morality and E-Morality

The common saying that the law is known by nature should not be understood
... as though actual and distinct propositions concerning things to be done
or to be avoided were inherent in men's minds at the hour of their birth. But
it means in part ... that at least the common and important provisions of the
natural law are so plain and clear that they at once find assent, and grow up
in our minds, so that they can never again be destroyed, no matter how the
impious man, in order to still the twinges of conscience, may endeavor to blot
out the consciousness of those precepts. For this reason ... the law is said to be
"written in the hearts" of men. Hence, since we are imbued from childhood
with a consciousness of these maxims, in accordance with our social training, and cannot remember the time when we first imbibed them, we think of
this knowledge exactly as if we had it already at birth. Everyone has the same
experience with his mother tongue.
    – Samuel Pufendorf, *On the Duty of Man and Citizen*

Ronald Dworkin is one of the few early commentators on *A Theory of Justice*
who display any enthusiasm for Rawls' linguistic analogy. In his 1973 essay,
"The Original Position," later reprinted as Chapter 6 of his influential book
Taking Rights Seriously (1977), Dworkin refers at one point to "Rawls' exciting, if imprecise, idea" that the conditions embodied in the original position
are "constitutive of our moral capacity." Dworkin later suggests that the
"most profound" interpretation of Rawls' idea implies that certain principles
of justice are "innate categories of morality common to all men, imprinted on
their neural structure" (Dworkin 1973: 26).

Despite his initial enthusiasm for these ideas, Dworkin is ultimately critical
of the substance of Rawls' linguistic analogy. He distinguishes two interpretations, or models, of Rawls' conception of moral theory, which he calls a *natural model* and a *constructive model*. According to Dworkin, the constructive
model is analogous to one interpretation of common law adjudication: it is
what a judge who is faced with a novel claim does when she attempts to reach
an accommodation between a judgment on this claim, a set of precedents,

and a set of principles that justify both the judgment and the precedents. By contrast, the natural model pursues a more "scientific" course: moral principles represent "laws" that are "discovered," and moral judgments represent "observational data" that are thereby "explained" (Dworkin 1973: 27–29).

Dworkin's main claim of relevance to our topic is that the conception of moral theory that Rawls describes in *A Theory of Justice* is inconsistent with the natural model but compatible with the constructive model. Dworkin supports this claim with a variety of arguments, some of which he elaborates at great length. He then concludes that Rawls' method is not only incompatible with the natural model, but, in fact, presupposes the constructive model. In reaching these conclusions, Dworkin does not explicitly reject Rawls' linguistic analogy. His objections to the natural model, however, appear to be directed toward any conception of moral theory that takes itself to be a branch of empirical science, and this is how they have often been interpreted (see, e.g., Daniels 1989; Fischer and Ravizza 1992). Consequently, his objections would appear to constitute a significant challenge to both Rawls' conception of moral theory, as we interpreted it in Part One, and the naturalistic research program in moral psychology that we began to develop in Part Two.

In my opinion, Dworkin's natural model is based on a series of confusions about both Rawls' conception of moral theory and the philosophy of science. These not only vitiate Dworkin's discussion of the linguistic analogy but also render his defense of human rights in *Taking Rights Seriously* weaker than it needs to be. In this chapter, in order to defend these claims, I first summarize the relevant parts of Dworkin's essay. I then explore how certain key features of his natural model appear to rest on a serious misunderstanding of these issues, particularly the conception of moral theory that Rawls describes in *A Theory of Justice.*

At the outset, it is worth noting that the relevant parts of Dworkin's chapter on Rawls are not isolated in one or a few paragraphs, but rather stretch across many pages. Examining the merits of his arguments, therefore, requires more effort than was the case with Hare, Singer, and Nagel, whose criticisms of the linguistic analogy are more succinct. In what follows I quote Dworkin at length. This may try the reader's patience, but it is necessary given my aims. Dworkin's interpretations of Rawls have been highly influential among philosophers, political theorists, and legal scholars. Indeed, it seems likely that the publication of *Taking Rights Seriously* was at least one major factor that led Rawls to abandon the naturalistic interpretation he originally gave to his theory of justice in favor of the constructivism of his later works (see generally Rawls 1980, 1993, 2001b).[1] Nevertheless, as I will attempt to show, Dworkin's criticisms of the natural model appear to be deeply confused and to rest on

---

[1] Rawls credits Dworkin with being "the first to suggest that justice as fairness is constructivist," but he qualifies this statement by observing that Dworkin "understood [constructivism] differently than I do here" (Rawls 1993: 191).

a fundamental misreading of what Rawls actually says about the nature of moral theory in *A Theory of Justice*. In addition, Dworkin's remarks suggest that he misunderstands the implications of the linguistic analogy for a naturalistic project in jurisprudence, along with misconceiving how such a project might supply a more secure foundation for human rights.

9.1 DWORKIN'S ANALYSIS OF RAWLS' LINGUISTIC ANALOGY

Dworkin begins his discussion of Rawls' linguistic analogy by making the following general observations:

> Rawls describes his moral theory as a type of psychology. He wants to characterize the structure of our (or at least one person's) capacity to make moral judgments of a certain sort, that is, judgments about justice. He thinks that the conditions embodied in the original position are the fundamental 'principles governing our moral powers, or, more specifically, our sense of justice' (p. 51). The original position is therefore a schematic representation of a particular mental process of at least some, and perhaps most, human beings, just as depth grammar, he suggests, is a schematic presentation of a different mental capacity. (1973: 25)

These remarks lead Dworkin to distinguish what he calls the "surface argument" of *A Theory of Justice* from what he calls its "deeper theory." As indicated, Dworkin suggests that the most profound and exciting interpretation of that deeper theory implies that principles of justice are "innate categories of morality common to all men" (1973: 26). Here is how Dworkin puts the point:

> I must say a further word about Rawls' exciting, if imprecise, idea that the principles of this deeper theory are constitutive of our moral capacity. That idea can be understood on different levels of profundity. It may mean, at its least profound, that the principles that support the original position are so widely shared and so little questioned within a particular community, for whom the book is meant, that the community could not abandon these principles without fundamentally changing its patterns of reasoning and arguing about political morality. It may mean, at its most profound, that these principles are innate categories of morality common to all men, imprinted in their neural structure, so that man could not deny these principles short of abandoning the power to reason about morality at all. (1973: 26)

Dworkin's chapter on Rawls is divided into two parts. The two passages I have just quoted occur toward the end of part one. Dworkin divides the second part of his chapter into three sections, one for each of what he calls the "three features of the surface argument" of *A Theory of Justice:* "the technique of equilibrium," "the social contract," and "the original position" (1973: 26). His argument that the natural model is incompatible with Rawls' conception of moral theory appears in the first of these three sections, and it is this section that will be my main focus.

9.1.1 The Natural Model versus the Constructive Model

Dworkin begins his argument by trying to ascertain the precise character of Rawls' concept of reflective equilibrium. According to Dworkin, reflective equilibrium presupposes a "coherence" theory of morality, but philosophers "have a choice between two general models that define coherence and explain why it is required, and the choice between these is significant and consequential for our moral philosophy" (1973: 27). Dworkin explains that his aim will be to describe these two models and then to argue that Rawls' concept of reflective equilibrium makes sense on one model, but not the other.

Dworkin proceeds to characterize the two models he has in mind. The first is what he calls a *natural* model, the basic philosophical assumptions of which he summarizes as follows:

Theories of justice, like Rawls' two principles, describe an objective moral reality; they are not, that is, created by men of societies but are rather discovered by them, as they discover laws of physics. The main instrument of this discovery is a moral faculty possessed by at least some men, which produces concrete intuitions of political morality in particular situations, like the intuition that slavery is wrong. Those intuitions are clues to the nature and existence of more abstract and fundamental moral principles, as physical observations are clues to the existence and nature of fundamental physical laws. Moral reasoning or philosophy is a process of reconstructing the fundamental principles by assembling concrete judgments in the right order, as a natural historian reconstructs the shape of the whole animal from the fragments of bones that he has found. (1973: 27–28)

The second model is what Dworkin calls a *constructive* model. Its basic assumptions are quite different:

It treats intuitions of justice not as clues to the existence of independent principles, but rather as stipulated features of a general theory to be constructed, as if a sculptor set himself to carve the animal that best fit a pile of bones that he happened to find together. This 'constructive' model does not assume, as the natural model does, that principles of justice have some fixed, objective existence, so that descriptions of these principles must be true or false in some standard way. It does not assume that the animal it matches to the bones actually exists. It makes the different, and in some ways more complex, assumption that men and women have a responsibility to fit the particular judgments on which they act into a coherent program of action, or, at least, that officials who exercise power over other men have that sort of responsibility. (1973: 28)

As indicated, Dworkin compares the constructive model with one model of common law adjudication, in which a judge faced with a novel claim attempts to fit a series of diverse precedents into a coherent decision. "We might treat this judge as being in the position of a man arguing from moral intuitions to a general moral theory," he observes. "The particular precedents are analogous to intuitions; the judge tries to reach an accommodation between these precedents and a set of principles that might justify them and also justify further decisions that go beyond them" (1973: 28). However, such a judge does not assume

> that the precedents are glimpses into a moral reality, and therefore clues to objective principles he ends by declaring. He does not believe that the principles are 'instinct' in the precedents in that sense. Instead, in the spirit of the constructive model, he accepts these precedents as specifications for a principle that he must construct, out of a sense of responsibility for consistency with what has gone before. (1973: 29)

Building on these initial contrasts, Dworkin identifies four main differences between the natural and constructive models. First, although both models seek consistency between intuitive judgments and principles, the fact that they do so for different reasons implies that their response to anomalous intuitions differs as well. As Dworkin sees it, the natural model "supports a policy of following the troublesome intuition, and submerging the apparent contradiction, in the faith that a more sophisticated set of principles, which reconciles the intuition, does in fact exist" (1973: 29). Dworkin likens this situation to that of an astronomer who is unable to reconcile clear observational data in a coherent account of the origin of the solar system. Such an astronomer, he claims, would continue to assume that her observations are accurate and to utilize them in her computations, while simply placing faith in the idea that some coherent theoretical explanation of them exists, even though it has not yet been discovered. By contrast, the constructive model "does not support the policy of submerging the apparent contradiction" on the assumption that reconciling principles can be discovered. Instead, "it demands that decisions taken in the name of justice must never outstrip an official's ability to account for these decisions in a theory of justice," even when some of her intuitions must thereby be compromised (1973: 29–30).

Second, Dworkin contends that the two models adopt different approaches toward certain familiar questions of metaphysics and epistemology. The natural model presupposes a "moral ontology" that denies "skepticism" and "relativism" and that presupposes the "objective standing" of the moral intuitions it seeks to explicate. By contrast, the constructive model is neutral on these issues; it neither assumes nor denies skepticism or relativism, nor does it affirm or deny the objectivity of these intuitions. It is thus consistent with, but does not require, the moral ontology presupposed by the natural model (1973: 30).

Third, Dworkin observes that, in light of the foregoing considerations, the two models adopt what he calls "different standpoints" toward moral intuitions. The natural model looks at moral intuitions "from the personal standpoint of the individual who holds them, and who takes them to be discrete observations of moral reality." By contrast, the constructive model "looks at these intuitions from a more public standpoint; it is a model that someone might propose for the governance of a community each of whose members has strong convictions that differ, though not too greatly, from the convictions of others" (1973: 31).

Finally, Dworkin argues that only the constructive model "is well suited … to developing a theory that can be said to be the theory of a community rather than of particular individuals." One virtue of this model, for instance, is that the range of moral intuitions to be assessed "can be expanded or contracted to accommodate the intuitions of a larger or smaller group, either by including all convictions held by any members, or by excluding those not held by all, as the particular calculation might warrant." On the natural model, however, this process "would be self-destructive … because every individual would believe that either false observations were being taken into account or accurate observations disregarded, and hence that the inference to objective morality was invalid" (1973: 31).

9.1.2 The Natural Model and Reflective Equilibrium Are Incompatible

Having identified these key differences between the two models, Dworkin turns to his main argument, which asserts that the natural model and Rawls' concept of reflective equilibrium are incompatible. "Which of these two models," he asks, "better supports the technique of equilibrium?" Although he notes that some philosophers, such as Hare, assume that Rawls is committed to the natural model, Dworkin insists that "the alliance between that model and the equilibrium technique turns out to be only superficial." Indeed, he argues that "when we probe deeper" the natural model and reflective equilibrium turn out to be incompatible (1973: 31–32).[2]

Dworkin offers three reasons to support his contention that the natural model and reflective equilibrium are incompatible. First, he argues that the natural model cannot provide a satisfactory explanation of what he calls the "two-way feature" of reflective equilibrium. In particular, although the natural model can explain why a theory of justice must fit our intuitions about justice, it cannot explain "why we are justified in amending these intuitions to make the fit more secure" (1973: 32, 34). Such a maneuver, he contends, "would be nothing short of cooking the evidence, as if a naturalist rubbed out the footprints that embarrassed his efforts to describe the animal that left them, or the astronomer just set aside the observations that his theory could not accommodate." Dworkin accepts that scientists do sometimes "adjust their evidence to achieve a smooth set of explanatory principles" and that Quine and other philosophers of science might be correct to endorse the principle of confirmation holism, according to which scientists "might react to recalcitrant or surprising experience by making different revisions at different places in

---

[2] As these remarks imply, Dworkin's main argument actually consists of two different claims. The first is implicit: the constructive model supports the "technique of equilibrium" better than the natural model. The second is explicit: despite a "superficial alliance" between that technique and the natural model, the two are incompatible.

[their] theoretical structures." Dworkin insists, however, that "if this is true at all, their procedures are very different from those recommended by the technique of equilibrium," because the latter "argues not simply that alternative structures of principle are available to explain the same phenomena, but that some of the phenomena, in the form of moral convictions, may simply be ignored the better to serve some particular theory." In short, the practice of setting aside a particular moral intuition in order to achieve the harmony of reflective equilibrium is something quite different than the ordinary scientific practice of offering alternative theoretical explanations of a given body of available evidence (1973: 32–34).

Second, Dworkin argues that "the results of the [equilibrium] technique, at least in Rawls' hands, are necessarily and profoundly practical" because the parties in the original position must find principles that are easy to understand, publicize, and observe; principles otherwise appealing "are to be rejected or adjusted because they are too complex or are otherwise impractical in this sense." Furthermore, principles that are selected in this spirit "are compromises with infirmity, and are contingent in the sense that they will change as the general condition and education of people change." Dworkin claims that these features are "inconsistent with the spirit, at least, of the natural model, according to which principles of justice are timeless features of some independent moral reality, to which imperfect men and women must attempt to conform as best they can" (1973: 34).

Finally, Dworkin argues that the natural model would be "seriously compromised" by two forms of "relativism" that are inherent in the concept of reflective equilibrium, which, he says, is designed to produce principles that are relative in at least two ways. First, reflective equilibrium "is designed to select the best theory of justice from a list of alternative theories that must not only be finite, but short enough to make comparisons among them feasible." Second, this procedure "yields results that are relative to the area of initial agreement among those who jointly conduct the speculative experiments it recommends." As a result, reflective equilibrium is designed to produce "different results for different groups, and for the same group at different times, as the common ground of confident intuition shifts" (1973: 34–35).

These two forms of relativism, however, would seriously compromise the "authority" of the natural model for at least two reasons, according to Dworkin. The first is that the natural model, as Rawls characterizes it, is merely what we have labeled an *evaluation procedure* (Section 2.1.6) for moral principles:

If the equilibrium argument for Rawls' two principles, for example, shows only that a better case can be made for them than for any other principles on a restricted short list, and if Rawls himself is confident that further study would produce a better theory, then we have very little reason to suppose that these two principles are an accurate description of moral reality. It is hard to see, on the natural model, why then they should have any authority at all. (1973: 35)

The second reason why reflective equilibrium's implicit relativism would undermine the authority of the natural model concerns an issue we examined in Chapter 7: namely, *whose* judgments the model takes to be probative. Dworkin writes:

If the technique of equilibrium is used by a single person, and the intuitions allowed to count are just his and all of his, then the results may be authoritative for him. Others, whose intuitions differ, will not be able to accept his conclusions, at least in full, but he may do so himself. If, however, the technique is used in a more public way, for example, by fixing on what is common amongst the intuitions of a group, then the results will be those that no one can accept as authoritative, just as no one could accept as authoritative a scientific result reached by disregarding what he believed to be evidence at least as pertinent as the evidence used. (1973: 36)

In short, Dworkin offers three reasons why the natural model is incompatible with Rawls' concept of reflective equilibrium: first, the natural model cannot explain the mutual adjustment of judgments and principles that is implied by reflective equilibrium; second, the natural model is inconsistent with the contingent, practical character of principles of justice; and third, the natural model is incompatible with two forms of relativism that Dworkin claims are inherent in the concept of reflective equilibrium, both of which compromise the authority of its conclusions.

Having ascertained that the natural model and reflective equilibrium are incompatible, Dworkin turns his attention to the constructive model and offers two reasons why none of the foregoing difficulties arise if one assumes that reflective equilibrium is meant to be in the service of the constructive model. First, he observes that "even a powerful conviction" that cannot be reconciled with other such convictions can be rejected within the framework of the constructive model: "the conviction is rejected not as a false report," he explains, "but simply as ineligible within a program that meets the demands of the model." Second, neither respect in which reflective equilibrium is inherently relativistic is an embarrassment for the constructive model:

It is not an embarrassment that some theory not considered might have been deemed superior if it had been considered. The model requires officials or citizens to proceed on the best program they can now fashion, for reasons of consistency that do not presuppose, as the natural model does, that the theory chosen is in any final sense true. It does not undermine a particular theory that a different group, or a different society, with different culture and experience, would produce a different one. It may call into question whether any group is entitled to treat its moral intuitions as in any sense objective or transcendental, but not that a particular society, which does not treat particular convictions in that way, is therefore required to follow them in a principled way. (1973: 36)

In other words, the constructive model is able to avoid the difficulties of the natural model for two relatively simple reasons, according to Dworkin. First, unlike the natural model, the constructive model is consistent with the mutual adjustment of judgments and principles that is implied by the notion of reflective equilibrium. Second, neither form of relativism that Dworkin claims would seriously compromise the authority of moral theory is a problem for the constructive model. On this basis, Dworkin concludes that Rawls' conception of moral theory presupposes the constructive model but is incompatible with the natural model (1973: 37).

9.2 PROBLEMS WITH DWORKIN'S ANALYSIS

Thus far I have sought merely to summarize those parts of Dworkin's commentary on Rawls that bear directly on the main concerns of this book. Having done so, let me turn now to a critical appraisal of Dworkin's central arguments.

As I noted at the outset, Dworkin's interpretations of Rawls have been highly influential. In particular, his distinction between the natural and constructive models and his emphasis on the inherent limitations of the natural model have been taken by many observers to be a significant challenge to the idea that moral theory can be conceived of as a type of natural science. In addition, his objections to the natural model and his endorsement of the constructive model appear to have been a factor that led Rawls over time to move away from the naturalistic interpretation he originally gave to justice as fairness in *A Theory of Justice* (see, e.g., 1971: 504–512) and toward the sharply limited political conception of the doctrine that characterizes his later works (see, e.g., 1993: xv–xvi, 191). Dworkin's natural model, however, appears to rest on a series of confusions. For our purposes these can be conveniently divided into two main groups. The first are confusions about the conception of moral theory that Rawls actually describes in *A Theory of Justice*. The second are confusions about science.

Because the primary concern of this chapter is how Dworkin misinterprets Rawls, I will not dwell on his apparent misconceptions about science, beyond making a few brief observations. First, Dworkin repeatedly underestimates the degree to which scientific observations are theory-dependent (see, e.g., Hanson 1958; Kuhn 1970; cf. Boyd 1985, 1988; Harman 1977; Sturgeon 1984). Second, along the same lines, Dworkin mistakenly assumes that scientists do not regularly set aside or ignore certain observations that cannot be readily explained within the parameters of their explanatory models. Put differently, Dworkin is mistaken to assume that scientists never sacrifice mere coverage of data for explanatory depth. The reality is otherwise: even those scientists who work with what are perceived to be relatively "hard" data often act more like the epistemic agents in Dworkin's constructive model than their counterparts in the natural model (Daniels 1980; cf. Kuhn 1970; Polanyi 1958). Indeed, philosophers and historians of science might note with some irony Dworkin's assumption that scientists never simply ignore some of the phenomena "the better to serve some particular theory" (1973: 33), since the great scientific revolutions of the seventeenth century were often predicated on doing exactly that (see, e.g., Burtt 1992/1924; Chomsky 1980, 1988a; Cohen 1985; Kuhn 1957, 1970). Chomsky explains the dramatic shift in perspective that occurred during this period as follows:

[O]ne of the most striking features of the Galilean revolution was that, perhaps for the first time, those responsible for that revolution (that is, Kepler, Galileo, the major figures in what we now regard as that scientific revolution) recognized that depth of explanation could compensate for lack of coverage of data.

Let me be more concrete. If you go back to the time of Galileo and look at the array of phenomena that had to be accounted for, it seemed prima facie obvious that the Galilean theory, the Copernican theory, could not be supported. That is, there were just masses of unexplained, or even partially refuting data. Galileo plowed his way though this, putting much of the data aside, redefining what was relevant and what was not relevant, formulating questions in such a way that what appeared to be refuting data were no longer so, and in fact very often just disregarding data that would have refuted the system. This was not done simply with reckless abandon, but out of a recognition that explanatory principles were being discovered that gave insight into at least some of the phenomena. Now, a willingness to move towards explanatory principles that give insight into some of the phenomena at the cost of not being able to handle all of the phenomena: that I think was one of the most striking intellectual achievements of the great scientific revolution.

So, let's return to the matter of the restriction of the domain of investigation. If you take, say, the Aristotelian world view, the range of phenomena taken to fall within a theory of motion was vastly greater than what Galileo could consider. For example, the Aristotelian theory of motion included not only what we would call mechanics – that is, things bumping into each other, and so on – but also growth, perception, development, change. All sorts of phenomena fell together within this theory of motion. The Galilean theory threw out most of those phenomena, and in fact restricted itself to matter in motion. I think that what was dramatic about the development of physics in that period was that, within the domain on which it concentrated, explanatory principles were emerging which could integrate and connect, and give a kind of rationale for phenomena that could previously only be described. Now, as a descriptive system, the Ptolemaic system was no worse than the Galilean system, maybe even a bit better, but it lacked depth of explanation.

This shift of intellectual attitude from concern for coverage of data to concern for insight and depth of explanation, and the related willingness to deal with highly idealized systems in order to obtain depth of explanation – this shift of point of view has taken place very rarely, I think, in the history of thought. ... Until a shift in this direction takes place, I think it would be fair to say that linguistics will not have undergone something like the revolution of early modern science. (Chomsky 1988a: 242)

In short, what Chomsky and other commentators have called the "Galilean style" of modern science is characterized by a "readiness to tolerate unexplained phenomena or even as yet unexplained counterevidence to theoretical constructions that have achieved a certain degree of explanatory depth in some limited domain, much as Galileo did not abandon his enterprise because he was unable to give a coherent explanation for the fact that objects do not fly off the earth's surface" (1980: 9–10). Dworkin therefore gets things exactly backwards when he claims that scientists do not ignore observations that their theories cannot accommodate. As one might infer, but perhaps should be made explicit, the Galilean style also forms the backdrop to my own effort in Part Two to explain a few relatively simple moral intuitions in terms of basic rules of criminal and civil law in lieu of constructing a more comprehensive theory of moral cognition, which might take into account a much wider range of phenomena. To paraphrase Chomsky, this decision was not made with reckless abandon, but rather from the settled theoretical conviction that a systematic analysis of these intuitions and the cognitive capacities that enter into them might lead to the discovery of deep explanatory principles, thereby providing genuine insight into at least some of the phenomena, and paving the way for future investigations.

9.3 DWORKIN'S MISINTERPRETATIONS OF RAWLS

Although these issues in the philosophy of science are important, I do not wish to belabor them here, partly because other commentators have already drawn attention to some of Dworkin's principal misconceptions of this subject (see, e.g., Daniels 1980). To the best of my knowledge, however, no sustained treatment of Dworkin's mischaracterizations of Rawls' conception of moral theory exists in the literature. Hence, this issue will be my focus in what follows.

What I take to be Dworkin's misinterpretations of Rawls can be stated rather perspicuously. The first concerns what Rawls identifies as the *subject matter* of moral theory. The second concerns what Rawls identifies as the *goal* of moral theory in light of its subject matter. The third concerns what Rawls identifies as the *evidence* available to the moral theorist to achieve this goal. Finally, the fourth concerns what Rawls identifies as appropriate *method* for the moral theorist to adopt toward her evidence, goal, and subject matter.

As we have seen, Rawls identifies the proper subject matter of moral theory in *A Theory of Justice* to be what I have called *I-morality:* a particular moral capacity of the human mind, which the theorist approaches from an internal, intensional, individual, and ideal perspective, in the sense discussed in Chapters 2 and 3 (see, e.g., Sections 2.1.8 and 3.3). Further, Rawls identifies the goals of moral theory to be a correct description, explanation, and justification of the principles of I-morality. He identifies the primary evidence available to the moral theorist to achieve these goals to be the set of considered judgments in reflective equilibrium. Finally, Rawls characterizes the method that moral theorists should employ to achieve these goals as the hypothetico-deductive method, at least with respect to the problems of descriptive and explanatory adequacy.

In his chapter on Rawls, despite his evident concern with foundational questions Dworkin manages to distort each of these four features of Rawls' conception of moral theory. According to Dworkin's natural model, Rawls' conception of the subject matter of moral theory is not I-morality, but *E-morality:* that is, a mind-independent object of some sort, which Dworkin repeatedly refers to as an "objective moral reality," "objective moral universe," "independent moral reality," and similar characterizations (e.g., 1973: 27, 31, 34). Further, Rawls' conception of the goal of moral theory is a description of E-morality, so construed. Rawls' conception of the evidence available to the moral theorist to achieve this goal is limited to the theorist's own moral intuitions and positively excludes the intuitions of others. Finally, Rawls' conception of the appropriate method in moral theory is not the hypothetico-deductive method, but what Dworkin refers to as "the technique of equilibrium" (e.g., 1973: 27–37).

Turning to Dworkin's constructive model, Rawls' conception of the subject matter of moral theory according to this model is not a particular moral or mental capacity, but something else: the design of a "program of action" for "officials who exercise power over others" (1973: 28). The goal of moral theory on this model is to "fit the particular judgments on which these officials act" into a program that is "coherent" (1973: 28). Rawls' conception of the evidence that is available to accomplish this goal includes the convictions of judges and other officials that are "held with the requisite sincerity," along with legal precedents and other "independent reasons of political morality" (1973: 31). Finally, Rawls' conception of the appropriate method in moral theory on this model is, once again, what Dworkin calls "the technique of equilibrium" (1973: 27–37).

Table 9.1 is a useful summary of these four features of Rawls' conception of moral theory, together with Dworkin's interpretations of each of them. In what follows, I examine each feature in turn.

9.3.1 Subject Matter

Dworkin begins his analysis of Rawls' conception of moral theory by acknowledging that Rawls characterizes moral theory as "a type of psychology." He recognizes that Rawls seeks "a schematic representation of a particular mental process," just as "depth grammar" is "a schematic presentation of a different mental capacity." Further, he recognizes that on at least one interpretation of Rawls' linguistic analogy, which he calls the "most profound interpretation," that analogy might imply that principles of justice "are innate categories of morality common to all men, imprinted on their neural structure" (1973: 25–26). It seems clear, therefore, that Dworkin begins his analysis by recognizing that Rawls' topic is I-morality.

Nevertheless, once Dworkin begins developing his two competing interpretations of Rawls, this recognition disappears, and the subject matter of

TABLE 9.1. *Dworkin's "Natural" and "Constructive" Interpretations of Rawls' Conception of Moral Theory*

	Rawls' Actual Conception	Dworkin's "Natural" Model	Dworkin's "Constructive" Model
Subject Matter	I-morality	E-morality	The design of a program of action for officials who exercise power over others
Goals	1. Describe I-morality (descriptive adequacy) 2. Explain the acquisition of I-morality (explanatory adequacy) 3. Justify the principles of I-morality (normative adequacy)	Descriptive adequacy?	To fit the particular judgments on which officials act into a program of action that is coherent
Evidence	Considered judgments (in reflective equilibrium)	The theorist's own moral intuitions (excluding the intuitions of people)	The convictions of officials held with the requisite sincerity, along with legal precedents and other independent reasons of "political morality"
Method	Hypothetico-deductive method	"Technique of equilibrium"	"Technique of equilibrium"

moral theory abruptly changes. On Dworkin's natural model, Rawls' subject matter is not I-morality, but something different. Dworkin refers to this new focus of inquiry in a variety of ways: "moral reality," "the objective moral universe," "independent moral reality," and so forth. For example, in one representative passage he writes:

[T]he natural model ... presupposes a philosophical position that can be summarized in this way. Theories of justice, like Rawls' two principles, describe an *objective moral reality;* they are not, that is, created by men of societies but are rather discovered by them, as they discover laws of physics (1973: 27, emphasis added; see also 29, 31, 34–35)

As vague and unhelpful as the italicized phrase is, one thing is clear: whatever it and analogous phrases such as "objective moral universe," "independent moral reality," and the like refer to is a *mind-independent* object or entity of some sort, that is, something that exists "outside the head." Yet this means that Dworkin's natural model departs crucially from Rawls' stated framework, which does not presuppose any mind-independent conception of moral realism. The subject matter of Rawls' conception of moral theory is an aspect of human psychology: the human moral capacity or sense of justice, that is, a set of states or properties of the human mind/brain. The subject matter of Dworkin's natural model, on the other hand, is a *non*-mental object of some sort: a set of states or properties existing outside and independently of the mind/brain. Rawls' actual subject matter, in short, is I-morality; the subject matter of Dworkin's natural model, by contrast, is E-morality. Hence, whatever else is true of Dworkin's natural model, it is not an accurate interpretation of Rawls.

For Dworkin to remain faithful to Rawls' actual conception of moral theory when introducing the natural model, he should have said something along the following lines:

The 'natural model' can be summarized in this way. Theories of justice, like Rawls' two principles, describe a real object: a cognitive faculty of the human mind/brain. The properties of this faculty are not created by men of societies, but rather discovered by them, as they discover the laws governing their language faculty.

Alternatively, had Dworkin wished to distance himself from the linguistic analogy (which, although useful, is not an essential feature of an I-morality conception of moral theory), he could have introduced a serious naturalistic interpretation of Rawls' conception of moral theory by means of many other relevant comparisons: for example, by comparing the moral faculty to the faculty of vision, or the immune system, or the digestive system. Yet, instead of reproducing Rawls' actual analogy, or at least an analogy that preserves the critical fact that Rawls conceives of moral theory as a branch of human psychology (such as the analogy to vision) – or, at a further remove, an analogy that preserves the fact that Rawls conceives of moral theory as a branch of (theoretical) human biology, that is, a field whose subject matter, in the final analysis, is a natural property of human beings (such the comparisons to the immune system or digestive system) – Dworkin departs from Rawls' actual framework in at least two crucial ways. First, he introduces the "realist" assumption that if moral principles exist, they must exist outside and independently of the mind/brain ("out there," in the phrase Dworkin often uses in this context; see, e.g., Dworkin 1998: 1719; cf. Guest 1991: 147–148). Second, he draws the loosest, most inapt analogy of all: between moral principles and laws of physics.[3]

---

[3] Dworkin's physics analogy is exceedingly unhelpful. Perhaps the only relevant feature of Rawls' conception of moral theory it preserves is the fact that Rawls conceives of descriptive adequacy to be a problem of empirical science. Yet the physics analogy largely strips

When it comes to accurately representing Rawls' subject matter, Dworkin's constructive model does not fare much better. According to the constructive model, Rawls' subject is not a particular moral faculty or mental capacity; in fact, it is not an aspect of human psychology or even an object or "thing" at all! Instead, Rawls' actual topic disappears and is replaced with the following goal: to design a coherent framework of principles that can serve as a guide for political or legal officials who exercise power over others. Thus, as we have seen, Dworkin's constructive model does not assume

> that principles of justice have some fixed, objective existence, so that descriptions of these principles must be true or false in some standard way. It does not assume that the animal it matches to the bones actually exists. It makes the different, and in some ways more complex, assumption that men and women have a responsibility to fit the particular judgments on which they act into a coherent program of action, or, at least, that officials who exercise power over other men have that sort of responsibility. (1973: 28)

Moreover, this initial characterization of the constructive model is no mere verbal slip. On the contrary, the idea that the proper subject matter of moral theory is a "program of action" that can give advice to "officials" who are responsible for "governing the community" is a recurring feature of Dworkin's elaboration of the constructive model. The textual support for this conclusion is quite clear.[4]

9.3.2 Goal

During the early part of his career with which we are concerned (1950–1975), Rawls not only thinks that the proper subject matter of moral theory is I-morality; he also repeatedly makes clear that the provisional goal of moral theory is to achieve descriptive adequacy with respect to I-morality.

---

moral theory of any intelligible claim to be a science. On Dworkin's interpretation, moral philosophers are like astrophysicists, probing the universe for mysterious moral properties. Not surprisingly, this conception of moral theory has little to recommend it.

[4] Note that I do not wish to deny that *A Theory of Justice* addresses problems of governance or that Rawls hoped that his book would influence political or legal officials. Presumably, he did hope that it would do so. Indeed, as I note in Section 1.3, Rawls touches on a wealth of practical topics, ranging from the philosophical bases of constitutional liberties and problems of distributive justice to civil disobedience and conscientious objection. My point is the narrower one concerning what, strictly speaking, Rawls takes to be the *subject matter* of moral theory in *A Theory of Justice*. In Section 9, Rawls makes it quite clear that he conceives of moral theory as a theory of I-morality; that is, "a theory of the moral sentiments ... setting out the principles governing our moral powers, or, more specifically, our sense of justice" (1971: 50–51). Elsewhere, Rawls emphasizes that a theory of justice, so understood, must not be confused with either political science ("our discussion is part of the theory of justice and must not be mistaken for a theory of the political system"; 1971: 227) or economics ("It is essential to keep in mind that our topic is the theory of justice, and not economics, however elementary"; 1971: 265).

For example, in his remarks on moral theory in Section 9 of *A Theory of Justice,* Rawls writes:

Now one may think of moral philosophy ... as *the attempt to describe our moral capacity;* or in the present case, one may regard a theory of justice as *describing our sense of justice.* (1971: 46, emphasis added)

A conception of justice *characterizes our moral sensibility* when the everyday judgments we do make are in accordance with its principles. (1971: 46, emphasis added)

Only a deceptive familiarity with our everyday judgments and our natural readiness to make them could conceal the fact that *characterizing our moral capacities* is an intricate task. (1971: 46–47, emphasis added)

There is no reason to assume that *our sense of justice can be adequately characterized* by familiar common sense precepts, or derived from the more obvious learning principles. *A correct account of moral capacities* will certainly involve principles and theoretical constructions which go much beyond the norms and standards cited in everyday life. (1971: 47, emphasis added)

According to the provisional aim of moral philosophy, one might say that justice as fairness is the hypothesis that the principles which would be chosen in the original position are identical with those that match our considered judgments and so these principles *describe our sense of justice.* (1971: 48, emphasis added)

In *describing our sense of justice* an allowance must be made for the likelihood that considered judgments are no doubt subject to certain irregularities and distortions despite the fact that they are rendered under favorable circumstances. (1971: 48, emphasis added)

If we can describe one person's sense of grammar we shall surely know many things about the general structure of language. Similarly, if we should be able *to characterize one (educated) person's sense of justice,* we would have a good beginning toward a theory of justice. We may suppose that *everyone has in himself the whole form of a moral conception.* (1971: 50, emphasis added)

I wish to stress that a theory of justice is precisely that, namely, a theory. It is a theory of *the moral sentiments* (to recall an eighteenth century title) setting out *the principles governing our moral powers, or, more specifically, our sense of justice.* (1971: 51, emphasis added)

Compare fairly transparent remarks like these, of which there are many, with Dworkin's own characterization of Rawls' goals. On Dworkin's natural model, Rawls' objectives are descriptive, but the object that the moral theorist seeks to describe is not *I*-morality, but *E*-morality. Hence Dworkin repeatedly uses phrases such as "describe an objective moral reality" or "accurate description of moral reality" to characterize those objectives (1973: 27, 34). On Dworkin's constructive model, by contrast, Rawls' goals are not descriptive, even in part, since according to that model there is nothing for moral principles to describe. Instead, Rawls' goals and subject matter merge into a largely ideological enterprise whose ultimate purpose is apparently to rationalize and justify – that is, to render coherent – the particular judgments of judges and other government officials who exercise power over others. If we ask what on Dworkin's view coherence amounts to, we receive the following answer: it is a relation of logical consistency between moral intuitions and moral principles, subject to two basic constraints. First, the constructivist moral theorist (or the legal official to whom the theorist gives advice) "accepts [legal] precedents as specifications for a principle he must construct, out of a sense of responsibility for consistency with what has gone before" (1973: 29). Second, the theorist (or official) "takes convictions [of other officials] held with the requisite sincerity as given, and [she] seeks to impose conditions on the acts that these intuitions might be said to warrant" (1973: 31). The second requirement flows from what Dworkin calls "independent reasons of political morality," a concept left undefined (1973: 30–31).

   In sum, Dworkin offers two interpretations of the goals of moral theory, neither of which conforms to Rawls' actual remarks about moral theory in *A Theory of Justice*. On Dworkin's natural model, Rawls' goal is to solve the problem of descriptive adequacy with respect to E-morality. On Dworkin's constructive model, Rawls' goal is to legitimize the exercise of legal or political authority by judges or other government officials. On Rawls' *actual* model, the goal of moral theory is to solve the problems of empirical and normative adequacy with respect to I-morality, that is, with respect to a specific moral faculty or mental capacity of the human mind/brain.

9.3.3 Evidence

Dworkin repeatedly mischaracterizes the evidence available to the moral theorist in Rawls' conception of moral theory. To take one clear illustration, consider again the following passage:

> The natural model ... looks at intuitions from the personal standpoint of the individual who holds them, and who takes them to be discrete observations of moral reality. The constructive model looks at these intuitions from a more public standpoint; it is a model that someone might propose for the governance of a community each of whose members has strong convictions that differ, though not too greatly, from the convictions of others. (1973: 31)

By my count, this passage includes at least three crucial distortions of the conception of moral theory that Rawls actually describes in *A Theory of Justice*. The first is the one that we just discussed: namely, Dworkin's substitution of E-morality ("moral reality") for I-morality in his statement of the descriptive goals of the natural model.

   Dworkin's second mistake is one that we examined at length in Chapter 8: namely, the failure to distinguish clearly between moral intuitions, *simpliciter,* and what Rawls calls *considered judgments.* As we have seen, the notion of a considered judgment is a technical concept in Rawls' framework, corresponding in certain relevant respects to the role played by grammaticality judgments in generative linguistics. Throughout his chapter on Rawls, Dworkin repeatedly ignores this concept, preferring instead to refer to considered judgments in a variety of more casual ways – as "ordinary judgments," "unreflective moral beliefs," "immediate convictions," and so on (see, e.g., 1973: 22–23). The net result of this practice is to obscure the fact that the primary function of the concept of a considered judgment in Rawls' framework is to select, from among the moral judgments people *actually* make, those judgments that the moral theorist believes are truly evidential, insofar as they reflect the properties of an underlying cognitive competence.

Dworkin's third mistake is perhaps the most important. It is his failure to distinguish the standpoint a moral theorist adopts toward considered judgments from the nontheoretical standpoint an ordinary person (including, perhaps, the theorist herself) adopts when she applies her sense of justice to particular moral and social problems. Put differently, Dworkin's third mistake is his failure to distinguish properly between first-person and third-person points of view. On Dworkin's natural model, the moral theorist is limited to adopting a *first*-person point of view toward her *own* moral intuitions (from something like the standpoint of a phenomenologist). On Dworkin's constructive model, the moral theorist adopts a *third*-person point of view toward her own *and* other people's moral intuitions – not for the purpose of solving the problems of empirical and normative adequacy, but for the purpose of legitimizing the exercise of political power and authority. In Rawls' *actual* model, the moral theorist adopts a *third*-person point of view toward her own *and* others' moral intuitions (that is, toward those intuitions that qualify as considered judgments), but she does so from the standpoint of a cognitive scientist, who takes the judgments to be evidence for the properties of a particular cognitive system.

In *The Independence of Moral Theory* (1975) – Rawls' 1974 Presidential Address to the American Philosophical Association, which was written after Dworkin's essay on Rawls first appeared in the *University of Chicago Law Review* (1973), but before it was reprinted as Chapter 6 of *Taking Rights Seriously* (1977) – Rawls implicitly corrects Dworkin's failure to distinguish properly between first-person and third-person points of view. Without mentioning Dworkin by name, Rawls takes pains to emphasize that in attempting to construct an empirically adequate theory of the human moral sense, a researcher must carefully distinguish her standpoint as a moral theorist from her standpoint as a person applying her own moral beliefs to particular moral and social problems:

In order to [investigate the moral conceptions that people hold, or would hold, under suitably defined conditions], one tries to find a scheme of principles that match people's considered judgments and general convictions in reflective equilibrium. This scheme of principles represents their moral conception and characterizes their moral sensibility. *One thinks of the moral theorist as an observer, so to speak, who seeks to set out the structure of other people's moral conceptions and attitudes.* Because it seems likely that people hold different conceptions, and the structure of these conceptions is in any case hard to delineate, we can best proceed by studying the main conceptions found in the tradition of moral philosophy and in leading representative writers, including their discussions of particular moral and social issues. We may also include ourselves, since we are ready to hand for detailed self-examination. *But in studying oneself, one must separate one's role as a moral theorist from one's role as someone who has a particular conception. In the former role we are investigating an aspect of human psychology, the structure of our moral sensibility; in the latter we are applying a moral conception, which we may regard (though not necessarily) as a correct theory about what is objectively right and wrong.* (1975: 7, emphasis added)

Two paragraphs later Rawls reiterates that he conceives of the moral theorist as an observer whose aim is to characterize the implicit moral conceptions of people in general:

Furthermore, because our inquiry is philosophically motivated, we are interested in what conceptions people would affirm when they have achieved wide and not just narrow reflective equilibrium, an equilibrium that satisfies certain conditions of rationality. That is, *adopting the role of observing moral theorists*, we investigate what principles people would acknowledge and accept the consequences of when they have had the opportunity to consider other plausible conceptions and to assess their supporting grounds. (1975: 8, emphasis added)

Despite reasonably clear statements like these, Dworkin's mistaken assumption that a moral theorist is *restricted* to adopting the first-person point of view of a phenomenologist and *excluded* from adopting the third-person point of view of a cognitive scientist has become a prevailing view in the field. T. M. Scanlon, for example, aligns himself with Dworkin and departs from Rawls' stated conception when he observes: "The revisability of the class of considered judgments ... illustrates the fact that the search for Reflective Equilibrium is essentially a first-person enterprise; if the judgments in question were those of other people, treated as a kind of sociological fact, then they would not be susceptible to this particular kind of revision" (Scanlon 1992: 10). Likewise, Joseph Raz suggests that one of the "strengths" of Dworkin's interpretation is

to make clear an important difference between a psychological and a philosophical theory of our sense of justice. The former may take the form of correlations between, say, the level of sugar in one's blood and one's tendency to approve or reject certain moral propositions. Or it may relate one's experiences in infancy to one's views about authority. A philosophical description of a moral sense will not include such principles. A metaphor which comes to mind is that while psychology may describe a person's moral disposition from the outside, philosophy is confined to an insider's view of the sense of justice. A philosophical description takes the form of a set of moral principles, and they are principles which the person whose sense of justice is investigated would accept as valid. Not only do they represent his moral judgments as a coherent system, but they are acknowledged by him to do so. This guarantees that the principles do not merely match his moral judgments. They present them in the way that he perceives them, interrelated in the way that he himself (at least after achieving equilibrium) interrelates them. To distinguish a theory of the moral sense which is subject to these constraints from others I shall call Rawls' philosophical theory a theory of the internal constitution of the moral sense. The view I attribute to Rawls is that morality is the internal constitution of the moral sense, and that the method of wide reflective equilibrium is the one by which that internal constitution can be best ascertained. (Raz 1982: 316)

Remarks like Scanlon's and Raz's are telling in that they reproduce the very first-person limitations on theory-construction that Rawls warns moral theorists to avoid, but that Dworkin mistakenly imposes. Hence, they leave little room for the problems of empirical and normative adequacy as Rawls actually frames them. Indeed, they leave little room for these problems as they were framed by most classical British moralists, as well as by Kant and other major historical figures in the modern period (see, e.g., Schneewind 1998). Consider, for example, how Sidgwick summarizes his effort to characterize "the Morality of Common Sense" in Book III of *The Methods of Ethics,* widely recognized to be one of the most careful and systematic treatments of common morality in the literature:

We started with admitting the point upon the proof of which moralists have often concentrated their efforts, the existence of apparently independent moral intuitions. It seemed undeniable that men judge some acts to be right and wrong in themselves, without consideration of their tendency to produce happiness to the agent or others: and indeed without taking their consequences into account at all, except insofar as these are included in the common notion of the act. We saw, however, that in so far as these judgments are passed in particular cases, they seem to involve (at least for the more reflective part of mankind) a reference of the case to some general rule of duty: and that in the frequent cases of doubt or conflict of judgment as to the rightness of any action, appeal is commonly made to such rules or maxims, as the ultimately valid principles of moral cognition. In order, therefore, to throw the Morality of Common Sense into a scientific form, it seemed necessary to obtain as exact a statement as possible of these generally recognized principles. I did not think that I could dispense myself from this task by any summary general argument, based on the unscientific character of common morality. There is no doubt that the moral opinions of ordinary men are in many points loose, shifting, and mutually contradictory, but it does not follow that we may not obtain from this fluid mass of opinion, a deposit of clear and precise principles commanding universal acceptance. The question, whether we can do this or not, seemed to me one which should not be decided a priori without a fair trial: and it is partly in order to prepare materials for this trial that the survey in the preceding eight chapters has been conducted. *I have endeavored to ascertain impartially, by mere reflection on our common moral discourse, what are the general maxims, according to which different kinds of conduct are judged to be right and reasonable in different departments of life. I wish it to be particularly observed, that I have in no case introduced my own views, in so far as I am conscious of their being at all peculiar to myself: my sole object has been to make explicit the implied premises of our common moral reasoning.* (Sidgwick 1981/1907: 337–338, emphasis added)

As this passage suggests, contemporary philosophers who follow Dworkin, Scanlon, and Raz in imposing first-person limitations on theory-construction are departing not only from Rawls' stated framework, but also from the conception of moral philosophy espoused by Sidgwick.

Raz's distinction between moral philosophy and moral psychology and his understanding of the constraints under which each of these disciplines must operate are particularly striking. Not only do they represent a sharp departure from Rawls' own conception of moral philosophy and "the conception of the subject adopted by most classical British writers through Sidgwick" (Rawls 1971: 51). They also rest on a caricature of modern psychology. On Raz's view, apparently, a psychological theory of the moral sense must be either crudely psychoanalytic, relating "one's experiences in infancy to one's views about authority," or crudely behaviorist, taking the form of "correlations between ... the level of sugar in one's blood and one's tendency to approve or reject certain moral propositions" (Raz 1982: 316). Notably, one of the principal theoretical approaches to the study of the mind on which modern cognitive science actually rests, involving the descriptive study of mental rules and representations, is simply excluded from this picture.

There is a further point to make about Raz. As stated earlier, Dworkin does not explicitly reject Rawls' linguistic analogy. Nevertheless, his criticisms of the natural model are apparently meant, and in any case have been widely interpreted, to extend to that analogy, as well as to the substantive research program in moral psychology that we outlined in Parts One and Two. Raz goes further than Dworkin in this respect. Not only does he adopt Dworkin's mistaken assumption that on Rawls' view the moral theorist "looks at intuitions from the personal standpoint of the individual who holds them" (Raz 1982: 316). Raz actually *relies* on this mistaken assumption as the basis for establishing a disanalogy between moral theory and linguistics. According to Raz, "one important difference between the Rawlsian conception of morality as the internal constitution of our moral capacity and linguistic theory" is that

linguistic theory describes linguistic behavior from the outside. Language users are unaware of its theory and even linguists do not judge the grammaticality of sentences by the use of the theory (except when they wish to test the theory itself). We know which sentences are grammatical independently of linguistic theory. The theory predicts our judgments. It does not explain how we come to make them; it does not describe how we reason about questions of grammar. Moral theory provides us not just with principles from which we can infer which moral judgments we make. These very principles are also principles which we ourselves recognize as organizing our moral views in the best way we can think of. (Raz 1982: 321)

Several apparent confusions about linguistics are reflected in this passage. Setting these aside, what I wish to call attention to is that the bad spatial metaphor that began with Dworkin has now come full circle (no pun intended). According to Raz, Rawls' linguistic analogy is a poor analogy because linguistics studies language from "the outside," whereas moral philosophy is confined to "an insider's" point of view (1982: 316, 321). The restrictions imposed on moral theory by this metaphor, however, should not be imputed to Rawls. On Rawls' view, moral theory studies morality from the outside, just as linguistics does. What Raz rejects here is not *Rawls'* linguistic analogy, therefore, but a new analogy of his own making.

Returning to Dworkin and summarizing the main point of this section: when it comes to characterizing the evidence available to the moral theorist, Dworkin's natural and constructive models represent a false antithesis; moreover, neither model accurately reflects Rawls' own stated views of the matter. In Dworkin's natural model, the moral theorist is limited to adopting a first-person point of view toward her own moral intuitions, and she thereafter uses those intuitions as evidence to describe a mind-independent moral reality. In Dworkin's constructive model, the moral theorist adopts a third-person point of view toward her own and others' intuitions – not for the purpose of constructing a theory of the moral sense, but for the purpose of designing a coherent theory of government. In Rawls' actual model, the moral theorist adopts a third-person point of view toward her own and others' intuitions (that is, considered judgments), but she does so from the standpoint of a cognitive scientist, who takes those judgments to be evidence for the properties of a particular cognitive system (I-morality).

9.3.4 Method

Consider finally the issue of method. In both *Outline* and Section 9 of *A Theory of Justice,* Rawls identifies the method that moral theorists should use to solve the problem of descriptive adequacy as the hypothetico-deductive method. Rawls does not use the term "hypothetico-deductive method," of course; nonetheless, it is clearly implied by his characterization of the problem of descriptive adequacy in these early texts (see, e.g., Rawls 1971: 46; see generally Section 4.4.2). Nor is Rawls unusual in this regard. For example, both Kant and Sidgwick, along with most other major historical figures, also assume that the correct method for solving the problem of descriptive adequacy is the hypothetico-deductive method.[5]

---

[5] Rawls identifies both Kant and Sidgwick as precursors in this regard (1971: 51, 251–257). On Kant's and Sidgwick's use of the hypothetico-deductive method, see also Chapter 4, note 12, and the references cited there. If I am correct, one might justifiably ask why Rawls never uses the term "hypothetico-deductive method" to characterize his method. First, it should be recalled that Rawls deliberately avoids "extensive methodological discussions" in *A Theory of Justice* (1971: ix). Nevertheless, his most explicit discussions of method do seem to imply a hypothetico-deductive model (see, e.g., 1971: 19–21, 46–47, 577–581). Second, it seems likely that Rawls simply takes for granted that scientific claims are justified by the hypothetico-deductive method, subject to reflective equilibrium, in line with the philosophical common sense of this period (see, e.g., Carnap 1966; Hempel 1966; Nagel 1961). When Rawls uses phrases such as "rational inquiry," "natural methods of inquiry," "common sense methods of inquiry," and the like, as he frequently does, this seems to be the general

Despite his evident concern with issues of method, Dworkin does not directly engage with the hypothetico-deductive method in his chapter on Rawls. Instead, he focuses his attention throughout his essay on what he calls Rawls' "technique" of reflective equilibrium, a concept he elevates into his main topic of discussion. Indeed, while Dworkin's main criticism of the natural model is that it is incompatible with reflective equilibrium, the idea that reflective equilibrium is a "technique" of some sort takes on a life of its own in Dworkin's essay, as illustrated by the following passages:

The *technique of equilibrium* supposes what might be called a 'coherence' theory of morality. But we have a choice between two general models that define coherence and explain why it is required. ... I shall describe these two models, and then argue that the *equilibrium technique* makes sense on one but not the other. (1973: 27, emphasis added)

Which of these two models, then, better supports the *technique of equilibrium?* Some commentators seem to have assumed that the technique commits Rawls to the natural model. But the alliance between that model and the *equilibrium technique* turns out to be only superficial; when we probe deeper we find that they are incompatible. (1973: 31–32, emphasis added)

[T]he natural model turns out to be poor support for the *equilibrium technique.* None of the difficulties just mentioned count, however, if we assume the *technique* to be in the service of the constructive model. ... Nor does either respect in which the *technique* is relative embarrass the constructive model. (1973: 36, emphasis added)

I shall start by considering the philosophical basis of the *technique of equilibrium.* ... I must spend several pages in this way, but it is important to understand what substantive features of Rawls' deep theory are required by his method. (1973: 27, emphasis added)

This *technique* presupposes ... a familiar fact about our moral lives. We all entertain beliefs about justice that we hold because they seem right, not because we have deduced or inferred them from other beliefs. (1973: 27, emphasis added)

In the first place, the natural model cannot explain one distinctive feature of the *technique.* It explains why our theory of justice must fit our intuitions about justice, but it does not explain why we are justified in amending these intuitions to make the fit more secure. (1973: 32, emphasis added)

It is common to say ... that scientists also adjust their evidence to achieve a smooth set of explanatory principles. But if this is true at all, their procedures are very different from those recommended by the *technique of equilibrium.* (1973: 32, emphasis added)

[T]he natural model does not offer a satisfactory explanation of the two-way feature of equilibrium. Even if it did, however, it would leave other features of that

---

method he has in mind. Of course, one must distinguish between the "logic of justification" and the "logic of discovery" in this context, as emphasized by Popper (1958/1934) and others.

technique unexplained; it would leave unexplained, for example, the fact that the results of the *equilibrium technique,* at least in Rawls' hands, are necessarily and profoundly practical. (1973: 34, emphasis added)

If the *equilibrium technique* were used within the natural model, the authority of its conclusions would be seriously compromised by both forms of relativism. (1973: 35, emphasis added)

What exactly does Dworkin mean by the "technique" of reflective equilibrium? That is not altogether clear. As we have seen (Section 7.4.2), reflective equilibrium is a *technical* concept in Rawls' framework, which strictly speaking refers to a state of affairs rather than a method or technique: namely, the state of affairs in which moral principles and considered judgments coincide, and the researcher thus understands the principles to which those judgments conform, together with the premises of those principles' derivation (Rawls 1971: 20). Moreover, Rawls defines the meaning of reflective equilibrium in the context of a conception of moral theory whose principal aim is to solve the problems of empirical and normative adequacy with respect to I-morality. Hence, if phrases like "Rawls' technique of equilibrium" are to be used in a manner that is faithful to Rawls' original meaning, they must be understood to be elliptical for statements such as the following: "Rawls' technique of solving the problems of empirical and normative adequacy by using the hypothetico-deductive method to explicate the set of considered judgments in reflective equilibrium." Interpreted in this manner, however, Dworkin's main criticisms of the natural model become true *by definition.* This is because Rawls defines reflective equilibrium in the context of an I-morality conception of moral theory, whereas Dworkin defines the natural model as an E-morality conception of moral theory. On an accurate interpretation of reflective equilibrium, therefore, Dworkin's central claim, that the natural model (as he defines it) and reflective equilibrium are incompatible, would appear to be true for trivial reasons.

Dworkin's interpretation of reflective equilibrium, however, is not accurate. Instead, he reinterprets the meaning of this concept, often investing it with novel properties that are generally not found in Rawls' own explanations of this concept. For example, Dworkin assumes that the moral principles that explicate considered judgments in reflective equilibrium must be relatively simple and *"must have independent appeal to our moral sense"* (1973: 23, emphasis added); in other words, he apparently assumes that the principles must themselves be the object of moral intuition. In addition, Dworkin assumes that *"we are each able to arrange these immediate intuitions or convictions in an order that designates some of them as more certain than others"* (1973: 22, emphasis added). Yet Rawls does not necessarily share these assumptions. Rawls does not insist that moral principles must be simple or must themselves be the object of moral intuition. Instead, he remains largely neutral on these questions, in keeping with his conception of moral theory as a progressive scientific discipline (see, e.g., 1971: 47, 50–52).[6] In addition, Rawls does not assume that human mental activity is so transparent that each individual is capable of organizing her moral intuitions into some type of coherent order that designates their relative certitude. On the contrary, he repeatedly emphasizes that solving the problem of descriptive adequacy is *difficult* and

---

[6] By a progressive scientific discipline, I mean in part a discipline whose progress may result in its abandoning common sense or self-evident principles in favor of deep theoretical explanations whose expression requires the use of technical concepts that are unintelligible to commonsense (however common sense is offended in the process). To illustrate, consider the following passage from Chomsky, which purports to summarize part of a linguistic grammar:

> To summarize, we have been led to the following conclusions, on the assumption that the trace of a zero-level category must be properly governed. 1. VP is α-marked by I. 2. Only lexical categories are L-markers, so that VP is not L-marked by I. 3. α-government is restricted to sisterhood without the qualification (35). 4. Only the terminus of a Xo-chain can α-mark or Case-mark. 5. Head-to-head movement forms an A-chain. 6. SPEC-head agreement and chains involve the same indexing. 7. Chain co-indexing holds of the links of an extended chain. 8. There is no accidental coindexing of I. 9. I-V coindexing is a form of head-head agreement; if it is restricted to aspectual verbs, then base-generated structures of the form (174) count as adjunction structures. Possibly, a verb does not properly govern its α-marked complement. (1986c: 79; quoted in Pinker 1994: 104)

Let us suppose that this is a correct statement of principles of grammar, and that these principles generate predictions about an (ideal) person's linguistic intuitions. Now consider the linguistic analogue of what Dworkin seems to require of moral principles: that the principles "must have independent appeal" (Dworkin 1973: 23) to our language faculty. What does this mean? Apparently it means that the native speaker, using her language faculty, must have linguistic intuitions about these principles in the same way that she has linguistic intuitions about expressions such as "colorless green ideas sleep furiously" or "What did Mary think who saw." Clearly this is absurd. The principles of a linguistic grammar are not, in general, *themselves* special objects of linguistic intuition (other than in the trivial sense in which every linguistic expression is or can be the object of linguistic intuition). Yet this is what Dworkin, though not Rawls, appears to be requiring of moral principles. The principles of a descriptively adequate moral grammar, Dworkin implies, must *themselves* be the object of moral intuition. This might simply be another way of stipulating that moral principles must be introspectible. In any event, it simply rules out without adequate justification the possibility that future progress in moral theory might yield principles like the following:

If the B-descendant of [S's V-ing at t] I-generates [S's V-ing at t], and if [S's V-ing at t] I-generates TRESPASS, then [S's V-ing at t] is P-marked and the B-descendant of [S's V-ing at t] inherits the P-marker; if the B-descendant of [S's V-ing at t] K-generates [S's V-ing at t], and if [S's V-ing at t] K-generates TRESPASS, then [S's V-ing at t] is P-marked and the B-descendant of [S's V-ing at t] inherits the P-marker, unless the B-descendant of [S's V-ing at t] I-generates DUTY DISCHARGE, in which case inheritance is blocked ...

The point here is a general one: To the extent that moral theorists make progress in solving the problem of descriptive adequacy, they *may* find themselves unable to state descriptively adequate principles in simple, commonsense terms (an outcome that Rawls thinks is likely; see Rawls 1971: 47, observing that a solution to the problem of descriptive adequacy "may eventually require fairly sophisticated mathematics."). As a result, they *may* need to resort

that introspection and commonsense reflection are often theoretically inadequate in this regard (see, e.g., 1971: 46, 491; cf. 1950: 75; 1951b: 178, 186).[7]

Before leaving the topic of Rawls' stated method, I should perhaps clarify that I do not wish to deny that Rawls' epistemology can be considered "coherentist" in one familiar sense of that term, namely, the view according to which epistemic justification is ultimately holistic or nonfoundationalist rather than linear or foundationalist (see, e.g., Lehrer 1990; Rescher 1973). In the present context, to describe Rawls' epistemology as coherentist in this sense appears unnecessary, since this characterization is already encompassed by the meaning of reflective equilibrium and the theory-dependence of the competence–performance distinction (cf. Chapters 7 and 8). Yet it is important to emphasize that coherentism, so construed, is not incompatible with Rawls' reliance on the hypothetico-deductive method to solve the problem of descriptive adequacy, as Dworkin mistakenly implies. For example, both the science of language and the science of vision utilize the hypothetico-deductive method, yet each of them also relies on a theory-dependent competence–performance distinction, hence each is coherentist or nonfoundationalist in this sense. Dworkin's objections to the natural model notwithstanding, the same is true of the conception of moral theory that Rawls describes in *A Theory of Justice*. It can be coherently interpreted in a naturalistic fashion as a branch of cognitive science without thereby rendering it incompatible with reflective equilibrium, coherentism, or the hypothetico-deductive method.

9.4 OBJECTIONS AND REPLIES

I have been arguing that Dworkin's analysis of Rawls' conception of moral theory in *Taking Rights Seriously* rests on a fundamental equivocation.

to completely *non*-intuitive technical concepts to characterize these principles. If so, then the principles would no longer have the type of independent appeal that Dworkin's account appears to demand.

7 To be fair, in his discussion of universality and publicity, Rawls does state a simplicity requirement for moral principles: "I assume that each can understand [the principles of justice] and use them in his deliberations. This imposes an upper bound of sorts on how complex they can be, and on the kinds and number of distinctions they draw" (1971: 132). However, in his more general remarks about moral theory in Section 9, Rawls also leaves open the possibility that the theoretical machinery needed to solve the problem of empirical adequacy may turn out to be complex: "A correct account of moral capacities will certainly involve principles and theoretical constructions which go much beyond the norms and standards cited in everyday life; it may eventually require fairly sophisticated mathematics as well. ... Thus the idea of the original position and of an agreement on principles there does not seem too complicated or unnecessary. Indeed, these notions are rather simple and can serve only as a beginning" (1971: 47). Further, it seems likely that Rawls would place greater weight on accuracy than simplicity, insofar as the two are found to be incompatible, at least with respect to the problems of descriptive and explanatory adequacy. Recall the very first page of *A Theory of Justice*: "Justice is the first virtue of social institutions, as truth is of systems of thought. A theory however elegant and economical must be rejected or revised if it is untrue" (1971: 3).

Dworkin begins his analysis by recognizing that Rawls' stated topic in *A Theory of Justice* is an aspect of human psychology: namely, the human moral sense or sense of justice (or what I have labeled *I-morality*). Nonetheless, once he starts to develop his natural model interpretation of Rawls, this recognition quickly disappears, and thereafter Dworkin takes Rawls' topic to be a mind-independent "moral reality" of some sort (or what I have labeled *E-morality*). As a result, Dworkin's analysis is deeply confused and does not bear directly on the conception of moral theory that Rawls actually describes in *A Theory of Justice*. In particular, Dworkin's distinction between the natural and constructive models implies a false choice that can and should be avoided.

How might Dworkin respond to these criticisms? In this section, I consider several possible responses and provide a brief reply to each of them. I then conclude the chapter by offering some brief remarks about moral grammar and human rights in Section 9.5.

One possible response on Dworkin's behalf might begin with an important qualification that Rawls makes when he suggests that moral philosophy can be conceived as the attempt to describe our moral capacity. In identifying this objective, Rawls notes that one might adopt this conception "at first" and then adds parenthetically "and I stress the provisional nature of this view" (1971: 46). What does Rawls mean by "at first" and "provisional" in this context? Perhaps what he means is simply that while the *initial* objective of moral philosophy might be to describe an aspect of human psychology, its *ultimate* objective is not descriptive, but normative: to justify moral principles from the traditional normative standpoint of a moral philosopher, rather than the descriptive standpoint of a moral psychologist. If one adopts this normative perspective, so the objection might run, then perhaps Dworkin is correct to favor the constructive model over the natural model.

Although this line of reasoning might seem tempting, there are several problems with this objection. In the first place, the objection does not effectively respond to my main criticism of Dworkin in this chapter, which is that the conception of moral theory that Rawls actually describes in *A Theory of Justice* is an I-morality conception, rather than an E-morality conception. Indeed, the objection as I have framed it implicitly concedes this criticism, since it identifies two possible objectives of Rawls' project: a descriptive objective, which concerns an aspect of human psychology, and a normative objective, which concerns a nonpsychological topic of some sort. The question remains why Dworkin mischaracterizes the descriptive project Rawls actually recommends – a perfectly intelligible research program in the cognitive science of moral judgment – and replaces it with his "natural model" of moral theory, which is not only highly implausible on its own terms, but which Rawls does not in fact endorse.

A related problem with this objection is that it mistakenly assumes a sharp distinction between the descriptive and normative aspects of Rawls' conception of moral theory, a typical misreading of Rawls that we sought to correct in Chapter 7. In particular, the objection assumes that the division of labor implied by phrases like "at first" and "provisional" in Rawls' remarks on moral theory corresponds to the difference between a descriptive moral theory, on the one hand, and a normative moral theory, on the other. "We might think of moral philosophy at first as a type of descriptive moral psychology," the objection imagines Rawls saying, "but this is only a provisional conception of its subject matter. Insofar as moral theorists seek to attain wide reflective equilibrium, that is, a reflective equilibrium that satisfies certain conditions of rationality, we longer concern ourselves with describing an aspect of human psychology. Instead, our aim is to construct a sound theory of normative ethics. The initial effort to describe our moral capacity is merely a heuristic device that can be usefully relied upon to further this objective."

Again, the problem with this argument is that it contradicts what Rawls actually says about the nature of moral theory in both *A Theory of Justice* and *Independence*. First, as I noted in Section 9.3.2, Rawls repeatedly identifies the goal of moral theory in *A Theory of Justice* to be an accurate description of I-morality, as that concept has been defined and elaborated here. Further, it seems clear that one of Rawls' main reasons for highlighting the "provisional" nature of this characterization is to caution against disregarding the potentially transformative effects of the process of achieving reflective equilibrium on the sense of justice itself (1971: 48–50, 578–79).[8] In addition, Rawls emphasizes that if moral philosophers make sufficient progress on the problem of descriptive (and explanatory) adequacy, "then questions of meaning and justification may prove much easier to answer" and, in fact, "some of them may no longer be real questions at all" (1971: 51).

Second, Rawls clarifies in *Independence* that this goal belongs to wide, and not just narrow, reflective equilibrium. The proper standpoint of both narrow and wide reflective equilibrium is that of "observing moral theorists," who seek to investigate "an aspect of human psychology, the structure of our moral sensibility" (1975: 7–8). Moral theory can therefore be characterized as a "type of psychology," and Rawls repeatedly warns philosophers not to turn away from the enterprise on that basis (1975: 7, 9, 22). Commentators such as Daniels (1980) who resist this conclusion, and who seek to reinterpret narrow and wide reflective equilibrium in a manner that dissociates the latter from an I-morality conception of moral theory, thus appear to be engaged in a mere terminological maneuver (Section 7.4.2).

In addition, it seems clear that the concept of reflective equilibrium itself, as its basis in Goodman's (1983/1955) account of induction implies, is meant to relax any sharp distinction between describing and justifying moral principles. Consequently, the point of view Rawls adopts in this regard may be

---

[8] Singer (1974: 493–494) reaches a similar conclusion, interpreting Rawls' qualification "to be a reference to the fact that the procedure [of describing our moral capacity] is not as one-sided as the provisional idea indicates, since our moral capacity may itself alter under the influence of a plausible theory."

usefully compared with the relaxed distinction between ethics and psychology that one finds in Hume, Smith, and most other "classical British writers through Sidgwick" (1971: 51).[9] Finally, qualifications like "at first" and "provisional" in Rawls' remarks on moral theory can also be interpreted to refer to the fact that any proposed description and justification of the original position – a theoretical model that "tries to account for our moral judgments and helps to explain our having a sense of justice" (Rawls 1971: 120) – is fallible and revisable. A reflective equilibrium is always potentially unstable because the relevant judgments and principles can be modified as a result of further investigation.

In light of the foregoing observations, a second possible response to the criticisms of Dworkin I have advanced in this chapter might adopt a different tack. This response might concede that the interpretations of both Rawls and Dworkin I have offered are sound, but it might object that my criticisms of Dworkin focus too much on the descriptive, psychological element in Rawls' theory to the detriment of its more salient social, political, and institutional elements. Rawls' book, after all, is titled *A Theory of Justice,* not *A Theory of the Sense of Justice.* His clear overarching aim is not to solve the problem of descriptive or explanatory adequacy in Chomsky's sense, but to articulate a workable and systematic conception of social justice in all of its aspects – empirical, conceptual, normative, and practical – and to apply it to the basic structure of society, that is, its major social, political, and economic institutions. From this perspective, Dworkin is surely correct to argue that Rawls' liberal project is best interpreted along the lines of a constructive model, rather than on the model of the natural sciences. Principles of justice when viewed in this light are actively *made,* not discovered; this is Dworkin's essential point, in keeping with the general thrust of modern moral, legal, and political thought. As such, Dworkin's commentary on Rawls can be viewed as less a matter of crude misinterpretation than of insightful rational reconstruction. Along with many other readers, Dworkin identified a crucial unanalyzed tension in Rawls' book between its descriptive and normative aspirations. He therefore confronted Rawls with a stark choice between two very different approaches to moral philosophy, which Rawls had largely sought to avoid. Moreover, unlike Hare and Singer, Dworkin did so from a highly sympathetic

---

[9] Schneewind (1998: 393) provides a helpful explanation of this point of view with respect to Smith (1976/1759), the terms of which seem to apply equally well to Rawls:

> It is sometimes objected that precisely because his theory aims at being a science, it offers at best a psychological account of why we judge morally as we do. It cannot direct our sentiments because, so the objection goes, the theory fails to ground our judgments or to give any reason why we should consider them authoritative. But the criticism misses the force of Smith's theory of approval. To ask for a justification of a set of moral judgments just is to ask whether the impartial spectator would approve of them. An affirmative answer is all the justification for morality there can be. Smith thinks we cannot escape from our moral sentiments to some other level of warrant.

perspective, which pointed Rawls toward a creative reinterpretation of his own philosophical project, while showing how some of its controversial yet inessential features could be discarded. Further, Dworkin's effort was largely successful: although Rawls did not agree with Dworkin's critique in all its particulars, he did come to realize on the basis of these and other criticisms that his theory of justice was best interpreted as a constructivist theory of political liberalism, rather than a naturalistic theory of human moral sentiments, analogous to the science of natural language (see generally Rawls 1980, 1985, 1993, 2001b; cf. 1971: 46–53).

Is this line of argument convincing? While I am inclined to believe it has considerable merit, the point remains that Dworkin's creative reconstruction, so understood, rests on a fundamental misinterpretation of the naturalistic conception of moral theory that Rawls actually describes in *A Theory of Justice,* which, as we have seen, is mentalist, not realist. Put differently, this line of argument does not change the fact that Rawls' conception of moral theory is an I-morality conception, rather than an E-morality conception. It is one thing to point out a latent ambiguity in another philosopher's account of moral theory and to confront him with a choice between two plausible competing interpretations of that account. It is quite another to present a false choice between a plausible interpretation and a caricature. On reflection, it seems difficult to conclude that Dworkin's commentary manages to avoid the latter. His competing interpretations of Rawls' conception of moral theory, and his natural model in particular, display serious confusions about subject matter, goal, evidence, and method that are difficult to square with Rawls' actual text (see generally Section 9.3). In any case, what is important for our purposes is simply to recognize that Dworkin's criticisms of the natural model do not appear to pose any significant challenges to the actual research program in moral psychology that Rawls outlines in *A Theory of Justice,* which we have attempted to develop further in this book. Insofar as Rawls was led by sound arguments to abandon that research agenda, one must look for them elsewhere.

9.5 BRIEF REMARKS ABOUT MORAL GRAMMAR AND HUMAN RIGHTS

Even if one grants that Dworkin's objections to Rawls' conception of moral theory are unsound, it remains unclear why Dworkin seems so reluctant to embrace this naturalistic project. While this is a speculative question, the following explanation seems plausible.

From the start, Dworkin approaches Rawls' work as a legal philosopher who is interested in convincing other legal philosophers, lawyers, and judges of the importance of moral philosophy for legal policy analysis, particularly in the field of constitutional law. For the past century, this group of readers has been notoriously allergic to the concepts of natural rights and natural law.[10] Dworkin is no exception: although he is often thought to be a champion of human rights, his writings reveal a deep ambivalence toward natural law, natural rights, and related concepts. Moreover, much like his predecessor and jurisprudential rival, H. L. A. Hart, Dworkin often appears resistant to the Enlightenment idea that human rights can be grounded in a theory of human nature (see generally Mikhail 2007b).

To illustrate these claims, consider the opening paragraphs of Dworkin's influential essay on natural law, which appeared shortly after *Taking Rights Seriously* was published:

> Everyone likes categories, and legal philosophers like them very much. So we spend a good deal of time, not all of it profitably, labeling ourselves and the theories of law we defend. One label, however, is particularly dreaded: no one wants to be called a natural lawyer. Natural law insists that what the law is depends in some way on what the law should be. This seems metaphysical or at least vaguely religious. In any case, it seems plainly wrong. If some theory of law is shown to be a natural law theory, therefore, people can be excused if they do not attend to it much further.
>
> In the past several years, I have tried to defend a theory about how judges should decide cases that some critics (though not all) say is a natural law theory and should be rejected for that reason. I have of course made the pious and familiar objection to this charge, that it is better to look at theories than labels. But since labels are so much a part of our common intellectual life it is almost as silly to flee as to hurl them. If the crude description of natural law I just gave is correct, that any theory which makes the content of law sometimes depend on the correct answer to some moral question is a natural law theory, then I am guilty of natural law. I am not now interested, I should add, in whether this crude characterization succeeds in distinguishing natural law from positivist theories of law. My present concern is rather this. Suppose this *is* natural law. What in the world is wrong with it? (1982: 165)

As this passage implies, Dworkin ultimately defends a version of natural law in this essay. Yet the version he embraces is far removed from that found in Cicero, Aquinas, Grotius, and other classical writers on natural jurisprudence and the law of nations, all of whom take the principal natural law thesis to be an empirical proposition about the essential properties of the human mind and all of whom affirm that the human moral capacity rests on innate and universal foundations (see, e.g., Mikhail 2007b: 754, n. 168; see generally Crowe 1977; Schneewind 1998). Dworkin's defense of human rights is thus qualitatively different from that of most classical natural lawyers, who typically seek to ground human rights in "something which is implanted in us, not by opinion, but by a kind of innate instinct" (Cicero, *De Inventione;* quoted in Crowe 1977: 40), that is, in what Hume suggests is a moral sense or

---

[10] The gradual demise of natural law thinking in Anglo-American jurisprudence is a complex topic, which I cannot adequately address here. For some useful background, see, for example, Alschuler (2000), Cover (1975), Duxbury (1995), Ely (1980), Finnis (1980), Friedman (1985), Gilmore (1977), Herget (1990), Horwitz (1977, 1992), Mikhail (2007b, 2008c), Paul (1976), G. E. White (1978), M. G. White (1949), Winston (1981, 2001), and Wright (1931).

conscience "which nature has made universal in the whole species" (Hume 1957/1751: 6; cf. Burlamaqui 2006/1748; Hutcheson 2007/1747; Reid 1969/1788; Smith 1976/1759).

Returning to Rawls, where does *A Theory of Justice* fit into this picture? Does it defend or imply a theory of universal human rights? While the language of human rights was clearly not Rawls' preferred idiom in 1971, there is at least one passage in the book that suggests an affirmative answer to this question and implies that, at least at this point in his career, Rawls was inclined to interpret justice as fairness as a natural rights theory, universal in its scope. In Section 77 ("The Basis of Equality"), Rawls (1971: 505–506) assumes "that the capacity for a sense of justice is possessed by the overwhelming majority of mankind." He takes this capacity to be one of the two defining features of moral personhood (the other being the capacity for having a conception of one's own good, as expressed by a rational plan of life), and he defines moral personality "as a potentiality that is ordinarily realized in due course," insisting that "there is no race or recognized group of human beings that lacks this attribute." Further, he contends that "the capacity for moral personality is a sufficient condition for being entitled to equal justice." Rawls then explains that this conception of moral personality

can be used to interpret the concept of natural rights. For one thing, it explains why it is appropriate to call by this name the rights that justice protects. These claims depend solely on certain natural attributes the presence of which can be ascertained by natural reason pursuing common sense methods of inquiry. The existence of these attributes and the claims based upon them is established independently from social conventions and legal norms. The propriety of the term 'natural' is that it suggests the contrast between the rights identified by the theory of justice and the rights defined by law and custom. But more than this, the concept of natural rights includes the idea that these rights are assigned in the first instance to persons, and that they are given special weight. Claims easily overridden for other values are not natural rights. Now the rights protected by the first principle have both of these features in virtue of the priority rules. Thus justice as fairness has the characteristic marks of a natural rights theory. Not only does it ground fundamental rights on natural attributes and distinguish their bases from social norms, but it assigns rights to persons by principles of equal justice, these principles having special force against which other values cannot normally prevail. Although specific rights are not absolute, the system of equal liberties is absolute practically speaking under favorable conditions. (1971: 505–506, n. 30)

I suspect that when Dworkin read passages like this in *A Theory of Justice* (cf. 1971: 28, 32), they gave him pause. On the one hand, he clearly was attracted to Rawls' liberal moral vision and wished to persuade lawyers, judges, and policymakers of its importance for their own ongoing debates about justice (see, e.g., Dworkin 1977: 149). On the other hand, he presumably was keenly aware that the natural rights element of Rawls' theory would be unpalatable for many in the legal community. This helps to explain, I believe, the highly ambivalent and equivocal character of Dworkin's "naturalistic" interpretation of Rawls' conception of moral theory that we have uncovered in this chapter. It also sheds light on other notable features of Dworkin's discussion of Rawls, such as the complex and paradoxical attitude toward natural rights displayed in the following important passage:

> It seems fair to assume ... that the deep theory behind the original position must be a right-based theory of some sort. There is another way to put the point, which I have avoided until now. It must be a theory that is based on the concept of rights that are *natural*, in the sense that they are not the product of any legislation, or convention, or hypothetical contract. I have avoided that phrase because it has, for many people, disqualifying metaphysical associations. They think that natural rights are supposed to be spectral attributes worn by primitive men like amulets, which they carry into civilization to ward off tyranny. Mr. Justice Black, for example, thought it was a sufficient refutation of a judicial philosophy he disliked simply to point out that it seemed to rely on this preposterous notion.
>
> But on the constructive model, at least, the assumption of natural rights is not a metaphysically ambitious one. It requires no more than the hypothesis that the best political program, within the sense of that model, is one that takes the protection of certain individual choices as fundamental, and not properly subordinated to any goal or duty or combination of these. This requires no ontology more dubious or controversial than any contrary choice of fundamental concepts would be and, in particular, no more than the hypothesis of a fundamental goal that underlies the various popular utilitarian theories would require. Nor is it disturbing that a Rawlsian deep theory makes these rights natural rather than legal or conventional. Plainly, any right-based theory must presume rights that are not simply the product of deliberate legislation or explicit social custom, but are independent grounds for judging legislation and custom. On the constructive model, the assumption that rights are in this sense natural is simply one assumption to be made and examined for its power to unite and explain our political convictions, one basic programmatic decision to submit to this test of coherence and experience. (Dworkin 1973: 45–46, emphasis original)

This remarkable passage makes clear, I think, just how watered down Dworkin's defense of rights actually is in *Taking Rights Seriously*. The passage not only reflects the delicate balancing act that often characterizes Dworkin's legal philosophy throughout his career, moreover, but also the profound influence of his ideas on others. By drawing a contrast between a "metaphysically ambitious" conception of natural rights and less controversial "constructivist" conception that merely seeks to ground natural rights in the "best political program" that a political theorist can devise, Dworkin anticipates the decisive turn toward political philosophy that Rawls would later make in the 1980s and 1990s, including his interpretation of justice as fairness as "political not metaphysical" (Rawls 1985; see also 1980, 1993, 1999). Invoking Justice Black's famous dissent in *Griswold v. Connecticut* (1965), Dworkin also defends a constructivist theory of natural rights in this passage that seeks to affirm the existence of such rights while avoiding the brunt of Black's famous rebuke of the "natural law due process philosophy" (381 U.S. 516) underlying the right to privacy in *Griswold*.

Whether and if so how Dworkin manages to accomplish all these objectives are questions that fall beyond the scope of this book. The main point I wish to make here is that the ambivalent and defensive attitude toward natural rights exhibited in this passage may help to explain why Dworkin had difficulty constructing a coherent naturalistic interpretation of Rawls' conception of moral theory. Another likely influence is the long shadow cast on modern American legal thought by legal positivism, in particular its impulse to "externalize" and thereby caricature the common law as a "brooding omnipresence in the sky" (Holmes, J., dissenting in *Southern Pacific Co. v. Jensen*, 244 U.S. 205, 222 [1917]). Indeed, Dworkin's own habit of externalizing moral principles ("objective moral universe," "independent moral reality," and so forth) seems merely to recapitulate one of legal positivism's central tendencies in this regard. Finally, a third plausible reason why Dworkin appears to have misconstrued Rawls may be his mistaken impression (apparently shared by Hare and Singer; see Section 7) that justice as fairness must be *either* empirical psychology *or* normative ethics, but not both. If Dworkin's biographer Stephen Guest is correct, then this factor also may be relevant (see Guest 1991: 148, describing Dworkin's belief that Rawls' conception of moral theory "is insufficiently prescriptive and that it needs more bite than its appearance as a successful moral psychology"). As I have argued, however, Rawls seems correct to assume that a moral grammar can be part of a solution to the problems of empirical and normative adequacy simultaneously, once the theory-dependence of the competence–performance distinction, the unreasonableness of asking a moral theory to provide anything other than an evaluation procedure for moral principles, and the rational choice element of Rawls' conception of normative adequacy are taken into account and given due weight. In short, the deepest moral convictions of common sense can be justified, at least in principle, in the manner Rawls originally envisioned.

Although I cannot adequately discuss the matter here, I wish to conclude these remarks by briefly indicating how one might understand the connection between moral grammar and human rights with a modern scientific framework. In contrast to Hohfeld (1913, 1917), who held that "[t]he strictly fundamental legal relations are, after all, *sui generis*" (1913: 30) and who therefore did not offer any sustained foundational analysis of rights (see, e.g., Herget 1990), I am inclined to think that the proper standpoint from which to interpret and defend human rights is the computational and internalist theory of language and mind pioneered by Chomsky and other philosophers and cognitive scientists (see, e.g., Chomsky 1972, 1975b, 1980; Fodor 1979; Jackendoff 1992, 1994; Pinker 1994, 1997). In this framework, fundamental legal concepts like *right, duty, power, liberty,* and the like are properly understood as *derivative* concepts, whose ultimate origin resides in a paraphrastic analysis of more basic moral and legal judgments, such as the considered judgments explicated in Chapter 6 (cf. Bentham's paraphrastic analysis of rights and other legal "fictions" in Ogden 1932: 7–18, 118–121). From this naturalistic perspective, human rights are indeed "fictions" in more or less Bentham's sense – mental constructs that are largely indispensible for human thought and discourse, but that have no immediate referent in the mind-independent, external world – but are surely no worse off for that; for the same may be said of many if not most concepts of folk psychology and ordinary discourse, and the principles that generate these rights are, or at least can be, as much a part of a science of human nature as other principles of cognitive science are. Furthermore, although the existence and character of these principles is, or least can be, a problem of ordinary science, the discipline that studies them may justly be called "jurisprudence" as much as anything else. For it is a matter of no small importance to recognize that for centuries before legal positivism sought to redefine its subject matter (see, e.g., Austin 1995/1832: 18), the science of juris- prudence was directed toward elucidating "the commonsense morality of the human race with the aid of the civil law's technical apparatus" (Schneewind 1990: 88, paraphrasing Reid's description of Grotius; cf. Reid 1969/1788: 383), in roughly the manner I have sought to illustrate in this book: by identify- ing a class of considered judgments in which "our moral capacities are most likely to be displayed without distortion" (Rawls 1971: 47) and a set of rules and principles from which they can be derived. The historical evidence for this proposition is hardly unequivocal, but nonetheless it seems reasonably clear (see, e.g., Mikhail 2007b: 778, n. 285). Hence a careful study of classical accounts of natural jurisprudence and the law of nations from a contempo- rary scientific perspective may prove to be a highly profitable enterprise for philosophers, legal theorists, and cognitive scientists alike. With the dramatic success of Universal Grammar in the last 50 years, it is perhaps not too much to hope that a revitalized conception of Universal Jurisprudence (Bentham 1948/1789; Pufendorf 1931/1660), conceived along similar lines, may also make significant progress in the years that lie ahead, thereby supplying an increasingly globalized yet fractured world with a deeper and more durable understanding of universal human rights.

To make these reflections more concrete, consider the model of moral grammar outlined in Chapter 6, whose deontic rules included basic rules of civil and criminal law, along with the Principle of Natural Liberty, the Rescue Principle, and the Principle of Double Effect. By conjoining these principles with a set of logico-linguistic principles that formalizes Hohfeld's analysis of fundamental legal conceptions (Figure 9.1; cf. Kocourek 1927; Terry 1884; Salmond 1966/1902), one can arrive at a set of bridge principles such as the following (where "MP" stands for *moral patient*):

(18) (a) $[[S\text{'s } V\text{-ing at } t^{(a)}]^c \text{ is forbidden}] \supset [S \text{ } has \text{ } a \text{ } duty \text{ not to } [V \text{ at } t^{(a)}]^c]]$
(b) $[[S\text{'s } V\text{-ing at } t^{(a)}]^c \text{ is forbidden}] \supset [S \text{ } has \text{ } no \text{ } right \text{ to } [V \text{ at } t^{(a)}]^c]]$
(c) $[[S\text{'s } V\text{-ing at } t^{(a)}]^c \text{ is permissible}] \supset [S \text{ } has \text{ } a \text{ } (liberty/privilege) \text{ } right$ to $[V \text{ at } t^{(a)}]^c]]$
(d) $[[S\text{'s } V\text{-ing at } t^{(a)}]^c \text{ is obligatory}] \supset [S \text{ } has \text{ } a \text{ } duty \text{ to } [V \text{ at } t^{(a)}]^c]]$

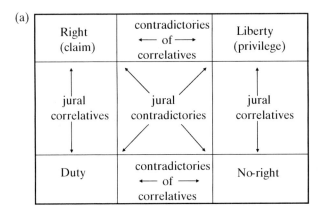

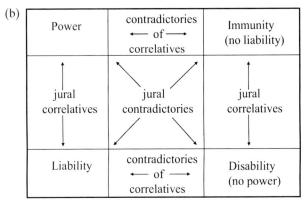

FIGURE 9.1. Hohfeld's (1913, 1917) Fundamental Legal Conceptions

(e) [[S's V-ing [MP] at $t^{(\alpha)}]^c$ is forbidden] ⊃ [[MP] *has a (claim) right* that S not [V at $t^{(\alpha)}]^c$]]

(f) [[S's V-ing [MP] at $t^{(\alpha)}]^c$ is permissible] ⊃ [[MP] *has no (claim) right* that S not [V at $t^{(\alpha)}]^c$]]

(g) [[S's V-ing [MP] at $t^{(\alpha)}]^c$ is obligatory] ⊃ [[MP] *has a (claim) right* that S [V at $t^{(\alpha)}]^c$]]

These principles, together with the rest of the moral grammar (plus a certain number of unspecified grammatical rules), can in turn generate expressions such as the following:

(19) (a) Hank has a right to throw the switch
(b) Ian has no right to throw the man
(c) The man has a right not to be thrown by Ian
(d) Ian has a duty not to throw the man
(e) Karl has no right to throw the switch

(f) Karl has a duty not to throw the switch
(g) Luke has a right to throw the man
(h) The man has no right not to be thrown by Luke
(i) Ned has no right to throw the switch
(j) The man has a right that Ned not throw the switch
(k) Oscar has a right to throw the switch
(l) The man has no right that Oscar not throw the switch

They can also explain why the following expressions are ill-formed (like the two prior lists, this list is illustrative, not exhaustive):

(20) (a) * Hank has no right to throw the switch
      (b) * The switch has a right not to be thrown by Hank
      (c) * Ian has a right to throw the man
      (d) * Karl has a right to throw the switch
      (e) * The switch has a right not to be thrown by Karl
      (f) * Luke has no right to throw the man
      (g) * Ned has a right to throw the switch
      (h) * The switch has a right not to be throw by Ned
      (i) * Oscar has no right to throw the switch
      (j) * The switch has a right not to be thrown by Oscar

In short, by employing various rules of logic and linguistic transformation, statements incorporating concepts such as *right, duty,* and the like can be rigorously derived and, in effect, proven as theorems in a computational model of moral cognition, much like considered judgments themselves. Within this framework, to have a right is typically to be the beneficiary of someone else's duty, and to be the beneficiary of someone else's duty is simply to occupy the structural position of a moral patient in a fully interpreted explanandum sentence, corresponding to a particular considered judgment (the explanandum phenomenon), for which a derivation can be given in reflective equilibrium (cf. Section 4.4.2). Conversely, to have a duty is to occupy the structural position of a moral agent in an explanandum sentence of like character.[11]

Although the matter clearly warrants more attention, it thus seems reasonable to infer that clear conceptual and empirical links between moral

---

[11] For purposes of this discussion, I assume that *moral agent* and *moral patient* are real psychological categories that are related to, but more restricted than, the more familiar grammatical categories of *agent* and *patient,* and that the former pair of categories can be given an adequate computational analysis that renders them distinct from one another and specifies their standard range of application. For example, it has seemed plausible to many observers that nonhuman sentient animals are moral patients, but not moral agents (cf. Bentham 1948/1789). The precise contours of these concepts and their proper role in the analysis of rights are important questions that demand careful investigation in their own right.

grammar and human rights can be formulated along the foregoing lines, as many jurists, philosophers, and cognitive scientists have often assumed. Indeed, one might go further and speculate on the basis of the foregoing analysis that many if not all of the specific human rights recognized by the Universal Declaration of Human Rights and other leading human rights instruments can in effect be proven as "theorems of moral geometry" (Rawls 1971: 126) in this manner, insofar as they depend on more basic moral intuitions that can be discovered and explained within the framework of the moral grammar hypothesis. Furthermore, this procedure need not be limited to so-called civil and political rights, but presumably could be expanded to include the full range of human rights recognized by international lawyers, nongovernmental organizations, and other progressive human rights advocates, including so-called social, economic, and cultural rights (such as those rights enumerated in Articles 22–27 of the Universal Declaration) and the right to be free from all unjustified forms of authority, exploitation, subordination, and dependency (cf. Mikhail 2007b). The fact that one can seriously contemplate this possibility – that cognitive science and human rights can be linked in this manner – is significant and worth reflecting upon. In the final analysis, the progressive development of these ideas may turn out to be the most important application of the research program outlined in this book.

9.6 SUMMARY

To summarize the main points of this chapter: Unlike Rawls' other early commentators, Dworkin initially appears enthusiastic about Rawls' linguistic analogy. Nevertheless, his criticisms of the natural model appear to have as their intended target any theory of moral cognition that conceives of itself as a branch of empirical science, such as Rawls' actual conception of moral theory and the substantive research program that we outlined in Parts One and Two. Dworkin's criticisms, however, are unsound. His main error is to make the unduly strong assumption that the subject matter of a naturalistic theory of moral cognition must be a mind-independent moral reality, rather than a cognitive faculty of the human mind/brain. Dworkin thus departs from both Rawls' stated framework and the research program developed in Parts One and Two (which, in this sense, is "Kantian," not "realist").[12] Put differently,

---

[12] As Scanlon (1982: 217) characterizes it, the Kantian approach holds that morality is "a sphere of objective, mind-dependent truths," that is, "objective truths about the mental constructions of which we are capable." Again, it seems worth noting in this context that both Rawls' framework and the research program outlined in Parts One and Two, but not Dworkin's "natural model" of moral theory, appear more or less consistent with the mainstream of the modern natural law tradition, as found in writers such as Grotius, Pufendorf, Leibniz, Hutcheson, Burlamaqui, Rousseau, Smith, and Reid, as well as Kant.

Dworkin's natural and constructive models represent a false antithesis. There is a genuine, mentalistic alternative to Dworkin's untenable version of naturalism, which deserves a more careful and sympathetic treatment than Dworkin manages to offer in *Taking Rights Seriously*. This naturalistic project, moreover, carries with it the potential to enrich and deepen our understanding of fundamental human rights.

PART FOUR

CONCLUSION

If we find that justice in the individual is something different [than in the State] we must go back to the State and test our new result. Perhaps if we brought the two cases into contact like flint and steel, we might strike out between them the spark of justice, and in its light confirm the conception in our own minds.

– Plato, *The Republic*

305

IO

Toward a Universal Moral Grammar

The moral sense is a distinct and original power of the human mind. ...
Our knowledge of moral philosophy, of natural jurisprudence, of the law of
nations, must ultimately depend, for its first principles, on the evidence and
information of the moral sense.
                                        – James Wilson, *Lectures on Law*

Hobbes ... [believes] that justice is founded on contract solely, and does
not result from the construction of man. I believe, on the contrary, that it is
instinct, and innate, that the moral sense is as much a part of our constitution
as that of feeling, seeing, or hearing. ... The moral sense, or conscience, is as
much a part of man as his leg or arm.
                                        – Thomas Jefferson, *Letter to Peter Carr*

Being men, they all have what Dr. Rush calls a *moral faculty;* Dr. Hutcheson a
moral sense; and the Bible and the generality of the world, a *conscience.*
                                        – John Adams, *Letter to John Taylor*

All human beings are born free and equal in dignity and rights. They are
endowed with reason and conscience and should act towards one another in
a spirit of brotherhood.
                                        – Article 1, *Universal Declaration of Human Rights*

The main arguments of this book have been relatively simple and straightforward. In Chapter 1, I began by asking whether the theory of moral cognition
is usefully modeled on aspects of Chomsky's theory of Universal Grammar.
I noted that while many authors have drawn a linguistic analogy or looked to
the comparison between moral theory and linguistics for inspiration, little
sustained attention has been given to examining what a research program in
moral cognition modeled on relevant aspects of generative linguistics might
look like. Although I have not provided an exhaustive treatment of this topic,
and probably have raised more questions than I have answered, I have nonetheless tried to show in a variety of ways that my initial question should be

answered affirmatively. At least in terms of its main questions, fundamental conceptual distinctions, key methodological commitments, and overarching theoretical goals, the theory of moral cognition would benefit from drawing on the basic terminology and theoretical apparatus of Universal Grammar. Chomsky and the community of scientists working within this basic paradigm have provided us with an exceptionally clear and compelling model of how a higher mental faculty can be studied. A moral theorist who, like Rawls, believes that humankind possesses a moral nature (1971: 580), and who seeks to understand the nature and origin of commonsense moral knowledge, would do well to pattern her investigation on aspects of Universal Grammar. More specifically, she would do well to build her research program on the foundation laid by Rawls in Section 9 of *A Theory of Justice* and, in particular, on those basic elements of Rawls' conception of moral theory that I have outlined and begun to develop in this book (see, e.g., Tables 2.1, 3.1, 3.2; Figures 4.1, 5.2).

Tables 3.1 and 3.2 represent the heart of what I have referred to in this book as Rawls' linguistic analogy. By drawing attention to these elements of Rawls' conception of moral theory in Chapter 3, I attempted to show that Rawls' analogy goes much deeper than has often been assumed. In point of fact, Section 9 contains almost the entire outline of a "generative" or computational approach to the study of moral judgment and moral cognition. The main points of comparison between this framework and Universal Grammar are relatively straightforward. Both frameworks begin from the fundamental empirical assumption that the mind/brain contains a particular cognitive system or mental grammar. Both defend this assumption by means of a version of the argument for mental grammar – in other words, by arguing that the domain in question is faced with a projection problem (cf. Chomsky 1957; Jackendoff 1994; Katz & Fodor 1963). Both frameworks focus initially on the problem of descriptive adequacy, which they distinguish from the problems of observational and explanatory adequacy. Both frameworks distinguish operative principles from express principles and, more broadly, competence from performance, while at the same time making allowance for the fact that the competence–performance distinction is theory-dependent, and thus can change over time. Finally, both frameworks adopt the standpoint of individual psychology, thereby taking their primary object of inquiry to be the cognitive competence of a single, idealized individual.

In Chapter 2, I suggested that while Rawls deserves credit for organizing his conception of moral theory in this way, his early approach to moral theory suffers from at least three main shortcomings, at least from the point of view of someone interested in using this approach to construct a naturalistic research program in moral cognition modeled on aspects of linguistic theory (see, e.g., Table 2.1). The first shortcoming concerns how Rawls conceives of the relationship between the moral principles that apply to institutional arrangements and those that apply to the actions of individuals. According to Rawls, the former set of principles is the more basic, and the latter set is derivative (1971: 108–110; cf. Hart 1973; Miller 1974). As I noted in Chapter 2, this assumption seems implausible from a naturalistic point of view. It seems more likely that the operative moral principles that generate considered judgments about the basic structure of society are themselves dependent on principles that apply to the acts of individuals, rather than the other way around. The second inadequacy concerns Rawls' conception of moral psychology and cognitive development. Rawls' early approach to these topics is not as sophisticated as it might be; in particular, he does not pay enough attention to the nativist (or classical rationalist) alternative to behaviorism and social constructivism. Among other things, this results in Rawls' defense of natural rights in *A Theory of Justice* being weaker than it needs to be. Finally, the third weakness of Rawls' early approach to moral theory is his failure to take his own meta-ethical requirements seriously enough. In particular, while Rawls articulates ambitious computational goals for moral theory in *A Theory of Justice* and his other early works, such as *Outline,* he does not actually attempt to satisfy those demanding objectives. All three shortcomings are perhaps understandable in light of the practical aims of Rawls' moral and political philosophy; nevertheless, they must constitute serious deficiencies for the cognitive science of moral judgment.

These perceived inadequacies formed the backdrop to the second part of this book. In Part Two, I attempted to put the theory of moral cognition on a sounder footing by using the trolley problems invented by Foot (1967) and Thomson (1986) to demonstrate that ordinary individuals possess a complex moral grammar that enables them to judge the deontic status of actions in a manner roughly analogous to how native speakers intuitively recognize the grammaticality of sentences. I also proposed a solution to the problem of descriptive adequacy with respect to a carefully controlled class of trolley problems, which I designed to study the computations underlying the ordinary exercise of moral judgment.

Unlike Kohlberg's (1981, 1984) dilemmas, the moral judgments occasioned by the trolley problems examined in Part Two are spontaneous, stable, rapid, intuitive, involuntary, and stringent, and made with a high degree of certitude – all properties one associates with probes used in linguistics and elsewhere in cognitive science, such as vision, musical cognition, numerical cognition, and face recognition. Moreover, the judgments appear to be widely shared among demographically diverse populations, including young children; even in large cross-cultural samples, participants' responses to these problems cannot be predicted by variables such as age, sex, race, religion, or education. Furthermore, individuals typically have difficulty producing compelling justifications for these judgments; trolley problem intuitions thus exhibit an apparent dissociation between judgments and justifications, thereby illustrating the distinction between operative and express principles. These findings are also predicted by the linguistic analogy; just as normal persons are typically unaware of the principles guiding their linguistic intuitions, so too are they often unaware of the principles guiding their moral intuitions. Finally, it is clear on analysis that it is difficult if not impossible to construct a descriptively adequate theory of these intuitions – and others like them in a potentially infinite series – based exclusively on the information given. Although each of these intuitions is triggered by an identifiable stimulus, how the mind goes about interpreting these novel fact patterns, and assigning a deontic status to the acts they depict, is not something revealed in any obvious way by the scenarios themselves. Instead, an intervening step must be postulated: a pattern of organization imposed on the stimulus by the mind itself. Hence, a simple perceptual model seems inadequate for explaining these intuitions. Instead, as is the case with language perception, an adequate model must be more complex and must specify at least three elements: the deontic rules operative in the exercise of moral judgment, the structural descriptions over which those computational operations are defined, and the conversion rules by which the stimulus is converted into an appropriate structural description.

In Chapter 4, after noting that the properties of trolley problem judgments illustrate various aspects of the linguistic analogy, I sought to formulate the problem of descriptive adequacy with respect to these judgments. I also situated that problem within the contemporary cognitive sciences. Finally, I considered and replied to the objection that trolley problems are too unfamiliar and artificial, and the intuitive judgments they yield too uncertain, to be helpful in describing the properties of unconscious moral knowledge. In response, I observed that exotic and unfamiliar stimuli are used in theory construction throughout the cognitive sciences, including linguistics, and that these problems are a useful heuristic device for uncovering the implicit structure of common moral intuitions.

In Chapter 5, I sketched a provisional solution to the problem of descriptive adequacy with respect to these intuitions, thereby seeking to render them as "considered judgments in reflective equilibrium" (Rawls 1971: 46). I also briefly distinguished this proposal, which I labeled the moral grammar hypothesis, from the dual-process model of moral judgment advocated by many researchers, such as Joshua Greene. Unlike Greene, I argued that the critical issue in the theory of moral cognition is not whether moral intuitions are linked to emotions (which they clearly are), but how to characterize the appraisal system that those intuitions presuppose, and in particular whether that system incorporates elements of a sophisticated jurisprudence.

In Chapter 6, I outlined a formal model of the mental operations implied by the moral grammar hypothesis. Drawing on the philosophy of action, I began by devising a new notation for describing the complex action representations at issue in the trolley problems. Building on the legal philosopher Julius Stone's "residual negative legal principle" (1968: 195), I then drew on principles of deontic logic to state a *closure rule* for this formal model, which I first identified as a residual permission principle, and subsequently labeled the Principle of Natural Liberty. In his brief remarks on the principles of natural duty in Section 51 of *A Theory of Justice,* Rawls mentions but does not elaborate on the fact that a complete system of moral principles will contain a principle asserting its completeness (1971: 340). The Principle of Natural Liberty was offered in Chapter 6 as one illustration of the completeness principle or closure rule to which Rawls refers.

Chapter 6 also described several more elements of the postulated moral grammar, including common law norms against battery and homicide, the Rescue Principle, and the Principle of Double Effect, together with (i) a general computational principle capable of generating complex act-token representations by transforming one representation of an action into another, and (ii) a pair of technical notions, K-generation and I-generation, which were used to formalize the relations among purpose, knowledge or foresight, and various legal norms. In addition, the chapter advanced a provisional solution to the main theoretical problem implied by the moral grammar hypothesis, which is how people manage to compute a full structural description of the relevant action that incorporates properties like ends, means, side effects, and prima facie wrongs like battery, even when the stimulus contains no direct evidence for these properties. As I observed in Chapter 5, this is a distinct poverty of the stimulus of the problem, involving perception rather than acquisition, which is similar in principle to determining how people manage to recover a three-dimensional representation from a two-dimensional stimulus in the theory of vision, or how people manage to recognize the word boundaries in unmarked auditory patterns in the theory of language. In our case, the question is how people manage to make the particular inferences they do about the various agents and actions in the trolley problems, even if one deliberately deprives them of direct evidence of those agents' mental states and other morally salient properties.

In Chapter 6, I observed that this process can be subdivided into at least five parts. To compute an accurate structural description of a given action, the systems that support moral cognition must generate a complex mental representation of the action that encodes relevant information about its temporal, causal, moral, intentional, and deontic properties. I then described how a complete theory of the conversion rules that map the proximal stimulus into a morally cognizable structural description could be given along the foregoing lines. After a brief note on Enlightenment Rationalism, I concluded the chapter with some clarifications about the method of using act trees to diagram these structural descriptions.

In Part Three, I turned my attention to some influential criticisms of Rawls' linguistic that appeared soon after the initial publication of *A Theory of Justice.* In Chapter 7, I argued that those philosophers like R. M. Hare and Peter Singer who criticize Rawls' linguistic analogy on the grounds that the conception of moral theory that it presupposes is too empirical or insufficiently normative appear to be operating with an unduly narrow and impoverished conception of moral philosophy. In the first place, they have failed to recognize the centrality of the problem of empirical adequacy in the history of their subject matter. If one follows up Rawls' reference to "most classical British writers through Sidgwick" (1971: 51), for example, it becomes clear that these writers placed this problem at the very center of their inquiries.

Perhaps more importantly, critics like Hare and Singer have failed to come to terms with the meaning of reflective equilibrium in Rawls' framework. The theme of those pages of *Fact, Fiction, and Forecast* to which Rawls refers when defining this concept is the justification of induction. Goodman's main point in that discussion is that philosophers should be wary of expecting too much from the theory of induction. Instead, they should recognize that the "smug insistence upon a hard-and-fast line between justifying induction and describing ordinary inductive practice distorts the problem" of determining which principles of induction are justified (Goodman 1983/1955: 64). The best interpretation of *A Theory of Justice* suggests that Rawls views the relationship between the problems of empirical and normative adequacy in a similar fashion. Moreover, once the theory-dependence of the competence–performance distinction and the fact that the appropriate goal of metaethics is to provide an evaluation procedure for moral principles are taken into account and given their due weight, Rawls' assumption that the same set of moral principles can be part of a solution to the problems of descriptive, explanatory, and normative adequacy simultaneously seems plausible. Hence, the argument from insufficient normativity is not persuasive, especially when it is advanced as a criticism of Rawls' stated framework. It simply leaves unanswered all of the traditional problems about commonsense moral knowledge that a naturalistic theory of moral cognition, such as the research program outlined here, is designed to investigate.

In Chapter 8, I examined Thomas Nagel's objections to Rawls' linguistic analogy. I argued that Nagel's criticisms are untenable as they stand, and that even if one reconstructs them in a more favorable light, they fail to call into question anything that Rawls actually says in *A Theory of Justice*. Nagel's argument appears to turn on at least two crucial assumptions, both of which relate to the competence–performance distinction. First, Nagel (1973: 2, n. 2) assumes that Rawls takes "whatever ordinary men agree in condemning" to be the proper subject matter of moral theory. This assumption, however, fails to account for the fact that the only judgments Rawls (1971: 47) takes to be evidential are *considered judgments,* that is, "those judgments in which our moral capacities are most likely to be displayed without distortion." Second, Nagel assumes that the competence–performance distinction in linguistics is not theory-dependent; however, as I explain in Chapter 8, this assumption is also mistaken.

Thereafter I considered three plausible reconstructions of Nagel's argument: first, that Rawls overstates the theory-dependence of the competence–performance distinction in linguistics and understates the theory-dependence of the corresponding distinction in ethics; second, that native speakers are not likely to alter their linguistic performance by reflecting on grammar, whereas the analogous situation does not hold in moral theory; and third, that there is an aspect to the problem of justifying moral principles that has no analogue in linguistics. While I conceded the potential validity of these claims, I argued that the only way to discover whether the first two claims are true is to pursue Rawls' project of "exploring our moral sense as grammar explores our linguistic competence" (Nagel 1973: 2). Insofar as it gives us a clearer picture of what this project involves, Rawls' linguistic analogy is not false at all. As for the third claim, Rawls appears to share the view that the problem of normative adequacy has no clear analogue in linguistics. Consequently, the relevance of Nagel's objection, so interpreted, seems limited.

In Chapter 9, I examined Ronald Dworkin's objections to Rawls' linguistic analogy. I began by noting that Dworkin does not, strictly speaking, reject the linguistic analogy; instead, he initially appears enthusiastic about it, describing as "exciting" and "profound" what he takes to be its implication that principles of justice might turn out to be "innate categories of morality common to all men" (1973: 26). Nevertheless, Dworkin's subsequent analysis of what he calls the "natural model" interpretation of Rawls' conception of moral theory is apparently meant, and has been widely interpreted, to apply to any conception of moral theory that takes itself to be a branch of empirical science, including the research program developed in Parts One and Two. Dworkin's criticisms of the natural model, however, are unsound. His main error is to assume that the subject matter of a naturalistic interpretation of Rawls' conception of moral theory would be a mind-independent "moral reality," rather than a particular cognitive faculty of the mind/brain. Dworkin's distinction between natural and constructive models of moral theory therefore, is a false and misleading contrast. There is a genuine, mentalistic alternative to Dworkin's untenable version of naturalism, which moral theorists interested in Universal Moral Grammar can seek to develop.

Having summarized the principal themes of the book let me also highlight some of its main limitations. There are many issues and topics surrounding the linguistic analogy that are not addressed in this book. For example, I have not discussed or quickly passed over many significant disanalogies between moral theory and linguistics. These include the role of factual beliefs, the possibility of logical error, the significance of probabilistic reasoning, the role of affective, emotional, and motivational systems, the impact of education, socialization, and situational cues, the plausibility of adaptationist-based evolutionary explanations, and the precise manner in which each discipline draws the competence–performance distinction. All of these topics warrant further study in light of the investigation of moral competence pursued here.

In addition, I have not tried to respond to all of the criticisms of Rawls' linguistic analogy in the literature. Instead, I have focused my attention on several of the most prominent criticisms that appeared from 1972 to 1974, shortly after *A Theory of Justice* was first published, which have strongly influenced subsequent discussions of the linguistic analogy since that time. Nevertheless, it seems likely that many of the arguments I have sketched in this book can provide a sound basis for responding to other familiar criticisms of Rawls' conception of moral theory. The distinction between operative and express principles, for example, appears to vitiate several of Bernard Williams' criticisms (1985: 93–99) of the linguistic analogy. Likewise, the competence–performance distinction, together with the three-way distinction among observational, descriptive, and explanatory adequacy, appears to undermine many of Shelly Kagan's (1989: 10–15) criticisms of Rawls' conception of moral theory. These conclusions require more sustained argument, however, and cannot be adequately defended here.

***

To conclude, it seems appropriate to offer a few remarks that might help to place Rawls' linguistic analogy in a broader historical and philosophical context. As has been implicit throughout this book, one of the many reasons why this analogy seems worth pursuing is that it provides a fruitful perspective from which to investigate the familiar idea that human beings possess an innate faculty of moral judgment.[1] This is partly because of the fact that, over the past five decades, Chomsky and other cognitive scientists have begun to offer a plausible interpretation of the parallel claim that humans possess an innate *language* faculty. Generative linguistics has contributed to a revival of interest in faculty psychology and lent credence to the view of a growing number of philosophers and cognitive scientists that the human mind is *modular,* that is, comprised of a series of distinct faculties, each with its own independent structure and developmental path (see, e.g., Fodor 1983; Gazzaniga 1992).

Among the most intriguing implications of the linguistic analogy are the existence and character of a distinct moral faculty. Although there are important ambiguities in what is meant by such a claim, the general notion that human beings possess such a faculty, whether labeled conscience, moral sense, faculty of moral intuition, or something else altogether, has a long and impressive intellectual pedigree (for some relevant background, both historical and analytical, see, e.g., Bain 1868; Bonar 1930; Breasted 1933; Crowe 1977; D'Arcy 1961; Darwall, 1995; Darwin 1981/1871; Greene 1991, 1997; Hillman 1970; Mackintosh 1830; Pollock 1922; Potts 1980; Raphael 1947, 1969; Schneewind 1977, 1990, 1991, 1998; Sidgwick 1988/1902, 1981/1907; Tierney 1997; Whewell 1852; Wills 1978; Wood 1991). Contemporary discussions of the moral faculty, however, are relatively rare; those that do exist are mostly perfunctory and dismissive. Even though it is the common assumption of much of traditional moral philosophy and

---

[1] Peter Railton (1986: 206) expresses a common viewpoint when he remarks: "Intuitionist moral theories ... enjoyed some success in capturing normative features about morality, but they have been largely abandoned for want of a credible account of the nature or operation of a faculty of moral intuition."

jurisprudence, the idea of a faculty of moral judgment that is a common human possession is often met today with disbelief or derision. Whether because of unwarranted assumptions about the properties such a faculty must necessarily possess, or because of tacit commitments to epistemological empiricism, behaviorist or Freudian psychology, Marxism, or historicist philosophy of more recent vintage, many contemporary philosophers, psychologists, and legal scholars simply ignore the idea, or reject it out of hand.[2]

In my view, Gall's chapter "The Moral Sense and Conscience" in *On the Functions of the Brain and Each of Its Parts* (1835), Bain's chapter "The Moral Faculty" in *Mental and Moral Science* (1868), Darwin's chapter "The Moral Sense" in *The Descent of Man* (1981/1871), and Sidgwick's analysis of commonsense morality in the third book of *The Methods of Ethics* (1981/1907, originally published in 1874) represent in some respects the high-water mark of the theory of moral cognition in the mid-nineteenth century. In the 1870s, neurophysiology was transformed by the early experiments on cerebral localization by Fritsch and Hitzig and by Ferrier (Young 1970). Subsequently, many of the insights into moral cognition that emerged during the Enlightenment were lost, and the theory collapsed under the weight of various intellectual movements, including utilitarianism, positivism, and anti-psychologism in philosophy; behaviorism and psychoanalysis in psychology; and historicism, antiformalism, and social Darwinism in law and the social sciences.[3] A central early figure in this development was Bentham, who, unlike many of his predecessors, professed disinterest in the origin of moral ideas,[4] and who deeply mistrusted appeals to conscience and natural rights in political debate, viewing them as little more than attempts by disputants to impose their prejudices on one another in the place of more public and rationally defensible methods of argument (Bentham 1948/1789). A second likely source was Hegel

[2] For philosophers, see, for example, Baier (1965: 120–121), Brandt (1959: 469; 1979: 163–182), Brink (1989: 8–9, 109–110), Duncan-Jones (1952: 180f.), Harrison (1976: 117), Mackie (1977: 38–42), Moore (1903: x), Nowell-Smith (1954: 260–269), Rorty (1984: 3–4), Singer (1974: 516), and Williams (1973: 230–249; 1985: 94). For psychologists, see, for example, Gardner (1996), Greene and Haidt (2002), and Kohlberg (1981, 1984). For legal scholars, see, for example, Ely (1980) and Posner (1999). Two notable exceptions to this pattern are Frankena's (1955) and Sturgeon's (1976) careful discussions of Hutcheson and Butler, respectively.

[3] A good intellectual history of the moral faculty that traces its gradual demise from around 1870 to 1960 does not yet exist. For some relevant background, see Hofstadter (1944), LaPiana (1994), Menand (2001), White (1949), and Young (1970).

[4] "But is it never, then, from any other considerations than those of utility, that we derive our notions of right and wrong?' I do not know; I do not care. Whether a moral sentiment can be originally conceived from any other source than a view of utility, is one question; whether upon examination and reflection it can, in point of fact, be actually persisted in and justified on any other ground, by a person reflecting within himself, is another: whether in point of right it can properly be justified on any other ground, by a person addressing himself to the community, is a third. The first two are matters of speculation: it matters not, comparatively speaking, how they are decided. The last is a question of practice: the decision of it is of as much importance as that of any can be" (Bentham 1948/1789: 19).

(Hegel 1991/1836; see generally Wood 1990). Whatever its precise causes, the fact is that by 1874, when Sidgwick wrote the first edition of *The Methods of Ethics,* scientific questions about the origin and nature of commonsense moral knowledge that had preoccupied the philosophers of the Enlightenment were already beginning to be replaced by different topics, such as whether, and if so how, rational limits to utilitarianism could be found.[5]

Moore's *Principia Ethica* (1903) initiated a further shift of attention away from the moral faculty. Although Moore is often classified as an intuitionist,[6] and although the "naturalistic fallacy" and "open-question" arguments that he popularized mostly recapitulated certain familiar arguments that Butler, Hume, Price, and other eighteenth-century writers had made in the context of the moral faculty, Moore disavowed any use of "intuition" that might imply the existence of a faculty of moral intuition (1903: x; cf. Raphael 1947). So, too, neither Prichard (1968/1949) nor Ross (1988/1930) identified their brand of ethical intuitionism with inquiry into the moral faculty.[7] During this period, only lesser known works, such as Westermarck's *The Origin and Development of the Moral Ideas* (1908) and Rashdall's *Is Conscience an Emotion?* (1914), continued to frame the investigation into the character of the mental act that takes place during moral judgment in a manner reminiscent of the earlier moral sense theorists.

Under the influence of logical positivism, with its verificationist criterion of meaning, Moore's arguments against naturalism were soon converted into noncognitivism. In their taxonomy of propositions, positivists operated with a limited menu of options: synthetic (or empirical), analytic, or meaningless. Since the propositions expressed or implied by intuitive moral judgments were correctly taken to be neither analytic nor empirical, they were assumed to be cognitively meaningless, a species of what was pejoratively termed *metaphysics*. While Stevenson's (1944) emotivism and Hare's (1952,

---

[5] Sidgwick provides the following unsatisfying explanation of his lack of interest in the problem of explanatory adequacy in the preface to the first edition of *The Methods of Ethics:* "I have avoided the inquiry into the Origin of the Moral Faculty – which has perhaps occupied a disproportionate amount of attention of modern moralists – by the simple assumption (which seems to be made implicitly in all ethical reasoning) that there is something under any given circumstances which it is right or reasonable to do, and that this may be known. If it be admitted now that we have the faculty of knowing this, it appears to me that the investigation of the historical antecedents of this cognition, and of its relation to other elements of the mind, no more properly belongs to Ethics than the corresponding questions as to the cognition of Space belong to Geometry" (1982/1907: vii). In a subsequent edition he observes: "This statement now appears to me to require a slight modification (1884)" (1982/1907: viii), but he does not elaborate on the meaning of this comment.

[6] Moore is classified as an intuitionist by Brink (1989: 2), Darwall, Gibbard, and Railton (1992: 115f.), and Williams (1985: 213), among others. However, Urmson (1974) relates that when he (Urmson) was an undergraduate attending Prichard's lectures, Moore, because he was a utilitarian, was regarded as the chief living opponent of intuitionism. Urmson therefore argues that it is a mistake to label Moore an intuitionist.

[7] However, some intuitionists, such as Broad (1952), did draw this connection.

1963) prescriptivism may be thought of as careful refinements to the more severe, less differentiated noncognitivism of figures like Schlick (1939/1930), Ayer (1936), and Reichenbach (1951), the former nonetheless remained non-cognitivist insofar as they held, together with the latter and with Hume, that ethical propositions do not admit of truth-value in the manner of genuinely empirical statements, despite their property-ascribing surface grammar. In this respect, noncognitivism appears to have added rather little, other than perhaps unprecedented negative emphasis, to what was already understood by Hume to be the nonreferential character of ordinary moral discourse.

Since the 1950s, academic moral philosophy has been characterized by at least two main trends. At the normative level, it has consisted of the continued development and evaluation of competing normative systems, such as various forms of consequentialism and deontology (including act-utilitarianism, rule-utilitarianism, and contractualism) and, more recently, of neo-Aristotelian ethical theories, such as virtue ethics and particularism. At the metaethical level, it has consisted largely of a series of sophisticated challenges to noncog-nitivism, including challenges to the very distinction between levels of inquiry that the notion of metaethics implies. In neither case has much attention been given to the moral faculty. I believe this pattern of neglect is unfortunate, for several reasons. First, this faculty was a common topic of discussion dur-ing the period in which many contemporary philosophical problems, such as the naturalistic fallacy and the is-ought problem, first emerged, and these problems are ultimately less intelligible in its absence. Second, many popular controversies about ethics, such as the possibility of moral objectivity, the per-sistence of moral disagreement, and the truth of moral relativism, are likewise less adequately understood without reference to the moral faculty. Finally, the very idea of such a faculty – part of what is distinctively human about each human being, and a source of individual dignity and human rights – is arguably what forms the most coherent philosophical basis for a democratic society, as John Adams, Thomas Jefferson, James Wilson, and other leading architects of American constitutional democracy, themselves heavily influ-enced by Hutcheson, Hume, Smith, Reid, and other moral faculty theorists of the Scottish Enlightenment, well understood (see, e.g., McCloskey 1967; Wills 1978; Wood 1991; cf. Mikhail 2007b, 2008c).

The relevance of Rawls' linguistic analogy for broader topics like these might not be obvious, but I believe its potential implications are profound. Linguists and cognitive scientists have argued that every normal human being is endowed with innate knowledge of grammatical principles – with a specific genetic program, in effect, for language acquisition. Both the classical under-standing of the law of nature and the modern idea of human rights – "the idea of our time" (Henkin 1990: ix) – rest at bottom on an analogous idea: that innate *moral* principles are a common human possession. Linguists and cog-nitive scientists have also argued that knowledge of language is not an aspect of general intelligence, but the product of a distinct mental faculty, with its own, largely predetermined developmental path. Again, classical natural law theory and modern human rights theory are ultimately predicated on a similar belief: that every human being possesses a faculty of moral judgment – a conscience – whose normal development is largely unaffected by racial, cultural, or even educational differences.

Whether these traditional ideas about natural law and human rights are true, and what their implications may be for political, social, and legal theory, are in my view the questions of ultimate significance that are raised by Rawls' linguistic analogy. In this book, I have not taken up these questions directly. Rather, I have concentrated my efforts on the much narrower issue of clarifying and defending what I take to be Rawls' proposal for how certain questions of moral theory should be investigated. One of the main points that I have attempted to convey is that these problems need not be shrouded in mystery and obscurity. The existence and character of a natural moral law, which ancient belief held is written in every heart, is, or can be, a problem of ordinary science. It belongs in principle in the cognitive and brain sciences, and it can be studied there in much the same way that natural language is studied. Whether it can meet with the same success is, of course, another question. Perhaps, if philosophers, linguists, cognitive scientists, and legal scholars would join forces and devote their talents and energy to pursuing this topic, they would discover that the concept of a Universal Moral Grammar has a rich empirical content and is more than a mere play on words. If so, then the simple but powerful conviction that animated the author of *A Theory of Justice* – that all humankind shares a common moral nature – would be vindicated.

Appendix: Six Trolley Problem Experiments

This appendix describes six of the original trolley problem experiments that my colleagues Cristina Sorrentino and Elizabeth Spelke and I conducted from 1995 to 1999, when I was a visiting graduate student, research affiliate, and lecturer in the Department of Brain and Cognitive Sciences at the Massachusetts Institute of Technology. Our findings were first presented at the Cognitive Science Society in 1998, the Society for Research in Child Development in 1999 and 2001, and various department seminars and colloquia from 1998 to 2002. The experiments were initially summarized in a 92-page manuscript, *Aspects of the Theory of Moral Cognition: Investigating Intuitive Knowledge of the Prohibition of Intentional Battery, the Rescue Principle, the First Principle of Practical Reason, and the Principle of Double Effect*, which I wrote in the spring of 2002 as part of my J.D. thesis at Stanford Law School, under the direction of Professors Tom Grey and Mark Kelman. A revised and expanded version, *Aspects of the Theory of Moral Cognition: Investigating Intuitive Knowledge of the Prohibition of Intentional Battery and the Principle of Double Effect*, Georgetown University Law Center Public Law & Legal Theory Working Paper No. 762385 (Mikhail 2002a), was published on the Social Science Research Network (SSRN) in July 2005 and is available for download at the following web site: http://papers.ssrn.com/abstract=762385. Both manuscripts have circulated for many years and have been assigned in graduate seminars at leading research universities. As a result, there are by now quite a few references to them in the literature (see, e.g., Cushman et al. 2006; Nichols 2005; Prinz 2007; Sinnott-Armstrong et al. 2008).

At the outset of our investigations, we were interested in a wide variety of empirical questions about the trolley problems and the moral intuitions they elicit, including most prominently the following questions: First, are these intuitions widely shared? Are they shared across demographic categories like gender, race, nationality, age, culture, religion, or level of formal education? Second, what are the operative principles? How precisely can we characterize the relevant mental operations, and to what extent are these computations open to conscious introspection? Third, how are the operative principles learned or acquired? What might cases like these teach us about moral development and the child's acquisition of a sense of justice or moral sense? Fourth, how are the operative principles physically realized in the brain? How and where are these moral computations actually implemented in human neuropsychology? Fifth, if there is a Universal Moral Grammar, which maps early childhood experience into a system of moral competence that in turn generates moral intuitions like these, how did this innate function or "morality acquisition device" evolve in the species? Could trolley problems and similar thought experiments be used to improve our understanding of the mental and moral (or proto-moral) cognition of other primates and other nonhuman animals?

I. EXPERIMENT I

Our first experiment attempted to address only a subset of these questions, including (i) whether and to what extent these intuitions are widely shared; (ii) what are the operative principles; and (iii) whether the operative principles are open to conscious introspection.

1.1 Method

1.1.1. Participants
Participants were 40 adult volunteers from the MIT community between the ages of 18 and 35. The group consisted of 19 women and 21 men.

1.1.2 Stimuli and Procedure
Eight cases were used, all of which were adapted from Foot (1967), Thomson (1986), and Harman (1977) (see Mikhail 2002a for the actual texts of these scenarios). In all eight scenarios, an agent must choose whether to perform an action that will result in one person being killed and five other persons, who would otherwise die, being saved.

The cases were divided into two groups. Four scenarios, modeled on the Transplant and Footbridge problems, described a choice between (i) committing a purposeful battery in order to prevent five people from dying, knowing that the battery would also constitute a knowing but nonpurposeful homicide, and (ii) refraining from performing this action, thereby letting the five die. Four other scenarios, modeled on the Trolley and Bystander problems, described a choice between (i) doing something in order to prevent five people from dying, knowing that the action would constitute a knowing but nonpurposeful battery and a knowing but nonpurposeful homicide, and (ii) refraining from performing this action, thereby letting the five die.

The hypothesized difference between the two sets of cases, in other words, concerned the type of battery embedded in the agent's action plan. In the first group of scenarios, the battery was specifically intended or *I-generated,* embedded within the agent's action plan as a means (henceforth "Purposeful Battery"). In the second group, the battery was merely foreseen or *K-generated* (but not specifically intended), embedded within the agent's action plan as a side effect (henceforth "Knowing Battery") (see generally Section 6.2.2).

Each participant received a written questionnaire containing only one scenario. The participant was first instructed to read the scenario and to decide whether or not the proposed action was "morally permissible." The participant was then asked to provide reasons explaining or justifying his or her response on a separate page of the questionnaire. Twenty participants were given a Purposeful Battery scenario. The other 20 participants were given a Knowing Battery scenario. The assignment of participants to scenario type was random.

1.2 Results

1.2.1 Judgments

The main results of Experiment 1 are presented in Figure A.1. Ten percent (2/20) of participants in the Purposeful Battery condition judged the action constituting purposeful battery to be permissible. By contrast, 95% (19/20) of participants in the Knowing Battery condition scenario judged the action constituting knowing battery to be permissible. This difference is significant: χ^2 (1, $N = 40$) = 28.96, $p < .001$, implying that the scenarios evoke different structural descriptions whose properties are morally salient.[1]

Male and female responses in Experiment 1 are presented in Figure A.2. Twenty percent (2/10) of the men in the Purposeful Battery condition judged this action to be permissible, while the other 80% (8/10) judged it to be impermissible. Meanwhile, 100% (10/10) of the women in this condition judged this action to be impermissible. By contrast, 100% (11/11) of the men and 89% (8/9) of the women who were given a Knowing Battery scenario judged the action constituting knowing battery to be permissible. These differences are also significant, χ^2 (1, $N = 19$) = 15.44, $p < .001$ (women) and χ^2 (1, $N = 21$) = 14.6, $p < .001$ (men), suggesting that there are no significant gender differences in how these actions are mentally represented and morally evaluated.

1.2.2 Justifications

Subjects' expressed principles – that is, the responses they provided to justify or explain their judgments – were also coded and analyzed. Three categories of increasing adequacy were used to classify these responses: (i) no justification, (ii) logically inadequate justification, and (iii) logically adequate justification. Responses that were left blank were categorized under the heading of "no justification." Responses that were not left blank but that failed to state a reason, rule, or principle, or to identify any feature whatsoever of the given

---

[1] An alpha level of .05 was used for all statistical tests in these experiments.

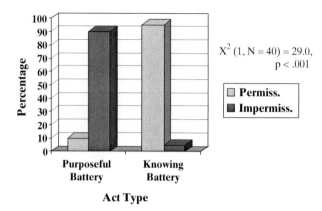

FIGURE A.1. Moral Judgments of Two Act Types in Experiment 1 (Purposeful Battery vs. Knowing Battery)

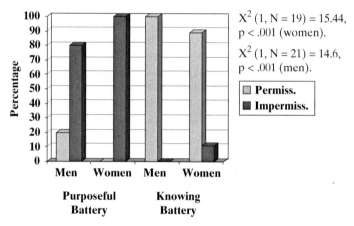

FIGURE A.2. Moral Judgments of Act Types in Experiment 1 by Gender (Purposeful Battery vs. Knowing Battery)

scenario that could in principle generate the corresponding judgment were classified as logically inadequate justifications. Finally, responses that did state a reason, rule, or principle, or did otherwise identify at least one feature of the given scenario – even one that was obviously immaterial, irrelevant, arbitrary, or ad hoc – that could in principle generate the corresponding judgment were classified as logically adequate justifications.

Using this taxonomy, two researchers independently coded a subset of justifications and achieved an interobserver reliability of 89% ($n = 36$). One researcher then coded the complete set of justifications collected in Experiment 1. Here 32.5% (13/40) of participants gave no justification, 17%

(7/40) provided logically inadequate justifications, while only 50% (20/40) provided logically adequate justifications. Significantly, many of the logically adequate justifications consisted of simple deontological or consequentialist principles that appeared incapable on inspection of generating the correct pattern of intuitions in Experiment 1. These justifications thus failed the test of observational adequacy in the sense defined in Section 2.1.6. However, no attempt was made to quantify the number or proportion of these observationally inadequate justifications.

1.3 Discussion

Experiment 1 was designed to achieve several different objectives. First, it was meant to test some widespread empirical assumptions in the literature about how trolley problems are mentally represented and morally evaluated. For many years philosophers and legal theorists had simply taken for granted such assumptions (see, e.g., the collection of essays in Fischer & Ravizza 1992). Prior to our studies, however, no controlled experiments had directly tested these assumptions. The experiments by Petrinovich and colleagues (Petrinovich & O'Neill 1996; Petrinovich, O'Neill, & Jorgensen 1993), which we first encountered after our own studies commenced, do not adequately clarify this issue because they elicit behavioral predictions ("What would you do?") rather than deontic judgments ("Is it morally permissible for X to do Y?") (see Section 5.2.1). As we predicted, these widespread assumptions in the literature were confirmed, and the deontic intuitions themselves were widely shared.

Second, Experiment 1 was designed to investigate whether experimental subjects could, when asked, provide coherent and well-articulated justifications for their judgments. We predicted that most subjects would be incapable of doing so, and this prediction also held: even under an extremely liberal coding scheme, according to which a justification was deemed logically adequate if it picked out at least one distinguishing feature of the given scenario, even one that was obviously immaterial, irrelevant, arbitrary, or ad hoc, that could in principle "serve as part of the premises of an argument that arrives at the matching judgments" (Rawls 1971: 46), only 50% of the participants in our study provided logically adequate justifications for their judgments. Furthermore, many of these justifications were inadequate to account for the pattern of intuitions generated in Experiment 1, thereby failing the test of observational adequacy in the sense defined in Section 2.1.6. This suggested that a within-subject design would elicit fewer logically adequate justifications than a between-subject design. For this reason, we decided to utilize a within-subject design in Experiment 2.

A further objective of Experiment 1 was to investigate the moral grammar hypothesis: specifically, the assumption that ordinary individuals are intuitive lawyers who possess tacit or unconscious knowledge of specific deontic rules, such as the prohibition of intentional battery and the Principle of Double

Effect (PDE) (see generally Chapters 5 and 6). As we saw in Chapter 6, when these rules and their associated structural descriptions are suitably formalized and applied to the trolley problems, they imply that throwing the switch and turning the train in the Trolley and Bystander conditions are permissible, whereas cutting up the patient and throwing the man in the Transplant and Footbridge conditions are impermissible. The data in Experiment 1 fell into just this pattern, thus confirming to some extent our hypothesis about the correct operative principles.

Finally, Experiment 1 was also meant to begin testing the universality of considered moral judgments by determining whether men and women share the same moral intuitions about the trolley problems. We predicted that there would be no significant gender differences in these cases. This prediction also held – a finding that is at least potentially at odds with the idea that men and women reason differently about moral problems (cf. Gilligan 1978).

2. EXPERIMENT 2

In Experiment 1 we discovered an apparent difference between the way purposeful battery and knowing battery are mentally represented and morally evaluated, at least in certain cases of necessity, such as the trolley problems. We also discovered evidence to support the hypothesis that both men and women possess intuitive knowledge of the prohibition of intentional battery and the PDE. Experiment 2 was designed to bring additional evidence to bear on these hypotheses, in three different ways.

The first way was to investigate the concept of battery on which we relied in Experiment 1. In Experiment 1 we followed well-established legal doctrine in assuming that battery could be defined, for our purposes, as "unpermitted ... contact with a person," that is, of contact without consent (Prosser 1941: 43; see also Shapo 2003). Moreover, we assumed that the notion of contact "extends to any part of the body, or to anything which is attached to it" and includes any touching of one person by another or by "any substance put in motion by him" (Hilliard 1859: 191). In Experiment 2 we investigated intuitive knowledge of these concepts by taking one of the Purposeful Battery scenarios used in Experiment 1 and modifying it so that the primary act-type description, "throwing the man," would likely be represented as consensual. Specifically, we took the standard Bystander problem and turned it into the Implied Consent problem (see Table 5.1).

The second extension of Experiment 1 focused on our subjects' intuitive knowledge of the consequentialist component of the PDE. As we saw in Chapters 5 and 6, the PDE is a complex principle of justification, which requires, among other things, that an action's good effects outweigh its bad effects (Section 6.3.6). In Experiment 1 we assumed that this condition was satisfied. That is, we assumed that our subjects would compute structural descriptions of the relevant actions that effectively encoded the deaths of five people as a good effect that outweighed the bad effect of the death of one person.

In Experiment 2, we directly tested intuitive knowledge of this condition of the PDE by taking one of the Knowing Battery scenarios used in Experiment 1 and modifying it so that its good effects were outweighed by its bad effects. Specifically, we took the Bystander problem and turned it into the Expensive Equipment problem by substituting "five million dollars of new railroad equipment lying across the tracks" for "five men walking across the tracks" (see Table 5.1). We reasoned that most people would recognize that the moral worth of a person is greater than that of a valuable thing.

Finally, our third modification was to switch from a between-subject design, which we had used in Experiment 1, to a within-subject design. Although fully half of the participants in Experiment 1 gave logically adequate justifications of their judgments, it seemed clear on reflection that many of these justifications could not account for the alternating pattern of intuitions generated by the two conditions in Experiment 1. For example, many responses reduced to either simple deontological justifications (e.g., "killing is wrong") or simple utilitarian justifications ("five versus one") that could not adequately distinguish the two conditions. We therefore sought to examine this issue directly in Experiment 2, as well as to begin to explore related issues, such as framing effects.

2.1 Method

2.1.1 Participants
Participants were 65 adult volunteers between the ages of 22 and 35, 55 of whom were graduate students at the John F. Kennedy School of Government at Harvard University, and 10 of whom were employees of the Cable News Network in Washington, D.C. There were 33 women and 30 men. Two subjects did not provide information about their gender.

2.1.2 Stimuli and Procedure
Five scenarios were used, one of which was the Trolley problem (see Section 4.1) and the other four of which were the Bystander, Footbridge, Expensive Equipment, and Implied Consent problems, respectively (see Table 5.1).

Unlike Experiment 1, which used a between-subject design, Experiment 2 employed a within-subject design. Each of the 65 participants received a written questionnaire containing two scenarios, including one or more of the four scenarios reprinted in the preceding paragraph. Participants were first asked whether the proposed actions were "morally permissible" and then to explain or justify their responses. Twenty-five participants were given the Bystander problem, 25 were given the Footbridge problem, 25 were given the Expensive Equipment problem, and 25 were given the Implied Consent problem.

The Trolley problem was used as a control. The assignment of participants to scenario type was random.[2]

2.2 Results

2.2.1 Purposeful Battery vs. Knowing Battery

We present the main results of Experiment 2 in stages, beginning with the comparison between purposeful and knowing battery (Figure A.3). Eight percent (2/25) of subjects in the Purposeful Battery condition (Footbridge) judged the action constituting purposeful battery ("throwing the man") to be permissible. Meanwhile, 76% (19/25) of subjects in the Knowing Battery condition (Bystander) judged the action constituting knowing battery ("throwing the switch") to be permissible. This difference is significant: χ^2 (1, $N = 50$) = 24.4, $p < .001$.

Male and female participants who were given these two scenarios showed a similar pattern of responses (Figure A.4). Fourteen percent (2/14) of men and 0% (0/11) of women in the Purposeful Battery condition (Footbridge) judged this action to be permissible. Meanwhile, 85% (11/13) of men and 60% (6/10) of women in the Knowing Battery condition (Bystander) judged this action to be permissible. These differences are also significant, χ^2 (1, $N = 21$) = 11.4, $p < .001$ (women) and χ^2 (1, $N = 27$) = 13.38, $p < .001$ (men).

2.2.2 Good Effects Outweigh Bad Effects vs. Bad Effects Outweigh Good Effects

Next, we describe the results of Experiment 2 in terms of the weighing of good and bad effects (Figure A.5). As indicated, 76% (19/25) of subjects who were given the Bystander problem (recategorized in Figure A.5 as "Good Effects > Bad Effects") judged Hank's throwing the switch to be permissible. By contrast, 0% (0/25) of the subjects who were given the Expensive Equipment problem (here categorized as "Bad Effects > Good Effects") judged Karl's throwing the switch to be permissible. This difference is significant: χ^2 (1, $N = 50$) = 30.65, $p < .001$.

---

[2] The exact breakdown of participants and scenario pairs in Experiment 2 is listed below. Each participant received a questionnaire with one of the following 10 pairs, with the number of participants in each condition listed in brackets:

Pair #1: Bystander (Hank) and Problem (Ian) [10]
Pair #2: Bystander (Hank) and Expensive Equipment (Karl) [5]
Pair #3: Footbridge (Ian) and Implied Consent (Luke) [5]
Pair #4: Footbridge (Ian) and Expensive Equipment (Karl) [5]
Pair #5: Bystander (Hank) and Implied Consent (Luke) [5]
Pair #6: Expensive Equipment (Karl) and Implied Consent (Luke) [5]
Pair #7: Trolley (Charlie) and Bystander (Hank) [5]
Pair #8: Trolley (Charlie) and Footbridge (Ian) [5]
Pair #9: Trolley (Charlie) and Expensive Equipment (Karl) [10]
Pair #10: Trolley (Charlie) and Implied Consent (Luke) [10]

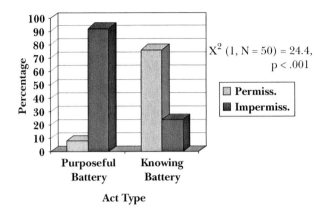

FIGURE A.3. Moral Judgments of Two Act Types in Experiment 2 (Purposeful Battery vs. Knowing Battery)

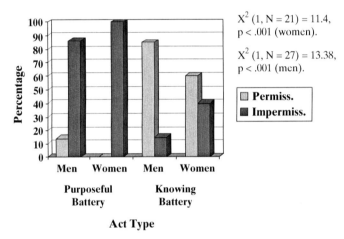

FIGURE A.4. Moral Judgments of Two Act Types in Experiment 2 by Gender (Purposeful Battery vs. Knowing Battery)

Men's and women's responses followed the same pattern (Figure A.6). Eighty-five percent (11/13) of men and 60% (6/10) of women judged throwing the switch to be permissible in the Bystander condition. By contrast, 0% (0/14) of men and 0% (0/11) of women held throwing the switch to be impermissible in the Expensive Equipment condition. These results are also significant, χ^2 (1, $N = 21$) = 11.4, $p < .001$ (women) and χ^2 (1, $N = 27$) = 19.99, $p < .001$ (men).

2.2.3 Purposeful Battery vs. Implied Consent
Third, we examine the comparison between purposeful battery and consensual contact (Figure A.7). As indicated, 8% (2/25) of subjects in the

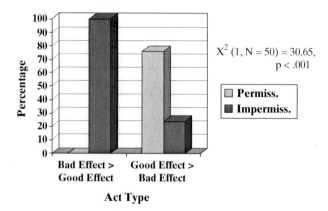

FIGURE A.5. Moral Judgments of Two Act Types in Experiment 2 (Good Effects vs. Bad Effects)

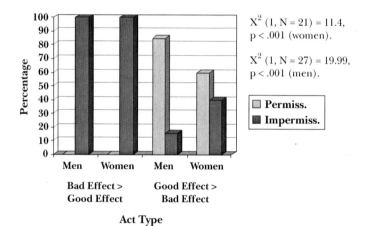

FIGURE A.6. Moral Judgments of Act Types in Experiment 2 by Gender (Good Effects vs. Bad Effects)

Purposeful Battery condition ("Ian") judged the action constituting purposeful battery ("throwing the man") to be permissible. By contrast, 96% (24/25) of subjects in the Implied Consent condition ("Luke") judged the same action to be permissible. This difference is significant: χ^2 (1, N = 50) = 38.78, p < .001.

Again, male and female responses conformed to the same pattern (Figure A.8). Fourteen percent (2/14) of men and 0% (0/11) of women in the Purposeful Battery condition judged throwing the man to be permissible. By contrast, 100% (7/7) of the men and 100% (16/16) of the women in the Implied

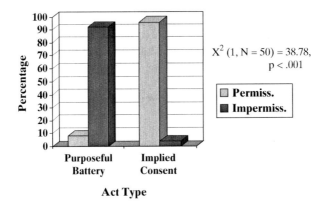

FIGURE A.7. Moral Judgments of Two Act Types in Experiment 2 (Purposeful Battery vs. Implied Consent)

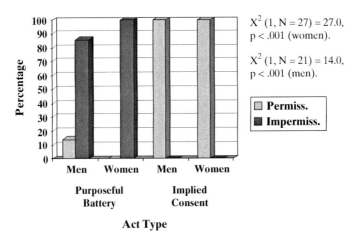

FIGURE A.8. Moral Judgments of Two Act Types in Experiment 2 by Gender (Purposeful Battery vs. Implied Consent)

Consent condition judged throwing the man to be permissible, χ^2 (1, N = 27) = 27.0, $p < .001$ (women) and χ^2 (1, N = 21) = 14.0, $p < .001$ (men).[3]

2.2.4 Justifications

Finally, we turn to our subjects' expressed justifications. Because we utilized a within-subject design in Experiment 2, we expected that these justifications

---

[3] Recall that two participants in Experiment 2 did not provide information about their gender. Both were given an Implied Consent scenario: one judged the action to be permissible and one held it to impermissible.

would be significantly less adequate than the corresponding justifications in Experiment 1, which relied on a between-subject design. In addition, we predicted that subjects presented with both the Footbridge and Bystander problems, in particular, would not be able to justify their conflicting intuitions.

Both of these predictions were confirmed. First, 35.4% (23/65) of participants gave no justification and 38.5% (25/65) provided logically inadequate justifications, while only 20.0% (13/65) provided logically adequate justifications. This contrasts sharply with the Experiment 1, in which 50% of subjects provided logically adequate justifications.

Second, only 10% (1/10) of those participants who were given both the Footbridge and Bystander problems and who attempted to explain their judgments provided logically adequate justifications. The other 90% (9/10) provided logically inadequate justifications. Further, as Table A.1 reveals, this group's expressed principles were widely divergent. Many participants merely restated the problem they were asked to resolve or otherwise provided answers that were nonresponsive. Moreover, several participants appeared puzzled by the nature and strength of their intuitions and by how those intuitions shifted as a result of minor and apparently inconsequential differences in the relevant action descriptions.

2.3 Discussion

The results of Experiment 2 corroborate and extend those of Experiment 1. First, they lend further support to the hypothesis that both men and women possess intuitive knowledge of the prohibition of intentional battery and the PDE. By postulating this knowledge, we can explain and predict their moral intuitions. Specifically, we can explain why their intuitions change so predictably when the Bystander problem is altered in such a way that the costs of throwing the switch outweigh its benefits, and when the Footbridge problem is altered in such a way that throwing the man no longer constitutes purposeful battery.

Second, Experiment 2 suggests that conscious access to these principles is limited. Even under a liberal coding scheme, only 20% of subjects provided logically adequate justifications. Further, only 10% did so when asked to explain the most challenging pair of moral intuitions, namely, the perceived contrast between the Bystander and Footbridge problems.

Third, Experiment 2 provides some initial evidence of framing effects. Most notably, only 76% (19/25) of respondents in the Knowing Battery condition judged Hank's throwing the switch to be permissible, a much lower percentage than the 95% (19/20) of participants who gave this response in Experiment 1. These effects were slightly less pronounced in male participants than in female participants, but they were discernible in both groups: 85% (11/13) of men gave this response, as compared with 100% (11/11) in Experiment 1, whereas 60% (6/10) of women gave this response, as compared with 89% (8/9) in Experiment 1. These sample sizes are quite small, and it therefore would be premature to draw any firm conclusions about these effects. It seems likely, however, that a more systematic investigation of framing effects in larger populations would yield significant results, perhaps including significant gender differences. Still, the dominant pattern of data in Experiment 2 fell in line with that of Experiment 1 for both men and women, in that both groups in the aggregate intuitively recognized the existence of morally relevant differences among the Bystander, Footbridge, Expensive Equipment, and Implied Consent problems. Hence Experiment 2 provides further evidence that at least some moral intuitions, presumably along with the unconscious principles that generate them, are widely shared, irrespective of gender.

3. EXPERIMENT 3

Participants in Experiments 1–2 and our other initial pilot studies included persons from countries or regions outside the United States, including Belgium, Canada, Colombia, Denmark, Egypt, France, Germany, India, Israel, Italy, Japan, Lebanon, Mexico, Puerto Rico, South Africa, and South Korea. Nonetheless, the majority of participants were inhabitants of the United States or other Western nations. Accordingly, Experiment 3 was designed to investigate the moral intuitions of a "non-Western" population.

3.1 Method

3.1.1 Participants
Participants were 39 adult volunteers ages 18–65 from the broader Cambridge, Massachusetts, community, all of whom had emigrated from China within the previous five years and most of whom had done so within the previous two years. The group included 19 women and 19 men; one participant did not volunteer information about his or her gender.[4]

3.1.2 Stimuli and Procedure
Same as Experiment 2, except that participants in this study were not asked to justify their judgments. Fourteen participants were given the Bystander problem, 16 participants were given the Footbridge problem, 15 participants were given the Expensive Equipment problem, and 16 participants were given the Implied Consent problem. The assignment of participants to scenario type was random.

3.2 Results

3.2.1 Purposeful Battery vs. Knowing Battery
Once again we present the results of Experiment 3 in stages, beginning with the comparison between purposeful and knowing battery (Figure A.9). Fourteen

---

[4] Our colleagues Fei Xu and Yaoda Xu were instrumental in helping us collect this data.

Appendix

TABLE A.1. *Justifications for the Bystander and Footbridge Problems by 10 Subjects in Experiment 2 (Within-Subject Design)*

Subject	Problem	Type of Battery	Judgment
1	Bystander	Knowing	Permissible
	Footbridge	Purposeful	Impermissible
2	Bystander	Knowing	Permissible
	Footbridge	Purposeful	Impermissible
3	Bystander	Knowing	Permissible
	Footbridge	Purposeful	Impermissible
4	Bystander	Knowing	Permissible
	Footbridge	Purposeful	Impermissible
5	Bystander	Knowing	Permissible
	Footbridge	Purposeful	Impermissible
6	Bystander	Knowing	Permissible
	Footbridge	Purposeful	Impermissible
7	Bystander	Knowing	Permissible
	Footbridge	Purposeful	Impermissible
8	Bystander	Knowing	Permissible
	Footbridge	Purposeful	Impermissible
9	Bystander	Knowing	Permissible
	Footbridge	Purposeful	Permissible
10	Bystander	Knowing	Impermissible
	Footbridge	Purposeful	Impermissible

Justification
"Very odd. I don't know why I chose differently in the second scenario. The end result is the same. I just chose my gut response – and now am intrigued with how to reconcile them."
"It's amazing that I would not throw a person but throw a switch to kill a person. I really wish there was more I could do for the [one] guy on the other track."
"In either case, the moral decision rule depends on how close to the active killing of the man is."
"Not acceptable to decide to risk someone else's life to save others."
"I know – five lives are five lives – it's all about the guts. That's what it comes down to. Blaise Pascal got it all wrong."
"The man, Hank can here actively influence a sequence of events which will limit damage (no. of deaths). In the second event, he cannot throw another man onto the tracks because he will actively and deliberately kill an innocent bystander. Really an impossible choice."
"Moral actors may be forced to make a decision between two passive choices where both will end rights. But to make action over passive choices requires another kind of analysis and degree of benefit."
"In the first scenario it would be permissible to act as a utilitarian optimizer. In the second rights come into question."
"I believe that the ultimate question is that of lives lost. Some would argue that Hank and Ian would be morally justified in not stopping the train. While this may be true, it does not necessitate that it be morally unjustified to stop the train."
"For the first scenario, I wanted to draw a distinction between 'is it permissible for him to throw the switch' and 'does he have a duty to throw the switch,' though I don't know if that would have changed my answer."

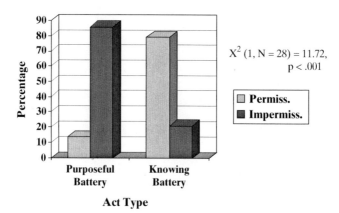

FIGURE A.9. Moral Judgments of Two Act Types in Experiment 3 (Purposeful Battery vs. Knowing Battery)

percent (2/14) of subjects in the Purposeful Battery condition (Footbridge) judged this action to be permissible. Meanwhile, 79% (11/14) of subjects in the Knowing Battery condition (Bystander) judged this action to be permissible. This difference is significant: χ^2 (1, N = 28) = 11.72, p < .001.

3.2.2 Good Effects Outweigh Bad Effects vs. Bad Effects Outweigh Good Effects

Because of the limited number of subjects in Experiment 3, we refrain from analyzing our responses by gender. Instead, we turn directly to the comparison between good and bad effects (Figure A.10). Seventy-nine percent (11/14) of subjects in the Bystander condition (here recategorized as "Good Effects > Bad Effects") judged throwing the switch to be permissible. Meanwhile, only 7% (1/15) of subjects in the Expensive Equipment condition ("Bad Effects > Good Effects") judged throwing the switch to be permissible. This difference is significant: χ^2 (1, N = 29) = 16.81, p < .001.

3.2.3 Purposeful Battery vs. Implied Consent

Third, we examine the contrast between purposeful battery and consensual contact (Figure A.11). Thirteen percent (2/16) of subjects in the Purposeful Battery condition judged throwing the man to be permissible. Meanwhile, 88% (14/16) of subjects in the Implied Consent condition judged throwing the man to be permissible. This difference is significant: χ^2 (1, N = 32) = 18.0, p < .001.

3.3 Discussion

The results of Experiment 3 suggest that the central findings of Experiments 1 and 2 are not limited to persons educated or raised in the United States or other Western nations. Instead, they suggest that at least some operative

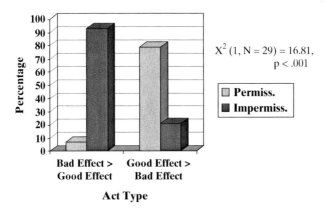

FIGURE A.10. Moral Judgments of Two Act Types in Experiment 3 (Good Effects vs. Bad Effects)

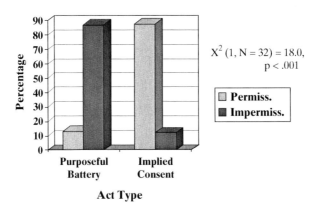

FIGURE A.11. Moral Judgments of Two Act Types in Experiment 3 (Purposeful Battery vs. Implied Consent)

principles of moral competence, including the prohibition of purposeful battery and the PDE, are transnational and possibly even universal or nearly so. While claims of universality are often controversial and should be considered cautiously, it is noteworthy that this hypothesis is consistent with the role already played by these principles in international humanitarian law. For example, the PDE's implied norm of noncombatant immunity – that is, its prohibition against directly targeting civilians, together with its qualified acceptance of harming civilians as a necessary side effect of an otherwise justifiable military operation – has long been part of customary international law and is codified in Article 48 of the First Protocol (1977) to the 1949 Geneva Conventions (see, e.g., Henkin et al. 1992: 364–365). Likewise, the PDE's implied norm of proportionality is also part of customary international law and is codified in Articles 22–23 of the Hague Convention of 1907 (see, e.g., Henkin et al. 1992: 368). Meanwhile, the prohibition of purposeful battery is, of course, a lesser-included offense of a wide range of human rights abuses involving unjustified aggression, including torture, mass rape, and genocide. It is perhaps not surprising, therefore, to discover that relatively simple thought experiments, such as the trolley problems, that implicate these basic legal concepts appear to elicit widely shared moral intuitions from individuals of different backgrounds (cf. Mikhail 2005, 2008a; see also Hauser et al. 2007; Miller 2008; Pinker 2008; Saxe 2005). Still, it is clear that more cross-cultural research is needed to investigate the potential universality of these intuitions.

4. EXPERIMENT 4

Experiments 1–3 support the hypothesis that the moral competence of adults, including non-Western adults, includes the prohibition of intentional battery and the PDE. By attributing intuitive knowledge of these principles to ordinary individuals, we can successfully explain and predict their moral intuitions.

TABLE A.2. *Explaining Six Trolley Problems as a Function of the Principle of Double Effect*

Problem	Homicide?	Battery?	Good Effects Outweigh Bad Effects?	Battery as a Means?	Deontic Status
Trolley	Yes	Yes	Yes	No	Permissible
Transplant	Yes	Yes	Yes	Yes	Impermissible
Bystander	Yes	Yes	Yes	No	Permissible
Footbridge	Yes	Yes	Yes	Yes	Impermissible
Expensive Equipment	Yes	Yes	No	No	Impermissible
Implied Consent	No	No	Yes	No	Permissible

As Table A.2 indicates, the computations presupposed by this explanation can be reconstructed in the simple form of series of yes–no questions or decision tree. Confronted with a presumptively wrong action, such as those homicides and batteries at issue in the Trolley, Transplant, Bystander, and Footbridge problems, the decision maker first asks whether the proposed action's good effects outweigh its bad effects. If the answer is no, then the decision maker concludes that the action is impermissible. If the answer is yes, then the decision maker next asks whether the action involves committing a battery (or homicide) as a means to achieve a given end. If the answer is no, then the decision maker concludes that the action is permissible. If the answer is yes, then the decision maker concludes that the action is impermissible.

Table A.2 illustrates that our central findings up to this point can be explained in the foregoing terms. However, these findings are also consistent with an alternative explanation, according to which trolley intuitions do not depend primarily on either the *mental state* (i.e., intentional) or *means-based* (i.e., causal/teleological) properties of an agent's action plan, but on its *temporal* properties, in particular on whether its bad effects or prima facie wrongs, such as battery, are mentally represented as occurring *before* or *after* its good effects. In particular, our central findings could be equally explained by the so-called Pauline Principle, which holds that "it is impermissible to do evil that good may come" (see, e.g., Anscombe 1970; Donagan 1977). Suitably formalized, a temporal interpretation of this principle would, in effect, calculate that any action plan in which either a bad effect or a battery occurs *before* a good effect is impermissible. As Table A.3 reveals, all but one of the impermissible acts examined thus far possess this property. The lone exception, Karl's throwing the switch in the Expensive Equipment problem, is explainable on other grounds. Hence the Pauline Principle (or some suitable formalization of it) also constitutes at least part of an observationally adequate explanation of the results of Experiments 1–3.

Experiment 4 was designed to explore this logically possible alternative. It was also meant to investigate a possible latent ambiguity in Judith Jarvis Thomson's original "loop" problem (Thomson 1985; see also Costa 1987b) and to provide an additional check on the abstract concept of battery utilized in Experiments 1–3. To accomplish these objectives, two new scenarios were constructed: the Loop Track (Ned) and Man-in-Front (Oscar) problems (see Table 5.1). In the former, battery is embedded within the agent's action plan as a means. In the latter, battery is embedded within the agent's action plan as a side effect. Unlike the scenarios used in Experiments 1–3, however, the Ned-Oscar pair is not distinguishable in terms of their morally neutral basic actions (e.g., "throwing the switch" vs. "throwing the man") or the temporal properties of their good effects, bad effects, and batteries. Instead, five fundamental properties are held constant between these two scenarios: (i) good effects,

TABLE A.3. *Explaining Six Trolley Problems as a Function of the Pauline Principle*

Problem	Homicide?	Battery?	Good Effects Outweigh Bad Effects?	Battery or Bad Effects Prior to Good Effects?	Deontic Status
Trolley	Yes	Yes	Yes	No	Permissible
Transplant	Yes	Yes	Yes	Yes	Impermissible
Bystander	Yes	Yes	Yes	No	Permissible
Footbridge	Yes	Yes	Yes	Yes	Impermissible
Expensive Equipment	Yes	Yes	No	No	Impermissible
Implied Consent	No	No	Yes	No	Permissible

(ii) bad effects, (iii) ultimate purpose or goal, (iv) morally neutral basic action ("throwing the switch" in each case), and (v) the temporal order of good effects, bad effects, and batteries. Further, although they were not designed with this feature in mind, both scenarios are "impersonal" scenarios in the sense defined by Greene and colleagues (2001; see Figure 5.3[b]). The Ned-Oscar pair is therefore the purest "minimal pair" of scenarios used thus far in our investigations.

4.1 Method

4.1.1 Participants

Participants were 309 adult volunteers ages 18–35 from the MIT community. Because the postulated difference between the relevant scenarios is quite subtle, we increased our sample sizes to be able to detect statistically significant differences in the two conditions. For the purposes of this study, we did not actively collect information on participants' gender. However, a retrospective analysis of participants' names indicated that at least 119 men and at least 117 women participated in this study. The gender of an additional 73 participants was not readily ascertainable in this manner.

4.1.2 Stimuli and Procedure

Two scenarios were used. In the Purposeful Battery condition (Loop Track/ Ned), battery was embedded within the agent's action plan as a means. In the Knowing Battery condition (Man-in-Front/Oscar), battery was embedded within the agent's action plan as a side effect. In both conditions good effects, bad effects, ultimate purpose or goal, and morally neutral basic action ("throwing the switch") were held constant. In addition, temporal order of good effects, bad effects, and batteries were also held constant.

A between-subject design was utilized. Each participant received a written questionnaire containing only one scenario, accompanied by a diagram designed to make the scenario fully comprehensible (on·file with author). The participant was instructed to read the scenario and to determine whether the proposed action it described was "morally permissible." Unlike Experiments 1 and 2, participants were not asked to provide justifications for their judgments; nevertheless, many did so on their own initiative, and these responses are analyzed below. We gave 159 individuals the Purposeful Battery scenario and 150 the Knowing Battery scenario. The assignment of participants to scenario type was random.

4.2 Results

4.2.1 Judgments
The main results of Experiment 4 are summarized in Figure A.12. Forty-eight percent (76/159) of participants in the Purposeful Battery condition judged throwing the switch to be permissible. Meanwhile, 62% (93/150) of participants in the Knowing Battery condition judged throwing the switch to be permissible. This difference is significant: χ^2 (1, N = 302) = 6.52, $p < .025$.

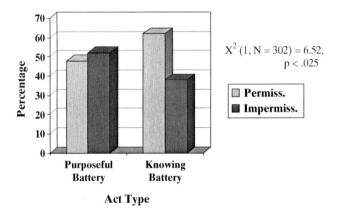

FIGURE A.12. Moral Judgments of Two Act Types in Experiment 4 (Purposeful Battery vs. Knowing Battery)

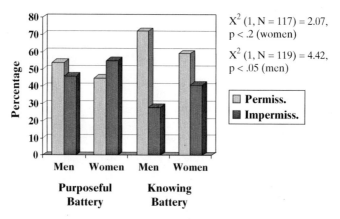

FIGURE A.13. Moral Judgments of Act Types in Experiment 4 by Gender (Purposeful Battery vs. Knowing Battery)

Judgments of men and women are presented in Figure A.13. Fifty-four percent (29/54) of men and 45% (32/71) of women in the Purposeful Battery condition judged throwing the switch to be permissible. Meanwhile, 72% (47/65) of men and 59% (27/46) of women held the same action to be permissible in the Knowing Battery condition. These contrasts are significant for men, χ^2 $(1, N = 119) = 4.42, p < .025$, but not for women, $\chi^2 (1, N = 117) = 2.07, p < .20$. Hence, based on these data, the null hypothesis that these scenarios are indistinguishable is falsified for men but not for women. However, larger sample sizes would presumably support the same conclusion with respect to women. These results also indicate a slight but discernible trend in which, in the aggregate, men appear more willing than women to permit throwing the switch in these circumstances.

4.2.2 Justifications
Although we did not ask for justifications, 49 subjects provided some sort of verbalized explanation of their judgments on their own initiative. Thirty of these 49 responses, or 9.9% (30/302) of the overall total, were logically adequate justifications, while 19 of these 49 responses, or 6.3% (19/302) of the overall total, were logically inadequate. Meanwhile, 83.8% (253/302) of subjects in Experiment 4 gave no justification.

4.3 Discussion
According to the moral grammar hypothesis, individuals who encounter the trolley problems spontaneously compute unconscious representations of the relevant actions in terms of ends, means, side effects, and prima facie wrongs, such as battery. They also distinguish battery as a means from battery as a

side effect, prohibiting the former but permitting the latter in the specific circumstances depicted by these problems (see Section 6.5). Consequently, we were led to make two related predictions about the Ned-Oscar pair of scenarios. First, we predicted that subjects would perceive an intuitive distinction between these scenarios, even though their overt differences are quite subtle, because in only one of these cases (Ned) does the agent specifically intend to commit a battery as a means of furthering his good end. In the Oscar condition, by contrast, we assumed that subjects would compute an unconscious representation according to which battery is not a means but a foreseen side effect. Second, we predicted that, on the basis of this distinction between means and side effects, subjects would judge Oscar's act of throwing the switch to be permissible but Ned's act of throwing the switch to be impermissible.

The results of Experiment 4 confirmed the first prediction. Although the differences between these fact patterns are extremely limited, our subjects did in fact distinguish the two scenarios to a statistically significant extent. That is, we were able to falsify the null hypothesis that these scenarios are intuitively indistinguishable. This implies that, despite sharing all of the properties described above, the Ned and Oscar scenarios trigger distinct mental representations whose properties are morally salient. This in turn lends at least some support to the hypothesis that the operative distinction between these scenarios is the distinction between battery as a means and battery as a side effect.

By contrast, the second prediction did not hold, or rather, it held only to a limited extent. Although a majority (62%) of those participants in the Knowing Battery condition held Oscar's throwing the switch to be permissible, while a minority (48%) of those in Purposeful Battery condition held Ned's throwing the switch to be permissible, the contrast between these percentages was less sharp than in our previous studies. Further, the Purposeful Battery responses were no different than chance in this regard. This was also a departure from our prior studies, in which the number of participants holding acts constituting purposeful battery to be permissible was small enough to warrant the claim that, as a general matter, individuals regard these acts to be impermissible.

Nevertheless, Experiment 4 did confirm an intuitive distinction between this pair of cases, despite their close similarities. Further, several explanations of these anomalous results suggest themselves and raise interesting problems for future research. We briefly mention two such possibilities here, leaving further investigation of them for another occasion.

First, although trolley intuitions are normally quite sharp (see, e.g., Thomson 1986), it is also a familiar and important observation that these institutions often "begin to fail above a certain level of complexity" (Nagel 1986: 174). Indeed, some trolley problems are so complex and elaborate (see, e.g., Unger 1996) that it seems doubtful whether they are particularly well suited for cognitive science or elicit considered judgments in Rawls' sense. While the Ned-Oscar pair arguably does not fall into the latter category, these probes are more complex and difficult to process than the problems used in Experiments 1–3. Indeed, we provided participants with a diagram to facilitate comprehension for just this reason. Consequently, these results could be the predictable effect of a kind of information overload, at least for some subjects. In the case of language, it is well understood that certain nonlinguistic factors, such as memory limitations and other performance variables, can interfere with the parsing of linguistic expressions. This, of course, is one reason why linguists draw the competence–performance distinction and distinguish grammaticality and acceptability judgments. A comparable situation presumably obtains in the moral domain. If so, then the best explanation of these results might rely on a moral competence–performance distinction (see generally Sections 2.1.4, 3.1.6, 8.2, and 8.3).

Second, a disparity between intended and actual result (LaFave 2003) may also help explain these findings. The standard operational test for distinguishing necessary means from unnecessary side effect is a counterfactual test, according to which one asks whether the actor would have acted differently if the negative result could have been avoided. By this measure, Ned but not Oscar is presumed to intend a battery as a means to achieving his end, because Ned's objectives include causing the train to hit the man, whereas Oscar's objectives do not. Put differently, if circumstances were altered and the man were no longer on the side track, then Ned would *not* throw the switch, because his immediate purpose in doing so is to cause the train to hit the man. By contrast, Oscar *would* still throw the switch in these circumstances, because his immediate purpose is to cause the train to hit the object, in front of which the man is standing.

The disparity between intended and actual result complicates this analysis. Although Oscar's purposes do not include saving the men by causing the train to hit the man, the *actual* result of his action will likely be just that, because unless the man jumps off the track in time, Oscar's throwing the switch will cause the train to hit the man *before* the train hits the object. From an ex post perspective, then, it may turnout to be true that Oscar committed a battery as a means to saving the five men, even though, from an ex ante perspective, it was not his specific intention to do so (see also Section 6.2.2).

Significantly, this disparity between intended and actual result is not present in any of the other Knowing Battery conditions. Instead, the intended good result of saving the five men necessarily occurs before, and independently of, the foreseen bad result of causing the train to hit the man in these conditions (and, it will be recalled, this temporal structure was one reason why the Ned-Oscar pair was constructed in the first place). Hence this important structural difference between the Man-in-Front problem, on the one hand, and the other Knowing Battery conditions utilized in our previous experiments, on the other, may also help explain the comparatively anomalous results of Experiment 4. This explanation is provisional, however, and more research is needed to clarify this issue.

5. EXPERIMENT 5

For our purposes, the PDE may be thought of as a complex principle of justification that holds that an otherwise prohibited action may be permissible if (i) the act itself is not wrong, (ii) the good but not the bad effects are specifically intended, (iii) the good effects outweigh the bad effects, and (iv) no morally preferable alternative is available. In Experiments 1–4, we focused mainly on the first and third provisions of this principle. In Experiment 5, we turned our attention to the second and fourth provisions.

5.1 Method

5.1.1 Participants
Participants were 60 adult volunteers ages 18–65 from the Washington, D.C., area. The group consisted of 32 women and 28 men.

5.1.2 Stimuli and Procedure
Four scenarios were used, one of which was the Bystander problem. The other three were the Intentional Homicide, Better Alternative, and Disproportional Death problems (see Table 5.1).

A within-subject design was utilized. Each of the 60 participants received a written questionnaire containing two scenarios, including (i) the Bystander problem and (ii) one of the other three scenarios. Thus, there were three conditions in this experiment, with 20 participants assigned randomly to each condition. Participants were asked to read the scenarios and decide whether the proposed actions were "morally permissible" and then to explain or justify their responses.

5.2 Results

5.2.1 Intentional Homicide vs. Bystander Problem
We present the results of Experiment 5 in stages, beginning with the comparison between the Intentional Homicide and Bystander problems (Figure A.14). Twenty percent (4/20) of subjects in this condition judged the action ("Mark's throwing the switch") constituting purposeful homicide in the former problem to be permissible. Meanwhile, 80% (16/20) of subjects in this condition judged the same action ("Hank's throwing the switch") constituting knowing homicide in the Bystander Problem to be permissible. This difference is significant: χ^2 (1, N = 20) = 14.4, p < .001.

5.2.2 Better Alternative vs. Bystander Problem
Because of the limited number of subjects in Experiment 5, we refrain from analyzing our responses by gender. Instead, we turn directly to the comparison between the Better Alternative problem and the Bystander problem

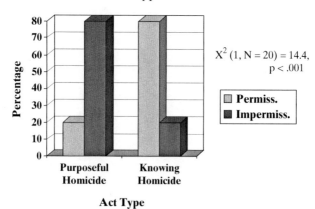

FIGURE A.14. Moral Judgments of Two Act Types in Experiment 5 (Purposeful Homicide vs. Knowing Homicide)

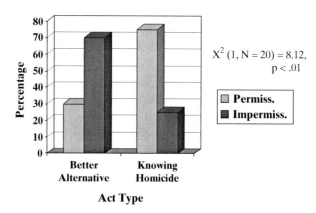

FIGURE A.15. Moral Judgments of Two Act Types in Experiment 5 (Better Alternative vs. Knowing Homicide)

(Figure A.15). Seventy-five percent (15/20) of subjects in this condition judged Hank's throwing the switch to be permissible in the Bystander problem. By contrast, only 30% (6/20) of subjects judged the same action ("Richard's throwing the switch") to be permissible in the presence of a better alternative. This difference is significant: χ^2 (1, $N = 20$) = 8.12, $p < .01$.

5.2.3 Disproportional Death vs. Bystander Problem
Third, we turn to the comparison between the Disproportional Death problem and the Bystander problem (Figure A.16). Fifteen percent (3/20) of subjects in this condition judged the action generating disproportional death ("Steve's throwing the switch") to be permissible. By contrast, 55% (11/20) of subjects judged the same action ("Hank's throwing the switch") to be permissible in

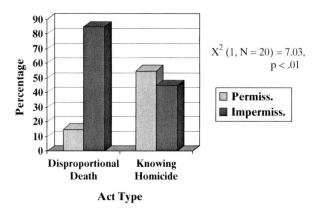

FIGURE A.16. Moral Judgments of Two Act Types in Experiment 5 (Disproportional Death vs. Knowing Homicide)

the Bystander problem in this condition. This difference is significant: χ^2 (1, $N = 20$) = 7.03, $p < .01$.

5.2.4 Justifications

Finally, we turn to our participants' verbalized justifications. The fact that we utilized a within-subject design in Experiment 5 led us to predict that these justifications would be less adequate than those in Experiment 1 (which used a between-subject design) and more like those in Experiment 2 (which used a within-subject design). This prediction was confirmed. Fifty-three percent (32/60) of participants gave no justification, 23% (14/60) provided logically inadequate justifications, while 23% (14/60) provided logically adequate justifications – a figure much closer to the percentage of logically adequate justifications in Experiment 2 (20%) than in Experiment 1 (50%).

5.3 Discussion

The results of Experiment 5 lend further support to the hypothesis that ordinary adults possess intuitive knowledge of the prohibition of intentional battery and the PDE. By attributing knowledge of this principle to our subjects, we can explain why their deontic intuitions change when the standard Bystander problem is modified such that (i) the bad but not the good effects are specifically intended, or (ii) a morally preferable alternative is available. Additionally, the results of Experiment 5 confirm our previous finding that individuals' deontic intuitions are also susceptible to the systematic manipulation of good and bad effects.

Experiment 5 also provides additional evidence of framing effects. For example, 80% (16/20) of participants in the Intentional Homicide condition (in which participants were given both the Intentional Homicide and Bystander problems in a within-subject design) and 75% (15/20) of participants in the Better Alternative condition (in which participants were given both the Better Alternative and Bystander problems in a within-subject design) judged throwing the switch in the Bystander problem to be permissible. Further, only 55% (11/20) of participants in the Disproportional Death condition (in which participants were given both the Disproportional Death and Bystander problems in a within-subject design) judged throwing the switch in the Bystander problem to be permissible. These percentages, and particularly the last figure, contrast sharply with the 95% of respondents who judged throwing the switch in the Bystander problem to be permissible in the between-subject design utilized in Experiment 1. This in turn suggests that whether individuals are prepared to permit knowing battery or knowing homicide on broadly utilitarian grounds in these circumstances may depend on how that question is framed, including the order in which multiple cases are presented. Because of the relatively few participants in this experiment, however, we refrain from drawing any firm conclusions about framing and ordering effects here, instead merely identifying them as important topics for future research.

6. EXPERIMENT 6

Experiments 1–5 were designed to investigate the moral competence of adults only. In Experiment 6, we extended this inquiry to include the moral competence of children ages 8–12. Our objectives in this regard were limited. First, we wished to determine whether children in this age group had moral intuitions about a pair of relatively simple trolley problems that were similar to adult intuitions. Second, and more generally, we wished to explore the potential of using these and similar thought experiments to investigate the moral competence of young children, perhaps including children much younger than eight years old. A central premise of both Piaget's (1965/1932) and Kohlberg's (1981, 1984) theories of moral development is that the moral conceptions of adults and children consist of fundamentally different principles. A corollary is the assumption that moral development is something that happens gradually over the course of one's lifetime, and thus should be investigated by means of longitudinal studies. In Experiment 6, we began testing these assumptions by presenting a group of children with two of the scenarios that we had previously used to study the moral intuitions of adults. Finally, we wanted to investigate whether these children's moral intuitions could be explained with reference to the prohibition of intentional battery and the PDE. That is, we wished to discover whether children, like adults, would treat these two cases of necessity differently, depending on whether battery is used as an intended means to a given end or as a foreseen side effect. In this manner we sought to ask whether these principles emerge and become operative relatively early in the course of moral development, thereby raising the possibility that specific poverty of the stimulus arguments related to these rules and their associated mental representations could be formulated in the moral domain.

6.1 Method

6.1.1 Participants
Participants were 30 children ages 8–12 who were recruited with parental consent from four metropolitan areas: Cambridge, Massachusetts; Knoxville, Tennessee; Toledo, Ohio; and Washington, D.C. There were 14 girls and 16 boys.

6.1.2 Stimuli and Procedure
Two scenarios were used. In the first scenario ("Dr. Brown"), which was modeled on the Transplant problem, battery was embedded within an agent's action plan as a means (henceforth "Purposeful Battery"). In the second scenario ("Charlie"), which was modeled on the Trolley problem, battery was embedded within the agent's action plan as a side effect (henceforth "Knowing Battery") (see Mikhail 2002b for the actual text of these scenarios).

A between-subject design was utilized. Each of the 30 children was given a written questionnaire containing either the Purposeful Battery or the Knowing Battery scenario. The child was first instructed to read the scenario and then to decide whether the proposed action it described was "wrong." For the purposes of this experiment, we took for granted the standard assumption in deontic logic that "wrong" is logically equivalent to "not morally permissible" (Prior 1955; Von Wright 1951), and we reasoned that the children would have an easier time answering a question using the term "wrong" than one using the phrase "morally permissible." Each child was also asked on a separate page to provide an explanation for his or her response. Fifteen children were given the Purposeful Battery scenario, and 15 were given the Knowing Battery scenario. Assignment of participant to scenario type was random.

6.2 Results

6.2.1 Judgments
The main results of Experiment 6 are summarized in Figure A.17. Forty percent (6/15) of the children in the Purposeful Battery condition judged this action to be permissible. By contrast, 93% (14/15) of the children in the Knowing Battery condition judged this action to be permissible. This difference is significant: $\chi^2 (1, N = 30) = 9.6, p < 0.01$.

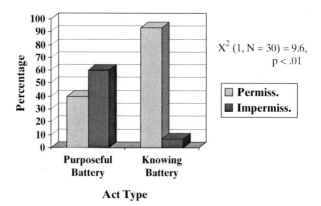

FIGURE A.17. Moral Judgments of Two Act Types in Experiment 6 (Purposeful Battery vs. Knowing Battery)

6.2.2 Justifications

Because of the limited number of participants in this experiment, we refrain from analyzing participants' responses by gender.[5] Instead, we turn to children's expressed justifications for their judgments. These justifications were categorized according to the same coding scheme used in our previous experiments. Here 46.7% (14/30) of participants gave no justification, 13.3% (4/30) provided logically inadequate justifications, and 40% (12/30) provided logically adequate justifications.

6.3 Discussion

Although the results of Experiment 6 are limited, they constitute initial evidence that the moral competence of 8–12-year-old children includes the prohibition of intentional battery and the PDE. Put differently, they suggest that simple deontological or consequentialist principles alone may be inadequate to describe the intuitive moral knowledge of children ages 8–12. More generally, these results support the utility of using trolley problems to investigate the moral competence of children, including even younger populations. This conclusion is significant in part because trolley problems are qualitatively

---

[5] Although we do not pursue the issue here, the breakdown of responses by gender did appear significant. Seven of eight girls and all seven of the boys in the Knowing Battery condition judged the action constituting knowing battery ("Charlie's turning the train") to be permissible. By contrast, one of six girls in the Purposeful Battery condition judged the action constituting purposeful battery ("Dr. Brown's cutting up the patient") to be permissible, but – surprisingly – a majority of boys (five out of nine) disagreed. These results suggest, albeit in a limited manner, that boys might be slower than girls to arrive at the standard adult view that certain deontological violations are impermissible. More research is needed to clarify this issue.

more complex than the questions used by researchers in the Piagetian tradition (see Section 7 and Mikhail 2002b for further discussion).

Turning to adequacy of justifications, it is notable that the justifications offered by children in Experiment 6 were only marginally less adequate than the corresponding justifications offered by adults in Experiment 1 (which also relied on relatively simple trolley problems presented in a between-subject design). In particular, the percentage of children who provided logically adequate justifications (40% or 12/30) compares favorably with the percentage of adults (50% or 20/40) of adults who did so in Experiment 1. Nevertheless, as was the case with adults, many of these logically adequate justifications were manifestly incapable of accounting for the divergent pattern of intuitions elicited in this experiment, in which saving five people at the cost of killing one person is felt to be permissible in one case, but not the other. Hence Experiment 6 provides further evidence that, like adults, children ages 8–12 possess unconscious moral knowledge that may be largely inaccessible to deliberate introspection (cf. Cushman et al. 2006).

Two further tentative conclusions may be drawn from Experiment 6. First, together with the results of our previous experiments, the results of Experiment 6 imply that at least some of the operative principles of moral competence, such as the distinction between intended means and foreseen side effect, are invariant throughout the course of moral development, at least between ages 8 and 65. This conclusion runs counter to one of the most basic assumptions of both Piaget's (1965/1932) and Kohlberg's (1981, 1984) approach to moral development, according to which the adult's and child's moral competence are comprised of fundamentally different principles. As indicated, a corollary of this proposition is the assumption that moral development is something that happens gradually over the course of one's lifetime, and thus should be investigated with longitudinal studies. The findings of Experiment 6 call at least some aspects of this framework and methodology into question, raising the possibility that, like language, vision, and other cognitive systems, the development of moral competence involves predetermined critical stages, after which this system more or less stabilizes.

Finally, the results of Experiment 6 also suggest, at least tentatively, that it may indeed be possible to formulate specific poverty of the stimulus arguments in the moral domain. While this possibility is theoretically intriguing, we refrain from drawing any firm conclusions about it here. Instead, we simply note that more experimental work must be done to determine whether certain complex moral principles, such as those investigated in these studies, are explicitly taught or otherwise available to the developing child during the acquisition process. Offhand, this seems unlikely, particularly in light of the discovery that adults do not explain or justify their own moral intuitions with reference to these principles. Indeed, the fact that at least some operative moral principles appear to be unconscious and nonintrospectible makes it plausible to suppose that these principles are not taught to successive generations explicitly. Hence we may reasonably assume, as a working hypothesis, that they are the developmental consequences of an innate cognitive faculty (see, e.g., Harman 2000; Mikhail 2000; Mikhail, Sorrentino, & Spelke 1998). However, this conclusion remains somewhat speculative, and the issue clearly calls for more intensive empirical investigation.

7. GENERAL DISCUSSION

Taken together, the studies presented here constitute significant evidence that adults possess intuitive or unconscious knowledge of complex moral principles, including the prohibition of intentional battery and the Principle of Double Effect. In addition, Experiment 6 provides some evidence for inferring that the same may be true of children ages 8–12. By attributing this knowledge to experimental subjects, we can predict and explain their moral intuitions. Because the imputed knowledge is *intuitive* and not fully open to conscious introspection, we can also advance a tentative explanation of why relatively few individuals appear capable of providing logically adequate justifications of their judgments, even on an extremely permissive interpretation of what counts as logically adequate, and why virtually no individuals appear capable of providing observationally adequate justifications, that is, justifications from which the systematic pattern of intuitions elicited by these experiments can be mechanically derived. The explanation, simply put, is that moral cognition appears to involve unconscious computations, that is, mental operations that are not consciously accessible. In this section, we elaborate on these findings and place them within a broader context by contrasting our approach to the theory of moral cognition with the approaches of Piaget (1965/1932), Kohlberg (1981, 1984), and Greene et al. (2001).

7.1 Contrast with Piaget: Complex versus Simple Acts

From the point of view of the theory of moral cognition and moral development, the trolley problems utilized in these investigations are fascinating for several reasons. Perhaps the most important reason is that these thought experiments are qualitatively more complex than the typical stimulus materials used by psychologists working within the Piagetian tradition. Piaget and his followers attempted to study moral competence by investigating the developing child's mental representations of the "subjective" and "objective" elements of moral judgment, the former consisting of the goals and intentions of an action, the latter consisting of an action's effects and material consequences. In Piaget's (1965/1932) original studies, children were found to base their moral judgments on mental representations of effects, not intentions, until around age nine. More recently, many investigators have suggested that these findings were an artifact of the methods and assessment procedures Piaget employed. Some researchers (e.g., Baird 2001; Berndt & Berndt 1975;

Costanzo, Coie, Grumet, & Farnhill 1973; Lilliard & Flavell 1990; Nelson 1980) have discovered that children as young as three use information about motives and intentions when making moral judgments, if that information is made explicit and salient. Moreover, a considerable body of research on infant cognition (e.g., Gergely, Nadasdy, Csibra, & Biro 1995; Johnson 2000; Meltzoff 1995; Woodward, Sommerville, & Guajardo 2001) suggests that even young infants are predisposed to interpret the actions of animate agents in terms of the agents' goals and intentions (cf. Heider & Simmel 1944).

Our research builds on these prior studies by asking how adults and children reconstruct and utilize information about intentions and effects when evaluating what might be called "morally complex acts" – that is, acts and omissions that are comprised of multiple intentions and that generate both good and bad effects. As indicated, Piaget's experiments focused attention on the subjective and objective elements of moral judgment. To this end, Piaget asked children to compare an action characterized by "good intentions" (e.g., helping mom to set the table) the negative consequences of which were significant (e.g., breaking 15 cups) with an action characterized by "bad intentions" (e.g., taking a cookie from the cookie jar) the negative consequences of which were slight (e.g., breaking one cup), and to determine which agent was "naughtier." Piaget discovered that until around age nine, children tended to judge the agent who was responsible for the "good intention/greater negative consequences" combination of factors to be "naughtier." After age nine, this response pattern changed: the older children tended to judge that the agent responsible for the "bad intention/slight negative consequence" combination was "naughtier." It was on this basis that Piaget concluded that children based their moral judgments on effects, not intentions, until around age nine (see, e.g., Piaget 1965/1932: 121–139).

As subsequent researchers noted, Piaget's conclusions were unjustified, because he used stories that co-varied two or more parameters at once. The exact role played by intentions and consequences in the children's judgments was therefore impossible to determine. To remedy this situation, later investigators modified Piaget's procedure by presenting children with stories that permitted the independent variation of intention and consequence parameters along two dimensions, "good" and "bad." In this way, the actions at issue could be characterized by one of four possible combinations of features: (1) good intention/good effect, (2) good intention/bad effect, (3) bad intention/good effect, and (4) bad intention/bad effect.

In one of Sharon Nelson's (1980) experiments, for example, children were given four different stories to evaluate. In the first, a boy, who sees his friend is sad because he does not have anything to play with, throws a ball toward the friend in order to play catch with him and cheer him up (good intention). The friend catches the ball and is happy (good effect). In the second, the boy throws the ball with the same intention (good intention) but ends up hitting his friend on the head and making him cry (bad effect). In the third, the boy is mad at his friend that day and throws the ball toward him in order to hit him with it (bad intention). However, the friend catches the ball and is happy (good effect). Finally, in the fourth, the boy again throws the ball at his friend in order to hit him with it (bad intention). This time he succeeds in hitting his friend on the head with the ball and making him cry (bad effect). When Nelson presented these four stories to her experimental subjects, she discovered that children as young as three years of age utilized information about intentions when making moral judgments (Nelson 1980).

Although experiments such as Nelson's, which permitted the independent variation of intentions and effects, were a substantial improvement on Piaget's original studies, they nonetheless limited their attention to what we might call "morally simple acts," that is, acts whose mental representations are characterized by only one morally salient (good or bad) intention and only one morally salient (good or bad) effect. By contrast, the trolley problems investigated in our studies are more complex, because they involve act-representations that are comprised of multiple intentions and other mental states and that generate both good and bad effects. Moreover, three of the four variables in the Piagetian framework – good and bad effects and good intention (i.e., ultimate aim, purpose, or goal) – are held constant in the Trolley, Transplant, Footbridge, and Bystander problems, whereas the fourth – bad intention – is not relevant. This suggests that some *other* property or set of properties is responsible for the divergent moral judgments generated by these examples.

The key insight of our research is that these intuitions can be adequately explained only by drawing on complex moral and legal principles, such as the prohibition of intentional battery and the Principle of Double Effect. Piaget (1965/1932: 13, 20) emphasized what he called the "juridical complexity" of children's moral judgments and observed that, to understand these judgments, psychologists must familiarize themselves with aspects of "the common law." Yet Piaget's own stimulus materials often failed to test for common legal distinctions, such as justification and excuse, recklessness and negligence, proximate and remote causation, or – what appears most relevant here – intended and foreseen effects.

Piaget is not alone in this regard. As Robinson and Darley (1995) have observed, many social scientists seeking to describe social norms and "the community's sense of justice" appear to rely on definitions and concepts that are both descriptively inadequate and legally inaccurate. As a result, they often underestimate the subtlety and complexity of laypersons' intuitive grasp of legal concepts and distinctions. And they often beg important questions about how moral knowledge is acquired. In a wide-ranging book criticizing the role of moral intuitions in legal policy, for example, Kaplow and Shavell (2002: 76) insist that norms "must be relatively simple because they must be imparted to children and applied without sustained analysis." Kaplow and Shavell's observation begs the question whether and to what extent norms are "imparted to children" in any meaningful sense. If morality is like language, then some of the principles generating human moral intuitions may turn out to be innate; indeed, as commentators such as Harman (2000) have argued, the Principle of Double Effect may turn out to be one such principle. From this vantage point, Kaplow and Shavell appear to have jumped the gun and inverted the proper relationship between descriptive and explanatory adequacy. The success of research programs in other cognitive domains suggests that the origin of moral intuitions can be adequately investigated only insofar as their acquired structure is clearly understood.

7.2 Contrast with Kohlberg: Operative versus Express Principles

Many research programs in moral cognition do not distinguish sharply between moral judgment and moral reasoning and tacitly assume that moral principles are introspectible. Perhaps the most influential research program of this type is the one developed by Lawrence Kohlberg (1958, 1981, 1984). On Kohlberg's view, Piaget was correct to assume that the capacity for moral judgment passes through a series of developmental stages. However, whereas Piaget proposed two broad stages, Kohlberg's theory postulates six.[6] Further, although Kohlberg's theory is partially based on Piaget's, his conclusions are far better supported empirically.

The aspect of Kohlberg's framework most relevant to our discussion concerns his focus on the explicit statements people make to justify or explain their moral judgments. Kohlberg assessed moral development by having trained researchers code an experimental subject's stated justifications for her decisions on a series of moral dilemmas. One of his best known puzzles is the "Heinz dilemma," which deals with the example of a man whose wife's life can be saved only by a medicine he cannot afford. Under these circumstances, would it be right for the man to steal the drug? Kohlberg and his associates put these and similar questions to children and adults of all ages, asking them to justify whatever decision they reached. By evaluating not the decision itself but the justification accompanying it, Kohlberg (1981, 1984) claimed to discover that moral development progresses through an unvarying sequence of six stages.

Kohlberg's overall theory is rich and complex, and we make no effort to evaluate it systematically here. Instead, we simply note that our investigations appear to confirm in rather dramatic fashion that those commentators who have questioned Kohlberg's methodological decision to focus on verbalized justifications rather than particular moral intuitions are correct to criticize this aspect of his framework (see, e.g., Darley & Shultz 1990; Haidt 2001; Kagan 1987; Macnamara 1990, 1999; Mikhail 2000, 2002b).

[6] Depending on whether one counts Piaget's "premoral" stage, his theory of moral development could also be said to consist of three stages, which Kohlberg subsequently expanded to six stages.

Unlike Kohlberg, we distinguished operative and express principles at the outset of our research and emphasized the importance of this distinction throughout our investigations. We also assumed that just as normal persons are typically unaware of the principles guiding their linguistic intuitions, so too are they often unaware of the principles guiding their moral intuitions. Further, based on both informal observation and a review of the relevant literature, we predicted that an empirical investigation of the trolley problems would reveal that our subjects' "locus of moral certitude" (Jonsen & Toulmin 1988) would be their intuitive judgments themselves, not their underlying justifications.

Our studies confirmed this prediction. When the participants in our experiments were asked to provide explicit justifications for their judgments, they were consistently incapable of articulating the operative principles on which their judgments were based. Indeed, in sharp contrast with Kohlberg's (1981, 1984) findings concerning the relevance of demographic variables like gender, race, nationality, age, and level of formal education, but in accord with our expectations, our subjects' moral judgments were widely shared, irrespective of these factors. Our subjects' *expressed* principles, however, were widely divergent. More importantly, our subjects consistently failed to state the operative reasons for their judgments in any theoretically compelling sense. They often said things that were incompatible with their own judgments, or even internally incoherent. And they often appeared puzzled by the nature and strength of their intuitions, and by how those intuitions shifted when we introduced small changes in the wording of the action-sequences they were given in order to evoke distinct mental representations.

A related point worth emphasizing concerns the methodology underlying Kohlberg's controversial findings about the role of gender and other demographic variables in moral development. As critics such as Carol Gilligan (1982) have observed, the original research from which Kohlberg derived his stage theory of moral development was based on a study of 84 American boys from suburban Chicago, whose development Kohlberg followed for a period of over 20 years. Although Kohlberg claimed universality for his stage theory, subsequent research revealed that girls, women, and other groups who were not included in Kohlberg's original sample tended to reach only the third or fourth stage of his six-stage sequence (Gilligan 1982; see also Edwards 1975; Holstein 1976; Simpson 1974). Critics like Gilligan have criticized these findings as the inevitable outcome of a research program that is insensitive to the fact that, in moral matters, men and women often speak "in a different voice" (Gilligan 1982). Generally speaking, however, these critics have not strayed far from Kohlberg's paradigm and have continued to "measure" or otherwise evaluate the character of an individual's moral judgment by looking to her actual utterances.

We think that the dissociation between moral judgments and justifications highlighted in our investigations calls into question the entire approach of both Kohlberg and many of his critics. Simply put, our studies suggest that these researchers may have focused their attention on the wrong phenomena. A comparison to the study of language and vision, neither of which constructs a theory of development based on expressed justifications, brings the point into sharper focus. Neither linguists nor vision theorists take the *post hoc* explanations of experimental subjects – for example, statements explaining or justifying the intuition that a particular utterance is ungrammatical – to be their primary source of data. Rather, their data are the subjects' intuitions themselves.

While our findings clearly establish a significant discrepancy between judgments and justifications, it would be a mistake to conclude from what has been said thus far that express principles have no evidentiary role to play in the theory of moral cognition. On the contrary, an individual's introspective reports may often provide important and even compelling evidence for the properties of her moral competence (cf. Chomsky 1965). Indeed, many of the justifications offered by adults and even some of the justifications offered by young children in our experiments were illuminating in that they revealed a strong intuitive appreciation for specific legal concepts and principles.

For example, several of the children who were given the Transplant problem and asked to explain their judgments in Experiment 6 referred on their own initiative to the crucial issue of lack of consent. One participant, an eight-year-old boy, who judged Dr. Brown's cutting up the patient to be wrong, made the following remark:

Okay, if given consent.

A second participant, an 11-year-old boy, commented:

I think that Dr. Brown should ask the person in Room 306 if they would like to be cut up to save the other peoples' lives.

A third participant, also an 11-year-old boy, said:

I said no because it never said that she gave permission to kill her; to give away her body parts .... I did not feel good about it because I would not like somebody to take my body parts.

Finally, a fourth participant, a 12-year-old girl, said:

I believe that it would be wrong to cut this 306 person up without them even knowing it. It would be different if Dr. Brown had asked this person if they would donate their organs and he had received their permission. That is why I would blame him if he took their life.

As these remarks suggest, the distinction between operative and express principles does not imply that researchers should simply disregard or automatically discount the significance of verbalized justifications. Although none of these children used the term "battery" to explain their judgments, their comments clearly suggest an impressive intuitive grasp of one of the key elements of battery, namely, lack of consent.

In sum, the distinction between operative and express principles appears to vitiate, or at least seriously compromise, the basic Kohlberg paradigm, which was the dominant approach to the psychology of moral development in the second half of the twentieth century (see generally Gilligan 1982; Haidt 2001; Kohlberg 1981, 1984; Rest 1983; Turiel 1983). Kohlberg's stage theory of moral development is one that primarily tracks the development of a person's ability to *express* or *articulate* moral reasons and principles. Although this is an important skill, which perhaps corresponds at some level with the ability to engage in more complex acts of moral reasoning, it does not necessarily reveal the properties of moral competence. On the contrary, as our subjects' responses to the trolley problems reveal, a person's introspective verbal reports and general viewpoint about her moral knowledge may sometimes be in error. Yet, at the same time, a subject's first-person reports *may* contain important evidence of the speaker's intuitive knowledge of a specific legal concept or principle, knowledge that runs the risk of being overlooked if the researcher is preoccupied with the search for global justifications in the manner advocated by Kohlberg. In the final analysis, the important point to note is that, as is the case with a theory of language or vision, the goal of the theory of moral cognition must be to account for a person's actual moral intuitions and the cognitive mechanisms that determine what she intuits, rather than to account for her own statements, explanations, or justifications of what she intuits and why. (For similar remarks on this apparent deficiency of Kohlberg's framework, see generally Darley & Shultz 1990; Haidt 2001; Kagan 1987; Macnamara 1990, 1999; Mikhail 2000. For parallel remarks with respect to language, see Chomsky 1965.)

7.3 Contrast with Greene: Computation versus Emotion

An important paper relying on trolley problems to investigate moral judgment, which appeared after the research described in this appendix was largely completed, was published in the journal *Science* in 2001 by Joshua Greene and colleagues (Greene et al. 2001). In this section, we briefly comment on this paper and contrast it with the investigation presented here.

To begin with, we note that Greene and colleagues have written a highly stimulating paper. They deserve credit for showing how a problem that has long preoccupied philosophers can be studied using the methods of brain imaging. The authors' conclusion that trolley problem judgments are caused by differences in emotional engagement, however, seems decidedly premature. Their research appears to have serious methodological flaws that suggest this conclusion may be overstated (see, e.g., Mikhail 2002b). More importantly, Greene and colleagues have given insufficient consideration to the competing hypothesis that their moral dilemmas elicit mental representations that differ in their structural properties. Put simply, a computational theory of moral cognition has been ruled out too soon.

The authors' central thesis is that "the crucial difference between the trolley dilemma and the footbridge dilemma lies in the latter's tendency to engage people's emotions in a way that the former does not. The thought of pushing someone to his death is, we propose, more emotionally salient than the thought of hitting a switch that will cause a trolley to produce similar consequences, and it is this emotional response that accounts for people's tendency to treat these cases differently" (Greene et al. 2001: 2106). They also advance a further generalization: "Some moral dilemmas (those relevantly similar to the footbridge dilemma) engage emotional processing to a greater extent than others (those relevantly similar to the trolley dilemma), and these differences in emotional engagement affect people's judgments" (Greene et al. 2001: 2106). Finally, on this basis, Greene and colleagues predict and then confirm that certain brain regions associated with emotion are more active when subjects respond to the Footbridge problem than when they respond to the Trolley problem.

These claims prompt three related observations. First, the authors' data do not exclude the possibility that the Footbridge and Trolley problems and related thought experiments engage perceptual and cognitive processing in systematically different ways, and that it is these differences, rather than (or in addition to) differences in emotion, that influence people's considered moral judgments. Rather, their data are consistent with assuming that people reliably distinguish permissible and impermissible actions for independent reasons and respond emotionally once these prior determinations have been made.

Second, on the authors' own view, some account of the process whereby subjects interpret the verbal stimulus and extract informational cues is not merely possible, but necessary. Indeed, Greene and colleagues presuppose just such an account, suggesting that people manage to conclude that it is acceptable to sacrifice one person for the sake of five in the Trolley problem but not the Footbridge problem by spontaneously analyzing these cases in terms of three features: "whether the action in question (a) could reasonably be expected to lead to serious bodily harm, (b) to a particular person or a member or members of a particular group of people (c) where this harm is not the result of deflecting an existing threat onto a different party" (Greene et al. 2001: 2107). Greene and colleagues purport to explain their subjects' moral judgments and predict patterns of brain activity on this basis.

Third, the authors' characterization of the function that maps verbal stimulus to moral response is neither complete nor descriptively adequate. It is incomplete because we are not told how people manage to recognize whether a given dilemma contains these features; surprisingly, Greene and colleagues leave this crucial first step in the perceptual process (the step involving conversion rules) unanalyzed. More importantly, the authors' account is descriptively inadequate because it cannot explain even relatively simple counterexamples to which any adequate theory of moral cognition must be responsive.

Consider, for example, two slight variations of the Footbridge and Bystander problems, which we investigated in Experiments 2–3 and Experiment 5, respectively. In the first problem (Implied Consent), a runaway trolley threatens to kill a man walking across the tracks. The only way to save him is to throw him out of the path of the train. Throwing the man, however, will seriously injure him. In the second problem (Disproportional Death), the same runaway trolley again threatens to kill a man walking across the tracks. This time, the only way to save the man is to throw a switch that will turn the trolley onto a side track, where it will kill five people.

Taken together, these two scenarios create an immediate problem for Greene et al. (2001). Throwing the man out of the path of the train is an action that "could reasonably be expected to lead to serious bodily harm to a particular person ... where this harm is not the result of deflecting an existing threat onto a different party" (Greene et al. 2001: 2107). On the authors' account, therefore, it should be assigned to their "moral-personal" category and judged impermissible. But a combined total of 93% (38/41) of participants in Experiments 2 and 3 thought this action was permissible. Conversely, while turning a trolley onto a side track where it will kill five people instead of one is an action that "could reasonably be expected to lead to serious bodily harm to ... a particular group of people," it is also "the result of deflecting an existing threat onto a different party" (Greene et al. 2001: 2107). On the authors' account, therefore, it should be assigned to their "moral-impersonal" category and judged permissible. Yet, 85% (17/20) of respondents in Experiment 5 thought this action was impermissible. How did our subjects manage to come to these conclusions? The answer cannot be the one proposed by Greene et al. (2001).

A better explanation of these intuitions is ready to hand, one that grows out of the classical rationalist and computational approaches that Greene and colleagues too hastily reject. We need only assume that people are "intuitive lawyers" (Haidt 2001) and have a "natural readiness" (Rawls 1971) to compute mental representations of human acts in legally cognizable terms. The operative reason why pushing the man in the Footbridge problem is impermissible is because it constitutes purposeful battery. The operative reason why turning the trolley in the Bystander problem is permissible is because the battery and homicide it generates are foreseen but nonpurposeful side effects that are outweighed by the good effect of preventing the train from killing the men. By contrast, the operative reason why turning the trolley in the Disproportional Death problem is impermissible is because its costs outweigh its benefits. Finally, the operative reason why throwing the man out of the path of the train in the Implied Consent problem is permissible is twofold: first, its benefits outweigh its costs, and second, this action is not a battery at all. In light of the reasonable presumption that the man would consent to being thrown and injured in order to save his life in these circumstances, his hypothetical consent to this harmful contact can be safely assumed in this situation (cf. Epstein 2004: 24).

Greene and colleagues raise an important objection to the computational approach. They observe that in an unusual variant of the Bystander problem invented by Judith Thomson (1985), in which the side track leading to the one person loops around to connect with the track leading to the five people, most people agree that it would be permissible to turn the trolley, even though doing so would appear to violate the Kantian injunction against "using" a person to achieve a worthy end (Greene et al. 2001: 2106). Yet the authors fail to note that the original Bystander problem and Thomson's looped track example differ in their temporal, causal, and counterfactual properties (see, e.g., Costa 1987b). More importantly, Greene and colleagues do not explain why one must accept their tacit assumption that the trolley would be turned in Thomson's looped track example for any relevant purpose other than the one motivating the agent in the original Bystander problem – to prevent the train from killing the men. If one refrains from making this assumption, then the intuition that turning the train is permissible in these circumstances can be explained along familiar lines.

Recall that the pair of "loop track" scenarios we invented in Experiment 4 was designed in part to investigate just this issue. In Experiment 4, we discovered that even in the context of this extremely minimal pair of vignettes, subjects remained sensitive to the distinction between intended means and foreseen side effect. Moreover, they did so even though the process of recovering these intentional properties from the impoverished stimulus is subtle and nontrivial. Further, the relevant data from this experiment cannot be readily explained by appealing to varying levels of emotional engagement (cf. Greene et al. 2001). These intuitions can be successfully explained, however, by invoking the operation of unconscious moral principles.

Finally, we emphasize that Greene and colleagues do not provide a clear procedure for determining whether the three features they identify are contained in (or otherwise derivable from) their stimuli. We are told that patterns of brain activity can be predicted on the basis of whether an action can "reasonably be expected to lead to serious bodily harm" to a person or group "where this harm is not the result of deflecting an existing threat onto a different party" (Greene et al. 2001: 2107), but we are not told how a given stimulus is to be analyzed in these terms. A further virtue of our computational hypothesis is that these crucial first steps in the perceptual process are fully analyzed. That is, not only can our subjects' judgments be generated by fixed and recognizable moral principles, once appropriate mental representations have been computed, but the mental representations themselves can be derived from their corresponding stimuli by a process that is largely mechanical. In short, a complete and explicit theory of the steps converting proximal stimulus to perceptual response can be given along these lines. In this sense, the theory of moral cognition presented here is at least observationally if not descriptively adequate. Greene and colleagues offer no comparable explanation of the conversion of proximal stimulus to perceptual response. Hence their theory is not even observationally adequate.

7.4 Conclusion

This appendix summarizes the results of six experiments conducted on a total 543 individuals, including 513 adults and 30 children ages 8–12. Our results constitute evidence that both adults and children ages 8–12 possess intuitive or unconscious knowledge of specific moral principles, including the prohibition of intentional battery and the Principle of Double Effect. Significantly, this knowledge appears to be merely tacit or otherwise consciously inaccessible: when participants were asked to explain or justify their responses, they consistently failed to provide adequate justifications for their judgments. Our findings also suggest that at least some moral intuitions and the principles that generate them are widely shared, irrespective of demographic variables like gender, race, nationality, age, and level of formal education. Finally, and perhaps most significantly, our findings imply that long-standing questions in moral epistemology may be fruitfully investigated within the framework of computational models similar to those utilized in the study of language and other cognitive systems. That is, we have shown how one may pursue a "Galilean" approach to scientific explanation in this domain, in which observable data are rigorously explained in terms of rules and representations (Chomsky 1980; Marr 1982). Having gathered evidence that individuals possess a specific type of intuitive moral knowledge, we are now in a better position to determine how this knowledge is acquired and whether or to what extent it may be innate. Our results thus pave the way for future investigations into the nature, origin, and use of human moral competence.

Bibliography

Alexander, R. (1987). *The Biology of Moral Systems*. Hawthorne, NY: Aldine de Gruyter.

Alicke, M. (1992). Culpable causation. *Journal of Personality and Social Psychology*, 63, 368–378.

Alschuler, A. (2000). *Law without Values: The Life, Work, and Legacy of Justice Holmes*. Chicago: University of Chicago Press.

Alter, A. L., Kernochan, J., & Darley, J. M. (2007). Morality influences how people apply the ignorance of the law defense. *Law and Society Review*, 41, 819–864.

American Law Institute (1938). *Restatement of the Law of Torts, as Adopted and Promulgated by the American Law Institute at Washington, D.C. May 12, 1938*. St. Paul, MN: American Law Institute.

(1965). *Restatement (Second) of Torts*. St. Paul, MN: American Law Institute.

(1985/1962). *Model Penal Code*. Philadelphia: American Law Institute.

Anscombe, G. E. M. (1957). *Intention*. Oxford: Basil Blackwell.

(1958). Modern moral philosophy. *Philosophy*, 33, 1–19.

(1970). War and murder. In R. Wasserstrom (Ed.), *War and Morality* (pp. 42–53). Belmont, CA: Wadsworth.

(1979). Under a description. *Nous*, 13, 219–233.

Aquinas, T. (1952/1274). *The Summa Theologica of St. Thomas Aquinas*. Chicago: Encyclopedia Britannica.

(1963/1274). *Summa Theologiae*. London: Blackfriars.

(1988/1274). *St. Thomas Aquinas on Politics and Ethics*. (P. Sigmund, Ed.). New York: W. W. Norton.

Aristotle. (1954). *Nichomachean Ethics*. (W. D. Ross, Ed.). Oxford: Oxford University Press.

(1988). *The Politics*. (S. Everson, Ed.). Cambridge: Cambridge University Press.

Austin, J. (1954/1832). *The Province of Jurisprudence Determined*. London: Hart.

Ayer, A. J. (1946/1936). *Language, Truth, and Logic*. London: Dover.

Baier, K. (1965). *The Moral Point of View: A Rational Basis of Ethics*. New York: Random House.

Bain, A. (1868). *Mental and Moral Science: A Compendium of Psychology and Ethics*. London: Longmans, Green.

361

Baird, J. (2001). Motivations and morality: Do children use mental state information to evaluate identical actions differently? Paper presented to Biennial Meeting, Society for Research in Child Development, Minneapolis.

Baker, M. (2001). *The Atoms of Language: The Mind's Hidden Rules of Grammar.* New York: Basic Books.

Banaji, M.R., Baron, A., Dunham, Y., & Olson, K. (2007). The development of intergroup social cognition: Early emergence, implicit nature, and sensitivity to group status. In M. Killen and S. Levy (Eds.), *Intergroup Relationships: An Integrative Developmental and Social Psychology Perspective* (pp. 87–102). Oxford: Oxford University Press.

Baron, J., & Ritov, I. (2009). Protected values and omission bias as deontological judgments. In B.H. Ross (Series Ed.) & D.M. Bartels, C.W. Bauman, L.J. Skitka, & D.L. Medin (Eds.), *Psychology of Learning and Motivation, Vol. 50: Moral Judgment and Decision Making.* San Diego, CA: Academic Press.

Baron, J., & Spranca, M. (1997). Protected values. *Organizational Behavior and Human Decision Processes,* 70, 1–16.

Barry, B. (1973). *The Liberal Theory of Justice.* Oxford: Clarendon Press.

Bartels, D.M. (2008). Principled moral sentiment and the flexibility of moral judgment and decision making. *Cognition,* 108, 381–417.

Bartels, D.M., & Medin, D.L. (2007). Are morally motivated decision makers insensitive to the consequences of their choices? *Psychological Science,* 18, 24–28.

Bennett, J. (1966). Whatever the consequences. *Analysis,* 26, 83–102.

     (1981). Morality and consequences. In *The Tanner Lectures on Human Values II* (pp. 45–116). Salt Lake City: University of Utah Press.

     (1995). *The Act Itself.* Oxford: Clarendon Press.

Bentham, J. (1948/1789). *An Introduction to the Principles of Morals and Legislation.* New York: Halfner Press.

     (1995/1843). *Works of Jeremy Bentham* (11 Vols.). (J. Bowring, Ed.). Bristol: Thoemmes Press.

Bergstrom, L. (1966). *The Alternatives and Consequences of Action: An Essay on Certain Fundamental Notions in Teleological Ethics.* Stockholm: Almqvist and Wiskell.

Berndt, T., & Berndt, E. (1975). Children's use of motives and intentionality in person perception and moral judgment. *Child Development,* 46, 904–912.

Bernstein, L. (1976). *The Unanswered Question: Six Talks at Harvard.* Cambridge, MA: Harvard University Press.

Blackburn, S. (1984). *Spreading the Word.* Oxford: Clarendon Press.

     (1993). *Essays in Quasi-Realism.* Oxford: Oxford University Press.

Blackstone, W. (1979/1765–1769). *Commentaries on the Laws of England* (4 Vols.). Chicago: University of Chicago Press.

Blair, J. (1995). A cognitive developmental approach to morality: Investigating the psychopath. *Cognition,* 57, 1–29.

     (2002). Neuro-cognitive models of acquired sociopathy and developmental psychopathy. In J. Glicksohn (Ed.), *The Neurobiology of Criminal Behavior: Neurobiological Foundation of Aberrant Behaviors* (pp. 157–186). Dordrecht: Kluwer Academic.

Bonar, J. (1930). *The Moral Sense*. London: George and Allen.

Botha, R. P. (1989). *Challenging Chomsky: The Generative Garden Game*. Oxford: Basil Blackwell.

Boyd, R. (1985). Observations, explanatory power, and simplicity: Toward a non-Humean account. In R. Boyd, P. Gasper, and J. D. Trout (Eds.), *The Philosophy of Science* (pp. 349–377). Cambridge, MA: MIT Press.

(1988). How to be a moral realist. In G. Sayre-McCord (Ed.), *Essays on Moral Realism* (pp. 181–228). Ithaca, NY: Cornell University Press.

Bradley, F. H. (1962/1876). *Ethical Studies*. Oxford: Oxford University Press.

Brandt, R. (1959). *Ethical Theory: The Problems of Normative and Critical Ethics*. Englewood Cliffs, NJ: Prentice-Hall.

(1979). *A Theory of the Good and the Right*. Oxford: Clarendon Press.

(1990). The science of man and wide reflective equilibrium. *Ethics*, 100, 259–278.

Bratman, M. (1987). *Intention, Plans, and Practical Reason*. Cambridge, MA: Harvard University Press.

Breasted, J. (1933). *The Dawn of Conscience: The Sources of Our Moral Heritage in the Ancient World*. New York: Charles Scribner's Sons.

Brentano, F. (1969/1889). *The Origin of the Knowledge of Right and Wrong*. (R. Chisholm, Ed.). New York: Humanities Press.

(1973/1952). *The Foundation and Construction of Ethics*. (E. Schneewind, Trans.). New York: Routledge.

Brink, D. (1987). Rawlsian constructivism in moral theory. *Canadian Journal of Philosophy*, 17, 71–90.

(1989). *Moral Realism and the Foundations of Ethics*. Cambridge: Cambridge University Press.

Broad, C. D. (1930). *Five Types of Ethical Theory*. London: Routledge and Kegan Paul.

(1952). *Ethics and the History of Philosophy*. London: Routledge and Kegan Paul.

(1985). *Ethics*. Dordrecht: Martinus Nijhoff.

Brown, D. (1991). *Human Universals*. New York: McGraw-Hill.

Bucciarelli, M., Khemlani, S., & Johnson-Laird, P. N. (2008). The psychology of moral reasoning. *Judgment and Decision Making*, 3(2), 121–139.

Burke, K. (1969/1945). *A Grammar of Motives*. Berkeley: University of California Press.

Burlamaqui, J. (2006/1748). *The Principles of Natural and Politic Law*. Indianapolis: Liberty Classics.

Burtt, E. A. (1992/1924). *The Metaphysical Foundations of Modern Science*. Atlantic Highlands, NJ: Humanities Press.

Butler, J. (1792/1726). *Fifteen Sermons Preached at the Rolls Chapel*. London: F. & C. Rivington.

(1983/1736). *A Dissertation upon the Nature of Virtue*. In S. Darwall (Ed.), *Five Sermons* (pp. 69–75). Indianapolis: Hackett.

Bybee, J., & Fleischman, S. (Eds.). (1995). *Modality in Grammar and Discourse*. Amsterdam: John Benjamins.

Cappon, L. J. (1959). *The Adams-Jefferson Letters: The Complete Correspondence between Thomas Jefferson and Abigail and John Adams*. Chapel Hill: University of North Carolina Press.

Cardozo, B. (1921). *The Nature of the Judicial Process*. New Haven, CT: Yale University Press.

Care, N. (1969). Contractualism and moral criticism. *Review of Metaphysics*, 23, 85–101.

Carey, S., & Spelke, E. (1994). Domain-specific knowledge and conceptual change. In L.A. Hirschfield & S.A. Gelmen (Eds.), *Mapping the Mind: Domain Specificity in Cognition and Culture* (pp.169–200). New York: Cambridge University Press.

Carnap, R. (1966). *An Introduction to the Philosophy of Science*. (M. Gardner, Ed.). New York: Basic Books.

Carruthers, P., Laurence, S., & Stich, S. (Eds.). (2005). *The Innate Mind: Structure and Contents*. New York: Oxford University Press.

    (2006). *The Innate Mind, Vol. 2: Culture and Cognition*. Oxford: Oxford University Press.

    (2007). *The Innate Mind, Vol. 3: Foundations and the Future*. Oxford: Oxford University Press.

Casebeer, W. (2003). *Natural Ethical Facts: Evolution, Connectionism, and Moral Cognition*. Cambridge, MA: MIT Press.

Castaneda, H. (1979). Intensionality and identity in human action and philosophical method. *Noûs*, 13, 235–260.

Chandler, M., Sokol, B., & Wainryb, C. (2000). Beliefs about truth and beliefs about rightness. *Child Development*, 71, 91–97.

Chomsky, N. (1957). *Syntactic Structures*. The Hague: Mouton.

    (1959). A Review of B. F. Skinner's "Verbal Behavior." In J. Fodor & J. Katz (Eds.), (1964), *The Structure of Language: Readings in the Philosophy of Language* (pp.547–578). Englewood Cliffs, NJ: Prentice-Hall.

    (1961). Degrees of grammaticalness. In J. Fodor & J. Katz (Eds.) (1964), *The Structure of Language: Readings in the Philosophy of Language* (pp.384–389). Englewood Cliffs, NJ: Prentice-Hall.

    (1964). *Current Issues in Linguistic Theory*. The Hague: Mouton.

    (1965). *Aspects of the Theory of Syntax*. Cambridge, MA: MIT Press.

    (1966). *Cartesian Linguistics*. Cambridge, MA: MIT Press.

    (1972). *Language and Mind*. (Enlarged Ed.). New York: Harcourt Brace Jovanovich.

    (1975a). *The Logical Structure of Linguistic Theory*. New York: Plenum Press.

    (1975b). *Reflections on Language*. New York: Pantheon.

    (1978). Interview with Noam Chomsky. *Linguistic Analysis*, 4(4), 301–319. Reprinted in N. Chomsky (1988a), *Language and Politics*. (C. P. Otero, Ed.). Montreal: Black Rose.

    (1980). *Rules and Representations*. New York: Columbia University Press.

    (1986a). *Knowledge of Language: Its Nature, Origin, and Use*. Westport, CT: Praeger.

    (1986b). Language and problems of knowledge. In A.P. Martinich (Ed.), *The Philosophy of Language*. (2nd Ed.) (pp.509–527). Oxford: Oxford University Press.

    (1986c). *Barriers*. Cambridge, MA: MIT Press.

    (1988a). *Language and Politics*. (C. P. Otero, Ed.). Montreal: Black Rose.

⸎ (1988b). *Language and Problems of Knowledge: The Managua Lectures.* Cambridge, MA: MIT Press.

▪ (1991a). Linguistics and adjacent fields: A personal view. In A. Kasher (Ed.), *The Chomskyan Turn* (pp. 3–25). Oxford: Basil Blackwell.

◂ (1991b). Linguistics and cognitive science: Problems and mysteries. In A. Kasher (Ed.), *The Chomskyan Turn* (pp. 26–53). Oxford: Basil Blackwell.

(1993a). *Language and Thought.* Wakefield, RI: Moyer Bell.

(1993b). Naturalism and dualism in the study of language and mind. *International Journal of Philosophical Studies,* 2, 181–209.

(1995a). Language and nature. *Mind,* 104(413), 1–61.

(1995b). *The Minimalist Program.* Cambridge, MA: MIT Press.

(2000). *New Horizons in the Study of Language and Mind.* Cambridge: Cambridge University Press.

(2002). *On Nature and Language.* Cambridge: Cambridge University Press.

(2009). The mysteries of nature: How deeply hidden? *Journal of Philosophy,* 106(4), 167–200.

Chomsky, N., & Halle, M. (1968). *The Sound Pattern of Modern English.* New York: Harper and Row.

Cicero. (1991/). *On Duties.* (M. T. Griffen & E. M. Atkins, Eds.). Cambridge: Cambridge University Press.

* Cohen, I. B. (1985). *The Birth of a New Physics.* New York: Penguin Books.

Cohen, M. R. (1916). The place of logic in the law. *Harvard Law Review,* 29, 622–639.

(1967/1933). *Law and the Social Order: Essays in Legal Philosophy.* Hamden, CT: Archon Books.

Cook, V., & Newson, M. (1996). *Chomsky's Universal Grammar: An Introduction.* (2nd Ed.). Cambridge, MA: Blackwell.

Copp, D. (1984). Considered judgments and moral justification: Conservativism in moral theory. In D. Copp & D. Zimmerman (Eds.), *Morality, Reason and Truth* (pp. 141–168). Totowa, NJ: Rowman & Allanheld.

Copp, D., & Zimmerman, D. (Eds.). (1984). *Morality, Reason and Truth.* Totowa, NJ: Rowman & Allanheld.

◂ Cosmides, L., & Tooby, J. (1994). Beyond intuition and instinct blindness: Toward an evolutionary rigorous cognitive science. *Cognition,* 50, 41–77.

Costa, M. (1987a). The trolley problem revisited. In J. M. Fischer & M. Ravizza (1992), *Ethics: Problems and Principles* (pp. 293–302). Fort Worth, TX: Harcourt Brace Jovanovich.

(1987b). Another trip on the trolley. In J. M. Fischer & M. Ravizza (1992), *Ethics: Problems and Principles* (pp. 303–308). Fort Worth, TX: Harcourt Brace Jovanovich.

Costanzo, P., Coie, J., Grumet, J., & Farnhill, D. (1973). A reexamination of the effects of intent and consequence on children's moral judgments. *Child Development,* 44, 154–61.

Coval, S., & Smith, J. (1986). *Law and Its Presuppositions: Actions, Agents, and Rules.* London: Routledge & Kegan Paul.

Cover, R. (1975). *Justice Accused: Antislavery and the Judicial Process.* New Haven, CT: Yale University Press.

Creel, A. (1972). Dharma as an ethical category relating to freedom and responsibility. *Philosophy East and West*, 22, 155–168.

Crowe, M. B. (1977). *The Changing Profile of Natural Law*. The Hague: Martinus Nijhoff.

Cudworth, R. (1996/1731). *A Treatise concerning Eternal and Immutable Morality*. (S. Hutton, Ed.). Cambridge: Cambridge University Press.

Cummins, D. D. (1996a). Evidence of deontic reasoning in 3- and 4-year-old children. *Memory & Cognition*, 24, 823–829.

(1996b). Evidence for the innateness of deontic reasoning. *Mind & Language*, 11(2), 160–190.

Cushman, F. A. (2008). Crime and punishment: Distinguishing the roles of causal and intentional analyses in moral judgment. *Cognition*, 108(2), 353–380.

Cushman, F. A., Young, L., & Hauser, M. D. (2006). The role of reasoning and intuition in moral judgments: Testing three principles of harm. *Psychological Science*, 17(12), 1082–1089.

* Damasio, A. (1994). *Descartes' Error*. Cambridge, MA: Harvard University Press.

⁎ Damasio, H., et al. (1994). The return of Phineas Gage: Clues about the brain from the skull of a famous patient. *Science*, 264, 1102–1105.

Dancy, J. (1983). Ethical particularism and morally relevant properties. *Mind*, 92, 530–547.

(1993). *Moral Reasons*. Oxford: Oxford University Press.

Daniels, N. (1979). Wide reflective equilibrium and theory acceptance in ethics. *Journal of Philosophy*, 76, 256–282.

(1980). On some methods of ethics and linguistics. *Philosophical Studies*, 37, 21–36.

(Ed.). (1989). *Reading Rawls: Critical Studies on Rawls' "A Theory of Justice."* Stanford, CA: Stanford University Press.

(1996). *Justice and Justification: Reflective Equilibrium in Theory and Practice*. Cambridge: Cambridge University Press.

Danto, A. (1965). Basic actions. *American Philosophical Quarterly*, 2, 141–148.

(1972). Role and rule in Oriental thought: Some metareflections on dharma and li. *Philosophy East and West*, 22, 213–220.

D'Arcy, E. (1961). *Conscience and Its Right to Freedom*. New York: Sheed and Ward.

(1963). *Human Acts: An Essay in Their Moral Evaluation*. Oxford: Clarendon Press.

Darley, J. & Shultz, T. (1990). Moral rules: Their content and acquisition. *Annual Review of Psychology*, 41, 525–556.

Darwall, S. (1995). *The British Moralists and the Internal 'Ought.'* Cambridge: Cambridge University Press.

Darwall, S., Gibbard, A., & Railton, P. (1992). Toward a *fin de siècle* ethics: Some trends. *Philosophical Review*, 101, 115–189.

Darwin, C. (1958/1859). *The Origin of Species*. New York: Mentor Books.

(1981/1871). *The Descent of Man, and Selection in Relation to Sex*. Princeton, NJ: Princeton University Press.

(1973/1872). *The Expression of the Emotions in Man and Animals*. New York: Appleton.

Davidson, D. (1963). Actions, reasons, and causes. *Journal of Philosophy*, 60, 685–700.

(1980). *Essays on Actions and Events*. Oxford: Clarendon Press.

Davidson, D., & Harman, G. (Eds.). (1975). *Semantics of Natural Language*. Dordrecht: D. Reidel.

Davis, L. (1979). *Theory of Action*. Englewood Cliffs, NJ: Prentice-Hall.

Descartes, R. (1985/1647). Comments on a certain broadsheet. In J. Cottingham, R. Stoothoff, & D. Murdoch (Eds.), *The Philosophical Writings of Descartes* (Vol. 1) (pp. 293–311). Cambridge: Cambridge University Press.

De Waal, F. (1996). *Good Natured: The Origin of Right and Wrong in Humans and Other Animals*. Cambridge, MA: Harvard University Press.

Donagan, A. (1977). *The Theory of Morality*. Chicago: University of Chicago Press.

(1994). *The Philosophical Papers of Alan Donagan* (2 Vols.). Chicago: University of Chicago Press.

Doris, J. (2002). *Lack of Character: Personality and Moral Behavior*. Cambridge: Cambridge University Press.

Doris, J., & Stich, S. (2005). As a matter of fact: Empirical perspectives on ethics. In F. Jackson & M. Smith (Eds.), *The Oxford Handbook of Contemporary Analytic Philosophy* (pp. 114–154). Oxford: Oxford University Press.

Dubber, M. D. (2006). *The Sense of Justice: Empathy in Law and Punishment*. New York: NYU Press.

Duncan-Jones, A. (1952). *Butler's Moral Philosophy*. Harmondsworth: Penguin Books.

Dupoux, E., & Jacob, P. (2007). Universal moral grammar: A critical appraisal. *Trends in Cognitive Sciences*, 11, 373–378.

(2008). Response to Dwyer & Hauser: Sounding the retreat? *Trends in Cognitive Sciences*, 12, 2–3.

Durkheim, E. (1997/1893). *The Division of Labor in Society*. New York: Free Press.

Duxbury, N. (1995). *Patterns of American Jurisprudence*. New York: Oxford University Press.

Dworkin, R. (1973). The original position. In N. Daniels (Ed.) (1989), *Reading Rawls: Critical Studies on Rawls' "A Theory of Justice"* (pp. 16–53). Stanford, CA: Stanford University Press.

(1977). *Taking Rights Seriously*. Cambridge, MA: Harvard University Press.

(1982). "Natural" law revisited. *University of Florida Law Review*, 34, 165–188.

(1998). Darwin's new bulldog. *Harvard Law Review*, 111, 1718–1738.

Dwyer, S. (1999). Moral competence. In K. Murasugi & R. Stainton (Eds.), *Philosophy and Linguistics* (pp. 169–190). Boulder, CO: Westview Press.

(2006). How good is the linguistic analogy? In P. Carruthers, S. Laurence, & S. Stich (Eds.), *The Innate Mind, Vol. 2: Culture and Cognition* (pp. 237–256). Oxford: Oxford University Press.

(2008). How not to argue that morality isn't innate: Comments on Prinz. In W. Sinnott-Armstrong (Ed.), *Moral Psychology, Vol. 1: The Evolution of Morality: Adaptation and Innateness* (pp. 407–418). Cambridge, MA: MIT Press.

(in press). Moral dumbfounding and the linguistic analogy: Implications for the study of moral judgment. *Mind & Language*.

Dwyer, S., & Hauser, M. D. (2008). Dupoux and Jacob's moral instincts: Throwing out the baby, the bathwater, and the bathtub. *Trends in Cognitive Sciences*, 12, 1–2.

Edel, A. (1970). Science and the structure of ethics. In O. Neurath, R. Carnap, & C. Morris (Eds.), *Foundations of the Unity of Science* (Vol. 2) (pp. 273–378). Chicago: University of Chicago Press.

Edwards, C. (1975). Societal complexity and moral development: A Kenyan study. *Ethos*, 3, 505–527.

Eldredge, L. (1941). *Modern Tort Problems*. Philadelphia: George T. Bisel.

Ellickson, R. (1991). *Order without Law: How Neighbors Settle Disputes*. Cambridge, MA: Harvard University Press.

Ely, J. (1980). *Democracy and Distrust: A Theory of Judicial Review*. Cambridge, MA: Harvard University Press.

Epstein, R. (2004). *Cases and Materials on Torts*. New York: Aspen Publishers.

Ferguson, A. (1966/1767). *An Essay on the History of Civil Society*. (D. Forbes, Ed.). Edinburgh: Edinburgh University Press.

Feuerbach, P. J. A. (1833). *Anselms von Feurbach kleine Schriften vermischten Inhalts*. Nuremburg: Otto.

Findlay, J. N. (1970). *Axiological Ethics*. London: Macmillan.

Finkel, N., Liss, M., & Moran, V. (1997). Equal or proportionate justice for accessories? Children's pearls of proportionate wisdom. *Journal of Applied Developmental Psychology*, 18, 229–244.

Finnis, J. (1980). *Natural Law and Natural Rights*. Oxford: Clarendon Press.
     (1995). Intention in tort law. In D. Owen (Ed.), *Philosophical Foundations of Tort Law* (pp. 229–247). Oxford: Clarendon Press.

Firth, R. (1952). Ethical absolutism and the ideal observer. *Philosophy and Phenomenological Research*, 12, 336–341.

Fischer, J. M., & Ravizza, M. (Eds.). (1992). *Ethics: Problems and Principles*. Fort Worth, TX: Harcourt Brace Jovanovich.
     (1992). Introduction. In J. M. Fischer & M. Ravizza (Eds.), *Ethics: Problems and Principles*. Fort Worth, TX: Harcourt Brace Jovanovich.

Fiske, A. P., & Tetlock, P. E. (1997). Taboo trade-offs: Reactions to transactions that transgress the spheres of justice. *Political Psychology*, 18, 255–297.

Flanagan, O. (1991). *Varieties of Moral Personality: Ethics and Psychological Realism*. Cambridge, MA: Harvard University Press.

Flavell, J. H., & Ross, L. (Eds.). (1981). *Social Cognitive Development*. Cambridge: Cambridge University Press.

Fletcher, G. (1998). *Basic Concepts of Criminal Law*. Oxford: Oxford University Press.

Fodor, J. (1970). Three reasons for not deriving "kill" from "cause to die." *Linguistic Inquiry*, 1, 429–438.
     (1979). *The Language of Thought*. Cambridge, MA: Harvard University Press.
     (1983). *The Modularity of Mind*. Cambridge, MA: MIT Press.
     (1985). Precis of modularity of mind. *Behavioral and Brain Sciences*, 8(1), 1–42.

Fodor, J., & Katz, J. (Eds.). (1964). *The Structure of Language: Readings in the Philosophy of Language*. Englewood Cliffs, NJ: Prentice-Hall.

Foot, P. (1967). The problem of abortion and the doctrine of double effect. In J. M. Fischer & M. Ravizza (Eds.) (1992), *Ethics: Problems and Principles* (pp. 60–67). Fort Worth, TX: Harcourt Brace Jovanovich. (Reprinted from *Oxford Review*, 5, 5–15).

Frankena, W. (1955). Hutcheson's moral sense theory. *Journal of the History of Ideas*, 16, 356–375.

(1963). *Ethics*. Englewood Cliffs, NJ: Prentice-Hall.

(1976). *Perspectives on Morality: Essays by William K. Frankena*. (K.E. Goodpaster, Ed.). Notre Dame, IN: University of Notre Dame Press.

Freeman, S. (2003). *The Cambridge Companion to Rawls*. Cambridge: Cambridge University Press.

(2007). *Rawls*. New York: Routledge.

Frege, G. (1980/1884). *The Foundations of Arithmetic*. (J. L. Austin, Trans.). Evanston, IL: Northwestern University Press.

Freud, S. (1994/1930). *Civilization and Its Discontents*. New York: Dover.

Fried, C. (1978). *Right and Wrong*. Cambridge, MA: Harvard University Press.

Friedman, L. (1985). *A History of American Law* (2nd Ed.). New York: Simon and Schuster.

Fuller, L. (1949). The case of the speluncean explorers. *Harvard Law Review*, 62, 616–645.

(1969/1964). *The Morality of Law*. (2nd Ed.). New Haven, CT: Yale University Press.

(1981). *The Principles of Social Order: Selected Essays of Lon L. Fuller*. (K. Winston, Ed.). Durham, NC: Duke University Press.

(2001). *The Principles of Social Order: Selected Essays of Lon L. Fuller*. Edited with a new introduction by Kenneth I. Winston. Oxford: Hart Publishing.

Gall, F.J. (1835). *On the Functions of the Brain and Each of Its Parts, in Six Volumes*. Boston: Marsh, Capen & Lyon.

Gallistel, R. (1999). The replacement of general-purpose learning models with adaptively specialized learning modules. In M. Gazzaniga (Ed.), *The Cognitive Neurosciences* (2nd Ed.) (p. 1179–1191). Cambridge: Cambridge University Press.

Gardner, H. (1996). Is there a moral intelligence? An essay in honor of Howard E. Gruber. In M. Runco (Ed.), *Perspectives on Creativity Series*. Cresskill, NJ: Hampton Press. Revised and reprinted in Howard Gardner, *Intelligence Reframed: Multiple Intelligences for the 21st Century* (1999). New York: Basic Books.

Gazzaniga, M.S. (1992). *Nature's Mind: The Biological Roots of Thinking, Emotions, Sexuality, Language, and Intelligence*. New York: Basic Books.

(2005). *The Ethical Brain*. New York: Dana Press.

Geach, P. (Ed.). (1991a). *Logic and Ethics*. Dordrecht: Kluwer Academic.

(1991b). Whatever happened to deontic logic? In P. Geach (Ed.), *Logic and Ethics* (pp. 33–48). Dordrecht: Kluwer Academic.

Geertz, C. (1973). Thick description: Toward an interpretative theory of culture. In *The Interpretation of Cultures: Selected Essays* (pp. 3–31). New York: Basic Books.

George, A. (Ed.). (1989). *Reflections on Chomsky*. Oxford: Basil Blackwell.

Gergely, G., & Csibra, G. (2003). Teleological reasoning in infancy: The naive theory of rational action. *Trends in Cognitive Sciences*, 7, 287–292.

Gergely, G., Nadasdy, Z., Csibra, G., & Biro, S. (1995). Taking the intentional stance at 12 months of age. *Cognition,* 56, 165–193.

Gert, B. (1998). *Morality: Its Nature and Justification.* New York: Oxford University Press.

Gilligan, C. (1982). *In a Different Voice: Psychological Theory and Women's Development.* Cambridge, MA: Harvard University Press.

Gilmore, G. (1974). *The Death of Contract.* Columbus: Ohio State University Press.

(1977). *The Ages of American Law.* New Haven, CT: Yale University Press.

Gimello, R. (1972). The civil status of li in classical Confucianism. *Philosophy East and West,* 22, 203–211.

Ginet, C. (1990). *On Action.* Cambridge: Cambridge University Press.

Gluckman, M. (1955). *The Judicial Process among the Barotse of Northern Rhodesia (Zambia).* Manchester: Manchester University Press.

(1965). *The Ideas in Barotse Jurisprudence.* Manchester: Manchester University Press.

Goldman, A. (1970a). *A Theory of Human Action.* Princeton, NJ: Princeton University Press.

(1970b). The individuation of action. *Journal of Philosophy,* 68, 761–774.

(1979). Action, causation, and unity. *Noûs,* 13, 261–270.

(1993). Ethics and cognitive science. *Ethics,* 103, 337–360.

Goldman, A., & Kim, J. (Eds.). (1978). *Values and Morals.* Dordrecht: D. Reidel.

Goodman, N. (1983/1955). *Fact, Fiction, and Forecast.* Cambridge, MA: Harvard University Press.

(1967). The epistemological argument. *Synthese,* 17(1), 23–28.

Gopnik, A., & Sobel, D. M. (2000). Detecting blickets: How young children use information about novel causal powers in categorization and induction. *Child Development,* 71, 1205–1222.

Gould, S. J., & Lewontin, R. C. (1979). The spandrels of San Marco and the Panglossian program: A critique of the adaptationist programme. *Proceedings of the Royal Society of London,* 205, 281–288.

Grady, M. (1989). Untaken precautions. *Journal of Legal Studies,* 18, 139–156.

Gray, J. C. (1972/1909). *The Nature and Sources of Law* (2nd Ed.), (P. Smith, Ed.). New York: Columbia University Press.

Green, L. (1928). The negligence issue. *Yale Law Journal,* 37, 1029–1047.

Green, S. (1998). The universal grammar of the criminal law. *Michigan Law Review,* 98, 2104–2125.

Greene, J. D. (2005). Cognitive neuroscience and the structure of the moral mind. In P. Carruthers, S. Laurence, & S. Stich (Eds.), *The Innate Mind, Vol. 1: Structure and Contents* (pp. 338–352). New York: Oxford University Press.

(2008a). The secret joke of Kant's soul. In W. Sinnott-Armstrong (Ed.), *Moral Psychology, Vol. 3: The Neuroscience of Morality: Emotion, Disease, and Development* (pp. 35–79). Cambridge, MA: MIT Press.

(2008b). Reply to Mikhail and Timmons. In W. Sinnott-Armstrong (Ed.), *Moral Psychology, Vol. 3: The Neuroscience of Morality: Emotion, Disease, and Development* (pp. 105–117). Cambridge, MA: MIT Press.

Greene, J., & Haidt, J. (2002). How (and where) does moral judgment work? *Trends in Cognitive Sciences,* 6(12), 517–523.

Greene, J.D., Cushman, F.A., Stewart, L.E., Lowenberg, K., Nystrom, L.E., and Cohen, J.D. (2009). Pushing moral buttons: The interaction between personal force and intention in moral judgment. *Cognition*, 111(3), 364–371.

Greene, J.D., Sommerville, R.B., Nystrom, L.E., Darley, J.M., & Cohen, J.D. (2001). An fMRI investigation of emotional engagement in moral judgment. *Science*, 293, 2105–2108.

Greene, R.A. (1991). Synderesis, the spark of conscience, in the English renaissance. *Journal of the History of Ideas*, 52(1), 195–219.

(1997). Natural law, synderesis, and the moral sense. *Journal of the History of Ideas*, 58(2), 173–198.

Gregory, R. (1970). The grammar of vision. In *The Listener*. Cited in N. Chomsky (1975b). *Reflections on Language*. New York: Pantheon.

Grey, T. (1983). Langdell's orthodoxy. *University of Pittsburgh Law Review*, 45, 1–53.

Grice, G.R. (1978). Moral theories and received opinion. *Aristotelian Society Supplement*, 52, 1–12.

Grotius, H. (1925). *On the Law of War and Peace*. (F. W. Kelsey, Trans.). Oxford: Clarendon Press.

Gruter, M., & Bohannan, P. (Eds.). (1983). *Law, Biology and Culture: The Evolution of Law*. Santa Barbara, CA: Ross-Erikson.

Guglielmo, S., & Malle, B. (2008). Can unintended side effects be intentional? Solving a puzzle in people's judgments of intentionality and morality. Paper presented to the Workshop in Experimental Philosophy at the 34th Annual Meeting of the Society of Philosophy and Psychology, Philadelphia.

Guest, S. (1991). *Ronald Dworkin*. Stanford, CA: Stanford University Press.

Haakonssen, K. (1996). *Natural Law and Moral Philosophy: From Grotius to the Scottish Enlightenment*. Cambridge: Cambridge University Press.

Haegeman, L. (1994). *Introduction to Government and Binding Theory* (2nd Ed.). Oxford: Basil Blackwell.

Haidt, J. (2001). The emotional dog and its rational tail: A social intuitionist approach to moral judgment. *Psychological Review*, 108, 814–834.

Haidt, J., & Joseph, C. (2004). Intuitive ethics: How innately prepared intuitions generate culturally variable virtues. *Daedalus*, 133, 4, 55–66.

Hale, M. (1668). *Preface to Rolle's Abridgement*. Excerpted in J. Hall (1938), *Readings in Jurisprudence* (pp. 341–343). Indianapolis: Bobbs-Merrill.

Hall, J. (1938). *Readings in Jurisprudence*. Indianapolis: Bobbs-Merrill.

(1947). *General Principles of Criminal Law*. Indianapolis: Bobbs-Merrill.

Hallborg, R., Jr. (1997). Comparing harms: The lesser evil defense and the trolley problem. *Legal Theory*, 3, 291–316.

Halle, M. (1962). Phonology in generative grammar. In J. Fodor & J. Katz (Eds.) (1964), *The Structure of Language: Readings in the Philosophy of Language*. Englewood Cliffs, NJ: Prentice-Hall.

Hamlin, J.K., Wynn, K, & Bloom, P. (2007). Social evaluation by preverbal infants. *Nature*, 450, 557–559.

Hampshire, S. (1972). A new philosophy of the just society. *New York Review of Books* (February 24), 34–39.

(1983). *Morality and Conflict*. Cambridge, MA: Harvard University Press.

Hannikainen, L. (1988). *Peremptory Norms (Jus Cogens) in International Law: Historical Development, Criteria, Permanent Status.* Helsinki: Lakimiesliiton Kustannus, Finnish Lawyers' Publishing.

Hansen, C. (1972). Freedom and responsibility in Confucian ethics. *Philosophy East and West,* 22, 169–186.

Hanson, N. R. (1958). *Patterns of Discovery.* Cambridge: Cambridge University Press.

Hare, R. M. (1952). *The Language of Morals.* New York: Oxford University Press.

(1960). Ethics. In J. O. Urmson & J. Ree (Eds.), *The Concise Encyclopedia of Western Philosophy and Philosophers* (pp. 100–109). London: Unwin Hyman.

(1963). *Freedom and Reason.* Oxford: Oxford University Press.

(1971). *Essays on Philosophical Method.* Berkeley: University of California Press.

(1973). Rawls' theory of justice. In N. Daniels (Ed.) (1989), *Reading Rawls: Critical Studies on Rawls' "A Theory of Justice"* (pp. 81–108). Stanford, CA: Stanford University Press.

(1981). *Moral Thinking: Its Levels, Method, and Point.* Oxford: Clarendon Press.

Harman, G. (1965). Inference to the best explanation. *Philosophical Review,* 65, 88–95.

(1967). Psychological aspects of the theory of syntax. *Journal of Philosophy,* 64, 75–87.

(1973). Review of language and mind. In G. Harman (1974), *On Noam Chomsky: Critical Essays* (pp. 201–218). New York: Anchor. Reprinted from *Language,* 49, 453–464.

(Ed.). (1974). *On Noam Chomsky: Critical Essays.* New York: Anchor.

(1977). *The Nature of Morality: An Introduction to Ethics.* New York: Oxford University Press.

(1989). A new paradigm. In C. Otero (Ed.) (1994), *Noam Chomsky: Critical Assessments. Vol. II: Philosophy* (pp. 486–491). New York: Routledge. Review of A. George. (Ed.). (1989). *Reflections on Chomsky.* Oxford: Basil Blackwell.

(1999). Moral philosophy and linguistics. Paper presented to the Twentieth Annual World Philosophy Congress, Boston. (Manuscript on file with author.)

(2000). *Explaining Value and Other Essays in Moral Philosophy.* Oxford: Oxford University Press.

(2008). Using a linguistic analogy to study morality. In W. Sinnott-Armstrong (Ed.), *Moral Psychology, Vol. 1: The Evolution of Morality: Adaptation and Innateness* (pp. 345–351). Cambridge, MA: MIT Press.

Harrison, J. (1976). *Hume's Moral Epistemology.* Oxford: Clarendon Press.

Hart, H. L. A. (1961). *The Concept of Law.* Oxford: Clarendon Press.

(1963). *Law, Liberty, and Morality.* Stanford, CA: Stanford University Press.

(1968). *Punishment and Responsibility: Essays in the Philosophy of Law.* Oxford: Oxford University Press.

(1973). Rawls on liberty and its priority. In N. Daniels (Ed.) (1989), *Reading Rawls: Critical Studies on Rawls' "A Theory of Justice"* (pp. 230–253). Stanford, CA: Stanford University Press.

(1982). *Essays on Bentham: Studies in Jurisprudence and Political Theory.* Oxford: Clarendon Press.

(1983). *Essays in Jurisprudence and Philosophy.* Oxford: Clarendon Press.

Hart, H.L.A., & Honore, A.M. (1959). *Causation in the Law*. Oxford: Oxford University Press.

Hauser, M.D. (2006). *Moral Minds: How Nature Designed Our Universal Sense of Right and Wrong*. New York: HarperCollins.

Hauser, M.D., Cushman, F., & Young, L. (2008a). Reviving Rawls' linguistic analogy: Operative principles and the causal structure of moral actions. In W. Sinnott-Armstrong (Ed.), *Moral Psychology, Vol. 2: The Cognitive Science of Morality: Intuition and Diversity* (pp. 107–143). Cambridge, MA: MIT Press.

(2008b). On misreading the linguistic analogy: A response to Jesse Prinz and Ron Mallon. In W. Sinnott-Armstrong (Ed.), *Moral Psychology, Vol. 2: The Cognitive Science of Morality: Intuition and Diversity* (pp. 171–179). Cambridge, MA: MIT Press.

Hauser, M.D., Cushman, F., Young, L., Jin, R.-X., & Mikhail, J. (2007). A dissociation between moral judgments and justifications. *Mind & Language*, 22, 1–22.

Hegel, G.W.F. (1991/1836). *Elements of the Philosophy of Right*. (A. Wood, Ed.). Cambridge: Cambridge University Press.

Heider, F., & Simmel, M. (1944). An experimental study of apparent behavior. *American Journal of Psychology*, 57, 243–259.

Helmholtz, H.V. (1962/1867). *Helmholtz's Treatise on Physiological Optics*. (J.P.C. Southhall, Ed. and Trans.). New York: Dover.

Hempel, C. (1955/1952). *Fundamentals of Concept Formation in Empirical Science*. Chicago: University of Chicago Press. Reprinted in O. Neurath, R. Carnap, & C. Morris (Eds.), *International Encyclopedia of Unified Science*, Vol. 2, No. 7. Chicago: University of Chicago Press.

(1966). *Philosophy of Natural Science*. Englewood Cliffs, NJ: Prentice-Hall.

Henkin, L. (1990). *The Age of Rights*. New York: Columbia University Press.

Henkin, L., Pugh, R.C., Schacter, O., & Smit, H. (1992). *Basic Documents Supplement to International Law: Cases and Materials*. St. Paul, MN: West Publishing.

Herget, J. (1990). *American Jurisprudence, 1870–1970: A History*. Houston, TX: Rice University Press.

Hilliard, F. (1859). *The Law of Torts* (2 Vols.). Boston: Little, Brown.

Hillman, J. (Ed.) (1970). *Conscience: Studies in Jungian Thought*. Evanston, IL: Northwestern University Press.

Hobbes, T. (1968/1651). *Leviathan*. (C.B. Macpherson, Ed.). New York: Penguin.

Hofstadter, R. (1944). *Social Darwinism in American Thought*. Philadelphia: University of Pennsylvania Press.

Hohfeld, W. (1913). Some fundamental legal conceptions as applied in judicial reasoning. *Yale Law Journal*, 23, 16–59.

(1917). Fundamental legal conceptions as applied in judicial reasoning. *Yale Law Journal*, 26, 710–770.

Holland, T.E. (1880). *The Elements of Jurisprudence* (10th Ed., 1906). New York: Oxford University Press.

Holmes, O.W. (1870). Codes, and the arrangement of law. *American Law Review*, 5, 1–13.

(1991/1881). *The Common Law*. New York: Dover.

Holstein, C. (1976). Development of moral judgment: A longitudinal study of males and females. *Child Development*, 47, 51–61.

Hornstein, N., & Lightfoot, D. (Eds.) (1981). *Explanation in Linguistics: The Logical Problem of Language Acquisition.* London: Longman.

Horwitz, M. (1977). *The Transformation of American Law, 1780–1860.* Cambridge, MA: Harvard University Press.

(1992). *The Transformation of American Law, 1870–1960: The Crisis of Orthodoxy.* New York: Oxford University Press.

Hourani, G. (1971). *Islamic Rationalism.* Oxford: Clarendon Press.

(1985). *Reason and Tradition in Islamic Ethics.* Cambridge: Cambridge University Press.

Hudson, W. (1967). *Ethical Intuitionism.* London: Macmillan.

Humboldt, W. (1971/1836). *Linguistic Variability and Intellectual Development.* (G. Buck & F. Raven, Trans.). Philadelphia: University of Pennsylvania Press.

Hume, D. (1978/1739–1740). *A Treatise of Human Nature.* (P.H. Nidditch, Ed.). Oxford: Clarendon Press.

(1983/1751). *An Enquiry Concerning the Principles of Morals.* (J.B. Schneewind, Ed.). Indianapolis: Hackett.

Hurd, H., & Moore, M. (2002). Negligence in the air. *Theoretical Inquiries in Law,* 3(2), Article 3 (1–79). Available at: http://www.bepress.com/til/default/vol3/iss2/art3.

Hutcheson, F. (1971/1728). *Illustrations on the Moral Sense.* Cambridge, MA: Harvard University Press.

(1993/1730). *Inaugural Lecture on the Social Nature of Man.* Reprinted in T. Mantner (Ed.), *Two Texts on Human Nature* (pp. 124–147). Cambridge: Cambridge University Press.

(2007/1747). *Philosophiae Moralis Institutio Compendis; with A Short Introduction to Moral Philosophy.* Indianapolis: Liberty Fund.

Hutcheson, J. (1929). The judgment intuitive. *Cornell Law Quarterly,* 14, 274–288.

Irwin, T.H. (1981). Aristotle's methods of ethics. In D. O'Meara (Ed.), *Studies in Aristotle* (pp. 193–223). Washington, D.C.: CUA Press.

(1995). *Plato's Ethics.* Oxford: Oxford University Press.

Isac, D., & Reiss, C. (2008). *I-Language: An Introduction to Linguistics as Cognitive Science.* Oxford: Oxford University Press.

Jackendoff, R. (1987). The status of thematic relations in linguistic theory. *Linguistic Inquiry,* 18(3), 369–411.

(1992). *Languages of the Mind: Essays on Mental Representation.* Cambridge, MA: MIT Press.

(1994). *Patterns in the Mind: Language and Human Nature.* New York: Basic Books.

(1999). The natural logic of rights and obligations. In R. Jackendoff, P. Bloom, & K. Wynn (Eds.), *Language, Logic and Concepts: Essays in Memory of John Macnamara* (pp. 67–96). Cambridge, MA: MIT Press.

(2007). *Language, Consciousness, Culture: Essays on Mental Structure.* Cambridge, MA: MIT Press.

Jackendoff, R., Bloom, P., & Wynn, K. (Eds.) (1999). *Language, Logic and Concepts: Essays in Memory of John Macnamara.* Cambridge, MA: MIT Press.

James, W. (1890). *The Principles of Psychology* (2 Vols.). New York: Henry Holt.

Johnson, M. (1993). *Moral Imagination: Implications of Cognitive Science for Ethics.* Chicago: University of Chicago Press.

Johnson, S. (2000). The recognition of mentalistic agents in infancy. *Trends in Cognitive Sciences*, 4(1), 22–28.

Jonsen, A. R., & Toulmin, S. (1988). *The Abuse of Casuistry: A History of Moral Reasoning*. Berkeley: University of California Press.

Jung, C. (1919). Instinct and the unconscious. *British Journal of Psychology*, 10, 15–26. Reprinted in J. Campbell (Ed.) (1971), *The Portable Jung* (pp. 47–58). New York: Viking Press.

— (1964). A psychological view of conscience. In J. Hillman (Ed.), *Conscience: Studies in Jungian Thought* (pp. 179–201). Evanston, IL: Northwestern University Press.

Kagan, J. (1987). Introduction. In J. Kagan & S. Lamb (Eds.), *The Emergence of Morality in Young Children* (pp. ix–xx). Chicago: University of Chicago Press.

Kagan, J., & Lamb, S. (Eds.) (1987). *The Emergence of Morality in Young Children*. Chicago: University of Chicago Press.

Kagan, S. (1989). *The Limits of Morality*. Oxford: Clarendon Press.

Kahneman, D., & Tversky, A. (1984). Choices, values and frames. *American Psychologist*, 39, 341–350.

Kamm, F. M. (1998). Moral intuitions, cognitive psychology, and the harming versus-not-aiding distinction. *Ethics*, 108, 463–488.

Kang J. (2005). Trojan horses of race. *Harvard Law Review*, 118, 1491–1593.

Kant, I. (1950/1783). *Prolegomena to Any Future Metaphysics*. (L. W. Beck, Ed.). Indianapolis: Bobbs-Merrill.

— (1964/1785). *Groundwork of the Metaphysics of Morals*. (H. J. Paton, Trans.). New York: Harper Perennial.

— (1965/1787). *Critique of Pure Reason*. (N. K. Smith, Trans.). New York: St. Martin's Press.

— (1991/1797). *The Metaphysics of Morals*. (M. Gregor, Trans.). Cambridge: Cambridge University Press.

— (1993/1788). *Critique of Practical Reason*. (L. W. Beck, Trans.). New York: Macmillan.

Kanwisher, N. (2000). Domain-specificity in face perception. *Nature Neuroscience*, 3, 759–763.

Kar, R. B. (2006). The deep structure of law and morality. *Texas Law Review*, 84, 877–943.

Kaplow, L., & Shavell, S. (2002). *Fairness versus Welfare*. Cambridge, MA: Harvard University Press.

Kasher, A. (1991). *The Chomskyan Turn*. Oxford: Basil Blackwell.

Katz, J. (1972). *Semantic Theory*. New York: Harper & Row.

— (1981). *Language and Other Abstract Objects*. Totowa, NJ: Roman and Littlefield.

Katz, J., & Fodor, J. (1963). The structure of a semantic theory. *Language*, 39, 170–210. Reprinted in J. Fodor & J. Katz (Eds.) (1964), *The Structure of Language: Readings in the Philosophy of Language* (pp. 479–518). Englewood Cliffs, NJ: Prentice-Hall.

Kaufmann, W. (1991/1980). *Goethe, Kant, and Hegel: Discovering the Mind, Vol. 1*. New Brunswick, NJ: Transaction Publishers.

Kelly, D., Stich, S., Haley, K., Eng, S., & Fessler, D. (2007). Harm, affect and the moral/conventional distinction. *Mind & Language*, 22, 117–131.

Kelman, M. (1981). Interpretive construction in the substantive criminal law. *Stanford Law Review*, 33, 591–674.

Kelman, M., Rottenstreich, Y., & Tversky, A. (1996). Context-dependence in legal decision making. *Journal of Legal Studies*, 25, 287–318.

Kemp, J. (1970). *Ethical Naturalism*. London: Macmillan.

Kenny, A. (1963). *Action, Emotion and Will*. London: Routledge and Kegan Paul.

(1995). Philippa Foot on double effect. In R. Hursthouse, G. Lawrence, & W. Quinn (Eds.), *Virtues and Reasons: Philippa Foot and Moral Theory: Essays in Honor of Philippa Foot* (pp. 77–88). Oxford: Clarendon Press.

Killen, M., & Smetana, J. (2008). Moral cognition, emotion, and neuroscience: An integrative developmental view. *European Journal of Developmental Science*, 2(3), 324–339.

Knobe, J. (2003a). Intentional action and side effects in ordinary language. *Analysis*, 63, 190–193.

(2003b). Intentional action in folk psychology: An experimental investigation. *Philosophical Psychology*, 16, 309–324.

(2005). Theory of mind and moral cognition: Exploring the connections. *Trends in Cognitive Sciences*, 9, 357–359.

Kocourek, A. (1927). *Jural Relations*. Indianapolis, IN: Bobbs-Merrill.

Koenigs, M., Young, L., Adolphs, R., Tranel, D., Cushman, F. A., Hauser, M. D., & Damasio, T. (2007). Damage to ventromedial prefrontal cortex increases utilitarian moral judgments. *Nature*, 446, 908–911.

Kohlberg, L. (1958). "The Development of Modes of Moral Thinking and Choice in the Years 10 to 16." Ph.D. dissertation, University of Chicago.

(1981). *Essays on Moral Development. Volume 1: The Philosophy of Moral Development*. New York: Harper and Row.

(1984). *Essays on Moral Development. Volume 2: The Psychology of Moral Development*. New York: Harper and Row.

Koller, J. (1972). Dharma: An expression of universal order. *Philosophy East and West*, 22, 131–144.

Kripke, S. (1980). *Naming and Necessity*. Cambridge, MA: Harvard University Press.

(1982). *Wittgenstein on Rules and Private Language*. Cambridge, MA: Harvard University Press.

Kropotkin, P. (1993/1924). *Ethics: Origin and Development*. (A. Harrison, Ed.). Bristol: Thoemmes Press.

Kroy, M. (1973). Ethics and conscience: A program. *Philosophia*, 3, 265–294.

Kuhn, T. (1957). *The Copernican Revolution: Planetary Astronomy in the Development of Western Thought*. Cambridge, MA: Harvard University Press.

(1970). *The Structure of Scientific Revolutions*. (2nd Ed., enlarged). Chicago: University of Chicago Press.

Ladd, J. (1957). *The Structure of a Moral Code: A Philosophical Analysis of Ethical Discourse Applied to the Ethics of the Navaho Indians*. Cambridge, MA: Harvard University Press.

Lamont, W. D. (1946). *The Principles of Moral Judgment*. Oxford: Clarendon Press.

LaPiana, W. (1994). *Logic and Experience: The Origin of Modern American Legal Education*. New York: Oxford University Press.

Lashley, K. (1951). The problem of serial order in behavior. In L. Jeffress (Ed.), *Hixon Symposium on Cerebral Mechanisms in Behavior* (pp. 112–146). New York: John Wiley & Sons.

Lasok, D., et al. (1980). *Fundamental Duties: A Volume of Essays by Present and Former Members of the Law Faculty of the University of Exeter to Commemorate the Silver Jubilee of the University.* Oxford: Pergamon Press.

Lawrence, R. (1972). *Motive and Intention: An Essay in the Appreciation of Action.* Evanston, IL: Northwestern University Press.

Leblanc, H., & Wisdom, W.A. (1993). *Deductive Logic.* Englewood Cliffs, NJ: Prentice Hall.

LeFave, W.R., & Scott, A.W. (1972). *Handbook on Criminal Law.* St. Paul, MN: West Publishing.

Lehrer, K. (1990). *Theory of Knowledge.* Boulder, CO: Westview Press.

Leibniz, G.W. (1981/1705). *New Essays on Human Understanding.* (P. Remnant & J. Bennet, Eds.). Cambridge: Cambridge University Press.

Lerdahl, F., & Jackendoff, R. (1983). *A Generative Theory of Tonal Music.* Cambridge, MA: MIT Press.

Leslie, A., Knobe, J., & Cohen, A. (2006). Acting intentionally and the side-effect effect: Theory of mind and moral judgment. *Psychological Science*, 17, 421–427.

Levi, E. (1949). *An Introduction to Legal Reasoning.* Chicago: University of Chicago Press.

Lewis, C. S. (1960/1943). *Mere Christianity.* New York: Macmillan.

Lewontin, R. (1990). The evolution of cognition. In D. Osherson & E.E. Smith (Eds.), *An Invitation to Cognitive Science: Vol. 3* (pp. 229–246). Cambridge, MA: MIT Press.

Lilliard, A., & Flavell, J. (1990). Young children's preference for mental state versus behavioral descriptions of human action. *Child Development*, 61, 731–741.

Locke, J. (1988/1660). *Essays on the Law of Nature and Associated Writings.* (W. von Leyden, Ed.). Oxford: Oxford University Press.

(1991/1689). *An Essay Concerning Human Understanding.* (P. Nidditch, Ed.). Oxford: Oxford University Press.

(1980/1690). *Second Treatise of Government.* (C.B. Macpherson, Ed.). Indianapolis: Hackett.

Loewer, B., & Rey, G. (Eds). (1992). *Meaning in Mind: Fodor and His Critics.* London: Wiley Blackwell.

Lombrozo, T. (2008). The role of moral commitments in moral judgment. *Cognitive Science*, 33, 273–286.

Lyons, D. (1965). *Forms and Limits of Utilitarianism.* Oxford: Clarendon Press.

(1975). Nature and soundness of contract and coherence arguments. In N. Daniels (Ed.) (1989), *Reading Rawls: Critical Studies on Rawls' "A Theory of Justice"* (pp. 141–167). Stanford, CA: Stanford University Press.

Machery, E. (2007). The folk concept of intentional action: Philosophical and experimental issues. *Mind & Language*, 23, 165–189.

MacIntyre, A. (1981). *After Virtue.* Notre Dame, IN: University of Notre Dame Press.

Mackie, J. (1974). *The Cement of the Universe: A Study of Causation.* Oxford: Clarendon Press.

(1977). *Ethics: Inventing Right and Wrong.* New York: Penguin.

Mackintosh, J. (1843/1799). *A Discourse on the Law of Nature and Nations.* Boston: Pratt.

(1862/1830). *Dissertation on the Progress of Ethical Philosophy.* Edinburgh: Adam and Charles Black.

Macnamara, J. (1986). *A Border Dispute: The Place of Logic in Psychology.* Cambridge, MA: MIT Press.

(1990). The development of moral reasoning and the foundations of geometry. *Journal for the Theory of Social Behavior*, 21, 125–150.

(1999). *Through the Rearview Mirror: Historical Reflections on Psychology.* Cambridge: MIT Press.

Mahlmann, M. (1999). *Rationalismus in der praktishen Theorie: Normentheorie und praktische Kampetenz.* Baden-Baden, Germany: Nomos Verlagsgesellschaft.

(2005a). The cognitive foundations of law. In H. Rottleuthner (Ed.), *Foundations of Law* (pp. 75–100). Volume 2 of E. Pattaro (Ed.), *A Treatise of Legal Philosophy and General Jurisprudence.* Dordrecht: Springer.

(2005b). Kant's concept of practical reason and the perspectives of mentalism. In Z. Bankowski (Ed.), *Epistemology and Ontology* (pp. 85–94). Stuttgart: Franz Steiner Verlag.

(2007). Ethics, law, and the challenge of cognitive science. *German Law Journal*, 8, 577–615.

(2008). *Elemente einer ethischen Grundrechtstheorie.* Baden-Baden, Germany: Nomos Verlagsgesellschaft.

Mahlmann, M., & Mikhail, J. (2003). The liberalism of freedom in the history of moral philosophy (reviewing John Rawls, *Lectures on the History of Moral Philosophy*). *Archiv für Rechts- und Sozialphilosophie*, Band 89/1, 122–132.

(2005). Cognitive science, ethics, and law. In Z. Bankowski (Ed.), *Epistemology and Ontology* (pp. 95–102). Stuttgart: Franz Steiner Verlag.

Mallon, R. (2008). Reviving Rawls' linguistic analogy inside and out. In W. Sinnott-Armstrong (Ed.), *Moral Psychology, Vol. 2: The Cognitive Science of Morality: Intuition and Diversity* (pp. 145–155). Cambridge, MA: MIT Press.

Mandelbaum, M. (1955). *The Phenomenology of Moral Experience.* Glencoe, IL: Free Press.

Mangan, J. (1949). An historical analysis of the principle of double effect. *Theological Studies*, 10, 41–61.

Mardiros, A. M. (1952). A circular procedure in ethics. *Philosophical Review*, 61, 223–225.

Marquis, D. B. (1991). Four versions of double effect. *Journal of Medicine and Philosophy*, 16, 515–544. Reprinted in P. A. Woodward. (2001), *The Doctrine of Double Effect: Philosophers Debate a Controversial Moral Principle.* Notre Dame, IN: University of Notre Dame Press.

Marr, D. (1982). *Vision.* San Francisco: Freeman.

McCloskey, R. (1967). Introduction. In R. McCloskey (Ed.), *The Works of James Wilson* (pp. 1–48). Cambridge, MA: Harvard University Press.

McDowell, J. (1979). Virtue, and reason. *Monist*, 62, 331–350.

McGilvray, J. (2005). *The Cambridge Companion to Chomsky.* Cambridge: Cambridge University Press.

McKie, J. R. (1994). Linguistic competence and moral development: Some parallels. *Philosophical Inquiry*, 26, 20–31.

Mead, G. H. (1956). *The Social Psychology of George Herbert Mead*. (A. Strauss, Ed.). Chicago: University of Chicago Press.

Meldon, A. I. (Ed.). (1958). *Essays in Moral Philosophy*. Seattle: University of Washington Press.

Meltzoff, A. (1995). Understanding the intentions of others: Re-enactment of intended acts by 18-month-old children. *Developmental Psychology*, 31, 838–850.

Menand, L. (2001). *The Metaphysical Club*. New York: Farrar, Strauss, and Giroux.

☐ Mikhail, J. (2000). "Rawls' Linguistic Analogy: A Study of the 'Generative Grammar' Model of Moral Theory Described by John Rawls in *A Theory of Justice*." Ph.D. dissertation, Cornell University.

(2002a). Law, science, and morality: A review of Richard Posner's "The Problematics of Moral and Legal Theory." *Stanford Law Review*, 54, 1057–1127.

(2002b). Aspects of the theory of moral cognition: Investigating intuitive knowledge of the prohibition of intentional battery and the principle of double effect. *Georgetown University Law Center Public Law & Legal Theory Working Paper No. 762385*. Available at: http://ssrn.com/abstract=762385.

(2005). Moral heuristics or moral competence? Reflections on Sunstein. *Behavioral and Brain Sciences*, 28(4), 557–558.

(2007a). Universal moral grammar: Theory, evidence, and the future. *Trends in Cognitive Sciences*, 11, 143–152.

(2007b). "Plucking the mask of mystery from its face": Jurisprudence and H. L. A. Hart. *Georgetown Law Journal*, 95, 733–779.

(2008a). The poverty of the moral stimulus. In W. Sinnott-Armstrong (Ed.), *Moral Psychology, Vol. 1: The Evolution of Morality: Adaptation and Innateness* (pp. 345–351). Cambridge, MA: MIT Press.

(2008b). Moral cognition and computational theory. In W. Sinnott-Armstrong (Ed.), *Moral Psychology, Vol. 3: The Neuroscience of Morality: Emotion, Brain Disorders, and Development* (pp. 81–91). Cambridge, MA: MIT Press.

(2008c). Scottish common sense and nineteenth-century American law: A critical appraisal. *Law and History Review*, 26, 167–175.

(2009). Moral grammar and intuitive jurisprudence: A formal model of unconscious moral and legal knowledge. In B. H. Ross (Series Ed.) & D. M. Bartels, C. W. Bauman, L. J. Skitka, & D. L. Medin (Eds.), *Psychology of Learning and Motivation, Vol. 50: Moral Judgment and Decision Making* (pp. 27–100). San Diego, CA: Academic Press.

Mikhail, J., & Sorrentino, C. (1999). Toward a fragment of moral grammar: Knowledge of the principle of double effect in children ages 8–12. Poster presented to the Society for Research in Child Development, Albuquerque, NM. (On file with author.)

Mikhail, J., Sorrentino, C., & Spelke, E. (1998). Toward a universal moral grammar. In M. A. Gernsbacher & S. J. Derry (Eds.), *Proceedings of the Twentieth Annual Conference of the Cognitive Science Society* (p. 1250). Mahwah, NJ: Lawrence Erlbaum Associates.

Mill, J. S. (1972/1861). *Utilitarianism*. (H. B. Action, Ed.). London: Guernsey Press. (1978/1859). *On Liberty*. (E. Rappaport, Ed.). Indianapolis: Hackett.

(1987/1843). *The Logic of the Moral Sciences.* (A.J. Ayer, Ed.). London: Duckworth.

Miller, G. (2008). The roots of morality. *Science*, 320, 734–737.

Miller, R. (1974). Rawls and Marxism. In N. Daniels (Ed.). (1989). *Reading Rawls: Critical Studies on Rawls' "A Theory of Justice"* (pp. 206–230). Stanford, CA: Stanford University Press.

(1992). *Moral Differences: Truth, Justice, and Conscience in a World of Conflict.* Princeton, NJ: Princeton University Press.

Moll, J., de Oliveira-Sousa, R., & Eslinger, P. (2003). Morals and the human brain: A working model. *NeuroReport*, 14, 299–305.

Moll, J., Zahn, R., de Oliveira-Sousa, R., Krueger, F., & Grafman, J. (2005). The neural basis of human moral cognition. *Nature Reviews Neuroscience*, 6, 799–809.

Moore, A., Clark, B., & Kane, M. (2008). Who shall not kill? Individual differences in working memory capacity, executive control, and moral judgment. *Psychological Science*, 19, 549–557.

Moore, G. E. (1903). *Principia Ethica.* Cambridge: Cambridge University Press.

Moore, M. S. (1982). Moral reality. *Wisconsin Law Review*, 1982, 1061–1156.

(1992). Moral reality revisited. *Michigan Law Review*, 90, 2424–2533.

(1993). *Act and Crime: The Philosophy of Action and Its Implications for Criminal Law.* Oxford: Oxford University Press.

Moravcsik, J. (1967). Linguistic theory and the philosophy of language. *Foundations of Language*, 3(3), 209–233. Reprinted in C. Otero (Ed) (1994), *Noam Chomsky: Critical Assessments. Vol. II: Philosophy* (pp. 173–197). New York: Routledge.

Much, N., & Shweder, R. (1978). Speaking of rules: The analysis of culture in breach. In W. Damon (Ed.), *New Directions in Child Development, Vol. 2: Moral Development.* San Fransciso: Jossey-Bass.

Murphy, D., & Bishop, M. (Eds.). (2009). *Stich and His Critics.* Oxford: Blackwell.

Nader, L. (1997). *Law in Culture and Society.* Berkeley: University of California Press.

Nado, J., Kelly, D., & Stich, S. (2006). Moral judgment. Forthcoming in J. Symons & P. Calvo (Eds.), *Routledge Companion to the Philosophy of Psychology.* New York: Routledge.

Nagel, E. (1961). *The Structure of Science: Problems in the Logic of Scientific Explanation.* New York: Harcourt, Brace & World.

Nagel, T. (1969). Linguistics and epistemology. In G. Harman (Ed.) (1974), *On Noam Chomsky: Critical Essays* (pp. 219–228). New York: Anchor.

(1973). Rawls on justice. In N. Daniels (Ed.) (1989), *Reading Rawls: Critical Studies on Rawls' "A Theory of Justice"* (pp. 1–16). Stanford, CA: Stanford University Press.

(1986). *The View from Nowhere.* In J.M. Fischer & M. Ravizza (Eds.) (1992), *Ethics: Problems and Principles* (pp. 165–179). Fort Worth, TX: Harcourt Brace Jovanovich.

Neale, S. (1992). Paul Grice and the philosophy of language. *Linguistics and Philosophy*, 15(5), 509–559.

Neisser, U. (1967). *Cognitive Psychology.* Cambridge, MA: MIT Press.

Nelson, S. (1980). Factors influencing young children's use of motives and outcomes as moral criteria. *Child Development*, 51, 823–829.

Nichols, S. (2004). *Sentimental Rules: On the Natural Foundations of Moral Judgment.* Oxford: Oxford University Press.

(2005). Innateness and moral psychology. In P. Carruthers, S. Laurence, & S. Stich (Eds.), *The Innate Mind, Vol. 1: Structure and Contents* (pp. 353–369). New York: Oxford University Press.

Nichols, S., & Mallon, R. (2006). Moral dilemmas and moral rules. *Cognition,* 100(3), 530–542.

Nielson, K. (1977). Our considered judgments. *Ratio,* 19, 39–46.

(1989). Reflective equilibrium and the transformation of philosophy. *Metaphilosophy,* 20, 235–246.

Nietzsche, F. (1967/1887). *On the Genealogy of Morals.* (W. Kaufmann, Ed.). New York: Random House.

Nisbett, R., & Cohen, D. (1996). *Culture of Honor: The Psychology of Violence in the South.* New York: HarperCollins.

Nowell-Smith, P. (1954). *Ethics.* Baltimore: Penguin Books.

Nozick, R. (1968). Moral complications and moral structures. *Natural Law Forum,* 13, 1–50.

(1981). *Philosophical Explanations.* Cambridge, MA: Harvard University Press.

Oakeshott, M. (1962). *Rationalism in Politics and Other Essays.* London: Methuen.

Ogden, C. K. (1932). *Bentham's Theory of Fictions.* London: Kegan Paul.

Olafson, F. A. (Ed.). (1961). *Justice and Social Policy.* Englewood Cliffs, NJ: Prentice-Hall.

Oliphant, H. (1928). A return to stare decisis. *American Bar Association Journal* 14, 71–76.

Otero, C. (Ed.). (1994). *Noam Chomsky: Critical Assessments. Vol. II: Philosophy.* New York: Routledge.

Paine, T. (1791). *Rights of Man; Being an Answer to Mr. Burke's Attack on the French Revolution.* London: J. S. Jordan.

Pareto, W. (1935). *The Mind and Society.* New York: Harcourt, Brace.

Paton, H. J. (1948). *The Categorical Imperative.* Chicago: University of Chicago Press.

(1964). Analysis of the argument. In H. J. Paton (Ed.), *Groundwork of the Metaphysics of Morals* (pp. 13–52). New York: Harper and Row.

Patterson, D. (2008). On the conceptual and the empirical: A critique of John Mikhail's cognitivism. *Brooklyn Law Review,* 73, 611–623.

Paul, A. (1976). *Conservative Crisis and the Rule of Law: Attitudes of Bar and Bench, 1887–1895.* Gloucester, MA: Peter Smith.

Pearl, J. (2000). *Causality: Models, Reasoning, and Inference.* Cambridge: Cambridge University Press.

Perrot, D. L. (1980). Has law a deep structure? – The origin of fundamental duties. In D. Lasok et al. (Eds.) (1980), *Fundamental Duties: A Volume of Essays by Present and Former Members of the Law Faculty of the University of Exeter to Commemorate the Silver Jubilee of the University* (pp. 1–18). Oxford: Pergamon Press.

Perry, R. B. (1954). *Realms of Value: A Critique of Human Civilization.* Cambridge, MA: Harvard University Press.

Petrinovich, L., & O'Neill, P. (1996). Influence of wording and framing effects on moral intuitions. *Ethology and Sociobiology,* 17, 145–171.

Petrinovich, L., O'Neill, P., & Jorgensen, M. (1993). An empirical study of moral intuitions: Toward an evolutionary ethics. *Journal of Personality and Social Psychology*, 64, 467–478.

Piaget, J. (1965/1932). *The Moral Judgment of the Child*. New York: Free Press.

Piatelli-Palmarini, M. (Ed.) (1980). *Language and Learning: The Debate between Jean Piaget and Noam Chomsky*. Cambridge, MA: Harvard University Press.

Peirce, C. S. (1955/1901). Abduction and induction. In J. Bucher (Ed.), *Philosophical Writings of Peirce* (pp. 150–156). New York: Dover.

(1955). *Philosophical Writings of Peirce*. (J. Bucher, Ed.). New York: Dover.

Pinker, S. (1994). *The Language Instinct: How the Mind Creates Language*. New York: HarperCollins.

(1997). *How the Mind Works*. New York: W. W. Norton.

(2007). *The Stuff of Thought: Language as a Window into Human Nature*. New York: Viking.

(2008). The moral instinct. *New York Times Magazine*, Jan. 13.

Pinker, S., & Bloom, P. (1990). Natural language and natural selection. *Behavioral and Brain Sciences*, 13, 707–784.

Pizzaro, D., & Bloom, P. (2003). The intelligence of the moral intuitions: Comment on Haidt. *Psychological Review*, 110, 193–198.

Plato. (1961). *The Collected Dialogues*. (E. Hamilton & H. Cairns, Eds.). Princeton, NJ: Princeton University Press.

Pocock, J. G. A. (1987/1957). *The Ancient Constitution and the Feudal Law: A Study of English Historical Thought in the Seventeenth Century*. Cambridge: Cambridge University Press.

Pogge, T. (2007). *John Rawls: His Life and Theory of Justice*. Oxford: Oxford University Press.

Polanyi, M. (1958). *Personal Knowledge: Towards a Post-Critical Philosophy*. New York: Harper Torchbooks.

Pollock, F. (1882). *Essays in Jurisprudence and Ethics*. London: Macmillan.

(1922). *Essays in the Law*. London: Macmillan.

Popper, K. (1945). *The Open Society and Its Enemies*. London: Routledge.

(1958/1934). *The Logic of Scientific Discovery*. New York: Science Editions.

Posner, R. (2007/1973). *Economic Analysis of Law* (7th Ed.). New York: Aspen Publishers.

(1981). *The Economics of Justice*. Cambridge, MA: Harvard University Press.

(1990). *The Problems of Jurisprudence*. Cambridge, MA: Harvard University Press.

(1995). *Overcoming Law*. Cambridge, MA: Harvard University Press.

(1998a). The problematics of moral and legal theory. *Harvard Law Review*, 111, 1637–1717.

(1998b). Reply to critics of "The Problematics of Moral and Legal Theory." *Harvard Law Review*, 111, 1796–1823.

(1999). *The Problematics of Moral and Legal Theory*. Cambridge, MA: Harvard University Press.

Postema, G. (1986). *Bentham and the Common Law Tradition*. Oxford: Clarendon Press.

Potts, T. (1980). *Conscience in Medieval Philosophy*. Cambridge: Cambridge University Press.

Pound, R. (1908). Mechanical jurisprudence. *Columbia Law Review*, 8, 605–623.

(1939). *The History and System of the Common Law*. New York: Collier.

Price, R. (1948/1759). *A Review of the Principal Questions of Morals*. (D.D. Raphael, Ed.). Oxford: Oxford University Press.

Prichard, H. (1968/1949). *Moral Obligation and Duty & Interest: Essays and Lectures by H. A. Prichard*. (W. D. Ross, Ed.). Oxford: Oxford University Press.

Prinz, J. (2007). *The Emotional Construction of Morals*. Oxford: Oxford University Press.

(2008a). Is morality innate? In W. Sinnott-Armstrong (Ed.), *Moral Psychology, Vol. 1: The Evolution of Morality: Adaptation and Innateness* (pp. 367–406). Cambridge, MA: MIT Press.

(2008b). Response to Dwyer and Tiberius. In W. Sinnott-Armstrong (Ed.), *Moral Psychology, Vol. 1: The Evolution of Morality: Adaptation and Innateness* (pp. 427–439). Cambridge, MA: MIT Press.

(2008c). Resisting the linguistic analogy: A commentary on Hauser, Young, and Cushman. In W. Sinnott-Armstrong (Ed.), *Moral Psychology, Vol. 2: The Cognitive Science of Morality: Intuition and Diversity* (pp. 157–170). Cambridge, MA: MIT Press.

(2008d). Against moral nativism. In M. Bishop & D. Murphy (Eds.), *Stich and His Critics* (pp. 167–189). Oxford: Blackwell.

Prior, A. N. (1955). *Formal Logic*. Oxford: Clarendon Press.

(1958). Escapism: The logical basis of ethics. In A. I. Meldon (Ed.) (1958), *Essays in Moral Philosophy* (pp. 135–146). Seattle: University of Washington Press.

Prosser, W. (1941). *Casebook on Torts*. Minneapolis: University of Minnesota Press.

(1971). *Casebook on Torts* (4th Ed.). Minneapolis: University of Minnesota Press.

Proudhon, P.J. (1994/1840). *What Is Property?* (D. R. Kelly & B. G. Smith, Eds.). Cambridge: Cambridge University Press.

Pufendorf, S. (1931/1660). *The Elements of Universal Jurisprudence, in Two Books*. (W. A. Oldfather, Trans.). Oxford: Clarendon Press.

(1934/1672). *On the Law of Nature and Nations, in Eight Books*. (C. H. Oldfather & W. A. Oldfather, Trans.). Oxford: Clarendon Press.

(1990/1673). *On the Duty of Man and Citizen*. In J. B. Schneewind (Ed.), *Moral Philosophy from Montaigne to Kant* (2 Vols.). Cambridge: Cambridge University Press.

(2003/1691). *The Whole Duty of Man, According to the Law of Nature*. (A. Tooke, Trans. 1691; I. Hunter & D. Saunders, Eds.). Indianapolis: Liberty Fund.

Putnam, H. (1975). The innateness hypothesis and explanatory models in linguistics. Reprinted in *Mind, Language, and Reality*. Cambridge: Cambridge University Press.

(1988). *Representation and Reality*. Cambridge, MA: MIT Press.

Quine, W. V. O. (1960). *Word and Object*. Cambridge, MA: MIT Press.

(1961/1953). *From a Logical Point of View*. (2nd Ed.). New York: Harper Torchbooks.

(1972). Methodological reflections on current linguistic theory. In D. Davidson, & G. Harman (Eds.) (1975), *Semantics of Natural Language* (pp. 442–454). Dordrecht: D. Reidel.

(1978). On the nature of moral values. In A. Goldman & J. Kim (Eds.), *Values and Morals* (pp. 37–45). Dordrecht: D. Reidel.

Quinn, W. S. (1993). *Morality and Action*. Cambridge: Cambridge University Press.

Rachels, J. (1975). Active and passive euthanasia. *New England Journal of Medicine*. In J. M. Fischer & M. Ravizza (Eds.) (1992), *Ethics: Problems and Principles* (pp. 111–116). Fort Worth, TX: Harcourt Brace Jovanovich.

Radin, M. (1925). The theory of judicial decision: Or how judges think. *American Bar Association Journal*, 11, 357–362.

Railton, P. (1986). Moral realism. *Philosophical Review*, 95, 163–207.

Raphael, D. D. (1947). *The Moral Sense*. New York: Oxford University Press.

(Ed.). (1969). *The British Moralists* (2 Vols.). New York: Oxford University Press.

Rashdall, H. (1914). *Is Conscience an Emotion?* Boston: Houghton Mifflin.

Rawls, J. (1950). "A Study in the Grounds of Ethical Knowledge: Considered with Reference to Judgments on the Moral Worth of Character." Ph.D. dissertation, Princeton University.

(1951a). Outline of a decision procedure for ethics. *Philosophical Review*, 60, 177–197.

(1951b). Review of Stephan Toulmin, *An Examination of the Place of Reason in Ethics*. *Philosophical Review*, 60, 572–580.

(1955). Two concepts of rules. *Philosophical Review*, 64, 3–32.

(1957). Symposium – Justice as fairness. *Journal of Philosophy*, 54, 653–662.

(1958). Justice as fairness. *Philosophical Review*, 67, 164–194. Reprinted, with minor changes, in P. Laslett & W. Runcimen (Eds.) (1962), *Philosophy, Politics and Society* (Second Series). New York: Barnes and Noble.

(1963a). Constitutional liberty and the concept of justice. In C. Friedrich & J. Chapman (Eds.) (1963), *Justice: Nomos VI* (pp. 98–125). New York: Atherton Press.

(1963b). The sense of justice. *Philosophical Review*, 72, 281–305.

(1967). Distributive justice. In P. Laslett & W. Runcimen (Eds.) (1967). *Philosophy, Politics and Society* (Third Series) (pp. 58–82). London: Basil Blackwell.

(1968). Distributive justice: Some addenda. *Natural Law Forum*, 13, 51–71.

(1971). *A Theory of Justice*. Cambridge, MA: Harvard University Press.

(1975). The independence of moral theory. *Proceedings and Addresses of the American Philosophical Association*, 48, 5–22.

(1978). The basic structure as subject. In A. Goldman & J. Kim (Eds.) (1978), *Values and Morals* (pp. 47–71). Dordrecht: D. Reidel.

(1979). A well-ordered society. In P. Laslett & J. Fishkin (Eds.), *Philosophy, Politics and Society* (Fifth Series) (pp. 6–20). New Haven, CT: Yale University Press. Originally published as A Kantian conception of equality. *Cambridge Review*, 96: 94–99.

(1980). Kantian constructivism in moral theory. *Journal of Philosophy*, 77(9), 512–572.

(1985). Justice as fairness: Political not metaphysical. *Philosophy and Public Affairs*, 14(3), 223–251.

(1993). *Political Liberalism*. New York: Columbia University Press.

(1999a). *A Theory of Justice* (Rev. Ed.). Cambridge, MA: Harvard University Press.

(1999b). *The Law of Peoples*. Cambridge, MA: Harvard University Press.

(2000). *Lectures on the History of Moral Philosophy*. (B. Herman, Ed.). Cambridge, MA: Harvard University Press.

(2001a). *Collected Papers*. (S. Freeman, Ed.). Cambridge, MA: Harvard University Press.

(2001b). *Justice as Fairness: A Restatement*. (E. Kelly, Ed.). Cambridge, MA: Harvard University Press.

(2007). *Lectures on the History of Political Philosophy*. (S. Freeman, Ed.). Cambridge, MA: Harvard University Press.

Raz, J. (1970). *The Concept of a Legal System*. Oxford: Clarendon Press.

(1982). The claims of reflective equilibrium. *Inquiry*, 25, 307–330.

Reichenbach, H. (1951). *The Rise of Scientific Philosophy*. Berkeley: University of California Press.

Reid, T. (1969/1785). *Essays on the Intellectual Powers of Man*. Cambridge, MA: MIT Press.

(1969/1788). *Essays on the Active Powers of the Human Mind*. Cambridge, MA: MIT Press.

Rescher, N. (1973). *The Coherence Theory of Truth*. Oxford: Oxford University Press.

Rest, J. (1983). Morality. In J. Flavell & E. Markman, (Eds.), *Manual of Child Psychology, Volume 3: Cognitive Development*. (4th Ed.). New York: Wiley.

Rey, G. (2006). Conventions, intuitions, and linguistic inexistents: A reply to Devitt. *Croatian Journal of Philosophy*, 18, 549–569.

Richards, W. (1988). *Natural Computation*. Cambridge, MA: MIT Press.

Richardson, H. (1990). Specifying norms as a way to resolve concrete ethical problems. *Philosophy & Public Affairs*, 19, 279–310.

Richardson, H., & Weithman, P. (1999). *The Philosophy of Rawls* (5 Vols.). New York: Garland.

Robinson, P., & Darley, J. (1995). *Justice, Liability, and Blame: Community Views and the Criminal Law*. San Francisco: Westview Press.

Robinson, P. H., Kurzban, R., & Jones, O. D. (2008). The origins of shared intuitions of justice. *Vanderbilt Law Review*, 60, 1633–1688.

Roedder, E., & Harman, G. (2008a). Moral theory: the linguistic analogy. Forthcoming in J. Doris, S. Nichols, & S. Stich (Eds.), *Empirical Moral Psychology*. Oxford: Oxford University Press.

(2008b). Moral grammar. Forthcoming in E. Bocardo (Ed.), *Cognitive Ethics*.

Rorty, R. (1982). *Consequences of Pragmatism*. Minneapolis: University of Minnesota Press.

(1992/1984). The priority of democracy to philosophy. In G. H. Outka & J. P. Reeder (Eds.), *Prospects for a Common Morality* (pp. 254–278). Princeton, NJ: Princeton University Press.

Rosenberg, J. F. (1988). About competence and performance. *Philosophical Papers* 17, 33–49.

Ross, W. D. (1939). *Foundations of Ethics*. Oxford: Clarendon Press.

(1988/1930). *The Right and the Good*. Indianapolis: Hackett.

Rousseau, J. (1979/1762). *Emile: Or, On Education*. (A. Bloom, Ed.). New York: Basic Books.

(1987/1749). *Discourse on the Sciences and the Arts.* In D. A. Cress (Ed.), *Jean-Jacques Rousseau: The Basic Political Writings* (pp. 1–21). Indianapolis: Hackett.

(1987/1754). *Discourse on the Origin and Foundations of Inequality Among Men.* In D. A. Cress (Ed.), *Jean-Jacques Rousseau: The Basic Political Writings* (pp. 25–109). Indianapolis: Hackett.

(1987/1762). *On the Social Contract.* In D. A. Cress (Ed.), *Jean-Jacques Rousseau: The Basic Political Writings* (pp. 141–227). Indianapolis: Hackett.

Russell, B. (1977). On the relative strictness of negative and positive duties. In J. M. Fischer & M. Ravizza (Eds.), *Ethics: Problems and Principles* (pp. 121–133). Fort Worth, TX: Harcourt Brace Jovanovich.

Ryle, G. (1949). *The Concept of Mind.* Oxford: Oxford University Press.

(1958). On forgetting the difference between right and wrong. In A. I. Meldon (Ed.), *Essays in Moral Philosophy* (pp. 147–159). Seattle: University of Washington Press.

(1968). The thinking of thoughts: What is 'Le Pensuer' doing? In *Collected Papers, Vol. 2: Collected Essays.* London: Hutchinson.

Sadat, L. (2002). *The International Criminal Court and the Transformation of International Law: Justice for the New Millenium.* Ardsley, NY: Transnational Publishers.

Salmond, J. (1966/1902). *Salmond on Jurisprudence* (12th Ed.) (P. J. Fitzgerald, Ed.). London: Sweet & Maxwell.

Savigny, F. C. von (1881/1814). *On the Vocation of Our Age for Legislation and Jurisprudence.* (A. Hayward, Trans.). London: Littleward.

Saxe, R. (2005). Do the right thing: Cognitive science's search for a common morality. *Boston Review,* Sept.–Oct.

Saxe, R., Carey, S., & Kanwisher, N. (2004). Understanding other minds: Linking developmental psychology and functional neuroimaging. *Annual Review of Psychology,* 55, 87–124.

Sayre-McCord, G. (Ed.). (1988). *Essays on Moral Realism.* Ithaca, NY: Cornell University Press.

Scanlon, T. M. (1982). Contractualism and utilitarianism. In J. Rachman & C. West (Eds.) (1985), *Post-Analytic Philosophy* (pp. 215–243). New York: Columbia University Press.

(1992). The aims and authority of moral theory. *Oxford Journal of Legal Studies,* 12(1), 1–23.

(1998). *What We Owe to Each Other.* Cambridge, MA: Harvard University Press.

Scheffler, S. (1988). *Consequentialism and Its Critics.* Oxford: Oxford University Press.

Schlick, M. (1939/1930). *Problems of Ethics.* (Trans. D. Rynin). New York: Prentice-Hall.

Schnall, S., Haidt, J., Clore, G. L., & Jordan, H. (2008). Disgust as embodied moral judgment. *Personality and Social Psychology Bulletin,* 34(8), 1096–1109.

Schneewind, J. B. (1963). First principles and common sense morality in Sidgwick's ethics. *Archiv für Geschichte der Philosophie,* Bd. 45, 137–156.

(1977). *Sidgwick's Ethics and Victorian Moral Philosophy.* Oxford: Clarendon Press.

(Ed.) (1990). *Moral Philosophy from Montaigne to Kant* (2 Vols.). Cambridge: Cambridge University Press.

(1991). Natural law, skepticism, and the methods of ethics. *Journal of the History of Ideas*, 52, 289–308.

(1998). *The Invention of Autonomy: A History of Modern Moral Philosophy.* Cambridge: Cambridge University Press.

Seok, B. (2008). Mencius's vertical faculties and moral nativism. *Asian Philosophy*, 18, 51–68.

Shapo, M. (2003). *Principles of Tort Law.* St. Paul, MN: West Group.

Shepard, R., & Metzler, J. (1971). Mental rotation of three-dimensional objects. *Science*, 171, 701–703.

Shweder, R., Mahapatra, M., & Miller, J. (1987). Culture and moral development. In J. Kagan & S. Lamb (Eds.), *The Emergence of Morality in Young Children* (pp. 1–83). Chicago: University of Chicago Press.

Shweder, R., Turiel, E., & Much, N. (1981). The moral intuitions of the child. In J. H. Flavell & L. Ross (Eds.), *Social Cognitive Development* (pp. 288–305). Cambridge, MA: Cambridge University Press.

Sidgwick, H. (1988/1902). *Outlines of the History of Ethics* (5th Ed.). Indianapolis: Hackett.

(1981/1907). *The Methods of Ethics* (7th Ed.). Indianapolis: Hackett.

Simpson, A. W. B. (1973). The common law and legal theory. In A. W. B. Simpson (Ed.), *Oxford Essays in Jurisprudence* (Second Series) (pp. 77–99). Oxford: Clarendon Press.

Simpson, E. (1974). Moral development research: A case study of scientific cultural bias. *Human Development*, 17, 81–106.

Singer, P. (1972). Famine, affluence, and morality. *Philosophy and Public Affairs*, 1(3), 229–243.

(1974). Sidgwick and reflective equilibrium. *Monist*, 58, 490–517.

Sinnott-Armstrong, W. (2008). *Moral Psychology* (3 Vols.). Cambridge, MA: MIT Press.

Sinnott-Armstrong, W., Mallon, R., McCoy, T., & Hull, J. (2008). Intention, temporal order, and moral judgments. *Mind & Language*, 23(1), 90–106.

Skinner, B. F. (1953). *Science and Human Behavior.* New York: Macmillan.

(1957). *Verbal Behavior.* Acton, MA: Copton.

Smart, R. N. (1958). Negative utilitarianism. *Mind*, 67, 542–543.

Smetana, J. (1983). Social cognitive development: Domain distinctions and coordinations. *Developmental Review*, 3, 131–147.

Smith, A. (1976/1759). *The Theory of Moral Sentiments.* Oxford: Clarendon Press.

Smith, M. B. E. (1977). Rawls, and intuitionism. *Canadian Journal of Philosophy*, Supp. Vol. 3: *New Essays on Contractarianism*, 163–178.

(1979). Ethical intuitionism and naturalism: A reconciliation. *Canadian Journal of Philosophy*, 9, 609–629.

Soames, S. (1984). Linguistics and psychology. *Linguistics and Philosophy*, 7(2), 155–179.

Solum, L. (2006). Natural justice. *American Journal of Jurisprudence*, 51, 65–105.

Spelke, E. (1998). Nativism, empiricism, and the origins of knowledge. *Infant Behavior and Development*, 21, 181–200.

Spelke, E.S., Breinlinger, K., & Jacobson, K. (1992). Origins of knowledge. *Psychological Review*, 99, 605–632.

Spencer, H. (1978/1897). *The Principles of Ethics* (2 Vols.). Indianapolis: Liberty Classics.

Sripada, C.S. (2008a). Nativism and moral psychology: Three models of the innate structure that shapes the contents of moral norms. In W. Sinnott-Armstrong (Ed.), *Moral Psychology, Vol. 1: The Evolution of Morality: Adaptation and Innateness* (pp. 319–343). Cambridge, MA: MIT Press.

(2008b). Reply to Harman and Mikhail. In W. Sinnott-Armstrong (Ed.), *Moral Psychology, Vol. 1: The Evolution of Morality: Adaptation and Innateness* (pp. 361–365). Cambridge, MA: MIT Press.

Sripada, C.S., & Stich, S. (2006). A framework for the psychology of norms. In P. Carruthers, S. Laurence, & S. Stich (Eds.), *The Innate Mind, Vol. 2: Culture and Cognition* (pp. 280–301). Oxford: Oxford University Press.

St. Germain, C. (1874/1518). *Doctor and Student, Or Dialogues Between A Doctor of Divinity and a Student in the Laws of England*. Cincinnati: Robert Clarke.

Stein, E. (1996). *Without Good Reason: The Rationality Debate in Philosophy and Cognitive Science*. Oxford: Clarendon Press.

Steinbock, B. (1980). *Killing and Letting Die*. Englewood Cliffs, NJ: Prentice-Hall.

Stevenson, C.L. (1944). *Ethics and Language*. New Haven, CT: Yale University Press.

(1963). *Facts and Values: Studies in Ethical Analysis*. New Haven, CT: Yale University Press.

Stewart, D. (1876/1793). *Outlines of Moral Philosophy*. (J. McCosh, Ed.). London: Elibron Classics.

Stich, S. (1993). Moral philosophy and mental representation. In M. Hechter, L. Nadel, & R. Michod (Eds.), *The Origin of Values* (pp. 215–228). Hawthorne, NY: Aldine De Gruyter.

(2006). Is morality an elegant machine or a kludge? *Journal of Cognition and Culture*, 6, 181–189.

Stone, J. (1968). *Legal System and Lawyers' Reasonings*. Stanford, CA: Stanford University Press.

Strawson, P. (1972). Grammar and philosophy. In D. Davidson & G. Harman (Eds.) (1975), *Semantics of Natural Language* (pp. 455–472). Dordrecht: D. Reidel.

Sturgeon, N. (1976). Nature and conscience in Butler's ethics. *Philosophical Review*, 85, 316–356.

(1984). Moral explanations. In D. Copp & D. Zimmerman (Eds.), *Morality, Reason and Truth* (pp. 49–78). Totowa, NJ: Rowman & Allanheld.

Suarez, F. (1944/1612). *De Legibus ac deo Legislatore*. (J.B. Scott, Ed.). Oxford: Clarendon Press.

Sullivan, R. (1989). *Immanuel Kant's Moral Theory*. Cambridge: Cambridge University Press.

Sunstein, C. (2005). Moral heuristics. *Behavioral and Brain Sciences*, 28, 531–573.

Terry, H. (1884). *Some Leading Principles of Anglo-American Law, Expounded with a View to Its Arrangement and Codification*. Philadelphia: T. & J.W. Johnson.

(1915). Negligence. *Harvard Law Review*, 29, 40–54.

Tetlock, P.E. (2003). Thinking about the unthinkable: Coping with secular encroachments on sacred values. *Trends in Cognitive Sciences*, 7, 320–324.

Thalberg, I. (1970). Singling out actions, their properties, and components. *Journal of Philosophy*, 68, 781–787.

Thomson, J. J. (1970a). The time of a killing. *Journal of Philosophy*, 68, 115–132.

(1970b). Individuating actions. *Journal of Philosophy*, 68, 774–781.

(1985). The trolley problem. In J. M. Fischer & M. Ravizza (Eds.), *Ethics: Problems and Principles* (pp. 67–76). Fort Worth, TX: Harcourt Brace Jovanovich.

(1986). *Rights, Restitution, and Risk*. Cambridge, MA: Harvard University Press.

(1990). *The Realm of Rights*. Cambridge, MA: Harvard University Press.

Tienson, J. L. (1990). About competence. *Philosophical Papers*, 19, 19–36.

Tierney, B. (1997). *The Idea of Natural Rights: Studies on Natural Rights, Natural Law, and Church Law, 1150–1625*. Atlanta: William B. Eerdmans.

Toulmin, S. (1950). *An Examination of the Place of Reason in Ethics*. Cambridge: Cambridge University Press.

Trivers, R. L. (1971). The evolution of reciprocal altruism. *Quarterly Review of Biology*, 46, 35–57.

Tuck, R. (1979). *Natural Rights Theories: Their Origin and Development*. Cambridge: Cambridge University Press.

Turiel, E. (1983). *The Development of Social Knowledge: Morality and Convention*. Cambridge: Cambridge University Press.

Unger, P. (1996). *Living High and Letting Die: Our Illusion of Innocence*. Oxford: Oxford University Press.

Urmson, J. O. (1968). *The Emotive Theory of Ethics*. Oxford: Oxford University Press.

(1974). A defense of intuitionism. *Proceedings of the Aristotelian Society*, 75, 111–119.

Valdesolo, P., & DeSteno, D. (2006). Manipulations of emotional context shape moral judgment. *Psychological Science*, 17(6), 476–477.

Vattel, E. (1863/1758). *The Law of Nations; or Principles of the Law of Nature Applied to the Conduct and Affairs of Nations and Sovereigns*. (J. Chitty, Trans.). Philadelphia: T. & J. W. Johnson.

Von Jhering, R. (1865–1869). *Geist des romischen Rechts*. Cited in M. R. Cohen. (1916). The place of logic in the law. *Harvard Law Review*. Reprinted in M. R. Cohen (1967/1933), *Law and the Social Order: Essays in Legal Philosophy*. New York: Archon Books.

Von Savigny, F. C. (1881/1814). *Of the Vocation of Our Age for Legislation and Jurisprudence*. (A. Hayward, Trans.). London: Littleward.

Von Wright, G. H. (1951). *An Essay in Modal Logic*. Amsterdam: North-Holland.

(1963). *Norm and Action*. London: Routledge and Kegan Paul.

Waldmann, M., & Dieterich, J. (2007). Throwing a bomb on a person versus throwing a person on a bomb: Intervention myopia in moral intuitions. *Psychological Science*, 18, 247–253.

Walzer, M. (1977). *Just and Unjust Wars: A Moral Argument with Historical Illustrations*. New York: Basic Books.

Warnock, G. (1967). *Contemporary Moral Philosophy*. London: Macmillan.

Warnock, M. (1978). *Ethics since 1900*. Oxford: Oxford University Press.

Watson, J. (1925). *Behaviorism*. New York: W. W. Norton.

Weinrib, E. (1980). The case for a duty to rescue. *Yale Law Journal*, 90, 247–293.

Wellbank, J. H., Snook, D., & Mason, D. T. (1982). *John Rawls and His Critics: An Annotated Bibliography*. New York: Garland.

Wellman, H., & Miller, J. (2008). Including deontic reasoning as fundamental to theory of mind. *Human Development*, 51, 105–135.

Westermarck, E. (1908). *The Origin and Development of the Moral Ideas* (2 Vols.). London.

Wheatley T., & Haidt J. (2005). Hypnotic disgust makes moral judgments more severe. *Psychological Science*, 16, 780–784.

Whewell, W. (1845). *Elements of Morality Including Polity*. Cambridge: Cambridge University Press.

(1852). *Lectures on the History of Moral Philosophy*. Cambridge: Cambridge University Press.

White, A. (Ed.). (1968). *The Philosophy of Action*. Oxford: Oxford University Press.

White, G. E. (1978). *Patterns of American Legal Thought*. Indianapolis: Bobbs-Merrill.

(1980). *Tort Law in America: An Intellectual History*. Oxford: Oxford University Press.

White, M. G. (1949). *Social Thought in America: The Revolt against Formalism*. New York: Viking Press.

(1956). *Toward Reunion in Philosophy*. Cambridge, MA: Harvard University Press.

Williams, B. (1973). *Problems of the Self*. Cambridge: Cambridge University Press.

(1985). *Ethics and the Limits of Philosophy*. Cambridge: Cambridge University Press.

Wills, G. (1978). *Inventing America: Jefferson's Declaration of Independence*. New York: Random House.

Wilson, E. O. (1975). *Sociobiology: The New Synthesis*. Cambridge, MA: Harvard University Press.

Wilson, J. (1967/1790–1791). *The Works of James Wilson* (2 Vols.). (R. McCloskey, Ed.). Cambridge, MA: Harvard University Press.

Wilson, J. Q. (1993). *The Moral Sense*. New York: Free Press.

Winston, K. (Ed.) (1981). Introduction. In K. Winston (Ed.), *The Principles of Social Order: Selected Essays of Lon L. Fuller*. Durham, NC: Duke University Press.

(Ed.) (2001). Introduction. In K. Winston (Ed.), *The Principles of Social Order: Selected Essays of Lon L. Fuller*. Edited with a new introduction by Kenneth I. Winston. Oxford: Hart Publishing.

Wolff, C. (1934/1740–1749). *The Law of Nations Treated according to a Scientific Method*. Oxford: Clarendon Press.

Wolff, R. P. (1963). *Kant's Theory of Mental Activity*. Cambridge, MA: Harvard University Press.

(1973). *The Autonomy of Reason: A Commentary on Kant's Groundwork of the Metaphysics of Morals*. New York: Harper.

(1977). *Understanding Rawls*. Princeton, NJ: Princeton University Press.

Wollstonecraft, M. (1995/1790–1792). *A Vindication of the Rights of Men, with A Vindication of the Rights of Woman, and Hints.* (S. Tomaselli, Ed.). Cambridge: Cambridge University Press.

Wood, A. (1990). *Hegel's Ethical Thought.* Cambridge: Cambridge University Press.

Wood, G. (1991). *The Radicalism of the American Revolution.* New York: Vintage.

Woodward, A.L., Sommerville, J.A., & Guajardo, J.J. (2001). How infants make sense of intentional action. In B. Malle, L. Moses & D. Baldwin (Eds.), *Intentions and Intentionality: Foundations of Social Cognition* (pp. 149–169). Cambridge, MA: MIT Press.

Woodward, P.A. (1997). The importance of the proportionality condition to the doctrine of double effect: A response to Fischer, Ravizza, and Copp. *Journal of Social Philosophy*, 28, 140–152. Reprinted in P. A. Woodward (2001), *The Doctrine of Double Effect: Philosophers Debate a Controversial Moral Principle* (pp. 211–227). Notre Dame, IN: University of Notre Dame Press.

(Ed.). (2001). *The Doctrine of Double Effect: Philosophers Debate a Controversial Moral Principle.* Notre Dame, IN: University of Notre Dame Press.

Wright, B. (1931). *American Interpretations of Natural Law: A Study in the History of Political Thought.* Cambridge, MA: Harvard University Press.

Wright, R. (1985). Causation in tort law. *California Law Review*, 73, 1735–1828.

Young, L., Cushman, F. A., Hauser, M. D., & Saxe, R. (2007). Brain regions for belief attribution drive moral condemnation for crimes of attempt. *Proceedings of the National Academy of Science*, 104(20), 8235–8240.

Young, L., & Saxe, R. (2008). The neural basis of belief encoding and integration in moral judgment. *NeuroImage*, 40, 1912–1920.

Young, R.M. (1970). *Mind, Brain, and Adaptation in the Nineteenth Century: Cerebral Localization and Its Biological Context from Gall to Ferrier.* Oxford: Clarendon Press.

Index

Note: Entries followed by a lowercase *f* or *t* represent subject material contained in figures or tables.

abduction, or inference to the best explanation, 17, 68–69
acceptability judgments: and competence–performance distinction, 232; and distinction with grammaticality judgments in linguistics, 233–235, 238–239, 248–251; and distinction with permissibility judgments in moral theory, 251–252
acquisition models, of language and morality, 88–91
act (action): basic, 176; and circumstances, 81, 86–87, 112f, 125–129, 132, 255; and consequences, 80–81, 86–87; definition of, 126; deontic status of, 85; descriptions of, in trolley problems, 81, 112t, 256; distinction with event, 87–88; and distinction between tokens and types, 111–117, 112f, 115–116f, 124–125, 130, 134–136; infinitely varying circumstances of, 81; mental representations of, 114–117; and plans, 118–120, 118–119f, 174f; as primary object of moral judgment, 87–88; structural descriptions of, 118–120; structural features of, 80–81, 85–86, 92–93; and tree diagrams, 39, 118–120, 126–128, 175–178; unconscious appraisals of, 82–85, 111–117, 118–120, 121–122, 162–175; voluntary, 88, 158. *See also* action plans; act trees; directly intended action; harm, and acts; permissible acts; possible acts
action-descriptions, 81, 256
action plans, 118–121, 128, 127–128f, 174f
act-token representation, 129, 176–177. *See also* complex act-token representation

act trees: definition of, 39; and explanations of variance in trolley problems, 126–8; and structural descriptions, 118–120, 175–178
Adams, John, 307, 317
Alexander, Richard, 24
American Law Institute, 130–131, 134
Anscombe, G. E. M., 6n7
appraisal theory, 111–117, 120–122, 162–174
Aquinas, St. Thomas, 148, 296
Aristotle, 7n8, 47, 132n4, 219
Asperger's syndrome, 121
Austin, John, 50n4, 176
autism, 121
Ayer, A. J., 4, 317

Baier, Kurt, 315n2
Bain, Alexander, 6n7, 8t, 83n5, 187, 315
basic action, 176
battery: definition of, 117, 133–137; derivation of, 171f, 173, 174f; distinction between harmful and offensive, 134n6; division of into purposeful (I-generated) and knowing (K-generated), 136, 146t, 154–156t, 159–161t, 319–350; location of in act trees as element of structural descriptions, 120, 174f; and means-side effect distinction, 118, 154–156t; and moral–conventional distinction, 104; multiple counts of as partial explanation of variance in trolley intuitions, 126–128; and Principle of Double Effect, 149–150; prohibitions of, 133–134, 135–136; and trolley problems generally, 324, 326, 327–329, 331, 334; voluntary act requirement for, 158

behavioral adequacy, 29
behaviorism: and competence–performance
distinction, xv, 17–19, 51–55; and contrast
with mentalism, 18–19, 236; damage to
moral theory caused by, 19; inability
to account for projection problem in
moral theory, 95; and Kohlberg's moral
psychology, 263n15; shift of focus of moral
theory away from, 19. *See also* mentalism
Bentham, Jeremy, 8t, 9n9, 129, 131, 133, 144,
299, 300, 315
binding theory, 70
biolinguistics, 23
Black, Hugo L., 298
Blackburn, Simon, 221
Blackstone, William, 133
Blair, James, 24
Bloom, Paul, 23
Botha, R. P., 69n10
Boyd, Richard, 221
Bradley, F. H., 20, 83nn4–5
Brandt, Richard, 5, 8t, 40, 97, 186, 247,
263, 315n2
Brentano, Franz, 20, 77, 83n5
Brink, David, 221, 315n2, 316n6
Broad, C. D., 191, 316n7
Bromberger, Sylvain, xii, 9n10
Burlamaqui, Jean Jacques, 303n12
Butler, Joseph, 88n8, 191, 244, 315n2, 316
"by" test, as a tool for constructing structural
descriptions and act trees, 119–120, 177–178

Carnap, Rudolf, 193
categorical imperative, 96, 133
causal structure, 86, 130–132, 134, 172
causation: and C-generation (causal
generation), 131–132; computational
theory of, 132; and definitions of battery
and homicide, 134–136; as element of
problem of descriptive adequacy and its
solution, 86, 117–122; as implied by notion
of K-generation, 132; and moral calculus
of risk, 135–144; and Periodic Tables of
Moral Elements, 154–156t, 159–161t; and
Principle of Double Effect, 148–152; and
Rescue Principle, 144–148; and Self-
Preservation Principle, 136–137; as a
universal feature of moral psychology and
legal systems, 104–105
certitude: as criterion of considered
judgments, 51–52, 245–246; and distinction
with certainty, 245; as property of

trolley problem judgments, 97–99.
See also uncertainty
ceteris paribus clause, 144
C-generation (causal generation), 131–132
children: intuitive jurisprudence of, 104;
linguistic abilities of, 4, 58–60, 70; moral
competence of, 258–264, 346–350; and
trolley problems, 82, 259–261, 346–350
Chomsky, Noam: and ambiguity in
Quine's notion of grammaticalness or
meaningfulness, 95–96; and analysis
of "knowledge of language," 24–25,
61–63, 68n9, 220; and argument for
linguistic grammar, 17, 46–47, 68, 189; and
competence–performance distinction,
17–19, 52–53, 231, 239, 240, 252–253, 255,
257n12; and considered judgments, 264n16;
and distinction between descriptive and
observational adequacy, 49; and distinction
between methodological and metaphysical
naturalism, 194n6; and generative grammar,
87, 89–90, 184, 204, 233, 314; and human
rights, 299; and I-language interpretations
of language, 24–25, 61–63, 211; and linguistic
analogy, 3, 8t, 9n9, 64, 98, 102, 104, 175, 229,
262n15; and linguistics and philosophy at
MIT, 9n10; and mentalism, 19, 236; nativist,
modular, and representationalist theory
of mind, 216n15; and new framework for
theory of moral cognition, 13–41, 307–308;
and problem of language acquisition,
69–70; and rationalism, 4, 48; and scientific
revolution, 275–276; and theoretical
grammar, 60–61; and transformation of
linguistics and psychology, 4, 6
Cicero, 126, 255, 296
circumstances: and acts as elements of
structural descriptions, 125–130; Bentham
on etymology of, 129; Cicero's list of, 126,
255; descriptions of in trolley problems,
111–112; as element of problem of
descriptive adequacy and its solution,
48–49, 85–86, 91–93; indefinitely varying
quality of, 81; insufficient information
about as illustration of poverty of
perceptual stimulus, 111–117, 120–121,
162–174; notation of in complex act-
token representations, 125; and question-
formation in linguistic theory, 255
closure rule, 132–133, 310. *See also* Principle
of Natural Liberty; Residual Permission
Principle

cognition, as substitute for "knowledge," 68. *See also* cognitive science; moral cognition

cognitive science: and artificial experiments, 94–96, 104; and computational theory, 36–38, 91–93, 102–104, 178; and framing the problem of descriptive adequacy, 87–93; and future of moral philosophy, 11, 317–318; and levels of empirical adequacy, 21–23; and mental representations, 46–48, 114–117; and modularity, 216n15, 314–315; and nativism, 35, 216n15; and Rawls' assumptions about moral development, 35–36; and unconscious inference, 175

Cognitive Science Society (CSS), 319

coherentism, 287. *See also* hypothetico-deductive method; reflective equilibrium

common law: and concepts of "intent," 130–132; and definition of act, 126; and definitions of battery and homicide, 133–136; and Dworkin's constructive model of adjudication, 266, 269–270; and particularism, 72–73; and Rescue Principle, 117, 144; and traditional model of adjudication, 93, 101; and trolley problems, 159–161t, 163–167t; and unreasonable risk (negligence), 140–141, 158, 159–161t

competence–performance distinction: and basic elements of Rawls' linguistic analogy, 51–56, 59t; in Chomsky's framework, 17–19; and Nagel's criticism of Rawls' linguistic analogy, 228–265; theory-dependence of, 55–56, 59t; and trolley problems, 342

competent judge: as element of Dworkin's interpretation of Rawls, 266–267, 269–270; as idealized component of explication, 196, 246

completion, rule for dating of action by time of, 125

complex action-description, 111. *See also* action-descriptions

complex act-token representation, 117, 124. *See also* act-token representation

complex omission-token representation, 144–145, 147. *See also* omission

computational theory, 36–38, 91–93, 102–104, 178

conceptual analysis, 4, 184, 192, 218–219

Confucianism, and concept of *li*, xv

conscientia (conscience), 93; and argument for moral grammar, 44; and distinction with *synderisis*, 93; and Universal Declaration of Human Rights, 307, 317–318

consent, concept of in definition of battery, 136–137

consequence, as element of problem of descriptive adequacy and its solution, 86–87

consequentialism: descriptive inadequacy of simple forms of with respect to trolley problems, 96; and trends in contemporary moral philosophy, 317

considered judgments: and competence–performance distinction, 51–52, 53; distinction between moral intuitions and, 282–283; distinction between reflective equilibrium and, 99–100; as evidence for moral theory, 236, 282–287; and explication, 196; moral competence and revisability of, 55–56; and moral intuitions of ordinary persons, 237; and Nagel's criticism of Rawls' linguistic analogy, 240–265; and prejudice, 162n11, 263; Rawls' use of concept, 40–41, 221–222; and trolley problems, 86t, 110, 111t

constituent questions, in linguistic theory, 255

constructive model (Dworkin), 266–267, 269–271, 273–274, 278t, 280, 294, 304

constructivism, Rawls on Dworkin's understanding of, 267n1. *See also* social constructivism

contact, and definition of battery, 134–165

contractual argument, in *A Theory of Justice*, 198–202

conversion rules, 117, 120–121, 162–174

cost-benefit analysis: and moral calculus of risk, 141–143, 158; and Principle of Double Effect, 150–152; and Rescue Principle, 147–148

criminal law: as element of moral grammar and intuitive jurisprudence, 102–103; and periodic table of moral elements, 158–162; universal grammar of, 105. *See also* battery; homicide; legal theory

Damasio, Antonio, 24

Damasio, Hanna, 24

Dancy, Jonathan, 48, 71

Daniels, Norman, 5, 30, 40, 44n1, 47, 52n5, 186, 198, 211–212, 237n5, 247, 293

Danto, Arthur, 176

Darley, John, 352

Darwall, Stephen, 6n7, 316n6

Darwin, Charles, 8t, 23, 24n7, 66, 183, 187, 315

decision procedure, 26, 27

deductive-nomological explanation, 91

degeneracy of stimulus, 70–71

deontic concepts and deontic modalities in natural language, 104, 105f

deontic logic: and periodic table of moral elements, 157; and square of opposition and equipollence, 104, 105f

deontic rules: 117–118, 132–152; and problem of descriptive adequacy, 225

deontic status: of acts and problem of descriptive adequacy, 85, 86; and periodic table of moral elements, 154t, 156t, 157; and simplifying assumptions in moral grammar hypothesis, 124–125

deontic structure, as feature of structural descriptions of trolley problems, 173–174

deontology, and trends in contemporary moral philosophy, 317

Descartes, René, xvii, 4, 17

descriptive adequacy: and cognitive science, 87–93; and normative adequacy, 223–224; problem of, 77–100, 195–197; and Rawls' linguistic analogy, 29–30, 37, 48–50, 51, 59t; and trolley problems, 78–82, 106–110, 111f; use of term, 21, 22–23, 28

descriptive ethics, 29n11, 48–49, 218. *See also* descriptive adequacy

De Waal, Frans, 24

dharma, Hindu concept of, xv

directly intended action, 149, 150. *See also* I-generation

discounted expected benefit, and cost-benefit analysis, 141

discovery procedure, 26, 27

Donagan, Alan, xvii, 8t, 97

Duncan-Jones, Austin, 315n2

Durkheim, Emile, 189

Dworkin, Ronald, 5, 7, 40, 41, 42, 58, 66, 186, 198, 204, 214, 266–304, 303n12, 313

Dwyer, Susan, 3, 8t, 64n7

Einstein, Albert, xvii

E-language, 62, 211. *See also* I-language

E-morality: distinction between I-morality and, 63–64, 266–304. *See also* I-morality

emotion: and considered judgments, 244–245; and Greene's dual process theory, 121–122; and intuitive appraisal theory, 111–117, 121–122; and overemphasis in recent moral psychology, 178

empirical adequacy: distinction between normative adequacy and, 183–227; and

formal model of moral grammar and intuitive jurisprudence, 123–179; and moral grammar hypothesis, 101–122; and new framework for theory of moral cognition, 21–23, 32; and problem of descriptive adequacy, 77–100, 223–224; use of term, 30n12

Enlightenment: and competence–performance distinction, 259; and discussions of moral psychology in treatises on moral philosophy, natural law, and law of nations, 5n4; and grounding of human rights in theory of human nature, 296; and moral cognition, 315; and noncognitivism in ethical theory, 218–219; and rationalism, 174–175; and theory of moral sentiments, 216

equipollence relations, 105f

ethical theory: and moral intuitions, 248–256; and particularism, 317; and Rawls' use of term "moral theory," 257; and virtue ethics, 317. *See also* descriptive ethics; metaethical adequacy; moral theory; normative ethics

evaluation procedure: for grammars, 26, 27; and reflective equilibrium, 213, 272

evidence, for moral theory, as element of Dworkin's misinterpretation of Rawls, 282–7. *See also* considered judgments, moral intuitions

evolution: and Darwin's theory of moral sense, 183, 187; of human language, 23–24; of human morality, 23–24, 258–264; and instinct for self-preservation, 172; and moral and intentional structure of trolley problems, 172–173; and origin of prejudice, 258–264

evolutionary adequacy, 29

explanandum phenomenon, 91

explanatory adequacy: and justice as fairness, 208; and Rawls' linguistic analogy, 29, 33, 51, 59t; and reflective equilibrium, 212–213; and trolley problems, 82; use of term in linguistics and cognitive science, 21–23, 28

explication, 191–195, 196–197

express principles, 19–21, 30, 50–51, 59t, 84–85. *See also* operative principles

extensionality, as property of E-language and E-morality, 62, 64

externalization, as property of E-language and E-morality, 62, 64, 299, 303

fairness, 201–202, 207, 208, 210, 297
Ferguson, Adam, 3, 7, 8t
Firth, Roderick, 64n8
Fletcher, George, 8t, 73n11
Fodor, Jerry, 35, 68, 149, 216n15
Foot, Philippa, xvii, 7, 38, 77, 309, 320
"for the purpose of" test, as tool for
    constructing structural descriptions and
    act trees, 119–120, 177–178
forbidden acts, 85, 105f, 124
framing effects, 345–346
Frankena, William, 8t, 315n2
Frege, Gottlob, 123
Freud, Sigmund, vi, xv, 35, 66
Fried, Charles, xxii, 9n10

Galileo, 275–276, 360
Gall, F. J., 315
Gardner, Howard, 315n2
generative grammar: Chomsky's concept
    of, 87, 89–90, 204; and competence–
    performance distinction, 233; and problem
    of descriptive adequacy, 87; requirement
    of perfect explicitness, 87; as theory of
    linguistic competence, 53–54; use of term, 14
generative linguistics: and basic elements
    of Rawls' linguistic analogy, 57; and
    competence–performance distinction, 236,
    238–240; use of term, 13–14
Geneva Conventions (1949), 335
Gert, Bernard, 8t, 234–235, 236
Gibbard, Allan, 6n7, 316n6
Gilligan, Carol, 354
Ginet, Carl, xviii, 124
goal: and action plans, 118–120, 176; and
    recursive definition of I-generation, 131
goal(s) of moral theory, 6, 14–15, 23–24,
    26–33, 48–49, 67t; as element of Dworkin's
    misinterpretation of Rawls, 276, 277,
    280–282, 293. *See also* descriptive
    adequacy; explanatory adequacy;
    normative adequacy
Goldman, Alvin, xvii, 3, 8t, 124, 125,
    130, 176
Goodman, Nelson, 31, 46, 188, 204n10,
    207–208, 209, 212–213, 293, 312
Gould, Stephen Jay, 23
grammar: argument for linguistic (Chomsky),
    17, 44–46; argument for mental
    (Jackendoff), 44; argument for moral, 17,
    43–48; argument for tacit knowledge of, 4,
    17, 44; different meanings of in generative

linguistics, 14, 58–60; distinction between
    theoretical and mental, 22n6, 60–61,
    250; distinction between theoretical and
    pedagogical, 58–60; distinction between
    universal and particular, 14–15; and
    grammaticality judgments of linguists
    versus acceptability judgments of native
    speakers, 232, 233–235, 237–240, 248–249,
    252, 256; and speaker's knowledge of
    language in Chomsky's framework, 15–16;
    as system of unconscious principles or
    rules, 15. *See also* generative grammar;
    linguistic grammar; mental grammar; moral
    grammar; Universal Grammar; Universal
    Moral Grammar
Green, Leon, 73n11
Greene, Joshua, 39, 102, 112, 113f, 121, 310,
    315n2, 338, 350, 356, 357, 358, 359
Griswold v. Connecticut (1965), 298
Grotius, Hugo, vi, xv, 5n4, 8t, 296, 303n12
*Grounds. See Study in the Grounds of Ethical
    Knowledge, A*
Guest, Stephen, 299

Haegeman, Liliane, 233, 239n7, 248–249,
    253n10, 256
Hague Convention of 1907, 336
Haidt, Jonathan, 39, 111–112, 113f, 315n2
Hall, Jerome, 73n11
Halle, Morris, 69
Hampshire, Stuart, 8t, 241
Hand Formula, 140–141
Hare, R. M., 5, 7, 29n11, 40, 42, 58, 96,
    97, 183–227, 229, 267, 271, 294, 299,
    311–312, 316
harm: and acts, 145–147, 146t; bodily,
    136; concept of in definition of battery,
    135–136; concept of in moral calculus of
    risk, 137–144; and contact requirement
    in definition of battery, 135–136; and
    distinction between harmful and offensive
    battery, 134n6; and omissions, 144–145,
    146t; and Principle of Double Effect,
    150–152; and Rescue Principle, 144–148
Harman, Gilbert, xxi, 3, 8t, 9n10, 220, 236,
    320, 353
Harrison, Jonathan, 315n2
Hart, H. L. A., 223, 296
Hegel, G. W. F., 315–316
Helmholtz, H. V., 83n5, 175
Hempel, Carl, 91, 134n5, 193
Henkin, Louis, 317

398 *Index*

Hilliard, Francis, 73n11, 135, 324
Hinduism, and concept of *dharma*, xv
Hobbes, Thomas, 50n4, 133
Hofstadter, Richard, 315n3
Hohfeld, Wesley Newcomb, 178, 299, 300, 301f
Holmes, Oliver Wendell, 84n5, 101, 176, 299
homicide: definition of, 117, 133–134; division of into purposeful (I-generated) and knowing (K-generated), 134, 146t, 154–156t, 159–161t, 319–350; location of in act trees as element of moral geometry, 120, 174f; and means-side effect distinction, 118, 154–156t; and Principle of Double Effect, 149; prohibition of, 104, 133–136, 172; as universal feature of legal systems, 104–105
human nature: and a common moral nature, 296–297, 308, 318; competing accounts of in Freud and St. Paul, xv; and human rights, 296; and mentalism versus behaviorism, 19
human rights, 57, 295–303, 317–318. *See also* rights; Universal Declaration of Human Rights
Humboldt, Wilhelm von, 35
Hume, David, xvii, 8t, 35, 42, 72, 187, 208, 294, 296–297, 316, 317
Hutcheson, Francis, 8t, 20–21, 259, 303n12, 315n2, 317
hypothetico-deductive method: and coherentism, 287; and common law adjudication, 93, 101, 266, 269–270; and deductive-nomological explanation, 91; and Dworkin's interpretation of Rawls, 289, 291; and medieval theory of conscience, 93; and problem of descriptive adequacy, 91–93; and Rawls' conception of scientific method, 287n5, 288; and reflective equilibrium, 291; use of by Chomsky, 287n5; use of by Kant and Sidgwick, 287n5

idealization: and considered judgments, 54; and linguistic competence, 233; and moral diversity, 56–57; as property of I-language and I-morality, 25, 26, 62; and Rawls' linguistic analogy, 56–57, 59t, 64–65
ideal theory, versus non-ideal theory, 199
I-generation: and act-token representations, 176; definition of, 130–132; and periodic table of moral elements, 154t, 156t; and Principle of Double Effect,

150; and recursive definition, 131. *See also* K-generation
I-language: Chomsky's interpretation of, 211; and competence–performance distinction, 233, 236; explanation of concept, 25, 62–63; and heart of Rawls' linguistic analogy, 67t; and metaethical adequacy, 219–221
immediacy, as property of moral judgments, 83n4
I-morality: and Chomsky's concept of I-language, 25–26; and difference between wide and narrow reflective equilibrium, 211; and distinction with E-morality in Dworkin's commentary on Rawls, 266–304; and heart of Rawls' linguistic analogy, 67t; and metaethical adequacy, 219–221; moral theory as theory of, 63–67; and subject matter of moral theory, 276–277
impartiality, as property of moral judgments, 244–245
implicit bias, 162n11. *See also* prejudice
"in order to" test, as tool for constructing structural descriptions and act trees, 119–120, 177–178
inaction, distinction with omission, 151
"Independence of Moral Theory, The" (Rawls 1975), 10, 49n3, 65, 66, 190, 198, 210–211, 213–217, 283, 293
individualization, as property of I-language and I-morality, 25, 62, 63
induction: and abduction, 17, 68–69; and explication, 192–193; and reflective equilibrium, 207–209
initial situation, role played by in Rawls' theory of justice, 198, 200, 201, 202
initial state, role played by in Chomsky's theory of language, 14–15n2
innateness: Descartes' and Chomsky's dispositional sense of, 17; different views of Reid and Mill on with respect to rules of justice and rules of grammar, 9n9; Dworkin's "profound" interpretation of Rawls and, 266, 268; and initial state of language faculty, 14–15; and language acquisition, 4, 69–71; of moral knowledge or moral principles, xv, 36n16, 82, 183, 187–190, 266, 268, 307, 317–318, 320, 346–350; and moral and intentional structure of trolley problems, 172–173; and nativism in cognitive science, 35–36; and poverty of the stimulus arguments, 14–17, 69–71, 82, 346–347, 349–350. *See also* explanatory

adequacy; poverty of the stimulus; Universal Grammar; Universal Moral Grammar
instantaneous language acquisition, idealization of, 69
intensionality: as property of I-language and I-morality, 25, 62, 63; and Rawls' conception of moral principles as functions, 64, 66
intention: in Anglo-American jurisprudence, 130–131; Bentham's distinction between direct and oblique, 131; computational theory of, 130–131; and construction of act trees, 175–178; and definitions of battery and homicide, 134–136; and distinction between intended and foreseen, 130–132; as element of problem of descriptive adequacy and its solution, 86–87, 117–122; and I-generation, 130–132; and means-side effect distinction, 118–121, 154–156t, 159–161t; ordinary language and, 130–131; and Periodic Tables of Moral Elements, 154–156t, 159–161t; and Principle of Double Effect, 148–152; recursive aspect of explication of, 131; and Rescue Principle, 144–148; and theory of mind, 143, 178; as universal feature of moral psychology and legal systems, 104–105; use of by children to distinguish two acts with the same result, 104. *See also* "for the purpose of" test; I-generation, "in order to" test; intentional structure
intentional structure, 172–173
internalism, as property of I-language and I-morality, 25, 62, 63, 220
intersubjective stability, 243
intersubjective validity, 223, 226
intuition(s), and linguistic judgments of native speakers, 232–236.
See also intuitionism; moral intuitions
intuitionism: and contrast with justice as fairness, 198; and descriptive adequacy, 133; and Moore, Prichard, and Ross, 316.
See also intuitions; social intuitionist model
intuitive jurisprudence: and appraisal theory, 111–117, 121–122; formal model of moral grammar and, 123–179; young children's possession of, 104
Irwin, Terence, xviii, 93n11, 241
Islamic rationalism, xv

Jackendoff, Ray, xxi, 17, 58, 68
Jefferson, Thomas, 307, 317

justice: and natural rights theory, 297; distinction between conceptions of and concept of, 199; sense of, 4, 65, 66; Rawls' two principles of, 31n13, 200.
See also fairness; social justice
justification: 191–192, 201–202, 219, 222; and trolley problem experiments, 321–323, 329–330, 332–333t, 340, 345, 348

Kagan, Jerome, 8t
Kagan, Shelly, 263, 314
Kant, Immanuel, 4, 8t, 13, 20, 35, 75–76, 93n12, 96, 123, 131, 191n4, 198, 285, 287n5, 303n12
Kaplow, Louis, 352, 353
Katz, Jerrold, 62–63, 64n7, 68, 124, 211
K-generation: and act-token representations, 176; definition of, 130–132; and periodic table of moral elements, 154t, 156t; and Principle of Double Effect, 148–152; and Rescue Principle, 146–147; and trolley problem experiments, 320–321.
See also I-generation; knowing battery; knowing homicide; knowingly harmful acts and omissions
knowing battery, representation of, 136
knowing homicide, representation of, 134, 148
knowingly harmful acts and omissions, 145, 146t, 147
knowledge: and competence–performance distinction, 18, 53; and distinction between knowledge how and knowledge that, 68; and justified true belief, 68; and possession of a mental structure, 61–62.
See also moral knowledge
Kohlberg, Lawrence, 8t, 11, 21, 34, 35, 66, 82n2, 84, 94n12, 96, 189, 243, 262, 263n15, 309, 315n12, 346, 349, 350, 353, 354, 356

labeled brackets, and linguistic structural descriptions, 253
language acquisition, psychological and logical versions of problem of, 69–70
LaPiana, William, 315n3
legal theory: and formal model of moral grammar and intuitive jurisprudence, 123–179; and human rights, 268, 295–303; and intuitive emotional appraisal, 121–122; and legal positivism, 50n4, 299–300; and moral grammar hypothesis, 101–104; and principle of natural liberty, 132–133; and rule of dating action by time of completion, 125; and structural

legal theory (*cont.*)
  descriptions of act-token representations,
    125–132; transformation of in past decade,
    xvi–xvii. *See also* criminal law; human
    rights; intuitive jurisprudence
Leibniz, G. W., 4, 20, 35, 36n16, 303n12
Levi, Edward, 73
Lewontin, Richard, 23
li (Confucian concept), xv
libertarianism, and principle of natural
    liberty, 133
linguistic analogy: basic elements of Rawls',
    42–73; concluding remarks on, 314–318;
    Dworkin's commentary on, 266–304;
    Hare's and Singer's criticisms of, 183–190,
    226–227; Nagel's criticism of, 228–258;
    place of within history of philosophy, 7–9;
    preliminary clarifications about, 27–33;
    and problem of empirical adequacy in
    moral theory, 77–179; question presented
    by, 1–12. *See also* moral theory; Universal
    Grammar, Universal Moral Grammar
linguistic competence: and competence–
    performance distinction, 18,
    233; Chomsky's use of term, 4.
    See also generative grammar
linguistic grammar, argument for, 44, 58
linguistic performance, 15
linguistic theory: and linguistic intuitions,
    248–256; and summary of Rawls' linguistic
    analogy, 67t; use of term, 13–14
linguistics: and competence–performance
    distinction, 54n6, 257–258; influence
    of Chomsky on, 6; initial comparisons
    between moral theory and, 14–27; and
    intuitions of native speakers, 232–236.
    See also generative linguistics; grammar;
    linguistic analogy; linguistic competency;
    linguistic grammar; linguistic performance;
    linguistic theory
Locke, John, 198
logical positivism, 316
Lorenz, Konrad, 66
Lyons, David, xviii, 200, 247, 263

Mackie, J. L., 220–221, 315n2
Macnamara, John, 3n1, 93n11
Mahlmann, Matthias, xix, 3, 8t, 9n10
Mardiros, A. M., 195n7
Marr, David, 103, 149, 178
Massachusetts Institute of Technology
    (MIT), xix, 9n10, 77–78, 319, 320, 338

"maximin" rule, 201
McDowell, John, 48
Mead, G. H., 189
means-based moral principles, and trolley
    problems, 96, 337. *See also* categorical
    imperative; "for the purpose of" test;
    I-generation; intention; intentional
    structure; "in order to" test
mental capacity: and moral sense as complex
    illustration of, 55; and Rawls on sense of
    justice as, 65, 281; and subject matter of
    Rawls' conception of moral theory, 277–280
mental chemistry, 127f, 129
mental grammar: argument for, 44, 58, 59t;
    distinction between theoretical grammar
    and, 60–61
mentalism: and contrast with behaviorism,
    18–19; and moral theory, 19, 224–225; and
    subject matter of linguistics, 19, 236
mental representation, and moral grammar
    hypothesis, 38, 114, 116–117
mental state attributions, and trolley
    problems, 337
metaethical adequacy: problem of, 31, 32,
    217–221, 223, 226–227; and reflective
    equilibrium, 212–213; use of term, 28, 29t.
    See also metaethics
metaethics, 9, 29n11, 217–221
metaphysics: and conceptions of naturalism
    and physicalism, 184; and Dworkin's
    interpretation of Rawls, 270, 296, 298; and
    independence of moral theory, 213, 216;
    and logical positivism's verificationist
    criterion of meaning, 316; and metaethics,
    217–222; and moral realism, 219; and Rawls'
    interpretation of justice as fairness, 298
method, as element of Dworkin's
    interpretation of Rawls, 287–291.
    See also hypothetico-deductive method;
    scientific method
Mikhail, John, 8t, 82n1
Mill, John Stuart, xvii, 8t, 9n9, 35,
    84n5, 127f, 129
Miller, Richard, 73n12
mind-independence, 220, 279.
    See also externalization
Model Penal Code, 158
modularity, and cognitive science, 216n15
modus ponens, 92
Moore, G. E., 4, 228, 315n2, 316
Moore, Michael S., 73n11, 176, 220
moral agent, concept of, 87–88, 302n11

Moral Calculus of Risk, 137–144, 148, 158
moral cognition: brain regions involved
  in, 105–106; modeling theory of on
  Universal Grammar, 3–12; and naturalism,
  34–39, 303–304, 313; new framework for
  theory of, 13–41; and nineteenth-century
  neuropsychology, 315
moral competence: of children, 346–350;
  as distinct from moral performance, 18,
  52; and parallel to linguistic competence,
  6; and rationality, 33; and Rawls' use of
  alternative terms for, 4n2
moral diversity: innate constraints on,
  15–17; problem of, 215; and Rawls' use of
  idealization, 56–57; significant influence of
  culture on, 90
moral faculty, xv, 44, 269, 276–287, 303–304,
  307, 314–318. *See also conscientia*
  (conscience); moral grammar; "Sense of
  Justice, The"
moral geometry: and mental representation
  of trolley problems, 119–120, 174f; Rawls
  on theorems of, 36–37
moral grammar: argument for, 17, 30, 43–48,
  58, 59t; and conversion rules, 120–121,
  162–174; and deontic rules, 117–118,
  132–152; and distinction between
  K-generation and I-generation, 130–132;
  as feature of Rawls' conception of moral
  theory, 43–48, 58, 59t; formal model of
  intuitive jurisprudence, 123–179;
  generative character of, 15; hypothesis of,
  38–39, 101–122, 310–311; and human rights,
  295–303; initial evidence for, 104–106;
  and intuitive legal appraisal, 121–122; and
  particularism, 71–73; and poverty of the
  perceptual stimulus, 111–117; and problem
  of descriptive adequacy, 30–31, 106–110,
  111f; and problem of normative adequacy,
  30–31; and simplifying assumptions,
  124–125; and structural descriptions,
  118–120, 125–132, 153–162; use of term, 16.
  See also Universal Moral Grammar
moral intuitions: and comparison with
  linguistic intuitions, 4–5, 16–17, 43–48,
  232–256; as data for moral theory, 236–238,
  240–256, 257–265; distinction between
  considered judgments and, 40–41, 51–55,
  282–283; as evidence of mental structure
  rather than as subject matter of psychology,
  236n4; malleability and revisability
  of, 229, 247–250; and Nagel's criticism

of Rawls' linguistic analogy, 236–238,
  248–256; and particularism, 71–73; and
  reflective equilibrium, 197–213; and trolley
  problems, 78–82, 82–86. *See also* considered
  judgments; moral judgment
moral judgment: and descriptive adequacy,
  82–85; expanded perceptual model of,
  114f; impartiality of, 51–55, 242, 244–246;
  intuitive character of, 16–17, 82–83,
  97, 246; and nature of explication, 194;
  novelty and unboundedness of, 72–73;
  properties of, 16–17, 72, 82–85, 242–246;
  spontaneous character of, 16–17, 83,
  97, 243; stability of, 72, 83, 97, 242–244.
  See also considered judgments; moral
  intuitions
moral knowledge: and competence–
  performance distinction, 17–19, 51–56,
  228–265; and main questions of the theory
  of moral cognition, 15, 24, 27, 29t; and
  skepticism, 68; and use of term, 61–67
morally preferable alternatives, 151–152
morally-worse-than relation, 138–139
moral patient, concept of, 299, 302
moral performance: and competence–
  performance distinction, 54n6; distinction
  between moral competence and, 18, 52;
  and use of moral knowledge, 15
moral personality, 297
moral philosophy: academic status of, xvi;
  and recent discussions of moral faculty, 44,
  314; and Hare's and Singer's criticisms of
  Rawls' linguistic analogy, 184, 186; main
  trends in since 1950s, 317; and problems
  of empirical and normative adequacy, 216;
  Rawls' distinction between moral theory
  and, 213–214; Rawls' knowledge of history
  of, 9n10; Raz's distinction between moral
  psychology and, 286
moral principles: comparative, 145–147;
  conditional, 81, 91–93; decision procedure
  for, 10, 27; and descriptive adequacy, 22–23;
  discovery procedure for, 27; evaluation
  procedure for, 27, 213, 217, 221–223,
  226–227; and explication, 191–196, 223;
  and metaethical adequacy, 28, 31–32;
  and normative adequacy, 28, 31–32; and
  particularism, 71–73; simplicity requirement
  for, 291n7. *See also* moral grammar
moral psychology: development of as an
  academic discipline, xvi–ii, 5n4, 19, 20–21;
  importance of for moral philosophy, 6n7,

moral psychology (*cont.*)
   41–49, 63–67, 77–179, 181–304; importance
   of for political, social, and legal theory,
   318; negative impact of behaviorism on,
   19, 20–21; Rawls' approach to cognitive
   development and, 35–36; Rawls'
   conception of moral theory and, 6; Raz's
   distinction between moral philosophy and,
   286. *See also* moral cognition; moral theory
moral realism, and metaethical adequacy,
   219–220, 270
moral reality, Dworkin's use of term, 278–279
moral relativism, and problems of
   empirical and normative adequacy, 216.
   See also relativism
moral structure, of trolley problems, 170f, 172
moral theory: features of Rawls' conception
   of, 43–57, 67t; goal of, 276, 277, 280–282,
   293; Hare's and Singer's criticisms of Rawls'
   conception of, 226–227; and I-morality, 63–
   67; initial comparisons between linguistics
   and, 14–27; and Nagel's criticism of Rawls'
   linguistic analogy, 228–229, 236–238, 252;
   noncognitivism and Rawls' conception
   of, 218–219; Rawls' distinction between
   moral philosophy and, 213; and Rawls
   on problems of empirical and normative
   adequacy, 213–217; and subjectivity, 222;
   subject matter of, 276, 277–280
motive, as element of problem of descriptive
   adequacy and its solution, 86–87
Mu'tazalites, xv

Nagel, Thomas, 5, 7, 40, 42, 58, 78, 228–265,
   267, 312–313, 341
nativism, in cognitive science and
   philosophy of mind, 35–36, 38, 216n15.
   See also innateness; Universal Grammar;
   Universal Moral Grammar
naturalism: and distinction between
   methodological and metaphysical, 194; and
   jurisprudence, xvi, 266–268, 295–303; and
   theory of moral cognition, 34–39, 303–304,
   313. *See also* physicalism
natural law: and Grotius, xv–xvi; and
   human rights, 296–297, 317–318; and
   jurisprudence, 266, 295–303; and
   Pufendorf, 266; and St. Paul, xv
natural liberty, principle of, 132–133.
   See also Residual Permission Principle
natural model (Dworkin), 266–267, 269–274,
   278t, 279, 283, 288, 289, 295, 303–304
natural rights, Rawls' theory of, 295, 297–299

necessity: as affirmative defense, 148, 158;
   cases of, xvi, 117
negative act, and complex omission-token
   representation, 144–145
negative utilitarianism, 158
negligence: common law of, 140–141, 158,
   159–161t; and Hand Formula, 140–141; and
   moral calculus of risk, 137–144; and trolley
   problems, 159–161t, 163–167t
Nelson, Sharon, 351, 352
neurocognitive adequacy, 23–24, 28–30, 29t
neuroscience: and brain regions involved
   in moral cognition, 105; and computing
   structural descriptions, 118–121, 162–174;
   and inadequate appraisal theory of
   trolley problems, 112–117, 121–122; and
   neurocognitive adequacy, 23–24, 28–30, 29t
Nietzsche, Friedrich, 8t, 33
noncognitivism, and metaethical adequacy,
   218–221, 316–317
normal form, of complex act-token
   representation, 124
normative adequacy: distinction between
   empirical adequacy and, 183–227; and
   Rawls' linguistic analogy, 29–30, 31; and
   descriptively adequate moral theory
   as a presumptive solution to problem
   of, 30, 40, 187, 192, 195–197, 215–217,
   221–222, 225–226; and problems of
   descriptive and explanatory adequacy,
   223, 225; and reflective equilibrium,
   31–33, 40; and requirement of rationality,
   32–33, 191, 230, 265, 313; use of term, 28.
   See also normative ethics
normative ethics, 29n11, 184, 186, 215, 218,
   219, 227, 292–293. *See also* normative
   adequacy
novelty: of linguistic expressions, 45–46,
   94–95; of moral judgments, 46–48, 72–73,
   78; and unfamiliarity of trolley
   problems, 95
Nowell-Smith P., 315n2
Nozick, Robert, 8t, 9, 54–55, 64n7, 98
nullum crimen sine lege (no crime without
   law) and *nullem peona sine lege* (no
   penalty without law), 132

obiter dictum ("something said in
   passing"), 20n4
objection from insufficient
   normativity, 188, 190
objection from prejudice, 40, 246–247
objective validity, 223, 226

objectivity, in moral judgment, 83.
    See also subjectivity
obligatory acts, 85, 105f, 124
observational adequacy: and problem of
    descriptive adequacy in moral theory,
    49–50, 59t, 252; use of term in linguistics
    and cognitive science, 21–23
omission: and complex omission-token
    representation, 144–145, 146t, 147; and
    equipollence relations, 105f; and periodic
    table of moral elements, 157; and Principle
    of Double Effect, 151–152
operative principles, 19–21, 30, 50–51, 59t,
    84–85. *See also* express principles
order of priority, and problems of descriptive
    and normative adequacy, 30, 197
original position, 198, 200–201
"Outline of a Decision Procedure for Ethics"
    (Rawls 1951), 10, 27, 40, 49n33, 66, 187,
    190, 195–197, 212, 217, 221, 242, 246

pacifism, and knowing homicide, 148
parsing problem, 16. *See also* perception
    problem
particularism, 71–73
Paul, St., vi, xv
Pauline Principle, 337, 338t
PDE. *See* Principle of Double Effect
perception problem: in linguistics and
    moral theory generally, 16, 17; in moral
    cognition
perceptual model, 88–91, 111–117
performance. *See* competence–performance
    distinction
periodic table, of moral elements, 153–162
permissibility judgments, 251–252
permissible acts, 85, 105f, 124
Perry, Ralph Barton, 25n8
personal-impersonal distinction (Greene),
    112–114, 113f, 121–122
Petrinovich, Lewis, 110n1, 323
philosophy of science, Dworkin's
    misconceptions about, 276.
    See also scientific method
physicalism, distinction between
    methodological and metaphysical, 194.
    See also naturalism
Piaget, Jean, 8t, 11, 21, 34, 35, 82n2, 84, 96,
    189, 243, 346, 349, 350, 351, 352, 353
Pinker, Steven, 8t, 23, 50n4, 57
P-language, 62–63
Plato, 4, 305
P-morality, 63, 64

political philosophy, of Rawls in 1980s and
    1990s, 298
political science, and Rawls' theory of justice,
    280n4
Popper, Karl, 288n5
Posner, Richard, 8t, 224–225, 315n2
possible acts, 85
Potts, Timothy, 93n11
Pound, Roscoe, 73
poverty of the stimulus: as argument for
    innate knowledge, 17, 70–71, 82, 90;
    and distinction with degeneracy of the
    stimulus, 70; and moral perception,
    111–117. *See also* innateness; Universal
    Grammar; Universal Moral Grammar
prejudice: and competence–performance
    distinction, 258–263; and considered
    judgments, 162n11, 263. *See also* implicit
    bias; objection from prejudice; racial
    discrimination
prescriptivism, and noncognitivism, 317
Price, Richard, 316
Prichard, H. A., 316
primary act-token and act-type descriptions,
    111, 114, 115–116t
primary agent-description, 111
Principle of Double Effect (PDE):
    decomposition of, 149; and deontic rules,
    117–118; and empirical adequacy, 148–152;
    historical roots of (Aquinas), 148; and
    negative utilitarianism, 158; and periodic
    table of moral elements, 154t, 156t; as
    principle of justification, 152, 158; and self-
    defense, 148; and trolley problems, 154t,
    156t, 324, 335, 336, 343
Principle of Natural Liberty. *See* natural
    liberty, principle of
probability, and Rawls on explication, 193.
    See also Moral Calculus of Risk
production problem, in linguistics and moral
    theory, 16–17
projection problem, 30, 46–47, 72–73, 78,
    94–96; and argument for moral grammar,
    30, 43–48; and novelty and unboundedness
    of moral judgments, 47–48
proper names, potential prejudicial effect of
    on moral intuitions, 162n11
properties of moral judgment, 51–55, 82–85,
    241–236
Prosser, William, 134, 324
provisional justification, 201–202
Pufendorf, Samuel, 8t, 266, 303n12
pure procedural justice, 201, 203, 207

purposeful battery, representation of, 136
purposeful homicide, representation
   of, 134, 148
purposely harmful acts and omissions, 145,
   146t, 147
Putnam, Hilary, 35

Quine, W. V. O., 8t, 9n9, 68, 95, 271
Quinn, Warren, 68n9

Rachels, James, 147
racial discrimination: and considered
   judgments, 258–261; and reflective
   equilibrium, 203. *See also* prejudice
Railton, Peter, 6n7, 314n1, 316n6
Rashdall, Hastings, 316
ratio decidendi ("reason for deciding"),
   20n4, 93, 101
rationality: compatibility of principles of
   moral competence with requirements of, 33;
   and Enlightenment, 174–175; and problem
   of normative adequacy, 209; and Rawls'
   approach to ethical theory, 191–192; and
   theory of rational choice, 31–33; and trolley
   problems, 97. *See also* rational judgments;
   reasonable men; rational reconstruction
rational judgments, and Rawls on considered
   judgments, 192, 242, 245–246
rational reconstruction (real and
   virtual), 191n4
Rawls, John: assumptions about cognitive
   development, 35–36; author's
   conversations with about moral theory,
   xvi, 36n16; and basic elements of linguistic
   analogy, 18, 21, 23, 26, 42–73, 308; and
   concluding remarks on linguistic analogy,
   307–318; and considered judgments, 97, 99,
   102, 110, 341; and contractual argument
   in *A Theory of Justice*, 198–202; and
   distinction between operative and express
   principles, 21; and Dworkin's commentary
   on distinction between I-morality and
   E-morality, 266–304; and eight reasons
   for pursuing moral theory, 215–217; and
   empirical and normative adequacy in
   Grounds, 191–195; and empirical and
   normative adequacy in *Independence*,
   213–215; and empirical and normative
   adequacy in *Outline*, 195–197; on
   explication of commonsense morality, xvii;
   Hare's and Singer's criticisms of linguistic
   analogy of, 183–190; and hypothetico-
   deductive method, 91–93; and lexical

order of moral principles, 146n7; and
   linguistics and philosophy at MIT, 9n10;
   and metaethics, 27, 217–221, 221–227; and
   modeling of theory of moral cognition
   on Universal Grammar, 3–12, 229; and
   Nagel's criticism of linguistic analogy,
   228–266; and outline of plan of book, 33–38,
   39–41; and preliminary clarifications about
   linguistic analogy, 27–33; and principle
   of natural liberty, 133; and problem of
   descriptive adequacy, 30, 78, 85–86, 88,
   89, 96, 221; and reflective equilibrium, 31,
   32, 99–100, 102, 179, 197–198, 202–212.
   See also "Independence of Moral Theory,
   The"; "Outline of a Decision Procedure
   for Ethics"; *Study in the Grounds of
   Ethical Knowledge, A*; *Theory of Justice, A*
Raz, Joseph, 5, 284–285, 286–287
reasonable men, Rawls' concept of in
   Grounds, 192, 242, 246
reflective equilibrium: concept of, 31, 32, 102,
   179, 202–213; and considered judgments,
   99–100; distinction between narrow and
   wide, 209–212; and Dworkin's constructive
   model, 273–274; and Dworkin's natural
   model, 271–274, 289–291; and Rawls on goal
   of moral theory, 293; and scientific method,
   31, 99–100, 291; Singer's commentary on
   Rawls' concept of, 188–189; as state of affairs,
   rather than method or technique, 204–205,
   289; in *A Theory of Justice*, 197–213
Reichenbach, Hans, 317
Reid, Thomas, xvi, 8t, 9n9, 187, 303n12, 317
relativism, and Dworkin on natural and
   constructive models, 270, 272–273.
   See also moral relativism
religious intolerance, and reflective
   equilibrium, 203
representationalism, in cognitive science,
   216n15
Rescue Principle, 117, 144–148, 151, 152
Residual Permission Principle, 124
Residual Prohibition Principle, 132–133
Restatement of Torts, 73n11, 158, 176
rewrite rules: and linguistic structural
   descriptions, 253; and moral structural
   descriptions, 129, 137
rights: Bentham's paraphrastic analysis
   of, 299–300; derivative status of
   in computational theory of moral
   cognition, 299; derived expressions
   about trolley problems incorporating,
   300–302; Hohfeld's analysis of, 299, 301t;

human or natural, 57, 295–303, 317–318.
See also human rights; natural rights

risk: gratuitousness of, 141; magnitude of, 140; marginal calculus of, 141; moral calculus of, 137–144, 148, 158; necessity of, 140–141; utility of, 140, 142–143

Robinson, Paul, 352

Rome Statute of the International Criminal Court, 57

Rorty, Richard, 9, 315n2

Ross, W. D., 8t, 68n9, 191, 316

Rousseau, Jean-Jacques, 8t, 20, 35, 36n16, 198, 303n12

Russell, Bertrand, xvii

Ryle, Gilbert, 8t, 68

Salmond, John, 178

Scanlon, T. M., xviii, 144, 284, 285, 286, 303n12

Schlick, Moritz, 181, 317

Schneewind, J. B., 21n5, 294n9

scientific method: and competence–performance distinction, 54–55; and Dworkin's interpretation of Rawls, 267, 269, 271–272; and "Galilean" style of inquiry, 275–276; and hypothetico-deductive method, 91–93, 287n5; and preference for explanatory depth to mere coverage of data, 274–276; and Rawls' notion of idealization, 54, 56, 65; and reflective equilibrium, 31, 99–100, 291; and scientific revolution, 275

secondary act-type descriptions, 111, 114, 115–16t

self-defense, and homicide, 148

self-preservation principle, 136–137, 172

semantic properties, and causal structure, 172

"Sense of Justice, The" (Rawls 1963), 66

Shavell, Steven, 352, 353

side-effect effect, 121, 143

Sidgwick, Henry, 5n4, 34, 35, 84n5, 93n12, 96, 131, 186, 187, 212, 219, 227, 285–286, 287n5, 294, 312, 315, 316

simple expected benefit, and cost-benefit analysis, 141

Singer, Peter, 5, 7, 34, 40, 42, 58, 144, 183–227, 267, 293n8, 294, 299, 311–312, 315n2

Sinnott-Armstrong, Walter, 11n12

skepticism: and Dworkin on natural and constructive models, 270; and use of term "knowledge" to describe linguistic or moral principles, 68

Skinner, B. F., 95

Smith, Adam, xvi, 1, 7, 8t, 187, 294, 303n12, 317

Soames, Scott, 62–63

social constructivism, 35, 189

social instincts, and moral structure, 172

social institutions, and Rawls on concept of justice, 199

social intuitionist model, of moral judgment (Haidt), 113f

social justice: no computational theory of, 37; Rawls' concept of in *A Theory of Justice*, 199

Social Science Research Network (SSRN), 319

Society for Research in Child Development (SRCD), 319

Sorrentino, Cristina, xix, 8t, 77, 82n1, 319

Spelke, Elizabeth, xvii, xix, 8t, 35, 77, 319

Spencer, Herbert, 84n5

spontaneity, as property of moral judgments, 83n4, 243

square of opposition and equipollence, 104, 105f. *See also* deontic logic

stability, as property of moral judgments, 83n4, 243–244

Stanley, Jason, xviii, 230n1, 237, 238, 258n13, 264n16

steady state, of language and moral faculties, 14–15n2

Stevenson, Charles L., 4, 316

Stich, Stephen, xxiii, 3, 8t, 11

Stone, Julius, 73, 134n5, 310

strong generation, 89n9, 252–256

structural features: of acts, 92, 118–120, 125–132; of omissions, 144–148; and periodic table of moral elements, 153–162

structure-dependent rules, of language acquisition, 70

Study in the Grounds of Ethical Knowledge, A (Rawls 1950), 10, 49n3, 66, 187, 190, 191–195, 196, 197, 212, 217, 219, 241–242, 246

Sturgeon, Nicholas, xviii, 221, 315n2

subjective stability, 243

subjectivity: in moral judgment, 83; and Singer's critique of Rawls, 222–223. *See also* objectivity; subjective stability

subject matter, of moral theory, as element of Dworkin's interpretation of Rawls, 276, 277–280. *See also* *conscientia* (conscience); moral competence; moral faculty; moral grammar; I-morality; "Sense of Justice, The"

Sunstein, Cass, 11n12

SVO hypothesis, 239n7
synderesis (first principles of practical
    reason), 93
Syntactic Structures (Chomsky 1957), 26,
    46–47, 49, 89, 253

Taking Rights Seriously (Dworkin), 291,
    296, 304
temporal structure, 171, 337
Tenenbaum, Josh, xix, 3n1
Terry, Henry, 176, 178
Theory of Justice, A (Rawls 1971), xvii, 3–12,
    21, 26–27, 31–38, 40, 42–43, 66–67, 73, 88,
    133, 183–190, 197–213, 215n14, 217, 228,
    241, 242, 249, 251, 253, 266–304, 308, 309,
    311, 312, 313, 318
Thomson, Judith Jarvis, xvii, xxiii, 7, 38, 77,
    158, 309, 320, 337, 359
thought experiments, xvi, 78–80, 96, 106–109t,
    163–167t
Toulmin, Stephen, 262
tree diagram, and linguistic structural
    descriptions, 253
Trivers, Robert, 24, 66
trolley problems: artificiality of, 94, 95–96,
    97; and cognitive mechanisms, 80–81; and
    considered judgments, 86t; and cost-
    benefit analysis, 142–143; description of
    experiments, 319–350; explanations of
    variance in, 126–128; and manipulation of
    structural features, 163–167; originating
    in the work of Foot and Thomson, 7,
    77–78; permissibility versus acceptability
    judgments in, 251–252; and problem of
    descriptive adequacy, 78–82, 94–100,
    106–110, 111t, 112t; racism and prejudice
    in moral judgments and, 259–261;
    structural descriptions of, 118f, 119f;
    unfamiliarity of, 94–95

unboundedness: of linguistic judgment, 46; of
    moral judgment, 72–73
uncertainty, of trolley problems, 94, 97–99
unconscious inference: Helmholtz's concept
    of, 175; and Leibniz's argument for innate
    moral knowledge, 36n16
Unger, Peter, 144
Universal Declaration of Human Rights, 57,
    303, 307
Universal Grammar (UG): and acquisition
    models, 90; and Chomsky, 3, 14; and
    criminal law systems, 105; and distinction

with particular linguistic grammar, 14;
    general introductions to theory of, 14n1;
    modeling of theory of moral cognition
    on, 3–12. *See also* acquisition models;
    explanatory adequacy; innateness;
    linguistic analogy; linguistic grammar;
    Universal Moral Grammar
Universal Jurisprudence, 300
Universal Moral Grammar (UMG): and
    acquisition models, 90; and author's
    overriding objective, 11; and a common
    human moral nature, 73, 317–318; and
    comparisons between linguistics and moral
    theory, 14, 15; and conclusions on theory of
    moral cognition, 307–318; and distinction
    with particular moral grammar, 15.
    See also acquisition models; explanatory
    adequacy; innateness; linguistic analogy;
    moral grammar; Universal Grammar
Urmson, J. O., 316n6
utilitarianism: descriptive inadequacy
    of simple forms of, 96; inadequacy of
    with respect to prohibitions of battery
    and homicide, 133; justice as fairness
    as a viable alternative to, 198, 210; and
    necessity defense, 158; negative version
    of, 158; Rawls and refutation of, 191, 198.
    See also consequentialism, cost-benefit
    analysis, necessity, negative utilitarianism

voluntary act, 87–88
Von Savigny, F. C., 8t, 9n9, 123

weak generation, 89n9, 252–256
Weinrib, Ernest, 144
Westermarck, Edward, 316
Whewell, William, 20, 21n5, 84n5
White, Alan, 315n3
Williams, Bernard, 5, 44n1, 186, 247, 314,
    315n2, 316n6
Wilson, E. O., 24
Wilson, James, 307, 317
Wittgenstein, Ludwig, 61
Wolff, Robert Paul, 31n14, 191n4
Wood, Allen, 9n9, 258n13

Xu, Fei, 331n4
Xu, Yaoda, 331n4

yes–no questions, and phrase structure
    in syntax, 255
Young, Robert M., 315